GREAT LIVES
FROM
HISTORY

GREAT LIVES FROM HISTORY

American Women Series

Volume 5
Rud-Z

Edited by

FRANK N. MAGILL

SALEM PRESS

Pasadena, California   Englewood Cliffs, New Jersey

Library of Congress Cataloging-in-Publication Data
Great lives from history. American women series /
edited by Frank N. Magill.
    p.   cm.
Includes bibliographical references and index.
    1. Women—United States—Biography. 2. Women—
Canada—Biography. 3. Women—United States—His-
tory. 4. Women—Canada—History. I. Magill, Frank
Northen, 1907-   . II. Title: American women series.
HQ1412.G74   1995
305.4'0973—dc20
ISBN 0-89356-892-9 (set)   94-38308
ISBN 0-89356-897-x (volume 5)   CIP

LIST OF BIOGRAPHIES IN VOLUME FIVE

LIST OF BIOGRAPHIES IN VOLUME FIVE

GREAT LIVES
FROM
HISTORY

MARGARET RUDKIN

Born: September 14, 1897; New York, New York
Died: June 1, 1967; New Haven, Connecticut
Area of Achievement: Business and industry
Contribution: The founder of Pepperidge Farm, producer of high-quality bakery
    products, Margaret Rudkin achieved business success at a time when such accom-
    plishments by women were rare. She wrote a best-selling autobiography/cookbook
    in 1963.

Early Life

Margaret Fogarty was born on September 14, 1897, the oldest of five children. She
grew up in a quiet neighborhood known as Tudor in New York City. Margaret's
grandmother, an immigrant from Ireland, had the strongest influence on her early life.
She lived with the family and introduced Margaret to cooking and to her Irish heritage.

In school, Margaret majored in mathematics and finance. She was the valedictorian
of her high-school class and later gained practical business experience working as a
bookkeeper at a bank. Four years later, Margaret joined the brokerage firm of
McClure, Jones and Company as a customer representative. There she met Albert
Rudkin, a broker and her future husband, who later left Wall Street to join Margaret
at Pepperidge Farm.

Margaret left McClure when she married in 1923. She became a homemaker and
the mother of three sons. In 1928, the Rudkins purchased their dream home, a
125-acre farm in Connecticut. One of the main attractions of the farm was its
pepperidge trees. Their home became known as "Pepperidge Farm."

During the 1920's, the Rudkins lived the life of the wealthy, owning five automobiles, hunting, and showing horses. An event in 1931, however, permanently altered
their lifestyle. Albert Rudkin suffered a serious polo accident that disabled him for six
months. Margaret was forced to sell their horses and four of their automobiles to raise
money. She also sought ways to make money with their farm.

The Rudkins were more than "gentlemen" farmers. Margaret raised fruits, vegetables, and poultry on the farm. Their first commercial venture was to plant an apple
orchard of five hundred trees. Later, Margaret raised turkeys, pigs, and cattle for sale
during World War II.

In addition to engaging in business activities, Margaret pursued her interest in
cooking. She prepared homemade jams, jellies, pickles, sauerkraut, and butter. She
ordered several free government booklets on food preparation and began a collection
of recipes. The business and cooking expertise she gained during her early years on
the farm would later aid her in the development of Pepperidge Farm, Incorporated.

Life's Work

In 1937, Margaret Rudkin launched a new business venture known as Pepperidge
Farm, Incorporated. Pepperidge Farm began when Rudkin's son, Mark, was diag-

nosed as having an asthmatic condition. A specialist believed that the chemical additives in commercially baked goods aggravated the boy's condition. For that reason, Rudkin began studying nutrition and holistic medicine. Soon thereafter, she began to bake with natural ingredients. Her specialty was whole-wheat bread made with fresh stone-ground wheat, butter, molasses, honey, and whole milk. The new diet and the bread seemed to help her son's condition improve. Therefore, the specialist ordered some bread for himself and other patients.

The specialist also wrote a letter recommending the bread for its nutritional content. Rudkin sold her bread to other doctors through a sizable mail-order business. She became so successful that she outgrew her kitchen, so she converted a horse stable and the garage into a bakery and hired a neighbor to help her bake. Two months later she began selling wholesale.

She persuaded new distributors to market her bread by giving them samples of bread to eat. Margaret would stroll into their shops with bread, butter, and bread knife in hand and offer them a taste. A local grocer was her first wholesale customer, and others followed. Later, a New York City specialty store, Charles and Company, began to purchase and sell twenty-four loaves a day. Although her product was expensive, twenty-five cents a loaf compared to ten cents a loaf for regular bread, consumers were willing to pay more for Rudkin's high-quality, tasty bread.

In November of 1937, Rudkin expanded her product line by producing old-fashioned white bread. She again used natural ingredients—unbleached white flour, honey as a sweetener, and grade-A butter. Her loaves were small but nutritional and delicious. People liked them. After only two years of being in business, Pepperidge Farm began producing 25,000 loaves of bread a week.

The huge success of Pepperidge Farm allowed Margaret Rudkin to open a plant in Norwalk, Connecticut, but it turned out to be too small. World War II broke out shortly thereafter, and Pepperidge Farm was forced to remain in the small plant until the war ended. In addition, Rudkin suffered other war-related problems. Butter became difficult to find. Instead, Rudkin used heavy cream, which cost a thousand dollars more a week. In addition, Pepperidge Farm workers began leaving the bakery for higher-paying jobs in the weapons industry. When the company was understaffed, Margaret kneaded bread to help out.

In 1947, Pepperidge Farm moved into a modern plant. The new bakery could produce as many as four thousand loaves an hour. Rudkin added sales staff and introduced new products in order to increase sales and production levels. Margaret Rudkin was determined to maintain the high quality of her products. She kept Pepperidge Farm under strict family control. Rudkin supervised the personnel and production functions, and Albert supervised all financial and marketing activities. To minimize outside influences, Rudkin financed plant expansions with company earnings.

Margaret Rudkin was a stern perfectionist when it came to production. Although it was more expensive to do so, she continued using natural ingredients and the hand-kneading process. She mainly hired women because she believed they were more gifted than men at breadmaking. The women, however, were to have no prior knowledge of baking bread. Rudkin wanted the women to learn only one way of making bread: her way.

Rudkin also utilized innovative management techniques. She required a full day's work from her employees. In return, she paid them above-average wages and instituted bonuses and insurance plans. Rudkin was known for rewarding faithful employees with job security, promotions, and Pepperidge Farm stock. Unlike other large bakeries, Pepperidge Farm had a somewhat relaxed environment, with Muzak playing in the background. Rudkin would comment to visitors that the "girls" would get up and dance with one another during breaks.

At the same time, Rudkin grew in popularity with the national press. She skillfully used television to advertise her products. Often she would appear in the commercials herself as "Maggie," marketing her bread for its "homey" and nutritional appeal. Enthusiastic newspaper articles and popular magazines such as *The New Yorker*, *Time*, and *American Home* touted Rudkin's success. The most significant article, however, was arranged by public relations expert Benjamin Sonnenberg. The article, "Bread, de Luxe," appeared in *Reader's Digest* and introduced Rudkin to the whole United States. Orders poured in from everywhere. Rudkin rewarded Sonnenberg by employing him on a user-fee basis and giving him 5 percent of the company.

Pepperidge Farm continued to grow over the years with the opening of a second bakery in Pennsylvania in 1949 and a third in Illinois in 1953. Rudkin continued to maintain the high quality of her products by using stone-ground wheat and unbleached flour. To ensure freshness, Rudkin decreed a two-day shelf life. Ingeniously, she solved the problem of losing money on unsold bread by making stuffing out of it and selling it at a profit.

Never tiring, Rudkin continued to expand the Pepperidge Farm product line. During a vacation to Europe, Rudkin and her husband tasted cookies at many large and small bakeries. On their return, Rudkin purchased Belgian cookie recipes from a European bakery and began to produce them. In 1958, a new plant opened in Dowington, Connecticut, to produce Rudkin's new frozen pastry line. By 1960, Rudkin's small company had grown to employ more than one thousand workers and had annual sales of $32 million.

In 1960, Rudkin sold Pepperidge Farm to Campbell Soup for $28 million worth of Campbell stock. She continued to run Pepperidge Farm as an independent subsidiary of Campbell Soup. In addition, she became a member of the board of directors of Campbell Soup.

Rudkin wrote a four-hundred-page best-selling autobiography/cookbook in 1963, which enhanced her image as successful homemaker and businesswoman. She included cooking tips and favorite recipes collected during her lifetime. She shared quips and recipes related to her Irish heritage, and included excerpts from famous ancient cookbooks. She stressed the importance of eating, sleeping, and exercising properly.

In 1962, Rudkin turned the presidency of Pepperidge Farm over to one of her sons and became the company's chairperson. She retired at the age of sixty-nine in 1966, when she became ill with breast cancer. Margaret Rudkin died a year later.

Summary

Margaret Rudkin achieved business success at a time when such accomplishments by women were rare, and she did so with the admiration and approval of the American public. During the 1940's and 1950's, the traditional role of the woman was home-maker, wife, and mother. The public, however, accepted Rudkin in her nontraditional role as a business executive. This was partly because of Rudkin's "homey" appeal and her line of business, which was viewed as domestic.

Rudkin was, however, more than just "mom" or "Maggie," as so many affection-ately called her. She was ambitious, determined, talented, and cunning—equal in ability and talent to her male counterparts. Her ingenuity, commitment to quality, and marketing skills made Pepperidge Farm into a multimillion dollar business.

Rudkin has been depicted in biographies as a nice woman who seemed to have stumbled into fame. The truth of the matter is that many women have baked bread, but Rudkin sold it to a nation. She was bright and a relentless worker, working until her death. She made the media work for her and used astute personnel policies. She stressed quality and was an exceptional production, personnel, and public relations manager.

Men and women alike have recognized Rudkin's great achievements. In 1955, the thirty-second Women's International Exposition presented Rudkin with the Distin-guished Award in Industry. Margaret Rudkin stands out as one of the most nationally prominent and successful business executives of the twentieth century.

Bibliography

Bainbridge, John. "Profiles—Striking a Blow for Grandma." *The New Yorker* 24 (May 22, 1948): 38-40. An excellent article containing in-depth discussion of Rudkin's business philosophy and unique business practices at Pepperidge Farm. Her manufacturing methods are discussed and compared with the industry norm.

Ingham, John N., and Lynne B. Feldman. *Contemporary American Business Leaders: A Biographical Dictionary*. New York: Greenwood Press, 1990. Discusses Rud-kin's popularity and acceptance by the public as a successful businessperson. Covers the history of Pepperidge Farm and Rudkin's accomplishments.

Lavine, Sigmund A. *Famous Merchants*. New York: Dodd, Mead, 1965. Part of a series of biographies for young people, this biography covers Albert Rudkin's early life to the success of Pepperidge Farm. It emphasizes Margaret Rudkin's accom-plishment of transforming herself from a housewife into a businessperson at a time when that was a rare feat.

Leavitt, Judith A. *American Women Managers and Administrators*. Westport, Conn.: Greenwood Press, 1985. A collection of biographies about twentieth century lead-ers in business, education, and government. The author gives an overview of Rudkin's accomplishments, awards, and involvement with Pepperidge Farm.

Rudkin, Margaret. *The Margaret Rudkin Pepperidge Farm Cookbook.* New York: Atheneum, 1963. A combination autobiography and cookbook by Rudkin. The four-hundred-page book contains information about her childhood and the evolution of Pepperidge Farm. Rudkin also took the liberty of writing about her own interests in ancient cookbooks and Ireland. She included many of her favorite recipes and cooking tips. The autobiographical sections of this book give the reader a sense of what Rudkin was like as a person.

Marsha M. Huber

WILMA RUDOLPH

Born: June 23, 1940; Bethlehem, Tennessee
Died: November 12, 1994; Nashville, Tennessee
Area of Achievement: Sports
Contribution: Despite her early physical handicaps, Wilma Rudolph overcame much
   adversity to excel as one of the fastest runners the world of track has ever seen. She
   established many track records and garnered numerous medals and awards.

Early Life

Wilma Glodean Rudolph was born on June 23, 1940, in the city of Bethlehem,
Tennessee. She was the fifth child of eight born to Ed and Blanche Rudolph. Weighing
only four and one-half pounds at birth, Wilma faced additional challenges to her
health when she contracted polio, double pneumonia, and scarlet fever at the age of
four. The severity of these illnesses made many doubt that she would survive childhood. Her mother, however, never wavered in her faith that Wilma would recover. She
fervently believed that her daughter would survive and regain the use of her left leg.
Wilma's own determination to overcome these childhood challenges provided her
with the resources necessary to accomplish her later athletic feats.

At an early age, Wilma was cognizant of the racial divisions in American society.
Her father was a railroad porter and her mother worked as a domestic in the homes of
white families. Wilma's extended family was a large one, since her father had eleven
other children from a previous marriage. As a consequence, Wilma resided with her
parents and a large number of siblings, with whom she shared household chores.
Wilma grew up in a Baptist home where discipline and God went hand in hand. Her
parents protected their children and encouraged them to stay out of trouble with the
law.

Physicians in Nashville encouraged Wilma's parents to massage her legs daily,
which they accomplished with the aid of the entire family. The doctors believed that
this physical therapy would help Wilma regain use of her left leg. Wilma's childhood
in Clarksville, Tennessee, was filled with many lessons. Her twice-weekly rides to
Meharry Medical College forced her to witness the pervasiveness of racial discrimination in the South. She traveled on a segregated bus where blacks were seated in the
rear and often were forced to relinquish their seats to whites. All facilities connected
with the bus, including ticket windows, toilets, and waiting areas, were segregated.
Only among the health care staff of Meharry's black teaching hospital did she witness
a level of dignity and equality.

When she was five years old, Wilma Rudolph began wearing a brace on her leg
daily, until bedtime. She resisted the limitations placed upon her by the steel brace.
Despite continued bouts with various illnesses and several surgeries before her tenth
birthday, Wilma often took off her brace and attempted to walk normally. Soon, she
progressed to wearing an orthopedic shoe.

Because of her many physical ailments, Wilma was forced to forgo the first two years of her formal education and entered second grade in 1947. Despite the inadequate educational resources available at Cobb Elementary School, Wilma was introduced to the basics of reading, writing, and mathematics. Her teachers also became a source of inspiration and motivation. They taught her self-respect, self-acceptance, and positive thinking. She was taught to "do" rather than simply wish. During her tenure at Cobb, Wilma learned about the accomplishments of many black heroes. The black history she was taught encouraged her to take pride in her heritage.

It was during her years at segregated Burt High School that Wilma's love of track was first instilled. She played basketball and was introduced to track by her basketball coach, Clinton Gray. During her time in high school, she competed in many different races, including the 50-, 75-, and 100-yard dashes and the relay. At the age of thirteen, she won all twenty races she entered. She excelled in basketball as well, leading her team to the Middle East Tennessee Conference title. It was at one of these competitions in 1955, that Rudolph met Tennessee State University track coach, Edward Temple. Temple wanted to coach Wilma and teach her the many techniques of track. Natural ability was not the only factor in track. The athlete, he advised, had to have more than the ability to run fast.

Eventually, Wilma entered a summer sports program at Tennessee State under the guidance of Coach Temple. Her high school coach drove her to Nashville, where she trained under Temple as a junior member of the Tigerbelle Track Club. At age sixteen, she qualified for the United States Olympic track team and traveled to the Olympic Summer Games held in Melbourne, Australia, in 1956. Being photographed with sports heroes such as Jackie Robinson and Don Newcomb filled Wilma with inspiration. Although an individual medal was to elude her, Wilma's performance as a member of the U.S. women's 400-meter relay team brought her a bronze medal. Undaunted, she vowed to return and garner gold at the next Olympic games.

Life's Work

After being graduated from high school in 1957, Wilma Rudolph entered Tennessee State University and decided to major in psychology and elementary education. She soon became an active member of the Tennessee State University Tigerbelles track team and worked to support herself while attending college. Choosing to supplement her income with work-study employment, Rudolph was required to work every day for two hours. In addition to completing her education, Rudolph aspired to participate in the 1960 Olympic games. She prepared for the Olympic tryouts with a competition in Texas. After this contest, the winning athletes were to be given the opportunity to try out for the Olympic team.

When she arrived in Rome for the 1960 Olympic games, Rudolph was filled with excitement and anticipation. Eager to fulfill a lifelong dream, she was not to be disappointed. Rudolph qualified easily in the preliminary races. She went on to win gold medals in the 100-meter and 200-meter dashes, and established a world record in the 200-meter event that was to stand for nearly a decade. Her performance as the anchor of the women's 400-meter relay team brought Rudolph a third gold medal and helped establish another world record.

After winning in Rome, Rudolph celebrated her victory with a Vatican visit to Pope John XXIII. Although it seemed impossible that Rudolph could top her Olympic performance, she managed to excel in every event she entered in her next track competition, held in London, England. She continued to tour Europe during 1960, entering races in countries such as Holland and West Germany. She was heralded and mobbed everywhere she went. She was given a variety of nicknames by the European press, including "La Perle Noire" (the black pearl) by the French media and "La Gazzella Nera" (the black gazelle) by the Italians.

She was given a hero's welcome in Clarksville upon her return from Europe. Thousands of individuals turned out to witness the twenty-year-old track sensation, and her arrival marked the occasion for Clarksville's first integrated event. She continued her nationwide trek with stops in Chicago, Detroit, Atlanta, Washington, D.C., and Philadelphia. In each city, she was hailed as America's sweetheart. She was honored by the White House with an invitation to meet President John F. Kennedy and Vice President Lyndon B. Johnson. She made speeches, signed autographs, made television appearances, and attended a variety of banquets in her honor. Rudolph was named the U.S. Female Athlete of the Year by the Associated Press in 1960 and won several awards, including the Helms World Trophy Award (1960) and the James E. Sullivan Memorial Trophy (1961) as the top amateur athlete in the United States. She competed in the all-male Millrose games (the first woman to have been invited in thirty years) and at the Penn Relays, Drake Relays, and New York Athletic Club Meet. She went on goodwill tours throughout the world, visited Africa and Japan, and carried herself with grace and poise.

Rudolph retired from competition in 1962 and was graduated from Tennessee State University in May of 1963. She eventually married a man whom she had known since childhood: Robert Eldridge, her boyfriend from high school. After moving to Indiana, she was offered the directorship of a community center. Social service seemed to be her calling, and she quickly became involved in the Jobs Corps program. Rudolph moved to Boston, Massachusetts, and later to Poland Springs, Maine. Her work came to the attention of Vice President Hubert Humphrey in 1967. He recruited Rudolph to work in his Operation Champion program. The program's purpose was to place star athletes in urban ghetto areas where they would work with inner-city children. Wilma Rudolph was targeted to be the track expert for the program along with another alumnus of Tennessee State University, Ralph Boston. When her work with Operation Champion ended, Rudolph went to St. Louis, Missouri, to work in the Job Corps. She later taught at Palham Junior High School in Detroit, Michigan.

Constant mobility became a hallmark of Rudolph's life. She truly epitomized her childhood nickname "Skeeter," given to her because she flitted around busily like a mosquito. She eventually relocated to California, where she worked in the Watts Community Action Committee. She moved back to Clarksville, Tennessee, in 1977 before ultimately taking up residence in Detroit, Michigan, with her family. During the course of her married life, she became a proud mother of four: two sons, Xurry and Robert, Jr., and two daughters, Yolanda and Djuana. Rudolph continued her activity in the Delta Sigma Theta sorority and other community-based programs in Detroit. In 1977, she published an autobiography entitled *Wilma: The Story of Wilma Rudolph*. The book later became a television film starring Cicely Tyson that provided inspiration to many physically challenged individuals.

In July of 1994, Rudolph nearly fainted while delivering a speech in Atlanta, Georgia. After consulting with physicians, Rudolph was diagnosed with brain cancer. Although she fought hard against the disease, Rudolph died at her home in Nashville, Tennessee, on November 12, 1994, at the age of fifty-four.

Summary

Wilma Rudolph's life exemplifies the human spirit. Her childhood battle with polio and paralysis did not deter her. She became a symbol of hope to many young people and adults who are physically challenged because she never permitted her handicaps to limit her achievements physically or mentally. Her dreams were lofty ones, and she worked hard to fulfill them.

Her Olympic triumphs and record-setting track achievements have earned for her a well deserved place in history. Using her personal triumphs as a springboard for continued success outside the sports arena, she turned her attention to providing service to her community. Rudolph's public service was varied, although most has focused on working with children. Her childhood determination to learn to walk without a brace epitomized the "I can do anything" sentiment she tried to instill in the children with whom she has worked. Her athletic achievements in track helped to open the doors to other African American female athletes, including Evelyn Ashford, Jackie Joyner-Kersee, and Florence Griffith-Joyner, to name only a few examples.

Bibliography

Biracree, Tom. *Wilma Rudolph.* New York: Chelsea House, 1988. A biographical account written for juvenile readers. Biracree provides a thorough overview of Rudolph's life, detailing her ailment-plagued childhood, her precocious athletic ability, and her astonishing Olympic career.

Jacobs, Linda. *Wilma Rudolph: Run for Glory.* St. Paul, Minn.: Eric Corporation, 1975. Another work aimed at young readers, this biography does a fine job of examining Rudolph's life outside the sports arena in addition to chronicling her Olympic victories and her significance in the history of women's sports.

Lanker, Brian. *I Dream a World: Portraits of Black Women Who Changed America.* New York: Stewart, Tabori & Chang, 1989. This beautiful coffee table book, based on a photographic exhibition held at the Corcoran Gallery in Washington, D.C., contains a number of interviews with prominent African American women. Lanker provides an incisive profile of Rudolph and her lifelong commitment to excellence in sports.

Rudolph, Wilma. *The Story of Wilma Rudolph.* New York: New American Library, 1977. Rudolph's autobiography provides the most complete account of her early life and her activities after her retirement from competition in 1962. Although Rudolph's account stops at 1977, her story articulates her personal philosophy regarding the usefulness of sports as an avenue for self-improvement.

Woolum, Janet. *Outstanding Women Athletes: Who They Are and How They Influenced American Sports*. Phoenix, Ariz.: Oryx Press, 1992. A well-researched collection of sports biographies that includes a sketch on Rudolph. The author notes that public fascination with Rudolph's accomplishments helped focus attention on and provide financial support for the growth of women's track and field competitions at amateur and professional levels.

Annette Marks-Ellis

ROSEMARY RADFORD RUETHER

Born: November 2, 1936; St. Paul, Minnesota

Areas of Achievement: Religion and social reform

Contribution: Positioning herself within the Roman Catholic church, Ruether has dedicated her life to fostering dialogue between opposites for the purpose of establishing "right relationships" in which all forms of oppression (racism, sexism, neocolonialism, anti-Semitism, classism, religious bias, and ecological destructiveness) are left behind.

Early Life

On November 2, 1936, Rosemary Radford was born to Rebecca Cresap Ord Radford and Robert Armstrong Radford in St. Paul, Minnesota. Her family moved to Georgetown, Virginia, where she was steeped in family traditions. Her maternal and paternal great-grandfathers had served in the Confederate Army, and letters the two exchanged hung on the Radford family's dining room wall, framed by swords. Despite this bond, the families provided different legacies.

The Radfords were of the Southern gentry, and, though poor, they instilled in Rosemary a sense of self-confidence. They also taught other lessons. One aunt's eccentricity as a spiritualist medium was acceptable; an uncle's theatrical career was not. Rosemary's father kept the family pew at Christ Church, Georgetown, but he rarely attended services.

Rosemary's mother also provided family values, which included the value of higher education and acceptance of differences. Her mother's family explored early California, and Rebecca had grown up speaking Spanish. Rebecca was descended from an English Catholic family that, atypically, encouraged intellectual pursuits, questioned authority, and interacted with individuals from various religions.

While her father was away in World War II, Rosemary lived with her mother, two older sisters, and her mother's women friends and attended a Catholic girls' seminary. An avid reader and painter, she spent much time alone or with adults. A favorite uncle, a Jew from New York, to whom a Radford aunt was married, encouraged her efforts in art and music.

After the war, her father's engineering work moved the family to Greece. There, with friends, Rosemary started a newspaper—her first writing venture. In 1948, after her father's death, the family moved back to Washington, D.C., where Rosemary met her first academic mentor, a history teacher who discussed racism and cultivated friendships with African Americans. Later, in La Jolla, California, Rosemary entered public school, edited the "subversive" school paper, and made her speaking debut at graduation.

In 1954, Rosemary entered Scripps College in Claremont, California. Robert Palmer taught her about religion as mythic poetry and symbols. With Philip Merlan, she studied the Neoplatonists and their influence on early Christian thought. Non-

Catholics said that she was too traditional, Catholics, that she was too educated. She came to distrust dualist thinking.

When a junior, she was married to Herman J. Ruether, a graduate student in political science. They shared a penchant for getting lost in the library stacks. Her religion and philosophy degree completed in 1958, she entered Claremont Graduate School. Three children were born while Rosemary and Herman completed advanced degrees without changing routines, which indicates the cooperative nature of their marriage. One young daughter would imitate her mother by sitting with two books, attending to one, then turning pages in the other—her version of Rosemary's translation process. In 1960, Rosemary obtained her master's degree in ancient history.

Life's Work

Shortly after her twenty-fifth year, Rosemary Radford Ruether became a social activist, which she attributes to her political scientist husband and daily reading of newspapers. Her first activism involved birth control and the Catholic church. In the hospital for the birth of her third child, she decided, despite Catholic teaching, to have no more. Next to her was a poor Hispanic Catholic woman named Concepción, who was having her ninth child and pleading with doctors to help stop more from coming. The injustice moved Ruether; she published several articles on birth control and the church.

At the same time, she found her new spiritual home—St. Andrews Priory in Valyermo—a Benedictine monastery run by Belgian monks ousted from mainland China. She was provided with a "religious experience in work and prayer in community" and "an environment that would not insult [her] intellect." Here she spent time completing her dissertation and discussing events of the 1960's—the Civil Rights movement, the anti-Vietnam War protest movement, the Catholic antiwar movement, the Second Vatican Council, and the new feminism.

After completing her doctorate in classics and patristics in 1965, she spent the summer working in Mississippi, and in 1966 she joined the Historical Theology faculty at Howard University's School of Religion, involving herself in conversations on black theology. She taught, wrote, and took part in demonstrations, even being arrested.

Her first book, *The Church Against Itself* (1967), urged the Catholic church to "bring forth the context that will permit human life to become more human and social life more social," what would later emerge as her concept of the creation of "right relationships."

Numerous early works by Ruether (1967-1968) recount concerns about the misogynism of the church and the struggle for women to become fully involved in the church and in society. She expanded her theories to include colonialism and Christian anti-Semitism. She developed a wide-ranging methodology and knowledge base to pose and answer questions. At Howard, Ruether refined her ideas on dualism and her ability to glean the positive from existing traditions. The university did not, however, provide her with a supportive environment in which to examine religion's sexist practices. Ruether found such an environment at Yale Divinity School (1973-1974) and Sir George Williams University (1974). Lecturing in theology and women's studies, Ruether clarified sexism as the primary oppressor/oppressed relationship; thirteen of the next twenty books she wrote dealt directly with women and religion. *New Woman/New Earth* (1975) is considered a classic. In it, Ruether uses the first millennium B.C.E. as a backdrop against which to understand Western patriarchal culture and its dualisms: women/men, body/spirit, reason/nature, black/white, and Jew/Christian. It was the first ecofeminist book, published before the concept had a name. This work has been compared to Susan Griffin's *Woman and Nature: The Roaring Inside Her* (1978); both works were instrumental in connecting violence against women with that against nature.

As Ruether's work, including that on woman-church (the transformation of religious liturgy and symbolism to include the female experience) drew the theological community's attention, Ruether was sought out by Garrett-Evangelical Theological Seminary in Evanston, Illinois to join a faculty creating a unique learning-teaching community. She relocated in 1976, and, despite other offers, she remained through the early 1990's. Ruether continued to speak and act out her convictions and develop her theories.

From 1976 to 1981, as author, coauthor, or editor, Ruether published sixty-one books, articles, and essays; the range of her topics reflects the breadth and depth of Ruether's work, from *Mary: The Feminine Face of the Church* (1977) to *To Change the World: Christology as Cultural Criticism* (1981).

Ruether's contributions continued to be recognized. In 1982, she received her first honorary doctorates and was named U.S. Catholic of the Year by *U.S. Catholic Magazine*. She also published three major works, including her influential *Disputed Questions: On Being a Christian* (1982), and she began writing columns for the *National Catholic Reporter*, which she continued until 1992, perhaps realizing a childhood dream of being a reporter.

Ruether was always interested in global issues, and she has lectured around the world. Her works have appeared in Spanish, German, French, and Dutch, and she went as a Fulbright Scholar to Sweden in 1984. In the winter of 1987, with her husband, she taught in Israel, an experience that resulted in their only joint publication, *The Wrath of Jonah: The Crisis of Religious Nationalism in the Israeli-- Palestinian Conflict* (1989). Ruether went on to produce two more publications on Middle East peace. In the summer of 1989, Ruether traveled in southern Africa, an experience discussed in "Black Women and Feminism: The U.S. and South African Contexts" (1990). At Garrett-Evangelical, she has regularly accompanied students abroad to meet others struggling with oppression and freedom.

With all of her travels and speaking engagements—more than 750 at major universities and church conventions between 1965 and 1993—she has remained involved in her local community, as her board positions with the Chicago Center for Peace Studies and Mary's Pence, a Catholic organization helping the poor in Chicago, demonstrate.

In 1992, Ruether released *Gala and God: An Ecofeminist Theology of Earth Healing*, a book heralded as "the culmination of Rosemary Radford Ruether's life-work." The work connects Ruether's varied interests: "liberation in general, ecumenical relations, liturgy, racism, language, ethics, history, Christology, and sexism." It defines sin as any wrong relationship between humans or between humans and the rest of nature. Ruether's work and life has not, however, reached its peak; there are still relationships, the Catholic church, and the world to transform.

Summary

Some people do not live to see their ideas accepted, but Rosemary Radford Ruether is not such a person: She is a woman who lives her ideals. A thoroughly skilled historian, she has at her command the tools with which to dismantle the father's house—namely, the patriarchal Roman Catholic church—a task she does not choose to undertake. Instead, as a result of her ecumenical and intellectual values, Ruether has the strength to live in the house and remodel it—a task other feminist theologians have found uninteresting or too frustrating. In the foreword to *The Inside Stories: Thirteen Valiant Women Challenging the Church* (1987), Ruether may have been speaking of herself when she asked why women stay in such a hostile environment. Her answer is that these women have claimed the Christian identity as their own, they wish to honor their roots, and, most powerfully, these women "sense they have clout precisely by remaining as dissidents within this particular church . . . [because] . . . power . . . lies in . . . the [ability] . . . to define the meaning of the community and its mission." That Ruether has succeeded in defining the meaning of her church's community and its mission is evident. In nearly every Catholic, theological, or ecofeminist scholarly work published after 1982, Ruether can be found quoted, her wisdom admired, or her ideas merely assumed. Ruether is a woman who, upon finding the feminine face of god, invited everyone to join in re-creating the wedding dance.

Bibliography

Baum, Gregory, ed. *Journeys: The Impact of Personal Experience on Religious Thought*. New York: Paulist Press, 1975. In this collection of reflections of modern-day theologians of note, Ruether traces her own political and philosophical development, connecting both with personal biography in the chapter "Beginnings: An Intellectual Autobiography." Through family anecdotes, she provides telling insights into her social convictions and academic pursuits.

Carr, Anne E. *Transforming Grace: Christian Tradition and Women's Experience*. San Francisco: Harper & Row, 1988. Carr examines themes and issues of concern to Christian women, exploring the debate from a feminist Roman Catholic perspective. Thirteen works by Ruether are listed in the bibliography, indicative that Ruether's ideas are integrated throughout, as are those of Mary Daly and Elisabeth Schussler Fiorenza, two other prominent feminist theologians. Actual references to Ruether, however, are minimal.

Hagen, June Steffensen, ed. *Gender Matters: Women's Studies for the Christian*

Community. Grand Rapids, Mich.: Academie Books, 1990. This text grew out of an introductory women's studies course at The King's College in Briarcliff Manor, New York, bringing together a wide spectrum of faculty members who were team-taught by ten Christians who identify themselves as biblical feminists. Although Ruether's work is dealt with only in brief, the materials presented here help to place her in the larger field of feminist theology.

Ramsay, William M. *Four Modern Prophets*. Atlanta, Ga.: John Knox Press, 1986. Ramsay explores and compares how four modern-day prophets have put forth "God's demand for justice." In addition to Ruether, Walter Rauschenbusch, Martin Luther King, Jr., and Gustavo Gutierrez are discussed. The author focuses almost exclusively on Ruether's call for an end to the oppression of women within Christianity and on ways in which her call can clarify issues in the third wave of feminism.

Ruether, Rosemary Radford. "A Wise Woman." *The Christian Century* 110 (February 17, 1993): 164-165. Ruether reflects on her mother as an early spiritual mentor. She credits her with the development of what some would call mutually exclusive characteristics—a "serious spirituality," beliefs in intellectual excellence and freedom, and ecumenicism, seeking to achieve worldwide unity among religions through cooperation and understanding.

Snyder, Mary Hembrow. *The Christology of Rosemary Radford Ruether: A Critical Introduction*. Mystic, Conn.: Twenty-Third Publications, 1988. The first chapter of this college text is an overview of Ruether's life. The history uses major life events as background against which to examine the forces influencing Ruether's philosophical development, specifically her dialectical and biblical foundations. The bibliography lists all major works through 1985.

Vaughan, Judith. *Sociality, Ethics, and Social Change: A Critical Appraisal of Reinhold Niebuhr's Ethics in the Light of Rosemary Radford Ruether's Works*. Lanham, Md.: University Press of America, 1983. In this highly theoretical work, Vaughan explores the philosophical underpinnings of Niebuhr and Ruether, both of whom have written of the need for social justice and social change. Because Ruether's ethical system stresses the essential nature of social interaction in human development, Vaughan evaluates it as being superior to Niebuhr's.

Su A. Cutler

MURIEL RUKEYSER

Born: December 15, 1913; New York, New York
Died: February 12, 1980; New York, New York
Area of Achievement: Literature
Contribution: Known as something of a veteran literary "freedom fighter," Rukeyser
   helped to promote social justice in many areas and showed women how they could
   improve their lives by improving the lives of others.

Early Life
   Muriel Rukeyser was born in New York City on December 15, 1913. Her father,
Lawrence B. Rukeyser, was a successful businessman, her mother, Myra Lyons
Rukeyser, was a former bookkeeper. She grew up surrounded by skyscrapers, facto-
ries, tenements, and machinery. Muriel's spare, functional poetry was to reflect this
cold, manmade environment. She entered Vassar College in the fall of 1930, when she
was only seventeen. Her main interests were literature and music. Later, she attended
Columbia University, but did not receive a degree.
   At Vassar, she served on the *Vassar Review* and the *Vassar Miscellany News*, the
two major student publications. She also had poems published in *Poetry* and in the
New York Herald Tribune. Like many intellectuals of her generation, she developed
strong left-wing political views in college. Most of her early poetry, however, was of
a strictly personal nature, and she continued to write about personal themes throughout her life. One of her outstanding characteristics as a writer was her tendency to
project her personality into her subject matter.
   Rukeyser admired poets such as John Milton, Percy Bysshe Shelley, and Walt
Whitman who wrote with the moralistic fervor of prophets. As a child, she told her
father that she wanted to be "someone like Joan of Arc." It was her belief that poets
were inspired leaders whose mission was to encourage humankind to realize its
highest potential. She did not believe that a poet should live in an ivory tower
producing art for art's sake but should be actively involved in worthy causes. As early
as the age of nineteen, she caught typhoid fever while being held in a police station in
Alabama, where she went to attend a protest meeting during the famous Scottsboro
trial, in which eight young black men were convicted of raping two white women and
sentenced to death.
   Little is known about Rukeyser's personal life except for the information she
revealed through her poetry. She was married for a short time and had one child by a
second man whom she did not choose to marry. Her poems suggest that she was
unhappy as a child and remained so most of her life. She was always remarkably
candid about expressing her personal feelings, and the following lines from a poem
entitled "Effort at Speech Between Two People" are quite revealing:

> When I was fourteen, I had dreams of suicide,
> I stood at a steep window, at sunset, hoping toward death:

> if the light had not melted clouds and plains to beauty,
> if light had not transformed that day, I would have leapt.
> I am unhappy.   I am lonely.   Speak to me.

Life's Work

Muriel Rukeyser's life and writings were dominated by her anger at social injustice and her desire to change the world through political activism. Her career as a published poet began in 1935, when her work *Theory of Flight* was published by Yale University Press after winning the Yale Series of Younger Poets competition. For the next forty years she produced a steady steam of poetry and translated poetry from French, German, Swedish, and Italian.

Rukeyser was a Marxist-inspired activist all of her life. As such, she aroused considirable hostility from conservative critics. Even after her death, attitudes toward her writing continued to be colored by readers' political persuasions.

The following lines from "Facing Sentencing" reveal much about Rukeyser's poetry and personality:

> But fear is not to be feared
> Numbness is   To stand before my judge
> Not knowing what I mean.

The indifference to orthodox punctuation, the gap in the second line indicating a pause similar to a rest in musical scoring, and the starkly prosaic diction exemplify her modernist technique; while the thought expressed represents the attitude she exhibited all of her life. She believed that a poet should be an activist, that poetry should be a way of life rather than a vocation or an avocation.

One of the most famous incidents in Rukeyser's life occurred when she went to South Korea to protest the imprisonment of the poet Kim Chi-Ha. When she was refused admission to see the condemned prisoner, she stood outside the prison gates in silent protest to draw attention to the reactionary government's suppression of free speech. This incident was expressive of Rukeyser's belief that a poet should be a social activist. She describes her experiences in South Korea in her last published book of poetry, *The Gates* (1976).

Rukeyser remained remarkably active even after she became seriously ill with diabetes and had suffered two strokes. Her outstanding qualities were her strength of purpose and her powerful drive. She aspired to be a prophet rather than a mere poet. She admired and wrote about people who were innovators and revolutionaries. Perhaps the literary figure whom she most closely resembles is the illustrious John Milton, author of *Paradise Lost* (1667, 1674), who continued writing poetry and essays in the service of the cause he believed in even after he had gone completely blind and was in danger of being prosecuted for treason by the vindictive inquisitors of the restored monarchy.

Rukeyser was an experimentalist in poetry. She wrote elegies, odes, lyrics, documentary poems, epigrams, and dramatic monologues. She was more intelligent than most of her contemporaries and could not be beguiled or coerced into following any established political line. She was guided by her own intelligence and her own conscience. This attitude made her a loner and an individualist; she did not have any faction to support, encourage, or defend her and, as a result, has tended to be ignored while inferior poets receive undue praise.

Rukeyser was a prolific writer. Her collected poems, published in 1978, fill a book containing 538 pages. She also wrote a novel, some plays, television scripts, juvenile books, biographies, and essays; it is as a poet, however, that she will be remembered. She also taught writing and poetry appreciation at Vassar, Sarah Lawrence College, and the California Labor School. She gave countless campus and public readings all over the United States before her death in New York City, her lifelong home, on February 12, 1980.

Summary

Muriel Rukeyser was a feminist poet who worked diligently on behalf of human rights. Unlike many feminists of the generation that followed hers, she did not display conspicuous hostility toward the male sex or express resentment of woman's historical role. She encouraged women writers to seek their unique feminine identities, not only through their writing but through taking active roles in the never-ending struggle for social justice. She had a strong impact as a writer, a teacher, a scholar, and a social activist. Her life demonstrated that she concurred wholeheartedly with Milton's sentiments expressed in his essay *Areopagitica* (1644):

> I cannot praise a fugitive and cloistered virtue, unexercised and unbreathed, that never sallies out and sees her adversary, but slinks out of the race, where that immortal garland is to be run for, not without dust and heat.

Rukeyser demonstrated through her life and work that writing, in order to be of value, must be an integral part of one's total life. Throughout her life, she struggled to find herself as an individual and to express that unique individuality in her writing—especially in her poetry. She believed that women had not only the ability but also the duty to influence the course of history through their activities in every field of human endeavor.

She was regarded as a courageous fighter, even by her bitter adversaries; she inspired many other women to follow her example and continues to be regarded as an influential figure in the feminist movement. Her refusal to follow any party line or subscribe to any dogma brought her into conflict with factions on both the left and right of the political spectrum. The final decision as to her importance as a poet remains unresolved, but she is sure to be remembered as an individualist with a powerful will who followed her own conscience and encouraged others to do the same.

Bibliography
Bernikow, Louise. "Muriel at Sixty-five: Still Ahead of Her Time." *Ms.* 7 (January,

1979): 14-18. An interview published in a popular feminist magazine not long before the poet's death. Rukeyser discusses her later poems and her views on recent developments in the feminist movement.

Gardinier, Suzanne. "A World That Will Hold All People: On Muriel Rukeyser." *Kenyon Review* 14 (Summer, 1992): 88-105. An in-depth discussion of Rukeyser's poetry as reflecting her life experiences and her political beliefs. Gardinier states that Rukeyser wrote "the poetry of a believer—in an age of unbelief." Many quotations from Rukeyser's early and later poems.

Kertesz, Louise. *The Poetic Vision of Muriel Rukeyser*. Baton Rouge: Louisiana State University Press, 1980. A comprehensive book about Rukeyser that traces the progress of images and themes in her work decade by decade. Explores her traditions and contemporaries and also records the critical reception of her published works over the years. Excellent bibliography and footnotes. Illustrated with photos of Rukeyser at various stages of her life.

Rich, Adrienne. "Beginners." *Kenyon Review* 15 (Summer, 1993): 12-19. In this beautifully written essay, Rich, a prominent poet herself, discusses Walt Whitman, Emily Dickinson, and Muriel Rukeyser, calling them all "beginners . . . openers of new paths . . . who take the first steps . . . and therefore seem strange and 'dreadful.'"

Rosenthal, M. L. "Muriel Rukeyser: The Longer Poems." In *New Directions in Prose and Poetry*, No. 14, edited by James Laughlin. New York: New Directions Books, 1953. A detailed examination of Rukeyser's longer poems. Rosenthal acknowledges Rukeyser's faults, such as her occasional "muddy emotionalism," but claims they are by-products of real achievements.

Rukeyser, Muriel. *The Collected Poems*. New York: McGraw-Hill, 1978. Rukeyser compiled and edited this collection of poems herself. They are drawn from twelve previously published books and represent the best single-volume collection of her poetry available. Index of titles and first lines. Some footnotes.

——————. *The Life of Poetry*. New York: Current Books, 1949. Rukeyser's explanation of her conception of the role of the poet in society, drawing on such diverse authorities as English mathematician/philosopher Alfred North Whitehead, Austrian psychoanalyst Sigmund Freud, German philosopher Georg Hegel, and American physicist Willard Gibbs. As the title suggests, Rukeyser believed that poetry should be a way of life.

Untermeyer, Louis. "The Language of Muriel Rukeyser." *Saturday Review* (August 10, 1940): 11-13. A distinguished American author and editor discusses the early career of the young Rukeyser, identifying what is unique in her use of language and comparing her with poets Hart Crane and W. II. Auden.

Ware, Michele S. "Opening 'The Gates': Muriel Rukeyser and the Poetry of Witness." *Women's Studies* 22 (June, 1993): 297-308. An extensive analysis of *The Gates* (1976), the last volume of Rukeyser's new poetry to be published before her death. Praises her oracular characteristics and lyricism while maintaining the integrity of her political and social messages.

Bill Delaney

FLORENCE SABIN

Born: November 9, 1871; Central City, Colorado
Died: October 3, 1953; Denver, Colorado
Area of Achievement: Medicine
Contribution: A graduate of The Johns Hopkins University Medical School, Sabin actually had three careers: teacher of anatomy and histology at Johns Hopkins, researcher at the Rockefeller Institute for Medicine, and volunteer in public health in Colorado.

Early Life

Florence Sabin's father, George Sabin, had studied medicine, like his father and brothers, but he had quit medical school and left Vermont for the gold mines of Colorado. Her mother, Serena Miner Sabin was a teacher from Vermont who had come to Colorado via Georgia. Florence was the second Sabin child, born two years after her sister Mary. When Florence was six, the Sabins lost an infant son. The following year, on Florence's seventh birthday, Serena Sabin died in childbirth. Within the year the second infant son was also dead.

George Sabin's engineering duties at his mining company prevented him from being home to care for his two young daughters, so he sent them to Wolfe's Hall, a boarding school in nearby Denver. The following school year, he arranged for the two girls to live with his brother Albert near Chicago. There they lived in a warm, nurturing environment. Albert Sabin encouraged Florence to study the piano, which nurtured her lifelong love of music. When Florence was ten, Albert took the girls to visit their Sabin grandparents in Vermont. Supposedly, the girls' grandmother told Florence that it was a shame that she had not been born a boy, since she would have made a good doctor, like her grandfather and her other two uncles.

Life's Work

The direction of Florence Sabin's life changed as the result of an unkind but true remark from a classmate at the Vermont Academy, where she and Mary continued their education. Albert Sabin had bought a piano for Florence, who planned to become a concert pianist. A student, irritated at her constant practicing of scales, told her that she would never be anything but an ordinary player. Sabin wanted to excel in whatever she did. She realized that what her classmate said was true and determined to switch to her second love—science. Once she made the switch, she found that science was easier and more enjoyable for her than playing the piano had been.

After her graduation from the Academy, Sabin followed her sister Mary to Smith College, where she became a protégée of Grace Preston, the college physician and a pioneer female doctor. It was Preston who told her about the medical school planned for The Johns Hopkins University, a medical school that would include women on an equal basis. The remarkable admissions policy was a result of the work of a group of Baltimore women headed by Mary Elizabeth Garrett, heir to the Baltimore and Ohio

Railroad fortune. Garrett and her group, later known as the Women of Baltimore, would provide the $500,000 needed to open the medical school if the university would agree to require the highest standards and to admit women on the same terms as men. The university agreed, and the door was open for women to be admitted to medical school.

After being graduated from Smith, Sabin returned to Denver, where she taught at Wolfe's Hall and at Smith in order to save enough money for her first year at Johns Hopkins. In 1896, she won a fellowship to Woods Hole, Massachusetts, a training ground for biologists. There she perfected her skills with the microscope. She had enough money from the fellowship to complete her savings for her first year.

The Women of Baltimore kept an interested eye on the female medical students. Because Sabin was one of the most talented students in her class, they expected much of her, and they were not disappointed.

Sabin soon became a protégée of professor Franklin Paine Mall, a brilliant anatomist who had trained at the University of Leipzig in Germany. Mall soon identified Sabin as the one student in ten thousand who could be a researcher. Her first research project was on the lymphatics, the system of fluids that bathe each cell of the body and cleanse the blood. In 1898, it was thought that the lymphatic system was independent of the blood vessels and was connected with them through open rather than closed ends.

Sabin's work convinced her that the lymphatic system budded out of the blood vessels and continued outward in channels by a process of further budding. She was certain that the system was a closed one. Because this contradicted prevailing medical opinions, Mall asked her to recheck her work. Her conclusions remained firm.

When Sabin was in her senior year, Mall suggested that she begin a study of the infant brain. With meticulous care she mapped the brain. Her notes and drawings were published in 1901 as *An Atlas of the Medulla and Midbrain*, which was the definitive work on the subject for the next thirty years.

A medical student's training does not end with graduation from medical school. He or she must then serve an internship in a hospital. There were three openings at The Johns Hopkins Hospital that were to be filled with the three best students from each graduating class. Sabin and another graduate, Dorothy Reed, were among the top contenders for the posts, but the hospital board did not want to fill two of the three positions with women. At Reed's urging, Sabin agreed that it was both of them or neither; they were awarded the internships. It was Sabin's first public support for a feminist cause.

With her internship finished, Mall offered Sabin a position in his lab, and the Women of Baltimore provided her with a seventy-five-dollar monthly fellowship so that she could afford to take it. She continued her work on the lymphatics, had a three-dimensional model of the brain built from the drawings of her *Atlas*, and still found time to work evenings in a dispensary for working women and girls.

In 1902, Sabin became the first female professor at Johns Hopkins, where she taught anatomy. That success was followed by a banner year in 1903, when she published her research papers on lymphatics. Nearly seventeen years later, the accuracy of her work was proved in a Johns Hopkins laboratory. Her work on lymphatics resulted in her being awarded a Naples Table Fellowship worth $1,000. A group of American women sponsored this award to enable American women scientists to study at the well-known research station in Naples, Italy. The final leg of her triad of achievements in 1903 was being appointed associate professor of anatomy with tenure.

When her mentor Franklin Paine Mall died, Sabin was passed over to take his place as head of the department of anatomy because she was a woman. A former male student of hers got the job instead, and she was given a consolation prize, the less prestigious post of head of the department of histology with the rank of full professor, another first for Johns Hopkins.

Although Sabin was a feminist and had marched in woman suffrage parades, other women advised her that her work as a researcher set such an example that it did more for the cause of women than marching in parades did. Sabin reluctantly took their advice and returned to her laboratory, although she did name her car *Susan B. Anthony* after the famous suffrage leader.

Honors continued to come Sabin's way, and 1925 was another banner year. She was named the first woman president of the American Society of Anatomists, the most prestigious organization in that field. Another honor was to be the first woman elected to the National Academy of Science. Her third honor was a request to join the Rockefeller Institute for Medical Research in New York. The head of the institute, Simon Flexner, considered Sabin the most eminent of all living women scientists.

During her years at the institute, Sabin studied monocytes (white blood cells) and how they combatted the tubercle bacillus, which causes tuberculosis. Although her retirement in 1939 at age sixty-eight occurred before she had solved this research problem, her work on monocytes still stands.

Returning to Denver to spend her retirement years with her sister, Mary, Sabin soon started on another career in public health. The governor of Colorado, John Vivian, had thought he was appointing a quiet, retired token woman when he asked Sabin to chair the Health Subcommittee of his Postwar Planning Committee. The Subcommittee on Health soon became Sabin's chief concern, because Colorado had one of the highest disease rates and the worst level of sanitation in the United States. Among the state's problems were high tuberculosis rates, livestock with brucellosis, bubonic plague, high infant death rates, tainted milk, and polluted streams. Sabin was soon involved in giving public speeches and lobbying the state legislature to get important health acts passed. This was an uphill task, since most legislatures were indebted to the cattle industry, which opposed anything which might cost them money. Those who opposed Sabin's efforts in 1946 were defeated, including the governor. In the 1947 legislature, Sabin got four of her six bills passed. She began to work to convince the cattle industry that, rather than costing them money, healthy livestock would boost their profits. The strategy worked, and the other two bills also passed. Her next appointment was as chair of the Interim Board of Health and Hospitals in Denver. She was soon traveling around Denver convincing people to get chest X-rays. The tuberculosis rate was cut in half.

At the age of eighty, in 1952, Sabin retired for the second time in order to care for her sister. That year, she received the Lasker Award of the American Public Health Association and the University of Colorado dedicated the Florence Rena Sabin Building for Research in Cellular Biology. The next year, the American Association of University Women established the Florence Rena Sabin Fellowship to honor exceptional work in the field of public health. Nearly one month before her eighty-second birthday, Florence Sabin died at home of a heart attack. A statue of her is one of two representing Colorado in Statuary Hall in Washington, D.C.

Summary

Florence Sabin strove all of her life for excellence in whatever she did. She was a meticulous researcher who set high standards for herself and others. She followed her mentor's method of teaching, which was to allow her students to solve their own research problems while she acted as a resource. She also followed Mall in giving students credit for what they had discovered. This included allowing them first place of authorship on any joint projects. Her research work on the brain, the lymphatics, and monocytes benefited generations of medical students and the patients for whom they cared. Her life as a researcher-teacher was outstanding, and she rightly received many honors for her achievements. When one considers the impact she had on the lives of the citizens of Colorado in her retirement years, it is evident that Sabin was one of the most outstanding scientists of her time, a truly outstanding example of what a woman can achieve in science.

Bibliography

Bluemel, Elinor. *Florence Sabin: Colorado Woman of the Century.* Boulder: University of Colorado Press, 1959. A biography that concentrates on Sabin the woman more than Sabin the scientist. Draws heavily from Sabin's correspondence as well as reminiscences from her sister Mary and others.

Haber, Louis. *Women Pioneers of Science.* New York: Harcourt Brace Jovanovich, 1979. Chapter 3 is on Sabin, and although it is only ten pages long, it does provide a good summary of her life. A portrait and a bibliography are included.

Kronstadt, Janet. *Florence Sabin.* New York: Chelsea House, 1990. An excellent basic summary of Sabin's life and work. Includes many excellent illustrations and pictures not found in other works.

Phelan, Mary Kay. *The Story of Dr. Florence Sabin: Probing the Unknown.* New York: Thomas Y. Crowell, 1969. Excellent on establishing historical background, such as the role of women at Johns Hopkins; some treatment of Sabin as a feminist.

Rossiter, Margaret W. *Women Scientists in America: Struggles and Strategies to 1940.* Baltimore: The Johns Hopkins University Press, 1982. A general history that helps to place Sabin in historical context.

Anne Kearney

SACAGAWEA

Born: c. 1788; central Idaho
Died: December 20, 1812; Fort Manuel, Dakota Territory
Area of Achievement: Exploration
Contribution: The only woman who accompanied the Lewis and Clark Expedition in exploring much of the territory acquired through the Louisiana Purchase, Sacagawea assisted as guide and interpreter.

Early Life

Sacagawea (also Sagagawea, Sakakawea) was born into a band of Northern Shoshone Indians, whose base was the Lemhi Valley of central Idaho. Her name translates as "Bird Woman" (Hidatsa) or "Boat Pusher" (Shoshonean). The Northern Shoshone, sometimes referred to as Snake Indians (a name given them by the French because of the use of painted snakes on sticks to frighten their enemies), were a wandering people, living by hunting, gathering, and fishing. As a child, Sacagawea traveled through the mountains and valleys of Idaho, northwest Wyoming, and western Montana. In 1800, at about age twelve, Sacagawea and her kin were encamped during a hunting foray at the Three Forks of the Missouri (between modern Butte and Bozeman, Montana) when they were attacked by a war party of Hidatsas (also called Minnetarees), a Siouan tribe; about ten Shoshone were killed and Sacagawea and several other children were made captives. Sacagawea was taken to reside with the Hidatsas at the village of Metaharta near the junction of the Knife and Missouri Rivers (in modern North Dakota).

Shortly after her capture, Sacagawea was sold as a wife to fur trader Toussaint Charbonneau. A French-Canadian who had developed skills as an interpreter, Charbonneau had been living with the Hidatsas for five years. At the time that Sacagawea became his squaw, Charbonneau had one or two other Indian wives.

All that is known of Sacagawea for certain is found in the journals and letters of Meriwether Lewis, William Clark, and several other participants in the expedition of the Corps of Discovery, 1804-1806, along with meager references in other sources. The Lewis and Clark party, commissioned by President Thomas Jefferson to find a route to the Pacific and to make scientific observations along the way, traveled on the first leg of their journey up the Missouri River to the mouth of the Knife River, near which they established Fort Mandan (near modern Bismarck, North Dakota) as their winter headquarters. The site was in the vicinity of Mandan and Hidasta villages. Here the expedition's leaders made preparations for the next leg of their journey and collected information on the Indians and topography of the far West.

Life's Work

Sacagawea's association with the Lewis and Clark Expedition began on November 4, 1804, when she accompanied her husband to Fort Mandan. She presented the officers with four buffalo robes. Charbonneau was willing to serve as interpreter, but only on condition that Sacagawea be permitted to go along on the journey. After agreeing to those terms, Lewis and Clark hired Charbonneau. At Fort Mandan on February 11, 1805, Sacagawea gave birth to Jean-Baptiste Charbonneau. Thus, along with the some thirty men, the "squaw woman" and baby became members of the exploring group.

The Lewis and Clark Expedition set out from Fort Mandan on April 7, 1805. Charbonneau and Sacagawea at different times were referred to in the journals as "interpreter and interpretess." Sacagawea's knowledge of Hidatsa and Shoshonean proved of great aid in communicating with the two tribes with which the expedition primarily had contact. Later, when the expedition made contact with Pacific Coast Indians, Sacagawea managed to assist in communicating with those peoples even though she did not speak their language. Her services as a guide were helpful only when the expedition sought out Shoshone Indians in the region of the Continental Divide in order to find direction and assistance in leaving the mountains westward. Carrying her baby on her back in cord netting, Sacagawea stayed with one or several of the main groups of explorers, never venturing out scouting on her own. Little Baptiste enlivened the camp circles, and Clark, unlike Lewis, became very fond of both baby and mother.

Several times on the westward journey Sacagawea was seriously ill, and once she and Baptiste were nearly swept away in a flash flood. In May of 1805, Sacagawea demonstrated her resourcefulness by retrieving many valuable articles that had washed out of a canoe during a rainstorm. Lewis and Clark named a stream "Sâh-câ-ger we-âh (*Sah ca gah we a*) or bird woman's River," which at a later time was renamed Crooked Creek. Not the least of Sacagawea's contributions was finding sustenance in the forests, identifying flora that Indians considered edible. She helped to gather berries, wild onions, beans, artichokes, and roots. She cooked and mended clothes.

Reaching the Three Forks of the Missouri, Sacagawea recognized landmarks and rightly conjectured where the Shoshone might be during the hunting season. A band of these Indians was found along the Lemhi River. Sacagawea began "to dance and show every mark of the most extravagant joy . . . sucking her fingers at the same time to indicate that they were of her native tribe." The tribe's leader, Cameahwait, turned out to be Sacagawea's brother (or possibly cousin). Lewis and Clark established a cordial relationship with Sacagawea's kinsmen, and were able to obtain twenty-nine horses and an Indian guide through the rest of the mountains. Coming down from the mountains, the exploring party made dugout canoes at the forks of the Clearwater River, and then followed an all-water route along that stream, the Snake River, and the Columbia River to the Pacific Coast. At the mouth of the Columbia River, just below present Astoria, Oregon, the adventurers built Fort Clatsop, where they spent the winter. Sacagawea was an important asset as the expedition covered the final phase of the journey. "The wife of Shabono our interpreter," wrote William Clark on October 13, 1805, "reconsiles all the Indians, as to our friendly intentions a woman with a party of men is a token of peace."

Besides her recognition of topography that aided in finding the Shoshones, Sacagawea's other contribution as guide occurred on the return trip. During the crossing of the eastern Rockies by Clark's party (Lewis took a more northerly route), Sacagawea showed the way from Three Forks through the mountains by way of the Bozeman Pass to the Yellowstone River. Lewis and Clark reunited near the junction of the Missouri and the Yellowstone. Sacagawea, Charbonneau, and infant Baptiste accompanied the expedition down the Missouri River only as far as the Hidatsa villages at the mouth of the Knife River. On April 17, 1806, they "took leave" of the exploring group. Clark offered to take Sacagawea's baby, whom Clark called "Pomp," with him to St. Louis to be reared and educated as his adopted son. Sacagawea, who consented to the proposal, insisted that the infant, then nineteen months old, be weaned first.

With the conclusion of the Lewis and Clark Expedition, details about Sacagawea's life become very sketchy. In the fall of 1809, the Charbonneau family visited St. Louis. Charbonneau purchased a small farm on the Missouri River just north of St. Louis from Clark, who had been named Indian superintendent for the Louisiana Territory. In 1811, Charbonneau sold back the tract to Clark. Sacagawea yearned to return to her homeland. Charbonneau enlisted in a fur trading expedition conducted by Manuel Lisa. In April of 1811, Sacagawea and Charbonneau headed up river in one of Lisa's boats. One observer on board at the time commented that Sacagawea appeared sickly.

Sacagawea left Jean Baptiste Charbonneau with Clark in St. Louis. On August 11, 1813, an orphan's court appointed Clark as the child's guardian. Sacagawea's son went on to have a far-ranging career. At age eighteen, he joined a western tour of the young Prince Paul Wilhelm of Württemberg, and afterward went to Europe, where he resided with the prince for six years. The two men returned to America in 1829, and again explored the western country. Jean Baptiste thereafter was employed as a fur trapper for fifteen years by the American Fur Company. He later served as an army guide during the Mexican War. Joining the gold rush of 1849, Jean Baptiste set up residence in Placer County, California. Traveling through Montana in May of 1866, he died of pneumonia.

There has been a lively controversy over the correct determination of the date and place of Sacagawea's death. Grace Raymond Hebard, a professor at the University of Wyoming, published the biography *Sacajawea* in 1933, in which she went to great lengths to prove that Sacagawea died April 9, 1884. Hebard traced the alleged wanderings of the "Bird Woman" to the time that she settled down on the Wind River Reservation in Wyoming. Hebard made a substantial case, based on oral testimony of persons who had known the "Bird Woman"; the hearsay related to known details of the Lewis and Clark expedition. Hebard also relied upon ethnological authorities. At the heart of the controversy is a journal entry of John Luttig, resident fur company clerk at Fort Manuel. On December 20, 1812, he recorded: "this Evening the Wife of Charbonneau, a Snake Squaw died of a putrid fever she was a good and the best Women in the fort, aged abt 25 years she left an infant girl." It is known that

Sacagawea had given birth to a daughter, Lizette. The Luttig journal was not published until 1920. Hebard claimed that the death notice referred to Charbonneau's other Shoshone wife, Otter Woman. The issue, however, seems put to rest by the discovery in 1955 of a document in William Clark's journal dated to the years 1825 to 1828. Clark's list of the status of members of his expedition states: "Se car ja we au Dead." Nevertheless, the notion that Sacagawea lived until the 1880's continues to have support.

Summary

Sacagawea had a fourfold impact on the Lewis and Clark Expedition. Though she viewed much of the country the group traversed for the first time, her geographical knowledge was most important in locating the Shoshones in the Rocky Mountains and directing Clark's party through the Bozeman Pass. At crucial instances her services as a translator were essential, and she served as a contact agent. Perhaps, most of all, as an Indian mother with a young baby, she dispelled many of the fears of the Indians encountered on the journey, particularly the fear that the expedition might harm them. She may be credited as a primary factor in ensuring the success of the Lewis and Clark expedition. Sacagawea also contributed to the uplifting of morale. Throughout the venture she exhibited courage, resourcefulness, coolness, and congeniality. The presence of mother and baby encouraged a certain civilized restraint among the members of the party. Henry Brackenridge, who met Sacagawea in April of 1811, said that she was "a good creature, of a mild and gentle disposition." Clark expressed regrets at the end of the expedition that no special reward could be given to Sacagawea. In many ways she was more valuable to the expedition than her husband, who ultimately received compensation for their efforts.

Sacagawea's place in history was long neglected. Interest in her life, however, gained momentum with the centenary celebrations of the Lewis and Clark Expedition in the early 1900's and especially with the rise of the suffrage movement, which saw in Sacagawea a person of womanly virtues and independence. Eva Emery Dye's novel, *The Conquest: The True Story of Lewis and Clark* (1902), did much during the course of its ten editions to popularize an exaggerated role of Sacagawea on the famous journey of discovery.

Bibliography

Anderson, Irving. "A Charbonneau Family Portrait." *American West* 17 (Spring, 1980): 4-13, 58-64. Written for a popular audience, this article provides a thorough and reliable account of the lives of Sacagawea, her husband Toussaint, and her son Jean-Baptiste.

——————. "Probing the Riddle of the Bird Woman." *Montana: The Magazine of Western History* 23 (October, 1973): 2-17. A scholarly article that persuasively disputes the evidence gathered by Grace Hebard to argue that Sacagawea lived to be nearly one hundred years old.

Chuinard, E. G. "The Actual Role of the Bird Woman." *Montana: The Magazine of*

Western History 26 (Summer, 1976): 18-29. Emphasizes the role of Sacagawea as a guide and contact agent and challenges the exaggeration of her actual accomplishments.

Clark, Ella E., and Margot Edmonds. *Sacagawea of the Lewis and Clark Expedition.* Berkeley: University of California Press, 1979. Includes discussion of Sacagawea's life and the efforts made to popularize her legend. Although they provide a relatively accurate account, the authors choose to accept the discredited theory that Sacagawea lived until 1884.

Howard, Harold P. *Sacajawea.* Norman: University of Oklahoma Press, 1971. A balanced biography aimed at a general audience, this work attempts to sort out fact from legend in the life of Sacagawea.

Jackson, Donald, ed. *Letters of the Lewis and Clark Expedition, with Related Documents, 1783-1854.* 2d ed. 2 vols. Urbana: University of Illinois Press, 1978. Contains a variety of letters, journal entries, and other papers relevant to the activities of the expedition. Sheds some light on the contribution of the Charbonneau family.

Ronda, James P. *Lewis and Clark Among the Indians.* Lincoln: University of Nebraska Press, 1984. This scholarly study examines the contact made between the Lewis and Clark expedition and the Indians. Provides insights into Sacagawea's contributions to the success of the expedition. Includes an appendix that evaluates various books and articles about Sacagawea.

Harry M. Ward

RUTH ST. DENIS

Born: January 20, 1879; Somerville, New Jersey
Died: July 21, 1968; Hollywood, California
Area of Achievement: Dance
Contribution: One of the pioneers of American modern dance, St. Denis helped to popularize the art form in its infancy with exotic and lavish productions based on Asian and religious themes.

Early Life

Ruth Dennis was born to Ruth Emma Hull Dennis and Thomas Dennis on January 20, 1879, while they were residents of the Eagleswood artists' and intellectuals' commune near Newark, New Jersey. Thomas Dennis was a British inventor and machinist, an alcoholic whose effect on the family was negligible. Ruth Emma Hull Dennis was a determined and resourceful woman who was instrumental in shaping the patterns and direction of her daughter's life.

A practicing physician until a mental breakdown ended her career, Ruth Hull Dennis was an advocate for the women's health and hygiene reform movements that swept the country in the late 1800's. Determined that her daughter would not suffer from the same conditions that afflicted many of the young women of her generation, she reared young Ruth in accordance with the precepts of the dress reformers and proponents of physical culture. She taught her daughter the exercise system of François Delsarte, as popularized by Genevieve Stebbins, a New York Delsartean and author of exercise manuals.

Delsarte's system, while incorporating physical exercises and body postures, also claimed a spiritual philosophy—each part of the body had its counterpart zone: the head corresponded to "mind," the heart to "soul," and the limbs to "life." Beyond its attraction as a method of simultaneously improving one's physical and spiritual conditions, the Delsarte system appealed to the elder Dennis as a connection between her commitment to health reform and her religious ideals. Young Ruthie grew up on a diet of wholesome food, plain, loose clothing, religious tracts, and "aesthetic gymnastics."

Pivotal experiences during her childhood were seeing the theatrical spectacle *Nero and the Destruction of Rome* (P. T. Barnum's circus extravaganza) in 1886, reading Mabel Cook's Theosophist allegory *The Idyll of the White Lotus,* and attending a Delsarte performance given by Genevieve Stebbins in the 1890's. These experiences, combined with having seen *Egypt Through the Centuries* at the Palisades Amusement Park when she was thirteen, convinced Ruthie Dennis that she would be an actress/dancer. Theatrical spectacle, self-expression, spiritual themes, and the lure of exotic Asian cultures were the ingredients that she would later embody in her dancing. Undaunted by her lack of training, blessed with natural grace and athleticism, and beset by financial difficulties at home, Ruth, with her mother, set off to conquer vaudeville.

Life's Work

Ruth St. Denis' first job was "skirt dancing" for twenty dollars a week at Worth's "dime" Museum. She soon advanced to playing small vaudeville houses, but she quit in 1893 for a job as a cloak model in order to support her family. Her desire to perform was not extinguished, however, and after doing specialty spots in musical comedies such as *The Ballet Girl* and *The Runaway Girl*, in 1899 she landed a job with the famous impresario David Belasco, in his production of *Zaza*.

In the six years that she spent touring with Belasco's company, St. Denis (her stage name) discovered the powers of a lavish and large-scale dramatic fusion of design, movement, and expression. It is Belasco who is credited with popularizing her name, and his European tour of 1900 brought St. Denis in contact with Isadora Duncan and Loie Fuller. Under Belasco's tutelage, St. Denis learned stagecraft, acting, and other skills: how to construct a physical basis for dramatic action, how nuances in timing affect an audience, and how to connect sound, color, movement, and theme into a unified dramatic production.

St. Denis was also influenced by the writings of Mary Baker Eddy. Ever her mother's daughter, she wanted her work in the theater to be spiritually uplifting and self-expressive, as well as profitable. On tour in Buffalo, New York, in 1904, Ruth saw a poster for Egyptian Deities cigarettes, which changed the course of her life. Fascinated by the exotic and remote Isis of the poster, Ruth left Belasco's company when the tour ended, and began to compose her first dance/drama, *Egypta*.

To raise money for the grandiose concept of *Egypta*, St. Denis began to create short, exotic dance solos that could be performed in vaudeville houses. In 1905, *Radha* was born, the first of many dances that combined Oriental themes, Delsarte poses, skirt dancing, sensuous costumes, and a flair for the dramatic. For St. Denis, *Radha* was "a jumble of everything I was aware of in Indian art." Her information came from library books, Coney Island Hindus, photographs, sideshows, and her mother's religious tracts.

Radha received its formal public premiere at the New York Theater, New York, on January 28, 1906. The reviews were unequivocal: *Radha* and St. Denis' accompanying dance dramas *Incense* and *The Cobras* were sensational. Her career as a solo dancer was launched.

Seeking to widen her audience, St. Denis began a three-year European tour, beginning in London in 1906. By 1908, an enthusiasm for solo dancers was at its peak: St. Denis and her contemporaries Isadora Duncan, Loie Fuller, and Maud Allan were all performing to full houses in Europe. All four were shaped by an American aesthetic of self-expression, liberation, and unconventional beliefs. While they shared a conviction that movement could be expressive, they also embodied unique approaches to the art they were creating. Of the four, St. Denis was the least affected by European culture. By the summer of 1909, she had achieved her goals; now a glamorous dancer with Europe's stamp of approval, she returned home, famous and fashionable.

St. Denis was a rarity in American theater: A "class act" in vaudeville and a box-office bonanza in "legitimate" theater, she bridged the public conceptions of high and low art. More than any other American dancer, St. Denis popularized the new art of modern dance (then called aesthetic, barefoot, or interpretive dancing) and made it accessible to American audiences during her cross-country tours of 1909 through 1912.

By 1914, solo dances were no longer fashionable. Partner dancing, as exemplified by Vernon Castle and Irene Castle, was the vogue. As her audience eroded, St. Denis sought to include partner dancing in her act. What she got was more than she bargained for: a partnership with Ted Shawn that was to last decades.

Shawn, twelve years her junior, had seen St. Denis perform in Denver when he was a divinity student at the University of Denver. Her performance captivated him and began to connect for him his unfulfilled yearnings toward the arts, religion, self-expression, and the body. Their rapport was instant and mutual: A few months after meeting, Shawn and St. Denis were married at the Aeolian Hall in New York City, on August 13, 1914.

Marriage to Shawn provided St. Denis with new venues and new audiences. In the spring of 1915, they opened "Denishawn," a utopian school of dance on an idyllic Los Angeles estate. The curriculum included technique classes taught by Ted, inspirational lectures on religion, history, and philosophy by "Miss Ruth," and an emphasis on fresh air, unhampered bodies, and healthful living. Students performed choreography by St. Denis and Shawn in annual pageants and concerts. Hollywood studios sent their actors and actresses to Denishawn; students from all over the country flocked to the school.

Most important, Denishawn became the training ground for the next generation of American dancers. Martha Graham, Doris Humphrey, Charles Weidman, and others studied at the school and performed with the company. Although they ultimately rebelled against their mentors, each took from Denishawn the belief in the validity of dance as a legitimate art form.

The Denishawn partnership was turbulent. St. Denis felt trapped by the demands of the institution and deeply divided in her role as wife. Terrified by sexual intimacy and the possibility of becoming pregnant, possessive of her public reputation and star billing, and worn down by the constant touring needed to support the school financially, St. Denis grew increasingly unhappy. Annoyed by his second billing on the program and lack of recognition for his work, Shawn became discontented and was increasingly attracted to men. Yet no matter how destructive their personal life, they upheld the public image of a devoted couple.

The 1930's brought the dissolution of the Denishawn enterprise. St. Denis had never completely shared Shawn's vision for a Greater Denishawn, with branch schools and multiple companies; she wanted to concentrate on her art, to create dances that were expressive of the divine. In 1934, when the Denishawn House mortgage was foreclosed, St. Denis moved into a tiny loft offered by a friend, and Shawn retreated to Massachusetts, where he had formed an all-male troupe of dancers.

Shortly before the end of Denishawn, St. Denis founded a Society of Spiritual Arts, a discussion group that included poets, artists, dancers, and religious leaders. In 1934,

St. Denis presented her first "Rhythmic Choir," a liturgical dance pageant called *Masque of Mary*. St. Denis portrayed the Madonna, and scenes were acted out through mime and plastique by a small group of dancers. With these works, St. Denis felt that she was uniting the dance and her spiritual life.

In 1939, her autobiography *Ruth St. Denis: An Unfinished Life* elevated her to a new status, dancer emeritus, the "First Lady of American Dance." Titular head of a new dance program at Adelphi College, St. Denis received a second career boost when she joined Shawn at his Jacob's Pillow dance school in the summer of 1941 to perform revivals of her early solos. Although she moved to California in 1942, she continued her association with Adelphi and occasionally rejoined Shawn in fund-raising concerts. They celebrated their golden wedding anniversary together at Jacob's Pillow in 1964 amid great publicity and public adoration.

Ruth St. Denis spent the last years of her life in California, performing and lecturing on dance. The recipient of many awards attesting her accomplishments in dance, including the Capezio Award (1960), Dance Teachers of America (1964), and the *Harper's Bazaar* list of "100 Women of Accomplishment," St. Denis died on July 21, 1968, after suffering a heart attack.

Summary

Ruth St. Denis lived to see the art she pioneered flourish and diversify. The emergency of American modern dance at the beginning of the twentieth century would not have been possible without the trailblazing determination, creativity, and courage of St. Denis and her contemporaries, Loie Fuller and Isadora Duncan. Of the three, it was St. Denis who established an American audience for modern dance and made dance both legitimate and popular.

A lifelong feminist, St. Denis reflected her mother's social reform ideals and spiritual questing, and combined them with a "new American woman's" independence, physicality, and brashness. A charismatic performer, St. Denis inspired countless young women and men to seek dancing as a career. St. Denis and the Denishawn touring companies brought dance to thousands of Americans, who developed a respect and admiration for this new art form, while the Denishawn schools nurtured the next generation of dance pioneers.

Bibliography

Brown, Jean Morrison, ed. *The Vision of Modern Dance*. Princeton, N.J.: Princeton Book, 1979. A collection of essays by leading figures in modern dance, including "The Dance as Life Experience" by Ruth St. Denis. St. Denis' philosophy of the dance as a spiritual communication is evident; Brown's book contextualizes St. Denis' accomplishments.

Kendall, Elizabeth. *Where She Danced*. New York: Alfred A. Knopf, 1979. An exploration of the pioneers of modern dance with a special emphasis on the life and career of St. Denis. It offers important insights into the social, political, and artistic climate that existed in the United States when St. Denis forged her art.

Mazo, Joseph. *Prime Movers: The Makers of Modern Dance in America*. Princeton, N.J.: Princeton Book, 1977. An entertaining history of modern dance and its founders. Mazo's chapter on St. Denis, "Salvation Through Spectacle," discusses St. Denis' choreography, influences, and impact. Several photographs convey the glamour and charisma of St. Denis, while the text incorporates reviews, social history, and analysis of her contributions.

St. Denis, Ruth. *Ruth St. Denis: An Unfinished Life*. New York: Harper & Brothers, 1939. St. Denis' autobiography details her life from childhood through her fifties. Often self-aggrandizing, the book offers insights into how St. Denis perceived her art, and the spiritual connection she constantly sought between her art and life.

Shelton, Suzanne. *Divine Dancer: A Biography of Ruth St. Denis*. Garden City, N.Y.: Doubleday, 1981. This thorough biography of St. Denis as person, artist, and woman focuses on the influences that shaped her beliefs, the connections between her personal life and her stage persona, and her accomplishments. Includes photographs and an extensive listing of additional source materials.

Sherman, Jane. *Soaring: The Diary and Letters of a Denishawn Dancer in the Far East, 1925-1926*. Middletown, Conn.: Wesleyan University Press, 1976. A personal, behind-the-scenes look at the Denishawn era by a young dancer in the company. Her perspective on "Miss Ruth" is critical and reverential; the book gives the reader a clear sense of what it was like to be a Denishawn dancer in the 1920's.

Cynthia J. Williams

MARI SANDOZ

Born: May 11, 1896; Sheridan County, Nebraska
Died: March 10, 1966; New York, New York
Areas of Achievement: Historiography and literature
Contribution: A western regional historian and novelist, Sandoz wrote extensively on frontier family life, white settlement, and American Indian resistance to white encroachment on the Central and Northern Great Plains.

Early Life

Mari Sandoz was born Marie Susette Sandoz on May 11, 1896, on a homestead in northwestern Nebraska, a violent frontier region. Her father, Jules Ami Sandoz, who was French-Swiss, emigrated to the United States in 1881. Divorced three times, Jules Sandoz married a German-Swiss immigrant, Mary Elizabeth Fehr, in 1895. She remained with him until he died. Mari, called Marie in childhood, was the eldest of their six children.

The family homesteaded marginal land in an inhospitable climate, enduring over-work, poverty, isolation, and repeated physical violence from Jules Sandoz. Jules helped newcomers and enjoyed local feuds, politics, storytelling, hunting, and trapping. Mary did the outside work, and Mari resentfully watched the babies. One of Jules's beatings left Mari physically scarred for life; she also lost sight in one eye after becoming snowblind rounding up the family's cattle.

Mari started school at nine, speaking her mother's Swiss German and some "hybrid English." She soon began writing short stories. When one was published in an Omaha paper, Jules, who considered writers the "maggots of society," locked her in the cellar as punishment. Although her schooling was interrupted often, she had a rich education, learning from the mercurial but brilliant Jules; from the storytelling of visiting Indians, trappers, traders, and settlers; and from her voracious reading.

In 1913, at sixteen, Mari completed eighth grade and passed the examination for country school teaching. She taught intermittently from 1913 until about 1925. In 1914, she married Wray Macumber, supporting him on her teacher's salary. Mari divorced Macumber in 1919, complaining of his violent temper and constant verbal abuse. The divorce strained relations with her mother, who opposed divorce; Mari, representing a new generation of women, resolved to resist abuse and lead an independent life.

Mari moved to Lincoln, Nebraska's capital, in 1919. In 1922, lacking a high school diploma, she entered the University of Nebraska and took classes in education, history, and literature until 1933, but earned no degree. She supported herself with low-paying jobs; one at the Nebraska State Historical Society enabled her to do personal research.

Writing short stories as Marie Macumber until 1929, Sandoz was encouraged by the faculty and by a women's writing group. She had many short works published but had no major successes. In 1933, Mari burned her rejected stories, "gave up writing permanently and sneaked back to the sandhills." Within weeks, she was writing again, revising the manuscript that would be her breakthrough. Jules Sandoz had died in 1928. On his deathbed, he had asked Mari to "write of his struggles" as a pioneer; she had started immediately. In 1935, after fourteen rejections, she submitted *Old Jules* to the Atlantic Press Non-Fiction Contest and won.

Life's Work

The Atlantic Prize brought $5,000 plus publication; the selection of *Old Jules* by the Book-of-the-Month Club brought another $5,000, freeing Mari Sandoz to write full time. Except for teaching in writing workshops, including one at the University of Wisconsin for nine summers between 1947 and 1956, Sandoz supported herself by her writing until her death.

Old Jules was the first book in what Mari Sandoz envisioned as a historical series on the Great Plains, which eventually included *Old Jules*, *Crazy Horse* (1942), *Cheyenne Autumn* (1953), *The Buffalo Hunters* (1954), *The Cattlemen* (1958), and *The Beaver Men* (1964). *Old Jules* told of both Jules Sandoz and the turbulent settlement period of northwestern Nebraska, blending fictional and historical techniques into the terse, vivid narrative that characterized Sandoz's style. It was published to widespread critical acclaim, after Sandoz had had heated arguments with her editors over her concepts of her work; the authenticity of her information; and her colloquialisms, rhythms, and anti-eastern bias. Similar disagreements occurred regarding subsequent books.

Old Jules was followed by *Slogum House* in 1937. A grim novel of Gulla Slogum and her ruthless quest for power, it was an allegory of the Fascist dictators. A second allegorical novel, *Capital City* (1939), portrays a fictional midwestern capital dominated by parasitical upper classes and antilabor Fascists. Both books received mixed reviews and provoked hostility from Nebraskans, who believed that the books' unflattering characters and events were real. In 1940, Sandoz moved to Denver, largely to gain access to research collections, but also to obtain relief from debilitating migraine headaches and Lincoln's continuing hostility.

Mari's major achievement in Denver was the biography *Crazy Horse*, which was published in 1942, after editorial battles over issues ranging from accuracy to Indian rhythms in her writing. Her interest in the Sioux warrior began in childhood with Indian storytellers who told her that the young Crazy Horse had seen a burial ceremony on the Sandoz homestead. Sandoz studied the northern Sioux and Cheyenne during the 1920's and 1930's, using numerous archival collections, interviewing old Indians, and traveling the Crazy Horse country. *Crazy Horse* is one of her best works, a sympathetic portrait of a selfless leader betrayed by enemies among his own people as well as by whites.

In 1943, Mari Sandoz moved to New York City to be near her publishers and eastern archival resources. An established writer, she now was sought by editors and received numerous awards, including an honorary doctorate from the University of Nebraska in 1950. Completely focused on her writing and a loner by nature, Sandoz nevertheless had a vigorous social conscience. She was alarmed by the Fascist dictators Benito Mussolini and Adolf Hitler and supported Allied opposition to them. She used her writing to fight Fascist traits she perceived at home: the power of greedy, repressive eastern interests; intolerance of ethnic and labor groups; and, later, McCarthyism. These issues had appeared in *Slogum House* and *Capital City*; she repeated them in a third allegorical novel, *The Tom Walker* (1947). Sandoz also sharply criticized the government's American Indian policies, current and historical, and supported several Indian organizations.

The Tom Walker was Mari's only major publication between 1942 and 1951, a period of intensive research. In 1953 *Cheyenne Autumn* was published. A biography of the leaders Dull Knife and Little Wolf, it follows their small band of Cheyennes in an 1878 escape from Oklahoma Indian Territory to their homelands in the Yellowstone area. Sandoz had researched the book for decades; in 1949, she traveled from Oklahoma north along the Cheyenne route, and walked most of the battlefields. Although it is demanding for readers unfamiliar with its events, *Cheyenne Autumn* remains one of Sandoz's greatest achievements. Mari disavowed the 1964 film version as libelous.

Sandoz wrote four more Indian books. *The Horsecatcher* (1957) and *The Story Catcher* (1963), designed for young audiences, tell of two boys, a Cheyenne who tamed wild ponies and a Sioux who became his people's historian. *These Were the Sioux* (1961) is a sketch of the Indians Mari had known from her childhood. Partly reminiscence, it praises Sioux values and suggests that Sandoz's Sioux neighbors showed more affection for her than her parents did. *The Battle of the Little Bighorn* (1966) focuses on whites as well as Indians, arguing that Custer's presidential ambitions led him to the Little Bighorn in search of a quick and popular victory. Short and gracefully written, these four books were all highly praised, although the Custer story generated controversy regarding Mari's sources, techniques, and interpretations.

In 1954, Sandoz had her first encounter with cancer and had a mastectomy. That year saw the publication of *The Buffalo Hunters*, which told the story of the slaughter of the great bison herds. *The Cattlemen* (1958), a history of the cattle industry, and *The Beaver Men* (1964), the history of the fur trade, completed the plains series. Rich in detail but somewhat unfocused, all received mixed reviews. *Winter Thunder* also appeared in 1954. This popular novelette told the story of a young schoolteacher and her students who survived a blizzard after their school bus overturned. *Miss Morissa*, a novel about a woman doctor in western Nebraska during the gold rush days of the 1870's, was published in 1955. Problematic as fiction, the book is interesting because of its historical setting and the woman doctor whose unhappy marriage resembles Sandoz's own.

In 1959, Sandoz made a series for Nebraska Educational Television, explaining her visions of creative writing and of the West. *Hostiles and Friendlies* was published that year. A collection of early pieces, it includes an autobiographical sketch; Mari's first significant story, "The Vine"; and a tribute to her mother, "Marlizzie." *Son of the Gamblin' Man*, a critical failure, appeared in 1960. A biography of the boyhood of the artist Robert Henri, it is interesting as a portrait of frontier Nebraska and because the affection between Henri and his violent and visionary father suggests the relationship Mari had wanted with Jules. Sandoz's next publication was *Love Song to the Plains* (1961). A collection of new essays on plains life and personalities, it was warmly praised for its lyrical writing and diverse subjects.

In 1964, Mari's cancer reappeared. After recovering from a second mastectomy, Sandoz discovered that she had bone cancer. Although weakening rapidly, she edited *Old Jules Country* (1965), an anthology of earlier pieces, and finished the Little Bighorn book, which was published posthumously, as were *The Christmas of the Phonograph Records* (1966), a short nostalgic memoir, and *Sandhill Sundays* (1970), another collection. Mari Sandoz died on March 10, 1966. She was buried on the family ranch in Nebraska's sandhills.

Summary

Mari Sandoz's stature rests largely on her nonfiction, particularly *Old Jules*, *Crazy Horse*, *Cheyenne Autumn*, *Love Song to the Plains*, and *The Battle of the Little Bighorn*. Although it reflects many traditional western themes, such as heroic masculine individualism, Sandoz's work foreshadows interpretations of the new Western history. It transcends Eurocentrism, presenting the importance of Indians and diverse ethnic groups with sympathy and understanding. Sandoz emphasizes postfrontier issues in her fiction, carrying the West into the twentieth century. Other contemporary concerns include community violence; the calamitous human and environmental consequences of the conquest of the West; recurring disputes over land use and ownership; and the central role of families in western settlement.

Sandoz was a meticulous researcher with unique sources of information, particularly her interviews with old Indians and settlers and some archival material that has since been lost. Her historical writing, however, contains problems. Historians criticize her frequent use of "invented" scenes and dialogue. Researchers are unhappy with her infrequent footnotes and generally spartan bibliographies.

Sandoz has an important place as a woman in western historical writing. Admittedly "not much of a feminist," she did not consciously write from a feminist perspective. Yet she unself-consciously succeeded in the then male-dominated field of western history. Her pivotal book, *Old Jules*, portrays not only a visionary but also a brutal patriarch and violent abuser. Writing in 1935 of the power and freedom of males and the subordination and restriction of females, Mari Sandoz anticipated the concerns and conclusions of contemporary feminist scholars.

Bibliography
Clark, LaVerne Harrell. "The Indian Writings of Mari Sandoz." Parts 1 and 2. *American Indian Quarterly*, 1 (Autumn-Winter, 1974). A favorable assessment of Sandoz's presentation of Indians.
Downey, Betsy. "Battered Pioneers: Jules Sandoz and the Physical Abuse of Wives on the American Frontier." *Great Plains Quarterly* 12, no. 1 (Winter, 1992): 31-49.

Analyzes Jules Sandoz's violence toward his family in its late nineteenth century context, arguing that such violence was common in frontier families.

Rippey, Barbara Wright. "Toward a New Paradigm: Mari Sandoz' Study of Red and White Myth in *Cheyenne Autumn*." In *Women and Western American Literature*, edited by Helen Winter Stauffer and Susan J. Rosowski. Troy, N.Y.: Whitson, 1982. A fine analysis of Sandoz's view of the interaction of Indian and white values.

Sandoz, Mari. *Letters of Mari Sandoz*. Lincoln: University of Nebraska Press, 1992. Contains more than four hundred letters covering nearly forty years. This is an excellent representation of Sandoz's interests, personality, and publishing career, with a superb introduction.

Stauffer, Helen Winter. *Mari Sandoz*. Boise, Idaho: Boise State University, 1984. An excellent abbreviated version of Stauffer's full-length study.

_____ . *Mari Sandoz: Story Catcher of the Plains*. Lincoln: University of Nebraska Press, 1982. The essential resource on Sandoz, this book combines biographical information with critical analysis of her writing and has an extensive bibliography of works by and about Sandoz.

Villiger, Laura R. *Mari Sandoz: A Study in Post-Colonial Discourse*. New York: Peter Lang, 1994. Analyzes Sandoz's major works from a postcolonial, multicultural perspective.

Betsy Downey

MARGARET SANGER

Born: September 14, 1879; Corning, New York
Died: September 6, 1966; Tucson, Arizona
Areas of Achievement: Women's rights and social reform
Contribution: An early advocate of birth control, Sanger devoted her life to the
struggle for contraceptive rights.

Early Life

Margaret Louise Higgins was born on September 14, 1879, in Corning, New York,
the sixth of eleven children. Her father, Michael Hennessey Higgins, who was of Irish
parentage, owned a stone monument shop that he frequently neglected in favor of
debating great social issues and atheistic philosophy. Her mother, Anne Purcell
Higgins, remained faithful to her Irish Catholic background and struggled valiantly to
rear her eleven children on the inadequate financial resources provided by the Higgins
business.

Margaret attended St. Mary's parish school in Corning and, for two years, Claver-
ack College, a private boarding school whose tuition was paid by her older sisters,
Mary and Nan. Attractive and high-spirited, she made friends easily and performed
well academically. Soon after taking a teaching position in Little Falls, New Jersey,
Margaret was summoned home to care for her ailing mother. In 1899, Anne Higgins
died at age forty-nine of chronic tuberculosis and, in Margaret's opinion, sheer
exhaustion. Although fond of—and much influenced by—her nonconformist father,
Margaret never forgave Michael Higgins for burdening her mother with so many
children and so little support.

In 1900, Margaret enrolled as a probationer in the new nursing school at White
Plains Hospital. Her nurse's training was interrupted periodically by a series of
operations for tubercular glands, a condition that would plague her, off and on, for the
next twenty years. In spite of her delicate health and rigorous training schedule,
Margaret found time to develop an active social life, which included a romantic and
idealistic young architect, William Sanger. On August 18, 1902, Margaret was married to William and moved with him to a New York City suburb, Hastings-on-Hudson.
Six months later, she became pregnant with the first of their three children. The
pregnancy aggravated her tubercular condition, and she was confined to a sanatorium
until the birth of her oldest son, Stuart. A second son, Grant, was born in 1908, and a
daughter, Margaret (Peggy), two years later. In 1910, the Sangers moved into a flat in
Upper Manhattan. To make ends meet, Margaret took on part-time employment with
Lillian Wald's Visiting Nurses Association in New York's lower East Side immigrant
community.

Life's Work

Both Sangers were drawn to radical politics in the years prior to World War I. They
joined the American Socialist Party in 1910 and soon became involved in labor

organizing for the International Workers of the World (IWW). Margaret Sanger contributed articles on venereal disease, women's health, and sexuality to the Socialist newspaper *The Call*, and took an active role in the textile workers strikes of 1912-1913. Her circle of associates included the best-known figures of the radical movement, among them IWW organizers William (Big Bill) Haywood and Elizabeth Gurley Flynn, Socialist Party leader and women's rights advocate Eugene Debs, and the fiery anarchist Emma Goldman. Goldman's ideas on "voluntary motherhood" and female sexuality fulfillment provided a philosophical foundation for Margaret's own feminist stand on reproductive freedom for women.

Sanger's nursing specialty was obstetrical cases, in which she dealt primarily with poor, immigrant wives who, like her mother, had aged prematurely from too many pregnancies and too little sustenance. Many of her working-class clients begged her for the "secret" of how to prevent successive and unwanted pregnancies. In 1912, she watched one of these overburdened women, a truck driver's wife named Sadie Sachs, die from a self-induced abortion. The Sachs case haunted Sanger, who soon gave up nursing to devote her energies full time to making birth control (a term she coined) available to all classes.

Contraceptive devices and methods (condoms, "womb veils," early withdrawal, a "safe period," and spermicidal douches) were mentioned in nineteenth century marriage manuals, but any discussion of them in print was deemed "obscene" and therefore illegal under the 1873 Comstock Laws. Sanger was arrested and imprisoned on several occasions, the first time for publishing the militantly feminist journal *Woman Rebel* (1914) and an even more explicit pamphlet on contraception, *Family Limitation* (1914). In an attempt to avoid criminal prosecution in the *Rebel* case, she fled to Europe, spending the next year studying with the English sexologist Havelock Ellis and inspecting birth control clinics in The Netherlands, where the "Dutch Cap" diaphragm was already in general use. In 1916, she opened America's first birth control clinic in Brooklyn, for which she received a thirty-day jail sentence. Her deliberate violation of the anti-birth-control statutes made front-page news and established Margaret Sanger as the nation's leader in the fight for reproductive freedom for women.

Sanger's public activism and her insistence on personal sexual freedom placed a severe strain on her family life. She and William Sanger ceased living together in 1914 and were quietly divorced in 1920. The sudden death in 1915 of her five-year-old daughter Peggy brought her much public sympathy but left a legacy of remorse in the Sanger family. Marriage to a millionaire oil magnate, J. Noah Slee, in 1922, provided Sanger with the autonomy and financial security she had always wanted. Until his death in 1943, Slee willingly backed her crusade for contraceptive reform, at home and abroad.

After World War I, Sanger took an increasingly pragmatic approach to challenging the laws forbidding the dissemination of birth control devices and information. She sought backing from influential upper-class matrons, including Gertrude Pinchot, the noted philanthropist, and Katharine Houghton Hepburn, granddaughter of the founder of Corning Glass (and mother of an aspiring young actress). Through such associations, she was able to provide funding for clinical research and professional instruction. In 1921, Sanger organized a lobbying group, the American Birth Control League, which later became the Planned Parenthood Federation of America (1942). She also edited the widely read League journal *Birth Control Review* (1917-1940). With Noah Slee's help, Sanger smuggled European-made diaphragms into the United States for use in the network of women's health clinics she set up across the country. By the end of the decade, birth control had become a respectable—if still controversial—middle-class cause.

Downplaying the radical rhetoric of her youth, Sanger courted the male-dominated medical profession, thus turning birth control into a medical rather than a purely feminist issue. This approach set the stage for a series of legal battles culminating in the *United States v. One Package* case, which Sanger's Committee on Federal Legislation for Birth Control had initiated. In 1936, a federal court ruled unanimously that physicians could, under certain circumstances, provide contraceptive medical services to their patients. A year later, the American Medical Association formally approved the teaching of contraception in medical schools. Not until 1965, however, did the Supreme Court, in *Griswold v. Connecticut*, finally strike down the last state laws banning birth control.

In an attempt to internationalize the birth control movement, Sanger lectured extensively in Europe and Asia during the 1920's and 1930's. High fertility rates in India and Japan made these two countries especially receptive to her ideas on population control and family planning. After World War II, she and her local supporters convinced government leaders in both nations to initiate state-subsidized birth control programs based on the Sanger model. At age seventy-three, she organized the International Planned Parenthood Federation (1952), thus ensuring that her work in developing countries would continue.

Although Sanger played a less prominent role in the American birth control movement after 1940, she continued to raise huge sums for research into better contraceptive methods. Never satisfied with the diaphragm, she urged the development of a female-controlled physiological contraceptive. Antifertility research was still too controversial, however, and neither the government nor most philanthropic foundations would fund it. In 1952 she persuaded Katherine McCormick, heiress to the International Harvester fortune, to subsidize the work of biologist Gregory Pincus. Pincus, who had been experimenting with synthetic hormones, assembled a team of scientists to produce the first biochemical contraceptive. Following extensive clinical testing, "the pill" went on the market in 1960. Margaret Sanger remained a powerful voice for women's reproductive freedom until her death in 1966.

Summary

Margaret Sanger's role within the movement she founded was that of organizer and publicist. By temperament and training, she was uniquely suited to the task. Early in the twentieth century, government officials opposed birth control as obscene and subversive; the medical establishment refused to regard contraception as a medical responsibility; and religious leaders—in particular, the American Catholic church hierarchy—attacked her as immoral and antifamily. Sanger thrived on the controversy, using it to gain public support for birth control reform. In time, governmental authorities, health-care providers, and many religious denominations came to accept as legitimate her goal of enlightened family planning.

At the heart of her crusade was Sanger's belief that reproductive freedom was a woman's fundamental right. "No woman can call herself free who does not own and control her own body," she frequently asserted. Cooperating with conservative groups and taking a legal rather than a political approach was a matter of strategy, not a shift in philosophy. For her, birth control meant freeing women from dangerous or unwanted pregnancies and allowing them to enjoy sexual intimacy on an equal basis with men. It also meant ending the horror of back-alley abortions, which had cost the lives of so many desperate women. In her later years, she even urged that restrictions on medical abortions be eased. Throughout her long career, Sanger based her reform arguments on feminist principles, even when second-generation birth control advocates openly criticized her "feminist bias." At the time of her death, women in America still had not achieved complete control over their own bodies. Margaret Sanger, however, did more than any other individual to bring this feminist goal closer to reality.

Bibliography

Chesler, Ellen. *Woman of Valor: Margaret Sanger and the Birth Control Movement in America*. New York: Simon & Schuster, 1992. The most complete and balanced account of Sanger's life and work to date. This biography reveals Sanger as a complex and controversial figure who deserves her status as the founder and champion of a great movement. Included are an excellent section of photographs and an exhaustive bibliography.

Douglas, Emily Taft. *Margaret Sanger: Pioneer of the Future*. Garrett Park, Md.: Garrett Park Press, 1975. An uncritical but informative tribute by a former congresswoman who devoted considerable attention to Sanger's international legacy.

Gordon, Linda. *Woman's Body, Woman's Right: Birth Control in America*. New York: Penguin Books, 1990. This revised edition of the 1976 publication utilizes a feminist perspective. Gordon provides excellent coverage of the long struggle for reproductive rights, but she accuses Sanger of retreating from her early socialist politics and capitulating to the conservative groups with which she attempted to work.

Gray, Madeline. *Margaret Sanger: A Biography of the Champion of Birth Control*. New York: R. Marek, 1979. A chatty exposé of Sanger's private life that, despite numerous factual errors, does contain useful information regarding her close associates in the birth control movement.

Kennedy, David. *Birth Control in America: The Career of Margaret Sanger*. New Haven, Conn.: Yale University Press, 1970. A somewhat hostile interpretation of

Sanger's work that focuses on the years 1914 to 1940. Kennedy trivializes Sanger's importance and, curiously, portrays her as an obstacle to cooperative efforts on behalf of birth control reform.

Lader, Lawrence. *The Margaret Sanger Story and the Fight for Birth Control.* Garden City, N.Y.: Doubleday, 1955. A journalist's account that was edited by Sanger herself, this work reflects the subject's own version of events and personalities.

Sanger, Margaret. *Margaret Sanger: An Autobiography.* New York: Dover, 1971. This reprint of Sanger's 1938 self-aggrandizing memoir should not be trusted as a candid or even truthful account of her motives and actions. Her narrative does reveal, however, Sanger's ability to tell a good story and engage her readers' sympathy for her point of view.

Constance B. Rynder

JEANNE SAUVÉ

Born: April 26, 1922; Prud'Homme, Saskatchewan, Canada
Died: January 26, 1993; Montreal, Quebec, Canada
Area of Achievement: Government and politics
Contribution: As Canada's first female governor-general, Sauvé was a pioneer for
women and for French-Canadians.

Early Life

Jeanne Mathilde Benoît was born on April 26, 1922, in Prud'Homme, Saskatchewan. Her father, Charles, a building contractor, and her mother, Anna, were French
Canadians who were determined to preserve their culture in the midst of the English
majority. Although the Benoît family had moved from the Saskatchewan prairies to
the Canadian capital of Ottawa when Jeanne was three, they still felt surrounded by
English speakers. To compensate, Charles reared his children in a traditional French
cultural atmosphere, based on the Roman Catholic church. Jeanne attended church
school throughout her childhood and adolescence. She then attended the University
of Ottawa.

Jeanne Benoît left the somewhat stifling security of her childhood world behind
forever when she moved to Montreal in 1943. Montreal was then the leading city in
Canada, a multiethnic, cosmopolitan metropolis. Of greatest importance to Jeanne
was that Montreal was primarily French-speaking; there, she did not have to shelter
herself against the majority culture. As a member of Jeunesse Étudiante Catholique,
a liberal organization of young Quebecois, Jeanne made many contacts that were to
prove influential in the future, among them Pierre Elliott Trudeau, who years later was
to sponsor Jeanne's political career as prime minister of Canada. In 1948, Jeanne
married Maurice Sauvé, an economics student. The Sauvés went to Europe, where
Jeanne taught French in England and later received her baccalaureate degree at the
University of Paris. Educated on two continents, Sauvé throughout her career was to
impress Canadians as an unusually literate and intelligent politician and public figure.
In 1952, the Sauvés returned to Canada.

Life's Work

Jeanne Sauvé soon began a career as a journalist and television personality.
Fluently bilingual, Sauvé broadcast in both English and French on the best-known
Canadian and American networks. Sauvé's visibility and articulateness made her
ideally suited to symbolize the aspirations of Quebec society during the 1960's.
During this decade, in a process known as the "Quiet Revolution," Quebec was
transformed under the leadership of Liberal premier Jean Lesage from a largely rural,
conservative province to a progressive, assertive force that sought greater influence
within Canada and even independence for itself. Although the conservative Union
Nationale party had ruled Quebec during their youth, both Sauvés were enthusiastic
about the modernizing Liberals. As Jeanne rose to fame in the media sector, Maurice

was making equal headway in the political sphere, serving in prominent provincial and national posts. The Sauvés were becoming a true "power couple" in Quebec public affairs.

This career division between the couple was to end, however, when Maurice lost his seat in 1968. The national Liberal Party, Canada's governing party, which by now was headed by Sauvé's old friend Trudeau, asked Jeanne to run in his stead in the next election four years later. Sauvé won handily and moved to Ottawa to take her seat in the federal parliament for the next session. Sauvé's move into national politics paralleled a decision made earlier by Trudeau and many other Quebecois politicians of his generation to "go to Ottawa" rather than focus their governmental ambitions within the province of Quebec. The ultimate goal of this decision was to make virtually manifest the theoretical assertion of equality between French-speaking and English-speaking Canadians as the two founding languages of the Canadian confederation, to give French Canadians a position of leadership on the national scene. Trudeau, seeing in his old friend Sauvé a kindred spirit in this regard, almost immediately appointed her to a cabinet post in charge of issues relating to science and technology. Even though Sauvé was a political novice, she rose to the task impressively, exhibiting a technical proficiency and competence that went beyond mere execution of day-to-day policy. After Sauvé won reelection in 1974 in her home riding (the Canadian term for a parliamentary district) of Ahuntsic in Montreal, Trudeau promoted Sauvé to a position of more responsibility, that of minister of the environment. Sauvé's most challenging crisis in this capacity was a dispute between the American state of North Dakota and the adjoining Canadian province of Manitoba over irrigation runoff that threatened to dump excess water from the upper Mississippi watershed into the Red River of the North Basin, largely located in Canada. Sauvé held her ground, although the dispute was resolved only after she had left office.

Sauvé's rapid advance in prominence during the 1970's was assisted by factors external to her own performance. This decade saw the large-scale revival of feminism in North America, as women began to be perceived as an interest group demanding more influence in the political process and desiring public visibility commensurate with their demographic position. Sauvé was poised to benefit from the existing power structure's need to accommodate women's interests. This era also saw the crest of a renewed Quebec nationalism. Federally inclined politicians such as Trudeau had hoped that the economic prosperity that had accompanied the modernization launched by the Quiet Revolution would bind Quebec closer to the rest of Canada. Instead, it had the opposite effect, raising nationalistic expectations in the province and ushering in an unprecedented era of Quebecois self-confidence. This was expressed politically in 1976, when the Parti Quebecois, which openly demanded political independence from Canada, won the provincial election, led by the charismatic René Levesque. Because she was a Quebec native committed to the maintenance and revitalization of the federal idea of Canada, Sauvé's presence in the cabinet became all the more crucial for Trudeau.

By this time, in one of the frequent cabinet reshuffles characteristic of Canadian politics, Sauvé had become communications minister, a task for which her media background had prepared her. This position brought her into direct conflict with Quebec nationalists. The conflict quickly became representative of the general tension in the linguistically divided Canada of the late 1970's, as Quebec premier Levesque arranged a referendum, to be held in May of 1980, that would determine whether the province would secede from Canada.

For a brief time, it seemed that Sauvé and the Liberal Party would not be in office to meet this challenge. In elections held in May of 1979, the Liberals were swept out of office by the progressive Conservatives, led by an attractive young politician, Joe Clark. Clark possessed only a minority, however, and in new elections held the following February, the Liberals were returned to office with a majority. Three months later, the independence side lost the Quebec referendum, temporarily silencing the national aspirations of the Quebec people.

Sauvé had been very active on Trudeau's behalf in both causes, and the returned prime minister rewarded her with the post of speaker in the new parliament. Unlike the American Congress, in which the speaker is the leader of the majority party, the speaker in Canada is deliberately nonpartisan; the main function of the post is to maintain decorum and process in parliamentary discussion. Sauvé's performance in this role over the next three and a half years demonstrated that she could transcend the particularities of factionalism and party interest, thus paving the way for her next position.

In December of 1983, Trudeau made history by appointing Sauvé to the position of governor-general. When Canada had entered into confederation in 1867, it had been agreed that the British sovereign would rule Canada. Because of Canada's geographical distance from London, however, the sovereign needed a representative, the governor-general, to rule on his or her behalf. From the beginning, the post had been ceremonial, as the British monarchy itself was by this time, but it was very important symbolically, and when the first Canadian entered this post in the middle of the twentieth century, it was felt that Canada's colonial status was on its way to being changed. When Trudeau appointed Sauvé, Queen Elizabeth II was the nominal Canadian head of state, with Sauvé serving as her representative in Ottawa. Theoretically, Trudeau served at Sauvé's behest, though actually the elected prime minister had all the power; Sauvé's role was wholly ceremonial.

Canadians paid more attention than usual to the appointment of this governor-general, because Sauvé was the first woman to hold the post. Sauvé plunged into her duties with gusto, immediately winning respect from the Canadian people for her bearing and dignity. The national scene, however, was shifting under Sauvé's feet, because her old friend Trudeau resigned in February of 1984, to be succeeded as Liberal leader and prime minister by John Turner. Turner lost the next federal election, in September, 1984, to the Conservative Brian Mulroney. Sauvé swore both Turner and Mulroney into office in her constitutional capacity as prime minister, and she worked smoothly with the latter man for the remainder of her five-year term, even though he was of the opposing party. Most important for the strongly Roman Catholic

Sauvé, however, was the role she played in receiving Pope John Paul II when he made the first-ever papal visit to Canada in 1984.

The life of a Canadian governor-general is not particularly eventful, but Sauvé succeeded in making a marked impression on Canada during her five years in office. Remaining scrupulously nonpartisan throughout her term, Sauvé had occasion to swear in Mulroney again on his reelection in 1988. Sauvé's term ended in 1989, and she retired, spending most of her post-government years in support of the artistic charities to which she had always been dedicated. When she died in Montreal in January of 1993, she was mourned by all Canadians.

Summary

Jeanne Sauvé's role as governor-general may have been only ceremonial, but she turned this lack of political clout into a personal advantage on the strength of her ability to relate to the Canadian people without the obtrusion of ulterior motive or political agenda. Sauvé refined the role of the governor-general, sometimes thought to be outdated and superfluous, to what it should be at its best: a cheerleader for the potential of the peoples of Canada.

Sauvé demonstrated that women had the capacity to hold supreme office in Canada. Once in the shadow of her husband, she ultimately became far more prominent than he had ever been. Sauvé's experience prepared the way for a woman who was to exercise real political power, future Prime Minister Kim Campbell. Most important, Sauvé's soothing presence and bilingual cosmopolitanism helped heal the simmering wounds that remained after the defeat of the Quebec independence referendum in 1980. Although the relationship between English and French Canadians was still bitter and unresolved, the fact that Canada remained unified as a nation was largely the result of Sauvé's quiet but determined efforts.

Bibliography

Armour, Moira, and Pat Staton. *Canadian Women in History: A Chronology.* Toronto: Green Dragon Press, 1990. Accords Sauvé's odyssey a prominent role in its chronicling of the accomplishments of women north of the 49th parallel, though it tends to marginalize the importance of her Quebecois background.

Greenwood, Barbara. *Jeanne Sauvé.* Markham, Canada: Fitzhenry & Whiteside, 1989. This introductory book covers Sauvé in a thorough if noncontroversial manner. The spotlight is on Sauvé as female role model and as bridge-builder between the English and French communities in Canada.

Megyery, Kathy, ed. *Women in Canadian Politics.* Toronto, Canada: Dundurn Press, 1991. This comprehensive book situates Sauvé's career in the context of the possibilities and obstacles faced by politicians of her generation and gender.

Mollins, Carl. "A Quiet Revolutionary." *Maclean's* 106 (February 8, 1993): 17. This most generous and affectionate of Sauvé's obituary notices reflects on her constitutional role and the promise she held out to Canadian women.

Wearing, Joseph. *The L-Shaped Party: The Liberal Party of Canada, 1958-1980.* New

York: McGraw-Hill Ryerson, 1981. This book provides crucial background on the party in which Sauvé received her political baptism and through which she rose to national prominence.

Woods, Shirley. *Her Excellency Jeanne Sauvé*. Toronto, Canada: Macmillan, 1986. The most detailed and scholarly treatment of Sauvé's life available. Although this book eventually will be surpassed by a full-scale historical biography, it is a vital prerequisite to the serious study of Sauvé's career.

Nicholas Birns

AUGUSTA SAVAGE

Born: February 29, 1892; Green Cove Springs, Florida
Died: March 26, 1962; New York, New York
Area of Achievement: Art
Contribution: A black sculptor, Augusta Savage earned a reputation as an inspiring and devoted teacher. A central figure in the Harlem Renaissance, especially in the 1930's, Savage became nationally known when she courageously exposed racial discrimination.

Early Life

Augusta Christine Fells, the seventh of fourteen children, was born in Green Cove Springs, a small town in northern Florida, famous for its red clay and bricks. Augusta's parents were Cornelia and Edward Fells. Her father was a Methodist minister and earned his living as a carpenter, fisherman, and small farmer.

When Augusta was only fifteen years old she was married to John T. Moore, who died a few years later. Her only child, Irene Connie Moore, was born in 1908. Later, Augusta was married to James Savage, whom she divorced in the early 1920's. She was to marry a third and last time, in October of 1923, but her husband, Robert L. Poston, died after four months, in March of 1924.

As a child, Augusta had already discovered her ability to work clay into small animals, such as ducks and chickens. These were toys for herself and her siblings. Her father strongly disapproved of her artistic endeavor. She later recalled how he would beat her five or six times a week and almost succeeded in driving all the art out of her. She learned to keep her activity a secret.

When her father was transferred to a church in West Palm Beach, Augusta no longer had access to clay and ceased to sculpt altogether for several years. One day, a chance occurrence led Augusta to take up sculpting again. She came upon a small pottery owned by a man named Chase, whom she persuaded to give her a twenty-five-pound bucket of good clay. She could begin to sculpt again. Impressed by Augusta's ability, Mr. Mickens, the school principal, hired her to teach a class in clay modelling in the very school she was attending. Thanks to Mr. Mickens' encouragement, Augusta's father soon changed his attitude toward her art. The minister was particularly pleased with an eighteen-inch statue of the Virgin Mary that he watched Augusta create, especially because of the religious sensitivity that permeated the figure.

After high school, Augusta attended Tallahassee Normal School (later Florida A&M University) for awhile, but dropped out to devote herself full time to sculpting. At the 1919 Palm Beach County Fair, she was permitted to set up her own booth to exhibit her animal sculptures. George Graham Currie, superintendent of the fair, encouraged her to create a variety of clay animals to suit every pocketbook. Savage's works were offered at prices ranging from twenty-five cents to five dollars. The officials, at first disturbed that a black woman had her own booth, changed their minds when pleased tourists quickly bought all of Augusta's ducks and chickens. Augusta not only earned $175 from her sales but she also received a ribbon and a special prize of $25.

Life's Work

Heartened by this success, Augusta Savage decided to go to New York and develop her talent. George Currie wrote a letter of introduction for her to Solon Borglum, a sculptor teaching at the American Academy of Fine Arts in New York. In October of 1921, Augusta Savage arrived in New York City with very little money in her pocket. Unfortunately, Borglum could not take her as a student because she could not afford the high tuition fee. He suggested that she apply to the tuition-free Cooper Union and wrote a letter of recommendation to Kate L. Reynolds, the school's registrar.

In October of 1921, Savage was admitted to Cooper Union where in six weeks she mastered two years of course work. When Savage's meager funds ran out, Reynolds helped her to get a grant for room and board. This was the first time in the school's history that the council had voted to support a student in addition to providing free tuition. Savage could continue her training, focusing on academic portraiture under George Brewster, until her graduation in 1923.

She received commissions to portray several prominent black leaders, modeling busts of W. E. B. Du Bois and Marcus Garvey in 1922. The Du Bois bust, in particular, is regarded as one of her finest works. The artistic community soon recognized her as a good portraitist.

Despite her obvious talent, Augusta Savage had to overcome many obstacles placed in her way because of her race and gender. An incident that made her nationally known concerned a summer study grant to the Fontainebleau School in France. She had already booked passage when it was recalled. When the committee members were pressed for the reason, they revealed that some young white women from the South objected to sailing on the same ship as Savage and to studying with her at Fontaine-bleau. Members of the press learned of this incident from Alfred W. Martin, a leader of the Ethical Culture Society of New York. On April 24, 1923, *The New York Times* contained a story, under the headline "Negress Denied Entry to French Art School," listing the names of the committee members. Martin appealed in vain to the committee to reverse its decision and pressured the French government to use its influence. Eventually, she accepted sculptor Herman McNeil's invitation to study with him instead. Although the press coverage had been sympathetic, Augusta Savage was labeled a troublemaker for exposing the racism of many in the art world. Even though art galleries and dealers acknowledged her talent, they refused to show or sell her work.

In 1925, thanks to the efforts of W. E. B. Du Bois and the sponsorship of Countess Irene Di Robilant of the Italian-American Society in New York, Savage received a working scholarship to study at the Royal Academy of Fine Arts in Rome, Italy. Responsibilities for her family prevented her on two occasions from taking advantage of this opportunity, however, and she postponed her Italian trip indefinitely.

A change in Savage's fortune finally came in 1929. She was awarded her first Julius

Rosenwald Fellowship to study in Paris. Her sculpture *Gamin*, a portrait of her nephew Ellis Ford depicted as a perky little street urchin, had particularly impressed the committee.

In 1930, she traveled to Paris, where she studied with a variety of teachers, including Charles Despiau, a talented modeler. While in Paris she received her second Rosenwald fellowship and an additional grant from the Carnegie Foundation. These additional funds allowed her to travel and to see art, especially the cathedrals of France, Belgium, and Germany. The study years abroad, especially in Paris, gave Savage a sense of liberation from racism. *La Citadelle-Freedom* (c. 1930), a small sculpture of a confidently smiling young woman lifting an arm in salute, may be an expression of this freedom.

After two years, she returned to New York in 1932. Upon her return, she opened a studio in Harlem known as the Savage Studio of Arts and Crafts, located on 163 West 143rd Street. She devoted her energy to teaching and to stimulating Harlem youths' interest in the arts. There was still little demand for her sculpture, especially in the aftermath of the Wall Street financial crash of 1929 and the subsequent Great Depression.

Savage exhibited at a few galleries in New York, and works such as *Envy*, *Martyr*, and *Woman of Martinique* (1932) were favorably received by the critics. She became more and more involved in teaching but still found time to sculpt *Realization* (1934), a powerful work depicting two figures in poses of hopelessness and resignation.

With the launching of President Franklin D. Roosevelt's Works Progress Administration (WPA), Savage became one of the champions of the Federal Art Project (FAP), a branch of the WPA. In January of 1934, the first free class in Harlem was established. Savage informally ran one school, the Uptown Art Laboratory, from her garage, which had been transformed into a studio. Three months later she was Assistant Supervisor of the FAP in New York City. When the Uptown Art Laboratory developed into the Harlem Community Art Center, Savage was named its first director, and Eleanor Roosevelt came to the opening ceremony held on December 20, 1937.

Savage's interest in teaching black youth is reflected in one of her finest and best-known works, *The Harp* (1939). The composition is also known as *Lift Every Voice and Sing*, after James Weldon Johnson's poem. The sixteen-foot sculpture depicts young black men and women, probably modeled after her students, standing solemnly one behind the other with their heads lifted up to sing. Their slender bodies resemble Romanesque sculpture, such as the figures on the west front of Chartres Cathedral, which Savage could have seen a few years earlier when traveling in France. Together, they form the components of a harp: strings, pillar, and curved neck. The soundbox to which the "strings" are attached is shaped as a gigantic arm with an open hand supporting the last singer. In front of the harp, a kneeling figure holds a plaque with musical notes.

The Harp was commissioned for the 1939 New York World's Fair. Since there was no money to cast this fine work in bronze, bulldozers destroyed the plaster original once the exposition was ended. Small souvenirs of *The Harp* were produced in bronze and a few have survived, but they lack the fine detail of the original. A photograph of the original sculpture exists in the Beinecke Rare Book Library at Yale University.

While working on the World's Fair commission, Savage took a leave from her position as director of the Harlem Community Art Center. When the sculpture was completed, however, Savage did not regain her position, but became a staff consultant. For the next five years she attempted to run an art gallery and exhibited some works. In 1945, she left New York City and moved to upstate New York to live on a farm near Saugerties. She lived there in solitude, but did make some portrait busts of local people until she became ill with cancer. Savage then moved back to New York City to live with her daughter during her last year and died on March 26, 1962.

Summary

Augusta Savage's legacy is her teaching and her efforts to promote black artists. Her enthusiasm for her students gave many of them a boost in launching their careers. She vigorously encouraged, for example, the training of young Jacob Lawrence to become a painter. He later remembered that when he was too young to be accepted in the WPA, Savage kept track of his birthday and, as soon as he was eligible, made him reapply. The WPA gave him a steady weekly income, and since he was obliged to paint two paintings every six weeks, he learned to establish himself as an artist.

Savage's talent as a sculptor is indisputable, as seen in the few works of hers that have survived, such as *Gamin*, and in remaining photographs of those that have not survived, such as *The Harp*. She appeared on the artistic scene when political and social circumstances prevented her from gaining wider recognition. She was honored, however, by being the first black woman to become a member of the National Association of Women Painters and Sculptors.

Bibliography

Augusta Savage and the Art Schools of Harlem. New York: Schomburg Center for Research in Black Culture, The New York Public Library, 1988. Published in connection with an exhibition held between October 9, 1988, and January 29, 1989, at the Schomburg Center. Includes an essay by Deirdre L. Bibby and a thorough chronology of Savage's career by Juanita Marie Holland.

Bearden, Romare, and Harry Henderson. *Six Black Masters of American Art*. New York: Zenith Books, 1972. The essay, "Augusta Savage (1900-1962)," is the most comprehensive treatment of her life available. Has some factual errors that have later been corrected in the writings of others.

Bibby, Deirdre. "Augusta Savage (1892-1962)." In *Black Women in America: An Historical Encyclopedia*, edited by Darlene Clark Hine. Brooklyn, N.Y.: Carlson, 1993. Bibby, whose brief biographical essay appears in the exhibition catalog cited above, here provides a fuller account of Savage's accomplishments. Includes one illustration of a youthful looking Savage.

Bontemps, Arna Alexander, ed. *Forever Free: Art by African-American Women,*

1862-1980. Alexandria, Va.: Stepheson, 1980. A catalog produced by Susan Willand Worteck for a traveling exhibition that included four sculptures by Augusta Savage. The exhibition, organized by Jacqueline Fonvielle-Bontemps of Illinois State University, was shown at the University of Maryland Art Gallery, from October 29 to December 3, 1981, with David C. Driskell as guest curator.

Igoe, Lynn Moody, with James Igoe. *Two Hundred Fifty Years of Afro-American Art: An Annotated Bibliography*. New York: R. R. Bowker, 1981. This thorough reference work gives a full list of the periodical literature and cites eleven works by Savage.

Lewis, Samella. *Art: African American*. New York: Harcourt Brace Jovanovich, 1978. Includes a short sketch on Savage's life and career, with illustrations of two of her significant works.

Smith, Jessie Carney. "Augusta Savage." In *Notable Black American Women*. Detroit: Gale Research, 1992. Provides a good introduction to Savage's life, with one illustration of the sculptor looking at two of her small figures. Helpful in placing Savage within the context of achievements made by other African American women.

Elvy Setterqvist O'Brien

PATRICIA S. SCHROEDER

Born: July 30, 1940; Portland, Oregon

Area of Achievement: Government and politics

Contribution: As a leader of the liberal wing of the Democratic Party, Schroeder has given direction to the important issues of foreign and military policy, women's rights, and the American family.

Early Life

Patricia Nell Scott was born in Portland, Oregon, during the summer of 1940, the first child of Lee Combs Scott and Bernice Lemoin Scott. Her parents were thorough-going Democrats, committed to populism, and her paternal grandfather was an Irish immigrant who had served with three-time Democratic presidential candidate William Jennings Bryan in the Nebraska state legislature.

Her parents taught Pat (as she came to be called) and her younger brother, Mike, to be independent and self-reliant. Because the family moved often, she also learned to make friends quickly. She attended grade school in Texas, junior high in Ohio, and high school in Iowa, and went on to the University of Minnesota in Minneapolis. An exceptional student, she completed her studies there in just three years and was graduated magna cum laude in 1961 as a member of Phi Beta Kappa honor society. Her undergraduate major was history, with minors in philosophy and political science.

Pat Scott continued her education at Harvard Law School, from which she was graduated in 1964 with a J.D. degree. Her experiences at Harvard continued to shape those views which would later influence her work in the United States Congress. She was one of only nineteen women in a class of 554 students. A male classmate once told her that she ought to be ashamed of taking a man's place in the law school. She found friends anyway, and in one of her classes met James White Schroeder, a fellow law student, to whom she was married on August 18, 1962. Both planned careers in law, although Jim was also interested in politics.

After graduation, the Schroeders moved to Denver, Colorado, where Pat was admitted to the Bar Association in 1964 and was later hired as a field attorney for the National Labor Relations Board. She temporarily stopped working following the birth of her first child, Scott, in June of 1966, and then resumed private practice as an attorney while teaching courses at the Community College of Denver (1969-1970), University of Denver (1969), and Regis College (1970-1972). For a brief period, she also worked as a Democratic precinct committeewoman.

Pregnancies were difficult for Pat Schroeder. A second one ended sadly in a miscarriage at seven months when she lost twins. She had thought something was wrong all along, but her doctor dismissed her concerns. The woman who would later become the champion of women's issues as well as health-care reform said she wrongly allowed the doctor to intimidate her. In 1970, Schroeder delivered her daughter, Jamie, without complications, but was rushed back to the hospital with life-threatening hemorrhaging that lasted six weeks. Her husband juggled child care for their four-year-old son and newborn daughter, went to the office, and worried about Pat. She later told audiences that that was when her husband truly understood the kind of stress working mothers experienced every day. After her recovery, Pat Schroeder was back working full time, committed to helping others understand their rights and problems not only in her work as a hearing officer for the Colorado Department of Personnel but also as a legal counsel for Planned Parenthood of Colorado.

Life's Work

The early 1970's marked a turning point in the life of Pat Schroeder. After his defeat in a 1970 race for the Colorado state legislature, Jim Schroeder talked Pat into running for the seat in the U.S. House of Representatives occupied by heavily favored incumbent James D. "Mike" McKevitt. Relying on the assistance of grassroots volunteers and the management of her husband, Pat Schroeder's campaign rejected a safe, middle-of-the-road stance. Using hard-hitting, guerrilla-like political tactics, Schroeder spoke out against the Vietnam War and argued for a restructuring of national priorities and values that would place greater emphasis on education, child care, and protection of the environment.

Although Schroeder exhibited the kind of controversial, almost too shrewd style that characterized much of her subsequent political career, her audiences appreciated her ability to simplify the issues. On November 8, 1972, she won an upset victory over Congressman McKevitt, capturing 51.6 percent of the vote, and was elected to the Ninety-third Congress as a representative from Colorado's First Congressional District.

Pat Schroeder became a political pioneer inasmuch as she was the first woman Colorado had ever sent to the U.S. House of Representatives. In addition, she became one of only a handful of women among some four hundred men in the "clubby" atmosphere of the nation's capital. From her first day on Capitol Hill in January, 1973, she began to encounter an entrenched male chauvinism and sexist condescension that made her pro-underdog and pro-women positions all the more appreciated among her growing number of supporters. When a male colleague, on meeting her for the first time, asked how she could be the mother of small children and a member of Congress at the same time, she snapped back that she had a brain and a uterus and she used both.

Shortly after taking office, Pat Schroeder lobbied her way onto the powerful House Armed Services Committee and began denouncing the colossal waste that characterized most military expenditures—expenses that comprised some forty percent of the national budget. She said that as a representative of women with children, she believed there were things that could be done to make the United States strong other than simply building bigger bases and more destructive weapons. Annoyed by the committee's fixation with technology and its belief that being able to kill the enemy fifteen times over rather than only five times over made the nation safer, Schroeder attacked the Armed Services Committee in a scathing article entitled "A Freshman in the Weapons Club" that was published in the November 5, 1973, issue of *The Nation*.

To register their opposition to the rubber-stamp approval of annual increases in the defense budget, Pat Schroeder and a group of other representatives submitted an alternative defense proposal in 1975 that eliminated hundreds of millions of dollars from the Pentagon's 1976 request. Schroeder continued to vote down appropriations bills for expensive weapons systems, including the B-1 bomber and nuclear-powered aircraft carriers, saying she did not oppose reasonable strength, only unreasonable redundancy.

As chair of the House Armed Services Committee's Defense Burdensharing Panel in the 100th Congress, Schroeder led the first comprehensive committee effort to assess the costs and benefits of mutual defense agreements between the United States and its allies. She has continued to be one of the most outspoken advocates of defense burdensharing, calling on the nation's allies to contribute a greater amount of money and resources for their own defense.

During the next two sessions of Congress, Schroeder chaired the Subcommittee on Military Installations and Facilities and led efforts to improve neglected military base facilities and infrastructure. As the first woman to serve on the committee, she focused on cutting wasteful defense spending and improving benefits for military personnel and their families.

During this same period, Schroeder put herself at the center of a national debate on the way that the military treats women and homosexuals. She helped expose cases of sexual harassment and called on the military to end its discriminatory policies toward gays and women. She also became a strong advocate of allowing women to serve in combat.

Yet for all of her military expertise, Pat Schroeder has been best known for her advocacy of family issues. In 1977, she helped found and served as the cochair of the Congressional Caucus for Women's Issues, a bipartisan group of representatives devoted to advancing legislation to improve women's health policies, economic equality, child support enforcement laws, and child care policy.

In 1985, Schroeder first proposed legislation to provide all workers with a minimum of job-guaranteed, paid leave for the birth, adoption, or serious illness of a child or dependent parent, and for workers with a serious temporary health condition. In 1989, she reintroduced the Family and Medical Leave Act and pushed for its passage with fervor during 1989 and 1990, taking on President George Bush's vocal opposition to its passage. The bill passed the House on May 10, 1990, by a vote of 287 to 187. Although Bush vetoed the bill, it was later signed into law by his successor, Bill Clinton, in February of 1993. Schroeder also introduced the Child Support Economic Security Act, which provided states with assistance in enforcing the collection of child support payments.

Schroeder contemplated pursuing the 1988 Democratic nomination for the presidency and was considered a leading contender according to a poll conducted by *Time* magazine in September of 1987. Failing to be taken seriously by the press corps, who labeled Schroeder and her fellow hopefuls as "Snow White and the Seven Dwarves,"

Schroeder was also forced to field absurd questions such as "Are you running as a woman?" Ultimately, the issue of her gender proved to be an insurmountable stumbling block in attracting sufficient political support for a campaign in the primaries, and Schroeder held a press conference to announce her decision not to run. Her tearful display of emotion during the press conference nearly drew more publicity from the media than her announcement, a situation that added somewhat to her discouragement in trying to break through stereotypical opinions regarding a woman's fitness to serve in public office.

In February of 1991, Schroeder was appointed to chair the House Select Committee on Children, Youth, and Families to explore ways in which the public and private sectors could improve the condition of America's families and children. As a select committee chair, she was one of only four women up to that point to head a House committee in the twentieth century. In 1992, she won her tenth straight reelection victory by 69 percent over her challenger.

As a member of the House Judiciary Committee, Schroeder supported legislation to prohibit discrimination on the basis of sexual orientation, and became a sponsor of the Freedom of Choice Act, a bill that would put into federal law the principles of *Roe v. Wade*, securing a woman's right to choose to terminate her pregnancy. She also fought for the legalization of the French-developed birth control pill, RU 486.

Of the several publications authored by Schroeder on military and domestic policy issues, her magnum opus is a 1989 book entitled *Champion of the Great American Family*, which outlines a family policy agenda for the twenty-first century.

Summary

Pat Schroeder has always been a pragmatist, a leader, and a courageous advocate for justice and equality. By 1994, Pat Schroeder had become the dean of the Colorado congressional delegation as well as the most senior female representative in Congress. She has served in the House leadership as a Democratic whip since 1978, and was appointed deputy whip in 1987. In 1989, she became cochair of the Democratic Caucus' Task Force on National Security.

Pat Schroeder's top priorities, indeed her passions, as an extremely vocal lawmaker have been family and women's issues as well as sane military policy. In the face of powerful opposition, she has worked to divert what she considered to be excessive military spending in order to expand social welfare programs, curb the national debt, and strengthen the nation's human resources so that the United States can compete effectively in the twenty-first century.

Schroeder's voting record in Congress has proven to be as independent as her thinking. In 1989, she voted against positions taken by President Bush more than any other member of the House (79 percent of the time). At the same time, however, she was rated more fiscally conservative by the National Taxpayers Union than Republicans Jack Kemp and Newt Gingrich.

In the last two decades of the twentieth century, Pat Schroeder has consistently been regarded as one of the few realistically viable female presidential candidates. A 1988

Gallup poll rated her as one of the six most respected women in the United States. When the political history of twentieth century America is finally written, it could well be that Patricia S. Schroeder will have done more to encourage legislative momentum in addressing the concerns of women and the American family than any other female politician.

Bibliography

Ferraro, Susan. "The Prime of Pat Schroeder," *The New York Times Magazine*, July 1, 1990, pp. 12-15, 29-30. One of the few accessible articles detailing the rise, influence, and major contributions of Representative Schroeder. It emphasizes her expertise on military policy and her support of family-oriented legislation.

Kempton, Beverly. "Bowing out: A Tough Choice." *New Choices* 29 (October, 1989): 20-25. This article, written for a popular audience, describes Schroeder's qualifications to run for president and her choice not to do so in 1988. Discusses the possibility that she might run in the future.

Schroeder, Pat. *Champion of the Great American Family*. New York: Random House, 1989. One of the few book-length studies to discuss Schroeder's life is this autobiography. It contains personal and political anecdotes and her proposal for a comprehensive national family policy.

_____ . "Toward Effective and Family Friendly National Policies for U.S. Children and Their Families." *Denver University Law Review* 69, no. 3 (1992): 303-314. A well-written, nontechnical article that details the problem to which Schroeder has devoted much of her professional life. It describes why the economic conditions of the American family have spiraled downward and what the government has done and needs to do to help families meet future challenges.

Snell, Marilyn B. "From Star Wars to Child Care." *New Perspectives Quarterly* 7 (Winter, 1990): 9-11. Part of a special section on the needs of working families, this article describes Schroeder's views on the child care debate. States her belief that the family unit is in danger of breaking down unless society gives more support so women can take time to bear children and still contribute to the family's financial resources.

Witt, Linda, Karen M. Paget, and Glenna Matthews. *Running as a Woman: Gender and Power in American Politics*. New York: Free Press, 1993. This sweeping narrative of the experiences of female candidates in American politics is the result of a fruitful collaboration between a journalist, a political scientist, and a historian. Throughout this work, the authors use Schroeder's political career as an example of the crusading efforts made by women politicians in Congress during the 1970's and beyond. Touches briefly on her aborted campaign during the Democratic presidential primaries of 1988.

Andrew C. Skinner

SUSAN SEIDELMAN

Born: December 11, 1952; Abington, Pennsylvania

Area of Achievement: Film

Contribution: A leading director of offbeat comedies, Seidelman broke through the ranks of independent filmmakers to work successfully in commercial cinema.

Early Life

The oldest of three children, Susan Seidelman was born December 11, 1952, in Abington, Pennsylvania. Reared in the suburbs by her father Michael, a hardware manufacturer with a "Mel Brooks sense of humor," and her mother Florence, a special-education teacher with an *I Love Lucy* sense of life, Seidelman did not spend much time watching films. Back then, she later said, her idea of a great film was Disney's *The Parent Trap* and anything that starred Natalie Wood.

After high school, Seidelman went to Drexel University, a technical college in Philadelphia, to study graphic design. In her second year, uninterested in design classes and tired of sewing, she switched her major to film study, thinking it an easier way to get through college. What was initially a facile choice soon developed into a life-altering career move.

In 1974, she received her bachelor of arts degree from Drexel. After having worked on a local television show as a producer's assistant, Seidelman was accepted into the prestigious Graduate School of Film and Television of New York University (NYU). Leaving the suburbs for the city, she made Lower Manhattan her residence, the milieu to which three heroines of her films are impulsively drawn.

At NYU, Seidelman made three short films. The first, *And You Act Like One, Too*, won her a student prize from the Academy of Motion Picture Arts and Sciences in 1977. The second, *Deficit*, was funded by an American Film Institute grant. Her third short film, *Yours Truly, Andrea G. Stern*, won prizes at the Chicago Film Festival, the American Film Festival, and the Athens International Film Festival.

While attending NYU, Seidelman caught up on all of the classic German Expressionist and French New Wave films she had neglected to see in her formative years. Her admiration for the artistry of filmmakers such as Federico Fellini, François Truffaut, Jean-Luc Godard, Roman Polanski, and of NYU alumni Martin Scorsese and Francis Ford Coppola is evident in the exuberant, free-flowing style that animates all of her work.

Seidelman earned an M.F.A. degree from NYU in 1977. Nevertheless, it was not until 1980, after three years working on television commercials and as a freelance editor, that she finally had the wherewithal to independently produce and to direct her first feature film, *Smithereens* (1982).

Life's Work

Smithereens is based on an original story by Susan Seidelman and Ron Nyswaner (adapted for the screen by Nyswaner and Peter Askin). Set in the gritty subculture of New York City's lower East Side, it is an offbeat comedy about a fame-seeking but ultimately failed heroine named Wren. Seidelman financed the film with a $10,000 inheritance, her own savings, and investments contributed by family and friends.

Working with an impossibly tight budget of $80,000 and with a formidable production schedule plagued by delays, Seidelman completed the film in two years and brought it to the Cannes Film Festival in May, 1982. It was accepted in the main competition there, the first independently produced American feature to achieve that distinction, and was ranked tenth among the festival's twenty-three entrants. The film had a successful New York opening in November, despite mixed reviews, and played well nationally.

Seidelman's next film, *Desperately Seeking Susan* (1985), is unquestionably her finest work and the one for which she is best known. Leora Barish's original screenplay is a buoyant screwball comedy about a middle-class New Jersey housewife, Roberta (played by Rosanna Arquette), who is intrigued by a cryptic classified advertisement from which the film's title is derived. Prompted by the promise of adventure, Roberta escapes the suburban doldrums only to become an amnesiac who believes she is the East Village free spirit Susan (Madonna) whom she has been seeking. This far-fetched tale of mistaken identities perfectly suited Seidelman's deft use of irony and her talent for weaving contrasting plot strands into a neatly blended narrative that never reaches for sentimentality or stoops to condescension. With a $5 million budget, provided by Orion Pictures, Seidelman shot the film in nine weeks on location in the fall of 1984 and completed editing in four months. When it opened March of 1985, *Desperately Seeking Susan* was favorably received by both critics and audiences. By the end of its run, the film had grossed approximately $30 million at the box office.

Although the film is an apotheosis of Seidelman's cinematic skills, it owes a good part of its success to the ascending celebrity of pop star Madonna, whose club-kid, magpie persona, at that time, coincided with the morally and generally vacant character she portrayed.

The films that followed from the three-picture deal Orion made with Seidelman were middling and box-office disappointments. All comedies that mixed farce with social commentary, these pictures fell short of the expectations of excellence her earlier films had promised. Nevertheless, to Seidelman's credit, she infused these films with an energy and a sense of whimsy that turned the mediocrity of their scripts into good-natured fun.

Floyd Byars and Laurie Frank's screenplay sets *Making Mr. Right* (1987) in the flat, open spaces of Florida, giving Seidelman a new milieu to explore, but, unfortunately, none of the urban character which she had always used so well. The story concerns a scientist and the android he creates (both played by John Malkovich in one of his few comic performances), and an image consultant (played by performance artist and actress Ann Magnuson) who is hired to humanize the creation. Seidelman said that she tried to address in this film the problems men and women confront when looking for the ideal mate, and what happens when those least expected to connect with each other end up doing so. The critics saw otherwise and unanimously panned the film.

Cookie (1989), a takeoff of a mob film, reunites Seidelman with the familiar terrain of New York City. Its eponymous heroine (played by British-born actress Emily Lloyd) is a gum-chewing Brooklyn teenager whose morals are as slack as her tongue is sharp. She is the driver for a paroled mob boss, played by Peter Falk, and, predictably, turns out to be his daughter by his mistress, played to dizzy perfection by Dianne Wiest. Nora Ephron and Alice Arlen's screenplay, although not without some charm, merely rehashes an old formula which, at its worst, relies on broad stereotypes and clichéd one-liners. At its best, *Cookie* is a cream puff of a film, but offers only empty calories.

In *She-Devil* (1989), her third film for Orion, Seidelman said she wanted to explore "the politics of beauty." In fact, she wanted the film to bring together all of her ideas about the complexities of identity, of illusion and reality, and about the difficulty of being an outsider in life. These ideas, however, do not cohere in the screenplay written by Barry Strugatz and Mark R. Burns, an uneven, tepid adaptation of Faye Weldon's scathing profeminist novel, *The Life and Loves of a She-Devil* (A more faithful adaptation is the film made for British television in the mid-1980's.) The problem with Seidelman's *She-Devil* is that it forsakes Weldon's mordant wit and grim irony for the contrived situations and reassurances of television comedy. The story is about an attractive and successful romance novelist, Mary Fisher (Meryl Streep), who steals the husband of an overweight housewife, Ruth Patchett (Roseanne Barr). It is immediately apparent where the viewer's allegiance ought to lie. Nevertheless, Mary is delightfully outlandish and fun to watch, while Ruth is repulsive and hardly likable, even though her vengeance and triumph over Mary is supposed to be the film's coup de grâce. The real coup, as it turned out, was casting Streep in a comedic lead, but Barr, who had to carry most of the film and whose limited range as an actor was painfully obvious, proved to be a mistake, and critics and audiences agreed.

Summary

At the age of thirty-two with her second feature, Susan Seidelman broke through the ranks of independent filmmakers to work successfully in commercial cinema. Nevertheless, she has chosen to stay a Hollywood outsider, remaining in Lower Manhattan, where she has lived since her film school days. It is not surprising, then, that all of her films are about women outside the mainstream who are eccentric, rebellious, and fiercely independent. Seidelman's women do not seem to fit within the narrow boundaries of normalcy and conventionalism in modern life. The world around them moves too quickly, changes too fast for them to begin to understand who they are and know where they belong in it. Their wild behavior is, in a sense, how they manage to survive.

An originality of ideas about contemporary society, a fascination with how people speak, think, and live, and an imaginative visual style are the outstanding characteristics of Seidelman's work. Her singular achievement as director of major Hollywood productions has heartened other independents, especially women, many of whom—Amy Heckerling, Martha Coolidge, Penelope Spheeris—have achieved success working in commercial cinema. A smart, proficient filmmaker, Susan Seidelman has achieved the freedom to choose the films she wants to make.

Bibliography

Bernikow, Louise. "The Devil and Susan Seidelman: A Director Who's One Smart Cookie," *Lear's* 2 (January 1, 1990): 108. An interview with Seidelman after the release of her film *Cookie*. Bernikow explores a number of issues related to Seidelman's struggle to find support for her work in Hollywood.

"The Director: An Interview with Susan Seidelman." *Gannett Center Journal* 3 (Summer, 1989): 78. This interview, conducted after Seidelman had completed work on *Cookie* and *She-Devil*, provides useful insights into her rites of passage in the film industry and the challenges that faced her in seeking creative control of her projects as one of America's leading female film directors.

Fischer, Lucy. "The Desire to Desire: *Desperately Seeking Susan*." In *Close Viewing: An Anthology of New Film Criticism*, edited by Peter Lehman. Gainesville: University Presses of Florida, 1990. Theoretical yet synthetic analysis of Seidelman's second commercial film. Compares *Desperately Seeking Susan* to other films that also portray women in dual roles, including some as absurdly diverse as *Rebecca* and *Cobra Woman*.

Quart, Barbara K. *Women Directors*. New York: Praeger, 1988. Includes a chapter on Seidelman's first three feature films. The author's chatty discussion style fails to focus clearly on the essence of Seidelman's work and neglects to provide plot summaries.

Travers, Peter. "Women on the Verge: Four Women Attempt to Infiltrate a Stronghold— The Director's Chair." *Rolling Stone* no. 561 (September 21, 1989): 47-48. Film critic Peter Travers interviews Seidelman along with directors Lee Grant (*Staying Together*), Kathryn Bigelow (*Blue Steel*), and Nancy Savoca (*True Love*). Provides a capsule overview of Seidelman's career along with a brief review of *Cookie*. Travers helps place Seidelman's achievements within the context of Hollywood's tenacious resistance against women film directors.

J. Greco

ELIZABETH ANN SETON

Born: August 28, 1774; New York, New York
Died: January 4, 1821; Emmitsburg, Maryland
Areas of Achievement: Religion and education
Contribution: Mother Seton, founder of the American Sisters of Charity, was the first American-born saint of the Roman Catholic church. She was an influential educator, a pioneer in promoting the education of young women.

Early Life

Elizabeth Ann Bayley was born on August 28, 1774, in New York City, the second daughter of Richard Bayley and Catherine Charlton Bayley. She was two years old when the Declaration of Independence was signed. Her father was a physician and medical researcher dedicated to treating the illnesses of New York's immigrants. Her mother was the daughter of an Anglican minister who was an early advocate of racial integration. Both parents provided an example of compassion for the less fortunate that would be reflected in Elizabeth's lifework.

In 1777, following the birth of her third child, Catherine Bayley died, leaving the infant Catherine and two other daughters, Mary and Elizabeth, motherless. Young Catherine lived only two years after her mother's death.

The physician Richard Bayley married Charlotte Barclay in 1778, and she bore him seven children. While Bayley provided financially for his daughters by his first marriage, he was not an attentive father, preoccupied as he was with his medical work and his extensive travels. Although Charlotte Bayley looked after the physical needs of her two stepdaughters, she showed them no affection. Both girls received a good basic education, however, as well as training in French and music.

Young Betty was an affectionate child, with an abundance of physical energy and a vivacious personality. She suffered intensely from loneliness, however, and felt alienated from her father's second family. When she was eight, she and her sister Mary were sent to New Rochelle to live with their uncle William Bayley. During the next four years, in a rural home with a view of the sea, Betty learned the love of nature that would be a source of spiritual strength throughout her life.

The girls returned to their father's house in 1786, but, following a family disagreement in 1790, Betty again left the Bayley household and lived with a succession of friends and relatives. As an adolescent, she turned to the Bible and private religious meditations for comfort. She was a member of the Episcopalian faith, but Catholic biographers see in this early interest in religion the seeds of the Catholicism that would inform her life's work. Her letters to her father in these years reveal her warm, intense personality and their deep affection for each other, despite his earlier neglect.

In 1794, Elizabeth married William Magee Seton, a wealthy New York merchant six years older than she. As their letters show, this marriage was based on strong physical attraction and intense friendship. Elizabeth was a small woman less than five feet tall, noted for her beauty and charm. She loved dancing, the theater, and the busy life of a New York society matron. Between 1795 and 1802, she bore William Seton five children and dedicated herself to her family and to charity work in the city.

Early in their marriage, William Seton began to show signs of the tuberculosis (then called consumption) that would cause his early death. In these years, too, the Seton family business collapsed, leaving the family impoverished and dependent on relatives. In 1803, Elizabeth and William, seeking the warmer climate that they hoped would ease the ravages of his disease, sailed to Italy. William died not long after their arrival, and the happy family life that had sustained Elizabeth for nine years ended. Seton, like many saints of the Roman Catholic church, would be inspired by a personal crisis to begin her life's work.

Life's Work

The Filicchi family in Italy, friends and business associates of William Seton, helped Elizabeth Seton through the immediate crisis of her husband's death in a foreign land. Responding to the warmth and comfort of the Filicchis, and drawn to the beauty of Italian churches, she became interested in the Roman Catholic faith.

When Seton returned to the United States, she underwent a period of physical and mental suffering, including severe weight loss and crying spells that modern psychologists would call clinical depression. She also began to show symptoms of the tuberculosis that had killed her husband. This time of personal crisis ended in 1805 when Seton decided to profess the Catholic faith. Since most Catholics of the time were poor Irish, French, and German immigrants of low social standing, her conversion shocked her family and friends. Moreover, Seton was impoverished, and she faced the task of rearing five children without an adequate income. Although she received some financial help from loyal friends, many relatives abandoned her.

Seton kept her family together in New York by running a boarding house for students. She provoked the anger of the Seton family when her sister-in-law Cecelia also converted to the Catholic faith. With the financial support of Antonio Filicchi and the encouragement of Bishop John Carroll of Baltimore, Elizabeth Seton left New York for Baltimore in 1808 to found a religious school for seven pupils, three of them her own daughters. Her sons were enrolled at Georgetown, then a Jesuit school for boys.

Her intention to form a Catholic sisterhood was realized in 1809, when, assisted by the generosity of Samuel Cooper, a wealthy benefactor, she acquired property in Emmitsburg, Maryland, about fifty miles west of Baltimore. She professed vows of poverty, chastity, and obedience to archbishop John Carroll, and, with the five sisters who had joined her, founded the first American religious community, known then as the Sisters of Charity of St. Joseph.

These first sisters chose as their mission the education of young girls. In addition to the hardships of living in crowded conditions without enough heat in the severe winter weather, Mother Seton and her small community lived with the constant threat of serious illness, which was common in the early nineteenth century. Moreover, because she was bound by the vow of obedience to the men who led the Catholic church, she was embroiled in disagreements about the supervision of her community.

At issue, too, was the question of the rules governing the new community. The regulations of European religious orders were not easily applied to American life. According to the rules of the French Sisters of Charity, the religious order on which the American community was modeled, Seton would have had to give up her rights as guardian of her children. Among the many battles Seton fought against her male clerical superiors, her most successful was winning the right to found her community without giving up her children.

The American Sisters of Charity, as her order was eventually called, adopted the customary clothing of Italian widows that Seton had worn since the death of her husband. This habit was a plain black dress with a shoulder cape, with a white cap tied under the chin. The most famous portrait of Mother Seton shows her wearing this religious habit.

The Sisters of Charity took as their primary mission the education of girls and young women. In order to pay for the upkeep of the buildings in Emmitsburg, the sisters taught young women from wealthy families who could afford to pay for their education. Because of the poor roads and the distance between home and school, these students boarded at the school. Mother Seton believed in education for all, however, and she provided a free education for a number of local girls, including many black children.

Mother Seton's philosophy of education was revealed in her many diaries, journals, and letters. She believed in strictly regulating the lives of the girls in her charge. Students began their day with prayer in the chapel and continued with studies in mathematics, grammar, and music as well as religious studies. Mother Seton's ideals of self-discipline and peacefulness in education apparently served her students well, as their affectionate letters to her after leaving school attest. This philosophy of education is generally regarded as the model for the parochial school system that would flourish in later years.

The community grew and expanded its mission. In 1814, the sisters founded the first Catholic orphanage in the United States in Philadelphia, and in 1817 they founded a similar institution in New York City. The Sisters of Charity also founded the first Catholic hospital in 1823. At the time of her death, there were twenty communities based on Mother Seton's ideals.

Elizabeth Seton's physical and spiritual energy was astounding, since for most of her adult life she suffered the ravages of tuberculosis. She suffered terrible personal tragedies as well. Her oldest daughter, Anna Maria, died of tuberculosis in 1812 at the age of seventeen. The loss of this child, her dearest companion, was a severe blow that precipitated a period of despair. Four years later, her daughter Rebecca died at the age of fourteen of a spinal tumor. A number of the sisters of the community succumbed to tuberculosis and other illnesses as well. Despite these personal crises and the constant financial problems of maintaining her community, Mother Seton's letters and journals reveal her deep faith in God and her mission.

In addition to her work as a teacher and spiritual leader, Mother Seton wrote a number of textbooks and spiritual treatises, as well as English translations of religious works written in French.

Elizabeth Seton died in 1821 at the age of forty-six at her community in Emmitsburg, among the sisters whose lives she had directed for twelve years. She was survived by her daughter Catherine, who died at the age of ninety as a nun; her son William, an officer in the United States Navy; and her son Richard, who had joined the business of the Filicchi family. She was canonized as a saint of the Roman Catholic church in 1975.

Summary

It is significant that the Catholic church, which prizes celibacy, chose as its first American-born saint a widow and the mother of five children. Elizabeth Ann Seton's new community clearly established that the rules of the religion of the Old World must be adapted to the American ideal of independence.

Beyond her importance to religious believers, however, Mother Seton's life and work have a uniquely American significance. Education, she believed, must transcend the old distinctions of class and discrimination and must be available to all, especially young women.

As a woman of the nineteenth century, when women's public role was largely confined to marriage and motherhood, Elizabeth Seton offers a model to all women. As a Catholic sister, she had opportunities not available to other women of the time. She established the rules for her own community, was involved in meaningful work in society, and had the freedom to develop friendships with the women of her community and influential churchmen of the time. Her followers in her own and other religious communities became administrators of schools and hospitals and other charitable institutions and earned the respect of people of all religions. The work of Mother Seton and other religious women of the nineteenth century is a powerful example of the strength and conviction of American women as a force in improving society by serving the poor, the sick, and the uneducated.

Bibliography

Dirvin, Joseph I. *Mrs. Seton: Foundress of the American Sisters of Charity*. New York: Farrar, Straus & Giroux, 1962. Mother Seton's life is interpreted by a priest who, working from original sources, is especially interested in tracing the development of his subject's spiritual life.

Dolan, Jay P. "The Immigrant Church: Schools." In *The American Catholic Experience: A History from Colonial Times to the Present*. Garden City, N.Y.: Doubleday, 1985. A good explanation of the development of the nineteenth century parochial school system, the social movement in which Mother Seton was a pioneer.

Ewens, Mary. "The Leadership of Nuns in Immigrant Catholicism." In *The Nineteenth Century*. Vol. 1 in *Women and Religion in America*, edited by Rosemary Radford Ruether and Rosemary Skinner Keller. San Francisco: Harper & Row, 1981. A scholarly feminist survey of the subject, with emphasis on the achievement of women in a male-dominated society.

Knowles, Leo. "An American Woman: St. Elizabeth Seton." In *Saints Who Spoke English*. St. Paul, Minn.: Carillon Books, 1979. The author has compiled simplified biographies, including much anecdotal material (somewhat romanticized), of fourteen saints.

Maynard, Theodore. *Great Catholics in American History*. Garden City, N.Y.: Hanover House, 1957. Mother Seton's work is considered in the context of the lives of twenty other figures representing the historical contributions of American Catholics to the life of the nation.

Melville, Annabelle M. *Elizabeth Bayley Seton: 1774-1821*. New York: Charles Scribner's Sons, 1951. A scholarly investigation using Mother Seton's own writings as well as historical sources. It offers a realistic portrait of her character development against the background of early nineteenth century America.

Marjorie J. Podolsky

ANNE SEXTON

Born: November 9, 1928; Newton, Massachusetts
Died: October 4, 1974; Weston, Massachusetts
Area of Achievement: Literature
Contribution: Despite a modest education and her lifelong struggle with mental illness, Anne Sexton became a poet who was celebrated by critics, academics, and the public as a new voice in literature and the cause of feminism.

Early Life

Anne Gray Harvey was born on November 9, 1928, the youngest of three daughters born to Ralph Harvey and Mary Gray Staples Harvey. Although Ralph Harvey had only a high school education, he did well in the New England wool business and opened his own firm shortly after Anne was born. Anne's mother, Mary Gray Staples, was born into a Maine family whose members held important positions in state politics and journalism. An adored only child, Mary Gray was sent to boarding school and completed three years at Wellesley College.

The three Harvey daughters were never close, and Anne grew up a lonely child. Ralph Harvey was fastidious of appearances, and Anne's messy clothes and loud voice failed to please him. Years after her sisters were permitted to join their parents at the dinner table, Anne continued to eat in the breakfast room with the nurse. Her parents went out most nights, threw large parties, and drank constantly. Anne's only happy memories were of summers at the Squirrel Island, Maine, vacation home with her mother's extended family. A great-aunt, Anna Dingley, who had lived abroad and later become a reporter for her father's newspaper, provided Anne's greatest family affection. Despite her full life, Dingley, called "Nana" by the children, played the family spinster. She moved in with the Harveys when Anne was eleven, and Anne remembers her as the only person who provided a parent's unconditional love.

Anne bloomed during her teenage years. Her mother, hoping to remedy her "boy-crazy" behavior, sent her to Rogers Hall, a girls' boarding school in Lowell, Massachusetts. Although she was an indifferent student, Anne published early poems in the school yearbook. She went on to Garland School, a finishing school in Boston, and became engaged. While still engaged, she met Alfred Muller Sexton II, called "Kayo," a young man from a prosperous Boston suburb, and eloped with him on August 16, 1948. Their first daughter, Linda Gray Sexton, was born in the summer of 1953, and Joyce Ladd Sexton was born two years later. Kayo accepted a job as wool salesman from his father-in-law, and the young family settled down near Boston, close to their childhood homes.

Despite the idealized roles of housewife and mother in the 1950's, Anne was severely depressed after the birth of her second child. She suffered terrors and fits of rage during which she abused the children and even attempted suicide. Her family paid first for household help, then for psychiatric help. While the children lived with relatives, Anne began treatment first with Martha Brunner-Orne in 1955, and later with her son, Martin Orne. Recognizing Anne's creative potential, he encouraged her to write. After another suicide attempt in May, 1957, Orne told her that she couldn't kill herself; she had too much to give through her poetry. Anne Sexton, the poet, was born.

Life's Work

With Martin Orne's encouragement, Anne Sexton enrolled in an evening poetry workshop and began to send her poems out for possible publication. More important, however, was the bond she formed with another student in the workshop, Maxine Kumin, which was to become the most fruitful poetic relationship in Sexton's life. The well-educated Kumin was three years older than Sexton, also had small children, and published regularly. Her instant recognition of Sexton's gift cemented a friendship that would comfort Sexton for the rest of her life.

By spring of 1958, Sexton was taking a new antidepressant drug and felt well enough for her daughter, Joy, to come home to live. She received occasional acceptances from prestigious magazines such as *Harper's* and *The New Yorker*. Her poetry was developing in new directions, partly as a result of her encounter with "Heart's Needle," a poem by William DeWitt Snodgrass which was seminal in what was to become known as "confessional" poetry. This poetry addresses the "unpoetic" themes in a person's life: domestic struggles, personal failure, and mental illness. At its best, it is well crafted and formally polished. Sexton attended the Writer's Conference at Antioch College in Ohio, where Snodgrass led a week's workshop. This marked the start of a long correspondence in which Snodgrass helped her find an authentic voice and encouraged her tendency to use poems as vehicles of autobiography and self-analysis. Her connection with Snodgrass led to an acceptance in Robert Lowell's famous writing seminar at Boston University, where she became friendly with poet Sylvia Plath. It was here that Sexton started her first major poem, "The Double Image," which established her among the new "confessional" poets.

In May of 1959, Houghton Mifflin accepted Sexton's first book, *To Bedlam and Part Way Back*. Even before it appeared, Sexton was in demand for readings at Harvard and for a series of recordings at Yale. The book came out in April, 1960, and received wide attention, partly because of Sexton's honesty in speaking of her mental illness. On the strength of the book, she was one of the first to apply to a new program at Radcliffe College designed for women whose careers had been interrupted. When Sexton received an acceptance the day after her friend, Kumin, received hers, she was jubilant. An honorarium of $2,000 that came with it was used to convert the back porch to a study for her use, but the biggest difference was in her relationship to her family. They finally considered her work respectable. Sexton felt well during this period and started to enjoy being with her family, particularly around their new swimming pool. Kumin frequently joined her with her children, and their friendship deepened. In the fall of 1961, *Newsweek* featured Sexton in an article on Radcliffe's new program, and soon afterward *The New Yorker* offered her a coveted "first reader" agreement. Some of her strongest poems date from this time, including "The Fortress," which was written for her daughter Linda.

All My Pretty Ones, her second collection, came out in October of 1962 and won mostly rave reviews. On the short list for the National Book Award, it established the themes she was to write about for the rest of her life: mental illness, sexual love, and spiritual anguish. A new orientation to her themes was to come with her growing interest in the feminist movement, triggered by the landmark publication of Betty Friedan's *The Feminine Mystique* (1963).

The suicide of her friend Sylvia Plath in 1963 affected her badly, and to make matters worse, she became involved in an affair with her new therapist. She worked on a long-abandoned play, but broke down and was hospitalized briefly. Her doctor prescribed Thorazine, which produced severe, long-term side effects. Nevertheless, Sexton continued to write. A new poetry collection called *Live or Die* came out in September of 1966 to mixed reviews. That same autumn, Sexton's therapist, Ollie Zweitung, terminated their affair. Distraught, she fell down the stairs at home and broke her hip.

After a long winter of convalescing, Sexton received heartening news: She had won a Pulitzer Prize. During this period, Sexton completed work for her next collection, *Love Poems*, which appeared in 1968. The following year there was some interest in her play *Mercy Street*, and she received a Guggenheim Foundation award that would help fund production. The play opened in October of 1969 at the American Place Theater in New York to mixed reviews, and had a brief run. A more successful venture was *Transformations*. Intended to be a popular poetry book of black humor, it took the form of fairy tales that Sexton transformed from the traditional ones. In September, 1972, Sexton was appointed part-time professor at Boston University, and she also accepted an appointment in literature at Colgate University, which required a long weekly journey to teach two days of classes in New York. In spite of her teaching commitments, she completed *The Book of Folly* and continued to work on *The Death Notebooks*, which turned out to be the last collection published during her lifetime.

Professional success did not alleviate her inner turmoil. During twenty days in January, 1973, that included two days in a mental hospital, Sexton wrote thirty-nine poems that were to make up a posthumous volume: *The Awful Rowing Towards God*. The poems came from a sudden frenzy of energy that resulted in bursts of images, and it was Kumin's encouragement that guided Sexton in the editing that completed the book. During the same surge of energy, Sexton made a decision to divorce her husband, an act that enraged her family.

After the publication of *The Death Notebooks* in February, 1974, Sexton was bombarded with requests for personal appearances. The high point of that winter was a reading in March arranged by the Harvard Literary Club, which was to be the Boston debut of *The Death Notebooks*. It turned out to be a triumph. Nevertheless, she was becoming more unstable, and she made another suicide attempt. Increasingly isolated from her family and old friends, she began to drink heavily and engaged in casual affairs with strangers. On Friday, October 4, 1974, she had a last working lunch with Kumin, then went home and committed suicide.

Summary

Anne Sexton's poetry was particularly important to young women in the 1960's and 1970's because of its intimate nature and feminist themes. She illustrated the problematic position of women at the time, the struggle to create an identity beyond what was recognized as "women's place in society." Another important feminist theme grew from Sexton's relationship with her mother and daughters. Some of Sexton's poems suggest that a woman *is* her mother and open the way for a new evaluation of the mother-daughter connection. Sexton wrote of menstruation, abortion, incest, adultery, and drug addiction when such topics were not considered suitable for poetry, particularly by male critics. Always grateful for the support of other women poets, she had much in common with Sylvia Plath, Maxine Kumin, May Swenson, Adrienne Rich, and Denise Levertov.

Sexton's poetry often addresses the sexual stereotyping of women and other themes that were central to the emerging feminist movement. As Sexton struggled with these issues in her own life, she confronted problems that she could not solve, but she was able to use them in her art. Contemporary women's poetry owes a debt to Sexton's pioneering work, which gave women the courage to think about their own lives honestly and courageously.

Bibliography

George, Diana Hume, ed. *Sexton: Selected Criticism*. Urbana: University of Illinois Press, 1988. Hume has collected eighteen essays that represent diverse perspectives and conclusions, although they all approach Sexton's work from a feminist viewpoint. Some are published here for the first time.

Hall, Caroline King Barnard. *Anne Sexton*. Boston: Twayne, 1989. Part of Twayne's United States Authors series, this volume studies Sexton's poetry chronologically with the aim of acquainting the reader with the whole work of an important poet. Hall examines the poet as the subject of her poems. This volume is a useful introduction, providing a framework for more advanced study.

Markey, Janice. *A New Tradition? The Poetry of Sylvia Plath, Anne Sexton, and Adrienne Rich*. New York: P. Lang, 1985. This valuable textual analysis tries to fit the three poets' work into the literary tradition. The relationship between feminism and poetry that characterizes the work of all three poets is discussed at length.

Middlebrook, Diane Wood. *Anne Sexton: A Biography*. Boston: Houghton Mifflin, 1991. Both comprehensive and controversial, Middlebrook's sources include tapes from Sexton's psychotherapy sessions with Martin Orne. The biographer uses them to illustrate the inextricable connection between the poet's illness and her writing.

Sexton, Linda Gray, and Lois Ames, eds. *Anne Sexton: A Self-Portrait in Letters*. Boston: Houghton Mifflin, 1977. Among these letters are intimate writings to her family as well as more formal correspondence to some of the major figures of twentieth century literature. The editors provide a helpful commentary.

Sheila Golburgh Johnson

DONNA SHALALA

Born: February 14, 1941; Cleveland, Ohio

Areas of Achievement: Education and government and politics
Contribution: Shalala served as head of two educational institutions, Hunter College in New York City, and the University of Wisconsin, where she was the first woman to lead a Big Ten University and one of the first to head a major research university before being named secretary of Health and Human Services by President Bill Clinton.

Early Life

Donna Edna Shalala was born on February 14, 1941, sharing her birthday with her twin sister Diane. She was born in Cleveland, Ohio, to parents of Lebanese descent, James Abraham Shalala and Edna Smith Shalala.

Shalala's propensity for leadership was already illustrated during her childhood. When she was nine years old, her home in Ohio was threatened by a tornado. As the family ran for cover, all were accounted for except Donna. Searching desperately for her, the alarmed mother found that her daughter was at a nearby intersection, directing traffic.

Shalala's drive and energy seem to have come from her mother, a woman who, while juggling two teaching jobs and the care of her daughters during the early 1950's, worked her way through law school. Edna Shalala was also a nationally ranked tennis player; into her eighties she continued to practice law full-time and compete in national tennis tournaments for players over the age of seventy-five. Donna's leadership and civic commitment are also modeled on her father, who was a civic leader in their Lebanese-Syrian community in Cleveland.

As a child, Donna Shalala was an outstanding athlete. When she was eleven, she wanted to play first base for her local summer softball league. Although her coach said she was too small, she persisted until he relented and gave her the position, a decision he never regretted, since the team went on to win the Cleveland city championship. In her teens Shalala was also a city and state tennis champion.

She received her undergraduate education in urban studies at Western College for Women in Oxford, Ohio, graduating with honors in 1962. Next, she spent two years in Iran as part of the Peace Corps. After a trip around the world, Shalala returned to the United States and completed her graduate studies at Syracuse University. During the summers, she traveled to Lebanon and Syria, teaching English as a second language for the United States Information Agency. While in graduate school Shalala also became, in 1966, the assistant director of the university's urban community development program and the Peace Corps Training Project for Peru. In 1967, she was appointed assistant to the chair of the New York State Constitutional Convention's Committee on Local Government and Home Rule. She received her master of social science degree in 1968, and her doctorate in politics and economics in 1970.

Life's Work

After completing her graduate studies, Donna Shalala moved from Syracuse to New York City, hoping to become a reporter for *The New York Times*. Failing to achieve this goal, she chose instead to accept a post as an assistant professor of political science at Bernard M. Baruch College, a Manhattan campus of the City University of New York. She stayed at Baruch College until 1972, when she moved to a position as associate professor of politics and education at the Teachers College of Columbia University, also serving as a visiting professor at Yale Law School. Shalala's appointment at Columbia lasted until 1979, although meanwhile she was also involved in two governmental positions.

Much of Shalala's early academic research and publication dealt with New York City politics. This work led to her appointment, in 1975, as a director of the Municipal Assistance Corporation, a body established specifically to pull New York City out of a dangerous financial crisis. Although she was the youngest member and the only woman on the board, Shalala was named its treasurer, taking on the responsibility of issuing $6 billion in bonds to refinance New York City's debt, closing on bond sales to financial institutions, and lobbying in the state capital. Again, her extraordinary leadership style showed itself. In one incident, after being barred from entering a Chicago club because she was a woman, Shalala went in the back door and sold bonds anyway.

In 1977, while still part of Columbia's faculty, she left the Municipal Assistance Corporation to join President Jimmy Carter's administration as assistant secretary for policy development and research in the Department of Housing and Urban Development (HUD). Shalala immediately set out to remedy some of the injustices against women in the area of housing. She began a multimillion dollar project to teach women, who owned only eighteen percent of the homes in the United States, the advantages and disadvantages of homeownership and how to qualify and shop for a mortgage. She also developed a women's policy and program staff, a home-weatherization program for female homeowners, a funding program for battered women's shelters, and special studies of the housing needs of female-headed families. Her tenure at HUD marked the beginning of serious government attention to housing as a women's issue. In addition to this work, she also helped found a support system for women in government, called the Women's Network.

Despite these successes, the late 1970's were a difficult time for Shalala. Unprepared for the harsh competition and aggressive political turf-battles of the Washington scene, Shalala experienced emotional exhaustion. Never one to succumb to difficult circumstances, she learned valuable lessons and made it through those years, developing new political skills.

In 1980, Shalala was inaugurated as president of Hunter College, the largest campus of the City University of New York. Although her appointment was controversial because of her lack of academic experience, she remained for seven years. She was, at the age of thirty-nine, the youngest woman ever to head a college, and the youngest president that Hunter had ever had.

The school was troubled by declining enrollment and financial resources; during her time there, Shalala turned around both problems. As her first act, Shalala personally contacted all the college's department heads, many of whom had opposed her appointment, asking for their input on the college's needs. She then involved faculty members in recruiting students, meanwhile raising one million dollars in private gifts in 1980 alone. While at Hunter, she also doubled the physical plant of the college, tripled the size of the library, more than quadrupled the amount of research money, and increased the number of women on the faculty and administration of the college. Despite her heavy administrative duties, Shalala also found time to teach some courses.

In 1987, Shalala was named chancellor of the University of Wisconsin at Madison, becoming the first woman ever to head a Big Ten university, and one of the only two female heads of major research universities. During her time at Madison, Shalala was faced with a number of major crises. Even before taking office, she was aware of a racial crisis brewing on this 43,000 student campus (the nation's fourth-largest university). With a minority enrollment of only five percent, a case involving derogatory depictions of racial minorities by a fraternity had resulted in high tension. One month after arriving in Wisconsin, Shalala issued her "Madison Plan," designed to increase minority presence on campus by employing new recruitment and retention strategies to attract and maintain minority students and by hiring more minority faculty members. Her concern was not only fairness to minorities but also the need to provide all students with a racially balanced learning environment.

She also instituted programs to improve the morale of undergraduates (often ignored on this research campus), rebuild Madison's ailing athletic programs, combat alcoholism on campus, increase the quality of elementary and secondary education, and promote science in the public schools. In addition, she was involved in controversies about verbal harassment based on race, sex, and other categories, and about the refusal of the Reserve Officers Training Corp to accept homosexuals.

In the fall of 1992, Donna Shalala was asked to become secretary of Health and Human Services for President Bill Clinton's cabinet, putting her back in Washington, D.C. Shalala's appointment was controversial because she lacked direct experience in the health field. Her prodigious administrative ability, combined with her experience as head of the University of Wisconsin hospital system during her tenure as chancellor, played in her favor, and she won the necessary confirmation for the position. In this cabinet post, Shalala played a major part, with Hillary Rodham Clinton, in developing the Clinton Administration's plan for reform of American health care. Shalala's priorities as secretary of Health and Human Services included making serious changes in women's and children's health care, finding treatment for ovarian, cervical and breast cancer, increasing the immunization of children, and developing a comprehensive approach to the AIDS epidemic.

Summary

Donna Shalala's enormous energy, proven political and administrative skill, willingness to get involved personally and to insist that others do so, ability to face controversy head-on and make difficult decisions, and commitment to justice in issues of gender, race, and sexual orientation, have helped make her a woman of great influence and importance in the United States. Her accomplishments, each appropriate to the particular situation, have been enormous. As a member of the Municipal Assistance Corporation she applied her knowledge of urban politics—specifically, New York City politics—to help resolve the city's financial crisis. As a part of the Department of Housing and Urban Development, she initiated programs to improve women's opportunities to own their own homes, to maintain decent housing, and to escape domestic violence. As president of Hunter College, she not only resolved the financial crisis but also increased the size of the college, its library, and its endowment. As chancellor of the University of Wisconsin, she committed herself to encouraging racial diversity, and she rebuilt the ailing athletic program, among many other initiatives that will have a lasting effect on the state of Wisconsin and its university. These accomplishments prepared her for her role as a member of the president's cabinet, and she has approached the issues that have faced her as secretary of Health and Human Services with her usual energy, integrity, and skill. Whatever she is doing, Donna Shalala immerses herself completely, confronting and proposing strategies to cope with the particular issues before her, thus providing both a role model for others and a lasting bequest to every institution with which she is involved.

Bibliography
Angelo, Bonnie. "Big Campus, Big Issues." *Time* 135 (April 23, 1990): 11-19. An interview with Donna Shalala while she was chancellor of the University of Wisconsin. The article focuses on a variety of campus issues such as the athletic crisis, alcoholism, sexism, racism, and the value of large research universities.
Bennetts, Leslie. "Donna Shalala Takes on Big-City Finance, Big Government, and Now . . . Urban Education." *Ms.* 9 (December, 1980): 88-94. This article, published as she was about to become president of Hunter College, details Shalala's early life and career, especially her experience in the Carter Administration, and her administrative and political style.
Cleveland, Ceil. "Campus CEO." *Working Woman* 16 (December, 1991): 60-63. Profile of Shalala highlighting her experiences as chancellor of the University of Wisconsin. The author discusses Shalala's management style, assesses her skills as one of the top five administrators in higher education, and addresses many of the issues Shalala chose to tackle during her tenure as chancellor.
Kosterlitz, Julie. "Thunder on the Left?" *National Journal* 25 (May 29, 1993): 1292-1296. A discussion of Shalala's activities as secretary of Health and Human Services. Noted for her political adeptness, Shalala has endeavored to make her agency more responsive to the needs of the public by meeting with various interest groups to confront important issues such as health care reform and the fight against AIDS.
Toobin, Jeffrey. "The Shalala Strategy." *The New Yorker* 69 (April 26, 1993): 53-62.

Addresses Shalala's early performance as secretary of Health and Human Services in the Clinton cabinet. In addition to providing details about her relationship with Hillary Rodham Clinton and their work together on health-care reform, the article also discusses the various crises and situations Shalala faced at the University of Wisconsin, and her responses to them.

Eleanor B. Amico

ANNA HOWARD SHAW

Born: February 14, 1847; Newcastle upon Tyne, Northumberland, England
Died: July 2, 1919; Moylan, Pennsylvania
Area of Achievement: Women's rights
Contribution: The first American woman to hold divinity and medical degrees simultaneously, the Reverend Shaw was a central figure in the crusades for political equality and women's rights.

Early Life

Anna Howard Shaw was born on Valentine's Day, 1847, in Newcastle upon Tyne, England. As the sixth child of a fragile and despondent mother and a restless and irresponsible father, Anna was not a likely prospect for fame or fortune. At age four, Anna moved with her family to the United States, settling in New Bedford, Massachusetts. Shortly before the Civil War, the Shaw family moved to the Michigan frontier. Anna spent her early teens cutting firewood, digging wells, caring for her sickly mother, and generally overseeing the Shaw household while her father and older brothers were away at war.

Anna pitied her mother, viewing her as a weak, lonely woman, overburdened with meaningless household chores, embittered by her plight yet unwilling or unable to escape her oppression. As a youth, Anna dreamed that she would be different. After years of indecision, Anna marshaled the courage to defy family tradition and pursue a formal education. At the age of twenty-four, despite the protests of her father, she left home to attend a high school in Big Rapids.

While in Big Rapids, Shaw met the Reverend Marianna Thompson. Inspired by this new and unusual role model, Shaw decided that she also would prepare for the ministry. Embarrassed at her decision, yet knowing that his disapproval would not stop her, her father attempted to dissuade Anna by offering to send her to the University of Michigan if she agreed to abandon her ministerial ambitions. By now a young woman with growing self-confidence, Shaw rejected her father's offer, secured a Methodist preaching license, and enrolled at Albion College, a Methodist school in southern Michigan.

Without financial or emotional backing from her family, Shaw supported herself during her two years at Albion with occasional preaching and public temperance speaking. Buoyed by her success, Shaw left Michigan for the School of Theology of Boston University, becoming only the second female to enroll at the institution. After being graduated in 1878, she secured a pastorate in East Dennis, Massachusetts. In 1880, Shaw pursued full ordination within the Methodist Episcopal Church. Denied such ordination, she entered into fellowship with the smaller Methodist Protestant denomination, and, amid great controversy, she was ordained as an elder in October of 1880.

Having successfully entered one profession dominated by men, Shaw embarked in 1883 on a second "for men only" profession. Without giving up her pastorate, Shaw began part-time work toward a medical degree. After completing her studies in 1886, Shaw became the first American woman to hold divinity and medical degrees simultaneously.

Despite her accomplishments, Shaw in the 1880's was undergoing a midlife crisis. Sympathetic from her youth to the plight of the disadvantaged, Shaw had entered the ministry in hopes of elevating the discouraged from their spiritual poverty. Convinced later that she must do more to relieve human suffering, she returned to medical school, and, after her graduation, requested a temporary leave from the pastoral ministry in order to serve as a paramedic in the slums of South Boston. While ministering to the emotional and physical needs of women prostitutes, Shaw concluded that the solutions to many of their problems were political. Ministers and physicians could treat the symptoms, but legislatures responding to the demands of an enlightened electorate were needed to eliminate the root causes of social injustice, poverty, and sickness.

Life's Work

At age thirty-nine, Anna Howard Shaw left the preaching and healing ministry for another career. Joining first the Massachusetts Suffrage Association and later the American Woman Suffrage Association (AWSA), Shaw became a full-time organizer and lecturer for the causes of suffrage and temperance. At the urging of Frances Willard, a fellow Methodist preacher and president of the Woman Christian's Temperance Union (WCTU), Shaw accepted the chair of the Franchise Department of the WCTU. Her task was to work for woman suffrage and then to use the ballot to gain "home protection" and temperance legislation.

In 1888, Shaw was selected as a delegate to represent both the WCTU and the AWSA at the first meeting of the International Council of Women. While at the gathering in Washington, D.C., Shaw met Susan B. Anthony, the renowned leader of the more radical National Woman Suffrage Association (NWSA). Anthony, who at this time was looking for recruits to groom for leadership within the NWSA, was immediately impressed with Shaw's potential. As a sturdy, spunky young woman, Shaw had the stamina for travel; as a single person, Shaw had total control of her time; as an extemporaneous preacher, Shaw had impressive oratorial skills; and as a respected religious figure, Shaw had a reputation that would soften the NWSA's "irreligious and radical" public image.

During the convention, Anthony made Shaw her special project, flattering her and reprimanding her for not efficiently using her gifts for the cause. Unlike Willard and other "social feminists," Anthony viewed suffrage less as a means to an end than as a fundamental right that must not be denied. As a single-issue woman, Anthony challenged Shaw not to waste her talents on temperance, but to commit herself totally to full suffrage. In response to Anthony's challenge, Shaw shifted her allegiance from the AWSA to the NWSA and promised Anthony that suffrage would become her consuming goal.

The emerging Anthony-Shaw friendship had a profound impact on the suffrage movement. In 1889, Shaw helped to persuade the AWSA to merge with Anthony's and

Elizabeth Cady Stanton's NWSA, creating for the first time in two decades a semblance of organizational unity within the movement. Three years later, Anthony accepted the presidency of the unified National-American Woman Suffrage Association (NAWSA) and secured for Shaw the vice presidency.

The Anthony-Shaw tandem was inseparable—collaborating, traveling, even living together. An odd-looking couple, good-naturedly called by friends "the ruler and the rubber-ball," Anthony and Shaw were strikingly different in appearance, style, and talent: Anthony was tall and thin, an unconventional, religious agnostic and organizational genius; Shaw, a roly-poly Methodist preacher with a quick wit and golden tongue. Despite, or perhaps because of their differences, they were able to extend each other's outreach and effectiveness. Shaw, exploiting her religious reputation and church contacts, introduced Anthony into mainline Protestant circles previous closed to Anthony and "her girls." Anthony, in return, taught the inexperienced Shaw how to devise and execute a strategy for suffrage victory. Grooming Shaw for executive leadership, Anthony prodded Shaw to follow a strategy of moderate agitation, always pressing forward the cause of suffrage, yet never alienating the masses with unnecessary conflict. More traditional than Anthony, Shaw accepted her master teacher's pragmatism. By the time of Anthony's death in 1906, Shaw had learned her lessons well.

Between 1904 and 1915, Shaw served as president of the NAWSA. During this era, the organization grew from 17,000 to 200,000 members and superintended suffrage victories in eight additional states. As the organization grew, however, it also became more divided. The success of the militant suffragettes in England pressured Shaw to abandon the methods she had learned under Anthony for more militant tactics such as campaigning against the political party in power rather than individual candidates unfriendly to suffrage, picketing the White House, calling hunger strikes, and pressing for immediate suffrage elections, even if there was no prospect for victory. Although Shaw grew to accept "passive resistance," she refused to abandon her mentor's game plan. "I am, and always have been," Shaw asserted in 1914, "unalterably opposed to militancy, believing that nothing of permanent value has ever been secured by it that could not have been more easily obtained by peaceful methods."

Although Shaw's policy of moderation raised her stature among the rank and file of the NAWSA, it also cost her respect among the more aggressive members within her executive committee. In December, 1915, at age 68, Shaw stepped down as president of the NAWSA, a position she had held longer than any other woman, and accepted the lifetime honorary position of president emeritus. Although official NAWSA publications attempted to cover up the internal feud, and most members never realized the depth of the disharmony, Shaw's resignation was not voluntary. Leaving the administrative details to the returning president, Carrie Chapman Catt, Shaw began working full-time at what she did best—traveling, lecturing, and evangelizing for the suffrage cause.

In May, 1917, President Woodrow Wilson asked Shaw to head the Woman's Committee of the Council of National Defense. Always an American patriot, and, like

Wilson, mesmerized by the prospect of making the world safe for democracy, Shaw left the suffrage circuit to accept the appointment. For two years, she worked to mobilize American women to contribute to the war effort. Following victory in Europe, Shaw resigned as chair of the Woman's Committee. In appreciation for her war service, President Wilson awarded her the Distinguished Service Medal of Honor, an award never before bestowed upon an American woman.

Shaw's retirement from public service, however, was short-lived, for soon she returned to the lecture circuit—this time to win support for the League of Nations. Although her spirit was willing, the ailing Shaw was unable to withstand the strain of another campaign. Succumbing to pneumonia, Shaw died in her home in Moylan, Pennsylvania, on July 2, 1919.

Summary

A Methodist clergywoman who was persuaded that Jesus Christ embodied the best attributes of both man and woman, that in Christ there was neither male nor female, and that full suffrage would adorn the coming millennial Kingdom, Anna Howard Shaw was an eternal optimist who never doubted that suffrage victory would be won. Claiming the motto "Truth loses many battles, but always wins the war," Shaw spoke and acted as if the impossible was already a reality. For Shaw, full suffrage, like the coming Kingdom, could be delayed but not denied.

Shaw's religious reputation and noted nonmilitancy made her an ideal candidate to lead the counterattack against those who opposed suffrage rights for women. In virtually every address, Shaw hammered at the "ridiculous" arguments of those who insisted that woman's suffrage would destroy the home, the church, and the nation. Early in the campaign, her opponents often challenged Shaw to public debates. By 1913, however, the National Anti-Suffrage Association adopted a policy of prohibiting any of its speakers from debating Shaw. Their cause, they believed, was better served by ignoring rather than challenging the Methodist suffrage evangelist.

Following her death, newspaper editors, regardless of their stand on the woman question, united in their testimonials to Shaw. The *New Haven Register* eulogized Shaw as "the best beloved and most versatile of the suffrage leaders"; *The Nation* labeled her as "the ideal type of reformer. . . . the despair of the anti-suffragists because she was so normal and sane, so sound and so effective"; the *Philadelphia Press* praised the "sense, moderation and dignity in her methods which won and held respect even of those who opposed her cause"; and the more conservative *Atlanta Constitution* characterized Shaw as follows: "Though an ardent suffragist, her sense of justice was so impressed upon her records that anti-suffragists and suffragists alike trusted her." Such tributes from both suffrage friends and foes suggest that the woman widely known as the "Demosthenes of the suffrage movement" had become by the time of her death a national heroine. Despite these accolades, however, Shaw has been largely neglected by historians, and she remains the only central leader of the suffrage movement without a full-length biography.

Bibliography

Flexner, Eleanor. *Century of Struggle: The Woman's Rights Movement in the United States*. Rev. ed. Cambridge, Mass.: The Belknap Press of Harvard University, 1975. A revision of an original 1959 publication, this overview remains the standard textbook on the women's rights movement.

Linkugel, Wil A. *Anna Howard Shaw: Suffrage Orator and Social Reformer*. New York: Greenwood Press, 1991. This introduction to Shaw includes a collection of her speeches and is an extension of Linkugel's 1960 Ph.D. dissertation "The Speeches of Anna Howard Shaw."

Pellauer, Mary D. *Toward a Tradition of Feminist Theology: The Religious Thought of Elizabeth Cady Stanton, Susan B. Anthony, and Anna H. Shaw*. Brooklyn, N.Y.: Carlson, 1991. A monograph within the Chicago Studies in the History of American Women series, this volume analyzes Shaw's feminist theology and compares it with the theologies of other leading feminists of the period.

Shaw, Anna Howard. *The Story of a Pioneer*. New York: Harper & Brothers, 1915. In the absence of a full-length biography, this readable autobiography remains the best general introduction to the life of this suffrage crusader.

Spencer, Ralph W. "Anna Howard Shaw." *Methodist History* 13, no. 2 (January, 1975). This article, which is derived from Spencer's 1972 Ph.D. dissertation, sketches Shaw's career, emphasizing her Methodist contacts and experiences.

Terry D. Bilhartz

BEVERLY SILLS

Born: May 25, 1929; Brooklyn, New York

Area of Achievement: Music
Contribution: Beverly Sills ranks among the most successful opera stars of the twentieth century. She also served as a director of the New York City Opera Company.

Early Life

Beverly Sills, named Belle Miriam Silverman at birth by her parents, Morris Silverman and Shirley Bahn Silverman, was the youngest of three children. Her father emigrated from Romania, while her mother crossed the Atlantic from the Ukraine. Belle was known in her family as "Bubbles" because, at her birth, the doctor punctured a bubble in her mouth. When she reached three years of age and sported golden curls in the Shirley Temple mode then in vogue, her mother entered her in a contest for "Miss Beautiful Baby of 1932," and she won, after singing a song called "The Wedding of Jack and Jill."

Shirley Silverman, recognizing that her daughter might have musical talent, saw to it that she was given lessons in voice, dance, and speech (encompassing elocution). Belle manifested her interest in opera by learning to sing various Italian arias phonetically by listening repeatedly to her mother's collection of old 78-r.p.m. recordings of Amelia Galli-Curci, the reigning diva of the day. Belle Silverman studied every Saturday morning at a school that charged one dollar for weekly educational experience; the school also produced a radio show, "Uncle Bob's Rainbow Hour," on which talented pupils performed. At age four, she was a regular on Bob Emory's show, mainly because her verbal skills were so extraordinary. This exposure led to an appearance in Town Hall in New York with Uncle Bob's other talented youngsters, and in that venerable auditorium, she sang her first aria, "Il Bacio," which she had learned from the Galli-Curci records.

By the age of seven, "Bubbles" Silverman was transformed into Beverly Sills on the advice of a friend of Shirley Silverman's; the new name, it was held, would look better on a marquee. At about that time, Beverly made her cinema debut singing more Galli-Curci imitations in *Uncle Sol Solves It*, a film with educational overtones featuring Willy Howard. In 1936, the talented young lady auditioned for the noted singer and teacher Estelle Liebling, again singing "Il Bacio," whereupon she was admitted into Liebling's studio for a weekly lesson of fifteen minutes' duration. Sills's association with this famous mentor opened doors very quickly. After rendering "Caro Nome" from Giuseppe Verdi's *Rigoletto*, she was immediately made a regular member of Major Bowes's Capital Family Hour, a weekly radio program aired on CBS. There followed in rapid succession a nine-month stint on the perennial soap opera *Our Gal Sunday* and appearances on the *Cresta Blanca Carnival* show and on NBC television's *Stars of the Future*, a pioneering television effort. Morton Gould's orchestra played for the Cresta Blanca program, and, as a result, Beverly sang with Gould's musicians and with a male singer named Merrill Miller, who later emerged as the operatic baritone Robert Merrill. After a childhood filled with professional successes, Beverly "retired" at the age of twelve. She was graduated from Brooklyn's Public School Number 91 as "Most Likely to Succeed." During her high school years, she continued vocal study with Liebling, but on a daily basis; she also added piano lessons once a week and daily lessons in French and Italian. By age fifteen, she had learned twenty operatic roles, with an emphasis on the bel canto repertoire. This predilection derived from her early worship of the coloratura soprano Lily Pons. In 1945, Beverly was graduated from high school at the Professional Children's School in Manhattan after spending the bulk of her teen years at Erasmus Hall High School in Brooklyn.

Life's Work

Through the connections of Estelle Liebling, Beverly Sills met producer J. J. Shubert, who promptly made her part of a touring company performing Gilbert and Sullivan operettas. After a year, she was singing the lead in such staples of the operetta repertory as *The Merry Widow* by Franz Lehar. Sills's dream of singing opera was realized when, in February of 1947, she made her debut as Fresquita in Georges Bizet's *Carmen* with the Philadelphia Civic Opera. Following a period of reflection after her father's death in 1949, during which she sang in private clubs, she went on a national tour with the Charles L. Wagner Opera Company in 1951 and 1952. One-night stands singing such standard roles as Violetta in Giuseppe Verdi's *La Traviata* and Michaela in *Carmen* prepared her for the difficult road to success that awaited her. On September 15, 1953, she made an auspicious debut with the San Francisco Opera Company, singing the role of Helen of Troy in Arrigo Boïto's *Mefistofele*. Three years of unsuccessful auditions for Joseph Rosenstock, music director of the New York City Opera, finally resulted in her signing a contract with that enterprising company. Her debut there on October 29, 1955, as Rosalinde in *Die Fledermaus* by Johann Strauss, was a veritable triumph. From that moment, Sills's career was made.

On November 17, 1956, Beverly Sills married Peter Greenough, whose family owned the Cleveland *Plain Dealer*; she immediately became stepmother to his two children, Nancy and Lindley, from an earlier marriage. This change in lifestyle resulted in a hectic commuting schedule, first from Cleveland to New York, and then, when the couple moved to Boston in 1959, from that city to New York. Sills's performance on April 3, 1958, in Douglas Moore's opera *The Ballad of Baby Doe* at the New York City Opera established her as a superb singing actress (acting is an area in which many a diva has been found deficient). Sills's penchant for trying new and/or unusual roles resulted in a repertory that included such diverse characters as Madame Goldentrill in Wolfgang Amadeus Mozart's *The Impresario*, the Prima Donna in Hugo Weisgall's *Six Characters in Search of an Author*, and Milly Theale in Moore's *Wings of the Dove*. Her burgeoning success was marred, however, by tragedy. Her first-born child, Meredith ("Muffy"), was afflicted with severe hearing loss, and her second child, Peter, Jr. ("Bucky"), suffered mental retardation.

After a period of withdrawal, Sills, with the encouragement of her husband and the support of Julius Rudel, general manager of the New York City Opera, returned to the stage. During the 1960's, she established herself as a prima donna of the first magnitude. In January of 1964, for example, she sang the role of the Queen of the Night in Mozart's *Die Zauberflöte* with the Opera Company of Boston under the direction of Sarah Caldwell. A month later, with the New Orleans Opera Company, she sang all three female leads in Jacques Offenbach's *The Tales of Hoffmann*. In the fall of that year, she presented her first performances at the New York City Opera of two Mozartean roles, Donna Anna in *Don Giovanni* and Constanza in *The Abduction from the Seraglio*. Her greatest triumph came with her re-creation of Cleopatra in George Frideric Handel's *Julius Caesar*, a veritable tour de force, which firmly established Sills as a coloratura extraordinaire. Her unquenchable thirst for challenging roles that require acting ability as well as vocal virtuosity led her to such characterizations as the Queen of Shemakha in *Le Coq d'Or* by Nikolai Rimsky-Korsakov, Manon in the opera of the same name by Jules Massenet, Lucia in Gaetano Donizetti's *Lucia di Lammermoor*, and the three female leads in Giacomo Puccini's *Il Trittico*. Sills proved that an American singer could indeed have a highly successful career in the United States without a prior European stamp of approval. When, on April 11, 1969, she carried "coals to Newcastle" by singing Pamira in Gioachino Rossini's *The Siege of Corinth* at Milan's famed La Scala opera house, her international reputation was secured; indeed, Italian critics were especially moved by her bel canto singing, an art molded by the great Italian operatic tradition of the past. Not in Italy alone did "La Fenómena," as the Milanese proclaimed her, triumph. Covent Garden in London, where she sang Lucia (December, 1969), and the Deutsche Oper in Berlin, where she sang Violetta (January, 1970), were also the scenes of great successes for Sills.

Beverly Sills opted to focus her efforts in her native country, and she built on her already formidable reputation by bringing historical perspective to her roles; she conducted research into the historical personalities she portrayed musically. She also studied biographical details about the composers that might lend insight to her interpretation. A long overdue but not anticlimactic debut at the Metropolitan Opera took place April 8, 1975. Sills again sang the role of Pamira, which had so impressed the audiences at La Scala six years earlier, and she triumphed yet again, garnering an eighteen-minute ovation. The untoward delay in performing at the Met derived from a long-standing clash of personalities—those of Sills and of Rudolf Bing, the Met's general manager. Sills's later appearances at the Met included *Lucia di Lammermoor* in December of 1976 and *Thaïs* by Massenet in January of 1978.

Having achieved all that she desired as an opera singer, including singing the three Queen roles in Gaetano Donizetti's *Roberto Devereux, Maria Stuarda,* and *Anna Bolena*, the diva announced her impending retirement on January 9, 1978. When Julius Rudel resigned his post at the New York City Opera, Sills became sole director effective July 1, 1979. Her some one hundred performances a year were gradually phased out, but she did star as Juana, the Mad Queen of Spain, in Gian-Carlo Menotti's *La Loca* in June, 1979, at the San Diego Opera. *La Loca* was commissioned in celebration of Sills's fiftieth birthday. Assorted fund-raisers were promoted throughout the land, and the long string of farewells was officially concluded at Lincoln Center in New York on October 27, 1980, and televised on PBS. The event raised a million dollars.

Wearing her new hat as an opera administrator, Sills, seeking to stem the tide of sagging ticket sales and dwindling audiences that had begun to trouble the company in Rudel's last days, discounted subscriptions by 20 percent. She began to promote the New York City Opera Company as an alternative to, not a rival of, the Met. She saw it as a house that took risks and that would strive for innovation. In July of 1982, she announced that, instead of a fall and spring season, a single season running from July through December would yield a better share of the available audience and reduce the enormous expenditure involved in opera production. She was proved to be right in taking that approach. Furthermore, she showed true grit by alternating performances of opera with those of operetta; her view was that a performance of the highest quality is the ultimate aim, regardless of the genre into which the production falls. Her years as program chair for the Wolf Trap Festival outside the nation's capital, and her six-year tenure on the board of the National Endowment for the Arts, where she studied grant proposals and worked on budgets for assorted projects, gave her a glimpse of the administrative juggernaut that she had undertaken to tame.

While concentrating on nurturing native talent and developing an ensemble company, Sills advocated bringing in star performers. She also pioneered in the offering of opera in English and in commissioning operas by American composers. Her second career ended when she retired in 1988, a success once again.

Summary

Beverly Sills has had an enormous influence on the perception of opera in the United States and throughout the world. The fact that she, an opera star, has received honorary doctorates from Temple University, New York University, the New England Conservatory of Music, Harvard University, and the California Institute of the Arts and has received such awards as New York City's Handel Medallion for artistic achievement (1974), the Pearl S. Buck Women's Award (1979), and the Medal of Freedom (1980) indicates that her very special status in U.S. cultural life has been noted even during her active career. Sills has served as national chair of the March of Dimes Mother's March on Birth Defects, an area of concern for her because of the afflictions of her own children. She has been invited to perform at the White House under both Democratic and Republican presidents.

Sills has shown that an American-born and American-trained artist can reach Olympian heights in the world of opera. She was a recognized star when she performed for the first time at the Met; indeed, she had already achieved eminence when she made her debut at La Scala. Extraordinary talent, native intelligence, wit, and perseverance guided her through personal tragedies and professional obstacles.

Both at home and abroad, her influence has been little short of sensational. Sills, through her frequent appearances around the country and on television, as performer and interviewee, as speaker and fund-raiser, has become a household name. Her advocacy of American talent, both performers and composers, and her support of the use of supertitles during foreign-language operas have helped to cultivate a new generation of American opera lovers.

As a wife and mother, Sills has inspired many young women who wrestle with the problem of managing a career while devoting time and energy to raising a family. Beverly Sills has demonstrated that an American artist with a dream can reach the pinnacle of success on her own terms.

Bibliography

Hines, Jerome. "Beverly Sills." In *Great Singers on Great Singing*. Garden City, N.Y.: Doubleday, 1982. An insightful interview with the diva, filled with meaningful quotes relating to Sills's careers as singer and impresario.

Sargeant, Winthrop. "Beverly Sills." In *Divas*. New York: Coward, McCann & Geoghegan, 1973. Containing photos of Sills in some of her most famous roles, this essay portrays the star on both a personal and a professional level. It includes insights into her family relationships as they affect her career.

Sills, Beverly. *Bubbles: A Self-Portrait*. Indianapolis: Bobbs-Merrill, 1976. Dedicated to Sills's mother, husband, and children, this autobiography, filled with numerous photos of the star and many other personalities important in her life, presents a highly personalized account of Sills's career from childhood to the period of her debut with the Metropolitan Opera Company.

Sills, Beverly, and Lawrence Linderman. *Beverly: An Autobiography*. New York: Bantam Books, 1987. A major updating of the previous autobiography, this work takes the reader up to Sills's later years with the New York City Opera Company, both as singer and director. A very informative source.

Wills, Garry. "Here's Beverly Sills, Singing in the Reign." *Esquire* 82 (September, 1974): 80-82, 84, 188-190. An insightful article detailing Sills's rise to stardom. Includes details about the behind-the-scenes discussions/arguments that resulted in major decisions such as how Sills came to star in *Julius Caesar* at the New York City Opera Company.

David Z. Kushner

AGNES SMEDLEY

Born: February 23, 1892; Campground, Missouri
Died: May 6, 1950, Oxford, England
Areas of Achievement: Journalism, social reform, and women's rights
Contribution: As a newspaper correspondent and writer, Smedley reported on the Chinese Communist revolutionary movement and the Sino-Japanese War during the 1930's and 1940's.

Early Life

Agnes Smedley was born on February 23, 1892, in a two-room cabin outside of Campground, Missouri, the daughter of a tenant farmer, Charles Smedley, and his wife, Sara Ralls Smedley. Her father, after a brief absence in 1903, moved the family to Trinidad in the mining district of southeastern Colorado, where they lived for a time in a tent. Later, they lived in a small house where boarders were taken in. Agnes went to school and helped her family by working in the homes of neighbors and later in a tobacco store. In 1908, after the family moved again, to Tercio, Colorado, Agnes took a county teacher's examination in New Mexico; the prerequisite was an eighth grade education, and the pay was forty dollars a month. She taught school across the state border in Raton, New Mexico, for a year and a half before she returned home to nurse her dying mother and to take care of her younger sister and brothers and an infant nephew. After leaving her family again, she worked as a magazine agent traveling through Colorado and New Mexico. In 1911, she entered the Tempe Normal School in Arizona and wrote for the school's newspaper. After a six-month period, however, she was forced to leave in order to support herself. While at Tempe, she met Thorberg Brundin, a schoolteacher, and Brundin's brother, Ernest. When the Brundins moved to San Francisco in the summer of 1912, Smedley followed them. On August 24, 1912, Agnes and Ernest were married.

The couple's marriage was a stormy one. Agnes did not want children; she wanted more education and a career as a journalist. Entering the San Diego Normal School in 1913, she was graduated a year later and took a position in the intermediate level of the school as faculty secretary and typing teacher. In the spring of 1915, in San Diego, Smedley attended lectures by Dr. Keshava Shasti, an Indian campaigner for independence from Great Britain, and Emma Goldman, the anarchist and birth control advocate. The two speakers profoundly influenced Smedley's thinking and led her to join and later become secretary of the Open Forum, the sponsor of Goldman's speech. Upton Sinclair came to San Diego to participate in the lecture series, followed by Eugene V. Debs; these two socialists convinced Agnes to become a party member.

Moving with her husband to Fresno, California, Agnes was hired as a reporter by the *Fresno Morning Republican.* As part of her assignments, she was sent to cover a Hindu rally in September of 1916, where she again became conversant with the Indian nationalist movement. After her marriage ended in divorce in 1916, she went east to New York, where she settled in Greenwich Village. In March of 1917, Smedley attended a lecture by the Indian leader, Laipat Rai; she became his secretary and later worked with more radical Indian nationalists to secure recognition of the Indian national party by the United States government. Smedley was arrested by military intelligence officers in March of 1918, interrogated about the activities of Indian nationalists against British rule, and indicted for violation of the Espionage Act of 1917, and, to make matters worse, for defying a New York City ordinance against the dissemination of birth control information.

Birth control advocate Margaret Sanger rallied to Smedley's aid and raised the $10,000 bail, but in October of 1918, Smedley was returned to prison. During her incarceration, she met Roger Baldwin, later the founder of the American Civil Liberties Union, and Kitty Marion, a leading exponent of birth control. After her release, Smedley became Sanger's associate, managing the business of the *Birth Control Review*; she was also employed by the New York socialist newspaper, *The Call*, and in March, 1919, along with both Americans and Indians, helped to establish the Friends of Freedom for India. As secretary of the new political organization, she coordinated efforts to defend Indians in the United States from the threat of deportation, and to obtain support for the independence movement from American labor unions, and she wrote articles in *The Call* attacking British imperialism in India.

Life's Work

All this was preliminary to what became Agnes Smedley's most important part of her career as a journalist and writer. In 1919, she went to Germany and then to the Soviet Union, where she visited Emma Goldman, under house arrest by Russian officials. In 1923, after suffering from a nervous breakdown, she published an article in the November 28th issue of *The Nation*. This article, entitled "Starving Germany," described the rising unemployment and inflation that would later drive the country to accept the leadership of Adolf Hitler's Nazi Party.

Her first trip to China came in December, 1928. Smedley went initially to Manchuria, and her report about the status of women in the Chinese province appeared in *The New Republic*. She traveled to Peking, to Nanking, the capital of Nationalist China, and to Shanghai. (She was being followed by British intelligence which suspected her of being involved in anti-British agitation among the Chinese people.) She met, among others, Edgar Snow, a young American reporter for the *China Weekly Review*; Hu Shi, who was later the Nationalist ambassador to Washington; and Mme Sun Yat-sen. Smedley collected a series of her articles in a book, *Chinese Destinies*, and began a new work on the Chinese Communists, *China's Red Army Marches*. In 1933, she left China, traveling first to Moscow and Leningrad and then to the United States. Her autobiographical novel, *Daughter of Earth*, first published in 1929 and translated into Chinese, Japanese, and German, was reprinted in 1935 in an abridged edition.

Smedley was back in Shanghai in October, 1934. In Shanghai she made contact with Ling Ding, a Red Army veteran and Communist Party operative. In the summer of 1936, she was invited by Ling Ding to come to Sian, close to the Red Army base in northwest China. She was in Sian in December, 1936 when Chiang Kai-shek was arrested by the Manchurian warlord, Chang Hsuchang, and when the Chinese Communist leader, Chou En-lai, was brought to the city to enter into negotiations with the Nationalists, Smedley's broadcasts from Sian describing the negotiations and interviewing participants made her famous in both China and the United States. The broadcasts were also criticized for their alleged favoritism toward the Chinese Communists.

At the beginning of the Sino-Japanese War in July, 1937, Smedley was in Yen-an, the headquarters of the Communist Party, located one hundred miles south of the Great Wall. She became acquainted with Chairman Mao Tse-tung and with Chu Teh, the commander-in-chief of the Red Army. She urged other foreign correspondents and doctors to come to Yen-an and Vincent Sheean, the later biographer of Mahatma Gandhi, and Norman Bethume, a Canadian surgeon, responded. She carried on a campaign against the rat-infested streets and caves where people lived in the mountain town. What she observed in Yen-an persuaded her—erroneously as it turned out—that the Chinese Communists were basically agrarian reformers and that, in land reform and in the first village elections that were held, she was seeing the future course of a revolution in China. She left Yen-an in the fall of 1937, spent three months with the Eighth Route Army under Chu Teh, and recorded her impressions of "the essence of the Chinese struggle for liberation" in *China Fights Back* published in New York the next year. She was in Hankow in 1938, organizing an effort to obtain medical supplies for both Communist and Nationalist troops through the Chinese Red Cross. She publicized the campaign in the British newspaper, the *Manchester Guardian*, and in the American magazines, *The Nation* and *Vogue*; she obtained donations from the American and British embassies, from Standard Oil, and from correspondents for American and British publications. She became a regular contributor to the *Manchester Guardian*, and in the summer of 1938, was given the position as a special correspondent to the British newspaper.

A few days before Hankow fell to the Japanese in October, 1938, Smedley left the city in a medical van, joined Communist guerilla units in the New Fourth Army, and for more than a year visited both Communist and Nationalist resistance units, writing articles and later *Battle Hymn of China* about Japanese atrocities and Chinese heroism. She continued to solicit contributions of medical supplies from the New Fourth Army and personally assisted in helping the wounded during Japanese bombing raids. She went to Chungking in March, 1940, headquarters of the Nationalist government, and in September, her health deteriorating, to Hong Kong for an operation.

After a period of convalescence, Smedley returned to the United States in May, 1941; she was never to see China again. She spoke at Pomona College in California, warning that the United States would soon have to confront the Japanese; later, she appeared at the Philharmonic Auditorium in Los Angeles on behalf of the Committee to Support China, arguing that the United States should declare war on all of the Axis powers. After Pearl Harbor, she emphasized the need for the Roosevelt Administration to accept China as an equal ally. In October, 1942, she crossed the country to New York and worked on the manuscript of *Battle Hymn of China*, completing it in January,

1943. In July of 1943, she became a resident at Yaddo, a retreat for creative artists located near Saratoga Springs, New York, supported by a private foundation. Associating with other writers and poets, including Carson McCullers, Langston Hughes, Jean Stafford, in a convivial atmosphere, Smedley was studying dramatic techniques for a play about China. She left at times on lecture tours, speaking at colleges and to women's clubs in New York, New England, and Canada and as far south as Georgia and west as Texas, publicizing the war in China and the fight of the Chinese people for freedom from all foreign domination, and incidentally attacking racial segregation in the American South.

It was Smedley's challenge to racism in the South that began FBI surveillance of her activities. Spied on by a secretary of Yaddo, hounded by the FBI, accused of being a Soviet agent (with no real evidence whatever), Smedley's income from lectures and her writing declined, and she became a pariah in the United States. Nevertheless, she continued to argue that the Communists had the support of the Chinese people; although she became concerned about Communist influence, she herself supported the Committee for a Democratic Far Eastern Policy and spoke at their rallies. In March of 1948, she was forced to leave Yaddo after a town protest (she had held a reception at the retreat for a New York Communist organizer). She was being heckled when she spoke in public about China, and some of her colleagues were avoiding her; she turned down invitations to speak because she feared that her reputation would injure the sponsors. In September, 1948, she decided to return to China, stopping first in London, but in April, 1950, her health failing, she entered the University Hospital in Oxford, England. On May 5, 1950, she underwent an operation for bleeding ulcers; her doctors believed that two-thirds of her stomach would have to be removed. The next day, with one friend at her side, she died of pneumonia, acute circulatory failure, and from the effects of the operation.

Summary

From obscurity and poverty, with sporadic formal education, Agnes Smedley became one of the premier journalists on the Chinese Communist revolutionary movement and the Sino-Japanese War during the 1930's and 1940's. Literally writing hundreds of articles and reviews and books in English and German, she publicized the cause of the Chinese people during World War II, and worked tirelessly to obtain financial assistance to maintain their armies in the field. Although she did not foresee the dictatorial intent of the Chinese Communists, she understood their popular appeal and she suffered opprobrium and ostracism because of her support of the Peoples' Republic of China. The list of her friends and acquaintances—Margaret Sanger, Emma Goldman, Pearl Buck, Edgar Snow, Katherine Ann Porter, Käthe Kollwitz, General Joseph Stilwell, Mao Tse-tung, Chou En-lai, Pandit Nehru—and of her political enemies—Henry Luce, Whittaker Chambers, Dr. Walter Judd, General Charles Willoughby—attest the importance and the controversial nature of her life and career.

Bibliography

Ma Haide. "A Woman Made by History and Who Made History." *Beijing Review* 33 (May 7, 1990): 33-36. Condensed from a speech made by a physician who became acquainted with Smedley in China during the 1930's, this article provides a firsthand account of Smedley's activities as a journalist and revolutionary.

MacKinnon, Janice R., and Stephen R. MacKinnon. *Agnes Smedley: The Life and Times of an American Radical.* Berkeley: University of California Press, 1988. A detailed and critical biography based in part on interviews with Smedley's contemporaries and with an extensive bibliography of her books and articles.

Milton, Joyce. *A Friend of China.* New York: Hastings House, 1980. Aimed at juvenile readers, this biography provides a good general introduction to the life of Agnes Smedley. Particularly useful in assessing her activities with Communist revolutionaries in China.

Smedley, Agnes. *Battle Hymn of China.* London: Gollancz, 1943. In a work that is autobiographical and anecdotal Smedley records her personal experiences in China from 1928 to 1941, describing among other things the arrest of Chiang Kai-shek and her contacts with Chinese guerilla troops in the New Fourth Army.

Snow, Edgar. *Red Star over China.* New York: Random House, 1938. A report by Smedley's friend and contemporary on the Chinese Communists before the Sino-Japanese War, with a recording of conversations with Mao Tse-tung about his youth and later career.

David L. Sterling

BESSIE SMITH

Born: April 15, 1894; Chattanooga, Tennessee
Died: September 26, 1937; Clarksdale, Mississippi
Area of Achievement: Music
Contribution: The first internationally popular female blues singer, Bessie Smith paved the way for later female blues and gospel singers such as Billie Holiday, Ella Fitzgerald, and Mahalia Jackson.

Early Life

Bessie Smith was born into abject poverty in Chattanooga, Tennessee. Her parents, William and Laura Smith, had a total of seven children in what Bessie later described as "a little ramshackle cabin." William was a part-time Baptist minister who ran a small mission but had to support his family by doing manual labor. He died shortly after Bessie was born, and her mother died by the time Bessie was eight or nine years old. Bessie and the other children were reared by their oldest sister Viola, who became an unwed mother at an early age, adding another hungry mouth to the family.

Bessie realized at an early age that she had an exceptional voice. She used to sing on the streets of Chattanooga with her brother Andrew accompanying her on the guitar. Then another brother got her a job with the Moses Stokes traveling minstrel show, and she began appearing with the legendary blues singer, Gertrude "Ma" Rainey. Their audiences were predominantly black because African American music was yet to be discovered by most white Americans. For many years, Bessie toured the South with the Rabbit Foot Minstrels under the tutelage of Ma Rainey, who is generally considered a blues singer second only to Bessie Smith.

It was a hard life, with exhausting schedules, segregated accommodations, humiliating encounters with bigoted white police officers, late hours, casual sex, gambling, fighting, and plenty of drinking. Bessie did not use hard drugs, but she enjoyed smoking marijuana, which was considered fairly innocuous and did not become illegal under federal law until 1937. Bessie picked up many bad habits from the people she associated with, who included gangsters, prostitutes, pimps, gamblers, dope peddlers, con artists, and assorted grifters, along with the hard-boiled booking agents who paid starvation wages to their overworked performers.

Bessie's early life taught her to be tough in a tough world. She was a big, strong woman who weighed approximately 210 pounds; she became notorious for her dangerous temper as well as her powerful voice. Her singing has been described as rough, coarse, low-down, and dirty, but her voice was a perfect instrument for the earthy blues songs that would eventually make her world famous.

Life's Work

Bessie Smith's big break came in 1923, when she was discovered by Frank Walker, a talent scout for Columbia Records. Her recording of "Downhearted Blues" sold three-quarters of a million copies, a fantastic achievement in those early days of wind-up phonographs and primitive recording equipment. In that one year she sold more than two million records. Some of her other famous recordings were "Jealous Hearted Blues" and "Jailhouse Blues." The power of Smith's singing is impossible to describe in words. Fortunately, her recordings are readily available throughout the United States, Europe, and elsewhere.

During the next decade, Bessie Smith recorded approximately 160 songs, accompanied by some musicians who also made music history, including trumpeter Louis Armstrong and pianist-bandleader Fletcher Henderson. At the peak of her career, during the Roaring Twenties, she was making as much as two thousand dollars a week from personal appearances and had a large additional income from royalties on record sales. It was her recordings that first brought her to the attention of white listeners in America and Europe; the affluence of this new audience made her rich and famous.

The titles of some of Smith's most popular songs provide an idea of the nihilistic philosophical background of the blues, which appealed so strongly to white audiences during the lawless Prohibition Era. One famous song was "'T'ain't Nobody's Biz-ness If I Do." Another was "Nobody Knows You When You're Down and Out." The standard twelve-bar form consisted of four bars per line, with the first line of the lyrics repeated, as in the following stanza:

> I cried and worried, all night I laid and groaned,
> I cried and worried, all night I laid and groaned,
> I used to weigh two hundred, now I'm down to skin and bone.

Many righteous and self-righteous citizens, both black and white, regarded the blues as "devil's music" because it seemed so hopeless and negative, and because it frequently celebrated such activities as drinking and having sex. Nevertheless, it appealed to many people who were disillusioned with traditional religion and were becoming pessimistic about the human condition in an era of gangsterism, predatory laissez-faire capitalism, and crooked politics. The blues had an influence not only on popular music but also on poetry, fiction, drama, and other art forms.

Bessie Smith lavished her money on her husband Jack Gee, an enormous man with a temper matching Smith's own. He had been a Philadelphia policeman but left the force to manage—or mismanage—his wife's business affairs. Jack was not faithful to his wife, and she was not faithful to him. She was sexually attracted to women as well as men and suffered many beatings from her husband, who was extremely jealous in addition to being concerned about guarding the source of his income. They separated in 1930 but remained on reasonably good terms until her death.

Bessie Smith's life ended abruptly in a tragic automobile accident on a narrow Louisiana road in the dead of night. The driver of her car did not see a truck that was blocking part of the road; they crashed into it at full speed, and the singer suffered numerous serious injuries, including a nearly severed arm. The aftermath has been the subject of many conflicting stories. Some people claim that Smith died from loss of blood because she was refused admittance at a racially segregated hospital. For more than thirty years she lay in an unmarked grave. Then in the 1960's, the famous white rock 'n' roll singer Janis Joplin, acknowledging her debt to Smith's inspirational example, paid to have a headstone created bearing the epitaph "The Greatest Blues Singer in the World Will Never Stop Singing."

When Bessie Smith died in 1937, her career was on the decline. Record sales had collapsed with the advent of the Great Depression after the stock market crash in October of 1929. New kinds of popular music were being developed to suit the younger generation and the more sophisticated, urbane spirit of the 1930's. Swing, as exemplified by such big bands as those of Glenn Miller, Count Basie, and Tommy Dorsey, had stolen the spotlight from blues and jazz, and Smith could not adapt to this type of music. Alcoholism was another important factor in destroying her illustrious career. She acquired a bad reputation for not showing up for engagements or for being too intoxicated to perform when she finally arrived.

Summary

Bessie Smith is generally considered the greatest blues singer who ever lived and is still referred to as the "Empress of the Blues." Before her time, most blues singers had been men. Smith not only became a great blues singer in her own right but also feminized the musical form so that the way was opened for many women to follow in her footsteps. Some of America's most famous popular female vocalists owe their success to the model provided by Bessie Smith. Among those others are Billie Holiday, Mahalia Jackson, and Janis Joplin, but there were also countless others whose careers were not as brilliant or dramatic. She also influenced the musical styles of such famous jazz musicians as Louis Armstrong, Bix Beiderbecke, and Jack Teagarden, among many others.

Bessie Smith was the first blues singer to achieve popularity with white audiences. This occurrence brought the wonderfully expressive musical form of the blues to the attention of the entire world. She introduced the blues to the new media of phonograph records, radio, and talking pictures, which had the capability of reaching vast numbers of people. Her recordings made white audiences in the United States and Europe conscious of the important contributions of African Americans to popular art and inspired musicologists to scour the South in search of great folk musicians who were still living in poverty and obscurity.

It was many years, however, before another new generation rediscovered Smith through her recordings and gave her the credit she richly deserved for her contributions to popular music. In 1970, Columbia Records initiated one of the biggest reissue projects in recording history. The company released Bessie Smith's entire output on five double albums. Two hundred thousand copies of these albums were snapped up within two years, and her recordings continue to be played on radio broadcasts and featured in record stores all over the world.

The blues expressed the suffering of African Americans and made other people more conscious of the injustice that this minority group had experienced since the settlement of the American Colonies began. Black women were an oppressed minority within a minority because they often bore the burden of providing all the financial and moral support for their families. Smith's beautiful blues songs carried the implicit message that racial injustice was responsible for much of the pain they expressed. Because of the many recordings Bessie Smith made during her lifetime, she became better known after her death than she was at the height of her career. Great art always has the power to bring people closer together, and Bessie Smith continues to influence people all over the world in that positive way.

Bibliography
Albee, Edward. *The Death of Bessie Smith*. London: S. French, 1960. This one-act play by a famous American author helped to spread Bessie's reputation to a wider audience and also helped to perpetuate the legend that she had died of injuries because she was refused admittance to a white hospital in Tennessee.
Albertson, Chris. *Bessie Smith, Empress of the Blues*. New York: Schirmer Books, 1975. A carefully researched biography written by an authority on Bessie Smith's music and told in an interesting, anecdotal fashion. Liberally illustrated with black-and-white photographs of Bessie Smith taken throughout her life. Contains a valuable discography of Bessie Smith's recordings as well as those of Ma Rainey and other significant blues artists.
Azerrad, Michael. "Rock and Roll Hall of Fame." *Rolling Stone* (February 9, 1989): 93. A section on inductees to the Rock and Roll Hall of Fame discusses the meteoric career of "the Empress of the Blues" and the great musical artists with whom she worked. Contains a portrait of Bessie Smith.
Brooks, Edward. *The Bessie Smith Companion: A Critical and Detailed Appreciation of the Recordings*. New York: Da Capo Press, 1982. This book represents many years of intense work by a Bessie Smith enthusiast who offers a detailed analysis of 159 recordings by the singer along with discussions of her life and the characteristics of her various accompanists. The best Bessie Smith discography available.
Feinstein, Elaine. *Bessie Smith*. New York: Viking, 1985. A short, well-written biography covering all the main details of Bessie Smith's life. This book is part of Viking's Lives of Modern Women series. Contains photographs, a chronology, a bibliography, and some information about available recordings.
Jones, Hettie. *Big Star Fallin' Mama: Five Women in Black Music*. New York: Viking Press, 1974. This excellent small volume contains chapters devoted to Ma Rainey, Bessie Smith, Mahalia Jackson, Billie Holiday, and Aretha Franklin, focusing on their influences on one another as well as their contributions to popular music. Contains good photographs of all five world-famous women.
Mezzrow, Milton. *Really the Blues*. New York: Random House, 1946. Reprint. New York: Limelight Editions, 1987. One of the best books ever written about the history and meaning of the blues. Mezzrow was a white musician who knew most of the early blues and jazz artists in Chicago and New York, including Bessie Smith. Discusses the early use of drugs by musicians and the precarious lives they led on the road.

Moore, Carmen. *Somebody's Angel Child: The Story of Bessie Smith*. New York: Thomas Y. Crowell, 1969. A short biography containing excerpts from the lyrics of Bessie Smith's blues songs. Emphasizes how the songs reflected her life experiences. Contains a discography and a bibliography.

Terkel, Studs. *Giants of Jazz*. New York: Thomas Y. Crowell, 1957. A famous American writer discusses the careers of thirteen great jazz artists with perception and sincere appreciation. He devotes one chapter to Bessie Smith.

Bill Delaney

MARGARET CHASE SMITH

Born: December 14, 1897; Skowhegan, Maine

Area of Achievement: Government and politics
Contribution: As the first leading American stateswoman to be elected in her own right to both houses of the United States Congress, Margaret Chase Smith focused her attention on improving the status of women, military preparedness, and defense of free speech and democratic values.

Early Life

Margaret Madeline Chase was born in Skowhegan, Maine, on December 14, 1897. Skowhegan, a mill and factory town in west-central Maine, provided a small-town atmosphere in which her parents George Emery and Carrie Murray Chase reared their six children. Margaret was the eldest of the four who survived. Her father, a barber from Irish and English background, was a hardworking family man whose own father had fought in the Civil War before taking his position as a Methodist minister in Skowhegan. Her mother took jobs occasionally to supplement family income while instilling in her children the importance of family life and independence.

While pursuing a commercial course of study in high school Margaret worked as a clerk in the local five-and-dime store, was employed as a telephone operator, and was hired to record tax payments in the town books during her senior year. She shook hands with President Woodrow Wilson on her senior class trip to Washington, D.C. After her graduation from Skowhegan High School in 1916, Margaret taught in the one-room Pitts School outside Skowhegan. Seven months later she returned to Skowhegan to accept a full-time telephone operator's job for Maine Telephone and Telegraph Company.

In 1919, she began an eight-year job at the town's weekly newspaper, the *Independent Reporter*, which Clyde Smith (her future husband) coowned. Rising to circulation manager, she continued to meet influential people and cultivate her skills in public relations. She drew on these skills in 1922, when she organized the Skowhegan chapter of Business and Professional Women's Club. Margaret was named president of the Maine Federation of the Business and Professional Women's Clubs the following year. In 1928, she served as Office Manager for the Daniel E. Cummings Company, a Skowhegan woolen mill. Her early working experiences not only taught her how to get along with people but also instilled in her a respect for working people that influenced her subsequent pro-labor record in the United States Congress.

In 1930, Margaret Chase married Clyde H. Smith, a respected and experienced Maine politician who was twenty-two years her senior. From 1930 to 1936, she supported his energetic public career while learning the basic skills for campaigning and public service. During this period, she also served as a member of the Maine Republican State Committee. Clyde Smith was elected to the United States House of

Representatives in 1936. Margaret served as his secretary in Washington, D.C., until his death in April, 1940.

Life's Work

Margaret Chase Smith won a special election in the spring of 1940 to fill her husband's vacated seat in the House of Representatives. As a candidate for the succeeding full term in office, Smith scored an impressive electoral victory in the September general election. Her eight years as the congresswoman from Maine's Second Congressional District are highlighted by her interest in military affairs. In her first term she broke with the Republican party and voted for the Selective Training and Service Act to draft men for the upcoming war. She was the only member of the Maine delegation to vote for Lend Lease in 1941 and she broke with her party to support a bill to arm American merchant ships. In 1943 she was appointed to the House Naval Affairs Committee which was later merged into the Armed Services Committee.

Many of Smith's concerns focused on the status of women in the civilian workforce and in the military. In 1944, she was appointed by Secretary of Labor Frances Perkins to serve as technical adviser to the International Labor Organization, which explored the role of women in employment planning after World War II. Smith worked to improve the status of women in the military by introducing the Army-Navy Permanent Nurse Corps Bill to grant women permanent status in the military. This bill was signed into law by President Harry S Truman in April of 1947. Smith toured the South Pacific naval bases and sponsored legislation which would permit women to serve overseas during war. She gained passage for the Women's Armed Services Integration Act of 1948 which gave women equal pay, rank and privileges. Her desire to see the United States exert leadership in world affairs enabled her to support U.S. membership in the United Nations and the European Recovery Plan.

Senator Smith favored domestic legislation to improve the conditions of the working class and women. She helped to defeat the Tabor Amendment which had proposed to halve the funds designated for community service programs such as child care. In 1945 and 1949 she cosponsored a proposed Equal Rights Amendment which did not get the necessary two-thirds majority votes in Congress to be submitted to the states for ratification. She voted with the Democrats against the Smith-Connally Anti-Strike bill. In economic matters she opposed a bill to freeze the social security tax and voted for federal pay raises. In 1947 she voted against a Republican proposal to cut President Truman's budget. That same year she voted with her party in supporting the Taft-Hartley Act, which placed specific limits on labor. She had been named chair of the Maine State Republican Convention in 1944 to prepare her to chair the national Republican Party conference in 1967.

Margaret Chase Smith ran for election to the U.S. Senate in 1948 winning by a record plurality. Though her opponents charged her with being a party maverick by calling attention to the votes that she cast contrary to her party, she produced a House voting record that aligned with her party ninety-five percent of the time. Her election to the United States Senate in 1948 made her the first woman in United States history to be elected in her own right without prior service by appointment to serve in the U.S. Senate and the first woman to be elected to both houses of Congress. Her four terms in the Senate from 1948 to 1972 acquainted her with six presidents among whom were Eisenhower and Kennedy.

In 1949 Senator Smith began a daily newspaper column, *Washington and You*, which was syndicated nationally for five years. She was named to the prestigious Senate Republican Policy Committee. She won the Associated Press award for Woman of the Year in politics in 1948, 1949, 1950, and 1957. She delivered her famous "Declaration of Conscience" speech on June 1, 1950 as a response to the abuses of Senator Joseph R. McCarthy's inquisitions into communism in the United States. She courageously opposed McCarthy's negativism and demeaning of Americans at a time when most Republicans in the Senate were either too afraid to oppose him or somewhat supportive of his extremist anticommunist activities. Her "Declaration of Conscience" speech still has appeal as a defense of American values and the importance of free speech to the maintenance of American democratic processes.

She traveled to Florence, Italy, in 1950 as U.S. delegate to the UNESCO conference. She was also appointed as a lieutenant colonel in the U.S. Air Force Reserves. After winning reelection to the Senate in 1954 she embarked on a twenty-three nation world tour to see how U.S. foreign aid money was being used. She interrupted her trip to return to the United States to cast her censure vote on Joseph R. McCarthy. In 1956 Senator Smith campaigned for Dwight Eisenhower, the Republican presidential candidate. She debated in his defense with Eleanor Roosevelt on CBS television's *Face the Nation*. As someone who enjoyed new experiences, Smith had by this time been the first woman to ride on an American destroyer in wartime, spend a day on an aircraft carrier at sea, and in 1957 to fly as a passenger in a F-100 jet fighter which broke the sound barrier.

In 1960, Smith won a hotly contested election over another female candidate, the first time two women had run against each other for a senate seat. That same year she won *Newsweek* magazine's press poll rating as Most Valuable Senator. Upon resuming her duties in the Senate, she agonized over her vote on Kennedy's Limited Nuclear Test Ban Treaty. Her concern for national security won out in her vote against both the treaty and most of her party. Her vote put her on the same side as Barry Goldwater, who became the Republican party presidential nominee for 1964. Although Margaret Chase Smith was touted as a potential candidate for vice president in 1964, she earned the distinction that year of becoming the first woman nominated for president by a major U.S. political party.

She supported the 1964 Civil Rights Act using her influence in the Republican Conference to keep the provision barring sex discrimination in employment in Title VII intact. Smith won an unprecedented fourth term for a woman to the Senate in 1966. In 1967 she was elected chair of the Conference of Republican Senators. The next year she had to miss her first roll call vote in her thirteen years in Congress because of hip surgery. She held the record for 2,941 consecutive roll call votes. In the remaining two years of her tenure in the Senate, Margaret Chase Smith cast important votes against President Richard Nixon's nominations of Clement F. Haynesworth and G. Harold Carswell for the U.S. Supreme Court. Demonstrations protesting the Vietnam War, especially on college campuses, led her to make her second "Declaration of Conscience" speech on June 1, 1970.

In her final campaign for reelection to the Senate in 1972, Smith was defeated by her Democratic opponent, William D. Hathaway. During her Senate career she served on the powerful Armed Forces, Appropriations, Government Operations and Rules Committees and showed strong support for the space program as a charter member of the Senate Aeronautical and Space Committee. She also sponsored legislation for government support of medical research. Senator Smith used her considerable influence to look out for the seafaring interests and industries of the state of Maine and to cast votes on issues critical to the well-being of the Republican Party and the future course in world politics for the United States.

After she left public office, Smith focused on a second career as a visiting professor and lecturer with the Woodrow Wilson National Fellowship Foundation and at numerous college and university campuses. In the course of her career, she has received ninety-five honorary doctoral degrees and more than 270 other awards and honors. In 1989, she was awarded the Presidential Medal of Freedom, the nation's highest civilian honor. The Northwood Institute, Margaret Chase Smith Library in Skowhegan, Maine, was dedicated in 1982 to serve as a congressional research library and archives. This library houses the papers, political memorabilia, and documents that Smith accrued in her thirty-two years in Congress. Her private residence adjoins the library on the historic Kennebec River. In 1990 she was honored by the dedication of the Margaret Chase Smith Center for Public Policy at the University of Maine.

Summary

Margaret Chase Smith's long and distinguished public service career furthered the interests of national security, especially military affairs. She pioneered legislation to further the status of women in domestic issues, military status, and internationally. She was a model of decorum and earned a reputation for integrity, honesty, and independence of judgment. As a servant of the people in Congress, she put first priority on her duties in office. She campaigned vigorously and without accepting campaign contributions.

Bibliography
Fleming, Alice. *The Senator from Maine*. New York: Thomas Y. Crowell, 1969. This is a well-written book highlighting the life of Margaret Chase Smith from childhood through her activities in Congress. Somewhat historically fictionalized, the book is suitable for grades six through eight.
Gould, Alberta. *First Lady of the Senate: Life of Margaret Chase Smith*. Mt. Desert, Maine: Windswept House, 1990. This work presents a juvenile level review of the public career of Margaret Chase Smith. The author emphasizes Smith's personal

values, public integrity, independent judgment, and contributions to public life.

Graham, Frank, Jr. *Margaret Chase Smith: Woman of Courage*. New York: John Day, 1964. This readable biography describes Smith's professional life in the Senate. The author emphasizes her accomplishments as a woman in national politics—at that time, an arena dominated almost exclusively by men. Presents clear explanations of how the U.S. government works.

Meisler, Stanley. "Margaret Chase Smith: The Nation's First Woman Senator Reflects Back over a Capitol Life." *Los Angeles Times*, December 8, 1991, p. M3. A brief interview with Smith in which she reminisces about her experiences as a politician in Washington, D.C. Places her accomplishments within the context of women's efforts to gain greater political representation during the 1990's.

Sherman, Janann. " 'They Either Need These Women or They Do Not': Margaret Chase Smith and the Fight for Regular Status for Women in the Military." *Journal of Military History* 54 (January, 1990): 47-78. A scholarly analysis of Smith's stance on the issue of equitable status and treatment for women in the military. Amplifies her views on a topic that continues to generate interest among American military leaders and the general public.

Smith, Margaret Chase. *Declaration of Conscience*. New York: Doubleday, 1972. This book, composed by Smith with the assistance of her legislative aide, William C. Lewis, Jr., focuses on her three decades of public service. It contains important source material including the text of her famous speeches and other important legislative statements.

Witt, Linda, Karen M. Paget, and Glenna Matthews. *Running as a Woman: Gender and Power in American Politics*. New York: Free Press, 1993. A journalist, a political scientist, and a historian collaborated on this sweeping narrative of the experiences of female candidates in American politics. Written from the vantage point of 1992's "Year of the Woman," the book contains various references to Smith's trailblazing efforts in Congress and a telling assessment of public opinion regarding her chances of becoming president in 1964.

Willoughby G. Jarrell

SUSAN SONTAG

Born: January 16, 1933; New York, New York

Area of Achievement: Literature

Contribution: One of the first American women to achieve eminence as a critical
essayist, Sontag became a spokesperson for 1960's radical intellectuals and a leader
in the antiwar movement that forced the United States to withdraw from Vietnam.

Early Life

Susan Sontag was born in New York City on January 16, 1933. Her parents were
fur traders working mainly out of Tianjin, China. During their formative years, she
and her younger sister were cared for by relatives. Her lonely, loveless childhood
shaped her bookish, introspective character. She always exhibited a high degree of
intelligence and found solace in reading matter that was often far beyond her years.

Her father died when she was only five. Her mother returned to the United States
and took the children to live in Arizona and later to the San Fernando Valley in
Southern California. Her mother, an alcoholic, gave the children little more than room
and board. Susan felt abandoned by both parents. She told an interviewer, "I still weep
in any movie with a scene in which a father returns home after a long, desperate
absence, at the moment when he hugs his child."

Susan was reading such difficult authors as literary and social critic Lionel Trilling
while still in high school. She entered the University of California at Berkeley when
she was only fifteen. By the age of eighteen, she was attending the University of
Chicago, where she met and married Phillip Rieff, who was to become a prominent
cultural historian and social psychologist. The couple were divorced in the late 1950's.
They had one child, who was reared by Sontag.

Sontag's early life, like her later life, was devoted to intellectual pursuits. She
enrolled at Harvard University, earning master's degrees in both English literature and
philosophy by 1954. She was a Ph.D. candidate at Harvard but did not complete her
dissertation. In 1959, after studying briefly at Oxford University and the University
of Paris, Sontag moved to New York City and obtained a job on the staff of
Commentary. Shortly thereafter, she began teaching at City College and Sarah
Lawrence College, and from 1960 to 1964 she taught at Columbia University.

In 1963, Sontag published her first novel, *The Benefactor*, and in 1967 she
published her second novel, *Death Kit*. Although her novels were well received, it was
the publication of her first book of nonfiction, *Against Interpretation, and Other
Essays* (1966), that made her famous. She has stated that she prefers to think of herself
as a fiction writer, but she attracts the most attention from the complex, modernistic
ideas expressed in her nonfiction books and essays.

Life's Work

Susan Sontag is invariably described as a "modernist." The opposite of a modernist is a "traditionalist," one who is concerned with styles and values of the past. There have been modernists and traditionalists in every age; in Sontag's age, modernism has included such interests as alienation, powerlessness, the search for new spiritual values, the decline of the West, and the conflict between capitalism and socialism. Sontag has always been fascinated with uniquely modern forms of expression such as cinema, while in literature she has championed unorthodox authors such as Franz Kafka, Samuel Beckett, and Nathalie Sarraute.

Sontag's most talked about essay continues to be "Notes on 'Camp.'" In it, she goes to great lengths to explain the concept, which was new to most readers at the time and is still a mysterious subject to many. The term was adopted from the homosexual subculture and originally referred to the exaggerated effeminate behavior many homosexuals affected before the advent of the gay liberation movement.

The essence of camp, according to Sontag, is its "love of the unnatural." She offers many examples of camp in art from the past and the present, giving special attention to Aubrey Beardsley, the Victorian English painter, and Oscar Wilde, the flamboyant English dramatist and poet of the same era, whose life was ruined by a famous trial in which he was exposed to public disgrace as a homosexual.

The concept of camp, since the publication of Sontag's essay, has become essential to evaluating modern art because so much of modern art is not meant to be taken at face value. One modern camp hero is Busby Berkeley, who designed the outrageous choreography for many Hollywood musicals during the 1930's; his trademark was using groups of scantily dressed chorus girls to make kaleidoscopic patterns.

Against Interpretation, and Other Essays made Sontag famous. She challenged the whole traditional idea that the function of art should be moral and intellectual edification. She asserted that art should be appreciated for its "sensory" qualities rather than for its "meaning." She was attacked by traditionalist scholars and critics, who had a strong vested interest in the matter because they had built their careers on explaining the "meaning" of works of art. They defended what Sontag called the "Matthew Arnold idea of culture," which the great English critic and poet had defined as "a pursuit of our total perfection by means of getting to know, on all the matters which most concern us, the best which has been thought and said in the world."

Sontag's essays appealed to the rebellious younger generation, who were questioning all the values they had been taught by their elders. Her notion of art as pure enjoyment seemed exactly suited to the spirit of the times. Later on, Sontag herself felt compelled to modify her views, having come to realize that too much freedom can be almost as harmful as too much control; in the meantime, however, she had succeeded in forcing a reexamination and reevaluation of traditional ways of thinking. She typified the uncompromising spirit of the 1960's. As Hilton Kramer wrote: "Hers was but one case among many in the sixties—a particularly distinguished one, of course—of intellectuals engaging in strenuous flights of cerebration on behalf of ideas that promised deliverance from the tyranny of cerebration."

Sontag has tried her hand at many artistic forms, including short stories, novels, biographies, and films.

She wrote and directed four feature-length films, but they did not enjoy enough success to encourage her to continue working in that medium. Pauline Kael, a brilliant motion picture critic for *The New Yorker*, criticized Sontag's films for lacking "dramatic sense" and noted the same fault in Sontag's novels. Many critics have stated that Sontag's expressionistic style of fiction is more suited to the short story form than to the novel.

In 1976, Sontag was hospitalized for breast cancer and told that she had two years to live. She made strenuous efforts to find effective treatment and eventually contacted a French doctor who brought the disease under control. Characteristically, she used the traumatic experience as a mental as well as a physical challenge and published *Illness as Metaphor* in 1978. Her intention was to expose the ways in which physicians and patients regard disease and the ways in which it is exacerbated by the workings of the imagination. The book brought its courageous author back into the limelight; it received a National Book Critics Circle Award for that year.

In 1988, Sontag published *AIDS and Its Metaphors*, which carries forward the ideas about illness expressed in *Illness as Metaphor*. She deplores the unjust stigma attached to victims of acquired immune deficiency syndrome (AIDS) because of false ideas about illness in general.

Sontag continues to be a leading, often highly controversial figure in the cultural and intellectual life of New York City. She is a member of the American Academy and Institute of Arts and Letters and the New York Institute for the Humanities. She leads an exceedingly quiet life and seldom grants interviews.

Summary

Susan Sontag's greatest impact has been as an essayist. Her short stories and novels might be said to illustrate the stylistic and intellectual ideas she has articulated in her nonfiction. As an essayist, she aroused great alarm and controversy in the intellectual world with *Against Interpretation, and Other Essays*. She did nothing less than challenge the basic assumptions of criticism that had been a guiding light of literature for centuries. She asserted that art did not need a moralistic or edifying purpose but should be appreciated for the pleasure it provides.

As a modernist and a feminist, Sontag brought a whole new perspective to a field that had been almost exclusively a male domain since the time of Aristotle. She naturally aroused hostility among conservative members of the entrenched establishment, most of whom were men. Their life work had been dedicated to interpretation—to finding and revealing the "meaning" of works of art to others—and Sontag challenged the notion that meaning was essential. Her views rapidly spread to Europe and the Soviet Union; they continue to influence artists, critics, and intellectuals all over the world.

Sontag made her appearance at exactly the right moment in history, during the romantic revolution of the 1960's, when people were looking for new ways of doing things. She helped to draw attention to avant-garde artists such as French filmmaker Jean-Luc Godard, who were creating some of the most important works of the century.

She is regarded as one of the intellectual leaders of 1960's revolution, which changed Americans and Europeans in every conceivable way. She vehemently opposed the repressive war that the United States was waging in Vietnam and was influential in changing public opinion so that the government was forced to find an honorable way of withdrawing from that exploited country.

Bibliography

Grenier, Richard. "The Conversion of Susan Sontag." *New Republic* 186 (April 14, 1982): 15-19. This essay discusses Sontag's confession in a famous speech in Town Hall in New York City that she had failed to understand "the nature of the Communist tyranny." Grenier looks back over Sontag's career and points out other ways in which she has modified her radical opinions.

Kramer, Hilton. "The Pasionaria of Style." *The Atlantic* 50 (September, 1982): 88-93. This is an article about Sontag's use of the publication of *A Susan Sontag Reader* as a springboard. Kramer calls Sontag "the critical spokesman of the sixties" because she gave intellectual support to the hedonism and loose morals that characterized that turbulent era.

Lacayo, Richard. "Stand Aside, Sisyphus." *Time* 132 (October 24, 1988): 86-88. An excellent short profile of Sontag that covers her career as a fiction and nonfiction writer over two decades and assesses her importance to American literature. Illustrated.

Sayres, Sohnya. *Susan Sontag: The Elegaic Modernist*. New York: Routledge, Chapman & Hall, 1990. An excellent critical study of Sontag's works. Contains extensive biographical notes as well as a fairly comprehensive bibliography of works by and about Sontag. The bibliography itemizes reviews of Sontag's essays, books, and films.

Sontag, Susan. *Against Interpretation, and Other Essays*. New York: Farrar, Straus & Giroux, 1966. A selection of critical essays described by Sontag as "case studies for an aesthetic," focusing on literature, theater, and film from the viewpoint of "the new sensibility" she championed. The book brought her worldwide attention as a brilliant iconoclast and is generally considered her most important publication.

_____ . *I, etcetera*. New York: Farrar, Straus & Giroux, 1978. A collection of eight unconventional, impressionistic short stories showing the author's versatility in that medium. Some critics have called the stories cold and unappealing, while others have described them as intelligent, witty, and inventive.

_____ . *A Susan Sontag Reader*. New York: Farrar, Straus & Giroux, 1982. This single volume offers a generous overview of Sontag's fiction and nonfiction written over a period of approximately a decade. It contains excerpts from some of her most famous essays, including an essay on camp that displays her modernism, her acute intelligence, and her enormous breadth of reading.

Bill Delaney

ELIZABETH CADY STANTON

Born: November 12, 1815; Johnstown, New York
Died: October 26, 1902; New York, New York
Area of Achievement: Women's rights
Contribution: Organizer of the 1848 Seneca Falls Convention, Stanton went on to serve as a major leader of the nineteenth century women's movement in the United States.

Early Life

Elizabeth Cady was born November 12, 1815, in Johnstown, New York, a town overlooking the Mohawk valley about forty miles from Albany, the state capital. Her early life was one of comfort, status, and privilege. Her father, Daniel Cady, was a leading lawyer who had become wealthy through real estate transactions; he was elected to the state legislature and to Congress, served for many years as a circuit court judge, and eventually became an associate justice of the state supreme court. Her mother, Margaret Catherine Livingston Cady, a highly capable and independent-minded woman, was descended from a Revolutionary War hero and more distantly from the old Dutch aristocracy of the Hudson River valley. Judge Cady was conservative in outlook, unsympathetic to abolition and other reform movements of the era; his wife often disagreed with him on such issues. They produced eleven children, of which only four daughters and one son lived to adulthood. Elizabeth was the "middle child." The son, Eleazar, died soon after graduating from college at the age of twenty, leaving an inconsolable father bereft of male progeny. Judge Cady's grief would become a major turning point in the outlook of his daughter Elizabeth.

In her memoirs, she recounted her heartfelt attempts to comfort her father and her sense of rejection when his reaction was "Oh, my daughter, I wish you were a boy." Eleven years old at the time, she determined to show him that she could do everything a boy could, beginning with horsemanship and Greek. She became proficient in both, secretly enlisting her clergyman neighbor as a Greek instructor. Later, she won a Greek prize at the coeducational Johnstown Academy. Her father was pleased, but his response was "Ah, you should have been a boy." He never did acknowledge Elizabeth as equal to his lost son. Nevertheless, she was permitted to spend time reading in the judge's office; overhearing his cases, she was impressed with the rights married men had over their wives' property, even the right to squander it on drink and impoverish the family. Discussing this situation with her father, she became convinced early that women's legal disabilities must be corrected.

Elizabeth's formal schooling was concluded at Emma Hart Willard's new Troy Female Academy, which offered a very respectable academic curriculum plus "finishing school" polish. While there, she was converted at one of Charles Grandison Finney's revivals, and for a while thereafter was haunted by fears of damnation. The end result, however, was to render Elizabeth a skeptic in religion. Upon graduating from the academy in 1833, she returned to the family home in Johnstown and an active social life. She was not yet consciously determined upon a career as a reformer, but the influences which were to make her the mother of American feminism were already part of her psyche.

Life's Work

In 1839, at the home of her cousin Gerrit Smith, a noted reformer, Elizabeth Cady met abolitionist activist Henry Brewster Stanton, handsome, personable, and a hero who had confronted angry antiabolitionist mobs. Pleasant acquaintance turned into romance. Judge Cady, an antiabolitionist, opposed the marriage, the more because Henry's finances were precarious. Nevertheless, the couple were married in May of 1840; the bride insisted, and Henry agreed, that the word "obey" be omitted from the ceremony. She also insisted on being known as Elizabeth Cady Stanton, not as Mrs. Henry Stanton with its implied loss of identity. A long trip abroad followed almost immediately, for Henry was a delegate to the World Anti-Slavery Convention in London. There, after an acrimonious debate, the more conservative abolitionist delegates won a ruling that women delegates were to sit apart from the men, along with guests such as Elizabeth, and not participate actively. Among the women delegates was Quaker leader and lecturer Lucretia Coffin Mott. She befriended Elizabeth, and the two discussed the need for changes in the status of women. Later they would be partners in launching the women's movement.

Meanwhile, back in Johnstown domesticity prevailed. Over a period of seventeen years, Elizabeth and Henry produced five sons and two daughters, all of whom lived to maturity. From 1840 to 1843, the family resided with Elizabeth's parents, for Henry recognized the need for family conciliation and settled down to read law with Judge Cady. Having passed the Massachusetts bar, Henry Stanton moved to Boston in 1843 with his wife and son. Two more sons arrived during the four Boston years. Elizabeth was a dedicated mother and recounted rather gleefully in her memoirs how much more she knew about infant care than did the doctors. Later, her growing boys gave her problems, to which boarding school became the eventual solution. Running a household she accepted as a congenial challenge. This responsibility included plenty of entertaining, for Boston was full of reform leaders and intellectuals, and she and Henry seem to have known them all. It was a very satisfying life. Judge Cady was partly responsible, for he had given the couple a house and would do so again for their next two moves. Henry never became financially affluent; Elizabeth had expensive tastes, but eventually income from her speaking engagements and writing, in addition to her inheritance from her father, helped keep the family in considerable comfort.

In 1847, the Stantons moved to Seneca Falls, in western New York State. Henry had political ambitions and thought the opportunities for his success would be better in a comparatively new and less populous area. His law business began to prosper, and he was elected to the state legislature.

Life in Seneca Falls was empty for Elizabeth, with Henry often absent and domesticity now seeming like drudgery. In July of 1848, however, she had occasion to renew her acquaintance with Lucretia Mott. Together with three mutual friends, they issued the call, via local newspapers, for a "women's rights convention" to be held a few days later in Seneca Falls. As preparation they drew up a "Declaration of Sentiments" based on the Declaration of Independence, stating "We hold these truths to be self-evident: that all men and women are created equal," and continued their arguments by substituting the word "men" for King George and the word "women" for the colonists. The conclusion was a series of resolutions to be voted on, covering among other things women's right to participate in all occupations, to obtain equal education with men, to speak in religious assemblies, and to exercise the "sacred right to the elective franchise." This last resolution was the most controversial and passed by a slim margin. The convention was a great success and received vast publicity, most of it sarcastic. Despite this negative reception, the women's rights movement had been launched, and Elizabeth Cady Stanton was its acknowledged leader.

From 1848 to outbreak of the Civil War in 1861, numerous women's rights conventions took place. Stanton could only occasionally participate; during the 1850's she gave birth to four more children. She did, however, write for various publications on temperance and women's rights and adopted the controversial "Bloomer costume," the first American trousers outfit for women. In 1851, she began a lifelong friendship and collaboration with temperance activist Susan Brownell Anthony, who had read with interest of the Seneca Falls Convention. Their partnership was to become the infrastructure of the women's movement, as Stanton gradually was able to become more active. Biographers have described the partnership as follows: Stanton was the creative one with the bright ideas, the writer and orator; Anthony, the researcher and organizer. As time went on, however, Anthony also did much lecturing. By the 1870's, significant differences of opinion created tension between them; but reconciliation followed, and the partnership continued until Stanton's death.

The Civil War brought a temporary halt to the women's movement; women's groups instead emphasized patriotism and abolition of slavery. They expected that at war's end they would be rewarded for their loyalty in the form of support from the abolitionists for woman suffrage along with votes for the freed slaves. Instead they were told, "This is the Negro's hour"—linking votes for the former slaves together with votes for women would generate such a backlash of opposition that perhaps neither group would get the vote. The women felt betrayed. After the passage of the exclusionary Fourteenth and Fifteenth Amendments, votes for women became the central focus of the women's movement. Stanton herself ran for Congress—the first woman to do so—on a universal suffrage platform. Her devotion to women's rights, however, exposed her to charges of xenophobia and racism: It was intolerable to her that uneducated male former slaves and immigrants could vote, but well-educated native-born white women could not. As more immigrants poured in, Stanton advocated the concept of "educated suffrage."

In 1869, two suffrage organizations were formed. The American Woman Suffrage Association (AWSA), led by conservative reformers such as Lucy Stone and Julia Ward Howe, concentrated single-mindedly on securing the vote on a state-by-state basis, ignoring other women's issues. In contrast, the National Woman Suffrage Association (NWSA), led by Stanton and Anthony, promoted simultaneously all the causes that had engaged them over the years: divorce rights, reform of organized religion, and employment rights, as well as suffrage by means of a federal amendment. Stanton could never agree to play down everything but the vote; she even expanded her causes to include birth control, unionization for factory women, and Irish Home Rule. In 1890, the two organizations merged to form NAWSA, the National-American Woman Suffrage Association, which would continue the suffrage fight (but not Stanton's other causes) until passage of the Nineteenth Amendment after World War I. Stanton and Anthony each served as president, briefly, of the merged association.

Stanton spent much of her time on lecture tours; and her contemporaries considered her a spellbinding orator. The fact that only a few states and territories actually enacted woman suffrage only showed the need to keep the issue before the public. Her lecturing provided her with money for her children's education, but even more with a satisfying sense of independence. Self-sovereignty became her guiding principle, but she also cultivated her image as mother of seven children.

Married life seems to have become increasingly difficult for her. Henry was away a great deal, so all the maintenance of the household fell to her. Furthermore, she herself was often away lecturing. Henry was not particularly sympathetic to the cause of women's rights. Elizabeth's biographers consider that by the 1880's, the marriage was essentially over—she and Henry lived apart, he in New York and she in New Jersey. Henry died in 1887.

Elizabeth Cady Stanton did maintain strong family ties to her children. Four of her children lived nearby. Her son Theodore had married a French woman, and her daughter Harriot had married an Englishman. During the 1880's, she made several trips to Europe, visiting her children and traveling about as a celebrity, for by this time many European women had taken up the cause of women's rights. The 1880's and 1890's were also filled with literary activity: the *History of Woman Suffrage* (1881-1882, volumes 1-3), *The Woman's Bible* (1898), and Stanton's autobiography, *Eighty Years and More* (1898).

As a young woman Stanton was petite (five feet, two inches) and active, with an attractive face and curly brown hair. In later years she was described as plump, with a halo of white hair, a rosy face, and jolly demeanor. In her last years she was seriously overweight, developing heart trouble and shortness of breath. Eventually she became blind. Until late in life, however, her health was robust. She was always considered a brilliant conversationalist who loved social life, especially with the intellectuals and reformers of Europe and the United States.

On the occasion of Elizabeth Cady Stanton's eightieth birthday in 1895, Susan B. Anthony and Theodore Stanton organized a mammoth celebration at the Metropolitan Opera House. In response to the acclaim which poured in, her speech acknowledged the progress since 1848, but showed her continuing pugnacity as she emphasized the need for changes in religious policies with regard to women. The speech was read for her, since by now it was difficult for her to stand.

Elizabeth Cady Stanton died peacefully on October 26, 1902, in the New York apartment which she had for some years shared with bachelor son Robert and widowed daughter Margaret. Family tradition had it that Elizabeth took her own life, having requested her doctor to provide her with a drug overdose when she could no longer enjoy living. Self-sovereignty was her principle.

Summary

Elizabeth Cady Stanton's major long-range contribution was as the originator of the organized women's movement in the United States and the major formulator of its policy in the early days. By stating her name as she did, rather than as "Mrs. Henry Stanton," she served notice of her continuing individuality, the self-sovereignty to which she referred in later years. Through her a host of other leaders, most notably Susan B. Anthony, were drawn into the movement. She exemplified for fifty years the leadership qualities of women and the removing of obstacles to women's full participation in the world.

Early in the twentieth century, Stanton's role was played down and Anthony's was pushed to the fore, so much so as to make Anthony seem like the originator. This shift occurred because a new generation was more conservative and favored emphasizing the vote as a goal, rather than the too-controversial societal changes promoted by the more radical Stanton. Recent biographers have made clear that indeed it was Stanton who started both the suffrage movement and a host of other changes proposed in the 1848 Declaration of Sentiments and later: equal rights in marriage, divorce, and child custody; the right of women to participate equally in religious affairs, to own property and make contracts, to enter the "trades, professions, and commerce"; equal access to higher education; and the post-1848 issues of birth control and unionization of women workers. In electing to pursue those same goals, the new feminist leaders of the 1970's and beyond have affirmed that Stanton's vision was true.

Bibliography

Banner, Lois W. *Elizabeth Cady Stanton: A Radical for Woman's Rights*. Boston: Little, Brown, 1980. A birth-to-death short scholarly biography, under 200 pages, with chapter-by-chapter essay on sources. The author carefully avoids canonizing Stanton. Banner's was the first work to discuss the reality of Stanton's marriage and family life and her rifts with Anthony, as well as her leadership of the women's movement.

Flexner, Eleanor. *Century of Struggle: The Woman's Rights Movement in the United States*. Rev. ed. Cambridge, Mass.: The Belknap Press of Harvard University Press, 1975. Classic history of the movement from pre-1848 stirrings through the passage of the Nineteenth Amendment. Several informative sections on Stanton. Excellent documentation and essay on sources.

Griffith, Elisabeth. *In Her Own Right: The Life of Elizabeth Cady Stanton*. New York: Oxford University Press, 1984. The best, most up-to-date, and most comprehensive scholarly biography. Exhaustive documentation. Includes genealogical material, an introduction with much information on sources and their location, and a particularly fine index. Discusses marriage and family problems as well as the rifts with Anthony. Excellent on Stanton as leader of the women's movement.

Hymowitz, Carol, and Michaele Weissman. *A History of Women in America.* New York: Bantam Books, 1978. A standard text on the subject, from colonial era to the 1960's, it presents much information about Stanton. Good documentation, extremely readable.

Lutz, Alma. *Created Equal: A Biography of Elizabeth Cady Stanton, 1815-1902.* New York: John Day, 1940. A readable semi-scholarly biography. Although it is not documented, this work has a secondary bibliography and a list of manuscript sources. Does not deal with the negative aspects of her marriage and family life, or with tensions between Stanton and Anthony.

Stanton, Elizabeth Cady. *Eighty Years and More: Reminiscences, 1815-1897.* London: T. Fisher Unwin, 1898. Reprint. New York: Schocken Books, 1971. Originally published 1898, this work is a spirited, highly readable memoir. Rather self-laudatory; according to recent biographers, Stanton wrote this work in a conscious effort to create an image for posterity. Shows her continuing ebullience in old age.

——————, et al., eds. *History of Woman Suffrage.* 6 vols. New York: Source Book Press, 1970. A reprint of the original edition, published between 1881 and 1922. Stanton served as an editor of the first three volumes. A classic primary source, the work is a collection of documents with narrative and commentary by the editors. Essential research source, but slow reading.

Stanton, Elizabeth Cady, and the Revising Committee. *The Woman's Bible.* Seattle: Coalition Task Force on Women and Religion, 1974. Originally published in 1898, Stanton's work discusses biblical passages and ideas from her feminist and rationalist viewpoint: creation of woman, marriage, the Commandments, Mary and Martha, Paul's pronouncements on women, the Virgin Birth doctrine as a slur on natural motherhood, and so forth.

Waggenspack, Beth M. *The Search for Self-Sovereignty: The Oratory of Elizabeth Cady Stanton.* New York: Greenwood Press, 1989. Begins with biographical chapter, followed by analysis of her speeches according to broad topical categories. Texts of several speeches, as well as a detailed description of primary sources.

Elizabeth C. Adams

GERTRUDE STEIN

Born: February 3, 1874; Allegheny, Pennsylvania
Died: July 27, 1946; Neuilly-sur-Seine, France
Area of Achievement: Literature
Contribution: A literary innovator, Gertrude Stein captured the dialogue of common
  people and significantly influenced the writing of post-World War I authors.

Early Life

Born into an affluent family that traded in imported fabrics, Gertrude Stein was the
last child of Daniel and Amelia Stein, who vowed to have five children. Gertrude
recommended being the youngest child in the family, contending that it saved one
considerable bother.

Daniel Stein, having quarreled with his brother and business partner Solomon, took
his family to Vienna in 1875, remaining abroad until Gertrude was five. She grew up
fluent in French and German as well as English.

In 1880, the Steins moved to Oakland, California, where Gertrude grew up. In
1888, Amelia Stein died, followed by Daniel in 1891. Gertrude's brother Michael
became her legal guardian. Her brother Leo, then nineteen, transferred from the
University of California at Berkeley to Harvard. Gertrude followed as soon as she
could, entering Radcliffe College (then known as "Harvard Annex") in 1893 as a
special student because she failed the entrance examination.

At Radcliffe, Gertrude studied philosophy and psychology with Harvard professor
William James, becoming his star student. She received the bachelor's degree magna
cum laude in 1898. Returning to Baltimore, where much of her family lived, Stein
began a medical degree at The Johns Hopkins University in 1897, continuing her
studies until 1901, whereupon, although she had succeeded during her first three years
as a medical student, she lost interest, failed courses, and left school a few months
short of receiving the M.D.

Gertrude Stein's life took its most significant turn in 1903, when she went to Paris.
There she fell in with the sisters Etta and Claribell Cone, textile heiresses who were
involved in the art world. Leo came to Paris where he and Gertrude, comfortable from
their inheritance, took an apartment at 27 rue de Fleurus. Gertrude lived there until
1937, when the owner reclaimed the apartment for a relative.

On September 8, 1907, Gertrude Stein met Alice Babette Toklas, newly arrived in
Paris from San Francisco. From that day until Stein's death almost forty years later,
the two were inseparable. Alice managed Gertrude's life, keeping house, shopping,
cooking, and guarding Gertrude's privacy so zealously that no one could see Gertrude
before passing muster with Toklas.

When interesting people arrived for the weekly salons at 27 rue de Fleurus, Toklas
shepherded away the women, whom Gertrude called totally uninteresting, so that
Stein could engage their men—including such luminaries as Pablo Picasso, Jo David-
son, Henri Matisse, Juan Gris, Ernest Hemingway, Ford Madox Ford, F. Scott

Fitzgerald, Thornton Wilder, and Sherwood Anderson—in animated conversation. Stein, who enjoyed husbands, found wives boring. When she toured America in 1934-1935, she stipulated that she would speak to no strictly female audiences.

Life's Work

Although Leo and Gertrude Stein were not enormously rich, Paris in the early twentieth century offered inexpensive living in a sophisticated European capital. The Steins lived from trust distribution to trust distribution, but after meeting their fixed expenses, they had enough left over to haunt the shops of art dealers and buy paintings that eventually were worth millions: works by Picasso, Matisse, Gris, and others who emerged as the most significant painters of the period.

Gertrude formed close friendships with the artists whose work she collected. Reflecting on the philosophy that underlay much Impressionist and post-Impressionist art, Stein began to transform elements of that aesthetic into a literary theory that determined the course her writing took.

Misunderstood by literary audiences that expected authors to tell their tales directly, presenting largely observable surface realities, Gertrude Stein moved in her own direction. By doing so, she led the way for more than a generation of later writers.

Stein's was a singularly original mind, given to abstraction. Her undergraduate work in psychology and her subsequent training in medicine helped Stein become attuned to nuances in human behavior—especially in the ways that people use language that few people perceived.

Just as the artists she admired distorted reality to achieve artistic ends, so did Stein begin to work with language in untried ways. Whereas most people are concerned with words as purveyors of meaning, Stein considered words also as sounds and shapes. That she became concerned with essences is evident in her line from "Sacred Emily" in *Tender Buttons* (1914), "Rose is a rose is a rose is a rose."

Hardly a horticultural description of a rose or a visual depiction of the color rose or an insight into a person named Rose, Stein's sentence forces conscientious readers to nudge into their consciousness all that they know about the word "rose." Stein plants a seed that she invites readers to cultivate.

Stein's first book, *Three Lives* (1909), is generally called a novel, although one must stretch the definition to call it one. This book contains sketches of three women, each a domestic servant. The first and third sketches, "The Good Anna" and "The Gentle Lena," are considerably shorter than the central sketch, "Melanctha," a name meaning "black earth." The good Anna is a German woman, bossy but with a kind heart. Lena is as submissive as Anna is domineering, but both women have two things in common: They work hard to survive, and they talk not as previous literary figures have spoken but as people of their social class actually talk. Their dialogue is filled with endless repetitions and non sequiturs, peppered with drivel—irrelevant details, middle-class moral judgments.

If readers object to this sort of dialogue (and most readers, on first exposure to *Three Lives*, find the dialogue bewildering), they should listen carefully to a typical conversation among working people riding home on a crowded bus or subway train after a day's work. Stein, who, as a medical student, did field work among Baltimore's working people, was attuned to their way of speaking. In *Three Lives*, she captures the everyday speech of common people with a verisimilitude that most authors of the day would have replaced with more conventional, literary dialogue.

Three Lives, using a stream-of-consciousness approach, broke new literary ground not only because it used three ordinary women as the protagonists of their respective stories but also because it devoted the longest of the three segments to a black protagonist, Melanctha Herbert, whom Stein presents not specifically as a black but as an ordinary working woman. Elements of Melanctha's black culture resonate in the story, but this segment is more than story of a working woman than that of a black woman—and "Melanctha" is the centerpiece of Stein's book.

Gertrude Stein's books seldom sold well. Some were printed at the author's expense. Publishers who accepted them usually ended up with mountains of copies that had not sold. *Tender Buttons*, a unique book of poetry employing collage and imposing the tenets of Cubism and Expressionism upon literature, and *Geography and Plays* (1922), a collection of short pieces, an almost surrealistic venture into the possibilities of language, followed *Three Lives*. Stein had also written a huge novel, *The Making of Americans* (1925), which traced three generations of a German American family not unlike her own.

No one wanted to publish this unwieldy book, which is still generally considered one of the most unreadable novels in the English language, although it is historically significant for its inventions in language and structure. In 1924, Ernest Hemingway, by now a close friend of Stein, persuaded Ford Madox Ford to serialize some of *The Making of Americans* in his *transatlantic review*, which ceased publication before Stein could be paid for her work. Finally, after years of trying, Stein got Robert McAlmon to publish her long manuscript in Paris.

Ten more of Stein's books were published before she experienced commercial success with *The Autobiography of Alice B. Toklas* (1933), which remains her most accessible book. It is fascinating for its glimpses into post-World War I Paris, culturally vibrant, filled with exciting American expatriates whom Stein labeled members of the "lost generation." Stein, who had always encouraged Alice to write her autobiography, finally did it for her in a book that is whimsical, factual, and delightful.

After three decades abroad, Gertrude Stein returned with Alice B. Toklas to the United States to lecture. They stayed from October, 1934, until May, 1935. Following *The Autobiography of Alice B. Toklas*, Gertrude published eleven more books. Gertrude and Alice sat out the Nazi occupation of France in the countryside where they usually spent their summers. The Nazis apparently overlooked Gertrude's Jewish heritage.

Gertrude developed cancer after the armistice. When her condition worsened, she was hospitalized in Paris, where she died in 1946, Toklas at her side. Alice remained in Paris, dying there on March 7, 1967, two months before her ninetieth birthday.

Summary

Some would say that Gertrude Stein had more impact as a personality than as a writer. Certainly, her force of personality drew people to her and, eventually, drove most of the same people away from her. It is the reflection of Stein's dynamic personality in *The Autobiography of Alice B. Toklas* that accounted for the initial success of that book and that accounts for its continued acceptance.

Like most highly original artists, Stein did not feel bound by what had gone before her. It is doubtful that she was well read in the classics, although she had a considerable understanding of modern literature, perhaps more through knowing its creators than through reading it systematically.

From 1903 on, Stein imbibed a way of life in Paris that stimulated all of her aesthetic sensibilities. She made a unique contribution in appropriating from the graphic arts ideas she could translate into her own form of artistic expression, writing. She also moved beyond writing when, with Virgil Thomson, she collaborated in setting her words to music, in producing with Thomson the opera *Four Saints in Three Acts* (1934).

Stein was forever attuned to nuances. Her field work in Baltimore exposed her to artistic possibilities in ordinary speech. Her understanding of the human brain provided her with insights into characters such as Melanctha Herbert, one of her most sensitively drawn protagonists.

Above all else, Gertrude Stein was her own person—brilliant, talented, prickly, self-assured, opinionated, and devoted to language in all its unique possibilities. Stein's advice to young writers, had she deigned to offer it, would probably have been "Live, live, live"; she would have followed this advice, however, with the admonition "Write, write, write!"

Bibliography

Bloom, Harold, ed. *Gertrude Stein*. New York: Chelsea House, 1986. Part of the Modern Critical Views series, this work contains fifteen essays on Stein, a chronology, and a bibliography. A balanced selection. A good starting point for beginners.

Bridgman, Richard. *Gertrude Stein in Pieces*. New York: Oxford University Press, 1970. Bridgman offers one of the fullest analyses of the overall structure and style of Stein's writing. The book is carefully conceived and clearly presented.

Hemingway, Ernest. *A Moveable Feast*. New York: Charles Scribner's Sons, 1964. Hemingway gives his side of the story about his relationship with Gertrude Stein and about its fracture. His view is biased but interesting.

Hobhouse, Janet. *Everyone Who Was Anybody: A Biography of Gertrude Stein*. New York: G. P. Putnam's Sons, 1975. This book gives a good rundown of the significant people who frequented 27 rue de Fleurus and both Stein and Toklas' opinions of them. Well illustrated.

Hoffman, Frederick J. *Gertrude Stein*. Minneapolis: University of Minnesota Press, 1961. This brief overview provides basic, salient details biographical and critical.

Mellow, James R. *Charmed Circle: Gertrude Stein and Company*. New York: Praeger,

1974. This book, rich with illustrations, captures the vibrant spirit of the exciting circle of painters, sculptors, writers, and fascinating passersby that came within the Stein-Toklas social orbit before and after World War I.

Miller, Rosalind S. *Gertrude Stein: Form and Intelligibility*. New York: Exposition Press, 1949. Miller presents the first sustained assessment of Gertrude Stein's conscious artistry in lucid detail. This book remains important despite its age.

Souhami, Diana. *Gertrude and Alice*. London: Pandora, 1991. The most frank account of Gertrude Stein's long-standing lesbian relationship with Alice B. Toklas, this book shows how strong Alice was and how she dominated many aspects of her forty-year marriage to Stein.

Sprigge, Elizabeth. *Gertrude Stein: Her Life and Work*. New York: Harper & Brothers, 1957. Like Mellow's book, this well-written biography is replete with excellent illustrations. It and Mellow's biography remain among the most valuable resources for Stein scholars and enthusiasts.

R. Baird Shuman

GLORIA STEINEM

Born: March 25, 1934; Toledo, Ohio

Areas of Achievement: Women's rights and journalism
Contribution: A leading proponent of the twentieth century feminist movement, Steinem was also a founder of *Ms.* magazine. Her outspoken advocacy for women has made her a nationally known figure.

Early Life

Gloria Steinem was born on March 25, 1934, to Ruth Nuneviller Steinem and Leo Steinem. Leo was a buyer and seller of antiques who traveled around the country with his family during the winter months. Their summers were spent at Ocean Beach Pier, an entertainment hall that Leo owned and managed at Clark Lake, Michigan. Before Gloria reached her teens, however, her parents separated and then divorced, and her older sister Sue went to college, leaving Gloria to take care of her mother, who was mentally ill with anxiety neurosis and agoraphobia. The two lived in the rundown little Toledo, Ohio, house in which Gloria's mother had grown up.

Gloria spent her teen years in Toledo, trying to balance schoolwork, social life, dancing lessons, and taking care of her mother, who was kept reasonably calm but also disoriented by tranquilizing drugs. When Gloria was seventeen, with their house increasingly dilapidated and their furnace condemned, she was feeling desperate until the church next door offered to purchase the house. After a great deal of persuasion, her father agreed to care for Ruth for one year so that Gloria could finish high school in Washington, D.C., where her sister Sue was living.

The following year, 1952, she entered Smith College, while Sue cared for their mother. After being graduated as a Phi Beta Kappa majoring in government in 1956, she broke a college engagement and went to India on a year's fellowship. Upon her return, unable to get a job as a writer, she spent two years working for the Independent Service for Information, a youth outreach organization that she later discovered was funded by the Central Intelligence Agency. Beginning in 1960, she worked in New York as a freelance writer and assistant for *Help!* magazine.

In 1964, she received national attention as a writer for the short-lived comedy television show *That Was the Week That Was.* She was still frustrated, however, because, although her interests were serious—politics, civil rights, the Vietnam War, world issues—she was limited because of her sex to writing about light topics such as fashion and celebrities. In 1968, however, she joined with Clay Felker in founding the magazine *New York,* becoming one of its writers and editors. Finally, she was able to write about political issues, and for that magazine she published articles about serious events in the country and the world.

Life's Work

Gloria Steinem's feminist consciousness began developing in 1969, when she realized that her concern with society's disenfranchised groups stemmed from the fact that she too was part of an oppressed group: women. She began in that year to talk with women who had experienced abortions, as she had herself before her trip to India, and she became an advocate for legalized abortion, coining the phrase "reproductive freedom."

In 1969, she won the Penney-Missouri Journalism Award for her article in *New York* entitled "After Black Power, Women's Liberation," one of the first serious journalistic reports on the new feminist movement. She marched in New York City's Women's Strike for Equality, a rally held in 1970 to celebrate fifty years of women's right to vote. Her writing became more and more focused on feminist issues, and she began lecturing with Dorothy Pitman Hughes, a black feminist, about the new movement and its importance. She became part of the National Women's Political Caucus, which had been founded in 1971 to try to involve women in politics and government.

In 1971, she became a cofounder, with Brenda Feigen, of the Women's Action Alliance, an organization whose purpose was to develop educational programs geared toward women's personal and economic equality. Members of the Alliance, meeting in Steinem's apartment, came up with the idea of a feminist-oriented national magazine for women.

At first, the women were unable to obtain funding for their venture, but then Clay Felker offered to put out a first issue as a supplement to *New York*. It was a great success, and with additional articles, it was republished as the preview edition of *Ms.* magazine, in January of 1972. In the midst of a publicity trip, Steinem began receiving complaints that the magazine was not available at newsstands. Assuming that it had not been delivered, Steinem called the home office, only to find that the entire first issue, three hundred thousand copies, had sold out in eight days. It was clear that Steinem and her associates were offering something that American women desperately wanted. Ultimately, Warner Communications agreed to finance *Ms.* while allowing the female editorial board complete control of the magazine. *Ms.* has the distinction of being the first national magazine to be run and controlled entirely by women.

Continuing her concern with politics, Steinem was elected in 1972 to the Democratic National Convention as a delegate for Representative Shirley Chisholm. That same year, she was chosen "Woman of the Year" by *McCall's* magazine. Still concerned that women would never be equal until the politics not only of the nation but also of their personal lives were changed, she and some of her *Ms.* colleagues founded the Ms. Foundation for Women, whose purpose is to provide grants to grass-roots, self-help projects for women. In 1974, she helped found the coalition of Labor Union Women. Gloria Steinem had become one of the most prominent spokespersons for the women's movement, and her name had become a household word.

In 1974, *Ms.* launched a television talk show called *Woman Alive*, which was hosted by Steinem. In 1975, she attended the International Women's Year conference in Mexico City, though not as a delegate. Like many others, she was disappointed that women's real concerns were largely ignored in favor of nationalistic issues and divisive propaganda. Two years later, as a member of President Jimmy Carter's national commission to organize an American Conference on Women to be held in Dallas in 1977, Steinem traveled the country speaking about feminist concerns and organizing state conferences that would elect delegates to the national meeting.

Throughout the 1970's, she was active in the effort to ratify the Equal Rights Amendment (ERA). It had passed Congress in 1972 and had received the ratifications of several states, but in an increasingly conservative time it failed to receive sufficient votes to pass by its original deadline in 1979 or even by an extended deadline in 1982. In 1978, in an effort to publicize the importance of the amendment and to extend the ratification period, Steinem helped to organize the extremely successful ERA Extension March in Washington, D.C.

In 1978, Steinem moved to Washington to research the effects of feminism on political theory, financed by a Woodrow Wilson Fellowship from the Smithsonian Institution. This fellowship gave her a chance to spend more time with her sister Sue, as well as her mother, who had finally received hospitalization and treatment and was now living independently.

In 1983, Steinem published her first book, *Outrageous Acts and Everyday Rebellions*, a collection of essays such as a feminist analysis of her mother's life, an undercover exposé of the Playboy Club written in 1963, and a fantasy about what life would be like if men could menstruate. Steinem had long encouraged women to commit "outrageous acts," no matter how small, to change the world, so the title was apt.

Ms. magazine, which had ceased publication in 1989, resumed in 1990 as a no-advertising, editorially free feminist publication, and it has been extremely popular despite the fact that the lack of advertising has increased the cost to subscribers. In the first issue, Steinem wrote an essay explaining the effect advertising has on women's magazines and the effect it had had in previous years on *Ms.* magazine, requiring the watering down of its message. Now published six times yearly, the new *Ms.* can include whatever its editors deem appropriate.

The year 1992 saw the publication of another book by Steinem, *Revolution from Within: A Book of Self-Esteem*. In this book, which utilizes some of the tools of the self-help movement that became popular in the 1980's, Steinem explores the issue of self-esteem for women, probing her own life as well as the stories of others to show the importance of high self-esteem for women as they struggle for equality in American society.

Summary

Gloria Steinem insists that she is an ordinary woman and that her concern has always been with ordinary women. Although she is a celebrity, she believes that the most important issues are those of the grass roots. She believes, passionately, that the personal is political, that changing the world begins by changing lives and the interactions of individuals, and that political power for women will mean nothing if their daily lives are filled with sexist oppression. Therefore, even as a celebrity, she is able to be a spokesperson for everyday people with everyday lives.

Her writing is insightful and brings readers frequently to the "click" experience (the "click" is a moment, identified and made famous in *Ms.* magazine, when the light comes on in one's mind and a new insight comes into focus—when something is thought about in a whole new way). Some of the phrases that she has coined have passed into the popular jargon and are considered part of the folk wisdom of the feminist movement. Some examples are "A woman without a man is like a fish without a bicycle." "We have become the men we wanted to marry." "Most of us are only one man away from welfare."

Although Steinem's time in the limelight was the 1970's, when she was most publicly active and at the helm of *Ms.* magazine, she is still known and respected as an outspoken leader of the second wave of the feminist movement.

Bibliography

Cohen, Marcia. *The Sisterhood: The True Story of the Women Who Changed the World.* New York: Simon & Schuster, 1988. This study of the feminist movement of the 1970's and beyond begins with an analysis of the post-World War II social factors that spawned the movement. It also weaves together biographical accounts of the lives of a number of feminist leaders, including several very informative sections on Gloria Steinem.

Davis, Flora. *Moving the Mountain: The Women's Movement in America Since 1960.* New York: Simon & Schuster, 1991. This history of thirty years of the feminist movement will help the reader understand the events and issues with which Gloria Steinem has been deeply involved. She is mentioned several times in the book, which illustrates how her journalistic and political work relates to the efforts of others.

Henry, Sondra, and Emily Taitz. *One Woman's Power: A Biography of Gloria Steinem.* Minneapolis, Minn.: Dillon Press, 1987. Written for younger students, this biography takes the reader from Steinem's childhood through her years as a young journalist, the founding of *Ms.*, and her political activism to the publication of *Outrageous Acts and Everyday Rebellions.*

Steinem, Gloria. *Outrageous Acts and Everyday Rebellions.* New York: Holt, Rinehart, and Winston, 1983. Steinem's first book, this is a collection of essays written at various points in her career as a journalist and feminist activist. Many of the pieces are personal and reveal a great deal about the author's own life. The thread binding these disparate essays together is Steinem's conviction that women matter and that women's needs are important.

_____ . *Revolution from Within: A Book of Self-Esteem.* Boston: Little, Brown, 1992. This book is an examination of the importance of self-esteem in women's lives. Using much of the language and many of the concepts of the self-help movement of the 1980's and 1990's, this book is self-revealing as well as analytical.

Yates, Gayle Graham. *What Women Want: The Ideas of the Movement.* Cambridge,

Mass.: Harvard University Press, 1975. This early analysis of feminist principles and activity includes a brief section on Gloria Steinem's ideals and her beliefs about the possibility of creating a feminist utopia in which men and women would be equal and gender differences would be minimized.

Eleanor B. Amico

MARTHA STEWART

Born: 1941 or 1942; Jersey City, New Jersey

Area of Achievement: Business and industry
Contribution: Known as the "guru" of home entertainment, Stewart has written books on entertaining, gardening, and cooking in addition to books on weddings and home remodeling.

Early Life

Martha Kostyra was born to Polish Catholic parents in Jersey City, New Jersey, sometime in 1941 or 1942, the second of six children. At the age of three, Martha's family moved, and she grew up in the suburban neighborhood of Nutley, New Jersey.

Martha's father was a pharmaceutical salesman, and her mother was a teacher. Although she was loved by both parents, Martha was her father's favorite child. He taught her how to garden and use tools, helped her in her public speaking, and taught her useful sales techniques. Most important, he instilled in Martha a sense of confidence and success by telling her she could accomplish anything she wanted.

Martha's mother and maternal grandmother also had an impact on Martha's early life. They taught her how to cook and entertain. The typical Kostyra family dinner each Sunday would include ten vegetable dishes and five fresh fruit desserts. As she grew up, Martha learned as much as she could about cooking, and her neighbors, who were retired bakers, taught her how to bake pies and tarts.

Even as a youngster, Martha liked to entertain others. She particularly enjoyed organizing birthday parties for the neighborhood kids. During her high school years, Martha catered a breakfast for the high school football team. Little did she know that one day she would become famous for her catering and cooking abilities.

In school, Martha was a straight "A" student who loved to read the classics. Upon graduation, Martha was offered scholarships to attend both Barnard College and New York University. Martha chose Barnard College and majored in art, European history, and architectural history.

During college, Martha began working occasionally as a model to earn extra income. She also met future husband, Andrew Stewart, who was a law student. They were married at the end of Martha's sophomore year. At that time, Martha was earning enough money from her modeling work to support them both. She appeared in advertisements and commercials for Clairol hair products and Lifebuoy soap. Martha graduated from college in 1963, and continued to model until she became pregnant.

In 1965, Martha Stewart gave birth to her only child, Alexis. She contemplated graduate school, but decided to work as a Wall Street stockbroker, the same occupation as her father-in-law. One of the few women to be working in the profession, Stewart learned quickly and became quite successful, eventually earning a reported $135,000 per year. Stewart later recalled that the 1973 recession made her a "nervous wreck," and she retired. She and her husband moved out of New York City that year, and purchased an old farmhouse in Westport, Connecticut. This move marked the beginning of Martha Stewart's entrepreneurial career.

Life's Work

In Westport, Martha and Andrew Stewart spent their first two years fixing up their old farmhouse. They had planned to restore and sell it at a hefty profit, but ended up keeping the home instead. Years later, Martha Stewart capitalized on her experiences on the project by writing a book on home restoration, using her home as an example.

In 1974, Stewart decided to launch a catering business with a friend. Although their business relationship later ended, Stewart continued to run the catering firm on her own. Aware of the pressures to entertain from her own experience as the wife of a successful attorney, Stewart became a popular caterer among her elite neighbors in Connecticut. Her business, Martha Stewart, Inc., grew into a million-dollar business over a period of ten years with many corporate and celebrity clients on the East Coast.

Stewart's husband, Andrew, left his job as a corporate attorney to become publisher and president of Stewart, Tabori, and Chang, a publishing company affiliated with Times-Mirror Books. Through him, Stewart learned about publishing and decided that she wanted to publish her own book. Acting as her agent, Stewart's husband assisted her in publishing her first coffee-table book with Crown Publishing. (The couple later divorced in 1989.) She wanted to produce a high-quality book and held to certain specifications despite publisher objections. Her publisher eventually conceded, and Stewart's book went on to become a best-seller. The book, *Entertaining* (1982), sold more than 750,000 copies by the early 1990's.

Although popular, the book had its critics. The food establishment criticized Stewart for plagiarizing recipes from popular cookbook authors such as Julia Child and Barbara Tropp, even though Stewart denied the charges and stated that recipes were in the public domain. *Entertaining* was designed to do more than just cite recipes. In the book, Stewart instructed women how to set a table and arrange flowers and how to hold a dinner party. The book called for entertainment that was informal and relaxed, but glamorous. Through example and style, Stewart sought to transform traditional homemaking chores, such as cooking, into enjoyable and rewarding pastimes. Since *Entertaining*, Stewart's name has become a household word to many American women.

In order to meet public demand for her entertaining expertise, Stewart produced eight additional books in the wake of her 1982 debut, including *Martha Stewart's Quick Cook Menus, Martha Stewart's Hors D'Oeuvres, Martha Stewart Weddings, The Wedding Planner, Martha Stewart's Christmas, Martha Stewart's Gardening,* and *Martha Stewart's New Old House*. Each book was priced near fifty dollars, primarily because of the oversize format and lavish use of color photographs, many of which featured Stewart herself in the process of gardening, entertaining, and cooking. Stewart's all-American good looks made her an attractive model, and her willingness to demonstrate her tips and techniques added a convincing air of authenticity to her recommendations. In addition to providing a wealth of advice, Stewart's works provided insights about her childhood and how her family did things, making her books both personable and informative.

Instead of advising readers to hire professional decorators, Stewart has advocated a "do-it-yourself" approach. She has recommended that readers use natural materials, such as potted flowers and fruit in baskets, as attractive dining centerpieces. She has also encouraged a mix-and-match approach to dinnerware—advising her readers on how to mix expensive formal pieces with more inexpensive items. According to Stewart, food preparation and an aesthetically pleasing environment are equally important to home entertainment.

Her book *Martha Stewart Weddings* was one of her most popular books. Illustrated with more than seven hundred photographs, the oversized book provided descriptions of two dozen actual weddings. Again, the book became a perennial best-seller, directing couples on every aspect of planning a memorable wedding.

Stewart's popularity became so widespread that corporate America took interest in courting her. The discount marketing chain Kmart signed Stewart to a $5 million, three-year contract to serve as a home entertainment consultant and spokesperson. The store soon began featuring a Martha Stewart line of products, including bed linens, flatware, and towels. Stewart also produced numerous television commercials to promote this new product line. Although many of her entertainment ideas appealed to an elite, well-to-do audience, Kmart was convinced that Stewart's homey appeal would draw middle-class baby boomers into their stores.

In 1990, Stewart embarked upon another ambitious project by signing a $15 million contract with Time-Warner. The agreement provided Stewart with the opportunity to publish a bimonthly magazine called *Martha Stewart Living*. Established Stewart followers and those who could not afford her coffee-table books were the proposed target market for the magazine, which was priced at three dollars per copy. Since its debut issue in 1990, the magazine has been a success, with circulation tripling to 750,000 readers. Plans were made to expand the magazine as a monthly publication in mid-1994. In addition, Stewart promised to publish additional books and tape various video projects and television specials for Time-Warner as part of the multimillion dollar deal.

In addition, Stewart launched other projects, including seminars and a weekly syndicated television show. Her popular seminars, which often have long waiting lists, provide a wealth of entertainment advice for a rather hefty $900 tuition fee. Stewart's television show has been syndicated on more than 140 television stations. The show, entitled *Martha Stewart Living*, covers many of the same cooking, gardening, and decorating tips found in her books and magazine. A typical show may include advice on cultivating hydrangeas, cooking a lobster dinner, and decorating Easter eggs.

Summary

Martha Stewart's phenomenal business success is a testament to her training on Wall Street. Her detractors, however, have noted that this same success seems to imply that a significant section of the female population embraces the "traditional" role of women rather than the "feminist" role. What happened to the liberating efforts of feminism? Why are women purchasing Martha Stewart books?

Some explained Stewart's success by noting that women of the 1980's and 1990's became frustrated with their progress in the working world and were returning to comfortable pursuits such as cooking, decorating, and entertaining. Unlike the woman of the 1950's, whose identity was primarily defined by her role as a homemaker, women of the 1980's and 1990's were attempting to juggle demanding jobs and kids and had minimal leisure time. As a result, homemaking activities such as gardening and entertaining became hobbies—a way for many working women to relax. These same working women had larger disposable incomes to spend on such activities. In fact, the trend for baby-boomers seems to be an increased focus on life at home for both sexes. Stewart's advice assists these families by making that time at home special.

Regardless of the verdict on her impact on feminist pursuits, Stewart has capitalized on the idea that women can "have it all." Women left homemaking in the 1960's and 1970's for the workplace. In the 1980's and 1990's, Stewart initiated a trend that brought women back to homemaking, but not as a full-time occupation. Rather, Stewart capitalized on the fact that many women found certain homemaking activities enjoyable and chose to offer her expert advice on the subject.

Bibliography
Gordon, Meryl. "Heart-Shaped Wreaths, Perfume-Sprayed Notepaper, Ribbon-Wrapped Linens—Is This What Women Want?" *Working Woman* 16 (September, 1991): 74-77. Stewart is profiled along with entrepreneurs Alexandra Stoddard and Mary Emmerling, who also focus on providing women with advice on home entertainment, interior decoration, and personal adornment. The author explores the way Stewart, in particular, caters to a certain image of femininity that became popular among her contemporaries in the baby-boomer generation during the 1980's and early 1990's.

Hitchens, Christopher. "Cultural Elite: Martha, Inc." *Vanity Fair* 56 (October, 1993): 80-89. A critical assessment of Stewart's popularity with the American public. Discusses the image Stewart has created for herself through her books, her videos, and her magazine *Martha Stewart Living*.

Hubbard, Kim. "Martha Stewart, the One-Woman Industry, Adds a New Line and Subtracts a Husband." *People Weekly* 30 (November 28, 1988): 118-121. A profile of Stewart that discusses the breakup of her twenty-seven year marriage as well as the success of her sponsorship agreement with Kmart.

Kasindorf, Jeanie. "Living with Martha—Can Decorating Dynamo Martha Stewart Make Herself a Permanent Cover Girl?" *New York* 24 (January 28, 1991): 22. Candid article and interview with Martha Stewart. Covers all aspects of her life including her upbringing, business affairs, and personal relationships. The author spent some time traveling with Stewart and integrated Stewart's day-to-day activities into this biographical sketch.

Stewart, Martha. *Entertaining*. New York: Crown, 1982. The famous coffee-table book that brought Stewart enormous public attention. Her first best-seller on home entertainment, this book contains an unusual amount of information about Stewart's personal life as well as her aesthetic taste.

Marsha M. Huber

LUCY STONE

Born: August 13, 1818; Coy's Hill, near West Brookfield, Massachusetts
Died: October 18, 1893; Dorchester, near Boston, Massachusetts
Areas of Achievement: Social reform and women's rights
Contribution: Stone committed her life to the struggle for woman suffrage and equal
   rights.

Early Life

Lucy Stone was born near West Brookfield, Massachusetts, on August 13, 1818, into a family whose ancestors were among New England's first settlers. Lucy's father, Francis Stone, tanned hides and served as the community's teacher until her birth, at which time he settled into farming. At home he commanded absolute authority, and discipline was swift, marked with severe whippings and humiliation.

Hannah Matthews Stone, Lucy's mother, was an obedient, hard-working housewife. Despite this outward docility, Lucy saw in her mother a quiet anger and resentment against male domination as prescribed by fundamental Christian ideology. Her father's control and her mother's grudging submission were such powerful influences that as a child Lucy swore never to marry or accept such a contemptible station in life.

Her developing objection to the status of women compelled Lucy to pursue a solid education and, in the process, to learn Greek so that she could verify the accuracy of biblical translations regarding a woman's position in society. At the age of sixteen, she was hired to teach at a local school with a salary of four dollars per month. The salary itself enraged Lucy because male teachers with the same credentials earned four times the money.

When not teaching, Lucy continued her studies at the local seminary for girls until 1843, when, at the age of twenty-five, she entered Oberlin college in Ohio, the only college that admitted female students and one that also supported the emancipation of slaves. Abolitionism was not new to Lucy. She had avidly read William Lloyd Garrison's *The Liberator* since it began publication, and she considered herself a "Garrisonian"—supporting a more radical antislavery stance than Oberlin College itself. While a student at Oberlin, Lucy taught former slaves, worked in the school cafeteria, learned Greek, founded the college's first women's debating society, and delivered her first public speech on women's rights and slave emancipation. Considered too radical by her peers and a potential troublemaker by the college, she nevertheless earned respect for her determination, intelligence, and ability to argue an issue soundly and convincingly. Following her graduation in 1847, she was hired by the Massachusetts Anti-Slave Society as a public speaker—a position considered socially improper for a woman.

Life's Work

Against her parents' wishes, Lucy Stone delivered her first public address on slave emancipation and women's rights in the summer of 1847. Stone possessed strong conviction, sound logic, and an eloquence in oratory which compelled even the most ardent opponent of women's rights to listen respectfully. Stone made frequent public lectures during that year, and most of these speeches concentrated on issues of women's rights.

By the end of the decade, New England had become the center of a growing social reform movement in the nation, and Stone was quickly emerging as one of the movement's most competent and committed proponents. She advocated the strict control of alcoholic beverages, arguing that liquor destroyed the fabric of the home and emboldened men to abuse their wives. She criticized Christianity for relegating women to a position of social inferiority and for not taking a stronger antislave position. She championed a woman's right to own property, to receive an advanced education, and to be granted equal status before the law. Without doubt, her arguments were sharply criticized by the male-dominated social order of the era, but the women who filled her lecture halls and whispered encouragement strengthened Stone's resolve to continue speaking for equality. She made women's rights her principal topic and was noted as the first woman speaker to do so. For her near solitary public position, she became known as the "morning star" of the women's rights movement.

Lucy Stone was the primary organizer of the First National Woman's Rights Convention, held in Worcester, Massachusetts, on October 23, 1850. More than one thousand participants listened to speakers such as Sojourner Truth, Sarah Tyndall, Frederick Douglass, and Stone present their calls for woman's equality. Although the Seneca Falls Convention of 1848 was the first such gathering, it had drawn a limited local audience of reformers. The 1850 convention, however, placed the issue of women's rights before a national audience and set into motion an annual conference largely directed by Stone who, at her own expense, published a report of the conference proceedings.

Stone's hectic lecture schedule took her across much of the nation pressing state assemblies for equal rights for women. In 1853, she endorsed a woman suffrage petition presented to the Massachusetts Constitutional Convention in Boston. From there, she spoke in Cincinnati, Pittsburgh, St. Louis, Louisville, and several other cities. Her presentations included specific points regarding women's equality in marriage—perhaps because of her developing relationship with Henry Blackwell, to whom she was married in May, 1855.

Symbolic of her expectations and demands for equality in marriage, Stone retained her maiden name and never did she refer to herself as Mrs. Blackwell, preferring instead Lucy Stone, wife of Henry Blackwell. Taking the husband's name amounted to the loss of a woman's identity, she argued. She further insisted that once married, a woman's property should remain hers, and the same should be true for the product of her labor and the guardianship of the children. According to Stone, a husband's control over a wife's property amounted to nothing short of legal theft. Moreover, nonconsensual sex was the equivalent of marital rape, she stated. She further demanded the abolition of the entire system of legal codes and customs that placed women under the care, protection, and exclusive control of their husbands. Personal independence and equal human rights, she maintained, could never be relinquished by a woman because of marriage, and the law should recognize the institution as an equal partnership.

Stone's arguments were certainly advanced for the era in which she lived. More often than not she was considered too extreme in her views. Typically, male listeners were outraged by Stone's speeches, and women found her ideas correct but impossible to attain. Despite the cool, and sometimes even hostile, response given her by the general public, Stone persisted in demanding equal rights in marriage.

The Civil War interrupted Stone's public lecturing. Also, the birth of her daughter refocused Stone's attention to child rearing and would have taken her from the lecture circuit even if the war had not erupted. Moreover, she started having severe headaches that occasionally confined her to bed for days.

Despite these interruptions, Stone resumed her active public life following the war. Increasingly, she emphasized woman's suffrage in her speeches—a right she believed was central to women's equality. She argued for suffrage in a series of lectures throughout New England and New York, coauthored a petition for Congress to consider women's right to vote, and helped organize a convention that led to the founding of the American Equal Rights Association. In March, 1867, Stone argued for black and woman suffrage before the New Jersey legislature stating that every person capable of rational choice was entitled to the right to vote. Democracy required equal suffrage. When a woman is denied the vote, she added, the very principle of democracy itself is violated. If women were indeed the natural possessors of morality, she concluded, then extension of the franchise would automatically bring a humane attitude to legislation. She spread her views throughout the North and again lobbied Congress, was instrumental in the formation of the New England Suffrage Association, and helped organize the New Jersey Woman Suffrage Association.

That women were not included in the Fifteenth Amendment only intensified Stone's battle for equal rights. Throughout 1869, she labored to publish *Woman's Journal*, with seven thousands copies of the first edition sold in early January, 1870. Voting rights was the primary focus of each edition, and this first issue highlighted Wyoming's new woman suffrage law. The *Journal* also addressed a variety of women's issues and concerns such as education, health, marriage, work, and the rearing of children.

Stone took residence on the floor above the *Journal*'s office and from there worked to gain advertisers, subscribers, and news stories. She spent hours managing the office, handling financial matters, and arranging for printing and distribution. Despite the hectic and consuming work, she maintained a lecture schedule that took her into Pennsylvania, Vermont, New York, and throughout Massachusetts. At the same time, she continued her active involvement in the American Equal Rights Association and in the creation of an amendment to grant woman suffrage nationally.

The 1870's were no less busy for Stone. Persons who could not vote, she consistently argued, were defenseless in society. Power rested in the ballot box, and once women received the franchise the ills of society would be remedied. To bring added pressure on state legislatures, Stone looked for untapped sources of support. The suffrage movement had relied upon a minority of women—those who were well educated, skilled at public speaking and organization, and not intimidated by the male population or by accepted norms for proper female behavior. In the late 1870's, Stone sought to include middle-class women by making the push for suffrage a socially acceptable position among women themselves. The formation of women's clubs in communities across the nation would afford women the opportunity to discuss the issue of suffrage and to chart a course of action locally to advance the cause. With clubs becoming fashionable outlets for middle-class women, Stone believed suffrage specifically, and the demand for equal rights in general, could be pressed forcefully by a new body of supporters. She imagined the widespread effect of such political action in every town and anticipated the strength such clubs could use in lobbying state legislatures. In one month she recruited almost 1,100 women into local clubs.

At the same time, Stone criticized government efforts to provide protective legislation for women in the workplace arguing that gender-based laws guaranteed unequal treatment for women, even if the intention of the legislation was positive. In addition, through the *Woman's Journal*, she championed better working conditions for all individuals, an end to inhumane conditions in reform schools, the elimination of government and business corruption, and she protested vigorously existing federal policy regarding American Indians. Before the decade ended, *Woman's Journal* was distributed in every state and in thirty-nine foreign countries.

Despite declining health throughout the 1880's, Stone remained as active as possible. In May, 1893, she attended the World's Congress of Representative Women at the World Columbian Exposition in Chicago. More than 150,000 people from twenty-seven nations assembled for a week-long convention. Among the slated speakers was Lucy Stone. Weak and frail, she took the podium and delivered her address entitled "The Progress of Fifty Years." She traced the course of the women's rights movement over five decades, praised the women who had unselfishly devoted themselves to the struggle, and clearly detailed the much improved status of women in contemporary America. She ended the speech with a reminder—much more work was needed, and the movement must continue until full equality was achieved.

Stone's speech in Chicago was her last. Five months later, on October 18, she died with her daughter Alice at her side. In commemoration of her life's work, university dormitories, city parks, and public schools were named in her honor. The suffrage movement persisted until passage of the twentieth amendment in 1919 which granted woman suffrage. The *Woman's Journal* continued publication until 1931, and, with each issue, echoed Lucy Stone's demand for gender equality.

Bibliography

Blackwell, Alice Stone. *Lucy Stone: Pioneer of Woman's Rights*. 2d ed. Norwood, Mass.: Alice Stone Blackwell Committee, 1930. Alice Stone Blackwell, Lucy Stone's daughter, presents an insightful and personal view of her mother's personal and public life.

Hays, Elinor Rice. *Morning Star: A Biography of Lucy Stone, 1818-1893.* New York: Harcourt, Brace & World, 1961. Hays portrays Stone as a solid, committed champion of women's rights and the emancipation of slaves—a model for contemporary feminists and reformers.

Kerr, Andrea Moore. *Lucy Stone: Speaking Out for Equality.* New Brunswick, N.J.: Rutgers University Press, 1992. Kerr presents a thorough and well-researched biography of Lucy Stone, and ranks Stone as one of the most powerful women reformers of the nineteenth century.

Lasser, Carol, and Marlene Merrill, eds. *Friends and Sisters: Letters Between Lucy Stone and Antoinette Brown Blackwell, 1846-93.* Chicago: University of Illinois Press, 1987. Lucy Stone's personal thoughts, views on women's rights, and half-century friendship with Antoinette Brown Blackwell, the first woman ordained into the Protestant ministry, is revealed through their private letters to each other.

Woloch, Nancy. *Women and the American Experience.* New York: Alfred A. Knopf, 1984. This publication surveys the history of women in America from the early seventeenth century through the late 1970's and places Lucy Stone in the broader context of the suffrage movement.

Kenneth William Townsend

HARRIET BEECHER STOWE

Born: June 14, 1811; Litchfield, Connecticut
Died: July 1, 1896; Hartford, Connecticut
Areas of Achievement: Social reform and women's rights
Contribution: Stowe's popular novel *Uncle Tom's Cabin* attacked slavery as a threat
   to the Christian family and helped to end this institution in the United States. In this
   and later novels, Stowe wrote as an early advocate for women—one who wished
   to help them by creating a "women's sphere" in the home.

Early Life
   Lyman Beecher, Harriet Beecher's father, was a stern New England Calvinist
preacher whose image of a God who predestined humans to heaven or hell left a mark
on his children. The fact that Harriet's mother died when she was four made Harriet's
father's influence even more important. By the age of six and a half, the young
"Hattie," as she was known to her family, had memorized more than two dozen hymns
and several long chapters in the Bible. As an adult, however, Harriet Beecher would
substitute for her father's dogmas a religion of hope that stressed the love and
compassion of Christ rather than the divine judgment that her father preached. Some
people hold that she "feminized" her father's religion. Throughout her life, she
retained a strong sense of religious mission and zeal for social improvement.
   At age twelve, Harriet moved to Hartford to live with her older sister Catharine, a
purposeful woman who had started the Hartford Female Seminary. Harriet attended
Catharine's school and stayed on as a teacher and guardian of young children. In 1832,
she moved with her family to Cincinnati, Ohio, where her father had been offered the
post as president of the new Lane Theological Seminary. Three years after arriving
in Cincinnati (in January, 1836), Harriet Beecher married Calvin Stowe, a Lane
professor.
   These years in the West prepared Stowe for her later career. She had eight children
between 1836 and 1850, and if she and Calvin had not alternated taking "rest cures"
in Vermont over the years, she might have had more. In 1834, Harriet won a
fifty-dollar prize for "A New England Sketch," which was published in the *Western
Monthly Magazine.* From that point on, the members of her family saw her as a person
of literary promise, even though she claimed that this activity was only a way of
supplementing the always meager family income. In 1842, Calvin wrote to his wife,
"[My] dear, you must be a literary woman. It is written in the book of fate."
   While in Cincinnati, Harriet also experienced the intense emotions aroused by the
slavery issue during these years. On one visit to a Kentucky plantation, she saw slaves
whom she later used as models for some of the characters in *Uncle Tom's Cabin.* In
1836, a local mob attacked the print shop of an abolitionist in the city, and the struggle
between the abolitionists and the moderates at Lane eventually drove her father to
retire and her husband to take a job at Bowdoin College in Maine in 1850.

Life's Work

When President Abraham Lincoln met Harriet Beecher Stowe in the fall of 1862, he greeted her as "the little lady who made this big war." He was not alone in believing that Stowe's *Uncle Tom's Cabin* (1852) had been a crucial event in arousing the antislavery sentiments that led to the outbreak of the American Civil War in 1861. Although *Uncle Tom's Cabin* was not the best novel of the nineteenth century, it certainly had the greatest impact. *Uncle Tom's Cabin* sold 300,000 copies the year it was published, and Stowe's great work helped to end slavery by personalizing that "peculiar institution." Slavery was wrong, the novel argued, because it was un-Christian. More specifically, slavery tore children from their mothers and thus threatened the existence of the Christian family. It has been said that *Uncle Tom's Cabin* was "a great revival sermon," more effective than those of her father. Harriet herself later wrote that the book was written by "the Lord Himself. . . . I was but an instrument in his hands."

Each of the main characters in this melodramatic novel displayed virtues and vices that were important to Stowe. The main character, Tom, was sold by a kind master, Mr. Shelby, to a second one, Augustine St. Clare, who had ambiguous feelings about slavery and planned to free Tom. Before he could do so, St. Clare was killed and Tom was sold to a singularly evil man, Simon Legree, who finally beat Tom to death when the slave refused to tell him the hiding place of two slaves who were planning to escape.

Aside from Tom, the strongest characters in the novel were female. The slave Eliza, also sold by Mr. Shelby, escaped with her son (who would have been taken from her) by jumping across ice flocs on the Ohio River. She and her husband George were finally reunited in Canada. Little Eva, the saintly and sickly child of Augustine St. Clare, was a Christ-like figure who persuaded her father to free Tom before she herself died. Mary Bird, the wife of an Ohio senator, shamed her husband into helping Eliza when she sought comfort at their home. Senator Bird violated the Fugitive Slave Law of 1850—which he had helped to pass and which required Northerners to return escaped slaves—by helping Eliza. Ophelia, a cousin of Augustine St. Clare who came from Vermont to help him care for his invalid wife and child, was the model of a well-organized homemaker who was especially proud of her neat kitchen. Another courageous female was the slave Cassy, who quietly poisoned her newborn with opium after she had had two other children sold away from her.

It was no accident that so many of the heroes in *Uncle Tom's Cabin* were women motivated by a Christian love of neighbor or that the most dramatic events in the novel focused on the way slavery destroyed families. *Uncle Tom's Cabin* was particularly effective in arousing antislavery sentiment and particularly infuriating to Southern defenders of slavery, precisely because it dramatically attacked one of the strongest arguments of slaveholders, the religious one that saw slavery as an essential part of the patriarchal system of authority established by God and sanctioned by Scripture. For Stowe, Christianity began at home with a strong family. Any institution that undermined the family was necessarily unchristian.

In many ways, Harriet Beecher Stowe was a lay preacher whose writings were sermons. Like some other nineteenth century advocates of women's rights, Stowe believed that women were morally superior to men. She did not believe that women should govern the country or replace men in the world of business, but rather that they should set a moral example for society through their control of the "domestic sphere," where they could influence society by shaping the lives of their children. Stowe advocated greater equality between the men's sphere and the women's sphere. Women deserved greater respect because most of them—slave or free—were mothers, and therefore they had a greater understanding of both love and the "sacredness of the family" than men did.

In some of her later novels, especially *Pink and White Tyranny: A Society Novel, My Wife and I* (both 1871) and *We and Our Neighbors* (1875), Stowe continued to argue that women could improve the world by being guardians of morals in the home. She was not a "radical" advocate of full social equality for women, and she was critical of reformers such as Elizabeth Cady Stanton and Susan B. Anthony. Yet, despite her active professional career as a writer, which made her the principal wage earner in the family after 1853, Stowe continued to maintain that she wrote only to supplement the family income. She also continued to write novels in which strong women—for example, Mary Scudder in *The Minister's Wooing* (1859) and Mara in *The Pearl of Orr's Island* (1862)—acted as female ministers who taught their families the path to salvation from the well-ordered kitchen that was, in effect, a domestic pulpit.

This complex woman continued to publish until she was nearly seventy. Although *Uncle Tom's Cabin* had a greater impact on American history than any other single novel, Harriet Beecher Stowe's literary reputation rests on those novels that portrayed life in the New England villages of her youth: *The Pearl of Orr's Island*, *Oldtown Folks* (1869), and *Poganuc People: Their Loves and Lives* (1878). Although peopled by stern Calvinist ministers and wise, compassionate women, these works were not consciously written to correct a social injustice, as was *Uncle Tom's Cabin*. In 1873, Stowe used some of her income to buy a large home in Hartford, Connecticut, where she and Calvin spent their last years. Calvin died in 1886, ten years before his sometimes controversial wife.

Summary

Harriet Beecher Stowe will always be remembered primarily as the author of *Uncle Tom's Cabin*, which helped to end slavery in the United States and to spark the bloodiest war in American history. In the 1850's and 1860's, she remained one of America's most popular writers. Many of her works were first serialized in *The Atlantic Monthly* and then published as books, which earned her a steady and comfortable income.

Historians now recognize that Harriet Beecher Stowe's contribution to American history goes beyond these accomplishments. Although one cannot view this tradition-ally religious woman as a modern feminist, she did play an important role in women's history. Writing was one of the few "respectable" careers open to women in nineteenth century America, since women could write at home and legitimately argue that their work was necessary to supplement family income. It is somewhat ironic that Stowe's fiction, which powerfully affected the course of events outside the "domestic sphere," was written to earn greater respect for women as leaders of the home and family. It is also interesting that a century after Stowe's reputation was at its peak, Betty Friedan's pathbreaking book *The Feminine Mystique* (1963) would attack the central idea of Harriet Beecher Stowe: that women's primary role should be to lead and shape the home and family.

It is a tribute to Harriet Beecher Stowe that Friedan's work was necessary. Stowe softened the harsh Calvinism of her father by emphasizing a religion of love more congenial to women; she also defended a separate "sphere" for female activity in American life. It can be argued that both of these things were necessary to raise the status of women in America. That, in turn, made it easier for other women to demand later the greater freedom that women enjoy in the United States a century after Stowe's death.

Bibliography
Adams, John R. *Harriet Beecher Stowe.* New York: Twayne, 1963. This short biography emphasizes the connection between Stowe's personality and her writings. Adams sees Stowe as a subservient person who finally declared her independence from domestic restrictions by writing *Uncle Tom's Cabin.*

Ammons, Elizabeth, ed. *Critical Essays on Harriet Beecher Stowe.* Boston: G. K. Hall, 1980. This useful collection contains essays on Stowe by literary critics and modern feminist scholars. Dorothy Berkson's essay "Millennial Politics and the Feminine Fiction of Harriet Beecher Stowe" is particularly good.

Crozier, Alice. *The Novels of Harriet Beecher Stowe.* New York: Oxford University Press, 1969. This study provides the best synopses of Stowe's works. The author stresses Stowe's religious motivation and notes that most of her novels were widely read and respected by educated readers of her day.

Degler, Carl N. *At Odds: Women and the Family in America from the Revolution to the Present.* New York: Oxford University Press, 1980. The passages on Stowe show a self-reliant woman who was equal to her husband in many ways. She managed her own financial affairs, was more interested in her writing than in routine domestic chores, and even gave her husband advice on how to control his sexual urges.

Douglas, Ann. *The Feminization of American Culture.* New York: Doubleday, 1988. The introduction to this work and a later section on Stowe show how she feminized the religion of the Calvinist preachers of her father's generation. Douglas sees Stowe's contribution to American life as an ambiguous one that both helped and hindered her twentieth century sisters.

Stowe, Harriet Beecher. *Uncle Tom's Cabin.* New York: Bantam Books, 1981. This famous work, always mentioned in textbooks but less often read, offers the best way to acquire an understanding of what was important to Stowe—and to many of her female readers in nineteenth century America. Many editions are available.

Wilson, Robert Forrest. *Crusader in Crinoline: The Life of Harriet Beecher Stowe.* Reprint. Westport, Conn.: Greenwood Press, 1972. This lengthy biography, originally published in 1941, remains the best single source for a full account of Stowe's life. It must be supplemented with some of the newer studies cited previously.

Ken Wolf

MERYL STREEP

Born: June 22, 1949; Summit, New Jersey

Areas of Achievement: Film and theater and drama
Contribution: Streep is a highly acclaimed actress who, in order to break stereotypes of women as weak, will only appear in films that depict women characters of many dimensions.

Early Life

In Summit, New Jersey, Meryl Streep, the oldest of three children, was born Mary Louise Streep on June 22, 1949. Her father, Harry Streep II, was an executive with Merck pharmaceuticals, and her mother, Mary, a commercial artist, shortened her daughter's name from Mary Louise to Meryl.

Meryl thought herself ugly during her childhood. She claimed that the other children did not like her because she was prim and bossy. At Bernardsville High School, however, Meryl decided to change her image. She replaced her corrective lenses with contacts, revealed a smile without braces, and lightened her hair. She dedicated herself to looking like a cover girl from *Seventeen* magazine. In addition, she took up drama and played Marian the librarian in *The Music Man*, Daisy Mae in *Li'l Abner*, and Laurie in *Oklahoma*. The transformation gained her the popularity that was missing in her childhood. She was a cheerleader, dated the star of the football team, and was chosen homecoming queen.

Only later, after entering Vassar, an all-female college, did Streep reflect on the shallowness of her high school years. At Vassar, she experienced a freedom she had never known at the coeducational high school where appearances were all that mattered. At Vassar, Streep developed depth of character; she expanded her mind and studied drama to perfect her art.

Streep performed in various productions at Vassar and, during a one-semester stay, at Dartmouth. After being graduated from Vassar, she performed with the Green Mountain Guild in Vermont and then went to graduate school at Yale, where she became the campus drama star. Meryl Streep received her M.F.A. degree from Yale in 1975.

After Yale, Streep went to Manhattan and was soon signed by Joseph Papp to appear with the New York Shakespeare Festival. Her great success on stage brought her to the attention of film producers. In March, 1977, she made her television debut in the CBS drama *The Deadliest Season*. In 1978, she appeared in NBC's *Holocaust*, for which she won an Emmy award. On the basis of that notability, Streep began to make films, performing in twenty-one films within fifteen years.

In September of 1978, Meryl Streep was married to sculptor Donald Gummer. They have one son, Henry, and three daughters, Mary Willa "Mamie," Grace, and Louisa. Streep claimed that motherhood was her primary role in life. Gummer and Streep decided that SoHo was not a suitable place to rear children, so they purchased a ninety-five-acre wooded mountaintop in Dutchess County, New York, where they could escape the stress of public life.

Life's Work

Meryl Streep has said she has a preference for performing live theater because she can put all her energy into plays; she can involve her whole body, open her mouth and scream. Her range of live performances includes musicals, comedy, and drama. Besides performing in the New York Shakespeare Festival, she has performed several plays on Broadway: *Trelawny of the Wells*, *Twenty-Seven Wagons Full of Cotton*, *Memory of Two Mondays*, *Secret Service*, *The Cherry Orchard*, and *Happy End*.

When Streep began to make films, she was determined to accept only roles that broke stereotypes of women as weak and that developed the multiple dimensions of women. She turned down exploitive roles in miniseries such as Sidney Sheldon's *Bloodlines* and Judith Krantz's *Scruples*.

Her film debut in *Julia* (1977) allowed her to make a political and social statement, because it cast a strong, positive light on women. She was particularly pleased that this film showed two women having a serious conversation, unlike the stereotypical female prattle in many films.

Streep was also excited to play the role of Susan Trahern in the film *Plenty* (1984). The character was a strong, unusual woman who was not afraid to express the depth of her anger. Streep admired this character, who demanded that the world live up to her ideal. On NBC's *Entertainment Tonight* (October 17, 1985), she made this comment about the movie *Plenty*:

> I think we've seen a lot of heroes in literature and in drama, men who ask a lot of their circumstances, and of society and the world, and who are demanding, aggressively so. I don't think that's unusual; what I think is unusual is that [in *Plenty*] it's a woman.

For similar reasons, Streep accepted the role of Karen Blixen in the film adaptation of Isak Dinesen's *Out of Africa* (1985). Blixen was a woman in turn-of-the-century Africa who challenged the restrictions of the male-dominated society. Blixen challenged the imposed female roles along with the harsh natural elements of the African landscape. She also had to remain strong after being abandoned by her husband and her lover.

These characters, along with the other roles chosen by Streep, reflect an ambiguous nature. They are struggling with the contradictions within their own hearts. Streep is capable of capturing the collage of feelings that exists inside individual characters with the use of her face, her body, and her voice.

Streep also selects quality productions that stimulate her creativity. She avoids boredom by choosing characters with multiple dimensions. This preference is best illustrated in her films *The French Lieutenant's Woman* (1981) and *Sophie's Choice* (1982). Both films involved complex characters. As Sarah and Anna in the film, *The French Lieutenant's Woman*, Streep had to shift back and forth between the roles of a contemporary actress and a woman in a mid-nineteenth century English seacoast town. She not only captured the dual characters with precision but also impressed the British cast with her mastery of the difficult dialect.

In *Sophie's Choice*, for which Streep won an Oscar, she portrayed the complexity of Sophie, a woman who endured a Nazi death camp. The memory that continually churns in the mind of Sophie is that while she was in the camp, she was forced to choose whether her son or daughter would die in the gas chamber. Although Sophie comes to the United States, where she seems to love and to laugh, Streep always reveals hidden pain in the depths of Sophie's heart. Her ability to portray multidimensional characters is the genius for which Streep has been praised. She always seeks challenges and takes risks, even with roles that might damage her acting career.

Streep is extremely devoted to her family. She took a year off from her career when her second child, Mary, was born. To those who questioned her decision, she responded, "Successful women are people whose life has more of an ebb and flow to it." She said that people who have long periods of activity need occasionally to break away. Life is not one continuous, steady flow of energy. At times, the energy needs rechanneling. Streep commented that she would never let her film career interfere with motherhood, because being with her husband and her family allows her to be her real self.

Streep is fanatical about separating her public figure from her private life. She accepts very few interviews, avoids questions about her private life, and does not permit the press to photograph her children. She does not want her family living with the self-consciousness of continually being under public scrutiny. She feels a great responsibility to perform her art to the best of her abilities, but she believes that film stars do not owe their public any part of the few private moments they have with family and friends. Streep draws a sharp line between her personal life and her public role.

Film critics and the public have praised her abilities in acting, in bringing out the intricate, sensitive, multidimensional aspects of her characters. She does not let her excellence in her art make her egocentric. Instead, she is a superstar who avoids the excesses of celebrity lifestyles. She chooses to be unpretentious, to be like other contemporary women who strive to combine career and family life. Streep is devoted to her marriage, which integrates the traditional values of love and commitment with modern ideas of male-female equality.

Meryl Streep dislikes being called a superstar. Instead, she reads and then forgets the comments of critics. She comes to each role with fresh dedication, untainted by praise or criticism of previous works. She also does not believe in the awarding of Emmys and Oscars, because one performance cannot be compared to another. Just as critics could not compare two shades of blue in a painting, performances should not be compared. She does not condone competing with other artists.

Summary

Meryl Streep's activism in nuclear disarmament earned for her the Helen Caldicott

Leadership Award from the Women's Action for Nuclear Disarmament in 1984. She has also gained for women more artistic freedom and more participation in writing, producing, and other creative aspects of film production. She has encouraged the presence of multidimensional female characters in films to replace the stereotypical weak roles of the past.

In addition, Streep has maintained a down-to-earth image rather than a superstar profile. This image has allowed women from all walks of life to identify with her. She has presented a success story of a woman who has combined career and family life. She has not indulged in the material excesses that might accompany her income, but has insisted on living a simple, ordinary life so that her family remains well adjusted.

Perhaps her philosophy can best be summed up by the speech she delivered at Vassar's 1983 graduation ceremony. She said that Vassar had taught her always to investigate her motives for taking particular actions, to continually evaluate her process for making choices, and to struggle to maintain her integrity. She spoke about finding an excellence for which she could strive even though the process might be a rigorous exercise of mind and heart. Individuals cannot sit back and accept mediocrity from themselves or from political leaders; they must become involved in the process as citizens of the earth.

Bibliography

Maychick, Diana. *Meryl Streep: The Reluctant Superstar*. New York: St. Martin's Press, 1984. An easy-to-read biography that covers Streep's childhood, high school and college years, early dramatic roles, her relationships with John Cazale and Donald Gummer, and her films until 1984. The book does not include a bibliography or chapter notes.

Pfaff, Eugene E., Jr., and Mark Emerson. *Meryl Streep: A Critical Biography*. Jefferson, N.C.: McFarland, 1987. An excellent study of Meryl Streep's early life, theater performances, television productions, and motion pictures. Included are many quotations by Streep and fine chapter notes that provide excellent sources for further study. Also includes a thorough filmography of Streep's work.

Skow, John. "What Makes Meryl Magic?" *Time* 118 (September 7, 1981): 38-41. An article that contains many quotations by Streep regarding her early interest in drama, her views about the Academy Awards, and her occasional self-doubts. This piece also includes comments by fellow students and college instructors regarding Streep's early performances.

Smurthwaite, Nick. *The Meryl Streep Story*. New York: Beaufort Books, 1984. This biography reviews Streep's early life along with her theatrical, television, and film accomplishments. Also includes a filmography of Streep's work and a fine collection of photographs of Streep.

Linda J. Meyers

BARBRA STREISAND

Born: April 24, 1942; New York, New York

Areas of Achievement: Music, film, and theater and drama

Contribution: As a critically acclaimed and commercially successful actress, singer, director, and producer, Streisand has paved the way for women in industries traditionally controlled by men.

Early Life

Barbara Joan Streisand was born in Brooklyn, New York, on April 24, 1942, the second child of Emanuel Streisand, a high school English teacher, and Diana Streisand. Her father died when she was fifteen months old. Streisand links both her artistic sensitivity and her far-reaching aspirations to an attempt to fill in the gap that came from growing up with a missing parent. Her father's death also created economic difficulties for the family. Streisand's mother initially used her brother's army allotment checks to support her baby daughter and nine-year-old son, Sheldon, and then found work as a bookkeeper. Streisand describes her family as "poor, but not poor poor. We just never had anything." When she was seven, her mother was married to Louis Kind, a real-estate dealer, which increased Streisand's feelings of isolation and rejection. In 1951, Roslyn, Streisand's half-sister, was born.

As a girl, Streisand was ostracized by other children as a result of her unconventional looks and extreme shyness. She found solace in films, and often re-created the roles she had seen in solitary games at her home. Instead of trying to fit in with her peers at school, Streisand accentuated her uniqueness by wearing peculiar outfits found at thrift shops. She avoided school activities and used her private time to prepare for her acting career: experimenting with makeup to create different characters, singing and rehearsing roles on the roof of her apartment building, and taking pictures of herself dressed up as various characters in the photo machines at the penny arcades.

At fifteen, she attended an acting camp in upstate New York, where she made her acting debut. Two years later, after being graduated with excellent grades from Erasmus Hall High School in Brooklyn, she moved to Manhattan, where she studied acting while supporting herself with a series of odd jobs. Despite a total lack of success in finding acting work, she resisted changing her unique looks and style, although she did alter the spelling of her name to the more distinctive "Barbra."

Although her mother tried to dampen her theatrical aspirations, Streisand has come to see the discouragement as beneficial to her career: "[B]y her not understanding me, she's responsible for my success. I had to prove to my mother that you don't have to be so beautiful to be a movie star . . . or conventionally beautiful. . . . Now I can look at her with enormous gratitude and I can feel love."

Life's Work

Discouraged after two years without acting success, Barbra Streisand decided to try using her singing voice to find work. She entered a talent contest at a Manhattan piano bar and won first prize: fifty dollars and a week's singing engagement. Her extraordinary voice, coupled with her flamboyant thrift shop costumes, created a sensation on the New York nightclub circuit. The Bon Soir, a Greenwich Village nightclub, signed her for a two-week singing engagement, which was extended to eleven weeks because of her popularity. Streisand remembers struggling with her singing success: "I thought, I'm an actress and what am I doing here singing? Until I realized each song is another play, another character."

After her smash engagement at the Bon Soir, she was cast in an Off-Broadway revue, *Another Evening with Harry Stoones*. The avant-garde musical opened and closed on October 1, 1961, a failure attributable to initial bad reviews and a format that was ahead of its time. Despite the musical's failure, many reviewers singled out Streisand's performance for praise.

Hired next to sing at one of New York's premier nightspots, The Blue Angel, Streisand was seen by director Arthur Laurents, who asked her to audition for a new Broadway musical that was being produced by David Merrick. Her audition made an impression not only on Merrick and the musical director but also on the male lead, Elliot Gould, who eventually became her husband. On March 22, 1962, at the age of twenty, Streisand made her Broadway debut as the lovelorn secretary Miss Marmelstein in *I Can Get It for You Wholesale*. Her bittersweet performance won her the New York Drama Critic's Award for best supporting actress in a musical and a Tony Award nomination.

After the show's nine-month run, Streisand embarked on a triumphant tour of the nation's leading nightclubs, receiving up to seven thousand dollars per night. She appeared on television variety shows hosted by Judy Garland, Dinah Shore, Bob Hope, and Ed Sullivan and was even invited to sing for President John F. Kennedy. After signing a record contract in 1963 with Columbia Records, she released a series of top-selling albums, including *The Barbra Streisand Album* (1963), for which she won two Grammy Awards. In December of 1963, *Cue Magazine* named her Entertainer of the Year.

Streisand's meteoric rise to stardom was crowned when she landed the starring role of Fanny Brice in the musical *Funny Girl*. The show opened at the Winter Garden Theatre on March 26, 1964, to rave reviews. Walter Kerr, of the New York *Herald Tribune* proclaimed: "Everybody knew Barbra Streisand would be a star and so she is." Streisand was nominated for the Tony Award for Best Actress, and the show became one of the most successful American musicals ever.

Meanwhile, Streisand had become the most popular singer of ballads since Judy Garland. In one week in 1964, five Streisand albums were on *Billboard* magazine's Top 100 albums charts, including *People* (1964), which reached number one on the charts, and *My Name Is Barbra*, which was on the charts for 101 weeks. She won the Grammy Award for Best Female Vocalist in both 1964 (for *My Name Is Barbra*) and 1965 (for *People*).

Expanding into television, Streisand signed an unprecedented $5 million contract with CBS to appear in a series of ten specials over a ten-year period. Rather than using the typical star-studded variety show format, Streisand daringly chose to start with a one-woman spectacular. "My Name Is Barbra" aired at 10:00 P.M. on April 28, 1965, to tremendous popular and critical acclaim. *Variety* exclaimed, "What counts on television is how the performer projects beyond the glass of the small home screen, and Miss Streisand burst through as though it were no more a barrier than the footlights of a Broadway stage. . . . She is destined to hit it big in all media." The show won five Emmy awards, including Outstanding Program and Outstanding Individual Achievement in Entertainment. Its acclaim allowed Streisand to take risks in her four subsequent specials, some of which were more successful than others.

When her eighteen-month Broadway contract ran out, she went to London for a sold-out fourteen-week limited engagement of *Funny Girl* in the West End. Soon after the opening, she and her husband Elliot Gould announced that they were expecting a baby. Jason Emanuel was born on December 29, 1966, when Streisand was twenty-four years old.

Streisand's fear of live performance and her boredom with the repetitiveness of theater pointed her career toward Hollywood. In 1968, she fulfilled her dream of becoming a movie star when she reprised her role of Fanny Brice in William Wyler's film of *Funny Girl*, for which she won an Oscar, tying with Katharine Hepburn for Best Actress of the Year. In 1969, she and Gould were divorced. During the same year, she was awarded a special Tony Award for "Star of the Decade." Her next film, *Hello Dolly* (1969), met with less success, and Streisand has called it "the worst mistake [she] ever made." Relations between Streisand and her fellow actors and director were stormy. On the set, Streisand was strident about her ideas, which contributed to her growing reputation as a controlling, temperamental actress. The overall reviews were mixed and the film lost money, but Streisand herself received relatively favorable press.

There was little conflict during the filming of her next picture, *On a Clear Day You Can See Forever* (1970), probably because of greater confidence on Streisand's part as well as increased tolerance for her perfectionism on the set. She succeeded in becoming one of the few female superstars whose connection with a project virtually guaranteed commercial success. Among the numerous films in which she has acted are *What's Up, Doc?* (1972), a screwball comedy with Ryan O'Neal; *The Way We Were* (1973), a sentimental love story with Robert Redford; *Up the Sandbox* (1972), a political film about a woman's dissatisfaction with being a housewife and mother, which was the first film developed by Streisand's own production company; *Funny Lady* (1975), a sequel to *Funny Girl*; and *A Star Is Born* (1976), a musical remake of the love story exploring the conflicts arising when a wife becomes more successful than her husband (played by Kris Kristofferson). Streisand became the first female composer to win an Oscar, for her song "Evergreen" from *A Star Is Born*.

In 1983, with *Yentl*, Streisand became the first woman to direct, produce, write, and star in a Hollywood film. The film recounts the story of a scholarly young woman who resists the gender restrictions of Orthodox Judaism by dressing as a boy so that she can study the Talmud. Her next directorial effort, *The Prince of Tides* (1991), in which she starred with Nick Nolte and also coproduced, was nominated for five Academy Awards, including Best Picture. Streisand's absence from the nominations for best director was attributed to sexism by many. Lynda Obst, producer of *The Fisher King* (1993), commented: "When you're celebrating a woman behind the camera, that's a woman in power, and people are still very uncomfortable with that. Streisand's a triple threat, a walking green light; she's a star, director and producer. She can get movies made and there are no other women in Hollywood who can say that."

Streisand herself sees some of the negative reaction to her work as part of a larger societal resistance to women who do not conform to traditional expectations. As she said in a 1992 *Newsweek* interview, "It's as if a man were allowed to have passion and commitment to his work, but a woman is allowed that feeling for a man, but not for her work." Nevertheless, Streisand has continued striving to fulfill her high professional goals. In 1993, she signed a $60 million film and recording contract with Sony. Among her diverse projects are Larry Kramer's *The Normal Heart*, a gay love story set in the early days of the AIDS epidemic; biographical films about photographer Diane Arbus, painter Jackson Pollock, and Lieutenant Colonel Margarethe Cammermeyer, the woman forced to retire from the Washington National Guard because of her sexual preference; and a romantic comedy entitled *The Mirror Has Two Faces*.

Throughout her career, Streisand has used her superstar status to contribute to a variety of liberal causes. Despite her discomfort with live performance, she has given concerts as political fund-raisers for the 1972 democratic presidential nominee George McGovern, for six 1992 female senatorial candidates, and for President Bill Clinton. The Streisand Foundation, her charitable organization, has donated more than $7 million to support projects related to the environment, AIDS, civil rights, and women's issues, including a fund for breast cancer research and education created in 1994.

Summary

Barbra Streisand has demonstrated that determination and talent can break down the barriers that women face in traditionally male-dominated fields. By 1994, she had starred in fifteen films, had recorded fifty albums and was the top-selling female recording artist in the world. She has been honored with every major entertainment award, including an Emmy, two Oscars, and eight Grammys. Success has spurred her to take risks by experimenting within fields and by expanding into new areas of artistic development. Despite receiving negative press for her adamant perfectionism, she has persevered in pursuing her artistic vision. Her desire to have control over her art led her from singing and acting into the traditionally male fields of directing and producing, and she has succeeded in becoming one of the most powerful women in the entertainment industry. Streisand not only has produced projects with strong women's roles but also has contributed to feminist causes with her time and money. She serves as a role model for others who are driven to pursue their dreams despite personal and social obstacles. Her tremendous popularity has shown the entertainment industry that a woman's vision can be commercially successful. As Streisand herself has said, "every woman's victory makes it easier for another woman." As a woman who has had a remarkable number of victories in a remarkable number of areas, Streisand has paved the way for many women in the arts and beyond.

Bibliography

Brady, Frank. *Barbra Streisand: An Illustrated Biography*. New York: Grosset & Dunlap, 1979. The limited written material is greatly strengthened by a wealth of photographs. The numerous film stills, along with photographs of Streisand on stage and on film sets, richly document her performance career. In addition, the images of her at events and with friends provide a few glimpses of the complicated woman behind the public personas.

Considine, Shaun. *Barbra Streisand: The Woman, the Myth, the Music*. New York: Delacorte Press, 1985. This 340-page biography, which includes twenty-four pages of photographs and a detailed index, explores every conceivable aspect of Streisand's life and work. The text is based on extensive research, including more than two hundred interviews with people who have known and worked with Streisand.

Jordan, René. *The Greatest Star: The Barbra Streisand Story*. New York: G. P. Putnam's Sons, 1975. The tone of this uneven biography alternates between worship and catty sensationalism. Nevertheless, the text is representative of one type of reaction to Streisand's story, and it provides insight into Streisand's importance to a wide range of people.

Spada, James. *Barbra, the First Decade: The Films and Career of Barbra Streisand*. Secaucus, N.J.: Citadel Press, 1974. This detailed biography focuses on the period from Streisand's Off-Broadway debut in 1961 through the release of *The Way We Were* in 1973. The four main chapters chronologically document Streisand's accomplishments in the various branches of the entertainment industry, under the headings "Broadway," "Recordings," "Television," and "Movies," providing complete information on every project, including casts and synopses of films, song titles on albums, and excerpts from numerous reviews.

Spada, James, with Christopher Nickens. *Streisand: The Woman and the Legend*. Garden City, N.Y.: Doubleday, 1981. This thorough biography breaks Streisand's life down into four parts: "Starting out 1942-63"; "Elegance 1964-60"; "The Experimental Years 1970-75"; and "Acclaim and Controversy 1975-81." Each well-documented section is complemented by numerous photographs of Streisand in her various incarnations.

Jennifer Burton

ELIZABETH SWADOS

Born: February 5, 1951; Buffalo, New York

Areas of Achievement: Music and theater and drama
Contribution: An innovative composer, Swados has combined world music with
  modern European compositional techniques to create important works at the famed
  La Mama Experimental Theatre in New York and other venues. She has adapted
  works as varied as classical Greek theater and *Alice in Wonderland* to create
  productions, and she has based works on current social themes.

Early Life

Elizabeth Swados was born in Buffalo, New York, in 1951, the second child of
Robert O. Swados and Sylvia Maisel Swados. The Maisel and Swados families were
filled with performers and writers. Although her early years were ones surrounded by
creativity, they were also marked by instability. Depression, dementia, alcoholism,
and even lobotomy occurred in her immediate family.

Elizabeth Swados' mother, a former actress and published poet, and her lawyer
father were the latest in a line that included the former concertmaster of a Russian
symphony, writers, musicians, and actors. Her father had been a frustrated actor
before turning to law school, and he later became influential in the development and
financing of the Studio Arena Theatre in Buffalo. Her beloved older brother Lincoln,
who was eight years her senior, profoundly influenced her life. Considered a genius
while growing up, Lincoln also exhibited erratic behavior, which led to his expulsion
from several schools. He had a charming, eccentric personality and often spoke of the
great writings he would one day produce. He would entertain at family gatherings
with musical comedy songs, stand-up comedy routines, and his collection of original
cartoons.

Elizabeth was an independent, solitary child who lived in an imaginary world
fueled by her brother's "lessons" in manners and behavior. She began her music
studies at age five with the piano and added the guitar at age ten. Soon she began
composing music on both instruments, beginning a lifetime of creativity that would
shield her to some extent from the problems of her family.

When Elizabeth was ten, Lincoln was diagnosed as paranoid schizophrenic during
his freshman year at Syracuse University. This diagnosis explained his violent mood
swings and the disappearances that his parents had attributed to his "artistic temperament." Lincoln began what would be years of hospitalization, medication, and shock
treatments. The prevailing view of mental illness at that time was that it was prevent-
able and shameful. The Swados' embarrassment about the lobotomy of Robert
Swados' mother had created a climate in which Lincoln's illness was rarely mentioned. Elizabeth's adored older brother simply disappeared from her life with no
explanation.

Elizabeth reacted to this continuing trauma by continuing her music studies, taking a special interest in the folk singers of the early 1960's. She began performing as a folk singer at age twelve for parties and bar mitzvahs, and she began to sing in small local clubs while she was still in high school. She also began writing seriously, and she had collected rejection slips from both *The New Yorker* and *Seventeen* by the time she left for Bennington College at age sixteen.

The strain of Lincoln's illness and their own demons began to take its toll on Robert and Sylvia Swados' marriage. Whereas Elizabeth took refuge in drugs and Robert Swados traveled continuously on business, Sylvia Swados was left alone and idle. Her difficult life worsened when Lincoln's debilitating condition culminated in a suicide attempt; he threw himself in front of a subway and severed an arm and a leg.

As her family coped with Lincoln's physical and mental problems, Elizabeth began her freshman year at Bennington College, where she studied both music and creative writing and was exposed for the first time to the Asian music that would influence her early works. She became involved in the sexual experimentation and drug culture of the middle 1960's, and she volunteered in Appalachia as a tutor and drama teacher. Believing that traditional studies had little to offer her, she dropped out of Bennington at age nineteen and began seriously to work on her composition at the avant-garde La Mama Theatre in the East Village of New York.

Sylvia Swados' illness and irrational dependence on her crumbling marriage swiftly led to alcoholism, institutionalism for depression, and eventually to her suicide by overdose when Elizabeth was twenty-three.

Life's Work

The La Mama Theatre was an avant-garde theatre company that experimented with various new forms and combinations of performing arts. Elizabeth Swados met director Andrei Serban there early in her career, which led to a fruitful collaboration. Serban's belief that drama should be viewed as ritual and was intended to evoke powerful emotions in the audience excited Swados. She began to combine the sounds and music of many cultures to create the effect desired by Serban. Together, they produced an adaptation of *Medea* (1972) using a combination of Greek and Latin words chosen for their sound rather than for their meaning. This work garnered a Village Voice Obie award for the twenty-year-old Swados' score.

Following this debut, Swados joined celebrated British director Peter Brooks's International Theatre Group as musical director and composer. She and Brooks toured Africa, where they performed improvisational theatre and gathered songs and folklore in local villages. The following year, they worked with El Téatro Campesino, which had been founded in California by Luis Valdez. In addition, the team collaborated with the National Theatre of the Deaf and a troupe of American Indian actors. These varied performing experiences further expanded Swados' knowledge and her use of alternative sounds and music.

In 1974, Swados created the score for *The Trojan Women*, which was performed along with either *Medea* or *Electra* (1973) and melded Asian and African music, American Indian laments, the ancient languages of the Mayan and Aztec cultures, and

Eastern European and Middle Eastern influences. In 1975, Swados worked on Bertolt Brecht's *The Good Woman of Setzuan.*

Anxious to incorporate what she had learned from Serban and move out on her own, Swados conceived and produced *Nightclub Cantata* (1976), a compilation of modern narrative poems interwoven with a startling variety of music, including ragtime, East Indian ragas, and rock and roll. Its successful run won for Swados not only good reviews but also a second Obie and an Outer Critics Circle award.

Swados' first Tony award-winning production was *Runaways* (1978), which was based on her own childhood and material she had collected by interviewing troubled adolescents. She decided to use nonprofessional teenage actors recruited from local schools. Initially, the play was a huge success, and it soon moved to an uptown Broadway theater. Unfortunately, the show floundered there when its casual, gritty look was deemed amateurish for the sophisticated uptown audiences. Yet *Runaways* received five Tony award nominations, and Swados was the first person ever to receive so many nominations. Her next show, *Dispatches* (1979), combined a reporter's view of Vietnam with a rock and roll score. She later collaborated with cartoonist Garry Trudeau on *Doonesbury* (1982), which was based on Trudeau's syndicated comic strip, and *RapMaster Ronnie* (1984), a play about President Ronald Reagan.

Not content to limit herself to composing and directing, Swados has also written several books, including *The Girl with the Incredible Feeling* (1977), *Leah and Lazar* (1982), *Listening out Loud* (1988), and *The Four of Us* (1991), which discusses her childhood and family. She has taught at Carnegie-Mellon University (1974), Bard College (1976-1977), and Sarah Lawrence (1976-1977).

Elizabeth Swados' relationship with her brother Lincoln worsened after their mother's suicide. Ultimately, he accused her of stealing his plays and wrote letters to newspapers denouncing her work. His life ended in 1987, when he died while being evicted from his condemned storefront room in New York.

Swados has prepared a production based on the Book of Job, featuring circus clowns, and a musical about a homeless man who sues the city of New York. She currently divides her time between Woodstock, New York, and an apartment in Manhattan.

Summary

Elizabeth Swados has turned a disturbing and unhappy childhood into a musical and literary career that transcends confusion and disillusionment. Her greatest contribution has been in the amalgamation of Asian, American Indian, Chicano, African, and Middle Eastern musical styles into a vital and coordinated sound. Her use of bird sounds and unusual percussion instruments has expanded her audiences' views of music. Traditionally, this type of music has been accessible only to audiences of twentieth century "classical" music.

Swados has also become known for presenting her views of societal problems such as the plight of runaway teenagers, the Vietnam War and its repercussions, and homelessness in a dramatic format that can be absorbed and understood by general theater audiences.

Bibliography

Bentsen, Cheryl. "Swados in Wonderland." *New York* 14 (December 29, 1980): 38-42. An in-depth interview with Swados conducted shortly after the debut of her revised version of *Alice*, a musical adaptation of Lewis Carroll's *Alice in Wonderland* directed by Joseph Papp and starring Meryl Streep. Good source of biographical information on her early life and her involvement in experimental theater.

Coven, Brenda. *American Women Dramatists of the Twentieth Century: A Bibliography*. Metuchen, N.J.: Scarecrow Press, 1982. A comprehensive listing of modern women playwrights that includes each artist's plays, their publishing dates, theaters of first productions, and dates of premier performances. The work also includes biographies of the playwrights and complete listings of reviews of their works. An excellent source of research material.

Crichton, Jennifer. "Elizabeth Swados." *Publishers Weekly* 221 (June 11, 1982): 8-9. Published after the debut of Swados' first novel, *Leah and Lazar*, this interview reveals Swados' evolution as a writer. Although she denies that the novel is autobiographical, Swados admits that she incorporates familiar details in her creative work.

O'Donnell, Monica M., ed. *Contemporary Theatre, Film, and Television*. Detroit: Gale Research, 1984. A companion volume to *Who's Who in Theatre*, this volume contains biographical sketches of people in these fields, with an emphasis on performers and directors. A cumulative index of *Who's Who in Theatre* is also included. These sketches, including the one on Swados, are brief and focus only on the creative affiliations, productions, and awards of their subjects. Personal information is limited to birth data, religion, and education. Related careers and union affiliations are also listed.

Swados, Elizabeth. *The Four of Us*. New York: Farrar, Straus & Giroux, 1991. A compelling and personal look at each member of Swados' nuclear family during and after her childhood years. The work is divided into four sections, each focusing on the story of one member and his or her influence on other family members. Swados' schizophrenic brother Lincoln is presented sensitively and compassionately. Her mother, a former actress and poet caught in a suburban lifestyle and an unhappy marriage, is presented in such a way as to make her eventual suicide understandable to the reader. Swados' father's obsession with sports, achievement, and work is tempered with his obvious pride and love for his daughter, and he is portrayed sympathetically. In discussing her own life, Swados is self-critical and revealing as she discusses her bisexuality, her substance abuse, and the psychological needs that her career has filled in her life. She presents her unusual background without self-pity, providing an interesting view of the influences and reactions that have contributed to her creative life.

Laurie Dawson

HENRIETTA SZOLD

Born: December 21, 1860; Baltimore, Maryland
Died: February 13, 1945; Jerusalem, Israel
Areas of Achievement: Social reform and education
Contribution: An author, teacher, Zionist, and health activist, Szold was the first president of Hadassah (the American women Zionists' organization), a founder of Hadassah Hospital in Jerusalem, and the director of Youth Aliyah, an agency devoted to saving Jewish children from Nazi Germany.

Early Life

Henrietta Szold was the oldest of six daughters born to Benjamin Szold and Sophie Schaar Szold after the couple had arrived in the United States from their native Hungary. Henrietta was reared in a home where learning was greatly valued. Her father, a rabbinic and Hebrew scholar, had been appointed rabbi of Congregation Oheb Shalom (Hebrew for "Lover of Peace") in Baltimore, Maryland, in 1859. As a young man, he had lived in two worlds of scholarship, memorizing long passages of Homer and learning the Hebrew Bible in its entirety. His first love, however, was God.

Henrietta's mother, Sophie, was the daughter of a prosperous Hungarian brewer and landowner and had been well tutored at home. Sophie was organized and meticulous, and she possessed a craving for excellence—qualities she passed on to her daughters.

As a young child, Henrietta was captivated by her beloved father and his erudition. She followed him around the house and was often found in his study, leafing through his many books. From her father, Henrietta learned French and Hebrew in addition to the household language of German. Most of all, she absorbed his love of God and God's creations. Whatever was important to Rabbi Szold was transmitted to Henrietta.

Although Henrietta's childhood and adolescent years coincided with the American Civil War (1861-1865) and the beginning of Reconstruction, in her memory she and her family lived out a succession of golden years on Lombard Street. In postwar Baltimore, the idea that newly emancipated slaves should be given an education was mocked, but Rabbi Szold became a leader in the Baltimore Association for the Education and Moral Improvement of the Colored People. Henrietta became her father's aide, secretary, and confidant. In 1877, at age seventeen, she was graduated from Western Female High School, where her academic record was never excelled.

College was not in Henrietta's immediate plans because of finances, discrimination (newly opened The Johns Hopkins University refused women), and self-imposed obligations to her father. Soon after her graduation, she began teaching (French, German, botany, and mathematics) at the Misses Adams' English and French School for Girls, where she stayed until 1893. The same year she was graduated from high school she also began to write for the New York *Jewish Messenger* as its Baltimore correspondent, under the name "Shulamith." Her voice as a social critic began to be heard, and by 1902 the *London Jewish Chronicle* was calling her the leading Jewish essayist in America.

After her upbringing, the crucial event in establishing the future direction of Henrietta Szold's life was the great influx of Russian Jews fleeing czarist-supported pogroms beginning in 1881. A group of Hebraists (Hebrew linguists) and intellectuals from the burgeoning Russian-Jewish ghetto in Baltimore organized the Isaac Baer Levinsohn Literary Society in 1888 and, at Henrietta Szold's urging, inaugurated a night school for immigrants in 1889. Szold taught and supervised the new education program until 1893, when she resigned from all of her teaching posts to become the executive secretary of the publication committee of the Jewish Publication Society in Philadelphia.

During this period of contact with Russian immigrants, Szold increasingly reflected on the terrible effects of anti-Semitism and became converted to the aims of Zionism. Before leaving for Philadelphia, she became a member of *Hebras Zion* (the Zionist Association of Baltimore), one of the earliest Zionist organizations in the United States.

Life's Work

A month before the publication of Theodore Herzl's Zionist classic *The Jewish State: An Attempt at a Modern Solution of the Jewish Question* (1896), Henrietta Szold composed an essay entitled "A Century of Jewish Thought." Delivered to the Council of Jewish Women in Baltimore, it was Szold's first public advocacy of Zionism, a cause to which she would devote the rest of her life. To Szold, Zionism was the vehicle by which the problems of Jews living in a hostile environment could be solved. In 1897, she joined the Federation of American Zionists, contributing speeches and articles to keep alive the hope of establishing a safe refuge for world Jewry.

Between 1893 and 1916, as she promoted Zionist causes, Szold simultaneously continued her work at the Jewish Publication Society. Beginning in 1895, she helped edit the *American Jewish Year Book* with Cyrus Adler, and from 1904 to 1908 she served as its sole editor. Between 1901 and 1906, she contributed articles to and collaborated on the *Jewish Encyclopedia*. During her twenty-three-year tenure at the society, she translated a dozen books, including Moritz Lazarus' two-volume work *Ethics of Judaism* (1900-1901) and Louis Ginsburg's *The Legends of the Jews* (1909).

In 1902, Henrietta Szold's father died, so she and her mother moved to New York, where Henrietta devoted some of her spare time to the study of Hebrew and the Talmud at the Jewish Theological Seminary, in addition to her Zionist pursuits. In 1907, Szold became an active member and leader of the Harlem study circle of the Daughters of Zion, one of a number of Zionist women's movements that began at the turn of the century. In 1909, after a painful, unrequited relationship with Professor Louis Ginsburg of the Seminary, Henrietta took a leave of absence from her work and made her first trip to the Holy Land—a trip that would change her life and thousands of others. She saw at first hand not only the beauty and desirability of the land but also the misery and disease among the settlers.

After her return to the United States in 1910, Szold began promoting the idea of forming an organization for the promotion of Jewish ideals, institutions, and enterprises in Palestine. On February 24, 1912, thirty-eight women constituted themselves as the Hadassah Chapter of the National Daughters of Zion; more chapters followed gradually in other cities. The name was changed to Hadassah in 1914 at the first convention of the young organization, and Henrietta Szold was elected its first president.

That same year, Szold was appointed by Supreme Court Justice Louis D. Brandeis to head the American Zionist Medical Unit for Palestine. Her party of forty-four doctors, nurses, and administrative personnel left for Palestine in 1918, along with supplies for a fifty-bed hospital. Funding for the first year was provided by Hadassah and other Zionist organizations in the amount of $250,000. In June of 1918, American Zionist groups were incorporated into the Zionist Organization of America; Henrietta Szold was placed in charge of educational and propaganda work.

At the end of 1919, Henrietta Szold learned that she was to be sent to Palestine as a representative of the American Zionist Organization attached to the medical unit. Her trip, beginning in February of 1920, marked the beginning of the most significant phase of her life, much of which was spent working in Palestine. She soon became the director of the medical unit; she also ran the newly established Nurses' Training School and directed health work in Jewish schools.

By the end of 1922, the medical unit was experiencing extreme financial difficulty, and it would have closed its doors had it not been for a gift from philanthropist Nathan Straus. Subsequently, the medical unit was enlarged and transformed into the Hadassah Medical Organization, with funding supplied by Hadassah. Twelve years later, in 1934, as a direct result of Henrietta Szold's bold and persevering leadership, the cornerstone was laid for the new Rothschild-Hadassah-University Hospital on Mount Scopus in Jerusalem—fittingly, by Szold herself.

In 1923, Henrietta Szold returned to the United States to visit an ailing sister. She again took up the presidency of a steadily growing Hadassah organization. In 1926, she resigned and was appointed honorary president. The following year, she was elected a member of the three-person executive committee of the World Zionist Organization and returned to Palestine as minister of health and education. In 1930, she was elected to the National Council of Jews in Palestine.

In 1933, when Henrietta Szold had decided to retire and return to the United States, Nazi rule caused the acceleration of German emigration. Szold was asked to help organize and direct a new agency called Youth Aliyah (*aliyah* is Hebrew for "immigration"), which would send German refugee children to Palestine. She threw herself into the work of making less tragic the plight of young people who had been uprooted from their homes and separated from their families. The first group of children arrived in 1934 to be greeted by Szold herself. In five years, 6,200 refugee children had moved to the Holy Land under her supervision; by 1948, 30,000 children had come under the care of the program.

In 1941, Szold was entrusted by the National Council of Jews in Palestine with the creation of the Fund for Child and Youth Care, designed to help children living in the country. In 1943 Szold supervised, with the help of her close associate Hans Beyth, the arrival of Youth Aliyah's best-known group of immigrants. These were Jewish children from all parts of Poland who had wandered war-torn Eastern Europe for three and a half years.

By 1944, Henrietta Szold was in poor enough health that she could not travel to the United States to accept an honorary Doctor of Humanities degree from Boston University. In August, she contracted pneumonia, and she died the following February in the very hospital she had been instrumental in creating.

Summary

On her eightieth birthday, Henrietta Szold addressed the schoolchildren of Palestine and encouraged them to accomplish noble acts, to think great thoughts, and to live wisely and energetically. She was the epitome of her own advice—the embodiment of selfless and dedicated creativity. Not only had she been a pioneer in establishing world-renowned humanitarian organizations, bringing a new level of health care to the Middle East—available to Jew and Arab alike—and helping to build a world-class hospital, but also she was responsible for rescuing, through Youth Aliyah, literally tens of thousands of young people from death.

Henrietta Szold, who had always wanted many children but had never married, had in effect become the mother of the *yishuv* (Hebrew for the Jewish settlement in the Holy Land). As a token of the high esteem in which Szold was held for her efforts, German-Jewish immigrants in Palestine founded a settlement in her honor—Kfar Szold.

Before her death, Henrietta Szold was cited by the Women's Centennial Congress (1940) as one of the one hundred outstanding women of the past century. Since that time, the magnitude of her vision and accomplishments has taken on even greater significance. At the end of her life, she focused her forward-looking concerns on Arab-Jewish relations. She joined Ihud, a movement devoted to achieving mutual understanding between Arabs and Jews. The influence of her life and work on behalf of Zionist and humanitarian causes continues to be felt worldwide.

Bibliography
Dash, Joan. *Summoned to Jerusalem: The Life of Henrietta Szold*. New York: Harper & Row, 1979. The detailed information in this biography is culled from an extensive list of archival sources. The work presents a substantial number of references for more specialized research. One of the best of many biographies, it provides a fairly complete picture of Szold's varied activities in a scholarly but readable style, giving some information that cannot be found elsewhere.
Decter, Midge. "The Legacy of Henrietta Szold." *Commentary* 30, no. 6 (December, 1960): 480-488. A succinct, factual, introductory biographical sketch that puts the most significant events of Szold's life in a chronological framework. It pays particular attention to her Zionist connections.
Fineman, Irving. *Woman of Valor: The Life of Henrietta Szold, 1860-1945*. New York:

Simon & Schuster, 1961. For many years the standard biography of Szold, this work presents many personal details about her activities taken from her own writings (including letters) and speeches. Its weakness for research is its lack of source notes or specific dates for certain events.

Krantz, Hazel. *Daughter of My People: Henrietta Szold and Hadassah.* New York: E. P. Dutton, 1987. This short book focuses on Szold's activities with Hadassah and Youth Aliyah after her 1909 trip to the Holy Land. Containing no notes, it uses many quotations and anecdotes to weave a biographical sketch in the popular style.

Levin, Alexandra L. *The Szolds of Lombard Street: A Baltimore Family, 1859-1909.* Philadelphia: Jewish Publication Society, 1960. Published by the scholarly society for which Szold worked, this volume presents a detailed portrait of Henrietta's family up to the time of her life-changing trip to Palestine. It places her in the context of the familial and social forces that helped shape her thinking.

Andrew C. Skinner

MARION TALBOT

Born: July 31, 1858; Thun, Switzerland
Died: October 20, 1948; Chicago, Illinois
Areas of Achievement: Education, sociology, and women's rights
Contribution: A leading authority on women's higher education, an author, the first
  dean of women in a coeducational institution, a cofounder of the American Asso-
  ciation of University Women, and a charter faculty member at the University of
  Chicago, Talbot was also a significant leader of women in sociology and home
  economics.

Early Life

Marion Talbot was born on July 31, 1858, while her American parents were visiting
Thun, Switzerland. Her father, Israel Tisdale Talbot, practiced homeopathic medicine
and served as the first dean of the medical school of Boston University. Her mother,
Emily Fairbanks Talbot, was a leader in the struggle for women's higher education
and women's work in the social sciences. She was active in establishing the Girls'
Latin School in Boston, an endeavor she began partly to secure a forum for her
daughter's training. The Talbots of Boston were located at the center of the city's
intellectual and cultural life. Marion, the eldest of their six children, was always
encouraged by her parents in her advocacy of women's rights in higher education.

After Marion's education at the Girls' Latin School, she was admitted conditionally
to Boston University, where she earned a B.A. degree in 1880. After several years of
social life and travel, she wanted more than the traditional life that was open to women
at that time. Probably at the urging of a family acquaintance and one of the founders
of human ecology, Ellen H. Richards, Marion was encouraged to study "domestic
science." After several years of sporadic study, she completed a B.S. degree from the
Massachusetts Institute of Technology in 1888.

In 1881-1882, Marion, her mother, Richards, and Alice Freeman Palmer, an early
president of Wellesley College, cofounded the Association of Collegiate Alumnae
(later renamed the American Association of University Women, AAUW). This organization spearheaded opportunities for educated women in the academy and in
society. Marion was its first secretary and was its president from 1895 to 1897.

In 1890, Talbot was appointed an instructor in domestic science at Wellesley
College (when Palmer was president).

Life's Work

In March, 1892, Alice Freeman Palmer met with W. R. Harper, president of the
University of Chicago, who offered her the position of dean of the women's colleges.
Palmer wanted to keep her presidency at Wellesley and work part-time at Chicago, so
she recommended Marion Talbot as her full-time assistant. With considerable anticipation mixed with fear, Talbot joined the University of Chicago faculty in 1892 as an
assistant professor in the Department of Sociology and Anthropology. Shortly there-

after, she became the first full-time women's dean in a coeducational institution.

Talbot was included within the structure, teaching, and practice of sociology at the University of Chicago as the head of "women's work" throughout the institution. In 1895, she became an associate editor of *The American Journal of Sociology*, a position she held until her retirement from Chicago in 1925. Talbot critiqued "women's work" in sociology and provided a "woman's perspective" for the most important journal in this discipline.

Talbot wrote in two major areas: the sociology of the home and the sociology of education. Talbot's study of the home was tied to its material reality, from its basic sanitary functioning to its aesthetic creation as an environment in which one lived. Thus, Talbot's pioneering work in women's education was complemented by her scholarly study of the application of science to the home.

Her study of the home was sparked by her association with Ellen H. Richards. Together, they edited *Home Sanitation: A Manual for Housekeepers* (1887) and wrote *Food as a Factor in Student Life* (1884), books that are now difficult to find and are outdated as sources of factual information. They were, however, crucial beginning steps in the study of nutrition and home economics. *The Modern Household* (1912), written with Talbot's former student Sophonisba Breckinridge, is an introductory text intended to help housewives and college students adapt to modern social changes affecting the home. The book covers a variety of topics, ranging from the mundane care of the house to ethics in consumerism and the community.

Anyone interested in the turbulent, innovative founding days of the University of Chicago will find Talbot's autobiography, *More than Lore* (1936), a delight to read. Talbot is forthright in her statements about discrimination against women professionals at the university. Unfortunately, this book is very hard to find and is out of print, so a brief summary is presented here.

Talbot's autobiography documents the segregation of the sexes at Chicago in 1902. Some professors wanted to "protect" young men against "dangerous" women. Her battle against this policy reflects her institutional struggle for coeducation and her bittersweet humor. Fortunately, the segregationist stance was never very successful, and it soon faded away.

Talbot's most important chapter on sexism at Chicago is called "The Weaker Sex." In it, she recounts women's long struggle to enter institutions of higher learning. Chicago was one of the few institutions that accepted women as graduate students in 1892, but few well-qualified women were hired over the next twenty-five years.

Although she was a powerful administrator, her intellectual leadership was severely limited at the University of Chicago. Talbot's continuing battles to make a department with its own funding, staff, journal, fellowships, library, and intellectual legitimacy is outlined in her personal papers at that institution, but this fascinating story has yet to be published.

Talbot was a charter member of the American Sociological Association and an early participant in the Lake Placid Conferences in Home Economics. She was also active in the American Historical Association, the American Public Health Association, the

Labor Legislation Association, and the National Federation of Women's Clubs. In 1904, Talbot was awarded an honorary doctor of law degree by Cornell College in Iowa.

Talbot lived a woman-centered existence. She was surrounded in her youth by notable women such as Emily Talbot, Julia Ward Howe, and Louisa May Alcott. She then worked with Richards, Palmer, and the social settlement leader Jane Addams. She trained and worked for many decades with Sophonisba Breckinridge, with whom she shared her life. For years, they lived in women's dormitories as leaders, friends, and bulwarks against a world hostile to educated women. Talbot built institutional structures for women and carved a place for them in the academy. She helped dozens and dozens of female professionals find their first jobs.

She continued her work as dean of women at Chicago until her retirement in 1925. In 1927, she served as acting president of Constantinople Women's College in Turkey for a year, and she did so again in 1931 and 1932. In 1948, Talbot's health and fortunes changed rapidly. Breckinridge died in July, 1948, and her death was a severe blow to Talbot. Within four months, Talbot also died, at the end of a very productive life.

Summary

Marion Talbot's administrative innovations at the University of Chicago and her analyses of women's work in that institution are major resources for scholars studying the history of women's higher education, especially in sociology. Talbot's policies on women's roles in universities laid the groundwork for similar programs throughout the country. Although she was not a radical, she consistently made decisions favoring equality between the sexes.

Concrete precedents favoring women are detailed in the administrative reports that Talbot made annually at the University of Chicago. In one report, for example, Talbot cited a number of statistics relating to women's low faculty status and the superior achievements of women students compared to those of men at Chicago. More women than men were also graduated Phi Beta Kappa. Female doctors (approximately 15 of graduates) were also very competitive in honorary awards and achievements. Women at Chicago built a sense of camaraderie through their participation in two organizations: The Club of Women Fellows for graduate women and The Women's Union for undergraduate women. These groups helped young women build social and professional networks when many people believed that women should not receive college degrees.

Despite Talbot's fights for women's equality, she believed that women should be "ladies," polite and well-bred, and that a higher education prepared women to be better wives and mothers. In this way, she supported the traditional roles of women. Her writings are interspersed, however, with an appreciation of women's contributions to society and the difficulty of managing a home, and these analyses sound similar to modern writings on housewives and housework. Most clearly, her critiques of discrimination against women in academia are still relevant and accurate.

Talbot was an immensely powerful woman who saw many of her dreams fulfilled during her lifetime. She helped establish the AAUW, with more than a hundred thousand members at the time of her death; saw women enter universities and college campuses across the country, and lived to see deans of women working on more than a thousand campuses. She was one of the recognized founders of home economics and had a pivotal role in the lives of early women in sociology.

Bibliography

Deegan, Mary Jo. "Marion Talbot, 1858-1947." In *Women in Sociology: A Bio-bibliographical Sourcebook*. Westport, Conn.: Greenwood Press, 1991. This entry is a more scholarly version than the one included here. A longer bibliography on Talbot and scholarship on her is included.

Fish, Virginia K. "'More Than Lore': Marion Talbot and Her Role in the Founding Years of the University of Chicago." *International Journal of Women's Studies* 8, no. 3 (May/June, 1985): 228-249. This is an excellent analysis of Talbot's autobiography and her central role at the University of Chicago. Because *More than Lore* is difficult to find in libraries today, this article allows more people to learn about the book.

Fitzpatrick, Ellen. *Endless Crusade: Women Social Scientists and Progressive Reform*. New York: Oxford University Press, 1990. Talbot and some of the women she trained are discussed here. The Progressive Era and these women's impact on it are examined.

Palmer, George Herbert. *The Life of Alice Freeman Palmer*. Boston: Houghton Mifflin, 1908. George Palmer was the husband of Alice Freeman Palmer, and his biography is particularly informative regarding Talbot's era and one of her closest friends. The biography refers to Talbot in several places.

Rosenberg, Rosalind. *Beyond Separate Spheres: Intellectual Roots of Modern Feminism*. New Haven, Conn.: Yale University Press, 1982. This is a fine account of Talbot's early life and family and of her work in social science. Other women in the social sciences from Talbot's era are also discussed.

Talbot, Marion. *The Education of Women*. Chicago: University of Chicago Press, 1910. This book describes the educational opportunities available to women in the United States in 1910. Talbot's defense of social hygiene, exercise, and training for rational thinking were "daring" ideas in her day.

_____ . *More than Lore: Reminiscences of Marion Talbot, Dean of Women, the University of Chicago, 1892-1925*. Chicago: University of Chicago Press, 1936. Although this book is hard to find, it is one of the most important books on women's entry into higher education and life at the University of Chicago from 1892 to 1925.

Talbot, Marion, and Lois Kimball M. Rosenberry. *The History of the American Association of University Women, 1881-1931*. Boston: Houghton Mifflin, 1931. This is a detailed account of the committees, work, and goals of the association that Talbot cofounded. It is a gold mine of information on the work and networks of early women professionals.

Wright, Gwendolyn. *Moralism and the Model Home: Domestic Architecture and*

Cultural Conflict in Chicago, 1873-1913. Chicago: University of Chicago Press, 1980. This excellent analysis of the ideal home and its physical construction is an important resource for understanding Talbot's environment and role in the exciting world of Chicago architecture. Wright also explains Talbot's work with Ellen Richards and some professors at the University of Chicago.

Mary Jo Deegan

MARIA TALLCHIEF

Born: January 24, 1925; Fairfax, Oklahoma

Area of Achievement: Dance
Contribution: Prima ballerina of the New York City Ballet for fifteen years, Tallchief symbolized American ballet for an entire generation of theater and television audiences.

Early Life

Elizabeth Marie (Betty Marie) Tall Chief was born on January 24, 1925, in Fairfax, Oklahoma, a small community on the Osage Indian Reservation. Oil discovered on the reservation—and the tribal leaders' insistence on holding their mineral rights in common—had made the Osage the wealthiest tribe in the United States. Betty Marie's father, Alexander Tall Chief, a full-blooded Osage, was a well-to-do real estate executive whose grandfather, Chief Peter Big Heart, had negotiated the tribe's land agreements with the federal government. Her mother, Ruth Porter Tall Chief, came from Irish, Scottish, and Dutch ancestry. Her paternal grandmother, Eliza Big Heart Tall Chief, often took young Betty Marie to secret tribal dance ceremonies (the government had outlawed these "pagan" rituals at the turn of the century), but it was Ruth Tall Chief's culture and ambitions that ultimately prevailed. Betty Marie began taking piano and ballet lessons at age three; by the time she started school, she was performing before nearly every civic organization in Osage County.

Concerned about the lack of educational and artistic opportunities on the reservation, Ruth Tall Chief convinced her easygoing husband to move the family to Beverly Hills, California, in 1933. There, Betty Marie began a rigorous program of piano lessons and ballet classes, the latter taught by Ernest Belcher (whose talented daughter Marge would later team up with dancer/choreographer Gower Champion). Ruth Tall Chief was determined to groom her daughter for a career as a concert pianist, but it was dance that captivated both Betty Marie and her younger sister Marjorie. In 1938, Betty Marie and Marjorie began intensive training with David Lichine, Lichine's prima ballerina wife Tatiana Riabouchinska, and Bronislava Nijinska. Sister of the legendary dancer Vaslav Nijinsky, Nijinska was one of the foremost ballet teachers and choreographers in the United States. Both Tall Chief sisters impressed Nijinska, who cast them in her ballet *Chopin Concerto*, which was performed at the Hollywood Bowl in 1940.

Life's Work

After her graduation from Beverly Hills High School in 1942, Betty Marie Tall Chief made her professional debut with the New York-based Ballet Russe de Monte Carlo, one of the two leading ballet companies in the country at that time. (The other, Ballet Theatre, hired Marjorie Tall Chief two years later.) Early in her five-year association with Ballet Russe, Betty Marie "Europeanized" her name to Maria

Tallchief. Advancing rapidly from the corps de ballet to solo parts, she attracted favorable critical notice in a variety of classical productions, including Bronisława Nijinska's *Chopin Concerto* in 1943 and, in 1944, Michel Fokine's *Schéhérazade* and George Balanchine's *Bourgeois Gentilhomme* and *Danse Concertante*. By 1946, Tallchief's repertoire also included principal roles in Leonid Massine's *Gaîté Parisienne* and two more Balanchine ballets, *Baiser de la Fée* and *Ballet Imperial*. Critics and audiences alike now recognized her as a rising star in the ballet theater.

Balanchine's brief stint as ballet master with the Ballet Russe (1944-1946) marked a turning point in Tallchief's career. Trained in the Russian Imperial School of Ballet, Balanchine was one of the most brilliant choreographers and teachers of the twentieth century. His School of American Ballet, founded in 1936, trained many of the best performing artists on the American stage. He quickly recognized the young dancer's potential, made Tallchief his protégée, and created roles designed to exploit her strength, agility, and great technical proficiency. On August 16, 1946, Tallchief was married to the forty-two-year-old Balanchine. The following spring, she made her European debut with the Paris Opera, where her husband was guest choreographer. When she returned to the United States, Tallchief joined Balanchine's new company, the Ballet Society, which in 1948 became the New York City Ballet (NYCB).

From 1947 to 1965, Tallchief was the prima ballerina of the NYCB and created roles in most of Balanchine's repertoire. Two of these roles were destined to become classics of the ballet theater. In 1949, composer Igor Stravinsky revised his score especially for Balanchine's new version of *The Firebird*, with Tallchief in the title role. Her electrifying performance as the mythical bird-woman dazzled critics and audiences alike; for the rest of her career, she would be more closely identified with this role than with any other. In 1954, Balanchine choreographed the NYCB's most popular and financially successful production, a full-length version of Peter Ilich Tchaikovsky's *The Nutcracker*, with Tallchief as the Sugar Plum Fairy, which is regarded as the most difficult role in a classical dancer's repertoire. Tallchief's Sugar Plum Fairy earned for her the title of "America's prima ballerina" and helped to establish *The Nutcracker* as an annual Christmas season favorite in cities all over the country.

During the 1950's and early 1960's, Tallchief reached the pinnacle of her success as a classical dancer. She toured Europe and Asia with the NYCB, accepted guest engagements with other ballet companies, and gave numerous television performances on programs such as *Omnibus*, *Hallmark Hall of Fame*, and *The Ed Sullivan Show*. She played the famous Russian ballerina Anna Pavlova in a 1953 film, *Million Dollar Mermaid*, dancing the Dying Swan role from Balanchine's version of *Swan Lake*. Among the many honors awarded her, none pleased her more than those conferred by her home state: June 29, 1953, was declared Maria Tallchief Day by the Oklahoma State Senate, while the Osage Nation staged a special celebration during which she was made a princess of the tribe and given the name *Wa-xthe-Thonba*, Woman of Two Standards. A triumphal tour of Russia in 1960 with the young Danish ballet sensation Erik Bruhn cemented her international stardom. In 1961, Tallchief won for a second time (the first came in 1949) the coveted annual Dance Award. She resigned from the NYCB in 1965 and retired from the stage a year later.

Tallchief's marriage to Balanchine (though not her friendship or their professional association) was annulled in 1952, on the grounds that he did not want children. By her own admission, their age difference and his obsession with Tallchief the artist rather than the woman doomed their marital relationship. A brief second marriage to airline pilot Elmourza Natirboff ended in divorce in 1954 when Natirboff insisted that she give up her career. In June, 1956, Tallchief was married to Henry D. Paschen, a Chicago construction company executive who accepted her career ambitions. She gave birth to their only child, Elise Maria, in 1959. Retirement in 1966 allowed Tallchief to settle permanently in Chicago with her husband and daughter.

During the 1970's and 1980's, Tallchief brought to the Chicago artistic world the same energy and determination that had characterized her own dancing. In 1974, she formed the Ballet School of the Lyric Opera, where she passed on to younger dancers the Balanchine techniques and traditions that had shaped her own success. The school's original purpose was to provide a corps of dancers for the Chicago Lyric Opera. When financial problems forced the elimination of ballet from the Opera's budget, Tallchief engineered, in 1980, the creation of the Chicago City Ballet (CCB), using $100,000 in seed money from the state of Illinois and a building donated by her husband. Marjorie Tallchief, retired from her own highly successful career in Europe, moved to Chicago to direct her sister's school, while Maria became artistic codirector (with Paul Mejia) of the new ballet company. Following the demise of the CCB in 1988, Tallchief returned to the Lyric Opera to direct its ballet activities. In 1989, she appeared in *Dancing for Mr. B.: Six Balanchine Ballerinas*, a documentary film for PBS.

Despite her assimilation into Euro-American culture, Tallchief remained proud of her American Indian heritage. In 1967, she received the Indian Council of Fire Achievement Award and was named to the Oklahoma Hall of Fame. A longtime member of the Association on American Indian Affairs, she frequently spoke to American Indian groups about Indians and the arts, and participated in university programs to educate students about the first Americans. In 1991, Maria Tallchief became a charter member of the Honorary Committee of the National Campaign of the National Museum of the American Indian, whose members raised funds to assist the Smithsonian Institution in building the new museum on the National Mall in Washington, D.C.

Summary

Maria Tallchief's primary contribution to American culture rests on her role as the first truly American prima ballerina. Four other American Indian ballet dancers enjoyed distinguished careers during Tallchief's era—Rosella Hightower (Choctaw), Yvonne Chouteau (Cherokee), Moscelyn Larkin (Shawnee), and Marjorie Tallchief— but none left her mark on the American ballet theater as did the elder Tallchief sister. Ballet as an art form in the United States was relatively new, and until the late 1940's, it relied heavily on European dancers. Even the Ballet Russe, with whom most of the "Indian ballerinas" began their careers, was a European company in exile, staffed largely with artists trained abroad. Not until the 1950's, when the NYCB came into its own as a major ballet company, did American ballet reach the standards set by the prestigious national ballets of Russia, France, and England. If it is true that George Balanchine and the NYCB created Tallchief's prima ballerina status, it is equally true that she, in turn, contributed significantly to that company's critical and financial success. American-born and American-trained, Tallchief fascinated audiences with her exotic beauty and her unmatched technical brilliance.

Gifted and driven, Tallchief made personal sacrifices in order to pursue her demanding career as a performing artist. Then, at age forty and still in peak form, she left the stage to devote more time to rearing her daughter. Like a number of Balanchine's former protégées, she ultimately went on to teach what she had learned from the master. She modeled her Chicago school after Balanchine's School of American Ballet in New York, and until his death in 1983, her former husband frequently hired dancers trained by Tallchief. A teacher, lobbyist, fund-raiser and publicist for the arts, Maria Tallchief remains a commanding force in the world of ballet.

Bibliography
Gruen, John. *Erik Bruhn: Danseur Noble*. New York: Viking Press, 1979. Somewhat gossipy in tone, this biography of the superb Danish dancer contains useful insights into the artistic partnership (and alleged personal relationship) of Tallchief and Bruhn in the 1960's. It is especially useful in the absence of any Tallchief biography assessing her off-stage persona and later ballet achievements.
_____ . "Tallchief and the Chicago City Ballet." *Dance Magazine* 58 (December, 1984): HC25-HC27. Examines the progress of the CCB as a major American ballet company in the Balanchine tradition, including Tallchief's work with her artistic codirector, Paul Mejia, and NYCB star Suzanne Farrell (Mejia's wife).
Hardy, Camille. "Chicago's Soaring City Ballet." *Dance Magazine* 56 (April, 1982): 70-76. Details the origins of Tallchief's ballet company, focusing on the CCB's premier of Mejia's *Cinderella*.
Kufrin, Joan. *Uncommon Women: Gwendolyn Brooks, Sarah Caldwell, Julie Harris, Mary McCarthy, Alice Neel, Roberta Peters, Maria Tallchief, Marylou Williams, Evgenia Zukerman*. Piscataway, N.J.: New Century, 1981. One of nine performing artists profiled through extensive interviews, Tallchief speaks candidly about her career as a dancer, her professional debt to Balanchine, and her continuing commitment to ballet through teaching and creating the Chicago City Ballet.
Mason, Francis. *I Remember Balanchine: Recollections of the Ballet Master by Those Who Knew Him*. New York: Doubleday, 1991. Tallchief's contribution to this collection reveals her undiminished admiration for Balanchine's genius. She discusses their early association at Ballet Russe, describes the creation of her most famous role, *The Firebird*, and incorporates anecdotes of their life together.

Maynard, Olga. *Bird of Fire: The Story of Maria Tallchief.* New York: Dodd, Mead, 1961. An incomplete and dated biography that lacks objectivity but gives the fullest account available of the dancer's early life and rise to stardom.

Myers, Elisabeth. *Maria Tallchief: America's Prima Ballerina.* New York: Grosset & Dunlap, 1966. A sentimental handling of Tallchief's stage career, based largely on the Maynard biography. Like Maynard's work, it reveals little about Tallchief the woman and nothing about her career after leaving the stage.

Constance B. Rynder

AMY TAN

Born: February 19, 1952; Oakland, California

Area of Achievement: Literature
Contribution: A superb storyteller, Amy Tan provides her readers with a portrait of the Chinese American experience, especially that of emigrant Chinese women and their American daughters.

Early Life

Amy Tan was born in 1952 in Oakland, California. Her father, John, who had been trained as an engineer in Peking, China, later became a Baptist minister in the United States. Her mother, Daisy, was reared in a well-to-do Shanghai family. Not until she was twelve years old did Amy learn that her mother had had another life—and another family—apart from one she knew. Daisy's first marriage produced three daughters. When the Japanese advanced on the city, she joined the thousands of others fleeing Shanghai for Chungking. Along the way, she was forced to abandon her daughters, hoping that whoever found them would reunite them with their parents. The death of her husband, the Communist Revolution, her marriage to second husband John Tan, and their emigration to America separated Daisy from her children, whose whereabouts were unknown to her. In the United States, Daisy and John Tan had three children; Amy was the middle child and the only girl.

Her childhood and adolescence brought Amy much conflict and pain. Growing up in San Francisco and later in suburban Santa Clara, Tan recalls that she often felt that "somehow I'd been born into the wrong family, that I went down the wrong chute and ended up in a Chinese family." She wished that she could undergo plastic surgery to westernize her Asian features. She even spent many nights as a child sleeping with a clothespin on her nose, hoping to awaken with a slim Anglo-Saxon one. During her fifteenth year, Amy lost both her older brother and her father to brain tumors.

Convinced that their Santa Clara home did not possess an auspicious balance of water and wind (*feng shui*), that the house was somehow bad luck, Daisy Tan moved her two remaining children to Switzerland. There, some of Amy's self-hatred and insecurities disappeared. In the United States, Tan notes, she had never felt attractive, had never been asked out on a date, and had never felt accepted. In Europe, however, she felt like a "novelty" because she was one of very few Asians there. Though "people stared," they wanted to know her, boys asked her out, and one almost convinced her to elope.

Amy began her university career at the College Monte Rosa Internationale in Montreux, Switzerland, and then returned to northern California with her family, where she earned her bachelor's degree in English and linguistics at San Jose State University in 1973. She received her master's degree in linguistics from that same university in 1974. It was there that she met Lou DeMattei, a law student, who was to become her husband on April 6, 1974.

Life's Work

Although her parents and her standardized test scores pushed her toward science and medicine, Amy Tan wanted to be a writer. She had won a writing contest at age eight but had set aside her aspirations until her freshman year in college, changing her major from premedicine to English. After she had spent one year in a doctorate program in linguistics at the University of California at Berkeley, a friend's murder evoked in her the grief and anger over the loss of her father and brother that she had long suppressed, emotions that ended her academic pursuits.

Tan worked with disabled children as a language development specialist for the Alameda County Association for the Mentally Retarded before turning to freelance business writing. When a supervisor suggested that she might do better as a project manager because he did not believe that she was a strong writer, she quit her job in protest. She now admits, "I didn't necessarily think I was the greatest writer in the world." Yet she knew she had to write. Around 1985 or 1986, she joined the Squaw Valley Community of Writers, a writing workshop in which she began sharing some of the stories she had begun to write. Several other events also began to shape her creative life. In 1986, busy with her freelance career, Amy received a telephone call: Her mother had just had a heart attack. Tan remarks, "At that moment, I realized I didn't know a lot about her. I made this pledge to myself if she lived, I would get to know her and write a book." Shortly thereafter, following her mother's recovery, Amy and Daisy Tan traveled to China to meet two of Daisy's lost Chinese daughters. At that moment, at age thirty-five, Amy was able to say, "I'm both Chinese and American. . . . Suddenly some piece fit in the right place and something became whole." She returned to begin work on *The Joy Luck Club*.

Amy Tan recalls that she once had a discussion with her mother, who asked, "If I die, what would you remember?" Amy told her that it would be the usual daughter memories: "You know, you're my mother, blah, blah, blah." Disgusted, Daisy Tan responded: "Well, I think you know a little percent of me." That prompted Tan's first novel. She states, "I wanted to write something that was not simply a recorded history of memories but something relived." She wanted to capture the difficulty that mothers and daughters share in trying to understand one another, especially as it is complicated by the emigrant experience.

Published in 1989, *The Joy Luck Club* became an immediate success, selling two million total copies upon its initial appearance, and staying on *The New York Times* best-seller list for nine months. The book's popularity surprised Tan in many ways. She observes, "What I wrote was so specific to how I felt about things that [the stories] were all about a Chinese mother. I thought maybe a few Chinese-Americans will read this. . . . But I had so many people tell me: 'This is the way it was between me and my mother.'" She also felt the burden of being held up as a "pioneer," just as Maxine Hong Kingston had after her 1976 memoir *The Woman Warrior*. "When *The Joy Luck Club* came out, I was Amy Tan, writer of ethnic literature, Amy Tan, writer of Asian-American literature, Chinese-American literature, immigrant literature. That stopped happening after the book became a mainstream success."

She originally conceived the book as a collection of short stories derived largely from her mother's life. Tan notes that her unique storytelling ability comes from both her father and her mother:

> My father was a minister, and his sermons were simple so that people could understand them and feel them. His way of telling stories was so full of feeling that I got a sense that you should care about who was listening to you and imagine what effect it might have on them. My mother's imagination . . . was full of all kinds of possibilities because she was not restricted to a particular religion or philosophy. She was open to anything that could work.

The Joy Luck Club follows the lives of two generations of women, Chinese emigrant mothers and their American-born daughters. Taking her mother's place at the East corner of the mah-jongg table three months after her mother has died and talking to her mother's oldest friends, central character Jing-mei Woo realizes the fears of these mothers and the loss that their daughters do not yet recognize: "They are frightened. In me, they see their own daughters, just as ignorant, just as unmind- ful of all the truths and hopes they have brought to America. They see daughters who grow impatient when their mothers talk in Chinese, who think they are stupid when they explain things in fractured English. . . . They see daughters who will bear grandchil- dren born without any connecting hope passed from generation to generation."

The novel is divided into four sections focusing on four families, four mothers and their four daughters. Each section moves from one family to the next, each mother and daughter telling her own story. There are two complete rounds of stories from mothers and daughters, with the exception of Suyuan Woo, who has died. Jing-mei speaks four times, providing her mother's story at the mah-jongg table and to her Chinese sisters when she finally meets them, the little girls her mother had to leave behind when fleeing Shanghai in 1949.

What we witness are mothers who are reluctant to let go of their daughters and daughters who are trying desperately to claim independence. The four older women gather each week at "The Joy Luck Club," founded in Shanghai by Suyuan Woo and continued in the United States, to play mah-jongg, to trade recipes, to invest the game winnings in the stock market, to tell stories, and to treat their children's accomplish- ments as a competition. Jing-mei (June) Woo must sort out the stories and the lives of these women as she tries to come to terms with those of her mother's contemporaries, their daughters, and herself. Bad relationships, unfinished college degrees, conflicts with parents, and struggles with their "Chineseness" typify the younger generation. Her mother once told Amy: "Make them cry. Nobody ever cried for my life when I went through it, so make them cry." *The Joy Luck Club* is sad, but it is also hopeful, amusing, and affirming. In it, Amy Tan establishes herself as one of America's finest contemporary writers.

Amy Tan's second novel, *The Kitchen God's Wife*, appeared in 1991. A traditional novel, it again depicts the lives of a mother and daughter. Tan knew she was taking a risk in revisiting the subject matter of her first book, but she believed that the task was unfinished. Pearl is the grown American daughter of chinese-born Winnie Louie. Each keeps a secret from the other: Pearl has multiple sclerosis, and Winnie has never told her daughter the truth about her Chinese life. Only when Aunt Helen, Winnie's closest friend, who is dying of cancer, threatens to reveal to Pearl Winnie's secrets before she dies does Winnie unveil that life. It is a tale of a mother with bound feet, a lonely childhood, a terrible marriage, and a world disrupted by domestic and political violence and war. The story is again based largely on her mother's life, and Tan is once again successful in revealing women's strength to survive. As Tan observes, "My mother's life is more strange than anything I could have made up," but she turned her mother's life in pre-World War II China into a masterpiece.

Summary

Amy Tan figures as a major and important voice in mainstream American letters. She has observed that "what enriches American literature is a diversity of voices. What people are beginning to recognize—and this is wonderful—is that all these different voices *are* American literature." Her novels, while revealing a unique experience in American life, also prove the universality of that experience.

In 1993, *The Joy Luck Club* was made into a feature film that has enjoyed both critical and popular success, which underscores the powerful emotional impact that Tan's work has had among readers and viewers.

Bibliography

Carabi, Angels. "*Belles Lettres* Interview with Amy Tan." *Belles Lettres* 6 (Summer, 1991): 16-19. A frank and honest discussion of *The Joy Luck Club*, touching on the major influences that shaped Tan's writing—her parents, especially her mother, the Chinese storytelling tradition, language, and her American childhood.

Cheng, Scarlet. "Amy Tan Redux." *Belles Lettres* 7 (Fall, 1991): 15, 19. A review of *The Kitchen God's Wife*. An insightful and detailed reading of Tan's second novel.

Ling, Amy. *Between Worlds: Women Writers of Chinese Ancestry*. New York: Pergamon Press, 1990. One of the very few book-length studies of Asian American women writers. An excellent analysis of the twentieth century Asian American female writing tradition, including a significant discussion of Amy Tan's first novel, placing it in the tradition of Kingston's *The Woman Warrior*.

Shear, Walter. "Generational Differences and the Diaspora in *The Joy Luck Club*." *Critique* 34 (Spring, 1993): 193-199. Comparing Tan's novel to Maxine Hong Kingston's *The Woman Warrior*, Shear maintains that each woman's story is an account of coming to terms with two cultures and that ultimately the isolated selves of the Chinese diaspora are able to return "home."

Tan, Amy. "Lost Lives of Women." *Life* 14 (April, 1991): 90-91. Taking an old family photograph taken in China in 1922 of women in her mother's family as a starting point, Tan traces many of the women's stories in *The Joy Luck Club* to these women.

Weinberg-Schenker, Peri. "An Interview with Amy Tan." In *Novel and Short Story*

Writer's Market '92. Cincinnati, Ohio: Writer's Digest Books, 1992. Provides insight into not only Tan's personal life but also her creative life, discussing what writers and people influenced her, how she writes, and how her publishing career began.

Laura Weiss Zlogar

JESSICA TANDY

Born: June 7, 1909; London, England
Died: September 11, 1994; Easton, Connecticut
Areas of Achievement: Theater and drama and film
Contribution: An extremely versatile actress, Jessica Tandy has repeatedly shown that
a superb talent, compelling stage presence, and dedication to craft can more than
compensate for a lack of superficial glamour.

Early Life

Jessica Tandy was born in London, England, on June 7, 1909, the sole daughter of
Harry and Jessie Tandy. Her father, a cordage manufacturer and merchant, died of
cancer when she was only twelve, and her mother, headmistress at a school for
retarded children, had to take on extra work as a clerk to make ends meet. Despite the
hardship, she gave considerable attention to her children and cultivated in Jessica and
the girl's two brothers, Michael and Tully, a taste for literature and art. She took them
to plays and museums, and during holidays she encouraged their efforts to produce
their own theatrical pieces.

As a child, Jessica attended Dame Alice Owen's Girls' School in London, where
her training in the classics was fairly rigorous. By the time she reached her teens, she
had already made up her mind to become an actress. She was encouraged in this
endeavor by her mother, who believed that the stage offered an avenue of escape from
material deprivation. Jessica began serious preparation for a stage career by taking
weekend acting lessons from a tutor and studying Shakespeare in night classes; then,
in 1924, at fifteen, she entered London's Ben Greet Academy of Acting.

Three years later, on November 22, 1927, Jessica Tandy made her stage debut at
Playroom Six, a small theater in London's notorious Soho district. She appeared as
Sara Manderson in a play called *The Manderson Girls*. It was an inauspicious
beginning, since she was paid very little and had to provide her own elaborate
costumes, which she had to fashion herself because she could not afford to have them
made.

The next year things improved. She joined the Birmingham Repertory Company
and toured for six months as an ingenue in Eden Phillpotts' *Yellow Sands*. In 1929, she
made her West End debut as Lena Jackson in *The Rumour* at the Court Theatre. Three
years later, in the role of Manuela in *Children in Uniform*, Tandy won considerable
critical acclaim and established her reputation as a solid actress.

Life's Work

Despite the fact that her growing stage fame rested on roles in modern plays, Jessica
Tandy's first love was the traditional drama of William Shakespeare, and during the
1930's she appeared in productions of several of his plays. Among her notable roles,
all on London stages, were Ophelia in John Gielgud's renowned 1934 production of
Hamlet at the New Theatre; Viola in Tyrone Guthrie's production of *Twelfth Night*,

which opened at the Old Vic in 1937; and Cordelia in *King Lear* and Miranda in *The Tempest*, both in 1940, with John Gielgud at the Old Vic. World War II intervened, however, and more than twenty years would pass before she again interpreted a Shakespearean role on stage.

The war and a failing eight-year marriage to actor Jack Hawkins induced Tandy to emigrate to the United States with her young daughter Susan. She arrived in America with very limited funds and without the hard-won reputation she had left behind in England. Although her goal was Hollywood, at first she stayed in New York, trying to make ends meet by taking a series of roles in minor Broadway productions. Initially, she became very discouraged. She was barely able to provide for herself and Susan, and she seriously considered giving up her craft. Then, in 1942, she met and married Hume Cronyn, whose love and support helped restore her professional self-esteem.

The Cronyns soon moved to Hollywood, where Tandy landed a contract with Twentieth Century-Fox, although her first American film, *The Seventh Cross* (1944), starring Spencer Tracy, was produced by Metro-Goldwyn-Mayer (MGM), which had her husband under contract. A series of bit parts followed, and it was not until 1947 that Tandy garnered a leading role in *A Woman's Vengeance*, an adaptation of an Aldous Huxley short story.

Determined to keep active in stage acting, in 1946 Tandy took the role of Miss Collins in Tennessee Williams' one-act play *Portrait of a Madonna*, which was directed by her husband at the Las Palmas Theatre in Los Angeles. Her strong performance persuaded the playwright to insist that she be cast as Blanche DuBois in the Broadway production of *A Streetcar Named Desire*, which opened at the Ethel Barrymore Theater on December 3, 1947. A major landmark in American theater, the production was directed by Elia Kazan and featured the young Marlon Brando as Stanley Kowalski, Blanche's crude brother-in-law and chief nemesis. Both Tandy and Brando won great critical acclaim for their portrayals. The work ran on Broadway for two years, and although in the 1951 film version the part of Blanche went to Vivien Leigh, Tandy's rendering of the role established her as a consummate stage performer.

Her success also convinced Tandy to keep on acting in stage plays, her avowed preference, but she did not again act in a Williams vehicle until 1970, when she played Marguerite Gautier in the surrealistic fantasy *Camino Real* at the Lincoln Center Repertory Theatre. In the interim, she and her husband worked together in several plays that they deliberately sought out as vehicles for their combined talents.

Their first famous performance together was as the husband and wife in Jan de Hartog's durable comedy *The Fourposter*, which opened in October of 1951 and ran for more than six hundred nights. For a time, the couple's efforts to repeat a joint-venture success were largely frustrated, and Tandy fared better on her own, particularly in the role of Louise Harrington in Peter Shaffer's *Five Finger Exercise*, which, under the direction of John Gielgud, enjoyed a long, critically acclaimed run beginning on December 2, 1959.

Tandy and Cronyn persisted in their efforts to work together, and they quickly became the new premier husband-and-wife acting team in contemporary American theater, inheriting the place long held by Alfred Lunt and Lynn Fontanne. New successes started with the parts of Agnes and Tobias in Edward Albee's *A Delicate Balance*, which opened in New York on September 22, 1966. It was followed by other widely acclaimed performances in Samuel Beckett's *Happy Days* (1972), Noël Coward's *Two Keys* (1974), D. L. Coburn's *Gin Game* (1977), and *Foxfire* (1982), coauthored by Hume Cronyn and Susan Cooper.

Because other opportunities challenged them, Tandy and Cronyn also worked apart, in both film and theater, both with great distinction. Tandy turned in brilliant stage performances as Marjorie in the New York version of David Storey's *Home* (1971), as Mary Tyrone in two Canadian productions of Eugene O'Neill's *Long Day's Journey into Night* (in 1971 and 1980), and as Amanda Wingfield in a revival of Tennessee Williams' *The Glass Menagerie*, which opened at the Eugene O'Neill Theatre in December of 1983. She also took the opportunity to perform in classic works, including various Shakespearean plays. She appeared as Lady Macbeth in *Macbeth* (1961), Cassandra in *Troilus and Cressida* (1961), Gertrude in *Hamlet* (1963), and both Hippolyta and Titania in *A Midsummer Night's Dream* (1976).

In cinema, Tandy, who lacked the superficial electrifying beauty and raw sex appeal of many Hollywood starlets, was for most of her career assigned only supporting roles as a character actress. She always turned in solid performances, appearing in diverse films, including *Dragonwyck* (1946), *Forever Amber* (1946), *The Desert Fox* (1951), *The Light in the Forest* (1958), *Still of the Night* (1981), and *The World According to Garp* (1981). Then, as if her stage reputation had finally caught on in Hollywood, Tandy garnered some major parts in *The Bostonians* (1984), *Cocoon* (1985) and its sequel *Cocoon: The Return* (1988), *Batteries Not Included* (1987), *Driving Miss Daisy* (1989), *Fried Green Tomatoes* (1991), and *Used People* (1992). For her superb depiction of the titular character in *Driving Miss Daisy*, Tandy won an Oscar for Best Actress, and she was nominated for Best Supporting Actress for her portrayal of the elderly nursing home resident in *Fried Green Tomatoes*.

Throughout their careers, Tandy and Cronyn tirelessly and unselfishly labored to advance and enrich theater in America. They worked in the regional theater movement to help new playwrights get started, often working for less pay than they could command in Broadway houses, and they also strove to keep the dramas of past eras before American audiences. Tandy, for example, acted in productions of works by Anton Chekhov, George Bernard Shaw, and William Congreve. Because their love of good literature was of primary importance to them, from time to time Tandy and Cronyn went on tour giving readings of both fiction and poetry. Together, they gave an aura of dignity and grace to their profession that has made them venerated by two generations of theatergoers in the United States.

After waging a four-year battle with ovarian cancer, Tandy died at her Connecticut home on September 11, 1994. Later that evening, presenters and winners at the 1994 Emmy Awards held in Pasadena, California, paid tribute to Tandy's impressive career and her performance in her last television film: Hallmark Hall of Fame's *To Dance with the White Dog* (1994), based on the 1990 novel by Terry Kay.

Summary

Jessica Tandy was often called a patrician among actresses in contemporary theater and film. Although fairly petite and never seductively beautiful, Tandy amply compensated for a lack of physical magnetism by projecting a stately dignity that has been her trademark for a generation. Although she played every conceivable sort of part, from vamp to wise matron, revealing great versatility, it was in her mature roles that she garnered the most applause and critical esteem. Her stage bearing, while aristocratic, was never haughty.

Tandy also had remarkable longevity as an actress, gracing the stage for more than sixty years. Through her wonderful talent, she avoided the curse of typecasting and the fading and aging starlet's fate—limited opportunities for older actresses and the fabled professional amnesia of casting directors. Few actresses in either film or on stage weathered so well in their careers, particularly in film, where for every durable Jessica Tandy, Katharine Hepburn, or Bette Davis there have been dozens of actresses who passed into career oblivion by age forty.

The honors bestowed on Tandy attest her achievements. In addition to her Oscar, she won three Tony Awards: for her portrayal of Blanche in *A Streetcar Named Desire*, of Fonsia Dorsey in *Gin Game*, and of Annie Nations in *Foxfire*. She also won other awards, including an Obie and various Drama Desk Awards.

Jessica Tandy serves as a role model for actresses determined to make their way in a world in which, all too often, advances are made through promotional hoopla rather than genuine acting skill. She demonstrated that real talent, hard work, and dedication can triumph over the bottom-line realities of commercial film and stage production.

Bibliography

Barranger, Milly S. *Jessica Tandy: A Bio-Bibliography*. New York: Greenwood Press, 1991. Number 22 in the Bio-bibliographies in the Performing Arts series, this is the only monograph devoted strictly to Tandy. It includes a biography, a professional chronology, a survey of all Tandy's stage, screen, and television work, and a fully annotated bibliography. It is the most valuable source work available.

Clarke, Gerald. "Two Lives, One Ambition." *Time* 135 (April 2, 1990): 62-64. This piece profiles Tandy and Cronyn and their professional life together. It notes their differences in style and makes some interesting observations about their skills never being compromised in a contemporary American theater that has insisted on mimicking television.

Cronyn, Hume. *A Terrible Liar: A Memoir*. New York: William Morrow, 1991. Although in his foreword Cronyn disclaims that this autobiography is about anyone but him, his intimate reflections on his courtship and marriage with Tandy and their professional career and relationship are both engaging and charming.

Spoto, Donald. *The Kindness of Strangers: The Life of Tennessee Williams*. Boston: Little, Brown, 1985. This highly regarded biography of Williams gives considerable coverage to the now legendary production of *A Streetcar Named Desire* and the principals in the cast. It is recommended for students who want an inside look at the productions of the great playwright's works, including Tandy's superb rendering of Blanche DuBois.

John W. Fiero

IDA TARBELL

Born: November 5, 1857; Erie County, Pennsylvania
Died: January 6, 1944; Bridgeport, Connecticut
Area of Achievement: Journalism
Contribution: Ida Tarbell became a prominent leader in American magazine journalism in a period when women were almost entirely absent from the field.

Early Life

Ida Minerva Tarbell was born on her grandfather's farm in western Pennsylvania four years before the Civil War began. Her father, Franklin Sumner Tarbell, had earlier struck out for Iowa and its richer farming prospects; he would not see his daughter until she was eighteen months old. Ida's mother, Esther McCullough Tarbell, was a descendant of Massachusetts pioneers and had taught school for more than a decade before her marriage. She would ultimately bear four children, of whom Ida was the eldest.

When Ida was three, her father moved the family to the Pennsylvania oil region to take advantage of financial opportunities there. After the Civil War, the family would follow the oil boom to several towns in western Pennsylvania, settling ultimately in Titusville when Ida was thirteen. While her father made an increasingly comfortable living building wooden oil tanks, Ida studied in the local schools and attended Methodist church services and revival meetings with her family. When the time came for her to continue her studies, her father naturally selected Allegheny College, the Methodist coeducational college in nearby Meadville.

For the next four years, Tarbell combined diligent study in biology and languages with social activities, class offices, literary magazine editing, and public speaking. She was romantically linked with at least one young man, but the relationship did not survive college and Ida never married. After her graduation, she embarked on a short-lived career as a teacher at the Union Seminary in Poland, Ohio. A low salary and high expectations placed on her ability to teach all subjects led to her return to Titusville after two years.

The opportunity that led to her career in journalism appeared a few months after her return. She was hired as an editor for the *Chautauquan*, a magazine published to promote adult education and home learning by the Chautauqua Literary and Scientific Circle. Although the editorial work she was assigned initially was stultifying, she gradually expanded her responsibilities to include translating, reviewing manuscripts, and writing her own articles. The workload at first was light, and the magazine was located in Meadville, which enabled her to complete a master of arts degree at Allegheny College.

When Tarbell left the *Chautauquan* in 1891, she had no intention of accepting a mundane editorial post. Instead, she sailed to France determined to immerse herself in Parisian culture, support herself by submitting articles to American newspapers, and write a biography of Mme Manon Philipon de Roland, a heroine of the French

Revolution. She did all of this and more. After reading some of her work, Samuel S. McClure, the publisher of *McClure's*, personally visited her in Paris to offer her a job. In the fall of 1894, she accepted his offer, which included money for the passage home.

Life's Work

Ida Tarbell's first work at the magazine was the surprising assignment of producing a series of articles on the life of Napoleon, whose hundred-year-old military exploits produced a flurry of activity in the popular press of the 1890's. She had not expected to do a work of that sort, and she was astonished to be asked, after returning from Paris, to undertake a biography of a French subject using the comparatively limited sources to be found in American libraries. Nevertheless, her labors at the Library of Congress resulted in a distinctive and popular *McClure's* series that was subsequently published as a book, as was the practice at the time.

The resources of the Library of Congress were excellent, as Tarbell discovered, and so were the human resources in the nation's capital. She remained in Washington, D.C., until 1899, during which time she met influential politicians and public servants. She wrote articles about them and ghost-wrote the memoirs of other famous men. Her major work during her Washington years was another *McClure's* assignment, a biography of Abraham Lincoln. She conducted interviews in Washington and Illinois and established a wide network of correspondents who provided her with information. Her study of Lincoln's early years was published in 1896, with a complete two-volume biography following in 1900, after its serialization in the magazine.

Called to the *McClure's* New York staff in 1899 as managing editor, Tarbell joined a talented group of writers and editors. Although McClure himself was seldom in the office, his partner, John Phillips, shrewdly managed the publisher's affairs. Among the writers McClure and Phillips published regularly were Ray Stannard Baker and William Allen White, both of whom were poised on the brink of fame as preeminent journalists of their time. Also on the staff then or shortly thereafter were Willa Cather, Finley Peter Dunne, and Lincoln Steffens. This group took the lead in a new journalistic enterprise—muckraking—and Ida Tarbell's series on the Standard Oil Company was in the forefront of that type of work.

The series that would later be published in book form as *The History of the Standard Oil Company* was launched in the November, 1902, *McClure's* magazine. Ida had undertaken it in response to Sam McClure's idea of detailing the rise of the trusts in the late nineteenth century; she had formulated the idea of tracing the history of one such enterprise and the great entrepreneur associated with it, John D. Rockefeller. Growing up in the oilfield districts had acquainted her with the industry and the geographic area in which the boom began. Her industrious methods of working and her indomitable spirit in researching her subject ensured a thorough product. If anyone in *McClure's* talented group of writers could master such a vast (and elusive) body of information, it was Ida Tarbell.

The Standard Oil series established two things: The first was that Ida Tarbell was a formidable author and one of the outstanding journalists of her time; the second was the fact that muckraking (as the reform journalists' movement was labeled in 1906 by Theodore Roosevelt) was a responsible enterprise that could produce thorough and dispassionate analyses of problems. Because of the efforts of Tarbell and her cohorts, *McClure's* became the leading voice of protest among the popular magazines.

This preeminence was short-lived, however, and Tarbell became the leader of a staff revolt against the magazine in 1906. At the center of the controversy was the mercurial Sam McClure. The publisher was famous for his ability to produce ideas for articles at a rapid-fire pace, but his erratic behavior in 1905 and 1906 seemed to Tarbell, Phillips, and others to threaten the magazine they had helped to build. They questioned his new, risky publishing ventures and wondered whether his commitment to reform had been undercut by his commitment to making money. Tarbell resigned from the magazine in April, 1906.

By June, the old *McClure's* group had formed a new venture. They founded the Phillips Publishing Company, raised money to purchase a failed magazine, and launched it in the fall as their own, *The American Magazine*. Tarbell remained a regular staffer and contributor until the group sold its interests in 1915, although she also submitted articles to other magazines. Her major series in *American Magazine* covered diverse topics: the protective tariff, the American woman, and the "golden rule" in business.

The first series highlighted the author at her best. She explained the complexities of the tariff to the general public, clarified controversies, and produced a reasoned analysis that clearly explained the costs of high tariffs to working people. Her golden rule series, her last extended writing for *The American Magazine*, was a defense of scientific management in industry, a work that demonstrated how efficiency could blend with humane treatment of labor. The third series—on the American woman— proved to be the most controversial and caused a rift between Tarbell and some of her suffragist friends.

Like may reformers during the early years of the twentieth century, Tarbell believed that the government, through protective legislation, could act in the general interest of laborers, women, and other minorities. Revolutionary change in the social or political system was not necessary. She was never truly a feminist. She did not support the woman suffrage movement, since she believed that a woman's influence was best exerted in the home, not in areas that were traditionally male preserves. Thus, for working women, she favored legislation that would limit their hours to allow them more time in the home. Raised by a suffragist mother, and herself a dominant force in a traditionally male profession, Ida Tarbell espoused an apparently contradictory philosophy relating to women and their roles in society.

After the sale of *The American Magazine* in 1915, Tarbell remained active as a freelance writer. She also traveled and lectured on topics about which she had written earlier. She worked briefly in Washington during World War I until she was side-tracked by a diagnosis of tuberculosis and by the subsequent treatment. She spent much time during her later years tending to family members, often at her farm in

Connecticut which she had purchased in 1906 with her book earnings. Projects she completed in her sixties and seventies included biographies of steel magnate Elbert Gary and General Electric head Owen D. Young, a history of American business during the late nineteenth century, and her autobiography, *All in the Day's Work*. Her major magazine writings were series on the Florida land boom and on Italian dictator Benito Mussolini.

Her work progressed more slowly as she aged, but she kept doggedly at it. In her eighties, she used her own declining health as the subject of a work she never completed, *Life After Eighty*. Old age, Parkinson's disease (diagnosed about two decades earlier), and pneumonia brought about Tarbell's death in early January of 1944. At her request, she was buried in Titusville.

Summary

Ida Tarbell exerted both a specific and a general influence on her times. The specific influence related to Standard Oil, whose illegal operations she documented as thoroughly as if she was preparing a legal brief. Legal action, in fact, was the result. When the attorney general filed a 1906 case against Standard Oil for violation of the Sherman Antitrust Act, the charges were essentially those that Ida Tarbell had made and documented in her book. The case was heard and appealed; when the Supreme court made its ruling in 1911, it ordered the dissolution of the giant corporation.

Tarbell's general influence concerned the status of women in public life. Although she, ironically, did not participate in feminist or suffragist activities, her whole career exemplified what activist women attempted to achieve—the opportunity for women to enter the professions.

Bibliography

Brady, Kathleen. *Ida Tarbell: Portrait of a Muckraker*. New York: Seaview/Putnam, 1984. The most thorough treatment of the contradictions in Tarbell's writings and of the contrast between her own achievements and her views on women and public life.

Conn, Frances G. *Ida Tarbell, Muckraker*. New York: Thomas Nelson, 1972. Written especially for juveniles, the book is anecdotal but informative. There is no systematic discussion of Tarbell's works, but there are numerous quotes from her writings.

Lyon, Peter. *Success Story: The Life and Times of S. S. McClure*. New York: Charles Scribner's Sons, 1963. Discusses Ida Tarbell's writings in the context of the magazine muckraking movement generally considered to have begun in *McClure's* magazine. Examines the complex relationship between Tarbell and McClure.

Tarbell, Ida M. *All in the Day's Work: An Autobiography*. New York: Macmillan, 1939. An unassuming autobiography made rather bland by the author's saccharine approach to describing the controversies in which she was involved.

_____ . *The History of the Standard Oil Company*. 2 vols. New York: Macmillan, 1904. Tarbell's magnum opus was not only the first great work of the muckrakers but also a solid history of the development of the oil industry in the

United States. It is the main work upon which her literary reputation rests.

Tomkins, Mary E. *Ida M. Tarbell*. New York: Twayne, 1974. This book in Twayne's United States Authors series mainly considers Tarbell's writings and evaluates her contributions to literature.

Richard G. Frederick

SARA TEASDALE

Born: August 8, 1884; St. Louis, Missouri
Died: January 29, 1933; New York, New York
Area of Achievement: Literature
Contribution: One of the best-selling poets of the early twentieth century, Teasdale used traditional verse forms to express her own attitudes toward love, beauty, and solitude.

Early Life

Sara Trevor Teasdale was born on August 8, 1884, in St. Louis, Missouri. At the time of her birth, St. Louis was experiencing a cultural and economic flowering, brought about in part by its mixed population of transplanted Easterners of Puritan ancestry and more recently immigrated Germans who stressed the importance of art and music. In 1884, the city was home to two universities, a museum, an art school, and numerous theaters where the great names in the acting and music worlds of the day sometimes performed.

The Teasdale family was of New England stock, descended from a dissenting Baptist who had emigrated from England in 1792. The poet's grandfather was a Baptist minister who had moved his family west to St. Louis in 1854. John Warren Teasdale, the poet's father, was a successful businessman. The ancestors of Sara's mother, Mary Elizabeth Willard, included the founders of Concord, Massachusetts, two presidents of Harvard, and a signer of the Declaration of Independence. Throughout her life, Sara would acknowledge the Puritan aspect of her character and its conflict with her more "pagan" poetic self.

Kept at home in early childhood because of her poor health, Sara began her formal education at the age of nine, attending a private school a block from her home, and she was graduated from a girls' school at the age of eighteen. In 1903, she became friends with an artistic and intellectual young woman named Williamina Parrish, with whom she and other friends formed a club called the Potters. These young women were products of the active women's club culture of the day and were themselves enthusiasts of and participants in the arts. For more than two years they produced a monthly hand-printed magazine known as *The Potter's Wheel.* Among their artistic influences were the Pre-Raphaelite poets and painters, particularly Christina Rossetti, the Celtic Revivalist Fiona MacLeod (actually, Scottish writer William Sharp), the Greek poet Sappho, and actress Eleonora Duse. Most of the poems in Sara's first book had originally appeared in *The Potter's Wheel.*

In 1905, Sara and her mother traveled to Europe and the Holy Land. Sara was depressed by the dirt and poverty of what was then Palestine but loved Seville, Spain, and Paris, France, where she pronounced the Venus de Milo "the most beautiful thing on earth." While in London, she sought out the homes of poets Elizabeth Barrett Browning and Algernon Charles Swinburne. The beauty that Teasdale found in Europe contributed subject matter for many of her later poems.

In 1906, *The Potter's Wheel* came to the attention of William Reedy, the publisher of a weekly newspaper known for its sponsorship of new artists. Reedy published one of Sara's prose sketches and a poem, thereby arousing her sense of professionalism and bringing her to the attention of poetry critics. The next year, the Poet Lore company published Teasdale's first book, *Sonnets to Duse and Other Poems*.

Life's Work

On the surface, Sara Teasdale's life changed little following her initial publications, but she experienced a growing dissatisfaction with life in St. Louis and in her parents' home. This period saw the beginning of her lifelong pattern of periodic "rest cures" (then prescribed for many ailments of women) at various sanatoriums and hotels. She was proposed for membership in the Poetry Society of America in 1910, and in January of 1911, she made her first visit to New York City for the meeting of the society. Her second book, *Helen of Troy and Other Poems*, was published by Putnam in October of that year.

Poetry Society membership brought Teasdale friendships with influential poets, editors, and critics. Her work also brought her into contact with John Hall Wheelock, the young poet who became the unrequited love of her life and the subject of many of her finest lyrics of frustrated love. Although he never reciprocated Teasdale's romantic affection, Wheelock became the person to whom she turned in many of the later crises of her life.

In 1913, Teasdale visited Chicago and met Harriet Monroe, editor of the recently founded magazine *Poetry*. Monroe introduced her to Illinois poet Vachel Lindsay, then just becoming famous as the author of "General William Booth Enters into Heaven." Lindsay's midwestern aesthetic was nearly the opposite of Teasdale's emphasis on careful craftsmanship in traditional verse forms, but he fell in love with his fellow poet and courted her with extravagant, lengthy letters and periodic visits. Teasdale remained fond of Lindsay throughout his life but found him exhausting and the prospect of a life of poverty with him terrifying. In December, 1914, she married St. Louis businessman Ernst Filsinger. Filsinger was passionately fond of the arts and a supporter of the twentieth century's new developments in poetry. In the early years of their marriage, he and Teasdale lived in St. Louis and occasionally wrote poetry together.

Teadale's 1915 volume *Rivers to the Sea* found her experimenting with free verse despite her original misgivings about the form. In this volume Teasdale found her poetic voice. *Sonnets to Duse* had been full of girlish enthusiasm, while *Helen of Troy* had consisted largely of dramatic monologues reminiscent of certain nineteenth century verse. *Rivers to the Sea* explored the moods of a love relationship from a woman's point of view and spoke as well of renunciation and of the need for solitude and natural beauty. The book was well received, and its first printing sold out in three months.

Ernst took a job in New York City, in late 1916, and he and Sara moved to the city where she would live for the rest of her life. To spare her the energy-sapping details of housekeeping, they lived in hotels, and she was able to devote herself exclusively to her writing and the promotion of her books. Her 1917 book, *Love Songs*, won the first Columbia University prize for poetry, an award that in 1922 would become the Pulitzer Prize. This volume contains some of her rare poems of fulfilled love; more important, however, the section "Interlude: Songs out of Sorrow" sounds a theme that would recur with increasing frequency in Teasdale's later work: that of using pain and grief as a means of attaining emotional independence from the accidents of life and love. In these poems, she also questions her Baptist upbringing, rejecting the notion of salvation through a personal god. The year 1917 also saw the publication of *The Answering Voice*, Teasdale's anthology of love poems written by women. The title is a clue to the volume's contents, largely poems detailing women's responses to men's love or lack of love. Most of the poets featured in the volume are such traditional favorites as Elizabeth Barrett Browning and Christina Rossetti, and even the more experimental writers sound the traditional women's themes of entrapment and escape.

Teasdale's next book, *Flame and Shadow* (1920), continues the development begun in *Rivers to the Sea* but adds the theme of the failure of love to provide meaning in life. Instead of seeking fulfillment through romantic love, the speaker in these poems banishes passion to the realm of memory and seeks salvation through beauty, conventional religions having failed. Beauty is perceived as the only meaningful thing that will outlast death, here seen as the great enemy of humankind. These poems also show Teasdale continuing to experiment with form, since even the seemingly conventional verses vary rhythms in unexpected ways.

The next five years were difficult ones for Teasdale because they held the deaths of both parents, a brother, and her friend Amy Lowell. The only book Teasdale wrote during this period, *Rainbow Gold* (1922), was an anthology of poetry for children. Teasdale's poor health and the overseas contacts required by her husband's business necessitated frequent separations, often of several months' duration. Despite Ernst's obvious devotion, marriage failed to provide an emotional foundation for Sara's life. Her 1926 publication, *Dark of the Moon*, expresses this darkening mood. Many of her familiar images—the sea, the stars, the wind—recur, but here they are not always positive. In one poem, the sea deceives humans into believing in their own immortality; in another, it erases all evidence of human presence. The speaker's attitude toward death changes in these poems as well; in "The Old Enemy" death is now, "save when he comes too late," a friend. The love poems here are calm and reminiscent, more recollections of past loves than celebrations of love's possibilities. Solitude is more and more accepted as the condition of life. Despite the book's essentially somber tone, its first edition sold out within two weeks.

This deepening solitude was typical of Teasdale's life as well as her work. She had long refused speaking engagements; now she no longer attended meetings of the Poetry Society. The death of longtime friend Marguerite Wilkinson in 1928 deprived her of an important daily contact. In 1929, she traveled to Reno, Nevada, and obtained a divorce; the news reached Filsinger on a business trip to South Africa. The divorce and a new friendship with college student Margaret Conklin, who eventually became her literary executor, brought some brief happiness to Teasdale, but these were not particularly productive years for her. Between 1926 and her death, she published only a revised and enlarged edition of *The Answering Voice* (1928) and a children's book, *Stars Tonight* (1930).

Possibly the most shattering event in Teasdale's life was the suicide of Vachel Lindsay in December, 1931. After a period of adjustment to Teasdale's marriage, the two had remained close friends, and the woman Lindsay married in 1926 had also become friendly with Teasdale. John Hall Wheelock, called by a hysterical Teasdale when she received the news of the suicide, viewed Lindsay's death as the event that inspired Teasdale to take her own life a little more than a year later.

Teasdale's last year found her writing poems again and working on a biography of Christina Rossetti. During a research trip to London, however, she became ill with pneumonia and was forced to return home still ill. Problems with high blood pressure and a broken blood vessel led her to fear that a stroke was imminent, and friends became concerned about her serous depression. On January 29, 1933, Sara Teasdale was found dead of an overdose of sleeping pills. Her last book, *Strange Victory* (1933), was published after her death.

Summary

Sara Teasdale's work explores the moods and thoughts of a woman who studies her own reactions carefully. Furthermore, her writing explores the dilemma of a traditional woman in a transitional time, a time when formerly conventional notions about women and love have not died but are being found inadequate. Even Teasdale's early, seemingly derivative work contains a questioning of the traditional view of her female heroes; her Helen and Guenevere are not simply the creatures of popular imagination. In addition, Teasdale's best work has the musicality that distinguishes all good lyric poetry; she often claimed that the most important trait of poetry was melody, and she referred to her own works as "songs." This aspect of her work began receiving critical attention in the late 1980's.

Although her once-popular verse has fallen into oblivion among most professional literary critics, Sara Teasdale has continued to speak to a popular audience. Evidence for this is the continued reprinting of her *Collected Poems* and of *Mirror of the Heart*, William Drake's 1984 edition of her work, which included previously unpublished poems. Even feminist anthologies, which originally excluded Teasdale, began including her work in post-1990 editions.

Bibliography

Carpenter, Margaret Haley. *Sara Teasdale: A Biography*. New York: Schulte, 1960. This early biography is particularly good in its treatment of Teasdale's early life, especially the Potter period. Its extensive use of letters to Teasdale also gives a vivid picture of her relationship with Vachel Lindsay.

Drake, William. *Sara Teasdale: Woman and Poet*. San Francisco: Harper & Row, 1979. This psychologically oriented biography attempts to place Teasdale in the context of the transitional period between Victorianism and modernism. Although its conclusions about her motivations are speculative, this book's attention to Teasdale as a product of her time and its conflicts offers a reading of her character that is less idealized than that of the Carpenter book.

Gould, Jean. *American Woman Poets: Pioneers of Modern Poetry*. New York: Dodd, Mead, 1980. This collection of biographical reviews of early twentieth century poets gives a sympathetic overview of Teasdale's life and places her in the first rank of lyric poets.

Mannino, Mary Ann. "Sara Teasdale: Fitting Tunes to Everything." *Turn-of-the-Century Women* 5 (1990): 37-41. This brief study of Teasdale's metrics places her in the context of turn-of-the-century experimentation and argues that the formal aspects of her work deserve more attention than they have so far received.

Schoen, Carol B. *Sara Teasdale*. Boston: Twayne, 1986. This chronologically ordered overview is the first book-length study of Teasdale's work. Essentially sympathetic, it focuses on her use of images and on the development of her ideas about love, solitude, beauty, and death, arguing that the critical neglect of Teasdale's work is unjustified.

Walker, Cheryl. *Masks Outrageous and Austere: Culture, Psyche, and Persona in Modern Women Poets*. Bloomington: Indiana University Press, 1991. Feminist in its focus, this study views Teasdale as representative of one reaction to nineteenth century views of women and women's poetry. It holds that her treatment of the conflict between independence and the desire for love is archetypal.

Rebecca Phillips

MEGAN TERRY

Born: July 22, 1932; Seattle, Washington

Area of Achievement: Theater and drama
Contribution: A founding member of the Open Theatre in the 1960's and playwright-in-residence at the Omaha Magic Theatre since 1974, Megan Terry is one of the most prolific American dramatists, having written more than sixty successful plays. She is one of the major pioneers in the development of transformational drama and is also considered one of America's first feminist dramatists.

Early Life

Megan Terry was born Marguerite Josephine Duffy on July 22, 1932, in Seattle, Washington, to Harold Joseph Duffy, Jr., and Marguerite Cecelia Henry Duffy. She later recalled her interest in a film career when she was four years old, although "it changed to theatre when I was seven"—the result of a visit to the Seattle Repertory Playhouse. Except for theatrical activities—grade school plays, amateur theatricals in the Duffy backyard—her childhood was uneventful until 1942, when her father left to fight in World War II. During the war, young Marguerite played at defending the Duffy home with toy guns and bullets. In the seventh grade, she wrote, directed, and acted in her first musical and became convinced that she was destined for the theater.

When Harold Duffy returned to Seattle after the war, he and his wife were divorced; when Terry was fourteen, she and her sister left Seattle to live with their father. Harold Duffy did not encourage his daughter's theatrical aspirations—he called her Tallulah Blackhead and Sarah Heartburn—but he did instill in her a love of the outdoors and taught her carpentry and bricklaying. Returning to Seattle to live with her grandparents during her last year in high school, she rediscovered the Seattle Repertory Playhouse and came under the tutelage of Florence James, a Stanislavsky-trained director, and her husband, actor Burton James.

Terry later described her time at Seattle Repertory as her upbringing. At the theater she learned design, studied the work of Gordon Craig and Adolph Appia, and discovered the links between theater and politics from Florence James, who combined her work in theater with running for public office as a Progressive Party candidate. During those years, Terry also discovered classical drama. She spent the summer of 1950 as a scholarship student at the Banff School of Fine Arts, where she took the stage name of Maggie Duffy and played Hermia in *A Midsummer Night's Dream.* From 1950 to 1951, she studied at the University of Washington in Seattle, and when Seattle Repertory was closed in 1951 by the House Committee on Un-American Activities, she moved to Canada to study at the University of Alberta.

Her two years in Canada widened Terry's theatrical experience by exposing her to the work of Antonin Artaud and giving her the extensive backstage work that led her to decide to become a playwright instead of an actor. Her grandfather's illness forced her back to Seattle, and she reenrolled at the University of Washington. From 1954 to

1956, she taught at the Cornish School of Allied Arts, where she reorganized The Cornish Players, a theater group composed of students from the school as well as any others who wanted to act. She also wrote four children's plays that were performed under her direction in the Seattle area. After her graduation in 1956, she returned to the Banff School of Fine Arts, where she earned certificates in directing, acting, and design.

At some point during the early 1950's, Marguerite Josephine Duffy—briefly Maggie Duffy—became Megan Terry, a name she chose in honor of her Welsh heritage. The name "Megan" came from the Celtic version of "Marguerite," and "Terry" was a reference both to the actress Ellen Terry and to "terra," or the earth.

Life's Work

In 1956, Megan Terry left the Pacific Northwest and moved to New York City. The move to New York unleashed Terry's playwriting talent, and for the next eighteen years she was a major figure in the New York theater scene. Her plays were produced by some of the major Off-Broadway and Off-Off-Broadway theaters—the Open Theatre, LaMama Experimental Theatre Club, Genesis Theatre, Cherry Lane Theatre, and the Manhattan Theatre Club, among others—as well as by the Firehouse Theatre in Minneapolis and the Mark Taper Forum in Los Angeles. She won the Stanley Drama Award for *Hot House* in 1965. Other fellowships and grants followed: two awards from the Office of Advanced Drama Research at the University of Minnesota (1965 and 1969), an ABC-Yale University Fellowship (1966), Rockefeller grants (1968 and 1974), and a National Endowment for the Arts literature fellowship (1972). Her plays won a number of awards, including a 1970 Obie for *Approaching Simone*.

During her New York years, Megan Terry became a founding member of the New York Open Theatre, the brainchild of Joseph Chaikin, who brought together a group of young writers and actors—Jean-Claud van Itallie, Sam Shepard, Richard Gilman, Roberta Sklar, and others, in addition to Terry. The Open Theatre, which was to become a major influence on both experimental and traditional theater, focused on improvisation as the first step to developing a script and, ultimately, a performance piece. The emphasis was on the ensemble and on acting that combined the ideas of Stanislavsky with Chaikin's own "psycho-physical" technique.

Megan Terry was playwright-in-residence for the Open Theatre from 1963 to 1968—five years during which she created or revised for production eight plays. An important play from the Open Theatre years is *Calm Down Mother* (1965), which is often cited in discussions of transformational drama as an excellent example of the genre. Transformational drama is what critic Robert Pasolli describes as "a theatre of abstraction and illusion," in which actors "[delineate], consecutively and concurrently, concrete objects, stereotyped individuals, human relationships, impartial observers and abstract actions." *Calm Down Mother* involves three actresses who play several roles, transforming themselves into different characters and acting out new relationships from scene to scene. The most significant of Terry's Open Theatre plays is *Viet Rock: A Folk War Movie* (1966). The play grew out of her Open Theatre workshop, in which the actors improvised scenes from newspaper stories and television coverage of the war. It opened at La Mama Experimental Theatre Club on May 21, 1966, in New York, and later it was produced at Yale and at other theaters around the United States.

Viet Rock was the Open Theatre's first full-length production, and, like *Calm Down Mother*, it is a transformational piece with shifting characterization, episodic structure, and the subsuming of individual identity into the collective creativity of the ensemble. The play, a series of variations on war, was intended as an antiwar piece and a commentary on American involvement in Vietnam. Theatrical experimentation aside, *Viet Rock* is historically significant in a number of ways: It was the first full theatrical treatment of the Vietnam War, the first commercial production of a transformational play, the first American rock musical, and the first American play in which barriers between stage and house were broken down when the actors left the stage to make physical contact with the audience.

Viet Rock was Megan Terry's only collaborative creation with the Open Theatre, although that group produced seven of her other plays. Her formal connection with the Open Theatre lasted until 1968, after which she went on to help found the New York Theatre Strategy and the Women's Theatre Council, both in 1971. Meanwhile, Terry continued to experiment with the role-shaping transformations that had become an integral part of her work, and her plays were given productions both on the stage and on television. The most important work of Terry's late New York period would prove to be *Approaching Simone* (1970), which is still one of Terry's best-known plays.

Throughout her career, Terry has stressed repeatedly the need for strong role models for women. *Approaching Simone* is a dramatized biography of French philosopher, theologian, and mystic Simone Weil, whose life ended tragically when at thirty-four she committed suicide by starvation. Terry portrays the gradual development of Weil's political and theological beliefs—from Judaism through socialism and communism and finally to Catholicism—by creating a series of evolving supporting roles against which the character of Weil remains fundamentally a woman seeking ways to continue being a strong and responsible citizen of the world. *Approaching Simone* premiered in Boston before moving to New York, where it was honored with the Obie Award for Best New Play of 1969-1970. For Megan Terry, the production of the play set in motion the next phase of her career. Playing the role of Simone was a young actress named Jo Ann Schmidman, who had already—in 1968, before she came east to study for a B.F.A. at Boston University—founded the Omaha Magic Theatre in Nebraska. Schmidman's performance in *Approaching Simone* earned for her a place with the Open Theatre, with which Megan Terry was still loosely connected, and the two future collaborators briefly became Open Theatre colleagues.

Since 1974, Megan Terry has lived and worked in Omaha, Nebraska. Several circumstances impelled her to move away from New York: The Open Theatre had disbanded in 1973; she was being blacklisted by Actors' Equity for withdrawing *Hothouse* from a showcase production; and, most important, she wanted to work with

Jo Ann Schmidman and the Omaha Magic Theatre. As playwright-in-residence at the Magic Theatre, Terry has been productive and innovative, continuing her work with transformational drama and moving into new thematic territory.

Babes in the Bighouse (1974) has been one of Terry's most popular Magic Theatre plays, with its combination of documentary with musical theater and cross-gender casting to explore the lives of women in prisons and reformatories. Other plays treat equally disturbing subjects: sexism in language, domestic violence, and teenage alcoholism, among others.

Another item on Terry's creative agenda at the Magic Theatre is the creation of plays that address society's need for appropriate female role models. *Mollie Bailey's Traveling Family Circus: Featuring Scenes from the Life of Mother Jones* (1983) has received critical acclaim for its juxtaposition of the imaginary Mollie Bailey, a nineteenth century housewife and the center of a traveling "family" circus, and the historical Mother Jones, a political activist from the same century.

Summary

Megan Terry's dramatic achievement is unique in the American theater. In her three decades as a playwright, she has produced a body of work that can be read as a history of American drama in the second half of the twentieth century. Her plays range from the realism of her Seattle period to the avant-garde experimentation of her New York plays; she has created ensemble pieces, naturalistic drama, performance art, musical theater, and transformational drama. Although she developed her transformational techniques out of the need to discover a theater that was relevant to the concerns of a 1960's audience, her experiments in theatrical image-making and the use of language have proved valid even for audiences in the closing years of the twentieth century.

Terry's continuing commitment to social change through the agency of a strong people's theater is responsible for two forms of drama into which she puts a great deal of creative energy: role model plays and public service community dramas. Critic Helen Keyssar has called Megan Terry the mother of feminist drama, a label that is particularly apt for the woman whose pioneering work in transformational drama is a major step toward breaking down gender stereotyping and freeing actors to play more varied roles. In her plays that highlight the activities and achievements of strong women characters, Terry not only provides American theater with excellent female roles but also gives audiences strong women with whom to identify. In her work with the Omaha Magic Theatre and its outreach programs, Terry is effecting social change by sparking dialogue about community concerns and political issues.

Bibliography

Betsko, Kathleen, and Rachel Koenig, eds. *Interviews with Contemporary Women Playwrights*. New York: Beech Tree Books, 1987. Includes an informative inter- view in which Terry discusses her creative process, influences on her work, women in theater, sources of her ideas, and the state of American theater. In addition, she reminisces about her work with the Open Theatre and the Omaha Magic Theatre as well as with a number of America's most significant contemporary playwrights.

Fenn, Jeffery W. *Levitating the Pentagon: Evolutions in the American Theatre of the Vietnam War Era*. Newark: University of Delaware Press, 1992. Contains an excellent analysis of Megan Terry's *Viet Rock* as transformational drama and as political commentary. Fenn studies the play in the contexts of both the experimental theater of the 1960's and the earliest American plays that focused on the Vietnam War.

Hart, Lynda, ed. *Making a Spectacle: Feminist Essays on Contemporary Women's Theatre*. Ann Arbor: University of Michigan Press, 1989. A wide-ranging collection of essays that includes Jan Breslauer's and Helen Keyssar's "Making Magic Public: Megan Terry's Traveling Family Circus," an analysis of Megan Terry's *Mollie Bailey's Traveling Family Circus: Featuring Scenes from the Life of Mother Jones* as new feminist drama. The other essays are equally valuable in that they provide a theatrical context for Terry's work and ideas.

Savran, David. *In Their Own Words: Contemporary American Playwrights*. New York: Theatre Communications Group, 1988. Features an in-depth interview with Megan Terry in which she describes the plays that have influenced her work and the emotions that lead to ideas for plays. She discusses specific plays and the genesis of each one, and she identifies her favorites among her plays. The interview closes with her speculations on the future of the American theater and her work with the Omaha Magic Theatre.

Schlueter, June. "*Keep Tightly Closed in a Cool Dry Place:* Megan Terry's Transformational Drama and the Possibilities of Self." *Studies in American Drama, 1945-Present* 2 (1987): 59-69. A lucid and interesting treatment of one of Megan Terry's more significant transformational dramas as an example of the Open Theatre's contribution to redefining the creation of dramatic character. Schlueter points out that *Keep Tightly Closed in a Cool Dry Place* is a work that strongly represents Terry's transformational experimentation and its impact on the definition of self in American drama.

E. D. Huntley

TWYLA THARP

Born: July 1, 1941; Portland, Indiana

Area of Achievement: Dance

Contribution: An important choreographer in the field of modern dance, Tharp established an individualistic style that was unique in its combination of various dance and musical genres. Her commercial work included film and Broadway performances as well as the work of her company.

Early Life

Twyla Tharp was one of five children born to Lecile and William Tharp in rural Portland, Indiana. Lecile was so convinced of her daughter's eventual theatrical fame that she named her "Twila" for a local Muncie Fair Pig Princess and changed the "i" to "y" for greater marquee appeal. After the death of her infant brother when she was eighteen months old, Twyla began piano studies with her mother. Soon, the arrival of twin boys and a younger daughter forced Lecile Tharp to send Twyla to a private piano teacher, and by the age of seven she was winning local and state competitions.

Suddenly, in 1949, the eight-year-old Tharp was moved across the country to the California desert town of Rialto, where the family had built a drive-in theater. Tharp credits this unexpected and unsettling move with engendering in her a restlessness that led to her future attempt to understand life through motion. This move also launched her into a hectic schedule of diverse lessons that her mother believed would lead to her inevitable success. Twyla Tharp worked at the drive-in, did homework to maintain her straight-A average, and was shuttled around the Los Angeles area to ballet, tap, baton, and violin classes.

By the time Twyla was graduated from high school in 1958, she had discovered not only her love of dance but also her physical incompatibility with the demands of classical ballet. Her attendance at Pomona College was interrupted by her focus on further and more demanding dance studies. This interest led to her attendance at New York's Barnard College, where she soon became disgusted with the lack of sophistication of the dance department. Luckily, she was allowed to develop her own curriculum, using all the resources of New York City as her classroom. She began to question what was "pretty" and to experience the liberation that came from allowing the body to determine its own momentum and shapes.

Life's Work

In 1962, Twyla Tharp pursued her degree in art history while spending most of her time studying dance with some of the most highly skilled and innovative choreographers of modern dance, including Martha Graham and Merce Cunningham. She also continued to study ballet, tap, and jazz, which would become essential to the amalgamation of styles for which she would later become famous. When once asked why she did not study dance in college, she replied that she saw no place for a true dancer at that time. The only job opportunities were on Broadway, in film, in television, and in classical ballet. Her interests were larger—in an arena that she soon learned she would have to create for herself.

Tharp's first and only job with a dance company other than her own came in 1963 with the Paul Taylor Company. Taylor, a former Graham dancer, left Graham's company to focus on dances that dealt with reality and truth rather than the mythology and archetypal themes for which the Graham company was known. Tharp's first professional role was a crab-like crawl across the state in *Scudorama* (1963). As Taylor entered a new creative phase that utilized costumes, however, Tharp again felt that she had been thrust into a world of artificiality. She left to pursue her own work.

Her first dance, *Tank Dive* (1965), premiered in a room at Hunter College and lasted all of seven minutes. What Tharp had hoped would make the dance world sit up and take notice went by without a word in the press. This situation lasted for five years, and Tharp credits her early obscurity with giving her the time to develop a style according to her own rules independent of public opinion.

During these early years, she developed a performing group that stayed with her on and off for the next twenty years. All of her early works were based on the skills, eccentricities, and personalities of these dancers. In the early 1960's, it was thought that all art should be for the "people" and that virtuoso performances were elitist and pretentious. Tharp upset and challenged this idea at every turn and put her dancers through astoundingly difficult physical moves. Her first dance to receive much critical attention was *Re-Moves* (1966). Tharp is quoted as saying that she never heard of anyone loving it, but at least it caught their interest. Clive Barnes of *The New York Times* wrote that her choreography was "bad in a rather interesting way." The company believed that they had not embarrassed themselves and were encouraged to continue. In these early pieces, Tharp used no music: She wanted to see how far the body could move and how far she could stretch the limits of dance. Music, she believed, set up structure and emotion, and she wanted to explore pure bodily movement. After 1966, Tharp began to build a performing repertoire. She also married artist Bob Huot.

Tharp soon found herself at odds with the avant-garde art world because of her desire to provide a living wage for her seven dancers. At a time when most dancers lived on unemployment to pay for their lessons, Tharp's company became the first to be paid fifty-two weeks a year. It was common for professional dancers, even with the hugely successful ballet companies, to work only a few months a year and rehearse and be on unemployment for the rest of the time. In order to achieve her financial goal, it was necessary for Tharp to supplement the company's original work with commercial jobs: films, television, ballets, commercials, Broadway shows, and self-produced seasons. This commercial work was considered reason enough for the dance community to discredit her as a serious artist.

In 1969, Tharp had more critical success but still little security or money. She began creating dances to incorporate the audience's real world, and two products of this period, *Medley* and *Dancing in the Streets of London and Paris* (both 1969), were designed to be performed outdoors on public streets. Tharp had recently decided to attempt to attract an audience that dance had traditionally been missing, and to make this new dance relate to their everyday lives. In order to demystify the dance world, she would both teach audience members to dance with the company and also complete some choreography in a public forum.

Newly pregnant with her son Jesse, Tharp moved to upstate New York and began to work on new pieces. After Jesse's birth in 1971, Tharp's dances took on a new dimension when she decided to add music. She had rediscovered the music of two 1920's jazz artists, pianist Jelly Roll Morton and trumpeter Bix Beiderbecke, and she created *Eight Jelly Rolls* and *The Bix Pieces* in 1971, utilizing their work. Outstanding for their humor, difficult dancing, and joy, these pieces would become staples in Tharp's company for years to come.

Tharp's next great opportunity came when Robert Joffrey of the Joffrey Ballet commissioned her to create a work for his company in 1973. It was the first time a modern dancer had worked with a ballet company. The work was set to the music of the Beach Boys and was called *Deuce Coupe*. Tharp broke new creative ground, and the piece was an immediate success.

In 1976, the directors of the American Ballet Theatre (ABT) approached Twyla Tharp to commission an original work for a dancer who had recently defected from the Soviet Union: Mikhail Baryshnikov. Tharp approached this assignment with uncharacteristic timidity; Baryshnikov was the current wunderkind of ballet, and he spoke very little English. *Push Comes to Shove* (1976), the result of the two artists' collaboration, made Tharp famous.

Among the commercial jobs that Tharp has taken for the money as well as for the learning experience have been choreographing and performing in the film *Hair* (1978), creating choreography for the Olympics (1976 and 1980), and directing and choreographing a Broadway adaptation of *Singin' in the Rain* (1985). Responses to these ventures have ranged from dismay to outright ridicule, but through it all, Tharp has maintained her desire to try new ventures.

Tharp disbanded her dance company in 1988, citing an overwhelming schedule that was reducing her ability to produce pure dance. After working briefly with ABT, she continued to produce and develop new work.

Summary

Twyla Tharp's impact on the field of dance has been profound. Her presence has been felt in several areas: feminism, jazz, respect for dance as an art, and audience accessibility.

Tharp has been quoted as saying that dance is the "stepchild of the arts" and that modern dance has been relegated to a position even below that of ballet. One reason that women have succeeded as modern dance choreographers, in Tharp's opinion, is that there has been nothing for anyone to gain by holding them down.

Tharp's company eventually broke many barriers. Most noteworthy was the fact that hers was the first company to pay dancers on a fifty-two-week schedule instead of paying for rehearsals and performances only.

It was important to Tharp not only to give modern dance respectability but also to take it out of the elitist position it occupied and make it entertaining for ordinary people. Tharp was able to lure young people into the theater again by using popular culture, rock and roll scores, and current social themes.

Her choreography often evolved from a desire to shatter gender stereotypes. Her company was primarily female until 1973, and this choice was responsible for her use of unisex couples and females as lift partners.

Tharp's reintroduction of classic jazz music into the popular cultural scene was another valuable contribution. Until her production of *Ten Jelly Rolls* in 1971, only jazz fans knew of the masterly pianist Jelly Roll Morton. Her *Bix Pieces* (1971) and *Sue's Leg* (1975) likewise introduced general audiences to the work of Bix Beiderbecke and Fats Waller.

Twyla Tharp has not only expanded boundaries for women dancers and choreographers but also has opened the doors of the dance hall for new music, popular culture, and the average audience member.

Bibliography
Croce, Arlene. "Guest in the House (Twyla Tharp and Jerome Robbins)." *The New Yorker* 60 (July 2, 1984): 79-81. An article discussing the influence, collaboration, and friendship of Tharp and Broadway/ballet choreographer Jerome Robbins.
"The Pioneers (Merce Cunningham and Twyla Tharp)." *Theatre Crafts* 17 (October, 1983): 27-29. An article discussing the influences on and by Tharp and Merce Cunningham in the field of modern dance. Generally, *Theatre Crafts* is not known for its dance-related articles. It is usually devoted to technical achievements and designers in the areas of lighting, stage, and costume design.
Tharp, Twyla. *Push Comes to Shove*. New York: Bantam Books, 1992. In her honest and plainly written autobiography, Tharp does not stint on revelatory material, but she does not dwell on the emotional and personal part of her life. She stresses dance and her evolving career. Contains a detailed chronology of her works and a list of dancers in the company.
Vaughan, David. "Twyla Tharp: Launching a New American Classicism." *Dance Magazine* 58 (May, 1984): 54-58. An informative article on Tharp's style and influence on American dance. *Dance Magazine* is an unusually good print resource on dance of all styles.

Laurie Dawson

MARTHA CAREY THOMAS

Born: January 2, 1857; Baltimore, Maryland
Died: December 2, 1935; Philadelphia, Pennsylvania
Areas of Achievement: Education and women's rights
Contribution: As dean and president of Bryn Mawr College, Thomas helped to build an institution dedicated to providing nineteenth century women with an education equal to that available in the best men's colleges.

Early Life

Martha Carey Thomas was born on January 2, 1857, the eldest of ten children of James Carey Thomas, a successful physician, and Mary Whitall Thomas. Both parents came from distinguished Quaker families and were well known for piety and philanthropy. Minnie, as she was called as a child, grew up in a home that combined Quaker suspicion of materialism with a substantial lifestyle—a large town house, servants, and a country house for summer.

Minnie's childhood was marred by a nearly fatal accident. At the age of seven, she set herself on fire while playing cook, severely burning her torso and thighs. Expected to die, she suffered two years of pain while recovering. The accident left her with considerable scars and a noticeable limp.

Surrounded by books, she read widely and dreamed of a college education. Despite the opposition of her father, who doubted the value of higher education for women, she was determined to go to college and become a doctor. In 1872, with her father's consent, she entered the Howland Institute, a Quaker boarding school for girls near Ithaca, New York. She took the classical course, which was equivalent to the first two years of college, and shifted her ambitions from medicine to scholarship. It took a year-long campaign, with strong support from her mother, before her father agreed to let her continue her education at Cornell University.

Carey, as she now insisted on being called, completed her B.A. degree in two years, but that did not satisfy her. In 1877, she was admitted to graduate study in linguistics at newly opened The Johns Hopkins University in Baltimore. She was not permitted to attend classes that were open to male students, however, and she found it difficult to focus on her work in such isolation. Her emotional problems were intensified by religious doubts that provoked stormy scenes at home, and by a love affair that she deliberately broke off, believing that combining marriage and scholarship was impossible for a woman.

With the Johns Hopkins experiment a failure, Carey and her mother wore down her father's resistance until he finally agreed that she could go to Germany to study. In 1879, she enrolled in Leipzig for graduate work in linguistics. German universities permitted women to attend all classes and seminars but would not grant them degrees. Therefore, in 1882, she went to the University of Zurich, Switzerland. She passed a three-day written exam and defended her dissertation so effectively in a three-hour oral examination conducted in German that the faculty awarded her a doctorate summa cum laude. She was the first foreigner and the first woman to achieve such a distinguished rating.

Life's Work

While Martha Carey Thomas was earning her degree in Europe, a unique opportunity opened for her in America. In 1880, Joseph Wright Taylor had bequeathed funds to build a college for women under orthodox Quaker auspices at Bryn Mawr, Pennsylvania. Carey Thomas' father, an uncle, and two cousins were among the members of the board of trustees named in Taylor's will. It was an extraordinary coincidence that a Quaker college for women was about to open just as a brilliant, determined feminist Quaker woman returned from Europe certified as an outstanding scholar. She was determined to make the most of it: In 1883, after her triumph in Zurich, she wrote proposing herself as ideally qualified to be the president of a women's college dedicated to the highest standards of scholarship. The board was impressed by her letter, but not convinced. They appointed James E. Rhoads as first president and offered Thomas the position of dean and professor of English.

Many of the principles Thomas had proposed were put into practice at Bryn Mawr. To ensure that the college would start out at a high level, the entrance requirements were the same as those at Harvard and the curriculum was modeled on that of The Johns Hopkins University. Unique among women's colleges, Bryn Mawr included graduate instruction from the beginning. Faculty members were chosen with the understanding that they would be active in research and scholarship; fellowships and travel grants would attract and support outstanding students. Despite Bryn Mawr's small size and limited resources, Thomas intended to prove that a woman's college could match the quality of the best men's colleges and turn out graduates capable of competing with men on an equal basis.

Bryn Mawr opened in 1885 with thirty-six undergraduates and seven graduate students (four of whom had fellowships). In a faculty of seven men and two women, only Woodrow Wilson, the future president of the United States, did not yet have a doctorate. The college attracted ambitious young men to its faculty but could not keep them; by 1898, all the original men had left.

As President Rhoads's energy declined, Thomas took on more administrative duties. When Rhoads requested retirement in 1892, Thomas was in effect acting president during the two years in which the board of trustees debated her requests to succeed him. Her forceful personality had alienated several trustees, but more important was their concern that the college was becoming less and less a Quaker institution because Thomas insisted that intellectual distinction outweighed sectarian affiliation. Not until lengthy discussions brought agreement on policy, and after strong interventions by feminist friends and her father, was she elected, and then only by a one-vote majority.

Thomas was more notable as an administrator than as a scholar or teacher. Although she insisted on high standards for her faculty, she herself engaged in no further scholarly work and stopped teaching soon after 1894. Her writing was devoted to advancing and defending the cause of women's education. Typical of her position was her reply to the remarks of Harvard president Charles William Eliot at the inauguration of Wellesley College's new president in 1899. She resented Eliot's charge "that women's colleges simply imitated men when they used the same educational methods instead of inventing new ones of their own." No sooner had women proved their ability to match male intellectual performance than they were told that this accomplishment was not enough. "He might as well have told the president of Wellesley to invent a new Christian religion for Wellesley or new symphonies or operas," she responded. "It would be easier to do all this than to create for women a new science of geography, new Greek Tragedies, new Chemistry, new philosophies, in short, a new intellectual heaven and earth."

In 1885, Thomas helped to found the Bryn Mawr School for Girls in Baltimore to ensure the availability of rigorous college preparation. In 1889, she organized a campaign that forced The Johns Hopkins University Medical School to admit women on an equal basis with men. Until the trustees agreed that there would be no discrimination against women, her wealthy women friends withheld substantial gifts to the endowment, without which the school could not have opened.

Thomas' view of the intellectual capacity of women was egalitarian; the operation of her college, however, was seriously affected by her acceptance of the dominant racist ideas of her day. Black students were discouraged, Jewish students irritated her, and Jewish faculty found advancement difficult. Thomas' hereditarian views on race contrasted sharply with her environmentalist attitudes toward sex differences— she believed that social limitations, not biological inferiority, prevented female accomplishment.

Thomas never married, but she developed close relationships with her women friends. After retiring in 1922, she traveled restlessly around the world for most of the decade before returning to Philadelphia during the Depression. She lived to speak at the fiftieth anniversary celebration at Bryn Mawr in 1935, earning a standing ovation from those who remembered her and from younger women to whom she was already a mythical figure. One month later, shortly before her seventy-ninth birthday, she died of a heart attack.

Summary

At all times, Martha Carey Thomas was an ardent feminist. As a leader in the field of higher education for women, she demonstrated how much a woman could accomplish despite existing social obstacles. Her greatest achievement was at Bryn Mawr, where she built an institution that opened scholarly opportunities for many women.

Her feminism was not limited to her work at Bryn Mawr. Once the college was solidly established, she turned her attention from women's education to the suffrage movement. In 1906, she became an active leader of the College Equal Suffrage Association, speaking frequently and fervently across the country. In 1908, she became the first president of the National College Women's Equal Suffrage League. Commencing in 1910, she undertook various leadership positions in the National-

American Woman Suffrage Association (NAWSA). Even after the passage of the Nineteenth Amendment, which secured the vote for women, Thomas kept up her interest in feminism. Unlike most of her friends, who joined the League of Women Voters, she preferred the more radical National Woman's Party, which began a campaign for an Equal Rights Amendment to the Constitution.

Thomas devoted her life to feminist causes. First as an example of what a woman could achieve in a scholarly field previously limited to men, despite male skepticism and resistance, then as a builder of a first-rate college and graduate school run by a woman for women, and finally as an eloquent leader of the woman suffrage movement, she acted effectively to advance the status of American women.

Bibliography

Cross, Barbara M., ed. *The Educated Woman in America: Selected Writings of Catharine Beecher, Margaret Fuller, and M. Carey Thomas.* New York: Teachers College Press, 1965. A brilliant introduction puts Thomas in the context of the evolution of women's education in the nineteenth century and illuminates the selections from her most important articles and lectures.

Finch, Edith. *Carey Thomas of Bryn Mawr.* New York: Harper, 1947. This authorized biography, based on manuscript sources, is outstanding in its presentation of Thomas' family situation and the problems she faced in achieving a scholarly education and career.

Frankfort, Roberta. *Collegiate Women: Domesticity and Career in Turn-of-the-Century America.* New York: New York University Press, 1977. Focuses on Wellesley and Bryn Mawr, arguing that the colleges grew more like each other in the early 1900's, preparing for the domestic roles of women while still stressing scholarly achievement.

Horowitz, Helen Lefkowitz. *Alma Mater: Design and Experience in the Women's Colleges from Their Nineteenth-Century Beginnings to the 1930s.* New York: Alfred A. Knopf, 1984. Studies the architecture and landscapes of women's colleges and provides penetrating insights into both the ideals and the actual life of students and teachers. Thomas' Bryn Mawr is a major example.

_____ . *The Power and Passion of M. Carey Thomas.* New York: Alfred A. Knopf, 1994. Horowitz's biography analyzes Thomas from a feminist perspective and demonstrates her capabilities as an educational leader on par with male figures such as Harvard's Charles William Eliot and the University of Chicago's William Rainey Harper. Horowitz also examines Thomas' personal life and provides insights into her lesbian relationships with several women.

Kendall, Elaine. *"Peculiar Institutions": An Informal History of the Seven Sister Colleges.* New York: G. P. Putnam's Sons, 1976. An anecdotal history that focuses more on personalities than on ideas. The author explores the ways in which academic life and customs developed as the colleges evolved.

Meigs, Cornelia. *What Makes a College? A History of Bryn Mawr.* New York: Macmillan, 1956. Covering the terms of the first four presidents of Bryn Mawr, this detailed history shows how powerfully and effectively Thomas molded Bryn Mawr to match her ideal world of women scholars.

Woloch, Nancy. *Women and the American Experience*. New York: Alfred A. Knopf, 1984. Puts Thomas and Bryn Mawr into the context of the movement of women into the professions and their involvement in the crusades of the Progressive Era.

Milton Berman

DOROTHY THOMPSON

Born: July 9, 1893; Lancaster, New York
Died: January 30, 1961; Lisbon, Portugal
Area of Achievement: Journalism
Contribution: Thompson was one of the first female political columnists. Her fiery interpretations of world events kept the masses informed.

Early Life

Not allowed to drink, dance, play cards, or go to the theater, Dorothy Thompson, born on July 9, 1893, found other ways to amuse herself. This intelligent, imaginative, Methodist minister's daughter loved to daydream about exploring foreign countries. She also loved to read. Her punishment for misbehaving was often memorizing literature. She knew many of the classics by heart.

Peter Thompson and Margaret Grierson Thompson's oldest child began life in Lancaster, New York. She grew up in many small New York cities and in Chicago, Illinois. Ministers and their families moved to a new parish every few years.

Life was busy, but Thompson's father always found time to play with his three children. She described him as a saintly man who loved to read and garden, two affections they shared. Thompson adored him.

Two tragedies marred Thompson's childhood: her mother's death and her father's remarriage. She disliked her stepmother, who, according to Thompson, seemed to be allergic to children. Thompson became unruly and was sent to Chicago when she was fourteen to live with an aunt.

Her aunt boosted her self-confidence and enrolled her in the Lewis Institute, a school noted for its academic excellence. She proved herself to a demanding English teacher, Dr. Edwin Herbert Lewis, who spurred her by saying she would only be good in the kitchen. After she was graduated from the Lewis Institute, she attended Syracuse Methodist University, where she monopolized conversations and worked for the Syracuse Equal Suffrage Club. When she was graduated in 1914, she knew she wanted to be a writer. She found a job giving speeches and raising money at the woman suffrage headquarters in Buffalo, New York.

Life's Work

Dorothy Thompson's public speaking paid off in 1917, when New York State legislators took up one of her causes and passed the Nineteenth Amendment, giving women the right to vote. Although the amendment was not ratified until 1920, Thompson's work at suffrage headquarters was finished.

She and a friend went to New York City to become journalists. She got a low-level job in the *New York Evening Post* city room, but she soon left. After she left another dreary job, as a Bible publishing society publicist, she was hired as publicity director for an organization that helped the poor in urban areas.

She still wanted to travel and write. She and a friend convinced the *New York*

Evening Post to consider any European stories they wrote. With that promise of income and $500 between them, they sailed to Europe in 1920.

Thompson visited Ireland to find relatives. Instead, she interviewed Irish independence leader Terence MacSwiney, Lord Mayor of Cork, before he started his fatal hunger strike. She returned to London, and the International News Service (INS) bought her stories. INS did not give her a job, but it made her a correspondent—a valuable thing, since it gave her press credentials. She headed for Paris.

To earn money, Thompson took an American Red Cross publicity job. She wrote press releases for one cent a line, making her margins wide enough to get thirty lines to a page. After she covered a labor strike in Italy, INS sent her to Austria for a month to cover the chaos there. The situation was bleak. After World War I, the defeated country was no longer the economically stable area it had been under Habsburg rule. Those who lived near Vienna were hungry and unemployed. The League of Nations bickered over what to do.

In 1921, the *Philadelphia Public Ledger* hired Thompson as its Austrian correspondent. She continued working for the Red Cross, publicizing its relief program based in Budapest, a four-hour commute from Vienna. Through her Red Cross work, Thompson met Marcel Fodor, a Hungarian-born correspondent for the *Manchester Guardian*. He became her mentor.

Soon Thompson was covering not only Austria and Hungary but also Czechoslovakia, Yugoslavia, Albania, Romania, Bulgaria, Greece, and Turkey. She always seemed to be where the news was, thanks to a growing number of influential friends and keen news judgment.

In the fall of 1921, she and Fodor pulled off a worldwide scoop. King Charles, the former Habsburg ruler, had tried for a second time to regain the Hungarian throne. The plot failed, and the king and his wife were held captive. No interviews were granted. Thompson dressed up as a Red Cross nurse and Fodor donned a Red Cross badge. They insisted that they had to make sure the captives were safe. They were admitted and got the only interviews.

Thompson was finding the career success she sought, but she also wanted a personal life. She had many friends, but no one special. Josef Bard, a Hungarian Jew who had a law degree but sought a literary career, changed that. They were married in 1922.

In 1925, Thompson was named Central European bureau chief for the *Philadelphia Public Ledger* and the *New York Evening Post*—tying the *Chicago Tribune*'s Sigrid Shultz for the honor of becoming the first woman to head a major American bureau in Europe. It was still a volatile time, though American loans for rebuilding had become available. Adolf Hitler was implementing the early stages of his plan to make Germany a superpower. He persuaded thousands of unemployed men to follow him.

Thompson's career flourished, but her marriage died. Bard disliked Berlin and coming in second to his wife's work. They were divorced in 1927. She was not single for long. Thompson met the famous novelist Sinclair Lewis and married him in 1928. Determined to make the marriage work, she quit her job and returned to the United

States. She and Lewis bought a farm in Vermont and settled down. Their son, Michael, was born in 1930. Thompson was not happy. She had no patience for small children, and Lewis was an alcoholic who did not satisfy her social needs. She was lonely and longed for dinner parties and the opera. She also wanted to be more than merely the wife of a famous novelist. The excitement of world crisis looked inviting.

Leaving her baby with nurses, she spent the next two years traveling to and from Europe, reporting on world events. Hitler was becoming more powerful, mobilizing a private army that outnumbered the German government's forces and promising work and bread for all. Thompson interviewed Hitler in 1931 for *Cosmopolitan* magazine. Germany's future dictator did not impress Thompson. In fact, she found it hard to believe the German people would support him. Hitler became chancellor of Germany in 1933. Thompson was expelled from Germany in 1934.

Missing her son, Thompson had moved him to Vienna in August of 1932. Another marriage had gone sour, but again she was doing well professionally. Helen Reid, wife of *New York Herald Tribune* publisher Ogden Reid, asked Thompson to write a political column. She liked the idea, and "On the Record," her three-times-a-week column, began publication on March 17, 1936 The column attracted both men and women. Businessmen liked her cautious economic views. Anti-facists and Jews liked her anti-Nazi views. Besides world politics, she covered domestic events. She went to Washington, D.C., to examine the New Deal proposed by Franklin Delano Roosevelt. She disliked it and supported his first presidential challenger, Alf Landon. After a year, her column was carried in more than 130 newspapers. She also gave speeches, began a domestic issues column for the *Ladies' Home Journal*, and, in 1937, started a radio broadcast.

In 1938 Hitler took Austria. Britain and France signed the Munich Pact instead of stopping Hitler. In 1939, Hitler and Russian leader Joseph Stalin signed a pact and took Poland apart. Thompson's columns and broadcasts became relentless pleas to an unwilling United States to get involved and stop the madness. She refused to let Americans forget what was happening in Europe.

At home, Roosevelt was up for election for a third time. She supported his opponent, Wendell Wilkie, until a trip to Italy in 1940 convinced her it would be detrimental to remove Roosevelt. The Europeans saw him as their only hope, especially since Wilkie was supported by those who refused to get involved in the war.

Thompson changed her endorsement on October 9, 1940, and supported Roosevelt. On October 14, she wrote another column supporting him, but the publisher, a staunch Republican, pulled it. Her contract was not renewed in March of 1941.

She signed a contract with the Bell Syndicate, and the *New York Post* became her New York outlet. She continued to have many readers, but she lost the *Chicago Tribune*'s conservative audience, with whom she loved to argue.

America entered World War II on December 7, 1941. She assured her readers that the war was for a good cause. Thompson's influence was at its peak. Everyone wanted to hear her. President Roosevelt welcomed her views of world politics. Her name was a household word.

In the same way that Thompson disliked being known only as a great novelist's wife, Lewis, his new novels not doing well, resented being overshadowed. They were divorced on January 2, 1942. By fall, she found a new love—her last and best. She married Maxim Kopf, an Austrian artist, on June 16, 1943.

In April of 1945, she and Kopf flew to Europe to witness the final days of World War II. Thompson lost the topic that had appeared in the majority of her columns. She found new battles, but they found less favor with her readers. She disagreed with the Allied demand for Germany's unconditional surrender. She argued that there were many Germans who did not support Hitler and that they were victims. She eventually lost her Jewish audience when she wrote in support of the Arabs, arguing against the Jews' takeover of Palestine.

Thompson continued her *Ladies' Home Journal* column, but her last syndicated political column was published on August 22, 1958. The last years of her life were spent working on an autobiography that she never finished and doting on her two grandsons. She spent Christmas with her daughter-in-law and grandsons in Lisbon, Portugal, in 1960. She died there on January 30, 1961, of a heart attack.

Summary

Dorothy Thompson's life was full of drama and intrigue—exploring Europe, constantly moving, finally finding personal happiness after divorcing two husbands, meeting famous people, having her opinion sought by millions, and having audiences with world leaders. She had an illustrious professional life.

She believed that it was her mission to make sure that Americans were not kept in the dark about events leading up to and during World War II. Although other political writers were concerned about the approaching war, none kept pressing the point as vehemently as she did. Three-fifths of her columns from 1933 to 1940 attacked the Hitler regime.

She spoke for those who could not, such as the Jews of Hitler's Germany. She urged others to do the same. Her controversial columns were written with honesty and emotional conviction. A critic of a collection of her columns entitled *Let the Record Speak* (1939) said it should have been called *Let the Record Roar*.

She made a name for herself at a time when women were still identified by who their husbands were. She also made advances for women in journalism, becoming a foreign correspondent and tying for the honor of becoming the first female to head a European news bureau.

Dorothy Thompson broke ground in political column writing, an area monopolized by men. The editors of the Bell Syndicate wrote in a commentary accompanying her last column that her comments reached more people than did any other at that time on serious political issues. She was a good reporter but disliked reporting. She preferred her column work, in which she could concentrate on ideas and the search for justice.

Bibliography

Belford, Barbara. *Brilliant Bylines: A Biographical Anthology of Notable Newspaper-*

women in America. New York: Columbia University Press, 1986. An excellent condensed biography. Includes one of Thompson's columns.

Edwards, Julia. *Women of the World: The Great Foreign Correspondents*. Boston: Houghton Mifflin, 1988. A good condensed biography written by a woman who was a foreign correspondent.

Sanders, Marion K. *Dorothy Thompson: A Legend in Her Time*. Boston: Houghton Mifflin, 1973. A comprehensive look at Thompson's life, including some of her journal entries and comments from those who knew her. The book is confusing at times, using too many names, bouncing back and forth between dates, and failing to translate some of Thompson's journal entries that are written in French.

Thompson, Dorothy. *The Courage to be Happy*. Boston: Houghton Mifflin, 1957. A collection of Thompson's lighter columns, written for the *Ladies' Home Journal*.

——————. *I Saw Hitler!* New York: Farrar & Rinehart, 1932. Thompson's interview with Adolf Hitler and some background information about the man.

——————. *Let the Record Speak*. Boston: Houghton Mifflin, 1939. A collection of Thompson's political columns.

Julie Foegen Frederick

LILY TOMLIN

Born: September 1, 1939; Detroit, Michigan

Areas of Achievement: Theater and drama and film
Contribution: An award-winning actress who has had success on television, in films, and in the theater, Tomlin is especially known for her portraits of eccentric but sympathetic characters.

Early Life

Mary Jean (Lily) Tomlin was born on September 1, 1939, in Detroit, Michigan, where her parents had moved from Kentucky during the Great Depression. Her father, Guy, worked as a toolmaker and her mother, Lillie Mae, was a homemaker. Four years after Lily's birth, her only sibling, Richard, was born.

The family lived in a low-income neighborhood, and although Lily's mother hoped that they might achieve a higher social status than that usually associated with immigrants from the rural South, her father disliked pretense and preferred gambling and drinking to other pursuits. Both parents, despite their disagreements about money and status, had strong-willed and independent natures. They were unconventional parents who gave considerable freedom to their children.

Lily did well in school, although she preferred observing classmates and teachers to pursuing her studies. Her interest in entertainment emerged through cheerleading when she entered high school. Lily also developed a reputation for free-spirited behavior and would amuse her friends with creative dramatic impressions. She combined popularity with a willingness to stand out from the crowd. After she was graduated from high school, Lily enrolled as a premedical student at Wayne State University in Detroit, but she began to tire of studying science and became increasingly interested in acting. While a sophomore, she appeared in a small part in a college production and then earned a larger part in another college play. Her dramatic performances won Lily praise from her instructors and peers, but she first showed signs of the precise direction that her career would take when she next appeared in a student variety show at Wayne State. Improvising, Lily appeared as a Tasteful Lady with exaggerated manners and obvious snobbishness. The audience greatly enjoyed this comic characterization, and Lily decided to pursue a career in the theater by leaving school and moving to New York City.

Life's Work

Her first stay in New York, in 1960, was brief because Lily Tomlin could not find work as a performer; frustrated, she returned to Detroit after a few months and decided to pursue a theatrical career in that city. She took jobs as an office worker and began to develop comic and dramatic routines for local nightclubs and coffeehouses. Although she often performed material written by others, her flair for improvisation remained one of her most noteworthy attributes. Relying on her facial expressions, vocal inflections, and physical poses, Tomlin would create entire characters onstage and through them offer thoughtful and humorous comments about society.

Tomlin decided to return to New York City in 1964, and this time she successfully built a reputation as a talented comedian. Although she continued to work at odd jobs to support herself, she also performed steadily in nightclubs, and her character-based monologues became increasingly polished. Her repertoire of characters grew, with Ernestine, a wise-cracking telephone operator, joining the Tasteful Lady.

From 1966 to 1968, Tomlin expanded her career into television and the theater. She briefly appeared *The Garry Moore Show* and had small parts in *Below the Belt* and *Photo Finish*, both of which were theatrical musical comedy revues. A favorable review of her performance in the latter caught the attention of talk-show host Merv Griffin, who invited Tomlin to perform several times for his national television audience.

Then, in 1969, Tomlin earned two offers to appear as a regular on television shows; she accepted the first, joining the cast of *The Music Scene*, but it failed quickly, so she accepted the second, an invitation to join the cast of *Rowan and Martin's Laugh-In*, broadcast by NBC. The hour-long variety show featured short skits and comedy monologues, with guest stars joining a cast of regulars. Highly rated and an Emmy winner, the show brought Lily Tomlin to the attention of a huge and receptive audience.

She instantly won the audience's favor through her character portraits, with Ernestine, the telephone operator, leading the way. Ernestine's self-important posturing and snorting laugh quickly became familiar features of *Laugh-In*, as she "placed calls" to celebrities and public figures ranging from Frank Sinatra to then-President Richard Nixon. Television audiences laughed at Ernestine's side of the "conversation" as she offered advice and criticism to the various noteworthies.

Tomlin's second most popular character was Edith Ann, a messy five-year-old girl with a smug, confident manner. She deliberately portrayed Edith Ann as a forceful tomboy, in obvious contrast to the scrubbed prettiness and polite charm often associated with real-life child stars such as Shirley Temple. Edith Ann, like Ernestine, offered her opinions on a range of topics and embodied the ideal of an independent person—of any age—speaking freely and honestly.

Tomlin remained on *Laugh-In* until it left the air in 1973, but she also released two recorded collections of her monologues, *This Is a Recording* (1971) and *And That's the Truth* (1972), the latter named for Edith Ann's signature phrase. Both sold well, and the first won a Grammy as the Best Comedy Recording of 1971. Her recording success, combined with Tomlin's concern that her characters were overexposed on the weekly *Laugh-In* episodes, prepared her to develop new directions in her career when the show ended.

First, Tomlin appeared on CBS in 1973 in two television specials. Both *The Lily Tomlin Show* and *Lily* were designed to showcase her talents as a character-based comedian. In them, Tomlin offered audiences a stronger sampling of her own opinions and social perspectives than she had on *Laugh-In*. Some of her views, including a strong antiwar perspective, caused CBS censors to trim skits from the shows. Tomlin continued to include controversial materials related to topics such as drug abuse, and despite the worries of her network, *Lily* won two Emmy awards.

In 1975, Tomlin made two additional one-hour specials, both for ABC, released her third album, *Modern Scream*, and appeared in her first film role. The film, *Nashville*, was directed by Robert Altman and chronicled the lives of twenty-four different characters as they interacted through the country music industry and a fictional presidential campaign. Tomlin played Linnea, a wealthy, married suburbanite who sings with a black gospel group, is the mother of two deaf children, and is engaged in a tender affair with a folk-rock star. Her performance won glowing reviews and an Oscar nomination as best supporting actress.

This successful acting debut helped Tomlin move from television appearances to performances in the theater. In 1976, she did appear in an NBC pilot for a new series, *People*, modeled after the popular magazine and with Tomlin as the host. Its creator and executive producer was Jane Wagner, a writer whom Tomlin had met while working on *Laugh-In*. Wagner had become Tomlin's closest friend and writing collaborator. *People* did not win network approval, but with their next work, the partners were more successful. Wagner and Tomlin cowrote a one-woman play called *Appearing Nitely*, which featured Lily as fifteen different characters and opened on Broadway in 1977. The play enabled Tomlin, with Wagner's help, to expand her presentation of eccentric, thoughtful people, all of whom offered blunt but kind-hearted observations about life's injustices and little joys. It earned $2 million in that year, and Tomlin successfully revised and repeated it in the early 1980's.

Tomlin's film career also developed, although she experienced some setbacks after her success in *Nashville*. In 1977, she appeared in *The Late Show* with Art Carney and won strong praise from critics as a woman suddenly paired with an aging detective in the hunt for a murderer. *Moment by Moment* (1978), a romance featuring Tomlin and John Travolta and written and directed by Jane Wagner, failed miserably. In 1980, however, Tomlin bounced back in *Nine to Five*, a popular comedy with Jane Fonda and Dolly Parton. *The Incredible Shrinking Woman* (1981), written by Wagner, achieved modest success, and *All of Me* (1984), costarring Steve Martin, did even better. Although there was no single theme to Tomlin's characters in these films, essentially they were strong women who questioned, in various ways, the social stereotypes based on gender. Tomlin had always been strongly committed to femi-nism, and her choice of film parts reflected her values.

In the 1980's, Tomlin also appeared in several television specials, but her greatest success came in a one-woman play, *The Search for Signs of Intelligent Life in the Universe*, written by Jane Wagner. After testing pieces of the play in appearances around the country, Tomlin opened the show on Broadway in 1985. Critics applauded the show, and Tomlin won the 1986 Tony for Best Actress in a Play.

Like Tomlin and Wagner's earlier collaborations, the play featured gentle humor that emphasized the connections between people from all categories, classes, and backgrounds. Feminism informed the work, which suggested that all lines drawn to divide or control people are artificial and should be erased. Tomlin erased these lines herself by playing characters of all ages, both sexes, varying income levels, and different sexual orientations. Tomlin and Wagner took the play on a national tour in 1986 and 1987, and a film version, released in 1989, brought the play to an even larger audience. Wagner's script, published in book form, also made best-seller lists.

Tomlin continued her film career opposite Bette Midler in *Big Business* (1988) and as part of an ensemble cast in Robert Altman's *Short Cuts* (1993). Never casual about her choices of parts and projects, she moved away from television in the late 1980's and has been identified primarily as an actress, rather than a comedian, since the early 1980's.

Summary

Lily Tomlin's emphasis on character portraits throughout her performing career enabled her to broaden audiences' perceptions of women as entertainers and to challenge barriers between human beings. From her early improvisations in the 1960's and especially in her stage performances on Broadway, Lily Tomlin portrayed people of almost every type—poor and rich, old and young, male and female, straight and lesbian. She emphasized their shared fears, anger, and vulnerability.

Although Tomlin has consistently supported feminism, gay rights, and other public causes, her political messages have primarily taken form in her acting and humor. Through her work, Lily Tomlin has conveyed deep respect for the unique qualities of each human being and has portrayed the strong, steady efforts of individuals to add their voices to the human conversation.

Bibliography

Carr, C. "The Mirror Turned Lamp." *Art Forum* 25 (January, 1987): 80-85. This discussion of Tomlin's work in *The Search for Signs of Intelligent Life in the Universe* also examines her consistent use of characters throughout her career. Specific characters are described in detail, and the article includes discussion of Jane Wagner's work with Tomlin.

Dressner, Zita. "Whoopi Goldberg and Lily Tomlin: Black and White Women's Humor." In *Women's Comic Visions*, edited by June Sochen. Detroit: Wayne State University Press, 1991. This article analyzes the characters, language, and messages of Tomlin's monologues and plays, and compares them to Goldberg's work. It emphasizes Tomlin's ability to avoid attacking people with jokes and her efforts to convey humorous messages designed to connect people and emphasize the shared experiences of being human.

Dunne, Sara. "Women as Children in American Comedy: Baby Snooks' Daughters." *Journal of American Culture* 16, no. 2 (Summer, 1993): 31-35. Tomlin's famous character Edith Ann is carefully analyzed and placed in historical context as an example of a child character portrayed by a female comedian. The article also discusses Fanny Brice, Gilda Radner, and Whoopi Goldberg.

Phillips, Lynn. "All of Her." *American Film* 13 (May, 1988): 20-27. Tomlin's film career is described and reviewed, through her performance in *Big Business* in 1988. The article is accompanied by photographs of Tomlin in several of her films.

Sorensen, Jeff. *Lily Tomlin: Woman of a Thousand Faces*. New York: St. Martin's Press, 1989. This biography provides both information about Tomlin's life and extensive discussions of her performances and career. It does not list its sources, however, although many references in the text to reviews of Tomlin's work include critics' names. The book includes photographs.

Beth Kraig

SOJOURNER TRUTH

Born: c. 1797; Hurley, Ulster County, New York
Died: November 26, 1883, Battle Creek, Michigan
Area of Achievement: Social reform
Contribution: A featured speaker at abolitionist meetings before the Civil War, Truth worked initially to expose the immorality of the practice of slavery and later to ensure to welfare of emancipated African Americans.

Early Life

Sojourner Truth, originally Isabella Baumfree, was born into slavery in Hurley, Ulster County, New York, around 1797. Her parents were slaves owned by Colonel Johannes Hardenbergh, a prosperous farmer of Dutch descent. Her father, James, a tall man said to be "straight as a tree" (for which he received the Dutch surname of "Baumfree"), was of African and possibly American Indian descent. Her mother, Betsey, also known as "Mau Mau Bett," was of African lineage; through family and biblical stories, she instilled in Isabella and her ten siblings the value of family and spirituality. She assured Isabella she could always talk to God when there was no one else to turn to. Formal education was not available, but Isabella developed a self-reliance and strength in her young years that would preserve her through severe testing and make her work in social reform possible. Her childhood also provided the background from which the vivid and memorable anecdotes used in her lectures would later spring.

Isabella herself was sold at the age of nine. Although she was a diligent worker, she was beaten for her inability to communicate with her owners, the Neelys (Isabella spoke a Dutch dialect). Next, she was sold to the Schryvers, who owned a tavern. During her time with the Schryvers, her mother died, and her father soon followed. Eventually, Isabella was sold to the Dumonts, where she worked part-time as a field hand and helped in the kitchen. At this time, Isabella's greatest wish was to please; sometimes, she would stay up half the night working to gain favor with her master.

When grown, Isabella fell in love with Robert, a slave from a neighboring farm, but they were forbidden to marry because Robert's master disapproved of the match. After the couple continued to met secretly, Robert was severely beaten and made to marry another woman. Isabella, in turn, was given in marriage to another Dumont slave named Tom. She still had the youngest two of their five children with her as the date for her emancipation approached in 1827 (New York legislators had decreed that all slaves above the age of twenty-eight in that year would be emancipated; previous laws had freed slaves born after 1799).

The year 1827 marked a turning point in the life of Isabella Baumfree. Dumont had promised Isabella and her husband their freedom in 1826 and a log cabin in which to live in exchange for her hard work and faithfulness as a slave. Despite sustaining an injury to her hand, Isabella worked harder than ever for that year in order to fulfill her part of the bargain. When the time came for Dumont to deliver, however, he refused, knowing that he needed her labor in order to overcome losses from crop failure. Furthermore, he illegally sold Isabella's son Peter out of state after she escaped his farm.

Isabella sought help after her escape. Quaker friends sent her to live with Isaac and Maria Van Wagener. It was during this period that Isabella took her first successful political action, suing for the recovery of her son by entering a plea before the Grand Jury of Kingston, and winning; Quakers helped Isabella raise money to retrieve Peter and they were reunited. The fact that the Van Wageners insisted on being called by their names, rather than by "master," impressed Isabella, since she had always perceived slave holders as being innately better than slaves.

Isabella's religious conversion followed, as did the beginning of her life as Sojourner Truth. Truth recounts her conversion as suddenly being overcome by the feeling she was loved, and feeling love for everyone else—even people who had abused her. She also sensed the presence of someone between her and God (Jesus), and realized her mission in life was to preach the injustice of slavery until it had disappeared for good.

Truth moved to New York City in 1829 and worked there as a maid until 1843, when she left to begin her career as a lecturer for the abolition of slavery and human rights. Truth, who said she conversed with God as with another person, claimed that God himself had now given her the name of "Sojourner" because she was to be a traveler and "Truth" because that was what she was to spread throughout the land. This name change signaled Truth's break with her former identity as a laborer, a slave bearing her master's name, and marked the beginning of her lifelong dedication to the fight to recognize the rights of all human beings.

Life's Work

During the twenty-five years that followed, Sojourner Truth traveled thousands of miles, lecturing in twenty-one states and in the District of Columbia. She would routinely set up the white sash given to her by abolitionist women with texts written across it "proclaiming liberty throughout the land," begin singing, then preach about the injustice of slavery as people gathered around her. By the 1840's, Truth had become a popular figure and known to be an impressive speaker, six feet tall, clad in gray dress with a turbanlike scarf covering her head, and armed with a mind quick and courageous enough to adapt to, disarm, and delight audiences that were especially hostile to African Americans and women who supported abolition or women's rights. Many lecturers left the United States at this time, rather than face proslavery mobs who frequently threatened lives and broke up meetings. Truth also inspired a famous work of art by the American sculptor, William Wetmore Story, entitled "The Libyan Sibyl"; the statue, of marble, resulted in part from the description given to the sculptor by Harriet Beecher Stowe, and was known for its majesty and mysterious quality.

Truth lived for many years in Northampton, Massachusetts, where she had happened onto the Garrisonian abolitionists during her travels. The Garrisonians held the brotherhood and sisterhood of all people sacred; thus, slavery was a violation against

God, and the fight against it became a holy war. The group was resolved to overthrow the system of slavery through education and persuasion, and Truth demonstrated this after Frederick Douglass' declaration in a public meeting that the only way for African Americans to gain their freedom was by force, when she asked, "Frederick, is God dead?"

The Garrisonians believed that women were men's equals, and in this way were allied with the women's movement. In 1850, Truth attended the Worcester, Massachusetts, Woman's Rights Convention and participated in the Woman's Rights Convention in Ohio in May of 1851. In the refrain (also the title) of her famous speech, "Ain't I a Woman?" Truth addressed the white women present who wanted rights for women, but at the same time believed African American women to be inferior because of their race. Truth also related her own lifelong history of back-breaking labor, refuting the conventional ideal of women as being unaccustomed to labor or confrontation. Most notably, she addressed biblically based claims of the natural intellectual inferiority of women, countering them with biblical facts. For example, she noted that while men based their claims of superiority upon the fact that Christ was a man, Christ himself was the product of God and a woman, leaving men out of the picture altogether.

Truth's narrative was first written down in 1850 by Olive Gilbert, a white abolitionist. Gilbert's rendering offers vivid stories of Truth's early life and transformation into revivalist and abolitionist, including humorous anecdotes and instances of Truth's effective handling of audiences, but also masks much of her renowned enthusiasm and directness—especially where this directness clashes with the ideal of womanhood during her time. An example of Truth's direct approach which is not included in Gilbert's text is Truth's response to male hecklers who asked if she were a man or a woman; she bared her breasts in proof—not to her own embarrassment, but rather to their collective shame.

A second edition of Truth's narrative, published in 1878, included news articles and correspondence regarding Truth, as well as samples from her "Book of Life"—a book she carried with her, filled with signatures of authors, senators, politicians, and friends—including President Abraham Lincoln, whom she visited in Washington, D.C., in 1864. During the Civil War, Truth nursed soldiers, bringing them food and gifts, funding her work by lecturing, singing, and selling her own photograph on which was written: "I sell the shadow to support the substance." She also became a freedom rider on the street cars which she rode to take care of the soldiers. On one occasion after successfully fighting to remove the Jim Crow cars (cars reserved for African Americans, but often used by whites), Truth drew a crowd while voicing her desire for a ride, which was at last granted, and rode further than she needed to make her point definite.

After the Emancipation Proclamation was signed, in 1863, Truth stayed in Washington, D.C., to work with newly freed slaves whose children were being kidnapped and taken to Maryland—still a slave state—organizing posses and persuading mothers to swear out warrants, as she once had done, finding homes and jobs in the northern states for many others. Truth also produced fifty petitions at her own expense in 1870 (when she was nearly eighty years old) asking Congress for land in the western United States that could be used to resettle freed people who were elderly, homeless, or unemployed.

Truth believed strongly that unemployment robbed people of dignity and humanity; crime was becoming a problem among the homeless and unemployed. Truth endorsed a general plan to Christianize, educate, and provide land for freedmen, as well as prohibit the drinking of rum, another source of demoralization. Truth attempted to convince politicians that since the future of her people was at stake, money used to imprison vagabond children could be better used to give them homes, churches, and schools. Truth also believed that children would fare better if women were allowed political rights.

Truth died in Battle Creek, Michigan, in November of 1883, after almost a century of struggle for social reform. Her funeral was attended by more than a thousand people, and a marble monument was erected there in her honor in 1947.

Summary

At a time when the cooperation between white abolitionists and African Americans was limited, as was the alliance between the woman suffrage movement and the abolitionists, Sojourner Truth was a figure that brought all factions together by her skills as a public speaker and by her common sense. She worked with acumen to claim and actively gain rights for all human beings, starting with those who were enslaved, but not excluding women, the poor, the homeless, and the unemployed. Truth believed that all people could be enlightened about their actions and choose to behave better if they were educated by others, and persistently acted upon these beliefs.

Truth's written narrative is one of many narratives presented to the public by abolitionists as proof against proslavery advocates' claims that African Americans were content with slavery and incapable of caring for themselves. Her speeches were also an effective weapon against slavery and were especially successful in drawing crowds to antislavery meetings and opening eyes to the injustice and irrationality of slavery. Like other freed slaves, Truth was a primary witness who could testify to the real suffering of slaves as well as demonstrate to proslavery crowds that, contrary to popular belief, African Americans were thinking, feeling human beings. Sojourner Truth is considered, along with Harriet Tubman, to be one of the two most influential African American women of the nineteenth century. W. E. B. Du Bois conveyed the importance of her contribution best when he described Truth as "one of the seven who made American slavery impossible."

Bibliography

Campbell, Karlyn Kohrs. "Style and Content in the Rhetoric of Early Afro-American Feminists." *Quarterly Journal of Speech* 72 (November, 1986): 434-445. Campbell discusses the difficulties African American women abolitionists faced as public speakers, which Truth was successful in combating through the power of metaphor and personal experience in speaking.

Dick, Robert C. *Black Protest: Issues and Tactics.* Westport, Conn.: Greenwood Press, 1974. Dick describes Truth's work as an African American antislavery lecturer, demonstrating her charisma, humor, and strength, as well as discussing the significance of slave narratives, both written and oral, in the antislavery movement.

Fauset, Arthur Huff. *Sojourner Truth: God's Faithful Pilgrim.* New York: Russell & Russell, 1971. This is yet another rendition of the narrative of Sojourner Truth as told to Olive Gilbert, made into factual fiction by Fauset. The narrator focuses on Truth's religious devotion and strength, as does Gilbert.

Gilbert, Olive. *Narrative of Sojourner Truth.* Edited by Margaret Washington. New York: Vintage Books, 1993. In the introduction to this edition of the *Narrative of Sojourner Truth,* editor Margaret Washington explores the Dutch culture in relation to slavery, the elements of culture and community in interpreting the effects of slavery upon African Americans, and the issue of gender in relation to the authorship of the narrative.

_____ . *Narrative of Sojourner Truth, a Bondswoman of Olden Time: With a History of Her Labors and Correspondence Drawn from Her "Book of Life."* New York: Oxford University Press, 1991. Introduced by Jeffrey C. Stewart, the prefacing material to Olive Gilbert's rendering (originally published in 1850) outlines Truth's contribution to African American women's literature beginning with Phillis Wheatley. This book is part of a series aiming to resurrect the literature of African American women by uncovering the genre's nineteenth century roots.

McKissack, Patricia C., and Fredrick McKissack. *Sojourner Truth: Ain't I a Woman?* New York: Scholastic, 1992. This juvenile biography provides a straightforward introduction to Sojourner Truth, clarifying the details of her early life in slavery, explaining her connection with early abolitionists, and providing insights into her efforts on behalf of women's rights. Includes a bibliography of sources for further study.

Jennifer McLeod

HARRIET TUBMAN

Born: c. 1820; Bucktown, Maryland
Died: March 10, 1913; Auburn, New York
Area of Achievement: Social reform
Contribution: A leading conductor on the Underground Railroad and a member of the
New England Freedman's Aid Society, Tubman devoted her life to delivering
African American slaves from bondage. She made nineteen forays into the South,
leading as many as three hundred people from bondage in the southern states
through the northern states into Canada.

Early Life

Araminta Ross, later known as Harriet Tubman, was born in Bucktown, Dorchester
County, on the eastern shore of Maryland around 1820. Tubman, the granddaughter
of native Africans, was born into slavery. She was proud of her African heritage and
often stated that not one drop of white blood flowed in her veins. She received no
schooling as a child and therefore could not read or write. Although her parents were
slaves and as such were not afforded the right of a legal marriage, they were devoted
to each other, and the family ties were quite strong.

As was typical during slavery, strong bonds of familial affection did not prevent the
sale of most of Tubman's brothers and sisters. Out of a total of ten children born to
Benjamin Ross and Harriet Greene, only Tubman and two of her brothers remained
on or in the vicinity of the plantation where they were born. When Tubman was six
years old, she was taken to the home of James Cook to learn the trade of weaving. She
was, however, given the task of watching muskrat traps, and after she became quite
ill from wading in the water, she was returned to her mother. Soon after she witnessed
the sale of two of her older sisters, Tubman was hired out as a nursemaid to a white
mistress who beat and abused her on a daily basis. The beatings Tubman received
usually took place in the mornings; therefore, the young slave prepared herself by
putting on as many layers of clothing as possible, and she cried loudly during her
period of punishment. Her preparations, however, did not deflect all the blows, and
she bore numerous scars on her neck and shoulders for the rest of her life.

At an early age, Tubman revealed the courage that was to characterize her life.
When she was thirteen years old, she was hired out as a field hand. She blocked the
doorway of a slave cabin in an attempt to prevent a plantation overseer from whipping
one of her fellow slaves. The overseer threw a two-pound brass weight at her, and it
struck Tubman in the forehead. The blow left a permanent scar on her forehead, and
it undoubtedly caused internal injuries. For the remainder of her life, Tubman suffered
from narcolepsy, a condition that caused her to fall asleep unexpectedly for indefinite
periods of time.

In her late adolescence, Tubman was hired out to John Stewart. Once again, she was
physically abused and treated cruelly. She drove oxen, carted, plowed, and performed
tasks that were usually assigned to male slaves. Her narcolepsy served only to

exacerbate her situation, because she was once severely beaten while she was unconscious. In 1844, Tubman married a free black named John Tubman. They never had any children, and the marriage was not a success.

Life's Work

In 1849, when Harriet Tubman was nearing her thirtieth year, her owner died. His slaves learned that they were to be sold and sent to the Deep South. The young woman decided to try to escape to freedom and did so with the help of Quakers. When Tubman began her journey north, she was accompanied by two of her brothers; however, they soon turned back, leaving their sister to continue alone. After an arduous journey of more than ninety miles, Tubman eventually arrived in Philadelphia. In 1850, she returned to the Baltimore area and was able to help her sister and her sister's two children escape to the North. Within the space of a few months, she returned to Maryland once more and freed a brother and two other men.

Tubman intended to help her husband travel North, but when she finally found him in 1851, he had already married another woman. She returned once again in 1851 and led out a group of eleven fugitives, including her brother and his wife. Because the Fugitive Slave Act of 1850 was being enforced in Philadelphia and Boston, she took this last party all the way to Canada and remained with them through the winter.

In the spring of 1852, Tubman returned to the United States. She worked as a cook in hotels and as a domestic servant in private homes in order to earn enough money to journey back to the South. In the fall of 1852, she returned to Maryland to lead nine more slaves to freedom. Tubman was aided by Thomas Garrett, a leader in the Underground Railroad efforts in Wilmington, Delaware, who is believed to have provided shoes, money, and support to as many as three thousand fugitives. Between 1852 and 1857, Tubman made only two journeys into the South to free slaves from bondage, but by this time she had earned the title of "Moses," a name given her by those whom she led from bondage.

In 1857, Tubman brought her parents out of bondage. She took them to Canada, where they spent the winter. Because they were extremely uncomfortable in the cold climate, Tubman decided to find her parents a better place to live. She found a small farm near Auburn, New York, and managed to purchase it from William H. Seward, secretary of state later in the Lincoln Administration. She settled her parents on the farm and made it her permanent home.

In the late 1850's, Tubman became well known to northern abolitionists such as Frederick Douglass, Wendell Phillips, and John Brown. Brown, in particular, proved to be a great admirer of Tubman, whom he always called "General Tubman." According to biographer Sarah Bradford, Tubman encouraged Brown in his plan to raid Harpers Ferry and aided him by supplying money and recruits from among her followers. Tubman made her last foray to Maryland in December, 1860, and delivered seven fugitives to freedom, including an infant who was drugged with opium to keep it from crying on the way.

Tubman relied on her ingenuity, intuition, and religious faith to support her in her dangerous missions into the South. She also carried a gun with her on her forays into slave territory. Her "passengers" knew that they had to keep up with the party or face the prospect of Tubman's gun. At one time, a reward of $40,000 was offered by slave owners for Tubman's capture. With such a price on her head, Tubman could ill afford to be stymied by fearful or exhausted fugitives. She once assured an inquiring reporter that if her charges could not keep up with the fleeing party, they would be shot. "Dead niggers tell no tales," she would tell anyone endangering her group. "You go on or die."

In the spring of 1860, Tubman was involved in a dramatic incident in Troy, New York. Tubman had stopped in Troy to visit a cousin. There she learned that a fugitive slave, Charles Nalle, had been taken prisoner and was about to be returned to the custody of his half-brother and master. Tubman went immediately to the office of the United States Commissioner and demanded Nalle's release. She wrested Nalle from his jailers, took him to the river, and put him in the boat that carried him across. Tubman followed the fugitive in another boat and then placed him in a carriage that took him to Schenectady, New York, out of harm's way.

During the Civil War, Tubman worked for the Union Army, nursing wounded soldiers and serving as a scout and spy. She nursed soldiers by day and baked pies and other goods at night. She sold the baked goods to support herself, for she received no money for her efforts from the United States government. Her knowledge of herbal medicine was especially helpful in nursing those soldiers who had dysentery. In 1863, Tubman accompanied Colonel James Montgomery on an expedition up the Combahee River. Tubman was used to convince the slaves along the river that the Union soldiers were coming to free them. Colonel Montgomery later wrote a letter commending Tubman's efforts as a scout.

After the Civil War, Tubman returned to her home near Auburn, New York. She discovered that her farm was in danger of foreclosure, and she was forced to appeal to friends and acquaintances for assistance. Sarah Bradford wrote the first account of Tubman's life, *Scenes from the Life of Harriet Tubman* (1869), in an effort to raise money to save Tubman's home.

Tubman did not retire after the Civil War. She continued to work actively for African Americans who had been freed by the war but were still suffering from the negative influences of a racist society. She opened her home to aged, indigent, and orphaned African Americans. Her last efforts on behalf of her people involved trying to build a hospital, the John Brown Home for the Aged. Since the government refused to give her a full veteran's pension, she sold fruit and authorized a second biography to raise money for the institution. Tubman remained active until the end of her life. She died in 1913 at her home near Auburn, New York.

Summary

The impact of Harriet Tubman's life far exceeds the number of people whose immediate lives she touched. Tubman was a heroine in every sense of the word. A woman of no pretensions, she took little thought for herself, but repeatedly risked her life, in the years before the Emancipation Proclamation, to bring slaves to freedom. During the Civil War, Tubman worked tirelessly as a nurse, scout, and spy on behalf of Union forces within the South. In the last years of her life, she devoted herself to building a home for the aged and indigent. She also spoke on behalf of woman suffrage. Tubman dedicated her life to a transformation of her society, a transformation that would benefit all Americans.

Bibliography
Blockson, Charles L. *The Underground Railroad*. New York: Prentice-Hall, 1987. A collection of narratives relating to the Underground Railroad that reveals the active roles slaves played in their own escapes. The material on Harriet Tubman is taken from interviews with her that appeared in the *Commonwealth* of July 17, 1863, from the first volume of the *Freedman's Record* of March, 1865, and from biographies written by Sarah Bradford and Earl Conrad.
Bradford, Sarah H. *Harriet Tubman: The Moses of Her People*. Reprint. Bedford, Mass.: Applewood Books, 1993. Tubman was personally known to Bradford, who first published this volume in 1886. It is a more complete follow-up to the author's first biography of Tubman, *Scenes in the Life of Harriet Tubman*, which was first published in 1869. Both volumes are currently available in reprint editions.
Buckmaster, Henrietta. *Let My People Go*. Columbia: University of South Carolina Press, 1992. An excellent overview of the activities of the Underground Railroad, this well-researched study details the exploits of the "conductors," including Harriet Tubman, who repeatedly risked their lives to bring their "passengers" to freedom.
Giddings, Paula. *When and Where I Enter: The Impact of Black Women on Race and Sex in America*. New York: William Morrow, 1984. This volume is a narrative history of African American women from the seventeenth century to the present. Although Giddings' information about Tubman is limited, it places her within the context of nineteenth century African American women's experience.
Starling, Marion Wilson. *The Slave Narrative: Its Place in American History*. 2d ed. Washington, D.C.: Howard University Press, 1988. Starling examines the voice of the African American slave, the voice that speaks through the translations of editors. She establishes the veracity of slave narratives. Among others, she examines the voice of Harriet Tubman, a voice that is recognizable through various written accounts.
Still, William. *The Underground Railroad*. Reprint. New York: Arno Press, 1968. An early organizer and leader of the Underground Railroad, William Still kept careful records and accounts of those who were brought to freedom. His original purpose was to provide documentation that would allow families to be reunited after the Civil War, but his account, first published in 1872, re-creates the life-and-death struggles, the hair's-breadth escapes, and the heroism of those involved in the work of the railroad.

Yvonne Johnson

BARBARA TUCHMAN

Born: January 30, 1912; New York, New York
Died: February 6, 1989; Greenwich, Connecticut
Area of Achievement: Historiography
Contribution: Recipient of two Pulitzer Prizes in history and one of the most widely read American historians, Tuchman helped reintroduce history as an art to the reading public.

Early Life

Barbara Wertheim would later recall having witnessed the first naval engagement of World War I when she was two years old. The event occurred in the Mediterranean as she traveled with her parents to visit her grandfather, who was then serving as U.S. Ambassador to Turkey. Her historical interests never wavered afterward, although they were reinforced during her childhood by the popular historical adventures recounted in Lucy Fitch Perkins' famous Twins series, as well as in books of the same genre by Sir Arthur Conan Doyle, Jane Porter, Alexandre Dumas, and George Alfred Henty. Her interests in place, imaginative research, and confident writing, however, required years of apprenticeship.

Wertheim's early background was marked by privilege and familial distinction. Maurice Wertheim, her father, was a leader in New York City's Jewish community, a successful international banker, publisher, and philanthropist. Her mother, Alma Morgenthau Wertheim, was a member of the prominent Morgenthau banking family. It was Henry Morgenthau, businessman turned diplomat, whom Barbara had been en route to see when elements of the British fleet attempted to intercept Germany's *Goeben* in August, 1914—one of the world's most memorable months, encapsulating the meltdown of a civilization whose ambience Barbara Tuchman later re-created in *The Guns of August* (1962). An uncle, Henry Morgenthau, Jr., served as Franklin Roosevelt's secretary of the Treasury, while cousin Robert Morgenthau gained repute as a U.S. federal attorney.

Barbara's formal education comported with her family's expectations and achievements: New York's Walden School and then, in 1929, Harvard's affiliate, Radcliffe College for women. In essays written decades later, she recalled the influences of Irving Babbitt, a specialist in French literature; Charles McIlwain, himself a Pulitzer Prize-winner for a historical study of American government; and John Livingston Lowe, an expert in comparative literature. Equally as memorable, she recounted, was her freedom to spend time in the magnificent stacks of Harvard's Widener Library, repository of one of the world's largest private book and manuscript collections. Meanwhile, her summers were spent with her family in Europe. Shortly after graduation, she joined her grandfather at the World Economic Conference of 1933.

Privileged as she was, Barbara Wertheim eagerly transmuted social advantage into cultivating her splendid background and temperament for historical writing. She commenced formal research working for the Institute of Pacific Relations soon after graduation. In 1935, she joined the staff of *The Nation*, which her father owned, writing on a variety of newsworthy subjects. The magazine dispatched her to Spain for coverage of that country's confused and savage civil war in 1937. Upon her return, she determined to work as a freelance correspondent for a British news journal. In the meantime, she witnessed the publication of her first book, *The Lost British Policy: Britain and Spain Since 1700* (1938), the precursor to eleven significantly better works.

Life's Work

As for everyone of her generation and age, war and family for a time preempted Barbara Wertheim's other affairs. In 1940, shortly after the outbreak of World War II, and the year prior to America's direct involvement, she married the president of New York City Hospital's medical board, Dr. Lester Tuchman. In the acknowledgments of her final work, *The First Salute* (1988), she not only thanked him for aiding her with her failing eyesight but also acknowledged him as being "the rock upon which this house is built." From 1943 until 1945, both Tuchmans performed national service, she at the Far Eastern Office of the Office of War Information. Some of Barbara Tuchman's initial curiosities about life in the Far East, subsequently fleshed out in her *Stilwell and the American Experience in China* (1971), took shape.

Despite these early publications, her "first" book, as she described it, did not appear until 1956—*Bible and Sword: England and Palestine from the Bronze Age to Balfour*, a study of British policy in Palestine. It was, by her own admission, incomplete. The last six months of her research dealing with events from 1918 until 1948, a period of British Mandate over Palestine, of Arab uprisings, the Arab-Israeli War, and reestablishment of the state of Israel in 1948, so overwhelmed her with a sense of disgust and injustice that, contrary to her editor's wishes, she destroyed them. Her emotions had victimized her perception of scholarly discipline. The study thus ended in 1918. The lesson this experience conveyed to her persisted: Stay within the evidence and let the emotions come to the readers insofar as possible from the presentation itself.

In this regard, Tuchman readdressed an earlier canon of major historians, which had been eclipsed somewhat by historical writing like that of the distinguished and enormously influential Charles A. Beard. Beard and his wife, Mary Ritter Beard, in company with James Harvey Robinson and other Progressives, conceived of history as an important force in effecting social change, of molding civilization. They wrote the "New History," which questioned the older standard of objectivity, and their works raised their banners around the qualified relativism that became the trademark of their school.

Tuchman agreed that the goal of absolute objectivity was unattainable by historians. Nevertheless, in essays explaining her philosophy of history, she placed herself in the tradition of German historian Leopold von Ranke, the figure generally credited with founding the modern school of objective historiography known as "Scientific History." Inserting one's opinions into the hunchwork guiding research, as well as imposing these opinions on one's selection of materials for writing, she believed, was highly undesirable. Rather, self-conscious striving for objectivity, recording history "how it really was," as Ranke stated it, was Tuchman's goal. Thus, for the most part, contemporary history—evaluations of headline events of her own day or of recent decades—by choice lay outside her intellectual bailiwick. Such events were too immediate and too emotion-charged for her to analyze calmly and reflectively.

In a few essays, Tuchman did indeed ignore these tenets, but not in her major works. *Bible and Sword* thus closed in 1918; *The Zimmermann Telegram* (1958), *The Guns of August* (1962), and *The Proud Tower: A Portrait of the World Before the War, 1890-1914* (1966) all focused on events and personalities of World War I. *Stilwell and the American Experience in China* examined occurrences from which the passage of a full generation buffered her. Likewise, *A Distant Mirror: The Calamitous Fourteenth Century* (1978) focused on the excitement and upheaval of a distant European past and *The March of Folly: From Troy to Vietnam* (1984) sketched the timeless absurdities of warfare, while her last book, *The First Salute: A View of the American Revolution* (1988), assessed the impact of foreign involvement on the American Revolution. She agreed that contemporary history could be written, citing William L. Shirer's *The Rise and Fall of the Third Reich* (1960) as a superior example, but not by her.

Musing further on her own historical approach and style, Tuchman emphasized her distaste for history "in gallon jugs." By that she meant history wrestled into the service of a historian's grand explanatory or philosophical schemes, and therefore girdled with sweeping generalizations. The historian who after 1934 and through the 1960's had most recently fit this description was the English historian Arnold Joseph Toynbee, whose *A Study of History* (1934-1964), a twelve-volume theoretical analysis of the rise and decline of more than a score of notable civilizations, had proved surprisingly popular, particularly as made accessible to general audiences in excellent abridgments. For Tuchman, however, climbing "those Toynbeean heights" would have required her to soar from the ground impelled by theories of her own invention. That sort of endeavor, as she saw it, was not what a historian should do. Besides, however grand the view from a Toynbeean perspective, Tuchman lamented the inevitable disappearance of detail.

It was indeed an eye for telling detail that characterized Barbara Tuchman's histories—"corroborative detail," in her words. Such detail, she insisted, restrained historians and forced them to adhere to as much truth as could be gleaned from their materials. It was her view that while corroborative detail might not produce glittering generalizations, it still might reveal historical truths in addition to keeping research anchored in reality.

Tuchman's final work, *The First Salute*, was published in 1988, some months before her death at her home in Greenwich, Connecticut, in February of 1989.

Summary

With the lengthy experience in research and writing that she had begun acquiring in her youth and with a firm grasp of the tenets of professional history, Barbara

Tuchman made straightforward narrative history her genre. She embellished it with brilliantly selected detail—one of her trademarks—that made events and personalities vital for her readers. When she began her major works, narrative history was out of fashion, particularly in academia, and interpretive history seemed the route to reputation. Worse, as far as many academics were concerned, much of the best narrative history, and certainly the most readable—with notable exceptions—had been produced by nonacademics.

Despite the authority of academic historians, which had grown with the expansion of American universities, mass education, and the importance of the doctoral degree beginning in the 1950's, Tuchman chose an alternate course for herself. She earned no higher degrees, and she was faintly bemused by the overwhelmingly male-dominated mandarinate represented by academic historians. She certainly respected the standards that academics had set for the collection and accuracy of their research. Yet, academics essentially wrote for one another. To the extent that this was the case, historical writing became a busy closet enterprise to which reading publics were not privy. Tuchman consciously returned to the older tradition of history, writing "objective" narrative with literary merit—a tradition that had included such notables as Allan Nevins, Samuel Eliot Morison, and Douglas Southall Freeman, all of whom urged that while history should be judged by rigorous standards of accuracy it should also join hands with literature. Capitalizing on this advice and following her own artistic predilections, Tuchman became one of the most widely read of modern American historians. A best-selling author, she was an important figure in reviving history for the public. Two Pulitzer Prizes are testimonials to the high abilities she brought to bear in scholarly realms that into the 1990's were still overwhelmingly dominated by men.

Bibliography

"Barbara Tuchman." *The Nation* 248, no. 9 (March, 1989): 252-253. A thoughtful, laudatory obituary by a periodical with which Tuchman was associated when she began her writing/research career, and one in which her family had owned an interest. This profile is valuable because while Tuchman's books were widely reviewed, there are few published materials about their author.

Beard, Mary Ritter. *Woman as Force in History: A Study in Traditions and Realities.* New York: Macmillan, 1946. Beard, who has been perceived as a founder of women's history and a champion of women writing history, was greatly admired by Tuchman. Neither Beard nor Tuchman fit into the academic historical guilds of their times. Brief annotated bibliography and useful index.

Hurwitz, Samuel T. "The Guns of August. Review." *American Historical Review* 7 (July, 1962): 1014-1015. Valuable as an appreciative academic review of Tuchman's first Pulitzer Prize-winning work. It credits Tuchman with vivid, imaginative, and passionate writing. It describes the work as a series of vignettes offering little new to professional specialists, but serving as a good example of how history can be written to appeal to a wide audience.

Marcus, Jacob R. *The American Jewish Woman, 1654-1980.* New York: Ktav Publishing House, 1981. Briefly places Tuchman as a member of the Morgenthau-Wertheim families in context with other notable Jewish women of her generation.

Tuchman, Barbara W. *Practicing History: Selected Essays*. New York: Alfred A. Knopf, 1981. A collection of frank, often charming commentaries and examples of Tuchman's work and views. All are articles or lectures rather than selections from her books. Essays in part 1 are especially interesting and revelatory. Few notes, no bibliography or index. Her historical views should be juxtaposed to those male academic historians who reviewed her work. On balance they credited her with striking prose and good "popular" history, making clear that it was less thoroughly researched, profound, or interdisciplinary than they expected "reliable" history to be.

Zinsser, Judith P. *History and Feminism: A Glass Half Full*. New York: Twayne, 1993. A clear, cogent survey and comparative analysis of men's history, women's history, and the impact of feminism on each. Useful for placing Tuchman in the broader modern context of women writing history. An excellent work with annotated suggestions for further reading and a valuable index.

Clifton K. Yearley

SOPHIE TUCKER

Born: January 13, 1884; Russia
Died: February 9, 1966; New York, New York
Areas of Achievement: Music and theater and drama
Contribution: Tucker's six-decade career as a comedian and singer centered on bawdy
songs, live audiences, and ethnic humor.

Early Life

Sophie Tucker was born Sophie Kalish, the daughter of Russian Jews emigrating
to America. According to her autobiography, her father, a military deserter, changed
his name to Charles Abuza in order to elude Russian authorities. His daughter grew
up as Sophie Abuza. She became Sophie Tuck when she married, and she later
modified her husband's surname when she entered show business as Sophie Tucker.

Sophie's father left Russia before her mother did. He sent back money so that she
could follow him, which she did—seventeen years old, pregnant, and with a two-year-
old son in tow. Along the way, she stopped at a farmhouse to give birth to her daughter.
Sophie wrote in her autobiography of her mother's "guts," her ability to "always do
what she had to do."

They arrived in Boston when Sophie was three months old and lived there during
her early childhood. Then, when she was eight years old, her father bought a restaurant
in Hartford, Connecticut, and moved there with his wife and four children (Philip,
Sophie, Anna, and Moses). Mother and children all worked long, hard hours to make
the restaurant a success, while Charles Abuza gambled upstairs, sometimes for days
at a time. Being so busy in the family restaurant kept young Sophie somewhat isolated
from other children and their play. It also instilled in her a loathing of poverty and
low-paid labor. She conceived a longing to free both herself and her mother from the
tyranny of the restaurant kitchen.

It was during her years in Abuza's Home Restaurant that Sophie began to dream of
a stage career. Traveling show-business people frequented the restaurant for the
cheap, plentiful Jewish food, and young Sophie listened to their shop talk. Eventually,
she began to sing for them as well, for tips and the occasional encouragement she
received. Because of the additional income her singing brought in, her family did not
object to her "making a show" of herself. Her mother even bought a used piano and
paid for music lessons for her. As it turned out, however, it was not the piano but the
voice that was to be her instrument.

Shortly after her graduation from high school, at the age of sixteen, Sophie was
married to Louis Tuck in a civil ceremony that was followed by the Orthodox wedding
on which her family insisted. They set up housekeeping, with Sophie still helping in
her family's restaurant, but after she became pregnant, the young couple moved back
in with the Abuzas. The marriage did not last long after the birth of Bert Tuck. Sophie
made the painful decision to leave her child with her parents and go to New York and
try her luck at show business.

Life's Work

In New York, Sophie Tucker "paid her dues." She made the rounds of Tin Pan Alley looking for songs, for work, for leads. Her voice was big, flamboyant, and brassy. She performed in rathskellers such as the German Village, where she sang fifty to one hundred songs a night for fifteen dollars a week and "throw money"—the tips thrown by the audience. She always sent a fraction of her pay home to her family. Another sizable fraction of her income was used to further her career; she established a lifelong pattern of investing heavily in songs and elegant costumes for her act.

While Tucker was trying to break into show business in New York, something happened that was to shape her early career. She auditioned for one of Chris Brown's "amateur nights," which were important because of the producers and booking agents that frequented them, scouting for talent. She was accepted, but Brown insisted that she sing in "blackface" because, he said, she was "so big and ugly." Painfully humiliated by Brown's assessment of her looks, Tucker allowed his assistant to blacken her face with burnt cork and paint exaggerated negroid lips on her with lipstick. She went onstage—and was a success. This success was to haunt her for some time; against her will, she became known as a "coonshouter" or "coon-singer," a performer of what were supposed to be southern black songs but generally were Tin Pan Alley's fantasy of such material. Even though she begged for the opportunity to go onstage in her own persona, once she had succeeded as a blackface performer, it was impossible to persuade producers to let her try things her own way. (She remained a "coonshouter" until much later, when the fortuitous loss of a trunk containing her stage makeup in Boston helped to free her from the mask.) Quite possibly, this early experience with the stage success of stylized ethnic stereotypes and dialects helped to prepare Tucker for her later, emphatically Jewish persona.

Eventually, Tucker broke into the vaudeville circuits. In 1909, she found a place in the Ziegfeld Follies. Her stint with the Follies did not last long. The intervention of jealous Ziegfeld stars Nora Bayes and Eva Tanguay brought her Ziegfeld career to an end. She went back out on the road and began to present more sexual material (songs such as "Make It Legal, Mr. Segal"). After she abandoned blackface, she began to incorporate more and more Yiddish humor into her act. The blended stereotypes of Jewish mother and sexually voracious woman-on-the-prowl became her signature. She became known as "The Last of the Red-Hot Mamas."

The rigors of touring kept Tucker from developing a settled network of friends who knew her as an individual separate from the fat, jolly stage personality she assumed in order to please audiences. After Louis Tuck died, she was married again, first to her pianist, Frank Westphal. After that marriage failed, she was married to her business manager, Al Lackey. That marriage also ended in divorce. The romantic longing in her songs ("Nobody Loves a Fat Girl, but Oh How a Fat Girl Can Love") paralleled a certain lack of fulfillment in her own life.

It was not until 1938 that Tucker appeared on Broadway, in Cole Porter's *Leave It to Me*. Broadway saw her again in 1941's *High Kickers*. Because her magic was so dependent on her charismatic interaction with live audiences, her film career was not distinguished. She appeared in *Honky Tonk* (1929), *Broadway Melody of 1938* (1937), *Thoroughbreds Don't Cry* (1937), *Sensations of 1945* (1944), and *Follow the Boys* (1944). The risqué nature of her act kept her from becoming known as a radio star, but television viewers saw a toned-down version of her work when she appeared on several episodes of *The Ed Sullivan Show*. When all was said and done, even after the passing of vaudeville, it was plain that live audiences were Sophie Tucker's forte. During last years of her career, she performed mainly in nightclubs and cafés. She continued to perform until about four months before her death from cancer in 1966. She left behind her the 1948 autobiography that bears the name of one of her most successful songs, Shelton Brooks's "Some of These Days."

Over the years, Sophie Tucker shared billings with many of the most important names in American entertainment, including Will Rogers, W. C. Fields, Eddie Cantor, Bea Lillie, Jimmy Durante, Judy Garland, Fanny Brice, Jack Benny, and Al Jolson. She performed the material of songwriting greats such as Jack Yellen, Shelton Brooks, Cole Porter, Irving Berlin, Henry Creamer, and Turner Leighton. With Lucille Ball, Dinah Shore, and Martha Raye, she shared the honor of being one of the very few women of her time ever to be honored by a Friar's Roast luncheon.

Summary

Sophie Tucker touched American popular culture through vaudeville, burlesque, the Ziegfeld Follies, films, television, and the nightclub circuit. In each of these venues, her bawdy humor and sexy personal style helped to bring feminine sexuality out of the Victorian closet. She lived her life at the intersection of categories that were devalued by the society around her: she was a woman; she was a Jew; she was fat; she did not fit the standards of what was called beauty in her time and place; and, for most of her career, she did not look or act young. Instead of deemphasizing these factors, she exaggerated them and built a long, successful performing career on them. Nevertheless, her triumph over marginalization was ambiguous; it was accomplished by inviting audiences to laugh at her womanliness, her Jewishness, her weight, her "ugliness," and her age. She strutted before youth-crazed American audiences in the persona of an aging woman who was still very much sexually alive, but she did so at the expense of presenting such a persona as comic.

Bibliography

Brown, Janet. "The 'Coon-Singer' and the 'Coon-Song': A Case Study of the Performer-Character Relationship." *Journal of American Culture* 7, nos. 1-2 (Spring/Summer 1984): 1-8. An excellent article exploring the politics of Tucker's performing persona. It gives a short history of performing in "blackface" and situates this tradition in the larger tradition of stage "fools" throughout history.

Cohen, Sarah Blacher. "The Unkosher Comediennes: From Sophie Tucker to Joan Rivers." In *Jewish Wry: Essays on Jewish Humor*. Bloomington: Indiana University Press, 1987. Views Tucker as the first in a tradition of female Jewish comedians that includes Belle Barth, Totie Fields, and Joan Rivers. Especially focuses on the important role of body size and body image in these entertainers' public careers.

Loy, Pamela, and Janet Brown. "Red Hot Mamas, Sex Kittens, and Sweet Young Things: Role Engulfment in the Lives of Musical Comedy Performers." *International Journal of Women's Studies* 5, no. 4 (September-October, 1982): 338-347. Women often enter show business seeking freedom and self-expression but find that they are forced by audience expectations to assume a stage persona similar to the stereotypical roles they sought to escape in the first place. This article examines three role types as they were embodied by Sophie Tucker, Anna Held, and Julia Sanderson.

Sochen, June. "Fanny Brice and Sophie Tucker: Blending the Particular with the Universal." In *From Hester Street to Hollywood: The Jewish-American Stage and Screen*, edited by Sarah Blacher Cohen. Bloomington: Indiana University Press, 1983. Compares the lives and careers of two Jewish female entertainers: Fanny Brice and Sophie Tucker.

Tucker, Sophie. *Some of These Days: The Autobiography of Sophie Tucker*. New York: Doubleday, Doran, 1945. A much-neglected gem of women's autobiography. Tucker's literary voice resembles her stage persona: jovial, philosophical, and positive.

Donna Glee Williams

TINA TURNER

Born: November 26, 1939; Brownsville, Tennessee

Area of Achievement: Music

Contribution: One of the most exciting and durable female rock singers, Turner first came to prominence during the 1960's.

Early Life

Tina Turner was born Anna Mae Bullock on November 26, 1939, in Brownsville, Tennessee. Her mother, Zelma Bullock, gave birth to Anna Mae in the basement of the Haywood Memorial Hospital, the only portion of the hospital where African Americans were allowed to be treated. Anna Mae's family lived in Nut Bush, Tennessee, where her father, Floyd Richard Bullock, was a manager of a cotton plantation. He also served as a deacon at the Woodlawn Baptist Church. Anna Mae had an older sister, Alline.

After the United States entered World War II in 1941, Anna Mae's parents moved to Knoxville, Tennessee, in order to find work in the defense industries. The girls had to remain behind, with Alline going to live with her maternal grandparents, Josephus and Georgianna Carrie, while Anna Mae was sent to live with her paternal grandparents, Alex and Roxanna Bullock. Grandmother Bullock was a very proper and religious woman who made Anna Mae attend church every Sunday. On occasion, the girls would get a chance to visit their parents, and during their parents' second year in Knoxville, Anna Mae and Alline lived with them for a few months.

When the factories finally shut down, the entire Bullock family moved to Flagg Grove, Tennessee, and, eventually, to the community of Spring Hill. Always a shy girl, Anna Mae found singing to be an excellent way of expressing herself. In addition to singing traditional hymns with the choir at the Spring Hill Baptist Church, Anna Mae began singing in school talent shows. Although she was capable of singing several musical styles, she particularly enjoyed singing blues songs.

Anna Mae's parents did not have a happy marriage, and the postwar years did not improve their relations. When she was eleven years old, they were divorced. In 1950, Zelma Bullock moved to St. Louis, Missouri, leaving her daughters in their father's care. Floyd Bullock married again, but the marriage did not last for very long. When Anna Mae was thirteen, her father moved to Detroit, Michigan, and the girls were forced to live with a cousin. The cousin, Ella Vera, was only willing to care for the girls as long as their father sent money for their support. Grandmother Roxanna Bullock took in the girls once the money was no longer forwarded. After graduating from high school, Alline moved to Detroit to live with her father. Soon, Anna Mae decided to go live with her maternal grandmother, Georgianna Currie. In 1956, Grandmother Currie died, and Anna Mae went to live with her mother and Alline in St. Louis.

Life's Work

Anna Mae Bullock was overjoyed to be living with her sister once again. Although she was merely sixteen, Anna Mae found the opportunity to attend various East St. Louis nightclubs with Alline and her girlfriends. One particular club, known as the Club Manhattan, featured the Kings of Rhythm, a popular band led by the charismatic guitarist Ike Turner. The band played in a number of clubs and had a large following, especially among women. The owner of the Club Manhattan was Booker Merritt, and his club became the home base for the Kings of Rhythm. Alline began dating the group's drummer, Gene Washington, and Anna Mae became good friends with several members of the band. Although she wanted a chance to sing on stage, no one believed that she was capable of performing. Anna Mae finally seized an opportunity and sang a B. B. King song on stage with Ike Turner playing organ during one of the band's breaks. Greatly impressed with her singing ability, Turner decided that he wanted her to join the band. Unfortunately, he would first have to convince Anna Mae's mother of the idea. Turner used all of his immense personal charm to negotiate with her mother, and finally Anna Mae joined the group and used the name "Little Ann."

After joining the act, Bullock became close friends with the band's saxophone player, Raymond Hill. In 1958, she had a son, Raymond Craig Hill, by him. At the time, Ike Turner served as more of a mentor to Bullock than anything else. Not too long after she was graduated from high school, she moved in with him. A native of Clarksdale, Mississippi, Ike Turner had grown up to be a very fine musician, but he also had a reputation for being a violent man. Although he was still married, Anna Mae Bullock fell in love with him. In 1960, she and Turner had a son, Ronald Renelle Turner. Sometime in 1962, they traveled to Tijuana, Mexico, to be married. There is some question whether the ceremony was legal, since Ike Turner did not officially divorce his previous wife until 1974.

A recording of Turner's song "A Fool in Love" was made with Anna Mae standing in for Art Lassiter on vocals. The song had been written for Lassiter, but he had some financial disagreement with Turner and decided not to show up at the recording session. One of the people to whom Turner later sent the recording was Henry "Juggy" Murray of Sue Records. Murray was impressed with the single and invited Turner to sign a recording contract. Turner had thought that the song would be recorded again with a male vocalist, but Murray believed that the song should be released as it was originally recorded. Turner signed with Murray for a $25,000 advance, and "A Fool in Love" was released in the summer of 1960, under the names Ike and Tina Turner. With her recording debut as a lead singer, Anna Mae Bullock had become Tina Turner.

She was not sure that the name change was a good idea, but she did not want to undermine her husband's vision of where they were going musically. The Ike and Tina Turner Revue began its first tour in 1960. By August of that year, "A Fool in Love" had reached the number two position on the rhythm and blues charts. The song also did well on the pop charts, reaching number twenty-seven, and it eventually sold eight hundred thousand copies. Ike Turner realized that Tina should serve not only as the lead singer but also as the focal point of the group. The newly expanded Ike and Tina

Turner Revue, which included female backup singers known as the Ikettes as well as the Kings of Rhythm, appeared on the popular television dance and music program Dick Clark's *American Bandstand*. Tina was an energetic singer and would dance in a sexually provocative way to excite the audience. With Ike at the helm, the Revue mixed rock, blues, and gospel music together to produce a dynamic sound.

The Ike and Tina Turner Revue toured the United States and Europe throughout the 1960's and even into the early 1970's. When the Rolling Stones began their 1966 European tour, the Revue had the privilege of being the opening act. Ike and Tina Turner had a number of top-selling songs during the 1960's, including "River Deep, Mountain High" and the Grammy Award-winning "Proud Mary." Although their initial success came in Great Britain, the Ike and Tina Turner Revue eventually made inroads among mainstream American fans. At the same time that their group was becoming more and more successful, Ike and Tina's marriage was falling apart. Tina Turner later stated in her 1986 autobiography, *I, Tina*, that her husband had regularly beaten her. In 1976, they separated and finally were divorced in 1978.

In the wake of her failed marriage and musical partnership, Tina Turner began to rebuild her life with the assistance of many wonderful musician friends she had met over the years. With the help of Mick Jagger and Keith Richards of the Rolling Stones as well as Rod Stewart and David Bowie, Tina Turner was able to start rebuilding her singing career. In 1979, she met a young Australian manager, Roger Davies. Through his direction, she was able to rediscover the raw energy within herself for singing rock and roll. The Rolling Stones asked her to be a part of their 1981 United States tour. Because of the exposure that the tour gave her, Turner was once again a singer who was in demand. Her own 1983-1984 European tour was a big success. In 1984, she released the album *Private Dancer*, which made her a superstar. Turner worked with four producers and eight songwriters in the course of making the album. It sold more than eleven million copies worldwide and garnered for Turner three Grammy Awards. The album included a number of hit songs: "Better Be Good to Me," "What's Love Got to Do with It?," and "Private Dancer."

In 1985, Turner appeared with Mel Gibson in the action film *Mad Max Beyond Thunderdome*. She had appeared earlier in the filmed version of the Who's rock opera, *Tommy* (1975). She continued to issue top-selling new record albums, including *Break Every Rule* (1986) and *Foreign Affair* (1989), as well as a greatest hits collection entitled *Simply the Best* (1991). In 1991, she was also inducted into the Rock and Roll Hall of Fame. A filmed version of her 1986 autobiography was released in 1993 as *What's Love Got to Do with It*. The critically acclaimed film starred Angela Bassett as Tina Turner and Laurence Fishburne as Ike Turner, both of whom received Academy Award nominations for their powerful performances. Tina Turner remained an international star by continuing to perform in her distinctive and sexually provocative style.

Summary

Tina Turner was a shy child who eventually was able to overcome her timid nature through singing and dancing. It was in a church choir that Turner first got the chance to express herself by singing traditional hymns. As a teenager, she gained the confidence to pursue a performing career as a rhythm and blues singer under the direction of her mentor and future husband, Ike Turner. It soon became evident that Tina Turner's raw vocal style and energetic stage presence could catapult her and her husband to music stardom. At the same time that her powerful voice and provocative image seemed to capture the liberating spirit of the 1960's, Tina Turner was imprisoned in an abusive relationship that marred her newfound fame. Finally, in the mid-1970's, she found enough inner strength to leave her husband and begin the process establishing herself as a solo artist. Through superb management of her talent and the support of friends, Tina Turner reestablished herself as a major rock star at a time when she was approaching her fifties. In addition to her electrifying performance style, Turner continued to be admired for her strength of character and ability to persevere against great odds.

Bibliography

Corliss, Richard, and Janice C. Simpson. "Aye, Tina!" *Time* 141 (June 21, 1993): 64-65. This article discusses the film biography of Turner's life, *What's Love Got to Do with It* (1993), particularly its portrayal of the abuse she endured at the hands of Ike Turner. She is portrayed as a true survivor, one who is at peace with herself and looking forward to a bright future.

Edwards, Audrey. "What Becomes a Sex Goddess Most?" *Essence* 24 (July, 1993): 50-55. In this article, Turner takes the opportunity to reflect on her life and what she has learned about herself. She does not think of herself as a victim, even though she had been abused for many years. Turner believes that the discipline of Buddhism has given her the needed inner strength to live with dignity and perform with the energy of someone much younger.

Gaar, Gillian G. *She's a Rebel: The History of Women in Rock and Roll.* Seattle: Seal Press, 1992. Appropriately, this excellent accounting of women in rock and roll includes a detailed commentary of Turner's career and her amazing ability to remain an exciting and vital performer.

Gates, David. "Will It Work Out Fine?" *Newsweek* 121 (June 21, 1993): 66. In addition to discussing the movie, *What's Love Got to Do with It*, there is mention of Turner's first United States concert tour since 1987 and of her new life in Germany.

Gundersen, Edna. "Tina Turner at 52: What's Age Got to Do with It?" *Ebony* 47 (January, 1992): 102-104. Turner speaks of her life in Germany with her boyfriend, German record executive Ervin Bach. She also reminisces about her early life and her struggle to survive. Turner expresses her interest in being able to act more often in the future and her intention to continue her singing career as long as she remains popular.

Hirshey, Gerry. "Woman Warrior." *GQ* 63 (June, 1993): 180-185. This article points out how courageous Turner was to leave her husband and strike out on her own.

She has remained youthful, even into her fifties, and popular throughout the world.

Orth, Maureen. "The Lady Has Legs." *Vanity Fair* 56 (May, 1993): 114-128. An extensive article that details Turner's harrowing life and reflects on how happy she is with her life in Europe. Even though Turner was in her fifties at the time of this interview, she continues to attract millions of fans who flock to see her in concert.

Turner, Tina, with Kurt Loder. *I, Tina*. New York: William Morrow, 1986. In this autobiography, Turner sets the record straight about her rise to fame and the abuse that she had to endure during her marriage to Ike Turner. Although somewhat dated, this book remains the definitive account of her life and of her amazing comeback as a solo artist.

Jeffry Jensen

CICELY TYSON

Born: December 19, 1939(?); East Harlem, New York, New York

Areas of Achievement: Theater and drama and film
Contribution: An actress of remarkable talent and conviction, Tyson brought perfection and idealism to the theater, by showing great sensibility to her characters, and by refusing to accept roles that are stereotypical and degrading to women and to African Americans.

Early Life

Cicely Tyson is believed to have been born on December 19, 1939, in the East Harlem district of New York City. The year of her birth is somewhat in doubt, since Tyson herself refuses to divulge her age. She was the youngest of three siblings, her sister Emily and a brother who only went by his last name, Tyson. Her parents, William and Theodosia (or Fredenika) Tyson, were immigrants from a small island in the West Indies called Nevis. They worked hard to support their children. While working as a carpenter and a painter, her father supplemented his income by selling fruits and vegetables from a pushcart. Theodosia was a domestic worker. Cicely contributed her share by selling shopping bags around the neighborhood from the age of nine. She was her father's favorite and was showered with love by him.

William and Theodosia were divorced when Cicely was eleven, and William later died in 1962. Following the divorce, the children lived with their mother, who was a strict disciplinarian. A devout Christian, Theodosia took her children with her to Saint John's Episcopal Church, ensuring that they adhered to her religious faith. The Tyson children were neither allowed to play with other children nor permitted to attend films or the theater.

As a schoolchild, Cicely sang with the choir and played the church piano organ. She attended Public School 121 and Margaret Knox Junior High School. She also taught Sunday school in the Episcopalian and Baptist churches. As a pianist and a member of the church choir, Tyson distinguished herself and was invited to give recitals at many concert halls in New York City.

When Cicely was graduated from Manhattan's Charles Evans Hughes High School, she worked as a secretary for the Red Cross while attending classes at New York University. She took an interest in modeling when her hairdresser requested her to model some wigs. Declaring that God "did not intend for her to sit at a typewriter," she set off to explore her talents and started modeling classes in the Barbara Watson modeling school. In 1956, she appeared on the cover of two of the foremost fashion magazines, *Vogue* and *Harper's Bazaar*, and became one of the top ten black models in the business. At a fee of $65 an hour, she was also one of the top models in the United States. Gifted and talented, her success was partly attributed to her arresting personality and natural elegance, her slender figure and striking bone structure along with her beautiful smooth skin and deep-set eyes. In addition, she was a perfectionist who took time in cultivating a certain level of professionalism in her work.

Cicely Tyson took an interest in acting when Freda DeKnight, a fashion editor for *Ebony* magazine, and actress Evelyn Davis encouraged her to audition for an independent black film called *The Spectrum*. Although she was cast in the film, it was never completed. Having decided to seek further training, she attended several acting schools in New York, including the Actor's Workshop and Paul Mann's workshop. While attending New York University, she also took classes at the Actors Studio under Lloyd Richards and Vinnette Carroll. She soon left New York University to launch her career in acting.

Life's Work

Cicely Tyson made her motion picture debut in 1957 in *Twelve Angry Men*, a United Artists production starring Henry Fonda. In 1959, she appeared in another United Artists production, *Odds Against Tomorrow*. Her actual acting talent was manifested on stage in 1957, when she was cast in the role of Barbara Allen in Vinnette Carroll's Off-Broadway production of *Dark of the Moon* at the Harlem Young Men's Christian Association (YMCA). The role was produced at the Equity Library Theater in 1959. Appearing with Tyson were James Earl Jones and Isabel Sanford. The play was choreographed by Alvin Ailey.

Having launched her acting career, Tyson appeared in several stage and television dramas. Among them were a variety showcase on Broadway called *Talent '59*; a television production of *Between Yesterday and Today*; and *For Camera Three*, a cultural series that ran on Sunday mornings on CBS television. Tyson made history on American television when she wore her hair natural on the Camera Three production. She appeared on a television special entitled *Americans: A Portrait in Verse* and in the 1959 Theater Guild production of *Jolly's Progress*. Tyson's success on stage and screen was discouraged by her religious mother, who considered acting immoral. Cicely Tyson's persistence in pursuing her career created a rift between the two that lasted for some time. Fortunately, they reconciled before Theodosia died in 1974.

In 1960, Tyson made a major appearance in a television adaptation of Paule Marshall's *Brown Girl, Brownstones*. Her next role came in 1961, in an Off-Broadway production of Jean Genet's *The Blacks* with a cast composed of James Earl Jones, Helen Martin, Maya Angelou, Roscoe Lee Brown, Godfrey Cambridge, and Louis Gossett, Jr. Tyson's brilliant performance as prostitute Stephanie Virtue Diop won her a Vernon Rice Award. Her performance resulted in an offer for a role in *Moon on a Rainbow Shawl* (1962), written by George Ray Hill. The play won an Obie Award and Tyson won her second Vernon Rice Award for her role as Mavis.

In 1963, Tyson landed a continuing role as George C. Scott's secretary on the short-lived television series *East Side/West Side* after being discovered by Scott during her performance in *The Blacks*. She gained national attention and broader acclaim as a brilliant actress and as a cultural icon for her distinct performance. She also became the first black woman to be cast in a recurring role on a prime-time dramatic television series. The year 1963 was a particularly good one for Cicely

Tyson. She was one of the cast of *Trumpets of the Lord* (1963), an Off-Broadway adaptation of James Weldon Johnson's *God's Trombones*. The play was choreographed by Donald McKayle. She later made a guest appearance on such television dramas as *Slattery's People* (1965), *I Spy* (1965), and *Medical Center* (1969). She appeared on stage in Lorraine Hansberry's *To Be Young, Gifted, and Black* (1969) and in the second revival of *God's Trombones* in 1968. She also had a unique opportunity to star opposite Sammy Davis, Jr., in the film *A Man Called Adam* in 1966.

Cicely Tyson, who exuded great pride in her race, refused to play demeaning roles even as she was climbing to the top. Her determination to stand firm on this issue resulted in fewer film roles in the 1970's, but she remained undaunted. After appearances in *The Comedians* (1967) and *The Heart Is a Lonely Hunter* (1968), she took a hiatus from films until 1972.

Sounder (1972) marked Cicely Tyson's return to the film screen. In the film, she played the character of Rebecca Morgan, a strong black woman struggling to survive in Depression-era Louisiana with her sharecropper husband and their children. She was nominated for an Academy Award in the Best Actress category. Although she did not win the Oscar, she was named Best Actress by the National Society of Film Critics and received an award as Best Actress from the Atlanta Film Festival.

Her next performance in the lead role in the television film *The Autobiography of Miss Jane Pittman* (1974) established Tyson as the leading black actress of her generation and as one of the best actresses in America. In playing the fictional protagonist, a former slave, from the age of nineteen until well beyond one hundred, Tyson showed her versatility and skill in the delicate portrayal of the different stages of life. The character was recognized as a black heroine for her struggles and tribulations in a racially segregated society and for defying that segregation by drinking from the "whites only" drinking fountain. Rex Collins, a New York critic, described Tyson's acting as "one of the most brilliant performances I have ever seen by a woman of any color, any age, any season." In recognition of her performance, Tyson won an Emmy award as the best leading actress in a television special. Her success was not without effort, however, since Tyson prepared for the role by spending part of her time with elderly women in a nursing home, studying in minute detail their every movement and gesture.

In the wake of her Emmy award, Tyson was courted by many magazines for interviews and appeared on the covers of *People*, *Ms.*, *Encore*, *Ebony*, and *Jet* magazines. Despite her exceptional performances in *Sounder* and *The Autobiography of Miss Jane Pittman*, Tyson, like many black actors, received offers for roles she considered to be undemanding for an actress of her caliber. Her insistence on performing only challenging roles brought less opportunities to her. She rejected most of the offers she received, but selectively played the roles of heroic women and black women of historic or contemporary importance. In December of 1976, she starred in *A Woman Called Moses* as Harriet Tubman, the black heroine who led more than three hundred slaves to safety on the Underground Railroad. This role was followed by her role as Coretta Scott King in the television film *King* (1978), and later as Marva

Collins, a Chicago educator, in *The Marva Collins Story* (1981). Also in 1981, she costarred with comedian Richard Pryor in the feature film *Bustin' Loose*.

On November 26, 1981, Tyson was married to her longtime friend Miles Davis in a ceremony performed by former Atlanta mayor Andrew Young and witnessed by entertainer Bill Cosby. After her marriage, she appeared less frequently on stage and screen. Evidently, the marriage was not a very happy one, and the couple divorced before Davis' death in 1991.

On August 12, 1983, Tyson starred as Miss Moffat in *The Corn Is Green*, a stage production by Zev Bufman and Elizabeth Taylor. The play received mixed reviews and closed on September 19, 1983. Other credits in the 1980's include *Benny's Place* (1982), *Playing with Fire* (1985), *Acceptable Risks* (1986), and *Cry Freedom* (1987). She costarred with Oprah Winfrey in *The Women of Brewster Place* (1989), a television drama produced by Winfrey.

In 1991, Tyson was featured in the film, *Fried Green Tomatoes*, and in 1993, in a television film *House of Secrets*. She had an important supporting role in the 1994 made-for-television film *The Oldest Living Confederate Widow Tells All*. Receiving star billing along with Melissa Gilbert in the 1994 NBC television series *Sweet Justice*, Tyson appeared in the role of a strong-minded woman defense lawyer heading up her own law firm in the Deep South. Despite her achievements as a highly talented and skilled actress, she continued to be offered roles that were not commensurate with her talent. Yet she continued to exhibit undaunted spirit in every role she played. Her determination to portray positive female and black images remained unchanged. Being an actress was important to her, and she was determined to give the best of herself. In an interview with *Redbook* in 1979, she expressed her wish "to get to a point where I am considered for a part simply because I'm a good actress rather than because I am a Black actress."

Summary

Cicely Tyson has established herself as a stage and screen legend and as a positive image for women and for the black race. Her refusal to play demeaning roles such as prostitutes, drug addicts, nannies, and gangsters is a protest against racism and injustice in America. Her persistence earned recognition and respect not only for herself but also for black theater and black artists.

When Tyson was not on stage, she was busy organizing and helping other people. In 1968, Tyson organized the Dance Theater of Harlem and served as the first Vice-President of the Board of Directors. She also served on the Board of Directors at Urban Gateway, an organization that exposes children to the arts. She is a trustee of the American Film Institute and the Human Family Institute.

Cicely Tyson owns several honors and awards for her artistic and humanitarian endeavors. She is a recipient of awards from the NAACP and the National Council of Negro Women. She was awarded an honorary doctorate of Fine Arts by Marymount College, a doctor of Humane Letters from Lincoln University, and other honorary doctorates from Atlanta and Harvard universities.

Tyson is a committed artist and a woman of social consciousness. She remains modest despite her accomplishments and considers her performance for two presidents, former U.S. president Jimmy Carter and Shehu Shagari of Nigeria, as "one of the highest compliments" she had ever received.

Bibliography

Andrews, Bert. *In the Shadow of the Great White Way: Images from the Black Theatre.* New York: Thunder's Mouth Press, 1989. This is a book of photography with a text on the history of black theater by Carter Harrison and an introduction by Cicely Tyson. Tyson discusses her friendship with Bert Andrews and their years in the entertainment industry. The photographs of Tyson's theater performances, including roles in *Moon on a Rainbow Shawl* and *The Blacks*, are documented in several pages of the book.

Angelou, Maya. "Cicely Tyson: Reflections on a Lone Black Rose." *Ladies' Home Journal* 94 (February, 1977): 40-41. Maya Angelou provides an insight into Tyson's childhood, her modeling and acting professions, and her determination in life.

Bogle, Donald. *Blacks in American Films and Television.* New York: Garland, 1988. Contains a section on Cicely Tyson that focuses exclusively on her career, starting from her graduation from New York's Charles Evans Hughes High School.

Hine, Darlene Clark, ed. *Black Women in America: An Historical Encyclopedia.* Brooklyn, N.Y.: Carlson, 1993. In a section dedicated to Cicely Tyson, Beverly Robinson provides a biographical description of the actress, stating her career achievements and evaluating her status as a black actress.

Robinson, Louie. "Cicely Tyson: A Very Unlikely Movie Star." *Ebony* 29 (May, 1974): 33-43. An exclusive interview with Tyson following her successful roles in films such as *Sounder* and *The Autobiography of Miss Jane Pittman.*

Smith, Jessie Carney, ed. *Notable Black American Women.* Detroit: Gale Research, 1992. In this biographical dictionary, Cicely Tyson's life and career are chronicled. Factual statements in the profile on Tyson are interspersed with direct quotations from the actress.

Nkeonye Nwankwo

YOSHIKO UCHIDA

Born: November 24, 1921; Alameda, California
Died: June 21, 1992; Berkeley, California
Area of Achievement: Literature
Contribution: An acclaimed writer, particularly of fiction, for both adults and young readers, Uchida is best known for her representations of the experiences of Japanese Americans in internment camps during World War II.

Early Life

Yoshiko Uchida (pronounced Oo-chee-dah) was born on November 24, 1921, in Alameda, California, to Dwight Takashi Uchida, a businessman with a Japanese import-export firm, and Iku Umegaki Uchida, a poet. As she was growing up in Berkeley, Yoshiko began writing stories and keeping a journal about her experiences. She and her sister Keiko were brought up with the cultural traditions of their Japanese parents, who reared their daughters according to a set of values Yoshiko later described as a mixture of Buddhist philosophy and Christian faith. Her parents were graduates of one of Japan's leading Christian universities and often entertained visitors from their homeland. They also took pride in their adopted country and encouraged their daughters to identify with American as well as Japanese culture.

Despite their loyalty to the United States, the Uchidas, along with other Japanese Americans, were regarded with suspicion. Just eight years before Yoshiko's birth, for example, the California legislature had passed the Alien Land Law that prevented Japanese residents and other "aliens ineligible to citizenship" from owning land in the state of California. When Uchida was just three, Congress passed the Immigration Act of 1924, stopping all immigration from Japan. The climate toward people of Japanese descent in the United States grew increasingly intolerant. As a youngster, though, Yoshiko wanted to fit in with schoolmates, and so she struggled with the double bind of cultural assimilation. By her high school years, Uchida found herself ostracized by her peers because of her race. Despite her experiences with racism, she completed her high-school degree in two and a half years and began her college studies at the University of California, Berkeley, when she was sixteen years old.

Life's Work

Near the conclusion of Yoshiko Uchida's senior year at the University of California, Berkeley, however, came the bombing of Pearl Harbor on December 7, 1941. Following that incident, American residents of Japanese heritage were evacuated and incarcerated by a United States federal government order (known as Executive Order 9066) issued by President Franklin Delano Roosevelt on February 19, 1942. Almost immediately after the Pearl Harbor bombing, Uchida's father, as a successful Japanese American businessman, was seized and detained by the Federal Bureau of Investigation. On April 21, 1942, Uchida's family (except for her father, who would be held in a prisoner-of-war camp in Montana) was ordered to relocate to Tanforan Racetrack in

California, where they were forced to live in a cramped, hastily converted horse stall.

Five months later, in September of 1942, Uchida and her family were moved to a guarded concentration camp in Utah known as Topaz. While at Topaz, Uchida served as a volunteer elementary school teacher until the spring of 1943. At that time, with the help of the National Japanese American Student Relocation Council, Uchida secured her release from the camp in order to conduct graduate study on a fellowship at Smith College in Northampton, Massachusetts. She received her master's degree in education from Smith in 1944. In December of that year, the United States Supreme Court would rule that loyal citizens could not be held in detention camps. This ruling helped bring about the end of Japanese American internment.

Emerging from the relocation centers were many talented Japanese American writers and journalists, such as Yoshiko Uchida. Even within the camps, internees managed to produce a great number of diaries, newsletters, journals, and literary magazines. When these Japanese Americans were released from the concentration camps, however, their poetry and fiction were seldom accepted for publication by American presses. Some authors were asked to write under pseudonyms to conceal their racial identities. Published Japanese American literature concerning the camp experience would not appear in the United States until the 1950's, and it would not be until June 1952 that Congress would pass Public Law 414, allowing Japanese aliens the right to become naturalized United States citizens.

During the early 1940's, Uchida began her professional career outside the camps as a teacher at Frankford Friends' School in Philadelphia, Pennsylvania (1944-1945). Uchida found that although she was qualified as a teacher, work as a secretary afforded her more time to devote to her writing. She served as the membership secretary for New York City's Institute of Pacific Relations (1946-1947) and later as the secretary to the United Student Christian Council, also in New York City (1947-1952). For a period of years, Uchida wrote in the evenings and sent out work to magazines. In time, she discovered success writing chiefly for young readers. She then became a full-time writer in 1952, and although she worked between 1957 and 1962 as a secretary at the University of California, Berkeley, she would work chiefly as a writer for the rest of her years.

In 1952, Uchida received a Ford Foundation Foreign Area Fellowship to collect Japanese folk tales. Her time in Japan, where she stayed for two years, heightened Uchida's racial awareness and pride. In addition to gathering tales, Uchida explored the rich traditions of Japanese folk art and craft. Crafts would remain an interest of Uchida's throughout her life. She authored more than twenty books dealing with Japanese and Japanese American culture. Several of these works draw from Uchida's own research or experiences, particularly her youth in the camps. When Uchida published *Journey to Topaz* (1971) in tribute to her late mother, her writing began to shift its focus from Japanese tradition to the issues facing contemporary Japanese Americans.

Uchida was a prolific writer for five decades. Her children's books include twenty-seven book-length works, the first of which had its origins in her research in Japan:

The Dancing Kettle and Other Japanese Folk Tales (1949). During the 1950's, Uchida published five volumes for children: *New Friends for Susan* (1951), *The Magic Listening Cap: More Folk Tales from Japan* (1955), *The Full Circle* (1957), *Takao and Grandfather's Sword* (1958), and *The Promised Year* (1959). She increased her output during the 1960's, releasing nine children's books during that decade, including *Mik and the Prowler* (1960), *Rokubei and the Thousand Rice Bowls* (1962), *The Forever Christmas Tree* (1962), *Sumi's Prize* (1964), *The Sea of Gold and Other Tales from Japan* (1965), *Sumi's Special Happening* (1966), *In-Between Miya* (1967), *Hisako's Mysteries* (1969), and *Sumi and the Goat and the Tokyo Express* (1969). During the 1970's, Uchida began to receive the most critical acclaim for her writing. In those years, she produced the following texts for young readers: *Makoto, the Smallest Boy: A Story of Japan* (1970), *Journey to Topaz: A Story of the Japanese American Evacuation* (1971), *Samurai of Gold Hill* (1972), *The Birthday Visitor* (1975), *The Rooster Who Understood Japanese* (1976), and *Journey Home* (1978). In the 1980's, she began preparing work for adult as well as young readers. Her children's books from the 1980's include *A Jar of Dreams* (1981), *The Best Bad Thing* (1983), *Tabi: Journey Through Time* (1984), *The Happiest Ending* (1985), and *The Two Foolish Cats* (1987).

Among Uchida's works for adults are *We Do Not Work Alone: The Thoughts of Kanjiro Kawai* (1953), *Desert Exile: The Uprooting of a Japanese American Family* (1982), and *Picture Bride* (1987). Uchida also wrote short stories, a regular column in *Craft Horizons* (1958-1961), copy for an Oakland Museum exhibit catalog (1976), and articles appearing in such periodicals as *California Monthly*, *Far East*, *Gourmet*, *Utah Historical Quarterly*, and *Woman's Day*. Continuing to work on projects, Uchida died at her home in Berkeley, California, in 1992 at the age of seventy.

Summary

As a distinguished woman writer of Japanese descent, Yoshiko Uchida's accomplishments demonstrate the way in which it was possible for her not only to survive racism and the experiences of internment camps in World War II but also to transcend these barriers and transform her experiences into literary texts that promote intercultural sensitivity. Uchida received many recognitions for her literary accomplishments and her contributions to intercultural understanding. Among these were the *New York Herald Tribune*'s Children's Spring Book Festival Honor Book in 1955, a silver medal for best juvenile book by a California author from the Commonwealth Club of California in 1972 and again in 1982, Award of Merit from the California Association of Teachers of English in 1973, a citation from the Contra Costa Chapter of the Japanese American Citizens League in 1976 for her outstanding contribution to the cultural development of society, the International Reading Association's Children's Choices awards in 1979 and in 1985, notable awards for children's trade book in the field of social studies by the National Council for Social Studies and the Children's Book Council (1979, 1982, and 1985). She also won the Morris S. Rosenblatt Award from the Utah State Historical Society in 1981 for her article "Topaz, City of Dust," received the University of Oregon's Distinguished Service Award in 1981, was given an award by the Berkeley Chapter of the Japanese American Citizens League in 1983, was cited by the Child Study Association of America among its Children's Book of the Year awards in 1985, and received the Friends of Children and Literature Award in 1987. Her works have been translated into Afrikaans, Dutch, German, and Japanese, among other languages.

Bibliography

Arbuthnot, May Hill, and Zena Sutherland. *Children and Books*. 4th ed. Glenview, Ill.: Scott, Foresman, 1972. This genre-based guide to children's literature incorporates numerous references to Uchida's work: *Dancing Kettle* and *Magic Listening Cap* listed as folk tales; *The Promised Year*, *The Forever Christmas Tree*, *Hisako's Mysteries*, and *Sumi and the Goat and the Tokyo Express* as realist texts; and *Journey to Topaz* as historical fiction.

Bacon, Betty, ed. *How Much Truth Do We Tell the Children?: The Politics of Children's Literature*. Minneapolis: MEP Publishers, 1988. Although this book does not address itself specifically to Uchida's texts, its chapter by Harue Palomino on political considerations surrounding the representation of the historical experiences of Japanese Americans in children's literature has considerable bearing on the balance of Uchida's work.

Butler, Francelia, ed. *Sharing Literature with Children: A Thematic Anthology*. New York: David McKay, 1977. This collection gathers texts thematically and features one section on "Fools"—straightforward, almost simple characters who prevail at story's end. Butler presents Uchida's story "The Sea of Gold" within a subsection devoted to folktales.

Chang, Catherine E. Studier. "Profile: Yoshiko Uchida." *Language Arts* 61 (February, 1984): 189-193. This article provides a literary biography of Uchida, centering around the writer's simultaneous efforts to preserve awareness of Japanese American culture and promote a vision of cultures coming together as one world. Also included is a selected bibliography of Uchida's works.

Hollowell, Lillian, ed. *A Book of Children's Literature*. New York: Holt, Rinehart and Winston, 1966. In addition to excerpting "Takoa's Big Surprise" from *Takoa and Grandfather's Sword*, Hollowell places Uchida's work in the company of another text concerning Japanese American internment, Florence Crannell Means's *The Moved-Outers* (1945). A brief profile of Uchida appears in the appendix.

Uchida, Yoshiko. *The Invisible Thread*. Englewood Cliffs, N.J.: Julian Messner, 1991. Aimed at juvenile readers interested in knowing more about the author, Uchida's memoir provides an account of the life experiences she had previously woven into her fictional works. A warmly nostalgic yet unflinchingly honest recollection of her childhood in Berkeley, California, and her family's wartime experiences living in the Topaz internment camp in Utah.

Linda S. Watts

GLORIA VANDERBILT

Born: February 20, 1924; New York, New York

Areas of Achievement: Fashion and art

Contribution: Gloria Vanderbilt, an innovative designer and brilliant entrepreneur, used her artistic abilities to create apparel and many other products and her business acumen to market her name and trademarks, thus gaining great wealth and world-wide name recognition.

Early Life

Gloria Laura Vanderbilt was born on February 20, 1924, at the Lying-in Hospital in New York City. Her father was Reginald Claypoole Vanderbilt, a great-grandchild of Cornelius Vanderbilt, who had amassed a vast fortune in the shipping and railroad industries and who was referred to as the Commodore. Her mother was Gloria Morgan, daughter of Harry Hays Morgan, an American career diplomat. Her maternal grandmother, Laura Kilpatrick Morgan, was present at young Gloria's birth and remained, until Morgan's death in 1956, an influential person in Gloria's life.

Reginald Vanderbilt, the youngest son of Cornelius Vanderbilt III, inherited $7.5 million outright and $5 million in an inviolable trust at the age of nineteen from his father's estate. When he turned twenty-one, Reginald received other inheritances from his grandfather and aunts. By his mid-twenties, however, it was evident that Reginald preferred alcohol, racetracks, and gambling houses to business and charitable enterprises. In 1915, all that was left of Reginald's fortune of approximately $30 million was the trust and the annual income from it. This inviolable trust was to be distributed to his children when they reached twenty-one.

Reginald Vanderbilt had two children. Mary Cathleen was born to his first wife, Cathleen Gebhard Neilson, in 1904. This marriage ended in divorce in 1919. A second marriage to Gloria Morgan, twenty-four years his junior, occurred in 1923. By the time his second daughter was born eleven months later, Reginald was a forty-four-year-old father who was terminally ill. On September 1, 1925, he died of internal hemorrhaging. His untimely death left his young widow penniless and his two daughters wealthy. Nineteen-month-old Gloria Laura Vanderbilt received $2.5 million to be held in trust until she reached twenty-one, at which time she would receive the principal. The trust came under the jurisdiction of the New York Surrogate Court, and dispensation of the trust income greatly influenced Gloria Vanderbilt's early life.

The role of caretaker for young Gloria was assumed by her maternal grandmother and nurse Emma Sullivan Keislich. Her mother retained legal custody and was granted a small allowance by the court for the support of herself and Gloria. Gloria's mother often petitioned the court for additional moneys for their upkeep. In Gloria's early years, her mother moved the household to many locations, including Paris, London, and New York. In addition to the many international settings, Gloria's memories of her early life are filled with images of a beautiful young mother immaculately adorned and always leaving for yet another social activity. Stability in Gloria's early years was provided by the ever-present and devoted nurse Keislich, whom she affectionately called Dodo, and by her grandmother Morgan. Yet it was her mother's lifestyle, great beauty, and taste that would have a significant impact on Gloria's professional life in the future.

In an effort to provide what she believed to be a better life for Gloria, Gertrude Vanderbilt Whitney went to court in 1934 to obtain custody of Gloria. Gertrude, an extremely wealthy and influential art patron and sculptor, was Reginald's older sister. The lengthy trial was played out in the media, and young Gloria learned early how to work the press, a skill that would help her in her life's work. Photographs of her along with the sordid details of the trial frequently appeared in the newspapers. In June, 1935, the Appellate Division of the New York State Supreme Court, in a unanimous decision, granted custody of young Gloria to Gertrude Vanderbilt Whitney.

During the next seven years, Gloria was exposed to the rich life of her aunt. Whitney, the founder of the Whitney Museum of American Art and benefactor of Whitney Studio Club (a haven for young artists), fancied herself an artist and shared this world with Gloria. The plush surroundings and various activities that were available in the midst of such wealth fostered Gloria's taste and creative talents. As early as age ten, she was painting and developing a keen awareness of the elements of design.

In 1941, Gloria left the Whitney estate and joined her mother in California. Reconciliation between Gloria and her mother did not occur, however, and at age seventeen, Gloria was married to Pat di Cicco, an agent for actors. The marriage ended four years later with Gloria paying di Cicco $200,000 (shortly after she had inherited some $4.5 million from her father's estate). The day after her divorce, Gloria was married to famed conductor Leopold Stokowski, a man forty-two years her senior. Gloria and Leopold had two sons, Stanislaus and Christopher, during their twelve-year marriage. It was during this time that Gloria suffered a nervous breakdown and, apparently on the advice of an analyst, began to express herself through art.

Life's Work

Gloria Vanderbilt's artistic talents began to publicly emerge during the 1950's. She spent a great amount of time writing, painting, modeling, and studying acting. *Love Poems* (1955), her first published book, was given high reviews. In 1955, Vanderbilt's first opening for her paintings was held; by 1962, there had been twenty five shows and three museum retrospectives of her paintings. In addition to painting and poetry, Vanderbilt had her first real acting experience in *The Swan* (1957). She later adapted the title of the play for use in her apparel logo.

Vanderbilt's energy during the fourth decade of her life seemed endless. Her published writings included a play, various short stories, and book reviews for *Cosmopolitan* magazine. By the late 1950's, she was often the topic of news articles including one in *Vogue* that featured Vanderbilt modeling the Mainbocher collection. Her alabaster skin, large brown eyes, and slender body captured and displayed the best features of the designer's clothing.

The successes of her thirties were not enough to hold Vanderbilt's second marriage together. She found herself in a New York court fighting for the custody of her two sons, in a battle much like the one that had raged two decades before on her behalf. Gloria eventually did receive custody. She was later married to Sidney Lumet, a film and television producer. This marriage lasted seven years as Gloria continued to work and receive much publicity as an artist. She starred in the film *The Rich Boy* (1961) and was featured modeling clothes and sharing her philosophy in numerous magazines.

Vanderbilt's life and successes took on a new dimension with her marriage to Wyatt Cooper, a writer from Mississippi, in 1964. She and he seemed on the same wave length, supporting each other's creative endeavors. The stability of home and secure family life became a reality for her. Two sons, Carter and Anderson, were born to Gloria and Wyatt.

Vogue often wrote about Vanderbilt and her family, her homes, and her artistic talents during the 1960's. Her home decorating skills along with photographs showing the work that she herself did was the subject of a feature article in a 1966 *Vogue* magazine issue. Her personal beauty secrets often made news as well. She seemed to be always available to the press, whether modeling Adolfo clothes, Kenneth Cave jewelry, her own collection of Mariano Fortuny dresses, or displaying any of her many other talents.

By the late 1960's, Vanderbilt was designing clothes for herself and continuing her work with other forms of art. In 1968, she held a one-woman show of paintings and collages at the Washington Gallery of Art. Reviewers recognized Gloria Vanderbilt's vivid and original convictions regarding fashion and art, and, by the early 1970's, she was to be described as a multifaceted artist.

Her first work as a commercial artist came in 1971, as a result of Don Hall of Hallmark seeing her drawings. He thought they would sell on paper products, puzzles, and do-it-yourself kits. And they did. It was then recognized by others that Vanderbilt's designs had decorative value that would sell. Bloomcraft fabrics along with manufacturers of wallpaper, china, glassware, flatware, towels, curtains, and numerous other products sought Gloria Vanderbilt's talents. The name that once was synonymous with money now was recognized as a leading designer.

Perhaps the capstone to her design work came through her association with Warren Hirsh, president of Murjani, in 1976. He was successful in convincing Vanderbilt to associate her name with a blouse collection produced by his firm. It was Murjani's Gloria Vanderbilt blue jeans with the swan logo on the front pocket, however, that provided her with a level of international recognition shared by only a few apparel designers. Her jeans were soon to outsell other major designer's lines. The success of the jeans was partially a result of her hands-on approach to their design and strategic marketing. Gloria became one of the first designers to do in-store appearances to promote a product.

In 1978, Vanderbilt's husband, Wyatt Cooper, died. Her work as an artist and designer continued, but she became more introspective. In 1979, Doubleday published her memoir, *Woman to Woman*. In it, Vanderbilt revealed details of how she became an artist and about finding the art of living. She continued to write. *Once Upon a Time* (1985) and *Black Knight, White Knight* (1987), the first two books in a projected five-part autobiographical series, were published by Alfred A. Knopf. She also carried her message of encouragement and design philosophy to women's groups as a speaker and in magazine articles.

Summary

Gloria Vanderbilt, the poor little rich girl, rose above the difficulties of her life to share her creative work and philosophy with millions of people, especially women. In doing so, she found her own life enhanced. She chose not simply to live a pleasure-filled life, but to strive for success. For this, she labored intensely. Her success may be measured not only in wealth but also in the many companies that selected a Vanderbilt design to enhance their products or Gloria's talent to create new products. The list of products that she has been associated with reads like a household inventory. More than things, Gloria Vanderbilt has offered to others inspiration about life and the impact of art upon life. She has shared herself through stories in magazines and books.

Bibliography

Goldsmith, Barbara. *Little Gloria . . . Happy at Last*. New York: Alfred A. Knopf, 1980. A well-researched biography that documents Gloria's place within the large Vanderbilt and Morgan families. The details of the Vanderbilt-Whitney trial over the custody of Gloria are presented as a gripping story exposing the follies and indiscretions of her patrician family.

Hellmann, Peter. "Sic Transit Gloria." *New York* 26 (February 15, 1993) 34-41. A lengthy article that provides a glimpse of Vanderbilt's business dealings and the advisers who evidently took advantage of her generosity in order to rake off healthy profits from her licensing agreements and other business transactions. Although somewhat less than flattering in its tone, the article does provide a concise summary of Vanderbilt's life and touches on a painful incident—the 1988 suicide leap of her son Carter from the balcony of her Manhattan apartment in her presence.

Patterson, Jerry E. *The Vanderbilts*. New York: Harry N. Abrams, 1989. This dynastic biography of the Vanderbilts examines the private and public lives of its members, including their marriages, divorces, financial dealings and business investments, and their patronage of the arts. Illustrated with numerous photographs of Vanderbilt residences and personal art holdings. Although it repeats much of what is known about Gloria Vanderbilt's early life, this work is useful for placing her within the larger context of her father's family and their lavish lifestyle.

Vanderbilt, Cornelius. *Farewell to Fifth Avenue*. New York: Simon & Schuster, 1935. This book provides an understanding of what it was like to be a part of the Vanderbilt family. From reading this work, one can better identify with Gloria Vanderbilt's own drive for success.

Vanderbilt, Gloria. *Black Knight, White Knight*. New York: Alfred A. Knopf, 1987. This is the second in a projected series of five memoirs by Gloria Vanderbilt focusing specifically on her own life. Vanderbilt tells of her early marriages and chronicles her teen years and early twenties as being experimental ones.

——————— . *Once Upon a Time*. New York: Alfred A Knopf, 1985. A memoir of Vanderbilt's childhood. She carries the reader back to her youth, vividly evoking the sights, sounds, and thoughts of her early years.

——————— . *Woman to Woman*. New York: Doubleday, 1979. A memoir of her thoughts and feelings, especially related to art. She shares her philosophies of work and creative talent. Readers may perceive Gloria Vanderbilt with a new understanding after perusing this book.

Sue Bailey

SARAH VAUGHAN

Born: March 27, 1924; Newark, New Jersey
Died: April 3, 1990; Hidden Hills, California
Area of Achievement: Music
Contribution: With her rich voice, Vaughan incorporated bebop into jazz singing.

Early Life

The only daughter of musical parents, Sarah Lois Vaughan was born on March 27, 1924, to Ada and Asbury "Jake" Vaughan. Devout Baptists, the family lived in a small apartment in Newark, New Jersey. Ada, a laundress and vocalist in the church choir, encouraged her daughter's early musical abilities, buying records for the Victrola whenever her meager earnings allowed. Ada also played the piano, and she set aside twenty-five cents a week for Sarah to begin lessons when she was seven years old; Sarah later attributed her ability to take apart music and put it together in a new way to her days as a pianist in the band at Arts High School. When Sarah was twelve, she became the organist at the Mount Zion Baptist Church and a soloist in the choir.

Sarah loved all kinds of music, but as a teenager she became obsessed with the popular songs of the day. Jake, a carpenter and guitarist, preferred religious music; he worried that popular music would have a negative effect on his daughter, so he held her to strict curfews and forbade her to attend dances. Defiantly, Sarah soaked up the nightlife by sneaking out at night to hear music at local clubs. She and her friends saw Billy Eckstine sing with the Earl Hines Band, heard the Erskine Hawkins band, and saw Josephine Baker. During the day, Sarah cut classes to hang out at a local record store, eavesdropping on musicians and listening to the latest releases. She would mimic the songs at home on the piano, playing and singing for friends all afternoon.

Sarah dropped out of high school during her junior year and began playing piano wherever she could, even when tips were her only payment. At fifteen, she was five feet, three inches tall, skinny, and unsophisticated looking in her modest clothes, but her impressive musicianship earned for her piano gigs in nightclubs where the legal age limit was twenty-one. Ada Vaughan found out about her daughter's night life when a club owner called, wanting to hire Sarah.

One night in October of 1942, Sarah ventured to New York City to compete in the amateur contest at the Apollo Theatre, a club made famous by the stars discovered on its stage. She won first prize, ten dollars, for her rendition of "Body and Soul" and was invited back for a week's engagement in a variety show. That week came in the spring of 1943, when Ella Fitzgerald was the headliner; Billy Eckstine, who was in the audience that night, was so impressed with Vaughan's voice that he recommended her to Earl "Fatha" Hines. After Hines heard her sing, he invited Vaughan to join his band as a second pianist and vocalist. At age nineteen, Vaughan packed her few belongings into a paper bag and arrived at Pennsylvania Station, ready to begin her professional singing career traveling with some of the most innovative jazz musicians of the twentieth century.

Life's Work

Sarah Vaughan regarded her year with the Hines band as an initiation period. The only woman traveling with sixteen men, she refused special treatment, preferring instead to dine with the band members at various clubs during the day, play dice and cards with them on the bus, and drink and smoke with them all night. The band members, including trumpeter Dizzy Gillespie and saxophonist Charlie "Bird" Parker, quickly learned to respect Vaughan for her tough, hard-working attitude and her amazingly versatile contralto voice. Around that time, pianist John Malachi nicknamed Vaughan "Sassy" for her independent, witty personality; she liked this playful description and let her friends call her "Sass" the rest of her life.

Hines's band is remembered for introducing bebop music to the jazz scene. Bebop, characterized by virtuosic instrumental improvisation, harmonic complexity, unpredictable rhythmic accents, and extremely fast tempos, was controversial when it was introduced but has since revolutionized jazz. Vaughan was the first female vocalist to master the form. In 1944, she joined Eckstine's big bebop band as a vocalist, and she made her first recording, "I'll Wait and Pray," in December of that year. Gillespie, an enduring fan of Vaughan's voice, passed this recording on to jazz musician and critic Leonard Feather, who produced her first two singles with Continental: four songs for twenty dollars apiece. She secured a three-year contract with Musicraft in 1945 and received national attention first for "Lover Man," recorded with Gillespie and Parker in 1945, and then for "Body and Soul," recorded in 1946.

In 1947, she met her first manager and first husband, trumpeter George Treadwell, who scheduled voice and elocution lessons for Vaughan, had music specially arranged for her, and secured performance dates at renowned clubs such as Birdland in New York and the Blue Note in Chicago. That year Vaughan recorded her first hit, "Tenderly," and in 1948 she recorded "It's Magic" for the film *Romance on the High Seas*, confirming her success as a pop star. The well-known Chicago radio and television personality Dave Garroway began featuring Vaughan's music on his widely aired shows; Garroway was the first to call her "The Divine One" for her operatic vocal range. She signed a five year contract with Columbia in 1949, producing primarily popular music with studio orchestras. By 1950, she was selling more than 3 million records and earning more than $1 million through royalties annually, and her music appeared on pop charts with increasing frequency.

Though Vaughan's popularity was made possible by her hits, she longed to pursue jazz again. In 1954, she signed with Mercury, and the company allowed her to pursue both types of singing. She continued to produce hits, including "Make Yourself Comfortable," "Whatever Lola Wants," "Mr. Wonderful," and her first million-album seller, "Broken Hearted Melody." She also recorded for Mercury's jazz subsidiary EmArcy, singing with the Count Basie Band, the Ernie Wilkins Orchestra, Clifford Brown, and other jazz artists, producing a total of 263 cuts by 1959.

Vaughan's voice and popularity continued to mature for the next thirty years. She performed at jazz festivals, nightclubs, and concerts around the world, satisfying audiences with her supple, innovative interpretations. She thrilled audiences at

Carnegie Hall numerous times, performing with Tony Bennett, George Benson, Joe Williams, and various trios and orchestras. She sang for presidents and prime ministers and was officially lauded in the Congressional Record. Music critics praised her three-octave range, the ease with which she jumped intervals to dress up a note, her use of both delicate coloratura passages and sultry, smoky baritone lines, and her voluptuous vibrato. Vaughan often said that she never sang a song the same way twice, and her favorite accompanists were those who knew how to change a complicated chord progression in order to challenge her improvisational skills. With its soft swoops and melodic leaps, Vaughan's voice was often compared to an instrument, particularly during scat singing (wordless singing). She reported that her singing was influenced more by horn players than by other singers, although she cited Judy Garland, Marian Anderson, and Leontyne Price as favorite vocalists.

The most critically acclaimed albums of Vaughan's career were produced in the late 1970's and early 1980's. *I Love Brazil* (1977), recorded in Rio de Janeiro with Brazilian composer Antonio Carlos Jobim, was nominated for a Grammy award. *How Long Has This Been Going On* (1978), which includes performances by Oscar Peterson, Ray Brown, Louis Bellson, and Joe Pass, was also nominated for a Grammy. In 1981, she received an Emmy award for her singing in a Public Broadcasting Special, *Rhapsody and Song—A Tribute to George Gershwin*. With the Los Angeles Philharmonic Orchestra, she performed a series of concerts and the televised *Gershwin Live!* (CBS, 1982); critics believed that Vaughan's voice imbued the show tunes with unsurpassable richness, and the album received a Grammy award for Best Jazz Vocal Performance. She also produced an album of Beatles songs and two albums of Duke Ellington songs. She recorded with the Jimmy Rowles Quintet, the Count Basie Orchestra, and the London Symphony Orchestra. In 1984, she recorded *The Planet Is Alive, Let It Live!*, singing poems written by Karol Wojtyla before he became Pope John Paul II. She sang Christmas carols with the Mormon Tabernacle Choir in 1988. She recorded several versions of "Send in the Clowns," which became her signature song. Finally, in 1989, after years of being compared to Ella Fitzgerald, Sarah Vaughan sang with her friend for the first time on an album for Quincy Jones, *Back on the Block*. It was the last recording of her prolific career.

On February 22, 1989, Vaughan was awarded her second Grammy, a Lifetime Achievement Award. At the ceremony, she sang "So Many Stars," demonstrating her undiminished vocal ability. Although she smoked most of her life and drank ice water during performances, her voice never lost its lush agility, and if it ever cracked during a performance, she covered it so well that her musicians did not hear it. Her accompanists called her a musician's vocalist because she understood music so well. If she forgot lyrics, she amused audiences by making up new ones, rhyming playfully or dropping in witticisms; she never forgot chords.

Sarah Vaughan was the fifty-sixth person to be inducted into the American Jazz Hall of Fame in New Jersey and the 1,808th person to be honored with a star on Hollywood's Walk of Fame. At various points in her career, she was named best female singer by readers of publications such as *Down Beat*, *Metronome*, *Billboard*, *Esquire*, and *Jazz Journal*. With her daughter, Paris Deborah, and her mother at her side, Vaughan died on April 3, 1990, at her ranch in Hidden Hills, California, of lung cancer. Thousands attended her funeral at the Mount Zion Baptist Church in Newark, New Jersey, while West Coast friends and musicians attended a memorial in California.

Summary

Sarah Vaughan confidently pursued a career as a serious vocalist and musician at a time when such opportunities were scarce for women, particularly women of African American descent. Her ceaseless improvisational abilities contributed to the development of jazz, and she was one of the few great female recording artists to provide vocals opposite primarily instrumental compositions.

When Vaughan began performing, many clubs admitted only whites; black musicians stayed with various families, including Vaughan's, because hotels discriminated as well. One Florida club owner was so enamored of Vaughan's voice that he asked what he could do to make her stay more comfortable; she requested that racial barriers be dropped for her performances, and they were. She cared deeply about her audiences, listening for their feedback and applause, singing for them with all of her heart. She was a tireless innovator, challenging her accompanists and earning the unyielding respect of the hundreds of musicians with whom she played. Scores of vocalists cite Vaughan as a major influence, and the fact that her music continues to be rereleased attests her continuing popularity.

Vaughan's formula for success was hard work and self-confidence; though she was shy with audiences during the beginning of her career, she never lost faith in her own ability to mesmerize them with song. She hired, married, lived with, fired, and divorced numerous managers over the years, and in the end she took care of herself and those most dear to her. Fans will long remember her earthy, unaffected personality, her tough spirit, and her elastic, powerful singing voice.

Bibliography
Feather, Leonard. *The Pleasures of Jazz*. New York: Horizon Press, 1976. Feather, jazz critic and longtime friend of Vaughan, gives a personal account of various musicians and vocalists, including Vaughan.
Gourse, Leslie. *Sassy: The Life of Sarah Vaughan*. New York: Charles Scribner's Sons, 1993. This detailed account of Vaughan's life incudes personal anecdotes, quotes from her accompanists and family, photos, a thorough discographical survey, a videography, and a bibliography.
Jones, Max. *Talking Jazz*. New York: W. W. Norton, 1987. This collection of interviews includes two with Vaughan combined into one article; the conversations about her career took place in 1973 and 1981.
Smith, Jessie Carney, ed. *Notable Black American Women*. Detroit: Gale Research, 1992. Includes a brief outline of Vaughan's life and career as well as anecdotes and quotes from critics who loved her voice.

Mary Pierce Frost

GWEN VERDON

Born: January 13, 1925; Culver City, California

Area of Achievement: Dance

Contribution: As a Broadway dancer and actress, Gwen Verdon refined musical theater dance to an art. She spent five years training film performers at Twentieth Century-Fox before rising to Broadway stardom in 1953. A versatile performer, Verdon has had a career encompassing television, theater, and film.

Early Life

Gwyneth Evelyn Verdon was born in Culver City, California, to Joseph William Verdon and Gertrude Standring Verdon. Both English-born, Joseph was a former gardener turned studio electrician for Metro-Goldwyn-Mayer studios, while Gertrude was a working vaudeville dancer. The couple had emigrated via Canada to California before the birth of their daughter. It soon became apparent that the infant's legs were so badly bent that a doctor advised breaking and resetting them. Gwen's mother refused the operation, put her daughter in corrective boots, and enrolled her in dancing lessons at the age of two. At the age of four, Gwen appeared with her mother in a Los Angeles dance recital, and by six was billed as "The World's Fastest Tapper" on the local vaudeville circuit.

Until the full popular acceptance of motion pictures in the 1920's, vaudeville was the most popular form of American theatrical entertainment. Appearing on variety programs of specialty dance, song, animal, acrobatic, or humorous acts, vaudeville performers worked on a week-by-week basis for a chain of privately owned theaters up and down both coasts and across the nation. These theater chains varied in terms of the prestige of their performers and the ticket prices charged to their patrons, and ranged from the Gus Sun circuit on the West Coast up to the elite Orpheum circuit. As a popular form of family entertainment, vaudeville was particularly open to juvenile acts. As the Depression hit, such "kiddie" acts not only were desired by the theater managers but also provided much-needed income for the performers' families.

Leaving the dance tutelage of her mother, Verdon began working with various teachers in the Los Angeles area, and eventually studied with Ernest Belcher and Carmelita Marrachi. Graduating from her child tap-dancing routines to other employment, Verdon became a bathing suit model during her teen years before moving on to become a dancer in nightclub choruses. During the 1920's through the 1950's, the nightclub provided an important venue for American entertainment and usually included a floor show with a dance band, a featured vocalist or singing group, a humorous master of ceremonies or comic, and a chorus of showgirls and dancers performing numbers with the singer or as a group with the band. Unlike nightclub dancers of the 1990's, chorus girls of this period were primarily dancers. Although they were often dressed in scanty costumes, they were not burlesque performers, but performed tap, popular social dances, and later jazz routines for the entertainment pleasure of the club's patrons. At the age of seventeen, Gwen interrupted her dance career to marry a Hollywood writer, James Henaghan, in 1942. When the marriage ended in 1947, she began her professional association with dance teacher and choreographer Jack Cole, one which would provide a vital link to her inevitable although elusive success.

Life's Work

Gwen Verdon and Jack Cole worked closely together during her early years as a dancer. She made her Broadway stage debut in 1948 in an abortive musical by Betty Comden and Adolph Green called *Bonanza Bound*. That same year, she assisted Cole with the choreography for Brazilian composer Heitor Villa-Lobos' Broadway production of *Magdalena*. By 1950, she was appearing in the line of Jack Cole's dancers in the short-lived Broadway production of *Alive and Kicking*.

Verdon also joined Jack Cole at Twentieth Century-Fox as his assistant dance director. For five years she taught such major Hollywood stars as Marilyn Monroe, Jane Russell, Lana Turner, and Betty Grable as they struggled to learn the choreography for dance numbers in their films. She often was given small dance parts in such films as *David and Bathsheba* (1952), but often found that her work was edited out of the film and left on the cutting room floor. The reason usually given was that Verdon stood out from the chorus within which she was supposed to be indistinguishable. She was also inadvertently attracting attention away from the star—an unconscious trait that would eventually lead to her success on the highest level of the dance world at that time, the Broadway stage in New York.

In 1953, Verdon was tired of working behind the cameras and in the chorus, and took the suggestion of choreographer Michael Kidd to audition for the musical *Can Can*. She was cast in the musical, but her outstanding presence and dance technique soon proved threatening to the show's French star, Lilo. Verdon's part was cut down during the show's out-of-town tryouts; discouraged by yet another instance of directors slighting her talent, Verdon gave her notice. She was persuaded, however, to stay through the show's Broadway opening. Cast as a can-can dancer who neglects her own career to support the sculptor she loves, Verdon performed only two dances: a sensuous Eve in Eden before and after the apple, and a stylized French waterfront seduction dance called an apache. The audience gave her a standing ovation, and she was forced back onstage in the middle of the show with their chants of "We want Verdon." She was acclaimed by reviewers the next day and received her first Antoinette F. Perry (Tony) award for her performance that season—the first of many such awards for Verdon.

Her triumph in *Can Can* was followed by Verdon's juicy role as Lola in the musical *Damn Yankees*, which opened on Broadway during the 1955-1956 season. Her portrayal of a devil's disciple who persuades a middle-aged baseball fan to sell his soul in exchange for the defeat of the New York Yankees, ran for more than 1,000 performances on Broadway and garnered her a second Tony award. She also reprised the role in the Warner Bros. adaptation of the musical that was filmed in 1958. Wary of landing on the cutting room floor again, Verdon stipulated that no part of her performance be altered without her permission.

From her earliest performances, the slender five foot, four inch dancer exhibited a charm that audiences responded to warmly. According to reviewers, Verdon appeared impish with her green eyes, pointed features, red hair, and smoky singing voice. As a dancer, she exhibited a joy of movement and a strong, brisk technical skill developed and honed to perfection by her work with Jack Cole and with her second husband, choreographer Bob Fosse, to whom she was married in 1960. Surmounting the technical demands and styles introduced by these choreographers, Verdon possessed a dynamic energy and a delight in her work that enchanted audiences for years.

In 1957, Verdon proved that her versatility and range extended beyond the limits of dance and musical comedy when she appeared in a dramatic musical based on Eugene O'Neill's *Anna Christie*. *New Girl in Town* told the bleak story of a Swedish tugboat captain and his unhappy daughter, a former prostitute named Anna. Although O'Neill's play was a dreary and strange choice for a musical, Verdon's Anna was a moving performance that was heralded by the critics and won her a third Tony. Her next Broadway success was in *Redhead* (1959). She was cast in the part of Essie, an English spinster who blossoms into a music-hall dancer. Verdon's dazzling nonstop athletic dance performance garnered her a fourth Tony award.

Several years elapsed until her 1966 appearance in the musical with which she is most identified by the modern generation of theatergoers, that of Charity Hope Valentine in *Sweet Charity*. Chronicling the lives of a group of taxi dancers in a New York dime-a-dance palace, the musical featured Verdon as the innocent Charity, who is searching for her true love amid squalor. Following that were *Children's Children* (1972), *Miliken's Breakfast Show Revue* (1973), a revival of *Damn Yankees* (1974), and *Chicago* (1975).

Verdon's career has also spanned television and films beginning with appearances in the 1950's on *Philco Playhouse* and the *Dinah Shore Show*. In the 1970's and 1980's, she appeared on a variety of television shows, including *M*A*S*H*, *Fame*, *Webster*, and *Trapper John, M.D.* On the popular series *Magnum, P.I.*, she was cast in a recurring role as Tom Selleck's mother. Her film appearances from the same period included roles in *Cotton Club* (1984) and *Cocoon* (1985). In addition, she worked from 1979 to 1980 as the production supervisor for the touring company production of *Dancin'*, a retrospective musical revue featuring Bob Fosse's choreography. In 1987, Verdon was involved in a revival of *Sweet Charity* produced by Fosse, her former husband. Unfortunately, Fosse died of a heart attack on his way to the Washington, D.C., opening night of the production. After his death, Verdon continued to maintain her ties to the theater and appeared in films, including *Cocoon II* (1988).

Summary

Gwen Verdon personified the perky, athletic female dancer that carried the classic Broadway musical through its heyday in the 1950's and 1960's. Her dynamic style, coupled with her charm and acting ability, helped make her one of the leading representatives of a golden era in American musical theater. Although Verdon was unable to fit into a Broadway stereotype of a slinky, long-legged femme fatale, she adapted her naturally ebullient personality to the technical demands of modern jazz dance as redefined by her husband Bob Fosse to create roles that exhibited her essential delight in movement.

Before the advent of modern Broadway choreographers such as Fosse, dance was based on synchronized chorus work often featuring dance partnership between principal characters. It was inserted as an interlude into the action of the plot instead of as a device to expand it. The choreography of the post-World War II musical theater placed more of a focus on technical skill and less on the classic beauty and uniformity of its dancers. It began to fit dance numbers into the plot of the entire production, and use them less as a showcase for chorus girls and songs. In this atmosphere, the small and slim Verdon could shine. With her winning personality and extraordinary technical skills, she was able to elevate Broadway dancing into this new arena. The choreography of Bob Fosse brought a new, sharp, show-stopping jazz style to the stage, and Verdon became its best known example as well as its ambassador.

Bibliography
Cohen-Stratyner, Barbara Naomi. *Biographical Dictionary of Dance*. New York: Schirmer Books, 1982. A dictionary of well-known and important figures in international dance focusing on ballet, jazz, and modern dance as well as dance performers on Broadway and film. The listings are brief but provide useful general information. The sketch on Verdon provides a good introduction to her accomplishments.

Gottfried, Martin. *All His Jazz: The Life and Death of Bob Fosse*. New York: Bantam Books, 1990. Gottfried, a drama critic, provides a starkly honest portrait of choreographer/director Fosse, who was married to Verdon for many years. While chronicling the couple's personal lives in detail, this biography also gives ample attention to their professional collaboration on a number of Broadway productions and film projects.

Grubb, Kevin. "Women Who Wow!" *Dance Magazine* 58 (August, 1984): 40-46. An article on dancers who are over the age of forty and still active in some area of dance. *Dance Magazine* offers the most current and accurate views on modern and classical dancers. It is a valuable resource for anyone interested in current choreographers, dancers, companies, and productions.

O'Donnell, Monica M. *Contemporary Theater, Film and Television*. Detroit: Gale Research, 1986. A multivolume series focusing on performers, directors, and playwrights in the theater, television, and film industries. The entries are brief but complete with short biographical data, principal film and stage appearances, related careers, and awards. A good source for modern performers whose careers cross media lines. The entry on Verdon takes her career up through the mid-1980's.

Rigdon, Walter. *The Biographical Encyclopedia and Who's Who of the American Theater*. New York: James H. Heineman, 1966. A brief but thorough biographical listing of prominent performers and playwrights in the American theater. In addition, this source includes complete listings of major New York productions by year, a list of premieres of American plays produced abroad, biographies of prominent theater groups, listings of current theater award recipients, and the architectural histories of famous American theaters. This is an extremely valuable general resource on the American theater, and it provides insights into Verdon's early career and the people with whom she worked.

Laurie Dawson

DIANA VREELAND

Born: c. 1903; Paris, France
Died: August 22, 1989; New York, New York
Area of Achievement: Fashion
Contribution: As fashion editor at *Harper's Bazaar* and editor-in-chief at *Vogue*, Vreeland directed America's fashion sensibility; as special consultant to the Metropolitan Museum's Costume Institute, she arranged enormously popular exhibits.

Early Life

Diana Dalziel (pronounced Dee-el) was born in Paris, France. In her autobiography, *D.V.* (1984), she winkingly hints at having been born in 1909 or 1910. The likely year is 1903, which would allow some credibility to her recollections of the demimondaines strolling along the Bois de Boulogne and the momentous change from Edwardian bustles and corsets to the outrageous hobble skirts of Paul Poiret that first shocked Paris in 1910.

Her father, Frederick Young Dalziel, was a dashing Scottish stockbroker, her mother a beautiful American named Emily Key Hoffman. On her mother's side, Diana claimed Martha Washington and Francis Scott Key among her ancestors. From both her parents she learned to live extremely well on relatively little, but Diana was not endowed with the family's striking good looks. Instead, Diana's gift appeared to be an unrestrainable imagination and a resourcefulness that buoyed her through the insecurities of adolescence and later made her an international cultural icon.

The Dalziels moved to New York in 1914. Diana was sent to the Brearley School, but lasted only three years in the disciplined environment. Discipline she eventually learned studying dance under Russian-born choreographer Michel Fokine. She loved to dance and was greatly influenced by Sergei Diaghilev and the Ballet Russe with its unabashed flamboyance. Excess, to Diana, was an art.

Rather than try to minimize her own heavy features, she exaggerated them. At sixteen, she powdered herself generously with calcimine— a theatrical makeup— which came off on her date's black dinner jacket. What for other young girls might have been a shattering experience was for Diana Dalziel something of a "coming out." Her exuberance and shamelessness lent her a charisma that mystified some and captivated others. On March 1, 1924, she was married to Thomas Reed Vreeland. Vreeland was older, handsome, and impeccably dressed—very important to the clothes-conscious Diana. Together they had two sons, Frederick (Frecky) and Thomas (Timmy), and despite her husband's frequent infidelities, she remained devoted to him until his death in 1966.

In 1929, the Vreelands moved from Albany, New York, to London. Diana opened a lingerie shop where, according to legend, Wallis Simpson acquired the nightgowns that would rob England of its king. Over the next few years, the Vreelands moved between England and the Continent and finally back to New York.

Aside from the lingerie shop venture, Diana had never worked, but Carmel Snow, editor-in-chief at *Harper's Bazaar*, offered her a job. "You seem to know a lot about clothes," Snow understated, and in 1936, Vreeland began writing "Why Don't You. . . ?", her much parodied column of helpful hints for the idle class. She was rapidly made fashion editor and became the leading voice in American fashion.

Life's Work

Diana Vreeland was not popular on Seventh Avenue—New York's fashion district—where American designers found her abrasive, critical, and contemptuous. She clearly preferred European design. When World War II broke out, however, the United States was cut off from Paris, and all the available fashion news came from Seventh Avenue. It was Vreeland who delivered (and to a large extent, dictated) wartime fashion. She taught the country to "make do" without compromising style. At her suggestion, for example, ballet slippers became chic when materials for shoes became scarce.

In the world of fashion, only Coco Chanel approached Vreeland's dynamism. Fashion photographer Richard Avedon later called her the "only genius fashion editor." Recognized as a fashion sybil, Vreeland herself declared that she "could only remember three months from now." When she decided to introduce the bikini to the American public, she demanded a model who could carry off the feat with a certain bravado (at the bikini's original debut in Italy, a stripper was employed because no professional model would wear it); Vreeland got a German baroness who agreed on the single condition that her name be used—Verushka.

Harper's Bazaar and *Vogue* were the leading fashion magazines in the United States for much of the twentieth century, *Harper's* having the edge on its rival with Snow, who had worked previously at *Vogue* and had accounted for much of its success then, and art director Alexey Brodovitch. It was Brodovitch who gave the magazine its arty layout, defining the look of fashion magazines that has persisted. The frenetic milieu of *Harper's Bazaar* was a noted feature of high society during the 1940's and 1950's and was even caricatured in the film *Funny Face* (1957).

Snow's health, however, declined in the late 1950's. Vreeland stood to inherit her mentor's position, but many believed that only Snow was capable of channeling Vreeland's reckless genius. Vreeland was passed over in favor of a safe and nepotistic choice. Slighted, she left *Harper's Bazaar* and moved to *Vogue*. She was hired as associate editor, but before long editor-in-chief Jennifer Daves was overwhelmed by Vreeland. Daves resigned and, in 1962, Vreeland replaced her.

At *Vogue*, there was no restraining Vreeland. In *Allure* (1980), Vreeland wrote that while she was at *Harper's Bazaar*, the only thing she had ever envied of *Vogue* was a portrait they had run of Brigitte Bardot. Bardot was as sexy—as excessive—as the 1950's could bear. "Her lips," Vreeland declared, "made Mick Jagger's lips *possible*." Outspokenness and experimentalism were just beginning to pervade the national spirit and, as the 1960's went on, so did an almost unprecedented cockiness. There were new materials to work with and an eagerness to shock—to make a "fashion statement." Vreeland reveled in the glossy new synthetics, the unembarrassed legs and navels of women, and the imperfect beauty of Cher and Barbra Streisand—and even Mick Jagger—all of which she presented in what had been a staid clothing magazine for the socially prominent. *Vogue* under Vreeland projected the high intensity of the era and imbued fashion with a whimsicality and daring that it had not enjoyed since the 1920's.

Vreeland spotted a waifish, wide-eyed young model, who, with her stick-thin limbs and almost adolescent figure, did not fit the classic image of the high-fashion model. Twiggy's became the most recognizable face (and body) in fashion journalism. Penelope Tree, Anjelica Huston, Marisa Berenson, and Edie Sedgwick headed a roster of women of peculiar and sensational beauty. They were photographed by the likes of Lord Snowdon and Cecil Beaton.

Vogue's photographers worked with Vreeland's almost mystical demands and brought to her much of the most stunning work done during that remarkably productive decade. On one occasion, she assigned a photographer to find an especially spectacular diamond. The stone was located—as a hunk of carbon—and was followed by the photographer for years while it was being cut. Vreeland considered the finished stone too garish on the model's perfect hands and so had the model's hands blackened with shoe polish. The effect was dramatic and singularly Vreelandesque. *Vogue* captured the camp and cant as well as the fervor and naïveté of the time. Vreeland's demands, however, were costly, and much of what she demanded was simply frivolous. In the 1970's, as fashion sobered and the publisher, Condé Nast, attempted to rein in her extravagant budgets, Vreeland refused to be conservative in either her vision or her spending. She was fired in 1971.

Over the next fourteen years, Vreeland would accomplish what many consider her best work. Theodore Rousseau, chief curator of the Metropolitan Museum of Art, suggested to Thomas Hoving, the museum director, that the still vital doyenne of fashion be made a special consultant to the museum's little known and underappreciated Costume Institute. Hoving was dubious until he was told that a group of enthusiastic supporters, which included socialite Babe Paley and former First Lady Jacqueline Kennedy Onassis, had already raised enough money to pay Vreeland's salary for two years.

Vreeland, with curator Stella Blum, arranged fourteen shows in fourteen years. The exhibits were enormously popular, though they suffered some criticism for being "unscholarly" and "entertaining." For example, Vreeland ordered new reproductions made of some garments because she did not believe the faded originals conveyed the designers' intended effect—a defensible argument if one considers that the whole point of haute couture is effect. Hoving himself later extolled Vreeland as one of his top three curators.

The premiere exhibit featured the work of Balenciaga, one of Vreeland's favorite designers. Among the most popular of these spectacular events were "Romantic and Glamorous Hollywood Design," most noted for its presentation of much of the wardrobe from *Gone with the Wind* (1939), and "The Glory of Russian Costume." In 1985, Vreeland declined at the last moment to attend the gala opening of "Costumes of Royal India." She instead retired, without explanation, not only from her work but also from society and eventually even from her friends. She spent the last four years of her life as a recluse in her famous red apartment, dying from heart failure in 1989.

Summary

Diana Vreeland's love of fashion began in childhood, when, as she wrote late in life, Paul Poiret "smashed the atom." It was his use of bold, bright colors and sumptuous textures as well as the immodesty of his designs that so appealed to her. The Orientalism and flamboyance of the Ballet Russe influenced her for the same reasons. It is impossible not to see the irony of so profound an appreciation for surface beauty in one who was unquestionably deprived of any of her own. Her trademark black lacquered hair and red lacquered nails, white powdered face, and unblended rouge—not only on her cheeks but also on her ear lobes—emphasized a homeliness that otherwise would have been unremarkable. Yet she did not powder her prominent nose to hide it or indulge in any foolish attempt to apologize for it by playing the clown. "I've always had a strong Kabuki streak," she wrote and illustrated her point by wearing a "Kabuki" face; the backdrop she provided for her astonishing visage, though, was an elegantly attired body, and the effect was one of unshakable self-confidence and an innate artistry.

For more than thirty-five years she dictated fashion from *Harper's Bazaar* and *Vogue*. The Kennedy's Camelot owed much of its elegance to Vreeland. The image of First Lady Jackie Kennedy with her prim handbag and pert pillbox hat is one of many indelible images from the reign of Vreeland. Twiggy's seductive, unblinking stare is another. Vreeland guided and promoted designers such as Oscar de la Renta and Carolyn Schnurer, introduced the bikini to America, and featured in her magazines the work of Richard Avedon, Irving Penn, Horst P. Horst, and other greats in twentieth century photography. When, in the 1960's, fashion became a driving cultural force Vreeland was there to give it its shape and momentum.

Vreeland's influence on the twentieth century was hardly subtle. Apolitical, she dressed politics and thereby helped to establish the ambience—the *Zeitgeist*—of four decades. Conservative in dress herself, she advocated radical styles and, in so doing, promoted the sexual revolution in a most effective way. Fashion, after her removal from *Vogue*, became staid, nostalgic—even regressive—and her vision and drive were sorely missed.

Bibliography

Collins, Amy Fine. "The Cult of Diana." *Vanity Fair* 56 (November, 1993): 174-184. A long article outlining Vreeland's life and achievements. A good source but sketchy on dates.

Snow, Carmel, with Mary Louise Aswell. *The World of Carmel Snow*. New York: McGraw-Hill, 1962. The memoirs of Vreeland's mentor and first editor written shortly before Snow's death. Offers an interesting perspective on Vreeland's tenure at *Harper's Bazaar*.

Steele, Valerie. *Women of Fashion: Twentieth-Century Designers*. New York: Rizzoli, 1991. A survey of twentieth century fashion focusing on the contribution of women. Chapter 10, "Think Pink," discusses the role of fashion magazines, *Harper's Bazaar* and *Vogue* in particular, and places Vreeland's career in context. Contains notes, bibliography, and a good index.

Vreeland, Diana. *D.V.* New York: Alfred A. Knopf, 1984. A witty and thoroughly unreliable recollection of the author's life. Seemingly woven from whole cloth, accounts of such unlikely events as Wallis Simpson's confidential tour of the Duke's bathroom might as well be true even if they are not. Valuable for getting a sense of Vreeland's life, if not the facts of it.

Vreeland, Diana, with Christopher Hemphill. *Allure*. Garden City, N.Y.: Doubleday, 1980. A collection of photographs admired and compiled by Vreeland, including many that appeared under her editorship. Vreeland's commentary is packed with the aphorisms for which she was famous. Indispensable for its insight into several successive but distinct eras of fashion and society.

Janet Alice Long

LILLIAN D. WALD

Born: March 10, 1867; Cincinnati, Ohio
Died: September 1, 1940; Westport, Connecticut
Areas of Achievement: Nursing and social reform
Contribution: Founder of the Henry Street Settlement and organizer of the first public health nursing system, Wald was a major social reformer during the Progressive Era.

Early Life

Lillian D. Wald was born in Cincinnati on March 10, 1867, one of four children in a Jewish family. Her parents, Minnie Schwarz and Marcus Wald, emigrated from Germany and Poland, respectively, fleeing revolutions in central Europe. Since her father traveled often, selling optical supplies, Minnie was the major influence on Lillian. Minnie loved all forms of beauty—flowers, music, furnishings—and she brought warmth and good taste into the household as well as devotion to family ties.

In 1878, the family moved to Rochester, New York. The city was a center for optical supplies, which made Max Wald's work easier, and family relatives were well established there, people of wealth and status. Like many upper-middle-class girls, Lillian attended a boarding and day school, the School for Young Ladies and Little Girls. The nonsectarian school prepared young women to be wives and mothers, but Lillian aspired to more than a conventional life.

At sixteen, Wald applied to Vassar but was rejected as too young, so she stayed two more years at school, feeling closed in—no profession, no career, no training. Isolated from the larger world, Lillian knew little of the growing social unrest and demands for reform.

Wald spent much time with her married sister, Julia Barry. During Julia's pregnancy a nurse was hired, and Lillian questioned her extensively about her training at Bellevue Hospital School of Nursing in New York City. Wald saw an opportunity for a noble career, and, in 1889, she applied to the New York Hospital's School of Nursing and was accepted. With limited training gleaned from lectures, Wald learned to make bandages and dressings, and to sterilize instruments. Her patients and colleagues alike found Wald a cheerful, dedicated person with extraordinary energy and ability. After her graduation in March, 1891, Wald helped to train incoming students.

In August, 1891, she began her new job as staff nurse at the New York Juvenile Asylum. One thousand children between the ages of five and eighteen were housed in the asylum. Outraged by the poverty, injustice, and abuses the children faced, Wald left after one year, and, in the fall of 1892, she enrolled at Women's Medical College, which was part of the New York Infirmary for Women and Children. Her studies and work made the poor very visible to Wald. She began a volunteer class, teaching home-care and hygiene to immigrant women. Based in the Louis Technical School at 267 Henry Street, Wald was exposed directly to scenes of poverty and degradation so intense that her life was changed.

Life's Work

Lillian Wald dropped out of medical college, determined to change the dreadful social conditions she encountered in New York's Lower East Side. She and a former schoolmate, Mary Brewster, planned to live among the poor, nursing them in their own homes. Support from wealthy patrons gave them economic security to do so. Wald and Brewster moved into a settlement house on Rivington Street with college graduates who were also willing to share their lives intimately with the poor. Classes were given in English, art, music, history, and economics, but Ward and Brewster focused on nursing the sick. The two nurses went from door to door in the tenements, handing out ointments, antiseptics, and advice. They wrote up their cases for a card file and reported monthly to their chief benefactor, Jacob Schiff, a senior partner in the international banking firm of Kuhn, Loeb, and Company.

Moving to a new address, the top floor of a six-story tenement, Wald and Brewster lived in the district in which they worked. They determined to remain independent and nonsectarian, resisting efforts to join forces with relief agencies. They visited homes, compiling statistics on the wretched situations and conditions they encountered. Immigrants poured into New York's Lower East Side. They clung together in religious and kinship groups, working twelve to fourteen hours daily, trying to survive. Wald wrote vivid reports to Jacob Schiff, describing these poverty-stricken people. Her experiences opened Wald to progressive thinkers and reformers such as Jacob Riis, Lincoln Steffens, and Josephine Lowell (founder of the Consumers' League of New York)

In April of 1895, Schiff bought a house on Henry Street that became Lillian's second home and the center for the Visiting Nurse Service. A second building next door was added later to accommodate the growing number of nurses asking to work with Wald. Henry House became a refuge for sick, needy neighbors who found nursing care as well as friendship there.

In 1900, the family of nurses grew to fifteen—an educated, middle-class, unmarried support network. Wald was the heart of this family, to which she also brought an executive ability to link Henry Street with the world of financial backers and with the larger reform movements. To save her patients' pride, Wald charged from ten cents to a quarter to those who could pay for personal health care, though no one was refused care. She wanted to treat the sick in their homes, referring only the extreme cases to dispensaries or the hospitals.

In 1899, the dynamic Florence Kelley joined Wald's inner circle of friends and advisers, becoming general secretary of the National Consumers' League. A lawyer and social activist, Kelley had served as special investigator of child labor conditions in Illinois. Wald and Kelley allied for social change, especially on behalf of children. Frequent visits by Jane Addams, head of Hull House Settlement, based in Chicago, further enlarged Wald's insights into the need for practical, political solutions to the economic and social problems of the day, which impinged heavily on health conditions. Addams' sharp mind and organizational skills were highly prized, and Wald and her coworkers often turned to her for advice.

Wald was moved particularly by the plight of children playing in crowded streets, attending crowded schools, and living in crowded homes. They faced hunger and disease daily, and Wald tried to awaken a social consciousness of their situation. She promoted neighborhood parks and more playgrounds, and she urged that public schools stay open after school hours and in summer as recreation centers. Wealthy patrons offered homes for day and weekend visits by the children, some bequeathing their estates as camps for Henry Street use.

Wald initiated the hiring of the first public school nurse. Worried that ill children were spreading contagious diseases, she offered to pay half the salary for a nurse if the Board of Education would pay the other half. A Henry Street nurse supervised four schools, identifying illnesses and visiting sick children's homes. When it was found that these schools had healthier children and better attendance than did all the others, the Board of Education agreed to make school nurses part of the system.

Forced to work to supplement their parents' wages, many children were not in school at all. In 1903, pressured by the National Consumers' League, settlement houses, and other reform organizations, New York established limits on child labor, although proper inspection was often absent. In 1905, Wald and Kelley proposed a federal bureau to care for the welfare of children. The proposal reached President Theodore Roosevelt, who discussed it with Wald and others. He supported a bill for a Federal Children's Bureau, and it was introduced in the 1906 Congress.

The bill was backed by prominent organizations and individuals such as women's clubs, state labor committees, newspaper publishers, and religious leaders. The bureau was envisioned as a national research center to collect and classify information on the nation's children. Because Congress refused to hold hearings on the bill, Roosevelt asked Wald to arrange what became, in January of 1909, a Conference on the Care of Dependent Children. When hearings on the bill began, Wald and Kelley testified in Washington, but Congress balked, and Wald and her colleagues kept up a barrage of writing and speaking to get the bill passed. In April of 1912, President William H. Taft signed the bill into law.

Expanding public health nursing into rural as well as urban areas, in 1908 Wald persuaded Schiff to give an initial grant of $10,000 to aid the Red Cross in establishing a Department of Town and Country Nursing. Realizing that there were too few nurses, she envisioned a corps of teachers to train more nurses. She persuaded another wealthy patron to bequeath a large sum to endow Teachers College of Columbia University with a postgraduate school for teacher nurses.

In 1913, the Henry Street Settlement and the Visiting Nurse Service celebrated twenty years of work in the Lower East Side. Wald could look back on twenty years of achievements, including improved status and increased self-esteem for all nurses.

The 1918 worldwide outbreak of influenza put new demands on Wald and her nurses. As head of the Nurses' Emergency Council, she created an effective administration to mobilize nurses, teachers, social workers, and volunteers to meet the health crisis. The Red Scare of 1919-1920, however, gripped the nation in a madness of violence, hatred, and intolerance. Dissent was dangerous, and Wald found herself censured as radical and unpatriotic because of her pacifist stand during World War I. Raising money became more difficult. Schiff died suddenly in September of 1920, ending the longest, steadiest, and most generous source of support for Wald's work.

The 1920's were a conservative age, and social reforms were not supported by the federal government as they had been in the past. Wald and her allies fought to retain progressive gains. She became vice president of the American Association for Labor Legislation, contributed to the American Anti-Imperialist League, and sponsored the American League to Abolish Capital Punishment. Wald remained very active on behalf of civil liberties, but her health declined with overwork.

During the Depression, Henry Street continued as a haven for the needy. The Visiting Nurse Service now had twenty centers, handling almost 100,000 cases annually. In 1933, Wald resigned as head of Henry Street but remained as president of the board of directors.

Wald died on September 1, 1940, and she was mourned by thousands. Her legacy would endure: the Visiting Nurse Service, the Henry Street Settlement, the Federal Children's Bureau, the public school nurse. Lillian Wald enriched the lives of many through her work as a pioneer public nurse, a settlement worker, a feminist, and a reformer—roles she imbued with a wealth of enthusiasm and charm.

Summary

Lillian D. Wald, through her many efforts to improve health care and remedy the societal ills of poverty, ignorance, and inequality, had an immense impact on U.S. society, the effects of which can still be perceived. Her initial interest in social reform was sparked by the misery she witnessed in poor neighborhoods, but her special contribution to the field was perhaps her identification of the root causes of the problems she saw around her. She did seek to solve the immediate problems of those who required help by providing health care and education, but she also went further, calling for the establishment and support of human rights, civil liberties, and opportunities for all citizens to live decent lives.

Bibliography

Daniels, Doris G. *Always a Sister: The Feminism of Lillian D. Wald*. New York: Feminist Press at the City University of New York, 1989. A selective biography centered on Wald's feminist thinking and actions. Chapter notes, a bibliographical essay, and an index are included.

Duffus, Robert L. *Lillian Wald, Neighbor and Crusader*. New York: Macmillan, 1938. Written with Wald's cooperation, this is a glowing tribute to her and her career. Includes an index.

Siegel, Beatrice. *Lillian Wald of Henry Street*. New York: Collier Macmillan, 1983. An excellent biography that captures the private Wald as well as the public figure. Chapter notes, sources, and an index are included.

Trolander, Judith A. *Settlement Houses and the Great Depression*. Detroit, Mich.: Wayne State University Press, 1975. The introduction and chapters one through three are superb regarding settlement houses and reform. Includes an appendix, chapter notes, and a bibliography.

Wald, Lillian D. *The House on Henry Street*. New York: Holt, 1915. An engrossing narrative of the famous settlement and its role in social reform. Many stories illustrate conditions among the poor. Includes an index.

Williams, Beryl. *Lillian Wald, Angel of Henry Street*. New York: Julian Messner, 1948. A lively biography meant mainly for young readers. Includes frequent dialogue and many anecdotes. A brief biography and an index are provided.

S. Carol Berg

ALICE WALKER

Born: February 9, 1944; Eatonton, Georgia

Area of Achievement: Literature

Contribution: Walker, winner of the Pulitzer Prize and the American Book Award, has dedicated her life to establishing a literary canon of African American women writers and to encouraging the "survival whole" of all women. She has actively sought to win recognition for literary "foremothers" such as Zora Neale Hurston and to place their contributions within the fabric of her own artistry.

Early Life

Alice Walker was born on February 9, 1944, into a family of sharecroppers near Eatonton, Georgia. Her father, Willie Lee Walker, was the grandson of slaves. Walker's enslaved paternal great-great-grandmother, Mary Poole, had walked from Virginia to Georgia carrying two of her children on her hips. Walker's relationship with her father became strained as she grew into adolescence and showed a proclivity for intellectual pursuits. Although her father was brilliant, his educational opportunities had been limited, and he feared that education would place barriers between him and his children. When Walker left her home for Spelman College in Atlanta, her relationship with her father ended.

Minnie Tallulah Grant Walker, Walker's mother, realized how important education was for her daughter. Minnie Walker, a farmhand and domestic worker, greatly desired an education for her daughter. She enrolled Walker in the first grade at the age of four and excused her from household chores so that she might have time for her reading and schoolwork. Minnie Walker saved the money she earned as a domestic in the town of Eatonton and bought several gifts that had a great impact upon her daughter's life. These gifts included a sewing machine that enabled Walker to make her own clothes, a suitcase, and a typewriter, of which she later made good use.

When Walker was eight years old, a shot fired from her brother's BB gun permanently blinded her right eye. Convinced that the resulting scar tissue in her eye was disfiguring and ugly, she retreated into solitude. She spent the next seven to eight years reading voraciously and writing poems. Walker was the valedictorian of her high school class, and when she was graduated in 1961, she was offered a scholarship to Spelman College in Atlanta. After traveling to Africa in 1964, Walker returned to the United States and entered Sarah Lawrence College. She soon discovered that she was pregnant, and just as quickly she found herself depressed and on the verge of suicide. Walker made a decision to end the pregnancy instead of her life and subsequently wrote her first published short story, "To Hell with Dying." She also produced *Once* (1965), her first published collection of poems, during her years at Sarah Lawrence.

While she was attending college, Walker spent her summers working for the Civil Rights movement in Georgia. She was graduated from Sarah Lawrence College in 1965, and after graduation, she became even more involved in the Civil Rights movement. In 1967, Walker was married to lawyer Mel Leventhal and moved with him to Mississippi. Leventhal worked as a civil rights attorney in the Jackson school desegregation cases, and Walker worked with Head Start programs and held writer-in-residence positions at Tougaloo College and Jackson State University. She subsequently taught at Wellesley College, the University of Massachusetts at Amherst, the University of California at Berkeley, and Brandeis University. In 1969, Walker's only child, Rebecca, was born.

Life's Work

In 1970, while she was working on her short story "The Revenge of Hannah Kemhuff," Alice Walker discovered the works of Zora Neale Hurston. Her discovery of Hurston had a profound effect on Walker. Walker described Hurston as her literary "foremother," and in her essay "Zora Neale Hurston" (1979), Walker states that were she condemned to spend her life on a desert island with an allotment of only ten books, she would choose two of Hurston's books: *Mules and Men* (1935) and *Their Eyes Were Watching God* (1937). In August, 1973, Walker traveled to Florida to locate Hurston's grave. She had a marker placed on the spot that was most likely Hurston's grave and then dedicated herself to calling attention to Hurston's genius. Through Walker's efforts, Hurston's work received the critical acclaim that it deserved.

In 1970, Walker published her first novel, *The Third Life of Grange Copeland*. Although Grange Copeland is the protagonist of the novel, Walker focuses on his treatment of African American women. Walker's main concerns in her novels are the powerlessness of African American women and sexist behavior on the part of men. In 1972, after the publication of *The Third Life of Grange Copeland*, Walker left Mississippi to teach at Wellesley College and the University of Massachusetts at Amherst.

The following year, Walker published a book of poetry, *Revolutionary Petunias* (1973), for which she won the Lillian Smith Award. This small volume of poems is a celebration of people who refuse to fit into other people's molds. She also published a book of short stories, *In Love and Trouble* (1973). The stories in this first collection depict African American women who are victimized by racism and/or sexism. They are women who are not whole, are often mute, and who are used and abused by the men they love.

In 1976, Walker published her second novel. *Meridian* is the story of a young woman's personal development in the midst of the Civil Rights movement. More autobiographical elements may be found in *Meridian* than in any other Walker narrative. Many of the struggles faced by Meridian were similar to struggles that Walker confronted in both her college years at a predominantly white women's college and in her interracial marriage to a civil rights lawyer. In 1976, Walker's marriage to Mel Leventhal ended in divorce, and two years later, Walker decided to move from New York City to San Francisco. A year after her move to the West Coast, Walker produced two more books. She published her second volume of African American women-centered poems, *Good Night, Willie Lee, I'll See You in the Morn-*

ing (1979), and she produced an anthology of Zora Neale Hurston's works, *I Love Myself When I Am Laughing* (1979).

Several literary critics, and even Walker herself, have compared Walker's stories and novels to crazy quilts. The bits and pieces that she weaves together have much in common; they originate in the South and they reveal the lives of African American women in various stages of development. In 1981, Walker produced *You Can't Keep a Good Woman Down*, a volume of fourteen stories that address the blossoming creativity of women. One year later, she produced her Pulitzer Prize-winning novel *The Color Purple* (1982). *The Color Purple* is a series of ninety letters that Celie, Walker's outwardly silent protagonist, addresses to God. These letters disclose Celie's development of self and voice, while providing the reader with a vision of how the societal intersection of sexism and racism affects the African American family.

The themes of forgiveness and reconciliation are prominent in Walker's writing. In Walker's next novel, *The Temple of My Familiar* (1989), her characters work toward forgiving one another. Walker reveals much of her personality in her book of essays *In Search of Our Mother's Gardens* (1983). Among other topics, she describes her discovery of and commitment to Zora Neale Hurston. Although Walker is a devoted mother, in her essay "One Child of One's Own," she openly and honestly describes her decision to have only one child. In *Living by the Word* (1988), her second volume of essays, her discussions range from the love she has for her daughter to her reactions to criticism of the treatment of men in her book *The Color Purple* (1985). In an interview with Oprah Winfrey in 1989, Walker discussed her critics' failure to recognize the development of nurturance and sensitivity in her male characters. In *The Color Purple*, Albert asks Celie to remarry him, and in *The Temple of My Familiar*, Suwelo realizes that Carlotta, and all women, are beings with feelings and spirits.

In several of her essays in *Living by the Word*, Walker moves her focus from the individual to larger issues between the peoples of this world—indeed, to unity within the universe. Walker's volumes of poetry *Horses Make a Landscape Look More Beautiful* (1984) and *Her Blue Body Everything We Know: Earthling Poems 1965-1990 Complete* (1991) reflect her larger concern for the cultures of this world and the planet itself. In her novel *Possessing the Secret of Joy* (1992), Walker moves from African American culture to detail the misogyny contained in the hideous practice of female circumcision. She continued her examination of that practice in the 1993 book *Warrior Marks: Female Genital Mutilation and the Sexual Blinding of Women*, which she wrote with Pratibha Parmas. Since the mid-1980's, Walker has lived in northern California. There she writes, communes with her friends, works in her garden, and prays to her Great Spirit.

Summary

Alice Walker has had a tremendous impact on the African American literary canon. In addition to being a major author of notable literature, Walker has enlarged the canon by bringing the works of Zora Neale Hurston before the public, and she has both written within and revised the tradition of African American women writers. Her literary contribution includes novels, short stories, essays, and poetry. Walker moved to the North and then to the West, but her writer's soul returned to the South of her childhood; thence, she has given voice to previously silent and unseen generations of African American women. She has recognized their artistry and praised their resiliency and strength. Walker writes to and for women of all colors and cultures, urging them to know their inner selves and to bind up wounds resulting from centuries of silence and abuse. Walker believes in change, for the individual and for society, and for the "survival whole" of the African American woman. Although Walker has been labeled a feminist writer, she prefers the term "womanist" rather than "feminist," for she believes that the term "womanist" captures the spirit of the African American woman. The spirit of the African American woman remains Walker's primary commitment.

Bibliography
Bloom, Harold, ed. *Alice Walker*. New York: Chelsea House, 1989. This volume includes much of the best current criticism of Walker's work. In his introduction, Harold Bloom discusses the impact of Zora Neale Hurston's work on Walker, and Dianne F. Sadoff and Deborah E. McDowell also discusses the import of the Walker-Hurston relationship.
Christian, Barbara. *Black Feminist Criticism: Perspectives on Black Women Writers*. New York: Pergamon Press, 1985. Christian includes two chapters about Alice Walker. "The Contrary Women of Alice Walker" is an analysis of the female protagonists of *In Love and Trouble*. "Alice Walker: The Black Woman Artist as Wayward" explores the ways in which Walker uses "forbidden" topics as a route to truth.
_____. *Black Women Novelists: The Development of a Tradition, 1892-1976*. Westport, Conn.: Greenwood Press, 1980. Barbara Christian traces the historical development of the literature of African American women. She then critically analyzes the works of three contemporary African American writers who are building from the earlier tradition that preceded them and are developing that tradition in a critical way. Chapter 6, "Novels for Everyday Use," is an analysis of the early novels of Alice Walker.
Gates, Henry Louis, Jr., and K. A. Appiah, eds. *Alice Walker: Critical Perspectives Past and Present*. New York: Amistad Press, 1993. The most complete collection of essays on Walker, this volume contains eleven reviews of her novels and sixteen critical essays on various aspects of her literature. The volume concludes with two well-regarded interviews in which Walker herself discusses her literary contributions.
Walker, Alice. *In Search of Our Mother's Gardens*. San Diego, Calif.: Harcourt Brace Jovanovich, 1983. A volume of Walker's essays in which she traces the development of her intellectual life, from her search for a literary model and gifts of empowerment, through the civil rights movement of the 1960's, toward what she terms "Breaking Chains and Encouraging Life." Her first essay deals with the

importance of models in an artist's life, and one of her last essays is an account of how she wrote *The Color Purple*.

Winchell, Donna Haisty. *Alice Walker*. New York: Twayne, 1992. Donna Winchell combines critical analysis with biographical information to provide a study of all Walker's works through 1991. Her comprehensive analysis includes Walker's novels, short stories, essays, and poetry.

Yvonne Johnson

MADAM C. J. WALKER
Sarah Breedlove

Born: December 23, 1867; Delta, Louisiana
Died: May 25, 1919; Irvington-on-Hudson, New York
Area of Achievement: Business and industry
Contribution: Madam C. J. Walker founded a successful business based on hair care for black women, then used her wealth to benefit others of her race.

Early Life

Sarah Breedlove was born on a farm in Louisiana on December 23, 1867. Her parents, Owen and Minerva Breedlove, former slaves, were poor sharecroppers whose only Christmas gift to Sarah's brother, Alex, and sister, Louvenia, was the new baby, as the cotton crop had failed that year. Theirs was the typical lot of sharecroppers, backbreaking labor that at each season's end never exceeded in profit the debt which they owed to their landlord.

In 1874, when Sarah was seven years old, she lost both her parents in a yellow fever epidemic. Although the older Breedlove children tried to work the land, they were not successful. Alex left to seek work in Vicksburg, Mississippi, and Louvenia took charge of the young Sarah. They moved to Vicksburg in 1878, and the two sisters worked as washerwomen to survive. Because they were so poor, Sarah was unable to go to school.

Sarah married Moses McWilliams, a laborer, in 1882, when she was fourteen years old. Her main objectives were to escape her sister's cruel husband and to have a home of her own. In 1885, she gave birth to her only daughter, Lelia. Two years later McWilliams died, and Sarah moved to St. Louis with her daughter. She labored as a washerwoman for eighteen years, managing to put Lelia through public school and then Knoxville College. She wanted a better life for her daughter, but it was difficult for a poor washerwoman to escape the drudgery of her occupation.

In 1905, when Sarah's brother died, she and Lelia went to Denver, Colorado, to join his family. At the age of thirty-seven and with only $1.50, about a week's wages for a washerwoman, to her name, Sarah began work on the hair care formula that would make her famous.

Life's Work

Sarah McWilliams suffered from thinning hair and sought a remedy for her condition. She began to experiment with available products but was not satisfied with the results. In later years, she claimed that she had had a dream or vision in which a black man appeared to her and gave her a formula that would restore her hair. Many of the ingredients could be obtained only from Africa, but she sent for them and mixed up the formula.

She found to her delight that after several weeks her hair showed marked improve-ment in health and growth. Eager to share her new and successful product, she began to sell the formula, which she named "Wonderful Hair Grower," in the African American community of Denver.

During her first year in Denver, Sarah married Charles Joseph Walker, a newspaperman, and changed her name to Madam C. J. Walker. Charles Walker contributed his knowledge of business to his wife's operations, which continued to expand. Unable to keep up with the demand for products and unwilling to limit her success, Walker herself assumed the role of manager.

More than simply offering cosmetic products for purchase, Madam C. J. Walker developed the "Walker System," which consisted of the application of her products and the use of hot-iron combs specially designed by Walker for the thicker hair of African American women.

Walker traveled extensively, giving demonstrations of her system, her own carefully coiffed hair a persuasive example of the system's effectiveness. She recruited African American women as Walker Agents to sell her products door-to-door and demonstrate the Walker System. With her training, these "hair culturists," as Walker named them, were able to open beauty parlors in their homes and earn much more than domestic service could bring them.

Moving to Pittsburgh in 1908, Walker opened Lelia College. Named for her daughter, Walker's school trained the growing ranks of women seeking to become hair culturists. The emphasis in training was to pamper the customer, providing a unique opportunity for black women to feel that their comfort and appearance mattered, to help them feel important in a world that devalued them. Yet Walker admonished her agents not to refuse to sell her products to a customer who was unable to afford the Walker treatment. Walker apparently never forgot her own impoverished roots.

As her fortune grew, Walker continued to travel extensively, selling her products and recruiting her sales force. Walker Agents, well-groomed women dressed in white blouses and long black skirts, became a common sight in cities throughout the United States. Realizing that black women elsewhere might desire her products, Walker also traveled to Central America and the Caribbean, discovering another market open to her products.

Along with her success came a growing influence in the black community. Walker addressed many African American organizations in her travels. At first frustrated in her attempts to address the National Negro Business League convention in 1912, Walker was championed by George Knox, a black newspaperman, who urged that she be heard. Booker T. Washington, who was in charge of the floor discussions, continued to pass her up and call on male speakers. This attempt to shut her out, because she was a woman and because many of the leading black citizens did not approve of her business, failed when Walker finally stood up and gave her speech without his recognition. (Washington later became one of her supporters.) Walker was a resounding success with the delegates, who plied her with questions later after dinner. She had become the richest woman in America, black or white, by her own efforts. That same year, she divorced Charles Walker, but maintained his name for business purposes.

In 1916, Madam C. J. Walker moved to Harlem, in New York City. She began to involve herself in the explosion of art and culture that became known as the Harlem Renaissance. Her brownstone residence served as the location for parties attended by leading figures in black politics and the arts. Walker took pains to ensure that each guest list included a lively mix of personalities and viewpoints.

Some sources have claimed that Walker quietly supported Marcus Garvey, whose followers charged that black intellectuals such as W. E. B. Du Bois were attempting to set up a black aristocracy based on lightness of skin color. It is true that Madam Walker used her own image, with its strong African American features, to sell her products.

The first annual Madam C. J. Walker Hair Culturists Union of America Convention was held in 1917. The convention gave further validation to the careers of Walker Agents nationwide and abroad, evoking a sense of pride and accomplishment.

That same year, Walker traveled with other concerned Harlemites to Washington, D.C., to visit President Woodrow Wilson. Her goal was to convince Wilson to back legislation making lynching a federal crime. Wilson declined to see her group, but a year later he issued a statement condemning racist violence. Unfortunately, nothing much was accomplished by Wilson's rather weak statement.

Although it was one of her best years, 1918 proved also to be one of her last. Despite poor health and against the advice of her physician, Walker continued to travel extensively to promote her products and to fulfill speaking engagements. She could not seem to slow down, even joking about this inability in the correspondence she sent to her business manager when she was supposed to be taking a break from her business concerns.

With her company's annual sales exceeding $250,000, Walker became a million-aire, and another round of travel and personal appearances began. The villa she had built on the Hudson River was completed that year, and she moved in, throwing a huge party that brought together all the notable figures of black culture.

Walker continued to contribute funds to various worthy causes in the black community. In 1919, she donated large sums to the National Association for the Advancement of Colored People (NAACP) to support its efforts at achieving antilynching legislation. On May 25, 1919, Madam C. J. Walker died at her Hudson River estate, Villa Lewaro. She left a will that divided her fortune between her daughter, who was the primary recipient, and the dozens of black organizations and charities which Walker supported.

Summary

Madam C. J. Walker's accomplishment in business was remarkable for her time, considering her race and gender. Yet she contributed much more than new products to the hair care industry and financial assistance to worthy causes. By establishing her own business, built by her own hard work and determined management, Walker provided an example for African American women, whose low social status often kept them in poverty. Her recruitment and training programs provided opportunities for black women to earn at least twice the wages they received as domestic workers and to become economically self-sufficient. Walker traveled widely, personally contacting potential employees and sometimes offering to let them start their business on credit, believing that they could become successful. Walker invested in people as well as causes. Besides her Walker Agents, she provided employment in her factories, even to the extent of using black architects and contractors to construct her facilities. The pride in appearance that she promoted through her products increased the self-esteem of black women, helping them to seek employment with greater self-confidence. Although Walker enjoyed the luxuries that her fortune could buy, she also contributed generously to many black organizations and causes. Even with her health declining, she continued to travel and promote such important civil rights issues as antilynching laws. She also opened up her home as a type of salon, providing a place where intellectuals and other figures in the arts and politics could mix in the vibrant culture that became known as the Harlem Renaissance.

Bibliography
Bird, Caroline. *Enterprising Women*. New York: W. W. Norton, 1976. This work challenges the assumption that women were not important in shaping the economic history of the United States. The author claims that Walker was one of many "cosmetic queens" who followed in the footsteps of Harriet Hubbard Ayer, and that Walker was a successful woman who found new ways to help other women solve the problems American culture had created for them.
Bundles, A'Lelia Perry. *Madam C. J. Walker*. New York: Chelsea House, 1991. Extensive, sympathetic portrait of Madam C. J. Walker detailing her accomplishments in business and philanthropy. Lavishly illustrated with contemporary photographs of Walker, her associates, and common, relevant scenes of the time.
Giddings, Paula. *When and Where I Enter: The Impact of Black Women on Race and Sex in America*. New York: William Morrow, 1984. Examines the evolving historical image of the black woman, from both internal and external viewpoints. Includes a discussion of Madam Walker's contributions to these images and refutes the claims that Walker undermined black pride by encouraging black women to attempt to "look white."
Huggins, Nathan Irvin. *Harlem Renaissance*. New York: Oxford University Press, 1971. Provides an elaborate background of Harlem in the days of Walker. Both concepts and figures in the arts and philosophy are examined thoroughly, providing an insight to the personalities and ideas that Walker brought together in her stimulating parties.
Lewis, David Levering. *When Harlem Was in Vogue*. New York: Alfred A. Knopf, 1981. Places Madam C. J. Walker in the ranks of the "New Negro," calling her "the richest self-made woman in America." Explains the post-World War I pride that moved many African Americans to actively seek their rights at home after fighting abroad for the rights of all Americans. Claims that Walker was a Garvey sympathizer. A sensitive look at the "New Negro."
Sterling, Dorothy, ed. *We Are Your Sisters: Black Women in the Nineteenth Century*.

New York: W. W. Norton, 1984. A compilation of oral histories that knits together the experience of black women. Provides an understanding of how difficult Walker's achievement was considering the racial and gender barriers which she faced.

Wells-Barnett, Ida B. *Crusade for Justice*. Edited by Alfreda M. Duster. Chicago: University of Chicago Press, 1970. Personal reminiscence and praise for Madam C. J. Walker from Wells, who moved in the same political circles. Readers can get an idea of the politics Walker supported once she became successful.

Patricia Masserman

MAGGIE LENA WALKER

Born: July 15, 1867; Richmond, Virginia
Died: December 15, 1934; Richmond, Virginia
Areas of Achievement: Business and industry and social reform
Contribution: The nation's first female bank president, Maggie Lena Walker worked
to create business opportunities to benefit African Americans.

Early Life

Maggie Lena Mitchell was representative of the generation of leaders born at the
end of the Civil War. She was born in Virginia on July 15, 1867, to a former slave,
Elizabeth Draper, and an Irish-born newspaperman, who worked for *The New York
Herald*. No official record of her birth exists and some scholars suggest that she might
have been born two or three years earlier. Her mother, Elizabeth "Lizzie" Draper, was
a cook's helper on the Van Lew plantation. In the spring of 1868, Elizabeth Draper
married William Mitchell, the butler to the Van Lew family. The Van Lew estate on
Church Hill, outside the city of Richmond, had a colorful history as a station on the
Underground Railroad. The Van Lews served as Union spies and harbored Union
soldiers during the Civil War. Thus, Maggie Lena Mitchell benefited from the social
and educational privileges afforded the servants at the Van Lew mansion in Richmond.

In order to achieve a greater sense of identity, the Mitchells left the Van Lew estate
and moved to two rented clapboard houses in College Alley in downtown Richmond,
close to William Mitchell's new job as head waiter at the St. Charles Hotel. Lizzie
Mitchell took in laundry and reared the children, Maggie and Johnnie (born 1870). In
February, 1876, Maggie's father disappeared and was found within a week in the
James River. The family believed the death was the result of a robbery, but the
authorities listed the death as a suicide. The loss of income caused Lizzie Mitchell to
expand her laundry business. A strict disciplinarian, her mother used Maggie as her
delivery person and babysitter.

Maggie received a segregated education from the public schools of Richmond. She
attended old Lancaster School, across from the jail, whose inmates educated young
Maggie about cursing. Her teachers were leaders of the black community. She
supplemented her education with the spiritual instruction from the Thursday night
"Sunday" school at the Old First Baptist Church (First African Baptist Church), the
oldest and largest black church in Richmond. She was baptized in the summer of 1878
during the Great Richmond Revival. Her financial education came at age fourteen,
when she participated in the black insurance business connected with the fraternal
organization the Independent Order of St. Luke (IOSL). Within two years, she
represented the IOSL as an elected delegate to the annual convention at Petersburg.

She finished at the head of her class at Armstrong Normal and High School in 1883,
a class that won national recognition for its attempts to lessen Jim Crow segregation.
For the graduation ceremonies, she led her senior class in requesting to join their white

counterparts at the Richmond Theater rather than accept their diplomas separately in the church hall. The school administration was willing to allow the joint ceremony only if it respected the Jim Crow norms requiring segregated seating of students and audience. The students rejected the choice to seat blacks in the balcony; instead, the students received their diplomas in the school auditorium.

After her graduation, she became a teacher for three years at the Lancaster School. During this time, she took classes in accounting and business management, skills she later put to use for the IOSL. Her teaching career ended when, on September 14, 1886, she married Armstead Walker, a former mail carrier and contractor who was active in her church. Thereafter she redirected her energies from teaching into her community organizations, especially the IOSL.

Life's Work

After the birth of her first son, Russell Eccles Talmage, in 1890, Maggie Lena Walker entrusted his care to household servants and ascended in the IOSL. Within a decade, she moved from executive secretary to grand secretary-treasurer, a position she held for thirty-five years. In 1893, she lost both her brother Johnnie and her infant second child Armstead. The Walkers adopted a daughter, Margaret "Polly" Anderson. Maggie Walker attended the 1895 convention of IOSL and submitted resolutions for the creation of a juvenile division managed by a council of matrons in each local council. By the time her son Melvin DeWitt was born in 1897, she had drafted the governing laws for administering juvenile circles, had formed the juvenile branch of the order, and had accepted the secretaryship of the St. Luke Endowment Department.

In 1899, she became the right worthy grand secretary, a secretary-treasurer with a salary of $100 a year. She found an organization in need of leadership with inadequate staff, no property, no reserve funds, and only 3,400 members, of whom only 1,080 were paying members. Only $36.61 remained in the treasury, and the organization's unpaid bills amounted to more than $400. She created a fraternal newspaper, the *Saint Luke Herald*, to establish communication and to market services. The managing editor, Lillian Payne, used editorials written by lawyer James Hayes to criticize lynching, politics in Haiti, racial discrimination, Jim Crow segregation, and subordination of black women. This newspaper stimulated the formation of a profitable printing business. In 1903, Walker organized a building project to erect a three-story brick hall that was then rented to the Right Worthy Grand Council, the central organization of the IOSL. Under her twenty-five-year leadership, the IOSL collected more than $3.4 million. Membership climbed to more than 100,000 in twenty-four states, and the organization had a cash reserve of $70,000, an office building worth $100,000, and a staff of 55 with 145 field agents.

The Walkers established their home on East Leigh Street, which was known as "the Fifth Avenue of Negro Society." This environment provided privileges and role models. Walker moved the IOSL from its initial goals of providing funeral/burial services and assistance for the ill and aged to the managing of savings and investments. She demonstrated her early religious training in the IOSL's slogan of "Love,

Purity, and Charity" and in the organization's "fraternal kindness." She made sure that a person had to declare belief in God before receiving coverage. Anyone could purchase a one-hundred-dollar policy without a physical examination. Her innovations produced many changes. Her suggestions to the Grand Council in 1902 led to the founding of a penny savings bank. In 1903, the St. Luke Penny Savings Bank became the St. Luke Bank and Trust Company, thereby making Maggie Lena Walker the first female bank president in the United States. She also started a short-lived department store on Broad Street, the St. Luke Emporium, to provide substantial employment for women. Walker became a well-known speaker on such topics as women in business, economic independence for the black community, cooperative enterprises, black consumers, and racial disfranchisement.

Walker not only created a financial empire but also served as a leader in the National Association of Colored Women. She founded the Richmond Council of Colored Women in 1912. She organized a fund-raising effort to raise money from the 1,400 members to buy the land for a girl's reformatory directed by clubwoman Janie Porter Barrett. As a result of these efforts, Maggie Lena Walker became a member of the board of trustees of the Virginia School for Girls and the Virginia Manual Labor School in Hanover County. Her club fund-raising also helped the tuberculosis sanatorium in Burkeville and a community center and a nursing home in Richmond. The community center on Clay Street evolved into an affiliate of the National Urban League, eventually became the first black library in Richmond, and, in 1991, became the Black History Museum. Walker served as a member of the board of trustees of the Frederick Douglass Home. She helped organize the local branch of the National Association for the Advancement of Colored People (NAACP) in 1917 and served on the national organization's board from 1923 until her death. Her leadership led to her appointment to the Virginia Interracial Commission. She became a founder of the International Council of Women of the Darker Races, an organization started by Margaret Murray Washington, whose goal was to join together in a global network all women of color.

Maggie Walker's professional achievements were marred by personal misfortune. Her son Russell, an accountant, was given a position at the bank. Said to be spoiled by his life of privilege, young Russell created tragedy for Maggie Lena Walker. In 1915, Walker's husband was shot to death by her son, who said he thought his father was a burglar. Since the story of an accidental shooting seemed implausible, Russell was arrested, brought to trial, and, after much anguished testimony, acquitted. Maggie Walker's enemies tried to remove her from her IOSL post to "safeguard" the order from scandal. She fought the removal during this time of personal tragedy by enumerating her achievements. She continued in her position.

As one of the wealthiest African American women of her day, Walker contributed to many charitable and educational projects. She established the St. Luke Educational Fund to help black youth receive an education. She served as a trustee of the National Training School for Girls in Washington, D.C., as both national director and a vice president of the Richmond branch of the NAACP, as a board member of the National

Urban League, and as a trustee of Hartshorn College.

The 1920's brought Walker honors and a series of personal losses. Her mother, Elizabeth Mitchell, who had been an active IOSL member, midwife, and resident in the Walker home, died in 1922. Walker's son Russell died in 1924. Virginia Union University awarded her an honorary degree in 1925. On the eve of the Depression, her financial organization absorbed other black banks to become the Consolidated Bank and Trust Company: Maggie Lena Walker served as chair of the board. This bank survived her death and continues to operate.

Walker's ill health during the Depression led to decreased activities. Already confined to a wheelchair as a result of complications from a 1907 fall that shattered her kneecap, Walker could barely get around as the years complicated her injuries. Her adopted daughter, Polly Anderson Payne, took care of Walker, who became known as the Lame Lioness. When she retired, Maggie Lena Walker's position at the IOSL was taken by her daughter-in-law Hattie, the widow of her eldest son. The city of Richmond praised Maggie Lena Walker in a Quarto-Centennial Service Celebration at the City Auditorium and also named a street, a high school, and a theater in her honor. The month of October, 1934, was declared Maggie L. Walker Month by African American organizations throughout the nation as a tribute to her life. Walker died a few months later on December 15, 1934, of diabetic gangrene. She was buried in her family's section in Evergreen Cemetery.

Summary

Maggie Lena Walker served as a model for racial solidarity. Her leadership of the IOSL provided evidence of black achievement as well as services for the black community and employment opportunities for both men and women. She lived a life that demonstrated service to the black community through her use of her organizational and business skills. Her life's commitment to racial progress relied on Booker T. Washington's emphasis on black business and racial uplift and W. E. B. Du Bois' advocacy of protest against injustices. Her organizations continue to serve the black community today: They are her living legacy.

The Walker home on Leigh Street has been restored and declared a national historic site by the United States Park Service. This Maggie Walker National Historic Site in Richmond, Virginia, contains her papers, diaries, and photographs.

Bibliography
Bird, Caroline. "The Innovators: Maggie Walker, Kate Gleason." In *Enterprising Women*. New York: W. W. Norton, 1976. This article analyzes Walker's leadership in business.
Brown, Elsa Barkley. "Maggie Lena Walker." In *Encyclopedia of Southern Culture*, edited by William Ferris and Charles R. Wilson. Chapel Hill: University of North Carolina Press, 1989. Brown's encyclopedia entry provides a brief overview of Walker's life and achievements.
Dabney, Wendell P. *Maggie L. Walker and the I.O. of Saint Luke*. Cincinnati, Ohio:

Dabney, 1927. This biography of Walker, written by a childhood friend of hers, serves to highlight the strengths of her leadership. It is, however, sometimes inaccurate, and it includes no critical analysis.

Daniel, Sadie I. *Women Builders*. Washington, D.C.: Associated Publishers, 1931. Written by a contemporary of Walker's, this book provides stories of successful women, including Walker.

Davis, Elizabeth L. *Lifting as They Climb*. Washington, D.C.: National Association of Colored Women, 1933. Places Walker's activities within the context of the club movement.

Duckworth, Margaret. "Maggie L. Walker." In *Notable Black American Women*, edited by Jessie Carney Smith. Detroit: Gale Research, 1992. A useful and informative article about Walker.

Ovington, Mary White. *Portraits in Color*. New York: Viking Press, 1927. Reminiscences by a white female reformer who helped to found the NAACP.

Dorothy C. Salem

BARBARA WALTERS

Born: September 25, 1931; Boston; Massachusetts

Area of Achievement: Journalism

Contribution: As the first female cohost of the *Today Show* and the first female network news anchor, Walters broke ground for women in the top echelons of network news.

Early Life

Barbara Jill Walters was born on September 25, 1931, in Boston, Massachusetts. She was the younger of the two daughters of Louis Edward Walters, a vaudeville booking agent, and his wife, Dena Seletsky Walters.

Lou Walters, of Lithuanian Jewish descent, had emigrated from London to the United States in 1910. The Seletskys were descended from Russian Jews who had come to the United States in the late nineteenth century. Although the Walters family was only minimally observant of major holidays, Barbara grew up in a succession of upper-middle-class Jewish milieus.

At the time of Barbara's birth, Lou Walters' highly successful booking business was failing as vaudeville disappeared with the advent of the talking motion picture. The family fortunes declined precipitously, and they would rise and fall several times during Barbara's youth.

Lou Walters was an energetic entrepreneur who founded and ran the celebrated Latin Quarter nightclubs, first in Boston, then in Miami, Florida, and New York City. The family moved from city to city, following Lou's successful and unsuccessful business ventures. Lou Walters was a celebrity, part of a vast entertainment network. Barbara grew up in a household where it was not unusual to be in contact with celebrities.

Barbara attended schools in Boston and Miami as well as the Fieldston School and Birch Wathen, private schools in New York. She is remembered by her peers as being shy and not particularly popular; she herself describes her youth as lonely. At Birch Wathen, Barbara showed a flair for writing and became active on the school literary magazine. Entering the elite and somewhat bohemian Sarah Lawrence College, Barbara set out to study acting, but she eventually turned to writing. She became the dramatics editor and theater and film critic for the college newspaper, as well as president of her dormitory.

Life's Work

After she was graduated from Sarah Lawrence in 1951, Barbara Walters took a copywriting job with an advertising agency. In 1952, she was hired by a local New York City television station to write press releases. During a taxi strike, she got her first news scoop when she obtained an exclusive interview with an official of the taxi association. Walters then produced a children's program, *Ask the Camera*, and did production work for a network panel show, *Leave It to the Girls*. When these shows were canceled, Walters found herself unemployed.

In 1955, Walters was hired by the *Morning Show*, CBS's competitor against the highly successful *Today Show*, where Walters would eventually make her name. On the *Morning Show*, Walters' job was to book unusual guests, but the gimmicky show lasted only six months. Taking the initiative in her desire to get on the air, Walters began to produce fashion segments, doing commentary despite her slight speech impediment, and even modeling clothing. When the show was replaced with *Good Morning*, Walters was rehired.

Television was in its earliest stages, and the directors and producers with whom Walters worked, who were impressed by her, were in the process of forming an old-boy network of contacts that would eventually achieve important positions on all three television networks (ABC, NBC, and CBS).

In 1957, *Good Morning* was canceled, and in 1958, Walters' father's nightclub failed. Needing to support herself and her family, Walters took a job in a public relations firm. There she worked with William Safire, who would become a speechwriter for President Richard M. Nixon.

In 1961, CBS veteran Fred Freed, now the producer of NBC's *Today Show*, hired Walters as a writer. Walters began a campaign to get on camera, initiating stories involving fashion shows and a beauty makeover. When Shad Northshield, another CBS alumnus, was hired to produce *Today*, Walters began to write and edit short features, and she made a trip to Paris to cover the fashion shows. Walters convinced Northshield that she should narrate the piece, and so, on August 29, 1961, Barbara Walters first appeared on *Today* as a commentator.

In 1962, Walters received a plum assignment from Northshield; she would cover First Lady Jacqueline Kennedy's goodwill visit to India and Pakistan. She had convinced him that the public would be interested in the woman's angle. When she managed to get a short interview with Jacqueline Kennedy, it was considered a journalistic coup, which gave Walters exposure and credibility.

The *Today Show* had a male host and a woman who was designated the "Today Girl." Since the show's inception, this position had been filled by a succession of thirty-three actresses or models. Walters had campaigned for the job but had been turned down by producer Al Morgan because of her "lateral lisp," which made it difficult for her to pronounce l's and r's. In 1964, Walters, with the help of *Today* host Hugh Downs, convinced Morgan to let her work several days a week on a probationary basis. In October of 1964, with no publicity and without any official designation, Barbara Walters appeared on the *Today Show*. She was the first woman not to be billed as the "Today Girl"; instead, she was referred to as "Today Reporter" Barbara Walters.

Morgan was not interested in promoting Walters, and Walters understood that her success depended on her being noticed. She hired a publicist to ensure that she was mentioned in the media. She also assembled a management team to represent her interests with the network. The publicity was successful, establishing Walters in her new position.

The persona that Walters created through her publicity efforts went beyond that of the anonymous journalist telling a story. She became a celebrity in her own right. Ironically, her own celebrity status aided in gaining access to the powerful and famous persons she would interview. Walters had an insider's view of publicity; she was never taken in by her own celebrity and treated herself as a working journalist. She is recognized in the industry for her preparation, persistence, and hard work, as someone who worked her way to the top.

In 1969, Walters was the first to interview former secretary of state Dean Rusk. The interview gave Walters credibility in Washington and led to more hard news assignments. In 1970, Walters published a book, *How to Talk with Practically Anybody About Practically Anything*, and took over a morning talk show, *Not for Women Only*, that focused on women's issues.

In 1971, Hugh Downs left the show to be replaced by NBC anchorman Frank McGee. Because he believed reporters should have a hard news background, McGee did not respect Walters, and his contract gave him control over interviews on the show. Walters could only question guests after McGee had asked three questions. When he was away from the show, he stipulated who would act as guest host, preventing Walters from performing that role.

Walters countered McGee by initiating her own interview segments, such as those with the Nixon Administration, in which he did not participate. Walters was well connected at the Nixon White House. Walters befriended National Security Adviser (later secretary of state) Henry Kissinger, whom she interviewed many times, as well as Nixon himself and Nixon's chief of staff H. R. "Bob" Haldeman. Walters broke the story of Nixon's 1972 trip to China and was invited to be one of the eighty-seven journalists to cover the historic opening of diplomatic relations with China.

The conflict ended when McGee died of bone cancer in 1974. Ironically, McGee's death led to Walters' becoming officially designated cohost of the *Today Show*. Her contract had stipulated that she would be promoted to cohost in the event that McGee left the show.

On April 22, 1976, Walters made television journalism history by signing with ABC to become the first woman news anchor. Her contract called for an annual salary of $1 million, half for her work on the *Evening News* and half for a series of four specials.

The publicity greeting the news of her salary was negative. Journalists publicly questioned her qualifications and decried the decline of journalism into show business. Even more of a problem was Harry Reasoner, who had been anchoring *ABC Evening News* alone. Like McGee, Reasoner had little respect for Walters, and the discord between the two was apparent to viewers. Eventually, they were never shown in the same camera shot. In June of 1978, Reasoner left ABC to return to CBS; Walters was assigned to special reporting assignments and interviews.

Although the anchor job was one of Walters' few failures, the *Barbara Walters Specials* were a huge success. The first program featured singer Barbara Streisand, President-elect Jimmy Carter and his wife Rosalynn, and a tour of Walters' own apartment. In November of 1977, Walters was the first to interview Israeli prime minister Menachem Begin and Egyptian president Anwar el-Sadat together. Barbara Walters' interviewing style, with its focus on the intimate revelations of celebrities and politicians, has influenced the direction of broadcast journalism. Walters' ingenuity, persistence, use of connections, and even her own celebrity have given her access to the powerful and famous that is unparalleled in the industry.

In addition to her specials, in 1981 Walters joined *20/20*, the ABC weekly news magazine program, as a regular contributor. In 1984, she was officially designated cohost of that show with Hugh Downs.

Summary

Barbara Walters made it to the top of broadcast journalism at a time when television news was essentially a man's domain. She was the first woman on *Today* to be treated as a serious journalist; before Walters, the role had essentially been decorative. As first woman news anchor at the national network level, she broke a barrier, achieving a position that was not matched by another woman until Connie Chung was named coanchor of the *CBS Evening News* in 1993. In 1976, critics questioned Walters' credentials, her high salary, and her show business orientation. In retrospect, most commentators believe that she was singled out for criticism because she was a woman entering a male preserve.

When Walters was passed over for promotion, she countered with hard work, initiating her own projects. When she was subjected to sexist dismissal of her work by critics and coworkers, she responded by going outside the system and producing her own interview segments. When she was given opportunities, she knew how to make use of publicity and a network of contacts that she cultivated throughout her career. Walters made sure that she understood how the system worked and used it to her own advantage.

Bibliography

Bonderhoff, Jason. *Barbara Walters: Today's Woman*. New York: Leisure Books, 1975. Containing short summaries of Walters' family background and early career, this biography ends before her move to ABC. It contains background information on many of her early interviews with such luminaries as singer Judy Garland, Great Britain's Prince Philip, and presidents Lyndon B. Johnson and Richard Nixon.

Lewis, Barbara, and Dan Lewis. *Barbara Walters: TV's Superlady*. New York: Pinnacle Books, 1976. This unauthorized biography provides inside information on Walters' career and the people with whom she worked through 1976, in a nonchronological format. It contains the complete text of the speech Walters gave to the ABC affiliates when she moved to that network.

Matusow, Barbara. *The Evening Stars: The Making of the Network News Anchor*. Boston: Houghton Mifflin, 1983. This analysis of the backgrounds and power struggles of news anchors contains a chapter on Walters and Reasoner that details the reasons for their failure. It also contains a good summary of Walters' career.

Oppenheimer, Jerry. *Barbara Walters: An Unauthorized Biography*. New York:

St. Martin's Press, 1990. Despite its somewhat negative tone, this biography documents Walters' career in detail and provides much material on her family background and personal life.

Powers, Ron. *The Newscasters*. New York: St. Martin's Press, 1977. This analysis of the network news as moving from journalistic to entertainment values places ABC's decision to hire Walters in context. It also contains sections in which Walters discusses her career.

Allison Carter

MERCY OTIS WARREN

Born: September 25, 1728; Barnstable, Massachusetts
Died: October 19, 1814; Plymouth, Massachusetts
Area of Achievement: Literature
Contribution: Warren was a leading figure during the American Revolution. As a pamphleteer and propagandist for the patriot cause, she wrote satirical plays attacking the corruption of the British government. She also wrote *A History of the Rise, Progress, and Termination of the American Revolution.*

Early Life

Mercy Otis was born on September 25, 1728, in Barnstable, Massachusetts, near Plymouth. Edward Dotey, her great-great maternal grandfather, came to America on board the *Mayflower* as a servant and signed the *Mayflower Compact*. Mercy's parents, James Otis and Mary Allyne Otis, settled on the farm at Barnstable, where James prospered as a merchant, farmer, and attorney for seventy-six years. He served as a judge of the court of common pleas for his county and as a colonel in the militia. It speaks for the prosperity of James and Mary Otis that they had their portraits done by John Singleton Copley in Boston; their portraits are regarded as some of the great artist's finest work.

Mercy was the third of thirteen children born to James and Mary and was their first daughter. Only seven of the children survived to maturity: James, Jr., Joseph, Mercy, Mary, Hannah, Elizabeth, and Samuel Allyne.

Mercy's father was a self-taught man with educational aspirations for his sons but no plans for his daughters' schooling. The oldest son, James, Jr., was taught by the Reverend Jonathan Russell. Mercy managed to sit in on her brother's lessons and learned how to read and write. James also instructed her, and they became fellow scholars and close companions. Several factors influenced Mercy's education. Her brother's tutor, the Reverend Russell, granted Mercy borrowing privileges in his library, and she absorbed Sir Walter Raleigh's *History of the World* (1614) and the classics with zeal. Because her father was involved in colonial affairs, she heard frequent political discussions within the family circle. As the oldest daughter in a large family, however, she could not neglect her household duties. She preferred needle-work, and a piece of her workmanship, a tablecloth, is exhibited at Pilgrim Hall in Plymouth.

At age sixteen, Mercy was introduced to James Warren, who was attending Harvard College. Their friendship evolved slowly into a courtship that lasted several years. Mercy Otis and James Warren were married on November 14, 1754. Three years later, James inherited a farm on the Eel River, near Plymouth, where he took Mercy, who was expecting their first child. They lived there for the rest of their lives. This home became a dramatic setting for many actors in the American Revolution, such as Samuel, John and Abigail Adams; John Hancock; and James Otis, Jr.

Mercy and James had five sons: James, born in 1757; Winslow, 1759; Charles,

1762; Henry, 1764; and George, 1766. Mercy's childbirthing was unusual because she got off to a slow start, three years into her marriage, and she seems to have spaced her pregnancies at regular intervals and to have lost no children in childbirth or infancy.

In the spring of 1762, she posed for John Singleton Copley. The resulting portrait is displayed at the Museum of Fine Arts in Boston. It portrays a petite, delicate woman with graceful hands and a fragile body adorned in elegant blue satin with pointed lace. Mercy's face looks at the beholder with lively, piercing eyes and a jaw set in a slight but determined smile.

Life's Work

As the wife of a country squire and public servant with five small boys to care for, Mercy Otis Warren still managed to find some quiet time to read and write poetry. She was inspired by the surrounding countryside, and her favorite themes were drawn from nature.

In the 1760's, as her husband and brother became involved in the growing conflict with Great Britain, her astute mind moved from poetry to politics. James Otis, Jr., was asked to defend a group of Boston merchants against the government's use of writs of assistance. Because these warrants were viewed as a violation of civil rights, Otis made a brilliant courtroom speech on February 24, 1761, in which he introduced the idea that taxation without representation is tyranny. He became a leading spokesman for the patriotic cause and was elected to the Massachusetts House of Representatives. He was joined in the legislature in 1765 by James Warren. In 1769, as the conflict with the Crown escalated, James Otis, Jr., became one of the first victims in the struggle when he was attacked and brutally beaten in a Boston tavern by Loyalists. He suffered a permanent brain injury and became a deranged invalid.

Mercy's close relationship with her brother took on a new form. Heartbroken over the loss of James's intellectual genius, she became committed to carrying on his work in the struggle in the form of pamphlet writing for the patriotic cause. Around the Warren fireside, many revolutionary plans were hatched. Mercy Warren became the muse of the circle of revolutionaries who met there. She also started writing satires and satirical plays in verse attacking the Tories, or Loyalists. As an upstanding New England woman of Puritan stock, she most likely never attended a play, and it is highly unlikely that her plays were ever performed, since they were intended for reading, not dramatizing. Her full-length play *The Adulateur* appeared in newspaper installments in 1772. This satire attacked the Royal Governor Thomas Hutchinson in the guise of a character named Rapatio. In a sequel entitled *The Defeat* (1773), she continued her attack against Hutchinson. In *Lamira*, she mocked the selfishness of the British aristocracy. Next, *The Squabble of the Sea Nymphs* celebrated the Boston Tea Party. Just before the Battles of Lexington and Concord, in 1775, she published her third full-length play, *The Group*, which criticized Tory leadership. She broke from her traditional style in *The Blockheads* in 1776, introducing female characters and writing in prose. The play that is regarded as her best was *The Motley Assembly* (1779), a drawing-room comedy that poked fun at the pretentiousness of Colonial society. As a woman, a patriot, and the wife of an officer, she was compelled to publish many of her plays anonymously, for her family's protection. Her plays were well received by Boston readers and American troops.

In 1775, the war struck the Warren household when Joseph Warren, James's brother, died at the Battle of Breed's Hill in Boston and James was asked to take his place as president of the Provincial Congress. General George Washington established a headquarters in Watertown and appointed James Warren as paymaster of his army. James Warren also served as a major general in the Massachusetts militia. As long as the army was nearby, Mercy was able to visit or stay with her husband. She spent many cheerful evenings with General and Mrs. Washington while they were encamped near Boston. James and Mercy also developed a long-lasting friendship with John and Abigail Adams. As ladies of learning, Abigail and Mercy adopted classical names. Mercy signed her letters "Marcia," and she addressed Abigail as "Portia."

By 1780, James Warren had lost his seat in the Massachusetts Assembly. After the war, the Warren family's political stature declined. Even Mercy Warren's attempts through political connections with John Adams to secure public offices for her sons failed. When Daniel Shays led an uprising of veterans in 1786, the Warrens were accused of supporting the rebels. None of the historical evidence suggests that the Warrens supported Shays's cause. In fact, their son Henry was among the troops dispatched to put down the rebellion. Moreover, in her *History of the Revolution* some years later, Mercy Warren sharply criticized Shays's Rebellion. It is likely that political conservatives accused the Warrens because of another issue. Mercy Warren, a Jeffersonian Democrat, had attacked the proposed new Federal Constitution of 1787 in the pamphlet *Observations on the New Constitution*. In 1790, she continued her plea for democracy and human liberty in *Poems Dramatic and Miscellaneous*, which included the poetic dramas *The Sack of Rome* and *The Ladies of Castile*.

She began her most ambitious project, *The History of the Rise, Progress, and Termination of the American Revolution*, during the war and published it in three volumes in 1805. It is valuable because of Warren's firsthand knowledge of revolutionary personalities. In her history, Warren stated that Federalist John Adams had "forgotten the principles of the American Revolution" and was "guilty of pride and ambition." Adams did not believe that ladies ought to write history, and he severely criticized Warren's account of the war as inaccurate. Eventually, their friendship was restored through the efforts of a mutual friend, Elbridge Gerry.

In her later years, Mercy Otis Warren maintained many friendships, continued to write poetry, and kept up a busy correspondence. When a Mrs. Ellet visited the Warren home, she described an aged Warren as still lively, eloquent, and elegantly dressed. Warren received foreign visitors from England and France in her later years as well. After his visit, the French Duke de Rochefoucauld-Liancourt included an impressive account of Warren in his book *Voyage in the United States of America*, stating that she was a talented, graceful woman of great sensibility despite her age. She remained strong and in good health for most of her eighty-six years, until just five days before her death on October 19, 1814, when she died of a sudden illness. She was buried alongside her husband James on old Burial Hill of the Pilgrims in Plymouth, Massachusetts.

Summary

   Some scholars have regarded Mercy Otis Warren as an early feminist. During the Constitutional Convention of 1787, Abigail Adams wrote to her husband John admonishing him to remember women's rights when crafting the new government. John Adams did not take this request seriously, so Abigail wrote to her friend Mercy, asking her to join in a petition-writing campaign to Congress on behalf of women. Warren's reply to Abigail no longer exists, but Abigail never followed through with her petitions to Congress. Mercy Warren's own writings seem to indicate that she saw her role as that of a traditional wife and mother. She once advised a friend to accept subordination as a woman for the sake of family order. Mercy's main concern for women was not their lack of political rights but their need for formal education. Considering all that she accomplished within the limited and traditional role of wife and mother in eighteenth and early nineteenth century society, Mercy Otis Warren was indeed an exemplary feminist.

Bibliography

Anthony, Katherine S. *First Lady of the Revolution: The Life of Mercy Otis Warren.* Garden City, N.Y.: Doubleday, 1958. A comprehensive study of Warren and the important figures of revolutionary Massachusetts. This biography provides a personal look at Warren, her family, and the lifestyle of colonial women.

Brown, Alice. *Mercy Warren.* New York: Charles Scribner, 1896. Reprint. Spartensburg, S.C.: Spartansburg Reprint Company, 1968. Alice Brown was regarded for several generations as *the* biographer of Mercy Otis Warren, and her book is still worth reading.

Evans, Elizabeth. *Weathering the Storm: Women of the American Revolution.* New York: Charles Scribner's Sons, 1975. A comprehensive study of the contributions of women in the war effort. Evans' work identifies Mercy Otis Warren as a significant activist during the American Revolution.

Fritz, Jean. *Cast for a Revolution: 1728-1814.* Boston: Houghton Mifflin, 1972. One of the best studies of Mercy Otis Warren to date. Fritz examines the inner workings of the Otis-Warren-Adams circle.

Marble, Annie-Russell. "Mistress Mercy Warren: Real Daughter of the American Revolution." *The New England Magazine* 28 (April, 1903): 163-180. One of the first examinations of Mercy Otis Warren, this article emphasizes her importance as a political activist.

Emily Jane Teipe

ANNIE DODGE WAUNEKA

Born: April 10, 1910; Navajo Nation, near Sawmill, Arizona

Areas of Achievement: Social reform and public health
Contribution: A Navajo health educator and leader in the implementation of Navajo
  health programs, Annie Dodge Wauneka helped to educate her people about how
  to eradicate tuberculosis, which was rampant on her reservation. Her advocacy of
  health reforms led to an expanded crusade to help improve the Navajo way of life.

Early Life

Annie Dodge was the daughter of Henry Chee Dodge, the first elected chairman of
the Navajo Tribal Council, and K'eehabah, a Navajo wife and mother. K'eehabah was
Chee Dodge's third wife, who took care of him in the absence of his second wife,
Nanabah. Nanabah had a large herd of sheep and was away for two years on business
and tending to her own herd. Annie was born in K'eehabah's hogan and her birth was
assisted by a Navajo medicine man. After Annie's birth, Nanabah returned and
K'eehabah went back to her own home taking Annie with her. When Annie was about
one year old, her father sent for her, and she began living with her father and her
half-brothers and half-sister. Chee Dodge had spent his youth at Fort Sumner, where
he learned to speak English and eventually went on to become a government interpreter, a tribal council head, and a rancher. Chee Dodge worked hard in his youth and
saved his money. By the time he was thirty years old, he was a wealthy man who
provided quite well for his family. Unlike other Navajos who lived in traditional
hogans, the Dodge family lived in a home, designed by a German architect, with many
rooms similar to a white man's house.

Chee Dodge was interested in his children's welfare and had progressive ideas
about the importance of education. Although he expected them to learn Navajo
customs, Chee Dodge also wanted his children to attend white schools. At the age of
eight, Annie began her education at the government boarding school located in Fort
Defiance. It was during her stay at this boarding school that Annie was exposed to
common white diseases such as flu and trachoma. Many of her friends died, and those
who did not were quarantined at the school with no classes. Annie helped the nurses
to care for her classmates, but it was a terribly long year and one that changed her life.
She came to know firsthand the pain and dangers of disease and knew then that she
wanted to help others. Later, Annie attended the Albuquerque Indian School. It was
here that Annie improved her fluency in English, since the Indian children were not
allowed to speak their native languages at this school.

One of Annie's happiest memories while at the Albuquerque Indian School was a
visit by her father and some other Navajo leaders. During this period, her father had
been elected the first tribal chairman and he came to give a speech concerning the
importance of their education. He told them to get as much education as possible, so
that they could use it to help their own people. Annie was very proud of her father,

and he remained a great influence in her life for many years to come. It was also during this time that Annie met a Navajo youth ten years her senior named George Wauneka, and they soon became close friends. At age eighteen, she left the Albuquerque Indian School and returned home to tend the family's flock of sheep.

Life's Work

While at home, Annie Dodge attended some of the important meetings that were going on between the Navajos and the officials of the Bureau of Indian Affairs (BIA). She came to understand the dynamics of tribal government and the courtesies involved in Indian and white negotiations. Her father came to rely on her more and more for her fine intellect, good education, and natural poise. She, in turn, respected her father for his forcefulness and energy and especially for his strong sense of fairness and justice, traits that she would later adopt as her own. It was also during this time, while traveling around the reservation with her father, that she learned the extent of her people's poverty. It was in witnessing this poverty that Annie would be spurred on to crusade for improving the Navajo way of life.

Annie Dodge and George Wauneka had discussed marriage while both were still in school. When they returned home, they decided to set a date for their wedding. What was unusual about Annie's marriage was that it was not arranged by her parents; Annie had chosen her own husband. There were Navajo rituals that did have to be followed, including the Navajo custom that the husband provided the materials for building the house, while the wife's family contributed the labor and the furnishings. Gifts are exchanged between the two families because the marriage not only united the couple but also the relatives. The only taboo that had to be carefully observed was the prohibition of marriage between members of the same clan. Navajo clans are made up of families that are related through the mothers of each family. George's mother and Annie's mother were of different clans, so it was permissible for them to marry. George and Annie were married in October of 1929, approximately one year after Annie left the Albuquerque Indian School. They lived in a modern house on the Dodge estate at Sonsela Butte for two years. After that time, Chee Dodge gave them his property in Tanner Springs. In return, Annie and George were to manage his huge cattle herd while also running their own herds. Although Annie and George lived with many modern conveniences, they continued to live the life of the Navajo. During their time at Tanner Springs, the couple reared six children: Georgia Ann, born in 1931; Henry, in 1933; Irma, in 1935; Franklin, in 1945; Lorencita, in 1947; and Sallie, in 1950. Annie also lost two children between the births of Irma and Franklin.

Annie Dodge Wauneka continued to attend the BIA meetings with her father in order to learn more about interpreting, and she accompanied him on visits to the hogans of those who requested his help. She continually witnessed the results of disease and despair among the poverty-stricken Navajos. She knew that her children were growing up strong and healthy, and she also knew that there were many mothers whose children were dying of malnutrition and disease. In recalling her days at the Fort Defiance School, Wauneka remembered how the white administrators had tried to keep the students very clean. As she visited the hogans of the Navajos with their dirt floors and roofs and lack of running water, she saw how impossible it was for them to keep their children clean. She set out to improve the living conditions for her people by educating them about germs and cleanliness. She began studying with the U.S. Public Health Service in order to gain more insight into the strategies she could use in implementing a health education program on the vast Navajo Reservation.

In 1951, Wauneka broke with tribal tradition and followed in her father's footsteps by being the first woman elected to the Tribal Council of seventy-four members. She competed against her husband in order to win her second term in 1954, and was reelected to a third term against another male opponent in 1959. Her work in public health made her the most obvious choice to head the council's Health Committee. This was the first time such an honor had been bestowed upon a woman. As she continued her work at the grassroots level with the Navajo Tribal Council Health Committee, Wauneka attended college and eventually earned her bachelor's degree in public health from the University of Arizona. In later years, she received an honorary doctorate from the University of Arizona. She was given the Josephine B. Hughes Memorial Award by the Arizona Press Women in 1958, was named Outstanding Worker in Public Health of the Arizona Public Health Association in 1959, and received the Indian Achievement Award of the Indian Council Fire of Chicago in 1959, the same medal her father received in 1945 in recognition of his achievements. In 1960, Wauneka began hosting a daily radio show from statio KGAK in Gallup, New Mexico. The program, which was broadcast in the Navajo language, covered health improvement information as well as topics of general interest to the Navajo Nation. During her years as health director among the Navajo, Wauneka not only witnessed the reduction of new tuberculosis cases but also worked to improve awareness of the dangers of alcohol abuse and the advantages of education and treatment before such abuse leads to serious illness.

In 1963, Annie Dodge Wauneka was one of thirty-one distinguished Americans selected to receive the Presidential Medal of Freedom Award. This prestigious award is presented to those who have made outstanding contributions to the national interest or the country's security, to world peace, or who have participated in cultural or other significant public or private endeavors. Wauneka was the first American Indian to receive this honor. This award was presented to Wauneka on December 6, 1963, sixteen days after President John F. Kennedy's assassination. At a White House ceremony President Lyndon B. Johnson presented the medal, a blue-and-white star on a red-and-gold background, to Wauneka. Wauneka's citation read: "First woman elected to the Navajo Tribal Council; by her long crusade for improved health programs, she has helped dramatically to lessen the menace of disease among her people and to improve their way of life."

Summary

Annie Dodge Wauneka faced many frustrating challenges throughout her life, but she learned to meet them fearlessly. As a mature Navajo woman, she possessed a deep knowledge of the political and financial realities of tribal life, yet even within the strong matrilineal traditions of her people there was little to encourage a woman to express openly her opinions about Navajo tribal government. Determined to follow the example of her father, Wauneka found the means to express herself. She was uniquely qualified to be the first woman elected to the Navajo Tribal Council because she was outspoken, brilliant, and did not flinch in the face of limitations placed on her because of her gender or race.

Wauneka was the daughter of a great chief and had a practical understanding of the complicated and often brutal "mechanics of politics." She often stated that one of her most difficult tasks was to win the confidence of her people and other Indians. Many traditional Navajos were openly hostile toward nontribal medicine, so she had to gain the trust of the medicine men and convey to them, in their own language the miracles of modern science. She took on the task of contacting runaways from the tuberculosis clinics on the reservation, convincing them to return because they were exposing their families to the dreaded disease. The greatest tributes to her work are the healthy Navajo men, women, and children who still live on the Navajo Reservation. Many of them would have died if it were not for Wauneka's efforts.

From her father, Annie Dodge Wauneka acquired strong moral beliefs, an attitude of complete honesty, and a serious mind. Chief Chee Dodge instilled in his daughter a sense of the urgent need for education and progress among her people. For the Navajo, she has made her life a total gift. She sees her work as building a bridge, a bridge of words that linked the Navajos together and helped the Navajos and the larger white community understand each other. The Navajos have been fortunate to have Annie Dodge Wauneka among them.

Bibliography

Bataille, Gretchen M., ed. *Native American Women: A Biographical Dictionary*. New York: Garland, 1993. A collection on notable American Indian women and the achievements in their life. Includes a profile on Annie Dodge Wauneka and her distinguished career.

Dennis, Henry C., ed. *The American Indian, 1492-1976*. 2d ed. Dobbs Ferry, N.Y.: Oceana Publications, 1977. An ethnic chronology and fact book that focuses attention on American Indian leaders from the advent of Columbus through the American Bicentennial. Wauneka is one of several Navajo leaders included.

Gridley, Marion E., ed. *Indians of Today*. 4th ed. Chicago: Indian Council Fire, 1971. Revised and updated since its 1960 original edition, this compilation of essays on Indian leaders places its emphasis on their life's work. Acclaimed for its insights into the intellectual American Indians.

Nelson, Mary Carroll. *Annie Wauneka*. Minneapolis, Minn.: Dillon Press, 1972. This is one of three titles by Nelson included in The Story of an American Indian series. An in-depth , scholarly portrayal of Annie Wauneka.

Waltrip, Lela, and Rufus Waltrip. *Indian Women*. New York: David McKay, 1964. A collective biography of thirteen American Indian women leaders. Contains an excellent chapter on Annie Dodge Wauneka depicting her youth, her family life, and her achievements.

Darlene Mary Suarez

LOIS WEBER

Born: June 13, 1881; Allegheny, Pennsylvania (later incorporated into Pittsburgh)
Died: November 13, 1939; Hollywood, California
Area of Achievement: Film
Contribution: As an actor, writer, and director, Lois Weber was the first American woman "auteur," the author of her own melodramatic films.

Early Life

Florence Lois Weber was born on June 13, 1881, in Allegheny, Pennsylvania. Her parents, George Weber and Mary Matilda Snaman Weber, observed the strict religious faith of their Pennsylvania German forebears. Although Lois was educated in schools in Pittsburgh, it was her training as a musician that influenced her film career. An accomplished pianist, she toured widely throughout the country while still in her teens. Her concert career ended, however, when a piano key broke off in her hand, thereby breaking her concentration and confidence. Her conservative religious background led her to apply her musical talents as a church missionary on the streets of Pittsburgh. When she had to find a job, she followed an uncle's advice and went on the stage; she said she "went on the stage filled with a great desire to convert my countrymen."

After working in musicals, Lois turned to melodrama, the genre she later worked with in film. While touring with *Why Girls Leave Home* in 1904, she met Phillips Smalley, the company's actor-manager. Some months later, the couple was married in Chicago. The pressures involved in pursuing their separate careers led Lois to give up hers in 1906 and establish a home in New York City. Two years later, however, she returned to work, this time as a film actor for Gaumont Studios. One biographer has attributed her decision to switch media to the potential the "evangelistic" Weber saw in film melodrama. Since she was also a playwright—*The Drunkard*, one of her melodramas, was quite popular—film offered her the opportunity to dramatize her messages by writing the script, acting as the lead, and directing the production. She later wrote that film gave her the opportunity to "preach to my heart's content."

Life's Work

When Lois Weber's husband returned to New York, he joined her in the writing-acting-directing venture at Gaumont. They began working with the Reliance Company in 1910, and left shortly after to work for Rex, Edwin S. Porter's film company. At Rex, Weber and Smalley acted as dramatic leads, scripted films, edited some films, and, under Porter's supervision, directed many films. After Porter left Rex to direct films for Famous Players, under the control of Adolph Zukor, Weber and Smalley were put in charge of production at Rex, which became part of Universal Pictures. Although she and her husband were a team, Weber was really the creative force in filmmaking and, by 1914, was the dominant partner. In 1913 and 1914, she wrote all the scripts, and the couple acted and codirected most of the two-reeler films, which appeared at the rate of two a month.

In the fall of 1915, despite an earlier notice about their directing independently, the couple moved from Universal to the Bosworth Company, where they codirected several feature films, among them the controversial *Hypocrites* (1915). The film's release was delayed because it featured a nude woman, unidentified but possibly Weber herself, as "The Naked Truth," the allegorical figure intended to reveal the corruption in the world. The film illustrates both Weber's desire to dramatize a message and her ability to sensationalize that message. Perhaps because of censorship problems, the film was a financial success.

When Weber rejoined Universal in 1916, she was arguably its most important director and enjoyed the status accorded D. W. Griffith and Cecil B. DeMille. She was in total control of her films and could write scripts and make films about any subject she wished. Her films, which were now known as "Weber Productions," rather than "Smalley Productions," included *The People vs. John Doe* (1916), an attack on capital punishment; *Shoes* (1916), an exposé of child labor; and *Hop, the Devil's Brew* (1916), a criticism of the liquor industry. These films paled in comparison, however, with *Where Are My Children?* (1916), a film that endorsed birth control but condemned abortion. Although Weber's script was based on an original story by Lucy Payton and Franklin Hall, the film is vintage Weber in its melodramatic plot, its religious overtones (souls of children in eternity, awaiting their birth), and its sensational subject matter. The film, which was well received critically and financially, succeeded, as one critic put it, in "driving home the lesson that it seeks to teach without being offensive." *The Dumb Girl of Portici*, another Weber film, opened at the same time. Although it featured Anna Pavlova in her only screen appearance, it played to mixed reviews, probably because it was a well-meaning studio assignment rather than a subject Weber herself had selected.

By 1917, Weber's status was such that she formed her own company, and she and Universal financed a studio, which doubled as her home, at 4634 Santa Monica Boulevard in Hollywood. Since she was still under contract with Universal, she did not shoot her first independent production, *To Please One Woman* (released in 1920), until 1919. After completing her six features for Universal, Weber signed an extremely lucrative contract with Famous Players-Lasky (later Paramount) that established her salary at $50,000 a picture and awarded her half the profits, making Weber the highest paid woman director of her era. When *To Please One Woman* was released, however, it was not the success, critically or financially, that the studio and Weber had anticipated. Her shifting emphasis from controversial films to "women's pictures," with religious conservatism and the sentimentality she herself condemned, was suddenly out of step with the mood and spirit of the 1920's—the jazz age.

The failure of *To Please One Woman* was followed by only four other independently produced films, all of which met similar fates in 1921. *What's Worth While?*, *Too Wise Wives*, *What Do Men Want?*, and *The Blot* all starred Claire Windsor, who was cast with Louis Calhern in all but one of these films. The problem with these films was not with the casting, but with Weber's use of themes, characters, and locales that had formerly been successful. Attacks on smoking, social gaffes, self-righteous small-town preachers—these simply were not acceptable to the urban audiences who saw themselves attacked in Weber's moralistic films. Good manners, proper behavior, etiquette—these were Weber's standards, and they were increasingly at odds with the standards of her audiences. The films were so unsuccessful that after releasing three of her films, Famous Players-Lasky relinquished rights to the last two, which were finally released by an independent distributor.

Domestic problems followed her cinematic failures; she and Smalley separated and were divorced in 1922. While Weber did direct *A Chapter in Her Life* (1923), it was essentially a remake of her 1915 film *Jewel*, which glorified Christian Science; the film failed at the box office. Weber, distraught over the crises in her life, suffered a nervous breakdown, and there were even rumors of an attempted suicide. In 1926, she was married to Captain Harry Gantz and resumed her career, returning to Universal to direct two feature films, *The Marriage Clause* (1926) and *Sensation Seekers* (1927), both of which indicted the lax moral standards of the age, especially those of the "flappers."

Weber's long career at Universal ended in 1927, when Universal asked her to write and direct a film adaptation of *Topsy and Eva*, a popular stage play filled with racial humor. Unwilling to make the film, she left the studio. Cecil B. DeMille soon enlisted her to direct *The Angel of Broadway* (1927), the story of actress and nightclub owner Texas Guinan's life. In the film, there is a parody of an innocent young Salvation Army woman. This parallel to Weber's own evangelistic past provides an appropriate frame for her silent film career, for *The Angel of Broadway* was her last silent film.

With her directing career apparently over, Weber found some work scripting films and then returned again to Universal, where her employment consisted of giving screen tests to aspiring actresses. In 1934, however, Pinnacle Studios, a Depression era production company, hired her to direct *White Heat*. Although it was an exploitation film set in Hawaii, the film review in *The Film Daily* paid tribute, of a sort, to the picture's "melodramatic qualities." She subsequently made futile attempts to use film's audiovisual potential in the public schools. When she died from a gastric hemorrhage on November 13, 1939, Weber was almost penniless and almost forgotten by film audiences. Her debts and funeral expenses were paid by scriptwriter Frances Marion, whom Weber had befriended early in Marion's Hollywood career.

Summary

Lois Weber was the first American woman to direct films and the most outstanding woman director of the silent film era. She encouraged the careers of many female stars, including Claire Windsor and Billie Dove. Because she wrote the scripts and acted as the lead in them, Weber was, like Charles Chaplin, an early auteur filmmaker, one whose complete control of the filmmaking process enabled her to put her own stamp on the films she made. Those films, which contained moral messages and which criticized the problems of the day (birth control, capital punishment, anti-Semitism, and so forth), at first reflected her audience's values; she fell out of favor, however, with the advent of the Roaring Twenties. A woman at once religiously conservative and politically and socially liberal, Weber was not willing to compromise on theme or subject matter; that unwillingness might not have proved fatal to her career if the motion-picture industry had not changed radically.

As the major studios came to control the industry, they began to emulate the specialized "factory" production methods of other industries, and the size of the financial commitment to films increased. Large sums of money were involved, and studios were less willing to take chances. As feminist film scholars have pointed out, there were several women directors in the early silent-film period. By the late 1920's, however, Dorothy Arzner was the only significant woman filmmaker in the industry. As was the case with midwives/doctors and nurse anesthetists/anesthesiologists, when large sums of money were involved, men tended to take control of the field. The fact that Weber's impact was not substantial is not attributable to the quality of her films, but to changing moral codes, increasing budget costs for films, and the emerging sexism in the industry. She has been rediscovered by film scholars, but efforts to assign her an appropriate role in film history have been hampered by the relative scarcity of her films. While many films directed by Charlie Chaplin and other male directors are available, only a few of the hundreds of films made by Weber are extant.

Bibliography

Haskell, Molly. *From Reverence to Rape: The Treatment of Women in the Movies.* New York: Holt, Rinehart and Winston, 1974. In her discussion of "The Twenties," Haskell comments on the absence of feminist films in that decade and states that Weber's supposedly "feminist" films have disappeared, leaving only commercial films. Using *Where Are My Children,* Haskell concludes that Weber's "sympathies were at the very least mixed, if not blatantly opposed to feminism."

Heck-Rabi, Louise. *Women Filmmakers: A Critical Reception.* Metuchen, N.J.: Scarecrow Press, 1984. Provides best overview of Weber's life and career. Heck-Rabi stresses Weber's role in nurturing Francis Marion as a scriptwriter as well as her role in furthering the careers of silent-era actresses such as Mildred Harris (Charlie Chaplin's first wife), Claire Windsor, and Esther Ralston. The chapter entitled "Moralist Moviemaker" contains plot summaries of Weber's films, contemporary critical responses to her works, a filmography, and copious notes.

Koszarski, Richard, comp. *Hollywood Directors, 1914-1940.* New York: Oxford University Press, 1976. Includes Weber in a section devoted to motion picture pioneers. Following a brief evaluation of her film career, Koszarski reprints an interview Arthur Denison conducted with Weber in 1917, shortly after she was granted a studio of her own. Weber distinguishes between films based on sentiment, her films, and those based on sentimentality.

_____ . "The Years Have Not Been Kind to Lois Weber." In *Women and the Cinema: A Critical Anthology,* edited by Karyn Kay and Gerald Peary. New York: E. P. Dutton, 1977. The best extended discussion of Weber, whom Koszarski regards as the "most respected woman director of the whole silent era." Koszarksi provides a short biography, analyzes several of her films, and accounts for her declining reputation. The book contains Weber's filmography and a helpful general bibliography.

Quart, Barbara Koenig. *Women Directors: The Emergence of a New Cinema.* New York: Praeger, 1988. Discusses Weber, as well as Alice Guy-Blaché and Germaine Dulac, in a section entitled "Antecedents." Quant provides a feminist account for the number of early women directors and for their subsequent disappearance as films became big business. The book contains a general bibliography.

Rosen, Marjorie. *Popcorn Venus: Women, Movies and the American Dream.* New York: Coward, McCann & Geoghegan, 1973. Informative, speculative analysis concerning Weber's post-1918 career, when she turned from controversial subjects to "traditional stories with a more compromising tone." Rosen suggests that as films required increasing amounts of money, studios were less willing to take chances.

Slide, Anthony. *Early Women Directors.* New York: Da Capo Press, 1977. Discusses the controversial nature of many of Weber's films, her concept of "missionary pictures," and her troubles with the censors over the film *Hypocrites.* Includes a helpful bibliography.

Smith, Sharon. *Women Who Make Movies.* New York: Hopkinson and Blake, 1975. Praises Weber as the first American woman filmmaker, stresses her treatment of marital problems, and discusses her problems with censors. Smith provides a bibliography, a directory of women filmmakers, and a listing of distributors of women's films.

Thomas L. Erskine

SARAH WEDDINGTON

Born: February 5, 1945; Abilene, Texas

Areas of Achievement: Law, government and politics, and women's rights
Contribution: As a twenty-six-year-old attorney, Weddington argued *Roe v. Wade* before the Supreme Court and has continued to work diligently as an advocate for women's rights.

Early Life

Sarah Ragle was born on February 5, 1945, in Abilene, Texas, to the Reverend Doyle Ragle and Lena Catherine Ragle. As the daughter of a Methodist minister, Sarah was conscious of being a "good" girl. She was active in the Methodist Youth Fellowship and assumed leadership positions in many school organizations; most notably she was the drum major for the junior high school band and the president of the Future Homemakers Association. At the age of seventeen, having skipped two grades in school, Sarah entered McMurray College, a small liberal arts college in Abilene where she continued her energetic participation in extracurricular activities. She acted in drama productions and served as the secretary of the student body while she secured teaching credentials for secondary English and speech. When Sarah discussed her intention of attending law school, the dean of the college discouraged her. Distressed by the continuing restrictions placed on her life simply because she was female, Sarah became even more determined to attend law school. She was graduated magna cum laude from McMurray College in December, 1965.

In June of 1965, Sarah entered the University of Texas Law School, where she was one of only five females among 120 men in the entering class. During her third year of law school, she was seriously dating Ron Weddington, an older student and Army veteran. After learning that she was pregnant and considering the impact of her pregnancy on her future career, Sarah decided that an abortion was the best answer to the dilemma. Since abortions were illegal in Texas at that time, Sarah sought Ron's assistance and traveled to Piedras Negras, Mexico, where she obtained an abortion.

Although Sarah was graduated in 1967 in the top quarter of her class and interviewed with law firms for months, she received no job offers. On August 25, 1968, Sarah and Ron Weddington were married. Ron had entered law school in June, and Sarah went to work assisting John Sutton, an attorney in San Angelo, with his work with the American Bar Association's Special Committee on the Reevaluation of Ethical Standards.

During these early years of employment, Sarah became involved in the Austin women's movement and its consciousness-raising groups. Discussions often focused on contraception and abortion, and Sarah researched legal questions to share with the group. Increasingly, the Austin women's movement spoke of overturning Texas antiabortion statutes dating from 1859, and Sarah soon became instrumental in their efforts.

Life's Work

Sarah Weddington was propelled into legal history when the Texas women's movement decided to file a lawsuit to challenge the constitutionality of the Texas antiabortion statute and asked her to handle the case. Weddington, in turn, asked Linda Coffee, her brilliant former classmate, to share the responsibility. Two lawsuits were filed on March 3, 1970, against the elected district attorney of Dallas County, Henry Wade. One suit, *Roe v. Wade*, was on behalf of Norma McCorvey, called Jane Roe—an unmarried pregnant waitress with one child. The other suit, *Doe v. Wade*, involved a married couple called John and Mary Doe who were concerned about their personal rights even though Mary was not pregnant. When the lawsuits were consolidated, the litigation expanded to that of a class action on behalf of all individuals in a particular situation who wanted to vest decision-making power in themselves, not in a state or federal law. Using both First and Ninth Amendments, Coffee and Weddington argued that the case concerned fundamental human freedoms of choice and privacy.

On June 17, 1970, the Fifth Circuit Court in Texas declared that its law in this matter was unconstitutional according to the Ninth Amendment and that, furthermore, the law was so ambiguous it was difficult for physicians to act responsibly and that the law deprived individuals of their right to choose not to have children. In its argument, the court affirmed the right of women and their families to be shielded from governmental interference in their personal decisions. The setback in this otherwise acclaimed decision was the judges' refusal to issue a directive ordering the state to stop enforcing its abortion law. As a result, confusion reigned: Were abortions considered legal in Texas? The district attorney's office stepped up its enforcement of existing antiabortion laws, making access to abortions even more difficult.

In an effort to achieve a meaningful and complete decision, Coffee and Weddington immediately filed an appeal in the Fifth Circuit and soon after with the Supreme Court, which agreed to hear the case. As the months passed without any preparation on the brief by Roy Lucas and the James Madison Institute, Weddington left her position as assistant city attorney for Fort Worth and moved to New York City with her husband, where they assumed total responsibility for writing the brief. Reputedly a pinch-hitter, Weddington wrote most of the women's history section, while Ron worked on the constitutional rights section. In preparation for the argument, Weddington rehearsed all details—specifically by participating in two moot courts where she tested her arguments and received valuable feedback. The day of the argument, December 13, 1971, was filled with a kind of electricity, and Weddington seized on it, demonstrating her oratorical skills, her quick mind, and her sophisticated poise to the seven sitting justices.

While they waited for a decision from the Supreme Court, Weddington ran for the Texas House of Representatives and on November 7, 1972, was the first woman elected from Travis County. Ann Richards, who later became governor of Texas, served as Weddington's campaign manager and was instrumental in generating political support for Weddington. Still focusing on antiabortion issues, Weddington introduced legislation in the 1973 session to repeal the Texas antiabortion statutes just in case the Supreme Court denied her case.

In the intervening months, politics among the Supreme Court justices intensified: there was talk of vote trading and of the need to protect President Richard Nixon, who had aligned himself with the antiabortion forces. Even though the justices had reached a decision, Harry Blackmun was convinced that the decision should be withdrawn and that the case should be reargued before a nine-man court, and William O. Douglas threatened to make public his memo outlining the sorry internal situation.

In compromise, the case was scheduled for reargument. Weddington prepared a supplemental brief on new developments concerning birth control and abortion and argued the case again before the Supreme Court with its two new justices, Lewis Powell and William Rehnquist, on October 10, 1972. Much of the questioning this time concerned the personhood of a fetus and various medical issues. Weddington emphasized that *Roe v. Wade* did not advocate abortion, but rather attempted to establish that an individual should be able to make the decision about continuing the pregnancy and, indeed, has a constitutional right to do so.

The Supreme Court ruled, 7-2, on January 22, 1973, that the Texas antiabortion statutes were unconstitutional because they violated the right of privacy and the due process clause of the Fourteenth Amendment. Justices who supported the majority opinion included Harry Blackmun (who wrote the decision), William Brennan, Warren Burger, William Douglas, Thurgood Marshall, Lewis Powell, and Potter Stewart. Dissenting from the decision were justices Byron White and William Rehnquist. The decision pointed out, however, that a woman's right to privacy is not absolute. In the dictum—advisory language not technically part of the opinion—the Supreme Court stated that some state regulations relating to access to abortions that fell within areas protected by the right of privacy would be appropriate, either for reasons of safeguarding health, maintaining medical standards, or protecting potential life. Going even further, the Court outlined a scheme for state regulation as well as procedures a state might use based on a trimester approach to pregnancy.

Weddington quickly grasped the significance of the decision. While she was excited that she had successfully argued an important case before the Supreme Court of the United States at such a young age, she realized that the court had qualified a woman's ability to make the abortion decision when it claimed that a state could regulate procedures. Thus, during the first trimester, according to the Court, a woman could make choices about abortion; in the later months, however, the state could restrict those choices to protect maternal health and fetus viability. As she feared, access to abortions did not materialize smoothly, even though the number of abortions increased. Within ten months, the antiabortion forces rallied, aided by religious institutions and the new political climate. As a result, in state after state, abortions became restricted—no public hospitals, no publicly employed physicians, no women more than twenty weeks pregnant could be involved.

Because of her legal success before the Supreme Court, Weddington gained national recognition, but her marriage suffered, and she and Ron divorced amicably in September, 1974. In 1977, while she was serving her third term in the Texas state legislature, Weddington accepted a position as general counsel to the Department of Agriculture, where she directed more than 200 attorneys. From 1978 to 1981, she served as special assistant to President Jimmy Carter on women's issues. When Carter lost his bid for reelection, Weddington became a lobbyist for the state of Texas and director of the Office of State and Federal Relations until 1986, when she returned to Austin to start her own law office. In the 1990's, Weddington lectured in history and government at the University of Texas and Texas Women's University and continued to speak to groups across the United States. As a speaker, she has been described as "dynamic and inspiring" in her commitment to developing leadership for the future. Weddington has continued to be actively engaged in legal and women's rights issues and in 1992 wrote *A Question of Choice*, a memoir of her experience as a lawyer on *Roe v. Wade*.

Summary

Sarah Weddington helped place the issue of woman's right to an abortion squarely before the American people. The publicity concerning the *Roe v. Wade* decision was muted because newspapers carried bold headlines announcing former president Lyndon B. Johnson's death. Although one poll indicated that 64 percent of Americans supported the decision at the time, abortion continued to be an inflammatory issue more than twenty years later. A significant faction of the public does not accept that the Supreme Court decided two issues: It clearly permitted individual choice while at the same time it continued the moral, legal, and medical tradition of thousands of years by affirming that legal personhood begins at birth. In the passing years, even the Court has shifted its position, as seen in its 1991 decision in *Rust v. Sullivan*, which prohibited doctors and employees in federally financed family planning centers from discussing abortion with patients. Despite the Court's wavering on the issue, Weddington herself has continued her bold support through her work in lobbying for the Freedom of Choice Act before Congress.

Freedom of choice emerged as a key issue in the 1992 presidential campaigns where it was embraced by the Democratic Party and excoriated by the Republicans. In general, however, the public has turned its attention to encouraging Congress to enact laws to ensure protected access to abortion clinics. In addition, President Bill Clinton appointed two new Supreme Court justices, Ruth Bader Ginsburg and Stephen Breyer, who were advocates of protections afforded by *Roe v. Wade*.

As he prepared to step down from the Supreme Court in 1994, Justice Harry Blackmun told reporters that *Roe v. Wade* was "a step that had to be taken as we go down the road toward the full emancipation of women." Because of Sarah Weddington's commitment and expertise, *Roe v. Wade* became a historic turning point in American history: it gave women, not the government or strangers, the right to make the most private decisions.

Bibliography

Faux, Marian. *Roe v. Wade: The Untold Story of the Landmark Supreme Court*

Decision. New York: Macmillan, 1988. One of the first works to provide a thorough exploration of this important legal case, this book examines the case's relevant issues in their original context and offers a perspective from 1988. The book explains behind-the-scenes political dynamics.

Garrow, David J. *Liberty and Sexuality: The Right to Privacy and the Making of Roe v. Wade*. New York: Macmillan, 1994. In an informative yet excessively detailed history, Garrow traces the social movement which led to the *Roe v. Wade* decision in 1973.

Hylton, Hilary. "Persistent Champion of Choice." *Los Angeles Times* 111 (September 17, 1992): E1. An interview with Weddington that appeared shortly after the publication of her work *A Question of Choice*. She discusses her concerns regarding the challenges being made to the *Roe v. Wade* decision and the activist role she has taken in keeping the issue of abortion rights before the public.

Krason, Stephen M. *Abortion: Politics, Morality, and the Constitution: A Critical Study of Roe v. Wade and Doe v. Bolton and a Basis for Change*. Lanham, Md.: University Press of America, 1984. Originally a dissertation, this encyclopedic book thoroughly examines the social history for the decisions, compares American and British law concerning abortion, studies the notion of privacy in history, and comments on the decisions.

McCorvey, Norma, with Andy Meisler. *I Am Roe: My Life*, Roe v. Wade, *and Freedom of Choice*. New York: HarperCollins, 1994. The plaintiff in *Roe v. Wade* tells her own version of the events that led to the landmark Supreme Court decision. Although she is highly critical of Weddington's handling of the case and alleges that Weddington failed to apprise her of the full consequences of trying to obtain a legal abortion through court action, McCorvey provides an interesting behind-the-scenes perspective on the battle for abortion rights.

Weddington, Sarah. *A Question of Choice*. New York: G. P. Putnam's Sons, 1993. Weddington explains her own personal involvement in the abortion issue, forces leading to the original lawsuit, and the progress of *Roe v. Wade* through the courts. Despite being labeled as an autobiography, the author pays remarkably little attention to her life; the case is the focus. Includes a plan for championing choice and pictures.

Deborah Elwell Arfken

IDA B. WELLS-BARNETT

Born: July 16, 1862; Holly Springs, Mississippi
Died: March 25, 1931; Chicago, Illinois
Areas of Achievement: Civil rights, women's rights, and journalism
Contribution: An organizer of the antilynching movement, Ida B. Wells was an
indefatigable crusader for equal rights for African Americans in the violent decades
around the turn of the century, working on issues of education, social services,
woman suffrage, and racial violence.

Early Life

Ida Bell Wells was the eldest of eight children born in slavery to slave parents who
were both of mixed racial parentage. (Her paternal grandfather was her grandmother's
white owner, and her mother's father was an American Indian.) Both had learned
trades during slavery—carpentry and cooking—which they were able to continue
after the Civil War. In the yellow fever epidemic of 1878, both parents and the
youngest child died, leaving Ida as the sole support of the younger children. Refusing
offers from relatives and friends to parcel out the children, sixteen-year-old Ida
decided to get a job as a schoolteacher. She had been educated at the Freedmen's
School in Holly Springs (later Rust College). She successfully took the teacher's exam
for the rural county schools and was able to "pass" for eighteen, teaching all week and
riding a mule six miles home for the weekend. (A family friend stayed with the
siblings during the week.) Later, she secured a better-paying position in Memphis. In
1886—after traveling to Fresno, California, with her aunt and siblings—she actually
taught school in three different states: California, Missouri, and Tennessee.

Her activist career began in 1884, when she was forcibly ejected from the ladies'
car on the Chesapeake and Ohio Railroad for refusing to sit in the segregated smoking
car (Jim Crow segregation of transportation facilities was just beginning then). She
sued the railroad and won $500 in damages; an appeal by the railroad to the Tennessee
Supreme Court reversed the decision, however, and she had to pay court costs.

Her interest in journalism began in Memphis, where she participated in a weekly
lyceum with other black schoolteachers, reading and discussing the weekly black
newspaper *The Evening Star*, among other things. When she saw how much influence
the newspapers had, she began writing a weekly column, which became popular and
was printed in many newspapers across the country. She signed her articles "Iola."
The name of the protagonist of fellow African American Frances Ellen Watkins
Harper's popular novel *Iola Leroy* (1892) may have alluded to Wells. In 1889, she
purchased a one-third interest in the Memphis *Free Speech and Headlight*, resigned
her teaching job, and began organizing, writing, and selling subscriptions for the
newspaper in black communities and churches throughout the South.

Life's Work

In 1892, three black men who owned a successful grocery store that competed with the white-owned store in the black neighborhood were lynched in Memphis, Tennessee. Ida B. Wells not only editorialized against the lynching in her newspaper but also counseled black citizens to leave Memphis and move west to Arkansas and the newly opened Oklahoma Territory. Thousands took her advice. Those who remained heeded her call to boycott the streetcar system. In 1892, therefore, Ida B. Wells organized a successful public transportation boycott, sixty years before Rosa Parks began the Montgomery bus boycott after she refused to vacate her seat in the back of the bus to let a white person take it. Thus began Ida B. Wells's life work—her crusade for justice.

When she left Memphis for a speaking and writing trip to Philadelphia and New York, angry whites destroyed her offices and press and published notices that if she returned she herself would be lynched. She was hired by the important black paper the *New York Age* to gather lynching statistics and expose the fallacy that black men raped white women. Only one-fourth of all those who were lynched were even accused of sexually accosting or insulting a white woman. Women and children as well as white men were victims of lynch mobs. Most lynchings, she found, were economically motivated, designed to intimidate the black community if it attempted to become financially independent. She used white newspaper accounts to gather her evidence, publishing in 1892 her first feature story (later a pamphlet): "Southern Horrors: Lynch Law in All Its Phases." She listed all lynchings by name, state, alleged crime, method of killing, and month, continuing this practice in the following years.

Even in the North, her speeches and writings exposing lynch law were not well covered by a frightened white press, and she despaired of making any changes. She knew that international pressure could aid the cause, so she took her antilynching crusade worldwide, traveling to England to 1893 and again in 1894. She was warmly received by former abolitionists, and she published her stories in the mainstream press, lectured daily, and founded the first antilynching organizations. Her strategy worked—the American press picked up the stories from England, and the antilynching story was disseminated to a wider audience. When she attacked well-known white Americans Frances Willard (the president of the Women's Christian Temperance Union) and evangelist Dwight L. Moody for addressing segregated white audiences in the South and not speaking out against mob violence, Wells became the center of an international controversy but gained much publicity for her cause.

In 1893, she returned from England and, along with the venerable former slave Frederick Douglass and Ferdinand Barnett (a Chicago attorney to whom she was later married), organized the protest of excluded African Americans at the Chicago World Columbian Exposition. The three activists wrote and distributed 20,000 copies of their pamphlet, *The Reason Why the Colored American Is Not in the Columbian Exposition*, to people from all over the world. Douglass, the ambassador to Haiti at that time, was the only African American who was officially a part of the exposition. The pamphlet pointed out that without blacks there would be neither American civilization nor the industrial miracle so celebrated at the fair.

Remaining in Chicago after her second trip to England, Wells was married to Barnett and eventually gave birth to four children, but she continued her political organizing and journalism in Chicago's black newspaper *The Conservator* (which she purchased from Barnett). Although she was criticized by other women activists such as Susan B. Anthony for marrying and thus having "divided duty," Ida B. Wells-Barnett managed to be both a mother and an organizer, often traveling to lectures with one or another child, nursing between meetings. In Chicago, she founded the first black woman's club (later named the Ida B. Wells Club), the Alpha Suffrage Club (the first black woman's suffrage organization), and the Negro Fellowship League (which set up a reading room, job referrals, and a rooming house for black men newly arrived in Chicago). She helped to found a black kindergarten and a black orchestra, and she worked as a probation officer.

Her political position was very much opposed to that of accommodationists such as Booker T. Washington. She espoused a radical view akin to that of W. E. B. Du Bois and later the pan-Africanism of Marcus Garvey. She believed that African Americans should use both the law and agitation to gain equal rights in all areas, and that nothing was impossible. Along with Du Bois, she was one of the founding members of the National Association for the Advancement of Colored People (NAACP) in 1909, but she later broke with the organization because of its timid stance on racial issues.

As an Illinois delegate to the national woman suffrage parade in Washington in 1913, Wells-Barnett refused to march with the black delegates at the back of the procession; she quietly integrated the ranks of the Illinois delegates as the parade moved down Pennsylvania Avenue. She helped Chicago elect its first black alderman in 1915 and continued to work within the political structure, running herself unsuccessfully for the state senate in 1930.

She continued her investigative work in the South with a campaign to give justice to the black soldiers involved in the 1917 24th Infantry rebellion in Texas during World War I. She personally investigated the causes of the East St. Louis and Chicago riots of 1919 (which she predicted in print two weeks before they occurred). In 1922, she visited and wrote an exposé of the prison conditions of the Arkansas black farmers who had formed a cooperative and were attacked by whites—and then were arrested for starting a riot. For this journalistic work, she was hounded by the Federal Bureau of Investigation as a dangerous subversive during the Red Scare of the early 1920's.

Ida B. Wells-Barnett labored to the end of her life, leaving her autobiography unfinished in mid-sentence when she succumbed to her final illness, dying of uremic poisoning at the age of sixty-eight.

Summary

Ida B. Wells-Barnett was radical, disputatious, angry, hard to get along with, and had arguments with nearly everyone with whom she worked. She said that she did not want publicity, but her autobiography makes it clear that she craved personal publicity. Still, she was a genius of an organizer: She had political savvy and a photographic memory. She was a powerful woman who played by the men's rules. She organized and carried out a successful economic boycott of public transportation facilities in the 1890's, she integrated the American woman suffrage movement, she single-handedly brought international attention to bear on the lynching scandal in the United States, and she kept the Chicago school system from being segregated by enlisting the help of social worker Jane Addams. She knew everyone and alienated everyone, and she took her issues personally to two presidents—William McKinley and Woodrow Wilson. She worked with, at various times, African Americans Booker T. Washington, W. E. B. Du Bois, Marcus Garvey, Madam C. J. Walker, Frederick Douglass, Anna Gaily Cooper, Fannie Barrier Williams, Mary Church Terrell, Mary McLeod Bethune, and many others. Although Wells-Barnett worked with whites when it was politically expedient to do so, she believed that a unified black community should band together for its own betterment. Her radical position and her refusal to compromise resulted in her near-erasure from American history, but Wells-Barnett has begun to garner more attention as the result of scholarly efforts in the fields of women's history and African American history.

Bibliography
Bedermank, Gail. "'Civilization,' The Decline of Middle-Class Manliness, and Ida B. Wells's Antilynching Campaign (1892-94)." *Radical History Review*, no. 52 (1992): 5-30. An analysis of the racist evolutionary rhetoric of the end of the century, with special reference to Wells-Barnett's work in England and at the Chicago World Columbian Exposition of 1893.
Giddings, Paula. *When and Where I Enter: The Impact of Black Women on Race and Sex in America.* New York: William Morrow, 1984. A history of black women in the United States, with large interpretive sections on Wells-Barnett's activist career, especially the antilynching campaign in England, the founding of the NAACP, and her activist work in Chicago. A good index and a bibliography are included.
Hendricks, Wanda. "Ida Bell Wells-Barnett." In *Black Women in America: An Historical Encyclopedia*, edited by Darlene Clark Hine. Brooklyn, N.Y.: Carlson, 1993. An important reference work that includes photographs and primary and secondary bibliographies.
Loewenberg, Bert James, and Ruth Bogin, eds. *Black Women in Nineteenth Century American Life.* University Park: Pennsylvania State University Press, 1976. Includes the introduction and a selection from Wells-Barnett's antilynching writings published in London in 1892.
Sterling, Dorothy. "Ida B. Wells: Voice of a People." In *Black Foremothers: Three Lives.* Old Westburg, N.Y.: The Feminist Press, 1979. A well-written and accessible narrative about all aspects of Wells's life. Contains a useful list of sources.
Wells, Ida B. *Crusade for Justice: The Autobiography of Ida B. Wells.* Edited by Alfreda M. Duster. Chicago: University of Chicago Press, 1970. This is Wells-Barnett's unfinished autobiography, which was edited and published by her daughter. It is the best source for biographical detail about Wells-Barnett's organizing and political work and is an important source for newspaper clippings and articles, many of which are printed verbatim.

Margaret McFadden

MAE WEST

Born: August 17, 1893; Brooklyn, New York
Died: November 22, 1980; Los Angeles, California
Areas of Achievement: Film and theater and drama
Contribution: A memorable screen presence and wit, Mae West was also a break-
through playwright in the handling of taboo subjects and a role model as a woman
in control of her own sexuality.

Early Life

Because her father was a prize fighter and her mother was a model, Mae West had
an early familiarity with show business. Indeed, since she began her stage career as a
child, she can hardly be said to have had an early life. By the time she left school at
thirteen, she was an established vaudeville performer. While on tour but still under
age (giving false information that has led to confusion about her age), she married a
dancer named Frank Wallace—by implication gay—apparently as a way of protecting
herself from scandal in the event of pregnancy. She never lived with Wallace—who
entered into a bigamous marriage with someone else—and denied for many years that
she was married.

When West made her Broadway debut in *À la Broadway* in 1911, she was already
a seasoned trouper. Alert to her unique style, she retailored her songs for her earthy
personality and was an immediate critical and popular success. Dividing her time
between vaudeville and Broadway, she had trouble with the police on more than one
occasion because of the suggestiveness of her dancing. In 1921, in *Sometime*, she
introduced the shimmy dance to white audiences, creating a particular sensation.

Life's Work

By 1926, Mae West realized that if she was to achieve star stature, she needed
material tailored to her special personality and good-humored view of sex. Since no
suitable star vehicle was available, she called upon her experience in writing her own
vaudeville sketches and fashioned a play by adapting John J. Byrne's *Following the
Fleet* (c. 1926). Even before opening, the show created more than one scandal, first
when New York newspapers refused advertising because of the title she chose, *Sex*
(1926), and then when the unprecedented enthusiasm of Yale undergraduates at the
tryout in New Haven, Connecticut, and of sailors at the tryout in New London,
Connecticut, caused the show to sell out even in previews. In New York, despite the
advertising blackout and a plagiarism suit from Byrne, the show ran to packed houses
for more than a year until suddenly the New York police decided that it was injurious
to the morals of minors. She was convicted on that charge and spent ten days in prison.

The play itself is innocuous by later standards, which it helped to forge. It has no
obscene language, nudity, or even suggested sex, all of which later became routine.
Sex, which concerns the lives of prostitutes on the Bowery in New York, is a
melodrama that presents a realistic view of sexuality with a light touch. The same

could be said of all West's later vehicles.

At about this time, she began a long-term relationship with James Timony, an attorney who worked for West's mother and who later became West's business manager. While she was still performing in *Sex*, she wrote and produced another play that created a scandal on a different front. *The Drag* (1926), which had to be performed in Paterson, New Jersey—to packed houses—because of censorship restrictions in New York, was the first substantial, realistic picture of male homosexuality in the theater. It presents a somewhat naïve view of homosexuals as men who want to be women and advocates restraint of this impulse because it disrupts family life, but there is no doubt that the theme was heartfelt on the author's part and ahead of its time in terms of tolerance.

West wrote and performed with great success in several more plays along the same lines as *Sex*, including a beauty contest exposé, *The Wicked Age* (1927), and *Diamond Lil* (1928), a nostalgic view of the Bowery in the 1890's. West also wrote but did not appear in another play dealing with male homosexuality, *The Pleasure Man* (1928). Less provocative than *The Drag*, this work simply included homosexuality as a fact of backstage life in a melodrama about other relationships. Nevertheless, the police closed the show shortly after its Broadway opening and prosecuted the author for immorality. This time, however, West won the case, striking a blow for artistic freedom. Unfortunately, it was too late for the production to be resumed.

West toured with some of her plays, but the death of her mother and the 1929 stock market crash profoundly disrupted her life, and she wanted a change. She wrote a novel called *Babe Gordon* (1930; later reprinted as *The Constant Sinner*), the first popular treatment of the social conditions in black Harlem. She also wrote a novelization of *Diamond Lil* (1932). Then, after a good Broadway run in a play she adapted from *The Constant Sinner* (1931), she accepted an offer from Paramount Studios to make films.

Allowed to rewrite her dialogue to fit her persona for her film debut in *Night After Night* (1932), West became an instant film star. Her next project was an adaptation of *Diamond Lil* into the legendary film *She Done Him Wrong* (1933), which featured Cary Grant in his first starring role. This film and its successor *I'm No Angel* (1933), for which she wrote the whole screenplay, were so successful that she brought Paramount Studios back from the brink of financial ruin. In *She Done Him Wrong* and *Belle of the Nineties* (1934; she also wrote the screenplay), she introduced costume drama to the talkies and started a Gay Nineties fashion trend. In the latter film, her insistence on using a black jazz band brought about the first instance of such integrated accompaniment.

At this point in her film career, however, West ran into the sort of trouble with the censors that had hounded her on the stage. The Hayes Office was introduced to monitor the language and plots of films while they were being made. *Klondike Annie* (1936), *Go West, Young Man* (1936), *Every Day's a Holiday* (1938), and other later pictures that West wrote and starred in were praised at the time for being clean yet amusing; most film historians, however, regard such later films as lacking the free spirit of her early ones. She was also banned from the radio for her supposedly too sensual reading of some innocuous lines in a sketch about Adam and Eve.

Her most memorable film, although not her best as either screenwriter or performer, is certainly *My Little Chickadee* (1940), costarring W. C. Fields, which she made for Universal. Although she found Fields unreliable because of his drinking and always maintained that he should not have been given a coauthor credit for the screenplay, the incongruous styles of the two meshed in this Western melodramatic spoof, apparently because she understood that giving Fields most of the laughs would mellow his usually misogynistic persona and because she saw that her eroticism could then effectively be directed away from her costar toward other men in the story.

Unhappy with the scripts she was offered and unable to convince anyone to finance a color costume epic of the Russian empress Catherine the Great, she was idle for several years. As a favor to actor-director Gregory Ratoff, she appeared in *The Heat's On* in 1943, but this unsatisfactory pastiche convinced her that she needed to return to the stage.

Turned into a play, *Catherine Was Great* received a lavish Broadway production from celebrated impresario Mike Todd in 1944. Critics found the play too historical and serious, but audiences loved it, and West followed the long Broadway run by taking the show on tour. She then adapted another play as *Come on Up* (1946) and played to great success in a production of *Diamond Lil* in the London West End, first on tour, and then in a revival on Broadway in 1949.

A number of scandals, personal problems, and lawsuits marred her later years. Frank Wallace surfaced and attempted to cash in on her fame, first by asking for separate maintenance, then by billing himself in a nightclub act as "Mae West's Husband," and finally by suing for divorce and alimony. She silenced him at last in 1942 in a divorce settlement by paying him an undisclosed amount of money. Her longtime companion James Timony died in 1954, as did Wallace. In 1955, *Confidential* magazine published a demonstrably untrue exposé. In 1950, 1959, and again in 1964, she was involved in complicated lawsuits in which she tried to defend the name Diamond Lil as a trademark, and two different writing teams accused her of plagiarism in *Catherine Was Great*.

Finally slowed down somewhat by advancing age and no longer able to carry a full play, West put together a nightclub act with a chorus of musclemen in 1954 and toured with great success, and she began a recording career. Yet there were troubles. Mickey Hargitay (Mr. Universe) and another muscleman in her act, Paul Novak, had a public fight over her when she played the Coconut Grove in 1955. When Hargitay turned his affections to Jayne Mansfield, a film star whose persona suggested West's sort of available sexuality but without the wit, West established a permanent liaison with Novak that was like the one she had had with Timony.

West made a spectacular television debut at the 1958 Academy Awards, singing "Baby, It's Cold Outside" (written in 1949, by Frank Loesser) with Rock Hudson, who was then at the height of his film career. Although a *Person to Person* interview with her on the occasion of the publication of her autobiography *Goodness Had Nothing to Do with It* (1959) was never shown because of the suggestiveness of some of her comments, she appeared on the television variety shows of Red Skelton and Dean Martin and as a guest star in the situation comedy *Mr. Ed.*

In 1970, the opportunity arose to return to film when a perfect part for her appeared in the screen adaptation of Gore Vidal's camp novel of sex change, *Myra Breckinridge* (1968). Her traditional parodic approach was exactly right for the material, and she was certainly the main reason people went to see the film. Excellent in parts and a *succès d'estime* for West, *Myra Breckinridge* was somewhat incoherent in its released form, since director Michael Sarne deleted most of the footage of rival auteur West. Its unauthorized use of clips of old films also caused legal trouble.

Nevertheless, the project convinced West that she still had a film public, and she set about refashioning a play adaptation she had appeared in briefly on tour into the film *Sextette* (1978). The time lag, however, was fatally damaging, and in the years between these last two films, anything that was left of her screen persona had passed with old age from parody and camp into caricature and grotesquerie. During the years between her two last films, she also wrote a novelization of *The Pleasure Man* (1975, "with the kind assistance of [her managing assistant] Lawrence Lee") and the self-help book *On Sex, Health and ESP* (also 1975), but both are believed to have been ghostwritten.

Although she was still active enough to record radio commercials in 1979, she died in 1980 after a series of strokes.

Summary

Only Jean Harlow rivals Mae West in creating an indelible screen presence in a short career as a film star. Like Harlow's, West's screen persona works because she manages to be sexy without taking herself seriously. The combination led to her more than once being compared to a female impersonator and made her popular with women as well as men because the parody removed any chance that she would permanently divert men's attention. The strong impact of her physical presence is, however, attested by the inflatable life preserver that bears her name.

Although she was most famous as a personality, her enduring mark on theatrical history was made as a writer. By introducing straightforward and unpunished sexual situations, her plays and films defied the taboos of the time. It is particularly interesting that it was a woman who brought the subject of male homosexuality to Broadway. Her work made it possible for later—perhaps more technically interesting—playwrights to treat sexual themes. She suggested that sex without guilt is possible, even for women and gay men.

Bibliography

Cashin, Fergus. *Mae West: A Biography*. Westport, Conn.: Arlington House, 1981. This unconvincing exposé maintains that West was a man or was at least somehow biologically deformed.
Eells, George, and Stanley Musgrove. *Mae West*. New York: William Morrow, 1982.

A scholarly biography that corrects some of West's autobiographical memories, this is the best narrative work on West's career.

Malachosky, Tim, with James Greene. *Mae West*. Lancaster, Calif.: Empire, 1993. This lavish picture book of candid photographs was compiled by West's private secretary.

Tuska, Jon. *The Complete Films of Mae West*. New York: Carol, 1992. A picture book that also contains full and remarkably accurate commentary on West's entire career, not only her films.

Ward, Carol M. *Mae West: A Bio-Bibliography*. Westport, Conn.: Greenwood Press, 1989. An annotated bibliography with a full career summary, this is the standard reference work on West.

West, Mae. *Goodness Had Nothing to Do with It: The Autobiography of Mae West*. New York: Avon Books, 1970. Although sometimes obviously protective of her reputation, West is candid but not salacious in this chronological review of her career and private life. She is, however, strangely unreflective, and the transitions are often abrupt.

Edmund Miller

EDITH WHARTON

Born: January 24, 1862; New York, New York
Died: August 11, 1937; St.-Brice-sous-Forêt, France
Area of Achievement: Literature
Contribution: Edith Wharton was a novelist who was noted for her portrayal of the decline of New York aristocracy and for her characters' trapped sensibilities.

Early Life

Edith Newbold Jones, the daughter of George Frederic Jones and Lucretia Stevens Rhinelender Jones, was born into a society of aristocrats who led a leisured, proper life and disdained business and politics. Wharton's family was a prime example of "old" New York: moneyed, cultivated, and rigidly conventional.

According to custom, young Edith was educated by tutors and governesses. She also spent much of her childhood abroad with her family. Edith was forbidden to read literary "rubbish," so she fell back on the classics on her father's bookshelves. Despite her culture and education, Edith was expected to excel primarily in society, which involved rigid adherence to proper manners, dress, and lifestyle.

In 1885, Edith was married to another American socialite, Edward Wharton, an easygoing and unintellectual man. The Whartons led an affluent, social life in America and in Europe, uninterrupted by children or financial concerns.

Although Edith Wharton performed her social tasks well, her duties were not enough for her hungry mind. She began writing poems, stories, books on interior decorating, and travel pieces. Her husband was embarrassed by his wife's writing, and her friends also did not approve. Fortunately, Edith Wharton made the acquaintance of writer Henry James. James not only supported her writing but also served as her confidant throughout periods of emotional turmoil. Although Edith claimed that she wrote for distraction, her diary notes that only by creating another imaginary world through writing could she endure the "moral solitude" of her marriage. Despite obvious incompatibilities, Edith and Edward lived together for twenty-eight years. That they did not divorce until 1913 is probably because of conservative class traditions.

Wharton's divorce plus other personal tensions spurred her to do some of her best work. She converted her anguish into writing about the corrosive effects of social class upon a woman's identity. Young Edith Wharton found her society's indifference to anything but forms stultifying. Much of her writing examines the superfluous details of a refined class frozen in convention. Wharton also portrayed struggling characters trapped by larger social forces and, sometimes, by morally inferior individuals. Nevertheless, when Wharton grew old, she concluded that the "Age of Innocence" in which she was reared was preferable to the modern world, which valued nothing.

The declining aristocracy became Edith Wharton's principal subject matter. She most often depicted the society of "old" New York in conflict with nouveau riche capitalists of the Gilded Age, who respected only money.

Life's Work

Edith Wharton's early literary output included poems, decorating books, short stories, and three novels. In 1899, a volume of short stories, *The Greater Inclination*, was published, followed by *The Touchstone* (1900). In 1901, *Crucial Instances* followed; these short books have a Jamesian influence. Wharton's three poetry collections are overserious and overornamented. Her first novel, *The Valley of Decision* (1902), another form of George Eliot's *Romola*, is notable because its descriptions capture the spirit of eighteenth century Italy. Wharton's novel *Sanctuary* (1903) and her short stories in *The Descent of Man* (1904) are still experimental. Nevertheless, in these early works appear two of Wharton's basic themes: the aristocratic, cold, egoistic male and the strong female, who eventually dominates the male.

The House of Mirth (1905) marked the beginning of Edith Wharton's mature artistic period. Wharton had discovered her medium and subject: the novel of manners and the invasion of old New York society by the millionaire "nouveau riche." Wharton indicated her realization that Knickerbocker society would eventually make peace with the "invaders." Her story concerned those who were trampled in this social clash. The novel's Lily Bart is similar to a Dreiser heroine in that she is doomed by heredity and a materialistic environment. Lily struggles to improve herself but is defeated by her embrace of a heartless social ideal and by scruples that prevent her from marrying only for money.

Despite the success of *The House of Mirth*, Wharton delayed for years before returning to the subject of society's clash with the invaders. *Madame de Treymes* (1907) is an innocents-abroad story with a Jamesian influence. *The Fruit of the Tree* (1907), a reform novel, considers labor reform and the morality of euthanasia, but it fails because of lack of unity. *The Hermit and the Wild Woman* (1908) is made up of slender stories of artists, but *Tales of Men and Ghosts* (1910) contains chilling ghost stories.

The novella *Ethan Frome* (1911) made Edith Wharton famous. Although *Ethan Frome* involves a poor New England farm family, Wharton's familiar themes predominate: a man under female domination and a human being crushed by circumstances and his own scruples. *Ethan Frome* is noted for its spare style, masterly details, tragic ending, and symbolism. Although Wharton used details, she did not often use symbolism. *Ethan Frome*'s theme is enhanced by landscape symbols that reflect Ethan's spiritual desolation. Suffocating snow symbolizes Ethan's financial and social trap, and withered apple trees on a slate hillside symbolize Ethan's emotional starvation.

The Reef (1912), although praised as a "Racinian" novel, puzzles readers because of its moral tone. The story involves a widow, who is at last to marry an old bachelor admirer, and her stepson, who is to marry the family governess. When she discovers that her fiancé and the governess have been lovers, the widow, Mrs. Leath, breaks her engagement. When she goes to the governess' sister's home to tell Sophy that she has given up her fiancé, she learns that Sophy has left for India in disreputable company. This departure leaves Leath free to return to her fiancé. The novel's problem is its

implicit sense that social class determines justice. The governess' fate is semiprosti-
tution precisely because she is a governess, but the bachelor's betrayal is forgivable
because he is a gentleman.

In *The Custom of the Country* (1913), Wharton returns to the theme of rich, old New
York and the "invaders." The heroine is not a delicate woman whom society crushes,
but a predatory female invader who victimizes the society she crashes. Undine Spragg
makes the same mistakes as Lily Bart, but unlike Lily, she uses street smarts and
amorality to extricate herself. Some people consider *The Custom of the Country* to be
Wharton's masterpiece because of its taut depiction of the invaders takeover of New
York society and the resulting social and moral emptiness.

In 1913, the year in which *The Custom of the Country* was published, the Whartons
were divorced. Edith Wharton, who had been spending most of her time in France,
now settled there. The new francophile wrote books meant for tourists, for whom she
had also written *A Motor-Flight Through France* (1908). Wharton also wrote about
France's involvement in World War I in *Fighting France* (1915), *The Book of the
Homeless* (1915), *The Marne* (1918), and *A Son at the Front* (1923), works more noted
for their support of France than for their literary merit.

Ironically, the war made Edith Wharton long for the vanished, quiet world of her
childhood. In "Autre Temps" (*Xindu*, 1916) and in *Twilight Sleep* (1927), Wharton
expressed nostalgia for the once despised conventions, believing that these instilled
fortitude and moral fiber.

In 1916 and 1917, Wharton published *The Bunner Sisters* and *Summer*. As in *Ethan
Frome*, the characters are poor and working class. *The Bunner Sisters* contains a
sensitive person trapped within an inferior human being, while *Summer* depicts
squalid lives and characters struggling in a battle destined for defeat. Again, as in
Ethan Frome, symbols signify the characters' fates, which are predetermined by
forces beyond their comprehension.

Wharton's nostalgia culminated in *The Age of Innocence* (1920), a Pulitzer Prize-
winning novel portraying the genteel New York of the 1870's and featuring characters
trapped by their environment. No matter how much Newland Archer and Ellen
Olenska are in love, society decrees that Archer shall marry May Welland, and so he
does. Later, Archer even approves his dull marriage as part of good, traditional ways.

Edith Wharton's best literary period ended with *The Age of Innocence*, for her work
declined after 1920. Wharton began publishing serial novels in American women's
magazines to earn money to sustain her expensive lifestyle. *Glimpses of the Moon*
(1922) shows a severe lapse in style and character. The short stories in *Old New York*
(1924) successfully evoke that period, but Wharton also wanted to depict her contemporary age. This ambition, coupled with her need for money, resulted in inferior
works. *The Mother's Recompense* (1925), *Twilight Sleep* (1927), and *The Children*
(1928) unconvincingly lay the causes of the era's ills at America's door. *Hudson River
Bracketed* (1929) and *The Gods Arrive* (1932), novels set in the Midwest, a region she
had never visited, make similar implausible criticisms.

Edith Wharton's posthumously published books are *Ghosts* (1937) and *The Bucca-*

neers (1938). *Ghosts* contains two superbly frightening stories, whereas *The Bucca-neers* turns back again to "old New York." This unfinished work revives Wharton's forceful style but lacks the bitterness of her earlier works. Some critics believe that this book would have been her best had she completed it.

Summary
    Edith Wharton's place in literary history is secured by *Ethan Frome*. She will also be remembered for her depiction of the high society of old Knickerbocker New York. These works are almost historical novels because of their accurate rendering of an age. Through her exquisite use of detail, Wharton delineated not only the conventions of an unadventurous society but also its moral ambiguity. The stifling conventions of upper-class New York trap its members and often annihilate those who aspire to its society. This demanding social code also, however, produces people who have a strong moral fiber. Ironically, these strong characters whose values have been shaped by "high society" sometimes make unnoticed, and often needless, sacrifices. Although some readers find Wharton's characters lifeless, she is considered a superb novelist of manners.
    Edith Wharton, though acclaimed in her lifetime, suffered from gender as well as class expectations. She began writing to escape her narrow social sphere as well as marital tensions. Edith Wharton endured artistic isolation partially because of her class. That class distrusted literature, particularly that written by women, because of the new and disquieting ideas that literature often advocated. That Edith Wharton's health improved and her publications increased after her divorce suggests that divorce separated her not only from a man but also from limiting gender roles. Edith Wharton triumphed over formidable obstacles of social position, wealth, and gender expectations. In this respect, she serves as role model for aspiring women with traditional familial and social obligations.

Bibliography
Auchincloss, Louis. *Edith Wharton*. Minneapolis: University of Minnesota Press 1961. This pamphlet covers Edith Wharton's biography and critically examines Wharton's plots, characters, themes, and style.
Bell, Millicent. *Edith Wharton and Henry James*. New York: George Braziller, 1965. This scholarly account of the friendship between Edith Wharton and Henry James includes many of their letters.
Benstock, Shari. *No Gifts from Chance: A Biography of Edith Wharton*. New York: Charles Scribner's Sons, 1994. As the first substantial biography of Wharton to appear in nearly two decades, Benstock's study is informed by her investigation of a variety of primary sources that have become available in recent years.
Howe, Irving, ed. *Edith Wharton: A Collection of Critical Essays*. Englewood Cliffs, N.J.: Prentice-Hall, 1962. This anthology contains articles dealing with Wharton's overall achievement and others centering on specific works or aspects of her writing.

Jessup, Josephine Lurie. *The Faith of Our Feminists*. New York: Richard R. Smith, 1950. A section on Wharton demonstrates how feminism is illustrated in Wharton's subtle portrayal of women's domination of men.

Lewis, R. W. B. *Edith Wharton*. 2 vols. New York: Harper & Row, 1975. This Pulitzer Prize-winning work is essential reading for those interested in Wharton's life and how it informed her work.

Lubbock, Percy. *Portrait of Edith Wharton*. New York: Appleton-Century-Crofts, 1947. This is an informal biography written by Edith Wharton's friend at the request of her literary executor. The biography portrays Edith Wharton through the perspectives of her friends as well as through the eyes of Percy Lubbock, with a nostalgic, sometimes gossipy tone.

Nevius, Blake. *Edith Wharton*. Berkeley: University of California Press, 1953. An excellent critical analysis of Wharton's works, plots, style, and themes—particularly the chapter "The Trapped Sensibility." The book follows Wharton's career chronologically, noting her artistic decline in the 1920's and her subsequent "tired writing."

Overton, Grant M. *The Women Who Make Our Novels*. New York: Moffat, 1922. Written while Edith Wharton was still alive, Overton's book pronounces Wharton's overall literary achievement brilliant but lifeless, but he exempts *Ethan Frome*, *The House of Mirth*, and *Summer* from this verdict.

Shapiro, Charles, ed. *Twelve Original Essays on Great American Novels*. Detroit: Wayne State University Press, 1958. This book is useful for Walter B. Rideout's essays on *The House of Mirth*. Rideout maintains that Edith Wharton has not received her just due because the major phase of her writing began just before World War I.

Mary Hanford Bruce

ELLEN G. WHITE

Born: November 26, 1827; Gorham, Maine
Died: July 16, 1915; St. Helena, California
Area of Achievement: Religion
Contribution: Cofounder of the Seventh-day Adventist church, Ellen G. White was a
   charismatic religious leader, a health reformer, and an educator.

Early Life

   Ellen Gould Harmon and her twin sister were the youngest children of Eunice
Gould Harmon and Robert Harmon, a hatter who employed his entire family in his
business. Ellen attended elementary school until a serious head injury forced her to
withdraw at age nine. Later, she studied for a brief time at Westbrook Seminary and
Female College in Portland, Maine, but she acquired very little formal education.
   The Harmons attended a Methodist church faithfully, and Ellen joined that congregation at her baptism in 1842. She cited a religious experience at a Methodist
campground meeting in 1840 as the occasion for her conversion. Soon after her
baptism, Ellen became attracted to the preaching of William Miller, a Baptist from
New York State who predicted that the return of Christ would occur in approximately
1843 and had acquired thousands of followers. When Ellen and her family embraced
Miller's Adventist teaching and disrupted their Methodist church by proclaiming it,
the congregation excommunicated them.
   When 1843 and 1844 passed and there was no Second Coming, many disillusioned
Millerites abandoned Adventism, but Ellen Harmon reported having a vision that
corrected Miller's error, and she thereby preserved a portion of his movement and
made it the basis for the Seventh-day Adventist church. Then age seventeen, Ellen
claimed that she saw heaven and that Jesus Christ directed her to seek the salvation
of souls. Soon she endorsed the view that Miller had been mistaken in his interpretation of prophecy and that in 1844 Christ had entered the sanctuary in heaven to
investigate the sins of God's people as a prelude to the coming end of history. This
became the official Seventh-day Adventist teaching. Another vision informed her to
adopt the Sabbatarian belief (observance of the Sabbath on Saturday) that Seventh-
Day Baptists had been proclaiming for some time. She began proclaiming her
prophetic message in Portland, where visionary religious activities had been occurring
at camp meetings.

Life's Work

   Convinced that she possessed the same gift of prophecy that had inspired seers of
the Bible, Ellen Harmon began preaching despite ridicule and attacks on her person.
On occasion, critics disrupted her meetings and threatened to harm her, but she
refused to be intimidated and continued preaching.
   Although most Millerites did not acknowledge Harmon's prophetic gifts, James
White, a preacher in that sect, became her collaborator and companion. Because they

expected the imminent return of Christ, they did not plan to marry, but their travels together caused gossip, so they wed in August of 1846. A year later, Ellen gave birth to Henry White, and the parents left him with friends so they could respond to a divine call to continue itinerant preaching of the Adventist message. When a second son, James, arrived in 1849, the Whites entrusted him also to the custody of a friend. James and Ellen White had four children altogether, two of whom died young. Ellen treated her sons' illnesses with home remedies, some which were of her own design, and both parents claimed that healings were the result of prayer.

James promoted his wife's revelations, but she often deferred to him when both received invitations to preach. They held that God had created the sexes equal but that the fall into sin had impaired that position. Women, because of the restorative power of the Gospel, could regain equality and preach. Ellen taught that the wives of pastors who assisted in their husbands' ministries should receive wages from the churches.

Through his printing enterprise, James White published Ellen's writings after she informed him that a vision had revealed to her that this was God's will.

By 1863, when Adventists numbered 3,500, the Whites formally organized the Seventh-day Adventist church, chiefly to ensure that control of the publishing house would remain in Adventist hands. Ellen White was a prolific author of more than 40,000 pages in print and another 50,000 in correspondence and unpublished compositions. Her emphasis was the interpretation of the Bible and of history, but her first publication was autobiographical: *A Sketch of the Christian Experience and Views of Ellen G. White* (1851). After experiencing a vision of the cosmic conflict of good and evil, she wrote *The Great Controversy* (1858), the first volume of a work known collectively as *Spiritual Gifts*, which she completed in 1864. *The Great Controversy* is her most significant book. In it, she argued that the Roman Catholic and Protestant churches had defected from Christ, and she cited the fourteenth chapter of the book of Revelation as predicting that that would occur. The Seventh-day Adventist church, in her view, restored Christianity to proclaim the Sabbath and the return of Christ during the last days.

White always asserted that her visions conveyed a correct understanding of the Bible, which she conveyed to her church. She believed that her revelations were necessary because Christians had far too long failed to study the Bible adequately. She did not regard her prophetic teachings as substitutes for the Bible, but as subject to its authority. The last of her daytime visions, which appeared to be trances, occurred in approximately 1879. After that, revelations came only in dreams, the final one of which occurred four months before she died. Some of her trances lasted several hours; others, only a few minutes. Sometimes she lost her sight during a trance and remained blind for a few days. White maintained that an angel delivered the revelations, through both trances and dreams.

Ellen G. White's thirty-five-year marriage ended with the death of James White in 1881. Intense grief kept her depressed for a year, until she learned in a dream that God had designated her son Willie to be her companion and spiritual adviser. He proved to be a skillful administrator, like his father.

White was not a learned theologian and therefore did not compose a systematic exposition of her distinctive beliefs. Her major doctrinal emphases are, however, clear. She believed that the charismatic practices of biblical times, such as prophecies, miraculous healings, and other channels of special revelation, would remain in effect until the Second Advent. This belief put her at odds with Protestant orthodoxy, which regards the Bible as God's last word until Christ returns. Although she regarded Roman Catholicism as a form of pseudo-Christianity, her belief in extrabiblical revelation is something she had in common with the papal church she appeared to despise.

Concerning the person of Christ, the influence of Ellen White led Seventh-day Adventists away from the Arianism of some of its early leaders (who believed that Christ and God were not made of the same substance) to a dogmatic affirmation of the Trinity. Her view of the work of Christ and the doctrine of salvation appeared in her book *Steps to Christ* (1892), in which she espoused a semi-Pelagian and Arminian understanding of sin and redemption (that is, she denied the concepts of Original Sin and absolute predestination), which put her at variance with the historic Lutheran and Reformed positions.

Regarding the social issues of her era, Ellen G. White was remarkably progressive. In addition to her belief in the equality of the sexes, she decried race prejudice and urged the abolition of slavery. Because she feared retaliation against black people, however, she did not encourage Seventh-day Adventists to form integrated congregations in the American South. She called on her followers to combat hunger, oppression, injustice, and destructive practices such as the use of tobacco, alcoholic beverages, and drugs. At her urging, Seventh-day Adventists founded sanatoriums, clinics, hospitals, and medical schools in many lands. White had once been a hydropathist who scorned conventional medicine—especially the use of toxic drugs. She sometimes branded resort to physicians as lack of faith in God, but she eventually modified her views and led the way in establishing the Western Health Reform Institute at Battle Creek, Michigan, the first of a network of such facilities that developed into respected centers of medicine and surgery. Seventh-day Adventists have continued to endorse White's prescription of a vegetarian diet and the avoidance of stimulants such as coffee and tea, a belief for which she claimed divine revelation.

Despite her many admirable accomplishments, the reputation of Ellen G. White remains sullied by accusations of plagiarism. Some of her ideas about hydropathy appear to have originated in the work of L. B. Coles, from whose *Philosophy of Health* White seems to have borrowed material without giving him credit. There is also evidence that she lifted material from the writings of Horace Mann. Her *Sketches from the Life of Paul* (1883), when compared with *The Life and Epistles of the Apostle Paul* (third edition, 1855) by W. J. Conybeare and J. S. Howson, shows much similarity that gives credence to the charge of plagiarism. When one compares her book *The Great Controversy* with J. A. Wylie's *History of the Waldenses* and J. H. Merle d'Aubigne's *History of the Reformation*, one finds further evidence of plagiarism. D. M. Canright, an Adventist for twenty-eight years who left the church and became a Baptist pastor, accused White of plagiarism and numerous inconsistencies in her practices. Although he was quick to discredit a cause he had once espoused, Canright was in a position to obtain information unfavorable to the founder of Seventh-day Adventism.

Ellen White encouraged reliance on divine intervention for deliverance from physical ailments, and when she agreed to resort to healing, she meant hydropathy. She learned about water-cures from James Caleb Johnson's article about treating diphtheria, which appeared in the *Yates County Chronicle* in 1863. She applied that treatment to her sons successfully. Her own health was, however, always fragile, and often she attributed her afflictions to attacks from Satan, who, she believed, wanted to kill her in order to terminate her preaching.

When she became an advocate of health reform, White announced that God had revealed his approval of her program. She warned that eating meat led to cancer, leprosy, and other diseases, but she ate meat on occasion herself. She maintained that, among the healing arts, hydropathy alone had God's approval, yet she later encouraged the practice of conventional medicine and promoted medical missionary work as a means by which Seventh-day Adventists could open doors for the preaching of their message. She told her disciples that the proclamation of the Gospel and the healing of bodies are inseparable ministries.

In *The Ministry of Healing* (1905), her last major writing about health, Ellen G. White omitted her earlier warning that meat and eggs excite sexual passions. In 1909, she permitted the consumption of eggs, butter, and milk, which she had earlier denounced. When she first heard of X-ray diagnosis, she denounced that too. Eventually, however, she supported the effort to make the Western Health Reform Institute a genuine medical and surgical facility of which Seventh day Adventists could be proud. John H. Kellogg was the first educated Adventist physician. He became director of the Western Health Reform Institute in 1875. Kellogg and White eventually quarreled, and he became one of those who accused her of plagiarism. In 1907, the Seventh-Day Adventist church excommunicated him for denying the validity of her prophetic gifts and for espousing a view of the Holy Spirit that seemed to imply pantheism.

Despite the inconsistencies in her teachings and practices, Ellen White exerted a strong influence on the development of medical education in particular and on education in general. Late in her life, she founded in California the College of Medical Evangelists, which became the highly acclaimed medical school of Loma Linda University.

Inspired by White, Seventh-day Adventists established schools for their children, even when that required the building of one-room schoolhouses. Battle Creek College was the first Adventist institution of higher learning, and from its opening in 1872 to the founding of Loma Linda University in 1910, White was the leader of her church's educational enterprise. She urged all the church's schools to maintain high academic standards, and they have done so.

Seventh-day Adventists have not attained their founder's goals for schools without controversy. One of White's *Testimonies for the Church* (1872) was a treatise entitled

Proper Education, which appeared in print when Battle Creek College enrolled its first class. In this and other essays, White warned against a curriculum in which classical rather than Christian subjects would predominate. She feared that professors and students would not be able to discern elements of truth in pagan authors without absorbing some of their anti-Christian philosophies. Although she asked for the maintenance of a biblical worldview in education, she unknowingly encouraged a sacred-secular dichotomy that placed traditional humanities in a category separate from religion. Instead of urging the integration of faith and learning, she sought to divorce Christianity from so-called secular subjects. Later Adventist leaders had to correct this approach to education.

Education was important to Ellen G. White because she believed that it was a means toward salvation; that is, that it aided in restoring the image of God, which had been marred by humanity's fall into sin.

In March of 1915, White fractured a leg, and she used a wheelchair thereafter until she died at age eighty-seven. By then, membership in the Seventh-day Adventist church had grown to 136,000, and the church was operating sanatoriums, clinics, and schools in many countries.

Summary

Ellen G. White lived at a time of energetic religious activity in the United States. Mormonism and Christian Science, as well as a number of charismatic movements, appeared in the same era. White's claim to be a prophet resembles claims of other religious leaders then and since, but she was distinctive in her teaching about the return of Christ, health reform, and the interpretation of Bible prophecies. She appears to have saved Miller's disheartened movement from extinction, and the international Seventh-day Adventist church bears witness to her success. Within that church, she continues to be the dominant influence, more significant to Adventism than Luther to Lutheranism or Calvin to Calvinism. Despite the charge of plagiarism, her books are, in the view of her disciples, inspired counsels from God.

The Seventh-day Adventist church recognizes a valid role for women as pastors and evangelists, and its medical schools have always admitted females on the same basis as males. The church employs women as counselors and medical missionaries. These policies, which conflict with the positions of more conservative denominations, are undoubtedly the results of the influence of Adventism's latter-day prophet. It is no wonder that Adventist literature refers to Ellen White as Messenger to the Remnant, Servant of God, the Lord's Messenger, and the Spirit of Prophecy.

Because she and her church suffered discrimination and some persecution, Ellen G. White was in the forefront of those who demanded freedom of religion for everyone, a position that her church continues to uphold vigorously. She urged her followers to work for God as a means to accelerate the fulfillment of prophecies and thereby to hasten the return of Christ. She taught that true Christians do not take up arms to fight, but she urged Adventists to affirm allegiance to the United States and to serve in its military forces in noncombatant roles. Many Adventists have put their training as health professionals to work in the hospital corps of the armed forces. Although Adventists have modified some of White's doctrines and abandoned others, her influence remains the chief authority and driving force in the denomination that she, as its prophet, helped to establish.

Bibliography

Anderson, E. Marcelle. "The Roles of Women in the Seventh-Day Adventist Church: Significance of Ellen G. White's Counsels." In *A Symposium on the Role of Women in the Church*. Washington, D.C.: General Conference of Seventh-Day Adventists, 1984. This essay carefully explains Ellen G. White's view of gender equality as a result of the restorative work of the Gospel, which allows women to participate in all phases of the ministry.

Butler, Jonathan M. "Adventism and the American Experience." In *The Rise of Adventism*, edited by Edwin S. Gaustad. New York: Harper & Row, 1974. This penetrating examination puts Seventh-day Adventism and Ellen G. White into historical context and relates the writings and works of the founder to those of other religious movements of the time. Contains an excellent bibliography.

Canright, D. W. *Life of Mrs. E. G. White*. Cincinnati: Standard, 1919. For twenty-eight years, the author was an Adventist minister. Disillusioned, he left to become a Baptist. His work is highly critical of James White and Ellen White; he denies Ellen White's prophetic gifts and accuses her of plagiarism.

Graham, Roy E. *Ellen G. White: Co-Founder of the Seventh-Day Adventist Church*. New York: Peter Lang, 1985. A thorough analysis of White's beliefs, this rather defensive study tries to accommodate some of her concepts to current theological and ecumenical opinions she would not have endorsed. Large bibliography.

Knight, Goerge R. "Ellen G. White: Prophet." In *Early Adventist Educators*. Berrien Springs, Mich.: Andrews University Press, 1983. Emphasizes Ellen White's influence on the founding of Adventist schools and colleges, and explains her philosophy of education from a sympathetic but not uncritical perspective. Important for a clear understanding of her role as an educator.

Numbers, Ronald L. *Prophetess of Health: A Study of Ellen G. White*. New York: Harper & Row, 1976. This thoroughly documented study is the work of an Adventist medical historian who is duly critical of his subject's inadequate understanding of medicine, although he supports her major doctrines. Invaluable for understanding White, this is the best biography available.

White, Ellen G. *Life Sketches of Ellen G. White*. Mountain View, Calif.: Pacific Press, 1915. This autobiography is indispensable. It is unfortunate that the coverage extends only to 1881; an unnamed editor compiled information about White for the subsequent period until her death.

James Edward McGoldrick

GERTRUDE VANDERBILT WHITNEY

Born: January 9, 1875; New York, New York
Died: April 18, 1942; New York, New York
Areas of Achievement: Art and patronage of the arts
Contribution: Whitney was a distinguished woman American sculptor of figures, monuments, and reliefs for the public domain and an art patron and founder of the Whitney Museum of American Art in New York.

Early Life

Gertrude Vanderbilt was born an heiress to the great family fortune established by her great-grandfather, Commodore Cornelius Vanderbilt. Gertrude was the second daughter and the fourth of seven children of Cornelius and Alice Claypoole Vanderbilt. Her father was a railroad magnate who indulged his interests as an art patron and collector. Gertrude was brought up in an atmosphere of wealth and luxury and spent most of her youth shuttling between her family's two homes: a luxurious mansion in New York City and a summer estate in Newport, Rhode Island. She was educated by private tutors both at home and in Europe. Later, she attended New York's exclusive, all-female Brearley School. During her youth, she wrote avidly in personal journals and showed promising skill in watercolor and drawing.

On August 25, 1896, Gertrude Vanderbilt was married to Harry Payne Whitney, an avid sportsman who spent his days traveling on hunting trips and playing polo. His father was William C. Whitney, a financier and secretary of the Navy under President Grover Cleveland. The couple maintained a town house on Fifth Avenue in New York City and a country estate at Westbury, Long Island. Gertrude bore three children, a son, Cornelius Vanderbilt Whitney, and two daughters, Flora Payne and Barbara. Over the years, Gertrude Whitney and her husband became estranged, yet they fostered a certain solidarity in times of crises and in relation to family obligations.

Gertrude Vanderbilt Whitney accepted the responsibility of rearing her three children and fulfilled her many social obligations. These obligations did not deter her from studying sculpture. She had three teachers from whom she learned her craft. The first was sculptor Hendrik Christian Andersen. Next, she studied with James Earle Fraser, who instructed her at the New Students League in New York City. Her last mentor, Andrew O'Connor, completed her education in Paris. Both Fraser and O'Connor were sculptors of public monuments and channeled her interests in the same direction. Her works soon became well known and highly regarded in the American and European art communities.

Life's Work

During the first ten years of her work as a sculptor, Gertrude Vanderbilt Whitney exhibited under a pseudonym. She believed that her famous family name would never allow her the freedom of unbiased criticism from her viewers. It was not until 1910, when her statue, *Paganism Immortal*, won a distinguished rating at the National

Academy that she began to exhibit under her own name. It was during these early years that Whitney set up her own studio in Greenwich Village. Though not taken seriously by the art community at first, she worked hard at perfecting her craft in her studio. Her dedication and perseverance soon won her the respect and companionship of other artists.

It was also during this time that Whitney became known as a patron of the arts. In 1908, when the "Eight of the Ash Can" group held an exhibit at the Macbeth Gallery, Whitney purchased four canvases from the exhibit. After witnessing the difficulties such young artists had in finding exhibition venues, she began to provide space in her studio where they could display their work. This temporary solution led her to establish the Whitney Studio in an adjacent building in 1914. It soon became a gathering place for various artists and developed into the Whitney Studio Club in 1918. Whitney stayed true to her original intentions for the gallery by continuing to exhibit and sell works by young artists who were either too poor or too unknown to afford dealers.

By this point, Whitney had built up her personal holdings in contemporary American art. In 1929, she chose to make her vast private art collection available to the public by offering her entire collection to New York City's Metropolitan Museum of Art, complete with an endowment to build a new museum wing in which to house her collection. After this offer was rejected, she established her own museum in 1931, known as the Whitney Museum of American Art. Whitney appointed Juliana Force, who had served as her assistant since 1914, as the museum's first director. For the remainder of her life, Whitney continued to make private gifts to young artists in the hope of advancing their study and work.

The camaraderie Whitney experienced during her early years in Greenwich Village helped her to become more focused on her art and gave her great self-confidence in her abilities as a sculptor. Others, too, increasingly recognized her talent. In 1912, she was hired to construct the terra cotta fountain in the Aztec style for the patio of the Pan American Union Building in Washington, D.C. Also, her marble sculpture entitled *Fountain of El Dorado*, which depicted man's frantic search for gold, won a bronze medal at the 1915 Panama-Pacific Exposition in San Francisco. This fountain was later erected as a permanent fixture in Lima, Peru.

Whitney's next large-scale work was the result of a 1914 competition in which she won the $50,000 *Titanic Memorial* commission. Her design and its execution are considered by many critics to be her most important work. This monument to American citizens who lost their lives in the famous sea tragedy is eighteen feet high and was installed on the banks of the Potomac in Washington, D.C., in 1931. A seminude figure of a man, carved in granite, takes the shape of a cross atop the sculpture's pedestal, thus contributing to the sculpture's powerful symbolism of sacrifice and resurrection. Critics contend that the work of French sculptor Auguste Rodin profoundly influenced Whitney in her execution of this monument.

As it did for many of her generation, World War I had a profound influence on Whitney. The awful realities of the war and the resulting bloodshed prompted her to establish a field hospital at Juilly, France, in the fall of 1914. She personally administered to the wounded soldiers until the spring of 1915, when exhaustion and anguish compelled her to return home. The war forced her to turn away from aesthetic abstraction in her art work, and her later works expressed greater realism, particularly her memorials to the soldiers of World War I. These pieces bore titles such as *At His Post*, *His Last Charge*, *Gassed*, *Blinded*, *His Bunkie*, *Private in the 15th*, and *The Aviator*. After she returned to New York, she had begun throwing together masses of clay to re-create images of the soldiers she had seen, and these statues formed the foundation for her larger war memorials of the 1920's. Whitney completed two panels for the Victory Arch in New York City as well as the Washington Heights Memorial at 168th Street and Broadway. The latter won the New York Society of Architects' Medal as the most meritorious work of 1922. In 1926, Whitney designed a large memorial for the harbor of St. Nazaire, France, to commemorate the 1917 landing of the first American Expeditionary Forces. Sadly, the Germans destroyed this monument during World War II.

Most of Whitney's later work of the 1920's and 1930's was completed at her studio in Paris. Whitney produced significant works during these two decades that diverged from the war theme. In 1924, she produced a larger-than-life bronze equestrian statue of Colonel William F. Cody, better known as Buffalo Bill, which was eventually installed in Cody, Wyoming. Whitney then created the Columbus Monument, a 114-foot statue that was placed at the port of Palos, Spain, in 1933.

In 1934, Gertrude Vanderbilt Whitney attracted national attention—not as a result of her work, but because of a highly publicized child custody case concerning her niece, Gloria Vanderbilt. Gertrude Vanderbilt Whitney fought for, and won, custody of Gloria. The stress and publicity surrounding the prolonged case greatly undermined Whitney's already failing health. She refused to give in to her illness, however, and continued to exhibit her work publicly until after the unveiling of her sculpture *The Spirit of Flight* at the New York World's Fair of 1939. Three years later Whitney died, reportedly of a heart condition, at the age of sixty-seven.

Summary

Gertrude Vanderbilt Whitney is one of the few American women to hold such a prominent position in the history of American art as a traditional sculptor of public monuments. Her work as an artist is often downplayed in light of her munificence as patron of modern American art. Ironically, the founding of the Whitney Museum is often viewed as her greatest creation. Although her work as a philanthropist was crucial in generating greater respect and attention for modern American artists and their work, Whitney is equally notable for her own struggle to establish herself as a sculptor of public monuments in an era when her gender and her social background made the realization of her dream nearly impossible.

Bibliography
Auchincloss, Louis. *The Vanderbilt Era: Profiles of a Gilded Age*. New York: Charles

Scribner's Sons, 1989. Novelist and biographer Auchincloss examines the lives and accomplishments of the Vanderbilts of the period from 1880 to 1920. Although not focused exclusively on Gertrude Vanderbilt Whitney, this family history provides lively anecdotes and places her within her familial and historical context.

Dunford, Penny. *Biographical Dictionary of Women Artists in Europe and America Since 1850*. New York: Harvester Wheatsheaf, 1990. This work contains a brief biography covering Whitney's main works as a sculptor and her significant contributions as an art patron.

Friedman, Bernard H. *Gertrude Vanderbilt Whitney*. Garden City, N.Y.: Doubleday, 1978. Biography of the sculptor written with the research assistance of the artist's granddaughter, Flora Miller Irving. This work is filled with many of Whitney's own writings but lacks much in the way of scholarly analysis and evaluation. The book details her life and relationships, but there is little information about her art.

Patterson, Jerry E. *The Vanderbilts*. New York: Harry N. Abrams, 1989. Released in the same year as Auchincloss' work, this dynastic biography of the Vanderbilts examines the private and public lives of various family members, including their marriages, divorces, financial dealings and business investments, and their patronage of the arts. Illustrated with numerous photographs of Vanderbilt residences and personal art holdings. Helps place Whitney within the context of her family background.

Rubinstein, Charlotte Streifer. *American Women Artists: From Early Indian Times to the Present*. New York: Avon Books, 1982. This collection of biographical sketches includes a readable, comprehensive, yet brief sketch on Whitney. Contains delightful anecdotes, including the fact that Whitney often worked in turkish harem pants, turban, and turned up shoes.

Whitney Museum of American Art. *Memorial Exhibition: Gertrude Vanderbilt Whitney*. New York: Whitney Museum of Art, 1943. The introduction to this catalog is written by Juliana Force, Whitney's administrative assistant and her chosen director of the Whitney Museum. Force emphasizes Whitney's career as a creator of monumental sculpture and focuses on the Whitney Museum's works from her collection.

Patricia McNeal

HAZEL HOTCHKISS WIGHTMAN

Born: December 20, 1886; Healdsburg, California
Died: December 5, 1974; Chestnut Hill, Massachusetts
Area of Achievement: Sports
Contribution: Labeled the "Queen Mother" of American tennis, Hazel Hotchkiss Wightman was a four-time national singles champion of the United States Lawn Tennis Association who paved the way for the acceptance of women's tennis as a reputable sport in the United States.

Early Life

Hazel Virginia Hotchkiss was born in the northern California town of Healdsburg in 1886. On her mother's side, she was the descendent of Virginia expatriates who had moved west following the Civil War. Her father's parents had moved from Kentucky and settled in California shortly after it was admitted to the Union in 1850.

Hazel's father, William Joseph Hotchkiss, a respected and successful Sonoma Valley rancher and owner of a cannery, encouraged Hazel to play aggressive sports (perhaps as an antidote for her poor health as a child) with her three older brothers and her younger brother. Although frail and petite, Hazel played baseball and football with her four brothers and more than held her own. She would later recall that her mother, Emma Groves Hotchkiss, worried that Hazel might become too much of a tomboy and admonished her never to forget to act like a lady. She was encouraged by her mother to give up the rough sports she played with her four brothers and concentrate instead on playing tennis.

Shortly after her family moved to Berkeley, California, in 1900 when she was fourteen, Hazel began playing tennis. Her style of play was established early. Most of her practice was on the makeshift gravel court at her home, since girls were not permitted on the single asphalt court at Berkeley after eight in the morning. Because of the challenges of playing on a gravel surface, she developed a game that depended on hitting the ball before it had an opportunity to bounce, and she soon became accomplished at this technique of volleying.

Life's Work

After six months of intensive preparation, Hazel Hotchkiss entered her first tournament. She and her partner, Mary Radcliffe, won the women's doubles championship in the Bay Counties tournament held in San Francisco. In the next seven years she not only helped change the prevailing belief that women should play a baseline rather than a volleying game, she also helped to popularize changes in tennis attire by wearing loose-fitting dresses when she played. She even popularized sleeveless dresses to provide greater freedom of movement for the arms. Combining tennis and academics while she attended the University of California at Berkeley, Hazel won the United States singles, doubles, and mixed doubles championships three consecutive years (1909-1911), an accomplishment equaled only by two other women (Alice Marble,

1938-1940; Margaret Osborne du Pont, 1948-1950). Her performance in the 1911 championships is even more remarkable because she won the singles, doubles, and mixed doubles championships on the same day. Her rivalry with May Sutton in the tournaments in California at this time was perhaps the first publicly recognized rivalry for women in tennis at the beginning of this century. Although she brought a strong spirit of competition to this intense rivalry, Hazel Hotchkiss quickly developed a reputation for authentic sportsmanship and was mentioned by subsequent women tennis players as a model they used in their careers.

Following her graduation from college in 1911, Hazel married George W. Wightman, a former Harvard tennis player and member of a prominent Boston family. The births of three children between 1912 and 1919 did not stop Hazel Wightman's activities as a competitive player on the national level. She resumed playing competitively after the birth of her first child, George, Jr., and added another United States Doubles Championship to her list of accomplishments in 1915. She also won the United States mixed doubles titles in 1918 and 1920, and in 1919, at the age of thirty-three, Hazel Hotchkiss Wightman captured her fourth and final U.S. National Championship singles title. She went on to win two more United States Doubles Championships in the 1920's, the last one coming in 1928 when at the remarkable age of forty-two she paired with twenty-three-year-old Helen Wills. Meanwhile, although she had become the mother of five children, Wightman captained the women's team in the 1924 Olympics, winning gold medals in the doubles and mixed double competition. She also demonstrated her skills in other racquet sports, winning the National Squash Singles and finishing as a finalist in the National Badminton Mixed Doubles championships in 1927.

Her contributions to tennis were not restricted, however, to her performances as an individual player. In 1919, Hazel Wightman donated a silver vase to the United States Lawn Tennis Association (USLTA), attempting to create an "international cup" for women comparable to the international cup for men inaugurated by Dwight F. Davis in 1900. She met implacable resistance to her proposal to International Lawn Tennis Federation and temporarily was forced to withdraw her offer. The creation of the West Side Tennis Club in Forest Hills, New York, however, provided an opportunity for a renewal of her dreams and the first Wightman Cup match was played at that facility in 1923. The United States team, captained by Wightman herself, defeated the British team 7-0. The following year, the Wightman Cup was played at the newly created Center Court at Wimbledon in Great Britain, and the British team won 6-1. The evenness of the competition in the next six years assured the success of the Wightman Cup. Even though the American teams dominated the British teams between 1931 and 1958, the Wightman Cup became a respected part of tennis competition and helped to improve the image of women's tennis in the world. The decision to move the competition indoors in 1974 coincided with the tennis boom of that decade and increased the appeal of the Wightman Cup competition; it was not uncommon for the matches to draw between ten and fifteen thousand spectators, figures that were comparable to Davis Cup matches.

Meanwhile, Wightman herself continued to remain involved with the promotion and development of tennis in the United States. She played on five Wightman Cup teams between 1923 and 1931, and she captained thirteen Wightman Cup teams in all, making her final appearance as captain in 1948. She continued to compete in national tournaments, playing in her last national championship when she was seventy-three years old.

Had these been her only accomplishments in tennis, Hazel Hotchkiss Wightman might still have earned her title as the "Queen Mother of Tennis," but she also contributed to tennis in several other ways. After her divorce from George Wightman in 1940, Hazel Wightman graciously opened her home near the Longwood Cricket Club in Chestnut Hill, Massachusetts, as a home away from home for aspiring women players who went east to prepare for the summer tournaments that culminated in the United States Nationals at Forest Hills. Wightman developed a reputation for a quick recognition of talent, and she aided several prominent tennis players, including Sarah Palfrey, Helen Wills, and Helen Jacobs. She became a respected tennis teacher and promoter, giving free clinics at the Longwood Cricket Club, running tournaments for players of all skill levels, and writing a manual which became a guide for many players.

As a tennis instructor, Wightman had a particular fondness for ordinary players. The awkward and shy players, she claimed, gained "confidence and poise" by being able to do "something well that other people admire." Her approach to the teaching of tennis emphasized the mental as well as the physical and technical sides of the game. She encouraged her students to "cultivate a buoyant spirit" as well as develop good footwork. She emphasized the fact that tennis was a sport that helped in the development of personal as well as physical grace. She always noted that she believed that ordinary players could gain as much from perfecting their skills as could the more accomplished players. Moreover, she argued long before the tennis boom of the 1970's that tennis should be a sport open to the entire public, not simply the wealthy members of elite private clubs. *Better Tennis* (1933), an instruction book that Wightman composed during the hours she waited in the car to pick up her children from school, became a standard teaching book during the 1930's.

Her contributions to tennis were recognized in 1957, when she was inducted into the Tennis Hall of Fame at Newport, Rhode Island. She also was recognized on the fiftieth anniversary of the Wightman Cup in 1973, when Queen Elizabeth II made Hazel Hotchkiss Wightman an honorary Commander of the British Empire. Wightman died in 1974 at the age of eighty-seven in Chestnut Hill, Massachusetts.

Summary

Hazel Hotchkiss Wightman's life mirrors in several ways the development of women's tennis in the United States. Her performance on the court as a national champion came at a time when few sports other than tennis were open to women. She excelled during an era in which women's tennis was dominated primarily by women whose wealth permitted them to have the travel and leisure time necessary for capturing championships. She changed the style of play for women by emphasizing a more aggressive game that combined volleying with the traditional ground stroke elements, and she was an active participant in the dress reform movement in women's tennis. She introduced the Wightman Cup during the Golden Age of Sports in the 1920's, supported and encouraged the development of international competition in tennis for women, advocated the acceptance of tennis as an Olympic sport, and helped nurse women's tennis through the Depression and World War II years. Although she at first was opposed to the professionalization of women's tennis, Hazel Hotchkiss Wightman became one of its strongest supporters. It was therefore appropriate that she was chosen to present the first monetary award for women that was equal to the men's prize—an award Wightman presented to Margaret Court at the United States Tennis Association championship in 1973.

Bibliography
Carter, Tom. "Stamp of Approval: Hazel Wightman Commemorated on Olympic Stamp." *Inside Tennis* (October, 1990): 28. A brief overview of Wightman's career is included in this column commenting on her selection as the first American tennis player to be featured on a stamp commemorating the participation of the United States in the Olympic Games.
Jacobs, Helen Hull. *Gallery of Champions*. Reprint. Freeport, N.Y.: Books for Libraries Press, 1979. Originally published in 1949, this collection of essays about many of the champion women's tennis players was written by Jacobs, a leading player who competed directly against many of the women she profiled. Includes a discussion of Hazel Hotchkiss Wightman's career during the years between World War I and World War II.
Klaw, Barbara. "Queen Mother of Tennis: An Interview with Hazel Hotchkiss Wightman." *American Heritage* 26 (August, 1975): 16-24, 82-86. Conducted only a few weeks before her death, Klaw's interview with Hazel Wightman reveals an individual who was capable of change but who remained true to the values which she had learned in the first quarter of the twentieth century.
Wightman, Hazel Hotchkiss. *Better Tennis*. Boston: Houghton Mifflin, 1933. Written in longhand while she juggled her roles as social director and chauffeur for her school-aged children, Hazel Wightman used this popular manual of the 1930's to promote the mental as well as the technical aspects of the game.
Wind, Herbert W. "From Wimbledon to Forest Hills: A Summer to Remember." *The New Yorker* 51 (October 13, 1975): 116-120. Although quite brief, this article was used by Wind as a means to reminisce about women's tennis in general and Wightman in particular.
Woolum, Janet. *Outstanding Women Athletes: Who They Are and How They Influenced American Sports*. Phoenix, Ariz.: Oryx Press, 1992. A thoroughly researched collection of sports biographies that includes a sketch on Wightman. Provides a thorough assessment of Wightman's career as a player and explains her role in popularizing a more aggressive style of play for women, in advocating dress reform

for women in the sport, and in promoting greater opportunities and equality for women in the world of tennis.

Robert L. Patterson

EMMA WILLARD

Born: February 23, 1787; Berlin, Connecticut
Died: April 15, 1870; Troy, New York
Area of Achievement: Education
Contribution: Emma Willard pioneered equal educational opportunity for women. Refusing to accept the idea that women could not study the same subjects as men, she learned history, geography, sciences and mathematics, and then taught them to other women. In the process she inculcated a desire to teach, thus preparing hundreds of disciples who carried forward her educational plans and ideals.

Early Life

Born to Captain Samuel Hart and Lydia Hinsdale Hart, Emma Hart was the ninth of seventeen children. Her father had served in the American Revolution as well as the Connecticut General Assembly. Growing up on a typical New England farm, Emma witnessed all the home manufacturing common to the late eighteenth and early nineteenth centuries. Because politics, religion, moral philosophy, and current events were discussed regularly around the Harts' dinner table, Emma learned early to form opinions regarding current issues and appropriate ways to express them. Emma's parents taught their children to read and discuss the best books. With this early preparation, Emma attended the local schools. At seventeen, she began to teach at the Berlin Academy at the same time that she continued her own education in Hartford.

Life's Work

Emma Hart left Berlin for Westfield, staying only a few months before moving on to Middlebury, Vermont, where in 1807 she took charge of the local girls' academy. At this time, education for women was severely limited. Most opportunities were for the daughters of well-to-do families who sent the girls to boarding schools where the education focused on "ornamentals" (subjects designed to prepare women for marriage and motherhood) as well as moral philosophy and domestic science. Painting, embroidery, French, singing, and playing the harpsichord were also considered central to the young woman's education, as these also would improve her marriageability.

After a few years of teaching in Middlebury, Emma Hart was married to physician John Willard, one of Middlebury's leading citizens who was twenty-eight years her senior. One son, John, was born to them in 1810.

During this time John Willard's nephew, who attended Middlebury College, boarded with them. Her nephew introduced Emma to the college curriculum available to men, which only reenforced her understanding of the deprivation women suffered relative to educational opportunity. She studied his notes and read his textbooks, including John Locke's *Essay Concerning Moral Understanding* and Paley's *Moral Philosophy*. With her nephew's help she renewed her interest in geometry, disregarding the current belief that such subjects were detrimental to a woman's health.

In 1815, John Willard's fortunes suffered a reversal. He and several associates lost money when a bank for which he served as director was robbed. Feeling responsible, John assumed and paid off the debt, forcing him into restricted financial circumstances. Emma Willard opened a boarding school for girls in their home in order to assist with the family finances.

At her Middlebury Female Seminary, Willard taught the ornamentals as well as the same subjects she had taught herself just a few years earlier. Her plan was to combine no more than three "hard" subjects with the lighter ones. As her father had done when she was a child, she read to the girls in the evenings from the classics. Academies such as Middlebury provided an education for women equal to that available to men in addition to establishing the foundation for colleges for women. Along with women such as Zilpah Grant and Catharine Beecher, Willard was one of many who opened such schools for women in the United States. They intended to teach traditional subjects deemed appropriate for helping prepare women for marriage as well as the curricula deemed more appropriate for young men. The growth of these schools indicated society's rising interest in women's issues.

Since Willard could not afford instructors, she first learned the subjects herself and then taught them to her pupils. She taught mathematics, a variety of sciences, philosophy, and history. She created new techniques for the teaching of history, geography, and mathematics. Her methods for teaching mathematics were particularly innovative: Since textbooks were generally unavailable, she cut out paper triangles for demonstration purposes. In teaching solid geometry, she carved shapes from vegetables.

In 1819, Willard moved her academy to Waterford, New York, at the behest of New York governor DeWitt Clinton, who hoped to persuade the state legislature to authorize funding. Many of her Vermont students followed her to Waterford, where interested townspeople leased a three-story brick building for the Waterford Academy. Soon she had twenty-two boarding students in attendance.

Governor Clinton's invitation was in response to Willard's pamphlet, *Address to the Public; Particularly to the Members of the Legislature of New-York, Proposing a Plan for Improving Female Education* (1819). She proposed an innovative curriculum, arguing that the education of women was in the best interests of the nation. In addition to a curriculum, she included a funding plan for Clinton to forward to the legislators. In 1819, Emma Willard journeyed to Albany to defend her proposals in person. Undoubtedly this was one of the first times that the New York legislature had been addressed by a woman. Despite two appeals from the governor and the apparent interest of a few legislators, the majority responded with ridicule and levity, contending her plan contravened God's will.

Within a few years, Willard's lease in Waterford expired. When the town of Troy, New York, offered her a building, she relocated there, opening the Troy Female Academy and enrolling ninety students in 1821. Her students were predominantly the daughters of the upwardly mobile middle-class business elite from some seven states, including pupils from as far away as Georgia. Continuing with her educational model, Willard offered, but did not require, ornamentals in conjunction with a traditional male curriculum. Her goals were utilitarian: She believed education improved a woman's ability to function within the bounds for her gender as set by society. She did not propose education as a method of social equality, but rather as a way for women to enhance their contribution to society, thus strengthening the state. She also focused on teacher training because she considered teaching to be a natural occupation for women. Although the Troy Female Seminary offered no instruction in teacher preparation, it turned out hundreds of teachers who spread Emma Willard's methods and philosophy throughout the United States.

In 1825, John Willard died. He had been a major influence in his wife's educational career, leaving his home in Vermont to follow her to New York. In addition to handling the business relations for her school, he served as the school physician, thus freeing her to devote time to education.

Suffering from ill health in 1830, Emma Willard went to Europe. She followed the traditional tour routes as well as going to Greece, where she opened a school for girls. Upon her return to the United States, she wrote of her travels and donated the proceeds from her work to the Greek school.

In 1838, Emma Willard turned over the active management of Troy Female Seminary to her son and his wife. In that same year, she married Dr. Christopher Yates, moving with him to Boston. The marriage was a disappointment to her and ended in separation within the year, when she returned to Connecticut to live with her sister, also an educator. In 1843, an act of the Connecticut legislature dissolved the marriage and granted Emma the right to retain the name Willard. The following year she returned to live in Troy.

After retiring from her leadership of the Troy Female Seminary, Willard devoted her time and talent to improving common schools, which would benefit women. She joined forces with Henry Barnard to work for better education in Connecticut. Traveling extensively, she used the Connecticut schools as models for other states. She called for higher salaries, more teaching opportunities for women, and better facilities for the students. As a result of her efforts, she generated a considerable amount of interest in education. Still with Henry Barnard, Willard attended the World's Educational Conference held in London in 1854, where she met several international educators. She spent several months in Europe before returning to Troy.

Because of her activity and society's rising interest in women's rights, the number of women's seminaries increased in the 1830's and 1840's. One of the most significant of the newer schools was Mary Lyon's famous Mount Holyoke Seminary, established in 1837. Also indicative of the rising tide of women's rights was the 1848 Seneca Falls Convention, at which Willard's former pupil, Elizabeth Cady Stanton, proposed the following: "Resolved, That it is the duty of the women of this country to secure to themselves their sacred right to the elective franchise." Interestingly, although she had been ridiculed by the all-male New York legislature, Willard did not actively campaign for the right to vote, nor did she lend her support to Stanton and the Seneca Falls Convention.

Throughout her life Willard wrote poetry, published history and geography textbooks, and submitted letters and articles to newspapers and magazines on topics of current interest. While her poetry is at best mediocre, her texts were innovative for their time. Among her letters and articles written in the days before the Civil War, she supported preservation of the Union at all costs, including giving tacit agreement to slavery. In fact, she found the Civil War so devastating that she renewed her interest in world peace. She revived her plans to convene an international peace conference in Jerusalem, but demurred because of her family's objections. Instead, she drew up a peace plan, similar to her *Universal Peace to be Introduced by a Confederacy of Nations, Meeting in Jerusalem*, which had been published in 1820. Her interest in peace came from her biblical studies and represented the only reform movement, other than education, in which she was involved. *Universal Peace* (1864) called for an international world court that could adjudicate disputes between nations.

During Willard's later years, the girls of the Troy Female Seminary would see her reading and writing in her study. Always encouraging and accessible, she was an affectionate and gentle woman whose very presence encouraged students. Willard died at Troy in April of 1870.

Summary

Emma Willard's Troy Female Seminary, renamed the Emma Willard School in 1895, later served as the model for coeducational collegiate education. She proved that women were capable of a demanding education and that they would benefit from the challenge and opportunity. Willard was among the first to break the traditional educational pattern for women, thus furthering the cause of women's rights by providing women with an educational framework. She trained hundreds of teachers who carried her ideas of an academic education for women to all parts of the nation. Even though she took an active interest in contemporary affairs, encouraging other women to expand their horizons, she herself was never an activist. She did not actively support women's rights, taking instead a deferential position in the hope that men would grant women equality. Her greatest contribution was serving as a role model for all Americans. Throughout her life, she proved women could study the same material men studied and achieve the same results.

Bibliography

Baym, Nina. "Women and the Republic: Emma Willard's Rhetoric of History." *American Quarterly* 43 (March, 1991): 1-22. Aimed primarily at a scholarly audience, this journal article explores the intellectual content of Willard's work as an educator and writer of history. Discusses Willard's approach to teaching and writing history not only as representative of the educational theories of her time but also as distinctive for its articulation of the concept that women had an important role in shaping the destiny of the American republic.

Fairbanks, Mary J., ed. *Emma Willard and Her Pupils: Or, Fifty Years of the Troy Female Seminary*. New York: Mrs. R. Sage, 1898. One of the earliest biographies written to honor the founder of the Troy Female Academy.

Hoffman, Nancy. *Women's "True" Profession: Voices from the History of Teaching.* Old Westbury, N.Y.: Feminist Press, 1981. Identifies Willard as one of the representative teachers who helped promote women's entry into the profession of teaching. Includes a biographical sketch that provides a good introduction to Willard's life and work.

Lutz, Alma. *Emma Willard: Daughter of Democracy.* Boston: Houghton Mifflin, 1929. Reprint. Washington, D.C.: Zenger, 1975. Lutz, a well-known historian and alumna of the Willard School, presents an admiring portrait of Willard. This work continues to serve as the definitive source on Willard and her career.

_____ . *Emma Willard: Pioneer Educator of American Women.* Boston: Beacon Press, 1964. Reprint. Westport, Conn.: Greenwood Press, 1983. A charming biography first published to mark the 150th anniversary of the Troy Female Academy (later known as the Emma Willard School). This work draws heavily on Lutz's earlier biography, cited above.

Townsend, Lucy F., and Barbara Wiley, eds. "Ever the Teacher, Even When Honeymooning: Emma Willard's Lost Geography Lesson." *The New England Quarterly* 64 (June, 1991): 297-308. A scholarly article that analyzes and discusses the educational content of a previously unpublished letter written by Willard. The authors include introductory comments and explanatory footnotes to the lesson that Willard sent back in a letter to students at her academy in 1838, while she was on her honeymoon with her second husband, Dr. Christopher Yates. Provides insights into Willard's teaching methods and educational philosophy.

Duncan R. Jamieson

FRANCES WILLARD

Born: September 28, 1839; Churchville, New York
Died: February 17, 1898; New York, New York
Areas of Achievement: Social reform and women's rights
Contribution: Willard was the major organizer of the Woman's Christian Temperance
   Union and a leading social reformer in the late nineteenth century.

Early Life

Born on September 28, 1839, in a village in western New York, Frances Elizabeth
Caroline Willard was the fourth of her parents' five children and only one of three to
survive babyhood. Her father, Josiah, was descended from Major Simon Willard, an
English Puritan convert and founder of Concord, Massachusetts. Willard's paternal
ancestors included ministers, educators, and public servants in Massachusetts. Her
father, a Baptist, married Mary Thompson Hill, a Scottish descendant of Congregationalists and Freewill Baptists, on November 4, 1831, in Ogden, New York.

In 1841, Frances' parents left the Baptists, joined the Congregationalists, and
moved to Oberlin, Ohio. Her father studied for the ministry and her mother enrolled
in college. In 1845, Josiah Willard developed tuberculosis; the next year, he moved
the family to a 360-acre farm in Wisconsin. The Willards converted once again, this
time to Methodism. Frances' father succeeded as both a businessman and a "gentleman farmer"; he dedicated much time to public service as a Free Soiler, Wisconsin
legislator, and natural science data collector for the Smithsonian Institution. Frances
had an older brother, Oliver, and a younger sister, Mary.

Frances thrived on the Wisconsin farm she called "Forest Home." Her parents
shared the care of the children, which was unusual at that time. Frances found her
father more difficult and distant than her mother. Mary Willard introduced her
children to works by many writers. Frances read voraciously; she loved poetry,
especially the works of Samuel Taylor Coleridge, William Cowper, and James Thomson. She wrote poetry, and she used her vivid imagination to design a plan for a "Fort
City" on a farm, complete with street names, bank notes, and laws. Lacking saloons
and billiard halls, it needed no jail.

At an early age, Frances showed her famous ability to build policy compromises.
One Sunday morning, when her parents forbade her to draw on her chalkboard, she
suggested that she be allowed to draw meeting houses. Her parents agreed. Her mother
often intervened with her father to permit "male activities" such as horseback riding.
Frances developed a reputation as a tomboy, and she showed much pride in accomplishments such as tree-climbing, shooting, and giving speeches.

The remote location of the Wisconsin farm barred Frances from any regular course
of study outside the home. Before she entered Milwaukee Female College at age
seventeen, Frances' formal education was irregular. At Milwaukee, she studied diligently and was happy. Much to her disappointment, however, her father, determined
to educate his children in a Methodist school, forced Frances after one year to enroll

in Northwestern Female College in Evanston, Illinois.

Frances completed the three-year college course in only three terms. During this time, she experienced much inner conflict about Christianity and refused to attend church services. After a bout of typhoid fever, however, Frances made a personal commitment to serve God and professed herself a Methodist. Her journals show that she considered all churches branches of the one church and that she dedicated herself to education in an "unsectarian spirit." She also disavowed female subordination. This affirmation of feminist and ecumenical attitudes at age twenty signaled much about the universality of her later reform aims as a temperance leader, suffragist, and proponent of social democracy.

Frances described her activities during the next fifteen years as those of a "roving teacher," and during that time she took teaching positions at nine different schools. She became engaged to the educator Charles Fowler but broke it off for fear of losing her independence.

After her father's death in 1868, Frances traveled abroad for two years with her friend and colleague Kate Jackson. The trip expanded Frances' view of the world and prepared her for both the rigors of travel and encounters with cultural diversity she experienced later in her career. In the meantime, her mother found that the family estate had evaporated. Frances returned to Evanston with Jackson, who sustained the household for a time with her own inheritance. Her journals show that Frances accepted the obligation to support her mother and herself financially. Despite her interest in "the woman question," she opted first for a career in education.

Life's Work

In 1871, Frances Willard was elected president of Evanston College for Ladies—the female branch of Northwestern—and she held that post until 1874. During the first year, she helped to develop the "annex plan," later used at Radcliffe and Barnard, for women's participation in male universities, developed an honor system to replace a cobweb of rules, incorporated the women's branch more fully into the university, and established herself as an independent authority. In 1872, however, Northwestern appointed Fowler, her former fiancé, as its new president. She immediately clashed with him over both rules for student life and her autonomous powers as dean of the women's college. Demoralized, Willard resigned her post in 1874, and soon thereafter she joined the temperance movement.

Mary Livermore, former editor of *The Woman's Journal*, encouraged Willard to devote her life to temperance reform in the Woman's Christian Temperance Union (WCTU). Willard reached the top of the WCTU hierarchy quickly. By 1875, she was elected president of the Chicago WCTU, secretary of the Illinois union, and corresponding secretary of the national union. With her innovative ideas and imaginative rhetoric, Willard quickly established herself nationally as a dynamic temperance speaker.

Willard first made a major contribution to the WCTU by publishing her pamphlet *Hints and Helps in Our Temperance Work* (1875). This blueprint for action emphasized temperance reform activities in local organizations but added common rules and shared ideas. This plan smoothed the transition that temperance reformers made from a spontaneous mass movement of protest into an organized pressure group.

Willard's second contribution was her "Home Protection Speech," which was presented to the Woman's Congress in November of 1876. Imitating the Canadian temperance reformer Letitia Yeomans, Willard used the phrase "home protection" to call women's attention to the threats that men's drinking of alcohol posed to women and children in the home. To Willard, drinking was the immediate cause of male violence. In her speech, she told women that "the rum power's overthrow" required "our thoughts as women and as patriots." Women should not put their trust for protection in men; instead, they should mobilize themselves to ensure the enactment of temperance. Willard initially avoided blending suffrage with temperance, probably because WCTU President Annie L. Wittenmeyer wanted to keep the two issues separate. She wedded the two reforms only after consulting Susan B. Anthony and experiencing a spiritual inspiration during prayer. The WCTU membership endorsed Willard's suffrage policy and elected her president of the national union in 1879.

Willard remained president of the WCTU until her death in 1898. During her tenure, the union expanded its efforts well beyond prohibition or restrictions on alcohol consumption. Although she considered white middle-class women her primary audience, Willard encouraged black women to form local branches of the WCTU for themselves and their children. She traveled widely in the United States and abroad, initiating the formation of "The World's WCTU" in 1883.

Willard clung to her home protection arguments throughout her career, but she embroidered on them aims for suffrage, an integration of the separate spheres of home and public life, and social democratic reforms—especially for political parties. In the late 1880's, she articulated her "Do Everything" philosophy: better police forces, help for indigent children, improved public health, and new forms of recreation.

By this time, the Knights of Labor were espousing temperance ideals. Amid controversy, Willard allied with that radical labor organization. Her ideas and symbols also found favor with the founders of the Farmers' Alliance and populist parties in states such as Colorado. Between 1889 and 1891, Willard tried but failed to fuse the organizational resources of like-minded labor, agrarian, suffrage, and temperance reformers. After she made her last valiant effort at the St. Louis Convention in 1892, Willard shortened her reform schedule in the United States, and she spent more time at the home of Isabel Somerset, a British temperance reformer.

While living in Britain, Willard decided that socialism offered the best hope for social progress. At the 1897 National WCTU Convention in Buffalo, New York, Willard identified herself as a "Christian socialist" and argued that "competition is doomed." Socialism, she believed, would "eliminate the motives for a selfish life" and "enact into our everyday living the ethics of Christ's gospel." The Woman's National Committee of the Socialist Party quoted Willard as saying, "[O]h, that I were young again, and it [socialism] would have my life!" In 1897, Willard became ill. She died in New York City on February 17, 1898.

Summary

Frances E. Willard was the most successful mobilizer of women in the nineteenth century United States. The membership of the WCTU and its juvenile affiliates grew during the 1880's from 27,000 to almost 200,000 members. (In contrast, the National-American Woman Suffrage Association had a membership of 13,000 in 1890.) In 1892, the local, state, and national WCTU treasuries totaled nearly $500,000. Although Willard's dream of a women's temperance movement at the center of a national social democratic reform effort never fully emerged, her ideas inspired many reformers, including Jane Addams and Carrie Chapman Catt. She unquestionably sharpened suffragists' rationales for giving women the vote. Without Willard's leadership, however, the WCTU returned in the early twentieth century to prohibition as its single issue. Willard's ability to attach a vision of social change to traditional values and hold the attention of her audience made her an innovative, pragmatic reform leader in American politics.

Bibliography

Bordin, Ruth B. *Frances Willard: A Biography.* Chapel Hill: University of North Carolina Press, 1986. A comprehensive biography that pays much attention to Willard's own sense of her identity and purpose as a women's rights reformer.

——————. *Woman and Temperance: The Quest for Power and Liberty, 1873-1900.* Philadelphia, Pa.: Temple University Press, 1981. The most thorough account of the formation of the WCTU, its course during the period of Willard's leadership, and its relationships with other movements.

Buhle, Mari Jo. *Women and American Socialism, 1780-1920.* Urbana: University of Illinois Press, 1981. This study portrays Willard as a major contributor to "gospel socialism" and her ideas as inspirational for female social democratic reformers, particularly populists, during the late nineteenth century.

Dillon, Mary Earhart. *Frances Willard: From Prayers to Politics.* Chicago: University of Chicago Press, 1944. This early psychological biography shows the close relationship that Willard perceived and tried to deepen between religion and politics in the United States.

Epstein, Barbara Leslie. *The Politics of Domesticity: Women, Evangelism, and Temperance in Nineteenth-Century America.* Middletown, Conn.: Wesleyan University Press, 1981. This book puts Willard's leadership in the context of evangelical reform and traditionalists' efforts to keep domesticity a central concern for women.

Marilley, Suzanne. "Frances Willard and the Feminism of Fear." *Feminist Studies* 19 (Spring, 1993): 123-146. This article shows that Willard's aims and ideology constituted a form of feminist dissent from the liberal assumption that men can be expected to protect women.

Willard, Frances E. *Glimpses of Fifty Years: The Autobiography of an American Woman.* Chicago: H. J. Smith, 1889. In her autobiography Willard provides a vivid account of her earliest childhood memories, transition into womanhood, the growth of the WCTU, and personal views about key issues such as corruption in political parties, the labor movement's potential, and abortion.

—————————— . "Woman in the Pulpit." In *The Defense of Women's Rights to Ordination in the Methodist Episcopal Church*, edited by Carolyn De Swarte Gifford. New York: Garland, 1987. This short book shows Willard's innovative arguments for the inclusion of women in the Methodist ministry.

Suzanne M. Marilley

MARY LOU WILLIAMS

Born: May 8, 1910; Atlanta, Georgia
Died: May 28, 1981; Durham, North Carolina
Area of Achievement: Music
Contribution: One of the great pianists in the history of jazz, Mary Lou Williams was
one of the few jazz musicians to master all the major styles of music that developed
during the fifty-year period in which she was an active player. Equally at home
playing ragtime, boogie-woogie, swing, and bebop, she was also a gifted composer
and arranger. In her later years, she created the Bel Canto Foundation, which was
dedicated to caring for jazz musicians who had fallen victim to alcohol and drug
addiction.

Early Life

The woman who was to become famous as Mary Lou Williams was born Mary
Elfrieda Scruggs on May 8, 1910, in Atlanta, Georgia. Her father deserted the family
shortly after his daughter's birth, and she only met him briefly in her later life. Her
mother remarried twice, and Mary took the names of her stepfathers, becoming known
first as Mary Lou Winn and then as Mary Lou Burley. She told jazz critic Whitney
Balliett many years later that she had no idea where the "Lou" came from.

When Mary Lou Burley was five or six years old, she moved, with her mother,
Virginia Burley, and her new stepfather, Fletcher Burley, to Pittsburgh, Pennsylvania.
By that time, Mary Lou was already an accomplished pianist. Her mother, who loved
to play a pump organ that she owned, had developed the habit of playing with Mary
Lou on her lap, and by the time the child was three, she had already begun to play
melodies on the keyboard. It was obvious that Mary Lou was musically gifted, and
Virginia Burley decided that she would encourage the child to develop her talent.

Virginia Burley had learned to play the piano by learning to read music; she had
not, however, learned to play by ear or to improvise, and she determined that her
daughter would learn those skills. Therefore, she would not allow Mary Lou to take
piano lessons. Instead, she invited excellent musicians to visit the family and arranged
for Mary Lou to watch, listen, and learn. The child learned rapidly, and by the time
she was six, she was playing at parties and various social gatherings. Fletcher Burley
was also extremely supportive of her playing, and he somehow found the money to
buy a player piano and piano rolls of such superb pianists as Fats Waller and James P.
Johnson. Like the great composer and pianist Duke Ellington, who had learned to play
piano by studying piano rolls, Mary Lou used her new instrument to further her
musical education. Supported by her mother and stepfather, Mary Lou often practiced
as much as twelve hours a day.

The young prodigy soon became a local celebrity, playing jazz, ragtime, and
boogie-woogie with the skill of an adult professional. The principal of the local school
sometimes took Mary Lou to play light classical music at afternoon teas at Pittsburgh's Carnegie Tech. She also occasionally took her to the opera to broaden her

horizons, but Mary Lou never developed a taste for opera. Her exposure to a wide variety of music, however, and her willingness to play almost all of it stood her in good stead in her later life.

Life's Work

By the time Mary Lou Burley had reached the sixth grade, many of the best jazz musicians in the area had become aware of her remarkable musical talent. Chu Berry, one of the best tenor saxophonists in the country, sometimes picked up Mary Lou and took her to play at local jam sessions, where she had the opportunity to play with fine musicians and further develop her playing skills.

Mary Lou Burley had been playing professionally for many years when, at age fourteen, she left home to travel on the vaudeville circuit so that she could help support her family. She worked with various acts, including the duo of Seymour and Jeannette. Of that period of her life, Mary Lou later said, "We toured carnivals and such, and it was an animal life. The *worst* kinds of people." Her stint with Seymour and Jeannette was significant primarily because one of her band mates was the saxophonist John Williams.

Williams befriended Mary Lou Burley, coming to her aid when musicians or managers objected to the presence of a woman in the band, and the two were married in 1927. The couple went to live in Memphis, Tennessee, but John Williams soon went on the road with Andy Kirk and the Twelve Clouds of Joy, leaving Mary Lou in Memphis temporarily. She worked there in various musical situations until John asked her to join him in Kansas City to travel with the band.

Initially, Mary Lou drove one of the band's cars. She was not a band member, although she was occasionally asked to play a boogie-woogie feature with the band when a performance was not going well; audiences always became enthusiastic when they heard and saw the slight, attractive young woman playing a driving number with the power of a man twice her size. One day, however, when a record company official had asked the Kirk band to audition for a recording contract, the band's regular pianist, Marion Jackson, failed to arrive. Mary Lou Williams took his place and played superbly, and the band was hired to make the record. At the recording session, Marion Jackson sat down to play the piano, but the record company's representative demanded that "the girl piano player" be brought back. Williams played on the record date and became the band's regular pianist.

Andy Kirk and the Twelve Clouds of Joy went on to become one of the best-known bands in the country, and Mary Lou Williams' thirteen-year tenure in the band made her famous. Williams began to write songs for the band, and she learned, with the help of Andy Kirk, who was a well-schooled musician, to arrange music. "Walkin' and Swingin'," "Cloudy," "Mary's Idea," "Froggy Bottom," and "Little Joe from Chicago" were among the works that she contributed to the band's repertoire. Williams went on to write for other band leaders, including Duke Ellington, for whom she wrote the popular "Trumpet No End," and Benny Goodman, for whom she wrote an arrangement of her original song "Roll 'Em."

As she traveled throughout the country with the Kirk band, Mary Lou Williams took every opportunity to meet the musicians she admired and learn from them. She played in jam sessions with virtually all the best musicians of the era, and she formed a strong friendship with Art Tatum, who is believed by many jazz experts to be the finest pianist the jazz tradition has produced. Williams said later that Tatum had taught her, among other things, how to control the tone of the piano without using the pedals, by keeping her fingers flat on the keys.

At some point in the early 1940's, John Williams and Mary Lou Williams went their separate ways. John left the Kirk band, and Mary Lou left somewhat later, in 1942, possibly because some new band members were receiving what she believed to be too many solo features. In 1942, Mary Lou Williams went back to Pittsburgh, where she formed a band that included the drummer Art Blakey. In the same year, after divorcing John Williams, she met and married trumpeter Harold "Shorty" Baker. She and Baker joined the Duke Ellington band in 1943, where she served as the band's arranger. Williams became restless, however, and she left the Ellington band after six months. Her marriage to Baker also ended at about that time.

Mary Lou Williams became active in New York City, where she often appeared as a solo artist in such clubs as the popular Café Society Uptown and Café Society Downtown. She also became excited about the new music of the era, bebop, which was being created at that time by such innovators as alto saxophonist Charlie Parker, trumpeter Dizzy Gillespie, and pianist Thelonious Monk. Although many players who had played in big bands hated the new music, which was more harmonically and rhythmically complex than the music of the swing era had been and was frequently played at difficult, breakneck tempos, Williams embraced it, finding it challenging and refreshing. Her study of bebop enabled her to become an even more skillful composer and arranger. Her song "Pretty Eyed Baby" became a pop hit that was sung by Frankie Laine and Jo Stafford. She also cowrote "The Land of Oo Bla Dee" for Dizzy Gillespie.

In 1945, Williams had her own show on radio station WNEW in New York City, and it was there that she first introduced *Zodiac Suite*, a twelve-part piece inspired by the signs of the Zodiac. She played the piece on the piano on the radio show, after which she orchestrated the work for eighteen instruments and performed it at Town Hall with members of the New York Philharmonic Orchestra. Williams remained active in New York, making recordings with various musicians and performing frequently.

In 1952, Williams traveled to Europe for what she thought would be a short visit. She was well received everywhere she went, but she was becoming disenchanted with the changing jazz scene. She was unhappy with much of the music that she heard, believing that it was superficial, and she was critical of audiences that did not pay close attention to her music, a phenomenon that was as common in Europe as it was in the United States. She became emotionally disturbed, stopped performing, and accepted the invitation of a French musician to recuperate in his country home. She stayed there six months and then returned to New York.

Williams did not resume her musical career when she arrived in New York. Instead, she became deeply involved in the Christian faith that she had rejected at an early age, and she decided that she would care for the indigent members of her community, particularly those jazz musicians who had fallen victim to alcoholism or drug abuse. She took the needy into her home, fed them, cared for them, and helped them find work. In order to finance this enterprise, which she called the Bel Canto Foundation, she opened a thrift shop and also used income generated by Mary Records, her own recording company. In 1957, she converted to Catholicism (her family had been Protestant), and the priest who served as her spiritual adviser, Father Peter O'Brien, convinced her to play and perform music once again. He told her, "Mary, you're an artist. You belong at the piano and writing music. It's *my* business to help people through the Church and your business to help people through music."

Williams began to perform again, and she wrote various pieces based on religious themes, such as the *Music for Peace* mass, which came to be known as *Mary Lou's Mass*. In 1977, she became artist-in-residence at Duke University in Durham, North Carolina, where she remained, teaching, writing, and playing, until she died of spinal cancer in 1981.

Summary

Mary Lou Williams' undeniable talent as a pianist and composer won for her a permanent place in the history of jazz. She had perfect pitch and was known for her flawless rhythmic sense, which gave her playing an urgency and passion that only a few great players on any instrument could match. Her song "Mary's Waltz" may be the first jazz composition to have been written in waltz time. She was praised and admired by such jazz luminaries as pianists Duke Ellington, Bud Powell, Thelonious Monk, Art Tatum, and Tadd Dameron, among many others. Ellington called her "soul on soul" and said that she was "perpetually contemporary." She was often praised for having mastered the styles of every era of jazz, a feat accomplished by very few musicians. Although she was critical of much of the avant-garde jazz she heard in her later years, she did not hesitate to perform in a special duo concert with Cecil Taylor, who is perhaps the most extreme pianist of the avant-garde. She consented to perform with Taylor because he, like Williams, had studied and absorbed the full range of the jazz tradition: She knew that his music was genuine.

Williams' example shows that gender need not hinder a talented woman who wishes to succeed in the traditionally male world of jazz. She believed that nothing could stand in the way of an excellent musician. In the liner notes for a recording she compiled called *Jazz Women: A Feminist Retrospective*, Williams wrote: "As for being a woman, I never thought much about that one way or the other. All I've ever thought about is music. No musician ever refused to play with me. No one ever refused to play my music or my arrangements. I was always accepted." In spite of her attitude regarding her own career, however, Williams always went out of her way to help women musicians be heard. As early as 1946, she recorded an album accompanied by an all-female quartet of superb musicians (Mary Osborne, guitar; Margie

Hyams, vibraharp; June Rotemberg, bass; and Rose Gottesman, drums).

When she created the Bel Canto Foundation, Mary Lou Williams provided an important service for both the jazz community and the larger community. She refused to coddle those who came to her for help; she helped to feed, clothe, and house them, but she also insisted that they make a serious effort to get back on their own feet. Her approach prefigured later trends in social work.

In the last years of her life, Mary Lou Williams did her best to teach those young musicians who would build the future of the jazz music she loved. She believed that much of the music that was being played at that time was superficial because it was not based on a knowledge of tradition. She believed that she had to do what she could to pass on the essence of that tradition—a tradition that she had mastered in every particular.

Bibliography

Balliett, Whitney. *Improvising: Sixteen Jazz Musicians and Their Art.* New York: Oxford University Press, 1977. In chapter 4, "Out Here Again," Balliett interviews Mary Lou Williams and discusses her playing style. The article contains much interesting information about Williams' life and career. Balliett is a superb stylist and a knowledgeable, perceptive jazz critic; this article is a delight.

Dahl, Linda. *Stormy Weather: The Music and Lives of a Century of Jazzwomen.* New York: Pantheon Books, 1984. Most of chapter 4, "The Ladies at the Keyboard," is dedicated to an examination of Mary Lou Williams' life and work. Although the section on Williams is relatively brief, it is filled with useful information and is sensibly arranged. A good place to begin a study of Williams.

Handy, D. Antoinette. "Mary Lou Williams." In *Black Women in American Bands and Orchestras.* Metuchen, N.J.: Scarecrow Press, 1981. Although the entry on Williams in this encyclopedia-like work is only three pages long, it contains various items of information, particularly regarding Williams' works, that cannot be found in other, longer articles.

McPartland, Marian. "Into the Sun: An Affectionate Sketch of Mary Lou Williams." In *All in Good Time.* New York: Oxford University Press, 1987. This article, written by a fine pianist who was Mary Lou Williams' friend, is exactly what its title says it is. It provides little hard information about Williams' life or career, but it does give the reader a feel for what Williams was like as a person and as a performer.

Russell, Ross. "Andy Kirk and the Clouds of Joy." In *Jazz Style in Kansas City and the Southwest.* Reprint. Berkeley: University of California Press, 1983. Although the Kirk band, not Mary Lou Williams, is the focus of Ross's article (originally published in 1971), Williams is discussed at various points. Ross states that Williams was the band's best soloist, and he discusses her contribution as a composer and arranger. The article is also useful in that it provides insight into the organization in which Williams came into her own and with which she stayed longer than any other.

Unterbrink, Mary. "Mary Lou Williams." *Jazz Women at the Keyboard.* Jefferson,

N.C.: McFarland, 1983. This extensive, well-organized, well-researched article is the best single source of information about Williams. Highly recommended.

Shawn Woodyard

OPRAH WINFREY

Born: January 29, 1954; Kosciusko, Mississippi

Areas of Achievement: Film and television
Contribution: A talk-show host, actor, producer, and one of the richest women in the entertainment business, Winfrey is the first African American to own a television and film studio.

Early Life

The Oprah Winfrey Show is watched every day by millions of people throughout the world. The woman behind the award-winning show is so famous and so popular that she is known as "Oprah" by her legions of fans, yet her position belies the struggles, heartaches, and disappointments of her past.

Oprah Gail Winfrey was born on January 29, 1954, in Kosciusko, Mississippi, the child of a young unmarried couple. Vernita Lee and Vernon Winfrey were barely out of their teens when they became parents. Vernon Winfrey was in the armed forces when a postcard from Vernita Lee notified him that he had become a father. Oprah Gail Winfrey's first name was to have been Orpah, but a misspelling on her birth certificate renamed the child Oprah.

Vernita Lee, who had become a single mother, began to seek employment. She opted to relocate to the North in an attempt to find work. Intent on settling in Milwaukee, Lee left Oprah in the care of the child's paternal grandmother. The influence of her elderly caretaker, according to Winfrey, is still an important element in her life. As Winfrey describes her, her grandmother was disciplined, strong, and religious. Oprah was reared to be a churchgoer. She proved herself to be intelligent, articulate, and animated. She learned to read early and became a voracious reader. Her quick mind was never idle; she craved mental challenges. Her school environment soon proved to be restrictive to the intelligent child, who found the lack of adequate mental stimuli stifling and confining.

At home, Oprah was under the strict care of her grandmother, whose caretaking techniques included living by the adage that children were "to be seen and not heard." The rod was not to be spared, if the occasion warranted its use. The strong-willed child resented her restrictive environment, and she began to believe that the best way out of her predicament was to become white. She believed that white children were adequately challenged and were not subject to corporal punishment. She fantasized about having lighter skin and a straight nose, and this fantasy was a source of comfort to her. She continued to be a high-spirited young girl, and ultimately she proved to be too difficult and recalcitrant for her grandmother to handle. Her grandmother decided that Oprah would have to move to Milwaukee to live with her mother.

Life in Milwaukee was very different from the kind of life Oprah had known in rural Mississippi. Vernita Lee, who had little money, lived an uncomfortable life in a single room. Living without enough money and the comforts of her grandmother's home made Oprah more rebellious. Vernita Lee soon decided that because both she and Oprah's paternal grandmother had been unable to handle what they deemed a recalcitrant child, it would be best for everyone for Oprah to live with her father. Oprah was to move yet again.

Life in Tennessee with her father and stepmother proved to be good for Oprah. They encouraged her in her academic work and provided a loving yet firm environment. Oprah thrived in her new surroundings, excelling academically and socially. After a year, Oprah went to visit her mother for summer vacation. When it was time for Oprah to return to Tennessee, Vernita Lee refused to permit her to return to her father. Vernita Lee wanted Oprah back. Reluctantly, Vernon gave in.

Life immediately turned sour for Oprah. Her self-esteem suffered badly. She felt unwanted and believed that her lighter-skinned sister was treated better than she was. She took refuge in reading books. The quality of Oprah's academic work never decreased, although she suffered from many years of sexual abuse by male relatives and acquaintances. She suffered in silence. She manifested her inner suffering and rage by lying and destroying property. Her mother's confusion and exasperation with Oprah increased, and soon it was decided that alternate living arrangements would have to be made. It was then decided that another visit to Vernon was needed. The move to back Tennessee in 1968, however, did not work out as well as the move in 1962 had. She had difficulty readjusting to her new environment.

In her senior year at Nashville's East High School, Oprah decided that she wanted her future to be in entertainment. Her aspirations were well on the way to being realized. She excelled academically and also won several titles, including that of Miss Black Tennessee. She read the news for the local radio station while she was still in her teens. Despite her decision to attend college outside Tennessee, her father insisted that she enroll in Tennessee State University in Nashville. With an oratorical scholarship in hand, Oprah entered Tennessee State as an English major.

Life's Work

During her college years, Oprah Winfrey worked for several media organizations. She was employed in Nashville by the radio stations WVOL and WLAC, and later she worked as a television reporter-anchor for WLAC-TV. Only a few months before she was to have been graduated from Tennessee State University, she accepted a position with WJ2-TV in Baltimore, Maryland. Her enthusiasm and personality attracted many admirers within the journalistic community, and she quickly became a favorite with the public. She became the cohost of a local morning show, *People Are Talking*.

Winfrey's popularity soon extended outside Baltimore. After having sent demo tapes to media markets throughout the country, Oprah was asked to host *A.M. Chicago*. She was now in the national arena, competing with television talk-show hosts such as Phil Donahue. She quickly won the ratings war against Donahue, who left Chicago in 1985 to relocate in New York.

It was at this time that Winfrey began to gain weight. She became concerned about her health and her appearance, and she tried many diets. Dieting, however, did not solve her weight problem. She found that she always regained any weight that she had been able to lose by dieting. Winfrey underwent extensive psychoanalysis, and she finally concluded that her weight problem was the result of her lack of a positive self-image, which in turn was the result of her childhood experiences. Despite the fact that she continued to be successful as a media personality, Winfrey continued to gain weight. Her popularity, Emmy awards, and increased respect within the industry did not halt her eating binges.

Winfrey soon decided that she wanted to work as an actor. In 1985, she requested a leave of absence from her show to costar in Steven Spielberg's film *The Color Purple*, which went on to garner extensive critical acclaim. The film, which was based on Alice Walker's novel of the same title, portrayed strong African American females but depicted many of its African American male characters as abusive and weak.

Winfrey was nominated for an Academy Award for her role in *The Color Purple*, and she followed that role with the role of the mother in a film version of Richard Wright's novel *Native Son*. Although the role was a relatively small one and the film was not widely distributed, Winfrey was satisfied with her performance. She hoped to continue portraying women of strength and character. Consequently, she pursued other acting projects in an effort to stretch her acting skills as well as to inform and educate her audience.

Because of Winfrey's popularity, *A.M. Chicago* was renamed *The Oprah Winfrey Show* and was widely distributed. By 1988, Winfrey was the most highly paid entertainer in show business. At that time, Winfrey also revealed that she had lost the weight she had wanted to lose for so long. Only a few months later, however, she had regained all of her former weight and more besides. The public became obsessed with her weight, and it became a frequent subject of tabloid journalism.

Yet Oprah remained the quintessential host and entertainer. She continued to break records in areas never before ventured into by any African American woman. In addition to owning and producing *The Oprah Winfrey Show*, Winfrey formed her own company, which she called Harpo (Oprah spelled backward), and purchased a studio. She ventured into film production, producing and costarring in African American author Gloria Naylor's *The Women of Brewster Place*, which was a ratings hit. The made-for-television film became a short-lived television series. Winfrey has won several Emmy Awards as Best Talk Show Host, and *The Oprah Winfrey Show* has won several Emmys as Best Talk Show.

Oprah Winfrey frequently gives lectures to youth groups and universities, and she has made multimillion-dollar donations to several causes. She supports the United Negro College Fund, and she has formed a Tennessee State University Scholarship Fund that awards ten students annually who are deemed economically disadvantaged as well as academically talented. She writes each student personally on a regular basis. She also serves as their mentor and provides them with moral as well as financial support, encouraging them to excel and to maintain grade-point averages of 3.0 or above. If they do so, she finances their education to its completion.

Winfrey also serves as a spokesperson against child abuse. A victim of sexual and mental abuse as a child, she has dedicated herself to helping those in similar situations. She has testified on the subject of child abuse in front of a congressional committee, and she continues to enlighten the public about the many problems that children face in the United States, such as abuse, homelessness, and illness.

Summary

Oprah Winfrey's rise to stardom may seem to many people to have been quick and easy. Despite her youth, however, Winfrey has paid her dues. Her achievements are the results of her effort and tenacity. Oprah has demonstrated that one's dreams and aspirations can be realized if they are supported by diligence and persistence. Her rise, despite seemingly insurmountable odds, has inspired many people. She affects millions of individuals daily through her television show, which has focused on a wide variety of topics. Her programs inform, enlighten, and influence a large sector of the populace. She has examined on her show such issues as racism, sexism, spousal abuse, acquired immune deficiency syndrome (AIDS), violence in schools, drunk driving, political corruption, and child abuse. She continues to make journalistic history by interviewing elusive luminaries. Her exclusive interview with superstar Michael Jackson in 1993 was a ratings coup.

Winfrey has expanded her business horizons by opening a restaurant in Chicago and by bringing to the screen inspiring stories such as *Kaffir* and *Beloved Boy*. She is always pursuing projects of substance and causes that will affect the masses. Still unmarried, Winfrey has been engaged for many years to entrepreneur Stedman Graham. She has also resolved the problem of her vacillating weight with proper nutrition, exercise, and medical supervision. Determined to keep the weight off, Winfrey has become an inspiration to many women who have experienced similar problems. Lauded by her employees for her generosity, Oprah Winfrey remains accessible to her public and continues to be one of the most famous people in the world.

Bibliography

King, Norman. *Everybody Loves Oprah!* New York: William Morrow, 1988. This book chronicles the life and work of Oprah Winfrey. It also deals with her ability to elicit admiration and love from those around her.

Long, Richard A. *African Americans*. New York: Random House, 1993. This text celebrates the role African Americans have played and continue to play in the history of the United States. Oprah Winfrey is discussed and analyzed in the chapter "The African-American Age."

Smith, Jessie Carney, ed. *Notable Black American Women*. Detroit: Gale Research, 1992. The biographical sketch on Winfrey contained in this book covers her life, achievements, and struggles in a definitive and informative manner.

Waldron, Robert. *Oprah!* New York: St. Martin's Press, 1987. A popular biography of Winfrey that includes a sixteen-page photograph section.

Woods, Geraldine. *The Oprah Winfrey Story: Speaking Her Mind, an Authorized*

Biography. Minneapolis, Minn.: Dillon Press, 1991. This biography, which bears Winfrey's stamp of approval, focuses on the significance of Winfrey's success as an African American woman. Includes an index and bibliographical references.

Annette Marks-Ellis

SARAH WINNEMUCCA

Born: c. 1844; Humboldt Sink, Nevada Territory
Died: October 17, 1891; Henry's Lake, Idaho
Areas of Achievement: Civil rights and social reform
Contribution: A Paiute Indian, Sarah challenged American officials and their policies
as she sought to maintain peace and ensure human rights for her people.

Early Life

Sarah Winnemucca was a Paiute Indian born sometime in 1844 in the Humboldt Sink, in what is present-day Nevada. The Numa, renamed Paiutes by white trappers, were a nomadic people and consequently, the exact day and place of her birth were not recorded. Her native name was Thoc-me-tony, or "Shell-Flower." Sarah's father, known as Old Winnemucca to distinguish him from a nephew of the same name, was a leader of several Paiute bands that were bound more by a common language than a tribal structure. Sarah was the fourth child of nine born to Tuboitonie, daughter of Captain Truckee.

As the leader of a separate Paiute band, Truckee was known for having served as a guide for several American emigrant groups in the 1840's. He accompanied General John C. Frémont to California, where he participated in the Bear Flag revolt, helping to wrest the territory from Mexico.

Sarah's early childhood was filled with troubling memories of the depredations of white invaders in the Great Basin area, including the murder of a favorite uncle. On one occasion, Sarah's mother buried her in the hot sand, covering her head with sagebrush in an attempt to hide the child from approaching whites. Tuboitonie returned that night to rescue Sarah, who was safe but traumatized by the ordeal. At the age of six, Sarah traveled with her mother, siblings, and Captain Truckee to California. The band found temporary work on a ranch north of Stockton, where Sarah observed white customs, learned rudimentary English and lost some of her fear of the whites. At the end of the work season, the Paiutes returned home only to discover that many of those left behind had succumbed to typhus. Truckee convinced the starving survivors that the whites had not poisoned the Humboldt River, as many believed, and further soothed their fears by obtaining flour for them.

Sarah traveled with her grandfather on several occasions to California, where she worked for and lived with various white families in the San Joaquin Valley. Truckee thought it important that the Paiutes assimilate. By the age of ten she had learned to speak Spanish. In 1857, she lived for about a year in Genoa, Nevada, with Major William M. Ormsby and his family. Sarah was the companion of the major's daughter, four years her junior. She worked in the family store as well and it was during this time that she refined her English-speaking skills and was renamed Sarah.

In 1860, to fulfill her dying grandfather's wish, Sarah and her younger sister Elma attended the Convent School of Notre Dame in San Jose, California. Sarah's formal education, however, lasted for only three short weeks. The Winnemucca sisters were forced to leave the school when some of the pupils' parents protested their daughters' association with the racially different Paiute students.

Life's Work

Although Sarah Winnemucca's formal schooling was short-lived, she had grasped enough rudimentary skills to master the written expression of English. Familiar with five languages—Paiute, Washoe, Shoshone, Spanish, and English—she began her career as an interpreter at the age of sixteen. In 1860, hostilities that had been induced by the discovery of silver and the subsequent influx of white miners into Paiute territory resulted in the Pyramid Lake War. Her role in the negotiations resulted in the creation of the Pyramid Lake Reservation.

In the face of continued encroachment by white squatters, Old Winnemucca and his daughter, Sarah, took their cause to the stage in 1864, giving speeches and performing costumed scenes from Indian life first in Virginia City and then in San Francisco. Unfortunately, their efforts, though entertaining, did little to change U.S. government policy regarding the Paiutes. Returning to the troubled reservation the following year, Sarah Winnemucca served as mediator between the army, the Indian agents, and the peaceful and hostile factions of the Paiutes. Despite her efforts, one of the Paiute camps was burned and women and children were killed, including her baby brother. The hostilities continued for a year, during which her sister and mother died.

Rather than starve on the reservation, many of the dislocated Paiutes settled near military forts where they could count on handouts from the military officials, who many believed were more trustworthy than the Indian agents. Sarah Winnemucca settled at Camp McDermitt, where she was hired as an official interpreter from 1868 to 1873, and in the process worked to smooth relations between the nine hundred Paiute encamped at the post and the McDermitt officials. This relatively tranquil period did not last long, as the federal government shifted its Indian policy in 1869 from the reservation system, managed by civilian agents, to one of individual land allotments administered by military personnel.

Winnemucca wrote a letter to the new Indian superintendent of Utah, Major Henry Douglass, endorsing the new assimilation policy as long as the Paiutes' rights and lands were protected from white encroachment. Her communiqué found its way to Washington, D.C., earning a level of notoriety that resulted in an 1870 article about her in *Harper's Weekly*. Riding this wave of popularity, she wrote directly to the Commissioner of Indian Affairs, Ely S. Parker, himself a Seneca Indian who had served as military secretary to Ulysses S. Grant during the Civil War. In her letter, Winnemucca complained about the deceitful and unscrupulous behavior of several Nevada agents. Such lobbying efforts on her part continued throughout most of her life.

The Malheur River Indian Reservation in Oregon was established in 1872. The agent, Samuel B. Parrish, hired Winnemucca as his interpreter in 1875. Again, she acted more as ambassador than translator. The two worked diligently to provide services for the residents and maintain peace between the various groups of Indians, white immigrants, and soldiers at the remote and difficult agency. Together they were able to establish some of the necessary ingredients for assimilation, including building a school for the children and training the men to farm. Parrish's sister-in-law taught the children while Winnemucca observed her teaching techniques. In her autobiography, Winnemucca held Parrish in great esteem and implied that he was the only agent that she ever completely trusted.

Parrish was replaced in 1876 by Major William V. Rinehart, throwing the agency into turmoil. Rinehart proved to be the worst kind of agent—miserly, inflexible when it came to Paiute infractions, oblivious when it came to white lawlessness. He did not anticipate dealing with Sarah Winnemucca, the educated, articulate, and determined young woman who did not hesitate to intercede with a report to Washington, D.C., on his misconduct. For her efforts, Winnemucca was banished from the reservation.

Meanwhile many of the Paiutes had fled the Malheur Reservation and were either living near Camp McDermitt back in Nevada or had joined their distant kin, the Bannocks, in Idaho. The Bannocks were increasingly discontent about their own mistreatment, and war broke out in 1878, pitting different Paiute factions against each other. Winnemucca volunteered her translating skills to the army in the hopes that she could help bring the war to a quick conclusion. Typically, she acted as envoy more often than interpreter. Learning that her father's band had been forced to join with the warring Bannocks, she set out alone in hostile territory to rescue him. She made the 223-mile round-trip, beginning late on the evening of June 13 and returning at 5:30 P.M. on June 15, to bring Old Winnemucca and his followers to safety. General Oliver Otis Howard, the commander in charge of the campaign, had nothing but praise for her actions during the hostilities.

Following the Bannock War, the Nevada Paiutes were ordered to the Yakima Reservation in Washington Territory. Winnemucca visited the reservation, where she discovered the Paiutes steeped in poverty and despair. She immediately traveled to Vancouver, Washington, to inform General Howard of the deplorable conditions and then to San Francisco to begin a lecture tour. She generated so much sympathy for the Paiutes' situation that in 1880, Carl Schurz, secretary of the interior, had her escorted to Washington, D.C., to meet with himself and President Rutherford B. Hayes. She secured the authorization for the Paiutes to return to Malheur in spite of a smear campaign conducted by her old nemesis, Rinehart. Returning to the West, she was reappointed as interpreter at the Malheur reservation despite Rinehart's presence. Unable to secure funds or protection to guarantee the safe conduct of the Paiutes from Yakima to Malheur, however, Winnemucca was forced to find other employment.

Sarah Winnemucca eventually moved to Fort Vancouver, where General Howard employed her as a teacher in the Indian school. During the year that she lived in Vancouver, she met and married her fourth husband, Lieutenant Lewis H. Hopkins. The following year, in 1883, she returned to the lecture circuit, speaking on behalf of native rights in Boston, a city traditionally known as a hotbed of reform. She was sponsored by Elizabeth Palmer Peabody, author of two pamphlets portraying the Paiutes, and Mary Peabody Mann, wife of the well-known education reformer Horace

Mann. Mary Mann became editor of *Life Among the Paiutes: Their Wrongs and Claims* (1883), written by Winnemucca to give an account of her own life and that of her people. These efforts secured thousands of signatures on a petition asking Paiutes be granted land in severalty. Though Congress passed the bill in 1884, Secretary of the Interior Edward Teller failed to implement it.

Sarah Winnemucca Hopkins returned to her brother's ranch in Lovelock, Nevada, where she started a school for Paiute children and taught with great success for three years. Her husband died of tuberculosis in 1886, and shortly thereafter she moved to Henry's Lake, Idaho. She resided there with her married sister, Elma Smith, until her own death in 1891.

Summary

Armed with her dexterity in languages and adroit skills in handling cross-cultural matters, Sarah Winnemucca labored to promote and maintain peace at a time in American history when that was a formidable task. Conflict between Indians and whites, whether civilians or soldiers, was inevitable when the U.S. government consistently failed to uphold its treaty obligations. Ignoring this historical backdrop, early historians, even those favorably disposed to her, judged Sarah Winnemucca a failure. Her critics focused on her personal life, some implying that she was of questionable morals due to her four marriages. She does not conform easily to heroic stereotyping. Sarah had not saved a white man as had Pocahontas, nor had she blazed a trail through her homeland for white men as had Sacajawea.

Recent historians have been more appreciative in their appraisal of her accomplishments. Their analysis avoids using the racial standard of the Noble Savage, or its female counterpart, the Indian Princess. Because of her personal accomplishments, charm, and intellect, Sarah became the spokesperson for all American Indians living in the Great Basin in the last half of the nineteenth century. She believed that the Paiutes' survival depended on their ability to become educated and to practice Anglo-style agriculture. Functioning more as envoy than interpreter, she worked for the human rights of the Paiute people.

Bibliography

Brimlow, George F. "The Life of Sarah Winnemucca: The Formative Years," *Oregon Historical Quarterly* 53 (June, 1952): 103-134. Although somewhat dated and containing historical inaccuracies, this article offers good examples of Winnemucca's letters, written to elicit government response to her activities.

Canfield, Gae Whitney. *Sarah Winnemucca of the Northern Paiutes*. Norman: University of Oklahoma Press, 1983. A complete biography that corrects many of the discrepancies and misconceptions about Sarah Winnemucca. Deftly weaving together her personal relationships with the concerns of her professional life, this scholarly work delves deeply into her motives and character.

Egan, Ferol. *Sand in a Whirlwind: The Paiute Indian War of 1860*. Garden City, N.Y.: Doubleday, 1972. Though Sarah Winnemucca receives little attention, this work provides the setting for the future problems with which Sarah would deal.

Howard, O. O., Major-General. *Famous Indian Chiefs I Have Known.* New York: The Century Company, 1922. This reprint of the 1908 edition contains separate chapters on each of the leaders that Howard knew while he was stationed in the West. Though historically naïve, this first-person account adequately represents the early favorable accounts of Winnemucca's endeavors.

Knack, Martha C., and Omer C. Stewart. *As Long as the River Shall Run: An Ethnohistory of Pyramid Lake Indian Reservation.* Berkeley: University of California Press, 1984. Sarah Winnemucca is curiously underrepresented in this thorough history of the people of the Pyramid Lake region.

Morrison, Dorothy Nafus. *Chief Sarah: Sarah Winnemucca's Fight for Indian Rights.* New York: Atheneum, 1980. This nonacademic work focuses on Winnemucca's career as an early spokesperson for Indian civil rights.

Peabody, Elizabeth P. *The Paiutes: Second Report of the Model School of Sarah Winnemucca, 1886-87.* Cambridge, Mass.: John Wilson and Son, 1887. This compilation of Winnemucca's 1883 Boston lectures is dripping with the sentimentality characteristic of Victorian America, but gives insight into her persuasiveness.

Stewart, Patricia. "Sarah Winnemucca," *Nevada Historical Society Quarterly* 14 (Winter, 1971): 23-38. A brief biography highlighting Winnemucca's achievements, the author emphasizes the need to evaluate those accomplishments with as little cultural bias as possible.

Rosanne M. Barker

ANNA MAY WONG

Born: January 3, 1905; Los Angeles, California
Died: February 3, 1961; Santa Monica, California
Area of Achievement: Film
Contribution: As one of the first Asian Americans to break through the film industry's
   general policy of racial exclusion Anna May Wong enjoyed a film career that
   spanned more than forty years. Especially for Chinese Americans, Wong came to
   represent opportunity and tangible success.

Early Life

Anna May Wong was born in Los Angeles, California, on January 3, 1905, the
second of eight children and the second daughter born to Wong Sam Sing and Lee
Gon Toy. At birth, Anna May Wong was given the Chinese name Wong Liu Tson
which means "frosted yellow willow." Little is known about her Chinese-descended
parents other than that they ran a laundry business. Wong attended Los Angeles public
schools while helping in the family's laundry, located in the city's Chinatown district.

Wong exhibited a fascination with film early in her life. As a child, she was often
truant from school, particularly Chinese language classes in the evenings, and spent
her time at picture shows or watching film crews at work. She was so full of questions
that film workers dubbed her the "Curious Chinese Child." Wong's interest in motion
pictures disturbed her father, who considered the film world disreputable and no place
for a proper Chinese American daughter. Instead, he wanted her to marry, have
children, and lead an honorable life. Despite his disapproval, Wong defied her father
and began to make the rounds of various casting offices. Her first film job came after
casting agent James Wang helped her find work as one of three hundred extras in *The
Red Lantern* (1919). She appeared in small roles in other silent films, such as *Bits of
Life* (1921) and *Shame* (1921), all of which featured sinister Asian characters. She
landed her first leading role in the minor film *The Toll of the Sea* (1922), playing a
Chinese Madame Butterfly who gives up her true love by committing suicide after he
finds a woman of his own race.

Life's Work

The year 1924 marked the ascent of Anna May Wong's star when she was cast as a
handmaid to a princess opposite Douglas Fairbanks, Sr., in *The Thief of Bagdad*, a
landmark in film history because of its lavish costumes and sets. The public eye was
irresistibly drawn to Wong's exotic beauty and grace. She was the darling of photographers, extremely photogenic with her ivory skin, deep brown eyes, and black hair
styled with sleek bangs. Wong did not play stereotypical roles such as the peasant
woman or the subservient geisha girl. Instead, she was known as the "Chinese
Flapper" and was hailed by Hollywood as its token Oriental siren. Recognized as one
of the most beautiful women on the screen, Wong quickly became a box-office
attraction.

Wong's success coincided with the rising popularity of numerous films, including *A Trip to Chinatown* (1926), that featured China, Chinatown, or London's Limehouse District as backgrounds for crime, mystery, and intrigue. Typically, the Chinese characters in these films were depicted as evil, treacherous, and often savage. By 1928, Wong had appeared in more than twenty silent films including *The Chinese Parrot* (1927), *Driven from Home* (1927), *Streets of Shanghai* (1927), *Old San Francisco* (1927), *Mr. Wu* (1927), *The Devil Dancer* (1927), and *Chinatown Charlie* (1928). Fellow players included Esther Ralston, Dolores Costello, Warner Oland, and William Boyd.

In 1928, Wong left Hollywood and spent three years in Europe. She went abroad under contract to independent German producer Richard Eichberg. Berlin critics praised Wong's performance in her first German film *Song* (1928). Overall, Wong's reception in Europe was a warm one. She landed several leading stage and screen parts, and her success peaked in the late 1920's and early 1930's. Between 1928 and 1930, Wong starred in German, English, and French productions, including the nearly silent film *Picadilly* (1929), which was nominated as one of the top ten films in Europe. The advent of talking pictures prompted Wong to learn German and French. In March of 1929, she made her stage debut in *The Circle of Chalk* opposite Laurence Olivier in London. Neither the play nor Wong's performance was favorably reviewed. In response to prevailing criticism, Wong spent some two hundred guineas on voice lessons in order to cultivate a British accent.

Thoroughly Anglicized, with her conversation liberally sprinkled with Briticisms, Wong returned to the United States in the fall of 1930. The Depression years proved to be Wong's most lucrative as a performer. In October of 1930, Wong made her first appearance on Broadway in Edgar Wallace's *On the Spot*, in which she played a wily, vengeful, half-caste Chinese moll. During Wong's European excursion, the United States had seen the rise in popularity of Sax Rohmer's novels featuring the sinister Dr. Fu Manchu. In 1931, under contract to Paramount Studios, Wong returned to Hollywood to star with Japanese actor Sessue Hayakawa in *Daughter of the Dragon*, based on Rohmer's *Daughter of Fu Manchu*. Wong's other American and British films during this period included Josef von Sternberg's *Shanghai Express* (1932), *Tiger Bay* (1933), the Sherlock Holmes picture *A Study in Scarlet* (1933), *Limehouse Blues* (1934), *Chu Chin Chow* (1934), and *Java Head* (1935). In 1935, Metro-Goldwyn-Mayer offered Wong a supporting role as a concubine in the screen adaptation of Pearl Buck's best-selling novel, *The Good Earth*. Wong turned down the part because she had wanted the lead role of O-lan instead. Unfortunately the role of the concubine was the only unsympathetic part in a film featuring an all-white cast portraying Chinese characters. Such use of Caucasians in Asian roles was typical in films during this time.

Wong sent her widowed father and several of her brothers and sisters to China in 1934, for a lengthy visit at her expense. In 1936, Wong made her first journey to China to spend a year observing the traditional culture of her parents' homeland. Although Wong had expected to receive cordial acclaim for her work, the Chinese government surprised and disappointed Wong by harshly criticizing her negative portrayals of

Chinese characters. She tried to explain that such roles were the only ones open to her in Hollywood. During her trip, the Sino-Japanese conflict escalated, and Wong returned to Hollywood to perform in the first film of her career that was sympathetic to the Chinese, *Daughter of Shanghai* (1937). Upon her return to the United States, Wong also wrote a series of articles for the New York *Herald-Tribune* that described her experiences on her trip to China.

In the late 1930's and early 1940's, Wong's major roles were all in forgettable B-films, including *When Were You Born?* (1938), *Dangerous to Know* (1938) and *King of Chinatown* (1939). Ultimately, the studios used Wong mainly as a coach or a consultant for films they made about Asians, films which primarily used Caucasian actors. During World War II, Wong appeared in a couple of Pacific War films, such as *Bombs over Burma* (1942). Offscreen, she devoted her time to raising money for United China Relief and working for the USO. In 1942, she went on an entertainment tour of Alaska.

Wong's career in the 1940's and 1950's faded into near obscurity with only intermittent minor television and film appearances. She made her screen comeback in the box-office success *Portrait in Black* (1960), in which she played Lana Turner's maid. Her last film, *The Savage Innocents*, was released later that year. Wong's career ended with a contract to play the part of the mother who sings "Chop Suey" in *The Flower Drum Song*, but she died before filming began. On February 3, 1961, Anna May Wong died in her sleep of a heart attack at the home she shared with her brother Richard in Santa Monica, California. Her survivors were listed as her brothers and sisters, since she had never married, claiming that she was wedded to her art. Even in her films, she rarely had a love interest and did not receive her first screen kiss until late in her career, opposite John Loder in the British film *Java Head*.

In 1973, the Asian Fashion Designers conceived the Anna May Wong Award. The designers saw Wong as a symbol of fashion inspiration, as she had moved through her long film career in an ever-changing series of cheongsam dresses and other Asian-influenced costumes with subtly refined styles that made her a standout among fashion clotheshorses such as Gloria Swanson and Greta Garbo. Through one fashion period to another, Wong maintained an individual and compelling sense of exquisite style, even in her public wardrobe.

Summary

Anna May Wong was one of the first Asian American actors to play an Asian on the screen, and she became the first actor of Chinese descent to achieve stardom. Typically, Caucasian actresses in heavy makeup and elaborate costumes had been cast in Asian roles. With her authentically beautiful ethnic features, Wong came to symbolize everything Oriental to a white audience at the same time that she became a success symbol to the Chinese American community. Although her career was considered a minor one in film history, Wong was much more to her fans of Asian descent. During Asian moon festivals and Chinese New Year events, Wong rode in a variety of parades as a bonafide box-office star. She lived her life as an American first and as a person of Chinese descent second, but was viewed as Chinese first and American second by her primarily white viewing public. Unfortunately many of the roles offered to this premiere Chinese American actress only served to reinforce unpleasant stereotypes. The actress who defied her father to pursue her dream found a career shaped by sex and race discrimination. Many of her own people were affronted by her screen caricatures. She, too, despised the negative racial stereotypes which, ironically, made her career possible. Remembered for her cheesecake sexiness and exotic sense of droll camp, Wong was unable to realize her true worth as an actress because she was always limited by the prejudices of her time.

Bibliography
Chu, Judy. "Anna May Wong." In *Counterpoint: Perspectives on Asian America*, edited by Emma Gee. Los Angeles: Asian American Studies Center, University of California, 1976. Gee's anthology features articles on Asian American themes such as history, labor, politics, education, and immigration. Chu's article, included in the section on communications and mass media, presents a thorough biography of Anna May Wong with details gathered from periodical articles and interviews.
Doerr, Conrad J. "Anna May Wong." *Films in Review* 19 (December, 1968): 660-662. Doerr chronicles the period from 1948 to 1956 when Anna May Wong was the landlady of his apartment in Santa Monica, California. Doerr reveals some amusing personal anecdotes about Wong's later years and includes specifics about her early life and the most productive years of her film career.
Keylin, Arleen, and Suri Fleischer, eds. *Hollywood Album: Lives and Deaths of Hollywood Stars from the Pages of The New York Times*. 2 vols. New York: Arno Press, 1977-1979. The editors have compiled obituaries from *The New York Times* that are quite detailed and full of biographical information. The listing for Anna May Wong is rich with detail about Wong's career and personal life.
Leibfred, Philip. "Anna May Wong." *Films in Review* 38 (March, 1987): 146-152. Leibfred provides an in-depth examination of Wong's career from her 1919 debut as an extra in *The Red Lantern* to final roles in 1960 as a character actress in the films *Portrait in Black* and *The Savage Innocents*. Covers many details about Wong's personal life and her relief activities on behalf of war-torn China during the 1940's. Includes a chronology of those films in which she received screen credits.
Stuart, Ray. *Immortals of the Screen*. Los Angeles: Shelbourne Press, 1965. Stuart features profiles of a range of film greats from Theda Bara to Al Jolson to Anna May Wong. Stuart includes biographical information, film credits, and photographs of the stars. The sketch on Wong places her career in silent and sound pictures within the context of Hollywood's perpetuation of negative stereotypes of Asians.

Jennifer Padgett Griffith

JOANNE WOODWARD

Born: February 27, 1930; Thomasville, Georgia

Areas of Achievement: Film and theater and drama

Contribution: A talented, award-winning character actress, Woodward has achieved critical and commercial success in films, on television, and on the stage. She is also an outspoken advocate for various social causes and is an important patron of regional theater and the ballet.

Early Life

Joanne Gignilliat Woodward was born on February 27, 1930, in Thomasville, Georgia, the second and last child of Wade Woodward, a school administrator, and Elinor Trimmier Woodward. The first child was named Wade for his father, but Elinor Woodward loved films so much that she named her only daughter for Joan Crawford. As a young girl, Joanne accompanied her mother when she went to see films, and the future Academy Award winner grew up wanting to be an actress.

The family relocated often but settled in Greenville, South Carolina, by the time Joanne was fifteen. Dreaming of the day when she would leave the South and go to New York or Hollywood, Joanne entered various beauty contests. Her mother supported Joanne's aspirations, but her father did not. There were other conflicts between her parents, and while Joanne was in high school, her parents divorced. This divorce had an impact on Joanne. She delayed her own marriage, and when it occurred, she vowed to make it last.

From 1947 to 1949, Joanne Woodward attended Louisiana State University, where she majored in drama. After leaving college, she worked as a secretary for a few months and then returned to South Carolina, where she appeared in several little theater productions, including one of *The Glass Menagerie*. Wade Woodward attended a performance one night, and although he had disapproved of her desire to be an actress, his opinion changed when he saw how good she was. After that, he financially and emotionally supported Joanne's dream, which by then had focused on going to New York City. Before making her big move, however, Joanne spent the summer playing starring roles in a little theater in Chatham, Massachusetts.

Life's Work

After arriving in New York City, Joanne Woodward entered the Neighborhood Playhouse School of the Theatre, where she studied drama. She concentrated on developing her acting skills and took speech lessons to eliminate her southern accent. Soon, she signed a contract with the theatrical agency Music Corporation of America (MCA).

In 1952, Woodward appeared in the title role of her first television production, *Penny*, for the program *Robert Montgomery Presents*. Other television work followed. During 1953 and 1954, Woodward understudied the female lead in *Picnic* on Broadway, where she came to know her future husband Paul Newman, another cast member.

Woodward became a member of The Actors Studio in New York and continued to work very hard at acting. Despite the support she received from her father, she was very poor. She lived in a one-room apartment and did her laundry in the bathtub.

At twenty-four, Joanne Woodward finally made it to Hollywood after getting the part of a teenager who was in love with an older man, played by Dick Powell, in the television production of *Interlude* (1954), a *Four Star Playhouse* episode. She was discovered in that role, and Twentieth Century-Fox Studios signed her to a contract that allowed her to appear in six television shows a year.

During the next two years, Joanne Woodward was much in demand, and she commuted between Hollywood and New York City to appear in such classic television programs as *Lux Video Theatre*, *Philco Television Playhouse*, *Studio One*, *Kraft Television Theater*, *The U.S. Steel Hour*, *Alfred Hitchcock Presents*, and *General Electric Theater*.

In 1955, she made her film debut in *Count Three and Pray*. Her performance as a strong-willed, independent orphan in post-Civil War rural America received excellent reviews. The next year, Joanne appeared in two disappointing productions, *The Lovers*, a Broadway play, and the film *A Kiss Before Dying*.

In the 1957 release *The Three Faces of Eve*, Woodward was finally given a part deserving of her talents. Her performance as Eve, the young schizophrenic with three separate personalities, earned for her the Academy Award for Best Actress as well as awards as best dramatic actress from *Film Daily*, the National Board of Review, the Hollywood Foreign Press Association, and the General Federation of Women's Clubs. Despite her success, however, Woodward never became involved in the pretentiousness of Hollywood. In 1958, when she received the Academy Award, she wore a green satin and velvet gown she designed and sewed herself.

Joanne Woodward's next picture was *The Long Hot Summer*, her first film with Paul Newman. Another hit, it was released in 1958, the same year in which Woodward and Newman were married. In 1958, she also appeared in *Eighty Yard Run*, a *Playhouse 90* episode and her first television production with Paul Newman. In that film, she played Louise Kelleher, a wife who gave up her career to be with her husband.

That fictional role did not mirror Woodward's real life. Although she made sacrifices, she managed to continue to act, rear a family, preserve her marriage, and support various causes. Joanne Woodward and Paul Newman had three children: Elinor Teresa in 1959, Melissa Stewart in 1961, and Claire Olivia in 1965. Joanne was also stepmother to Paul's three children (Scott, Susan, and Stephanie) from his first marriage.

Woodward continued to make films, including *Rally 'Round the Flag, Boys!* (1958), *The Sound and the Fury* (1959), *The Fugitive Kind* (1959), *From the Terrace* (1960), *Paris Blues* (1961), *The Stripper* (1963), *A New Kind of Love* (1963), *Signpost to Murder* (1964), *A Big Hand for the Little Lady* (1966), and *A Fine Madness* (1966). She also acted in another Broadway play, *Baby Want a Kiss?*, in 1964.

In 1968, *Rachel, Rachel* was released. For her performance as Rachel, an introverted New England spinster schoolteacher searching for broader horizons, Woodward received the Golden Globe award for best actress from the Foreign Press Association. The New York Film Critics' Circle also voted her best actress, and she was nominated for the Academy Award. After she made *Winning* (1969), Joanne Woodward was named the female box-office star of the year by the National Association of Theatre Owners.

Woodward became an outspoken advocate for social causes, especially birth control, abortion rights, racial equality, historic preservation, and protecting the environment. In 1969, she and her husband received the William J. German Humanitarian Relations Award of the American Jewish Committee.

More movies and more awards followed: *W.U.S.A.* (1970); *King: A Filmed Record . . . Montgomery to Memphis* (1970); *They Might Be Giants* (1971); *All the Way Home* (a 1971 television production); *The Effect of Gamma Rays on Man-in-the-Moon Marigolds* (1972), for which she received the Cannes Film Festival award as the year's best actress; *Summer Wishes, Winter Dreams* (1973), for which she won awards as best actress from the New York Film Critics' Circle and the British Academy and was nominated for the Academy Award; *The Wild Places* (a 1974 television documentary); *The Drowning Pool* (1976); two television films in 1977, *Sybil* and *Come Back, Little Sheba*; and a film, *The End*, and a television drama, *A Christmas to Remember*, in 1978. In addition, Joanne received an Emmy for best actress for her performance as a middle-aged divorced mother and marathon runner in the 1978 television film *See How She Runs*.

After her husband's son Scott Newman died of a drug and alcohol overdose in 1978, both Joanne Woodward and Paul Newman became actively involved in efforts to prevent drug abuse. They supported the Scott Newman Center for Drug Abuse Prevention and Health Communications Research and made a television documentary on the drug angel dust, *Angel Death*, in 1979.

For Woodward, three more films with social significance followed: *Streets of L.A.* (1979), a television feature about illegal aliens; *The Shadow Box* (1981), also for television, about terminally ill cancer patients; and *Crisis at Central High* (1981), a movie based on the 1957 integration of Central High School in Little Rock, Arkansas. For her performance as vice principal Elizabeth Huckaby, she was again nominated for an Emmy as best actress.

In the 1980's, Woodward directed the play *Golden Boy* in Massachusetts and episodes for both the *Family* and *Sense of Humor* television series. She also became a spokesperson for regional theater and actively participated in and directed actors' workshops in New York. In addition, she sponsored dance companies, financially supporting and becoming chairperson on the board of directors of Dancers, a New York ballet company.

Most of all, however, Joanne Woodward continued to act, starring in *Candida* (1982; both in summer stock and on Broadway), *Harry and Son* (1984), and *Passions* (1984), a television melodrama. For years, her mother had suffered from Alzheimer's disease, and in 1985 Woodward won her second Emmy as best actress for her performance as a victim of that destructive affliction in the television production *Do You Remember Love*. That year, Woodward was also the corecipient with Paul Newman of the Screen Actors Guild's highest honor, its Annual Achievement Award for outstanding accomplishments in the acting profession.

Woodward starred in a film version of *The Glass Menagerie* in 1987; she had appeared in summer stock productions of the play in 1985 and 1986. Another play, *Sweet Bird of Youth*, followed in Toronto in 1988, and in 1989 she made a television documentary on Group Theater. She also continued to act in films. *Mr. and Mrs. Bridge* was released in 1990, and in 1994 the Hallmark Hall of Fame television special *Breathing Lessons* aired.

Summary

Joanne Woodward is an intelligent, disciplined, talented, serious character actress with a personal commitment to perform meaningful roles. She has had critical and commercial successes in motion pictures, on television, and on the stage. She has excelled in a variety of challenging roles, bringing to life, among many others, a victim of multiple personalities (*The Three Faces of Eve*), a pathetic showgirl (*The Stripper*), an introverted spinster (*Rachel, Rachel*), a hateful, abusive widow (*The Effect of Gamma Rays on Man-in-the-Moon Marigolds*), a determined marathon runner (*See How She Runs*), and a victim of Alzheimer's disease (*Do You Remember Love*). In addition, many of the works in which she has performed have helped to raise the social consciousness of the public. Woodword has worked hard to perfect her craft and has shared her knowledge with aspiring youth by supporting, participating in, and directing actors' workshops. She has also used her position to support causes such as birth control, racial equality, historic preservation, and the protection of the environment. In addition, throughout her career she has protected her privacy and that of her family and has refused to fall prey to the typical superficial Hollywood lifestyle. Finally, she has preserved her marriage despite the stresses of her own career, personal tragedies, and the star status of her husband.

Bibliography

Brooks, Andree. "The Making of a Preservationist Starring Joanne Woodward." *Historic Preservation* 34 (November/December, 1982): 14-16, 57. A serious article about Woodward as social activist. Gives examples of her efforts to preserve historic theaters in New York City and other sites. Illustrated.

Morella, Joe, and Edward Z. Epstein. *Paul and Joanne: A Biography of Paul Newman and Joanne Woodward*. New York: Delacorte Press, 1988. A candid, illustrated biography that provides details about Woodward's early life and a reasonably complete analysis of her acting career, although more attention is given to Newman's accomplishments. The authors' liberal use of quotations is especially revealing. Includes an index.

Netter, Susan. *Paul Newman and Joanne Woodward*. London: Piatkus, 1989. Although this illustrated biography repeats much of the information in Morella and Epstein's work, additional material is included. Netter's feminine perspective also counters somewhat the other authors' emphasis on Newman.

Shalit, Gene. "Joanne and Paul: Their Lives Together and Apart." *Ladies' Home Journal* 92 (July, 1975): 70-71, 60-66, 94. A lengthy interview in which Joanne Woodward reveals her philosophy about acting and the difficulties caused by the explosive mix of stardom, career demands, and family responsibilities.

Weston, Carol. "Talks with Two Singular Women." *House and Garden* 153 (November, 1981): 128-130, 192. An interview in which Joanne Woodward reflects on her acting style and discusses how she created the complex characters she has often portrayed. She also discusses her commitment to regional theater and historic preservation

Judith A. Oliver

FANNY BULLOCK WORKMAN

Born: January 8, 1859; Worcester, Massachusetts
Died: January 22, 1925; Cannes, France
Areas of Achievement: Exploration, geography, and women's rights
Contribution: A tireless explorer and geographer, writer, accomplished linguist, feminist, and suffragist, Fanny Bullock Workman set international mountain-climbing records for women. Her enormous contribution to the body of geographical knowledge was acknowledged by numerous geographical societies around the world.

Early Life

Fanny Bullock was born into a wealthy family in Worcester, Massachusetts, on January 8, 1859. Her mother was Elvira Hazard Bullock. Fanny's maternal grandfather was Augustus George Hazard, a merchant and gunpowder manufacturer based in Connecticut, where he built up the family fortune. Fanny's father, Alexander Hamilton Bullock, was a politician who served as the Republican governor of Massachusetts from 1866 to 1868. Fanny had an older sister and brother. Her early education came from private tutors. After completing Miss Graham's Finishing School in New York, she spent two years in Dresden and Paris, where she became fluent in German and French. She returned to Massachusetts when she was twenty. At the age of twenty-two, on June 16, 1881, Fanny was married to William Hunter Workman, a physician. He was twelve years older than she was, had done his postgraduate studies in Munich, and had already traveled extensively in Europe. They had one daughter, Rachel, in 1884. Fanny began hiking with her husband in the White Mountains of New Hampshire. It was there that she climbed her first mountain, Mount Washington (6,293 feet), an unusual accomplishment for a woman of that time. In 1886, they began taking trips to Scandinavia and Germany. William Workman became ill in 1888, and since they were independently wealthy, he retired from his medical practice without causing them any economic hardship. The Workmans spent the next nine years in Europe, using Germany as their home base while they traveled, leaving their child in the care of nurses or at boarding school. It was during these years that Fanny did her first serious climbing.

Life's Work

Fanny Bullock Workman, who preferred to be called Mrs. Bullock Workman, began her adventurous career when her husband took her hiking in the White Mountains of New Hampshire. She climbed Mount Washington several times. After her husband retired and they moved to Europe, she began to make her first serious ascents.

Most of the climbing that Fanny did during their early years in Europe was in the Alps. With the help of guides, she scaled Zinal Rothorn (4,221 feet), the Matterhorn (14,780 feet), and Mont Blanc (15,781 feet). These were exceptional accomplishments, because it was unacceptable in the 1890's for women to do mountain climbing.

Amazingly, she made these climbs wearing the long skirts that were considered proper for women of that era. In fact, throughout the years of her exploring and climbing, she continued to wear skirts as a part of her outfit, though in later years she did begin to wear them shortened up to her boot tops.

Wearing skirts was Fanny Workman's only concession to the feminine role that was considered appropriate in the Victorian age. She and her husband were adamant in their belief in the equality of women with men. As their excursions grew longer and more complex, they began trading roles form year to year. One would organize the expedition, arranging for all the necessary supplies, pack animals, permits, workers, and guides. The other would be responsible for all the photography and record keeping. Both tasks were enormous. Their expedition parties grew to include more than a hundred people, and many arrangements had to be made long distance via mail and telegraph. The records that they kept during these expeditions included precise scientific readings of geographic location and altitude, mapping, and geological descriptions of the terrain. Hundreds of photos were taken with the best equipment then available—bulky, heavy cameras and tripods that had to be carried in cumbersome wooden cases.

In the early 1890's, Fanny and her husband began going on bicycle tours, first in Europe and then in North Africa. These journeys were not mere sightseeing trips; they were adventures. The Workmans faced attacks by wild dogs, journalists eager for interviews, bandits, extremes of weather, poor food, and water supplies, epidemics of malaria and the plague, and other problems that would have stopped less determined travelers. They began writing collaborative accounts of their adventures, and the first book they published was *Algerian Memories: A Bicycle Tour over the Atlas Mountains to the Sahara* (1895). In that same year, they took with them the recently invented Kodak camera to the Iberian Peninsula. The book that followed was *Sketches Awheel in Modern Iberia* (1897). The book recording their longest journey, which they took from 1897 through 1899, was *Through Town and Jungle: Fourteen Thousand Miles Awheel Among the Temples and People of the Indian Plain* (1904). This trip also involved traveling 1,800 miles in Ceylon and 1,500 miles in Java, Sumatra, and Cochin China (South Vietnam). These books all had many good reviews and were well received by a wide audience.

The part of this longest journey that had the most impact on them was a side trip that they took to escape the intense summer heat while in India in 1898. In Kashmir, they put aside their bicycles for a few weeks and proceeded on foot to see the Karakoram and Himalayan mountain ranges up close. They were so enchanted that they put together an expedition the next year, planning to return to Sikkim to spend two months hiking and climbing there.

The venture in Sikkim was beset by problems from the beginning. The Workmans had never arranged such a major venture before, were unaccustomed to the terrain and the climate, and were unfamiliar with the local customs and language. It had taken so long to arrange the expedition that, by the time they got started, the weather—which had already been unseasonably bad for some weeks—was worsening with the approaching winter, and the days were growing short. They were determined, however, and they set off with their large caravan and staff in October. The couple's eagerness and spirit of adventure were not shared by the porters and bearers. These workers were used to less-determined mountaineers who did not insist on risking the arduous journey under such dangerous weather conditions or traveling at such a fast pace.

Despite their convictions regarding the equality of women, the Workmans treated their hired workers with astonishing insensitivity. In the Workmans' account of this expedition, *In the Ice World of the Himálaya* (1900), they showed that they had not risen above the American social model of the time—racism. Not recognizing the impact of their lack of experience and the environmental conditions, let alone the devastating effects of their leadership style, they placed the blame for the nearly overwhelming problems of this expedition on their perception that the Asian workers were uncooperative and unmanageable.

The Workmans never modified their approach when working with their porters and bearers in any of their further ventures in the Karakoram or Himalayan ranges, and they suffered many enormous hardships because of it. In one expedition in the Karakoram, 150 of their workers deserted, taking huge amounts of staple foods with them.

The work that Fanny and her husband did in their seven expeditions in the Himalayas and Karakoram ranges was remarkable and invaluable, and it included many firsts. Fanny set altitude records—as high as 23,00 feet—for women that went unmet for decades. They mapped uncharted areas, including some of the largest nonpolar glaciers in the world. Their observations were essential to geological knowledge of glacial processes. Their maps were the first records of the watersheds for several rivers in the areas bordering Nepal and Tibet. They wrote five books recording these expeditions—the one previously mentioned and *Ice-Bound Heights of the Mustagh* (1908), *Peaks and Glaciers of Nun Kun* (1909), *The Call of the Snowy Hispar* (1910), and *Two Summers in the Ice-wilds of Eastern Karakoram* (1917). They also wrote articles for magazines such as *The National Geographic* and *Alpine Journal*.

Fanny's professional recognition by scholars and boards of geographical societies came slowly. It was not an era when women were accepted as knowledgeable or capable of such undertakings. It was not only the sheer volume of precise data that she had collected but also the documentation of the care that had been taken to collect it that won them over. They may have been swayed also by the length of her career in such daunting expeditions. The peak recognition that she received was from the Royal Geographic Society, where she lectured in 1905, becoming only the second woman to have done so.

After World War I, the Workmans retired for good in the South of France. Fanny was ill for several years before she died at the age of sixty-six in Cannes, France.

Summary

Fanny Bullock Workman excelled as an explorer, climber, and geographer at a time when women were expected to be fragile and helpless. Her accomplishments were recognized by geographic societies and academic institutions around the world.

Because Bullock Workman spoke several languages, she could usually communicate directly with people in many of the places she traveled. She delivered lectures in several countries in their national language. She was the first American woman to speak at the Sorbonne.

Honors from ten European nations' geographical societies were bestowed on Fanny. She was a member of the Royal Asiatic Society and was a fellow of the Royal Geographical Society and the Royal Scottish Geographical Society. In the United States, she was a Corresponding Member of the National Geographic Society and the Brooklyn Institution of Arts and Science. She was a charter member of the American Alpine Club and an Honorary Member of the Appalachian Mountain Club.

Fanny was an ardent feminist. In 1912, she was photographed at an altitude of 21,000 feet on the Silver Throne plateau in the Himalayas, reading a newspaper. Its headline proclaims "Votes for Women." She believed strongly in higher education for women, and to that end she willed a total of $125,000 to Bryn Mawr, Radcliffe, Smith, and Wellesley, which were then exclusively women's colleges. She believed that women should be granted equal status with men in the scientific, social, literary, and political fields.

In her private life, she and her husband were patrons of the arts. They were great fans of the music of Richard Wagner, literature, and art. The two were devoted to each other, and their marriage was a partnership in both their personal and professional lives.

Bibliography
Hamalian, Leo, ed. *Ladies on the Loose: Women Travellers of the Eighteenth and Nineteenth Centuries.* New York: Dodd, Mead, 1981. The chapter on Fanny Bullock Workman in this book provides limited biographical information and then an excerpt from *Through Town and Jungle,* which is about bicycling in India. It is the only book that Bullock Workman wrote without her husband. Her comments regarding the native peoples are careful, detailed, and objective.
McHenry, Robert, ed. *Liberty's Women.* Springfield, Mass.: G. and C. Merriam, 1980. This volume includes brief but detailed biographical information. No photos or maps are included. No specific information on any specific expedition is given.
Miller, Luree. *On Top of the World: Five Women Explorers in Tibet.* New York: Paddington Press, 1976. A balanced, very readable account. Discusses some of the controversy that surrounded the couple's treatment of the hired workers and guides during the 1898 expedition in Sikkim. Includes studio photos of Fanny Bullock Workman.
Workman, Fanny Bullock, and William Hunter Workman. *In the Ice World of Himálaya: Among the Peaks and Passes of Ladakh, Nubra, Suru, and Baltistan.* New York: Cassell, 1900. Their first book about the Workmans' Himalayan expeditions. The narration is uneven in content, though it is interesting. In it are harsh

comments about the workers they hired. Many photos and illustrations are provided. Includes a chapter in two parts, one by each author, detailing physiological responses to high altitudes.

—————— . *Two Summers in the Ice-wilds of Eastern Karakoram: The Exploration of Nineteen Hundred Square Miles of Mountain and Glacier*. New York: E. P. Dutton, 1917. The body of this book was written by Fanny, which may account for its warm, personal tone. It includes fine geologic and geographic observations and detailed descriptions. There are also numerous photographs, many of which are fold-out panoramas, of the expedition in progress. Several scientific tables are included.

Marcella Joy

CHIEN-SHIUNG WU

Born: May 29, 1912; Liu Ho, China

Area of Achievement: Physics

Contribution: Wu made significant contributions in the research of nuclear forces and structure, including experiments that overthrew the principle of parity, a basic principle of physics. She is one of the world's leading experimental physicists.

Early Life

Chien-Shiung Wu was born on May 29, 1912, in Liu Ho, China. Her father was a middle school principal, whom she described as always questioning and learning. Both characteristics were learned very well by his daughter. Despite the difficulties of growing up in rural China, Wu often described her childhood as a happy one. She and her two brothers were avid readers. Wu grew up in a small village near Shanghai, just after the fall of the Ching Dynasty and at the beginning of the Republican Era under the leadership of Sun Yat-sen.

Wu attended secondary school in Suchow, a beautiful city called the "Venice of China" by Marco Polo, and located about two hours outside of Shanghai. In secondary school, she studied English and became interested in physics. In China, it was not unusual for females to study science. Now as then females are proportionally more represented in the sciences and engineering in China than in the United States.

By the time Wu was ready to attend college, China was engaged in an armed struggle between nationalist forces under the leadership of Chiang Kai-shek against communist forces lead by Mao Tse-tung, various warlords, and increasing Japanese agitation. Nevertheless, she enrolled at the National Central University in Nanking, a city that later became the capital of China during World War II. Despite the upheaval in China, Wu completed her bachelor of science degree in 1936, only one year before the Japanese invasion of China in 1937.

After graduation, Wu moved to the United States to do graduate work at the University of California at Berkeley, under the direction of noted physicist Ernest Lawrence. Two years later, in 1939, Lawrence became the winner of the Nobel Prize in Physics for his invention of the atom-smashing cyclotron. Wu was an outstanding graduate student and was elected to Phi Beta Kappa. She completed her Ph.D. at Berkeley in 1940.

Life's Work

Following the completion of her doctoral degree in 1940, Chien-Shiung Wu stayed on at the University of California as a research fellow and lecturer until 1941, when she accepted a position as assistant professor at Smith College. In 1942, she was married to fellow physicist Luke Chia-liu Yuan. She taught at Smith for one year before she accepted a position as instructor at Princeton University for the 1943-1944 academic year (her husband had received an appointment at Princeton to work at the

RCA Research Laboratories). After leaving Princeton in 1944, Wu joined the faculty at Columbia University as a senior scientist at the Division of War Research to work on radiation detection. After the war, she remained at Columbia, becoming an associate professor in 1947. After only five years, she was offered a tenured post as a full professor in 1952. After the Communist Party came to power in China in 1949, she decided to remain in the United States and became an American citizen in 1954.

Wu devoted most of her early work to the study of nuclear forces and structure, in particular, beta disintegration. Because of her area of study and her expertise, Tsung Dao Lee, a colleague at Columbia, and Chen Ning Yang, a researcher at the Institute for Advanced Study at Princeton, invited Wu to conduct experiments designed to test their theory related to the principle of conservation of parity.

Parity is a type of symmetry represented by an object and its mirror image. Any system in which the principle of parity conservation is violated will not obey the same physical laws as its image. The only circumstance under which a violation of mirror symmetry can be detected is one in which there is a clear indication on physical grounds of whether the system is right- or left-handed.

This thought led Lee and Yang to propose an experiment involving the beta-decay of a nucleus to test this law. They had written and presented a paper in 1956, entitled "Question of Parity Conservation in Weak Interactions," where they questioned the law of parity. After working out the theoretical bases for a series of experiments to test their theory, they solicited a number of experimental physicists to conduct the actual experiments. As a colleague of Yang, Wu accepted the challenge.

The experiment was carried out in late 1956 by Wu and her associates from the U.S. National Bureau of Standards. Wu and her colleagues used an ultra low-temperature device that cooled radioactive cobalt 60 to a fraction of a degree above absolute zero (459 degrees below zero on the Fahrenheit scale). The physicists applied a magnetic field to the cobalt 60 that made the spinning nuclei align themselves parallel to the applied magnetic field. The aligned cobalt atoms continued to disintegrate, releasing electrons. According to the law of the conservation of parity, half of them should have released their electrons toward one end of the magnetic field and the other half toward the opposite end. Contrary to this hypothesis, however, more electrons were released in one direction than the other. According to Wu, "The results showed that the electrons were emitted preferentially in the direction opposite to that of the nuclear spin and therefore conclusively proved that the beta decay of Cobalt behaves like a left-handed screw." The electrons released more often against the conventional field direction than with it, which indicated a preference for left-handedness. After repeating the process numerous times, Wu and her colleagues successfully demonstrated that the law of the conservation of parity in weak interactions was a false concept. She demonstrated that particles have a "handedness."

With this experiment, Wu disproved what had been considered a basic law of physics, a law that had served as the basis for scientific inquiry for more than thirty years and was said to be a law of nature. Her experiment overturned this law. An article in the *New York Post* on January 22, 1959, described the results of Wu's experiments as "the most important development in nuclear physics since the actual unleashing of atomic energy."

Chien-Shiung Wu also made other important contributions to physics. She and two other colleagues at Columbia in 1963 experimentally confirmed Richard Feynman and Murray Gell-Mann's theory of conservation of vector current in beta decay. In 1966, she published *Beta Decay*, a summary of her research that became the authoritative work in the field. Wu also demonstrated that the electromagnetic radiation from the annihilation of positrons and electrons is polarized. Her experiments in this area confirmed Paul Dirac's theory, thus proving that the electron and positron have opposite parity. She studied the x-ray spectra of muonic atoms and certain biological problems, including the structure of hemoglobin. In 1972, she was named Pupin Professor of Physics, a position she kept until her retirement in 1981.

During and after her distinguished career, Wu held many other professional positions. She was a member of the Advance Committee to the Director of the National Institute of Health from 1975 to 1982. Wu held honorary professorships at Nanjing University, the Science and Technology University, Beijing University, Tsao Hwa University, and Nankai University in the People's Republic of China, and at Padua University in Italy. She also held membership in the National Academy of Science and was an Honorary Fellow in the Royal Society of Edinburgh. Wu was a member of the American Physics Society, where she was president in 1975; the Chinese Academy of Science; and was a fellow in the American Association for the Advancement of Science and the American Academy of Arts and Sciences.

Wu received numerous honorary degrees for her outstanding contributions to physics. She received a Doctor of Science from Princeton in 1958, thus becoming the first woman ever awarded this honor. She received honorary degrees from Smith College in 1959; Goucher College in 1960; Rutgers University in 1961; Yale University in 1967; Russell Sage College in 1971; Harvard University; Bard College, and Adelphi University in 1974; Dickerson College in 1975; and a Doctor of Laws from the Chinese University in Hong Kong in 1969.

Wu was awarded numerous awards during her outstanding professional career. She received the Research Award from the Research Corporation in 1959, becoming the first woman ever to win this annual award for outstanding scientist. She also received the American Asian University Woman Award in 1960, the Comstock Award from the National Academy of Science in 1964, the Achievement Award from the Chi-Tsim Cultural Foundation in 1964, the Scientist of the Year Award from *Industrial Research* magazine in 1974, the Tom Bonner Prize from the American Physics Society in 1975, the National Science Medal in 1975, and the Wolf Prize in Physics in 1978. She was honored at the Nishina Memorial Lectures at the Universities of Tokyo, Osaka, and Kyoto in 1983, and an asteroid was named in her honor in 1990.

Summary

In 1958, Chien-Shiung Wu was called the "world's foremost female experimental physicist" and later would be recognized as one of the world's leading experimental physicists. Her experiments on parity led to a Nobel Prize for the two theoretical physicists, Tsung Dao Lee and Chen Ning Yang, who developed the theory that her experiments verified. Lee and Yang were the first Chinese-born scientists to win the Nobel Prize and among the youngest winners to ever receive a Nobel Prize. Although Wu herself was not recognized by the Nobel committee, her contributions were essential in confirming the theoretical work for which the prize was awarded. As one of the few women to earn distinction in the field of experimental physics, Wu earned the respect of her peers and served to inspire many students—male and female—who studied under her direction. In the citation that accompanied her honorary degree from Princeton University, Wu was congratulated for proving "the unwisdom of underestimating the power of a woman" and for reasserting "the principle of intellectual parity between women and men."

Bibliography
Asimov, Isaac. *Asimov's Biographical Encyclopedia of Science and Technology*. Rev. ed. Garden City, N.Y.: Doubleday, 1972. Provides a brief but interesting and informative account of Tsung Dao Lee and Chen Ning Yang's theory, their lives, and the parity experiment.
Gardner, Martin. *The Ambidextrous Universe*. New York: Basic Books, 1964. Written in language accessible to the general reader, this work contains a thorough survey of the subject of parity. Illustrated.
Life. January 28, 1957, pp. 59-60. A description of Wu's experiment on parity with illustrations and pictures. Discusses the impact of her discovery.
Magill, Frank N., ed. *The Nobel Prize Winners: Physics*. Pasadena, Calif.: Salem Press, 1989. Volume 2 contains articles on 1957 laureates Chen Ning Yang and Tsung-Dao Lee, the two theoretical physicists who developed the theory disputing the conservation of parity. The article on Yang includes a thorough and accessible explanation of Wu's experiment.
Noble, Iris. *Contemporary Women Scientists of America*. New York: Julian Messner, 1979. A short but informative description of Wu and her work, placing her experiences within the context of other American women scientists.
Novick, Robert, ed. *Thirty Years Since Parity Nonconservation: A Symposium for T. D. Lee*. Boston: Birkhäuser, 1988. Wu is one of the contributors to this collection of lectures honoring Lee on the occasion of his sixtieth birthday. Although somewhat technical in its approach, Wu's firsthand account of the initial experiment with cobalt 60 provides a good introduction to the world of experimental physics as it existed in the 1950's.
Yost, Edna. *Women of Modern Science*. New York: Dodd, Mead, 1959. Although dated in tone, this compilation of sketches profiling prominent women scientists provides one of the best introductions to the life and career of Chien-Shiung Wu.

Gregory A. Levitt

HENRIETTE WYETH

Born: October 22, 1907; Wilmington, Delaware

Area of Achievement: Art

Contribution: As a member of the first rank of contemporary American artists, Henriette Wyeth is noted for her murals, her landscape and still life paintings, and her portraits.

Early Life

On October 22, 1907, Ann Henriette Wyeth was the first of five children born to Newell Convers Wyeth, perhaps the most noteworthy illustrator of his time, and his wife Carolyn Brenneman Bockius Wyeth, a beautiful young woman whom he had met during his studies in Delaware. Although the Wyeths' daughter had been named for her two grandmothers, she was known simply as Henriette (pronounced in the French manner as "On-ree-et"). She was born in Wilmington, Delaware, on her father's twenty-fifth birthday and received his special attention throughout her life. In November of 1908, during preparations for the family's Thanksgiving dinner, the young Henriette bit off a piece of an apple she had been playing with and began to choke. After being summoned from his studio, her father picked Henriette up by her ankles and shook her vigorously, dislodging the obstruction in a manner he had learned from his mother. The baby recovered with no aftereffects. About the time of her third birthday, however, she was stricken by poliomyelitis (then known as infantile paralysis). Her family feared for her life, as there was no known cure for the disease. Eventually, Henriette began to walk, talk, and laugh again, suffering only minimal secondary damage to her right hand.

Henriette and her siblings Carolyn, Andrew, Ann, and Nathaniel were reared on an old farmstead in Chadds Ford, Pennsylvania, not far from Wilmington. Life in the family household revolved around strict adherence to a daily schedule established by N. C. Wyeth, who prepared breakfast for the family, completed his own daily chores, and assigned duties to family members as part of each day's plans. After the mundane particulars of life were attended to, N. C. Wyeth turned to his studio work. Because of his own dislike of formal education, he had been sent to illustrator Howard Pyle for instruction. The sketching of geometric forms, plaster casts, and still life arrangements chosen from Wyeth's notable collection of costumes, weaponry, and other props formed the basis of instruction in drawing and painting that he provided in his home school for each of his five children once he believed they were ready to learn. To the discipline of the illustrator's technique, their father added the knowledge of painting that steered the children toward the creative lives they subsequently pursued. As his first student, Henriette impressed her father with her accomplished skill at drawing.

The Wyeth children learned much from their natural surroundings. Henriette was taken for long walks along the banks of the Brandywine River and learned about the historic stand by American forces who made a valiant attempt to rebuff the British advance on Philadelphia at the Battle of Brandywine in September of 1777. The beauty of the countryside, combined with the classics they read and the stories and legends their father recounted to them, served as inspiration to the young Wyeths' artistic sensibilities.

Many incidents from Henriette's childhood were recorded in hundreds of charming letters her father exchanged with his relatives in Needham, Massachusetts. He particularly commented on her untaught and, to use his term, "astounding" understanding of perspective and proportion as revealed in her early work. In turn, Henriette worshiped her father as an infallible instructor, even going so far as to destroy those works inspired by her interest in Impressionism after her father objected to her use of such techniques. She adhered closely to his artistic tastes, even when they bucked the popular tide as exemplified by the Modernist work of Pablo Picasso and his contemporaries. Her father directed the smallest details of her portrait work, counseling her never to paint a woman posed with her legs apart.

In 1921, Henriette began formal academic study at the school connected with the Museum of Art in Boston. Her family had returned to her father's boyhood home in Needham, and she stayed with them there until her courses began. At the age of sixteen in 1923, she enrolled as a student at the Pennsylvania Academy of Fine Arts in Philadelphia. In one of his letters, her father wrote that she was "working hard and doing excellent work" and that he was proud of her willingness to commute by train into the city at 7:00 each morning and return at 5:30 at night. Her apprenticeship at the school marked the beginning of her work as a professional artist.

Life's Work

While still a student, Henriette Wyeth began to accept professional commissions from residents of Wilmington to paint their portraits before branching out to seek commissions elsewhere. At the same time that Wyeth's career as an artist was being launched, she fell in love. On one of her train trips home from Philadelphia in 1924, she met Peter Hurd, a young art student from Haverford College. Hurd, who hailed from New Mexico, was traveling to Chadds Ford in the hope of becoming an apprentice to her father. He was successful in securing the apprenticeship and eventually joined Henriette as a student at the Pennsylvania Academy of Fine Arts. The two were married on June 28, 1929, in the Unitarian church in Wilmington.

Henriette gave birth to a son, Peter Wyeth Hurd, and a daughter, Carol, in the early years of her marriage. In 1932, Hurd was invited to exhibit his work at the Corcoran Gallery in Washington, D.C. Shortly thereafter, he received a commission to paint a mural in his native New Mexico. He accepted the commission and traveled to New Mexico, leaving his wife and their two children behind in Pennsylvania. Upon his arrival, he set about designing an art studio where Wyeth could paint in the clear desert light of the Southwest. Solicitous of his wife's needs, he supervised the construction of the studio himself in order to assure her of a suitable environment in which to work. The studio was nestled in the Hondo Valley along the Ruidoso River, surrounded by national forest lands and looking out on the majestic Centinela peak of the Capitan

Mountains. Wyeth and the children joined him at their new home on Sentinel Ranch in San Patricio, New Mexico. The couple's son Michael was born in New Mexico. Soon, many other artists discovered the attractions of the Southwest, and a thriving art community began to flourish in Santa Fe, New Mexico.

During World War II, Wyeth stayed home with their children while Hurd worked as a war artist and correspondent for *Life* magazine, covering the activities of the U.S. Army Air Force in England during 1942 and spending five months in Italy, South America, Africa, India, and Saudi Arabia with the U.S. Air Transport Command during 1944. While focusing on rearing her children, Wyeth worked on many of her paintings during this period.

Wyeth maintained a disciplined lifestyle, keeping to a daily schedule of painting in order to fulfill her commissions while at the same time running her household and caring for her family. She garnered acclaim for her portraits, and a number of prominent women chose to sit for her, including Helen Hayes, First Lady Pat Nixon, and Mrs. John D. Rockefeller III. Her work is perhaps best classified as super realism—a realism informed by Impressionism's preoccupation with light, Abstraction Lyrique's brush work, and Musee Imaginaire's symbols.

The 1960's were a busy time for Wyeth and her husband. In 1964, the couple was commissioned to make a cover portrait of President Lyndon B. Johnson for *Time* magazine's "Man of the Year" issue. The following year, Hurd was selected to paint the official presidential portrait of Johnson for the White House Historical Association. Although Johnson himself rejected the portrait as "the ugliest thing I ever saw," the portrait was eventually housed at the National Portrait Gallery in Washington, D.C. Wyeth accepted an individual commission from *Time* magazine in 1963 to produce a cover portrait of her brother Andrew Wyeth. Many members of the Wyeth family served as subjects in Henriette Wyeth's portraits.

As the area around Santa Fe and Roswell, New Mexico, continued to attract more art aficionados, the cities became distinguished art centers. Special exhibits of Wyeth's work and that of her husband appeared at the Roswell Museum and Art Center and at the Gerald Peters Gallery in Santa Fe. The Brandywine River Museum in her hometown of Chadds Ford, Pennsylvania, also launched a retrospective of her works. Her paintings hung in many private and permanent public collections, including those at the Art Institute of Chicago, the Carnegie Institute in Pittsburgh, the Columbus Museum of Art in Ohio, the Delaware Art Museum in Wilmington, the Foundation of New York State University, the Museum of Texas Tech University in Lubbock, the New Britain Museum of American Art in Connecticut, and the National Portrait Gallery in Washington, D.C. She earned special acclaim in her adopted state when she was given the Governor's Award by the state of New Mexico in 1981.

Wyeth's husband, Peter Hurd, died on July 9, 1984, in Roswell. After his death, Wyeth continued to live alone at their ranch in San Patricio. Two of her own children had become recognized as artists in their own right and the third a noted musician. She herself continued to work as an artist into the early 1990's, mastering the challenges of encroaching age by learning to paint using both of her hands.

Summary

As a member of a noted artistic family and the wife of a distinguished muralist, Henriette Wyeth found herself somewhat overshadowed by the accomplishments of her father, her brother, and her husband. Nevertheless, her work merits attention both for her ability to capture the vitality and warmth of her subjects and her determination to pursue her artistic career at the same time that she cared for her family. Following the example of her father, Henriette Wyeth found opportunities to encourage the artistic talents of her children. Having sought academic training in art at a time when many women were discouraged from pursuing such a bohemian career, Wyeth continued to seek commissions as a professional after marriage and motherhood. Although she supported a conservative view of women's purpose in life, believing that the demands of motherhood ought to be given precedence, Wyeth also voiced her conviction that women should be well educated in order to achieve their dreams and take full pride in their own accomplishments.

Bibliography

Corn, Wanda M. *The Art of Andrew Wyeth*. New York: New York Graphic Society for the Fine Arts Museum of San Francisco, 1973. The illustrations in this stunningly rendered collection of works by the artist's brother, Andrew, are accompanied by a written commentary with many quotations from Henriette Wyeth. Includes bibliography of additional sources on the Wyeth family.

Dallas Museum of Fine Arts. *Famous Families in American Art*. Dallas: Author, 1960. Fascinating study of the proclivity for creative expression through art among the carefully nurtured progeny of celebrated families. Includes profiles of Henriette Wyeth, her siblings, and their offspring.

Meryman, Richard. *First Impressions: Andrew Wyeth*. New York: Harry N. Abrams, 1991. This short work focuses on the career of Andrew Wyeth, as seen by his personal friend and longtime biographer, Richard Meryman. Includes commentary and recollections by Henriette Wyeth and her husband about family life with her father. Illustrated with photographs, reproductions of magazine art, and portraits of family members.

Meryman, Richard, and David Allen Harvey. "The Wyeth Family: American Visions." *National Geographic* 180 (July, 1991): 78-109. This survey of the lives of the amazing Wyeths begins with the immigrant Swiss parents of N. C. Wyeth and continues through his great grandchildren, particularly those who are actively involved in the creative art-world of the 1990's. Color photographs of family members and reproductions of their works make up approximately half of this thirty-two page article.

Wyeth, Newell C. *The Wyeths: The Letters of N. C. Wyeth, 1901-1945*. Edited by Betsy James Wyeth. Boston: Gambit, 1971. After his sudden death at a railroad crossing in Chadds Ford, N. C. Wyeth's daughter-in-law took on the massive task of sorting through Newell Wyeth's extensive correspondence. The resulting work chronicles his life from art school in Wilmington through the arrival of his grandchildren, one of whom was killed with him in 1945. Provides special insights into his daughter Henriette's childhood.

Betsey Pender

ROSALYN S. YALOW

Born: July 19, 1921; New York, New York

Areas of Achievement: Biochemistry and medicine
Contribution: Yalow was instrumental in the development of the radioimmunoassay
technique for the measurement of minute quantities of biological materials. For her
work, Yalow was awarded a 1977 Nobel Prize in Physiology or Medicine.

Early Life

Rosalyn Sussman was born on July 19, 1921, in the New York City borough of the
South Bronx. She was the second child, and first daughter, of Simon Sussman and
Clara Zipper Sussman. Neither of her parents had any significant level of formal
education. Simon Sussman, a Russian Jew born on the Lower East Side, never
finished grade school. He earned a living with a paper and twine business. Yalow's
mother, Clara, had emigrated from Germany at the age of four. Nevertheless, in a
scenario common to Jewish families in New York, the parents were determined that
both Rosalyn and her older brother Alexander would receive a good education.

Rosalyn Sussman was described by one of her biographers as a "precocious,
stubborn and determined child." Along with her brother, Rosalyn made frequent trips
to the local library, and she was a reader prior to even entering kindergarten. Her
formal schooling set the stage for her later work. Attending local public schools,
Rosalyn developed a strong interest in mathematics by the seventh grade, and in
chemistry while attending Walton High School.

While enrolled at Hunter College, Sussman read the recently published biography
of Marie Curie written by Eve Curie, the daughter of the great scientist. Sussman later
recommended the book to women interested in careers in science. A colloquium on
nuclear fission sponsored by Enrico Fermi and strong support from her professors
convinced Sussman that she should consider a career in physics. In 1941, Rosalyn
Sussman became the first graduate with a degree in physics from Hunter College.

Despite the reluctance of graduate schools to accept and support women in physics
(the message of Marie Curie often being forgotten), Sussman was offered a teaching
assistantship in that area of science at the University of Illinois in Champaign-Urbana.
She was the only woman among four hundred students and the first woman within
that college (engineering) since 1917. Ironically, on the first day of school, she met a
physics student named Aaron Yalow, whom she would marry in June, 1943. Rosalyn
Yalow received her Ph.D. degree in physics in 1945.

Life's Work

Rosalyn Yalow's graduate career in nuclear physics was strongly influenced by her
adviser, Maurice Goldhaber, and his wife Gertrude, who was also a physicist. Under
their direction, Yalow became competent in the safe handling of radioisotopes and in
the use of apparatuses for their measurement. Yalow's first job following her gradu-

ation was as an assistant engineer, and the only female engineer, at Federal Telecommunications Laboratory (FTL) in New York. Since Aaron Yalow had not yet completed the work for his thesis, Rosalyn returned to New York alone. Aaron Yalow joined her in late 1945, joining the staff at Montefiore Hospital as a medical physicist.

In 1946, with the closing of FTL, Yalow returned to Hunter College as a physics instructor for veterans returning from the war. During this period, Yalow also began developing an interest in medical research. Taking advantage of her husband's contacts, Yalow met Edith Quimby, a medical researcher at New York's Columbia College of Physicians and Surgeons. Since Quimby was interested in the application of physics to medical research. Yalow volunteered to work in Quimby's laboratory, gaining experience in the use of radioisotopes for such research.

During the early postwar period, Yalow's expanding knowledge and experience in this particular scientific field was a rare commodity. In December, 1946, she was hired as a "part-time" consultant in the newly opened Radioisotope Section of the Bronx Veterans Administration (VA) Hospital, a place that Yalow considered to be the first organization to "recognize the importance of radioisotopes in medicine." The facilities at the hospital were crude, to say the least. One portion of the facilities was located in a converted janitor's closet. Of necessity, Yalow was forced to design and build much of the equipment for the laboratory. Yalow's research at the VA Hospital focused on the application of nuclear materials to medical diagnosis and therapy. She was highly successful in this endeavor, producing numerous publications and receiving official support and recognition from the Veterans Administration.

By 1950, Yalow had resigned her position at Hunter College to become a full-time member of the VA staff. That same year, a thirty-two-year-old resident at the VA Hospital, Solomon Berson, was appointed to Yalow's group, becoming chief of the service four years later. Berson and Yalow began an extensive collaboration, each supporting the other: Yalow provided the experience in mathematics and nuclear medicine, and Berson provided the necessary clinical expertise. Their collaboration continued for more than two decades, ending only with Berson's death in 1972.

Yalow and Berson began their collaboration by attempting to improve the application of radioisotopes in the clinical diagnosis of disease. Specifically, they developed a method for measuring the rate at which a radioactive isotope of iodine (Iodine-131) is metabolized. When their first publication on the subject appeared in 1952, it was hailed as an important contribution to the use of diagnostic tracers in medicine.

Shortly thereafter, Yalow and Berson began applying their techniques to the analysis of proteins in blood serum. Their initial investigations centered on the metabolism of insulin, the protein hormone in the blood which regulates sugar levels. The researchers observed the abnormally slow disappearance of injected insulin from the blood of patients with adult-onset diabetes and correctly deduced that the cause was the binding of antibodies directed against the foreign molecules of injected insulin obtained from cattle or pigs. The result of such antibody production was the binding and retention of insulin molecules. Ironically, this early work was initially rejected for publication.

In order to carry out this research, it was necessary to be able to measure minute quantities of insulin protein. Existing procedures, however, were inadequate for such fine measurements. For that reason, Yalow and Berson developed the technique of radioimmunoassay (RIA) for the measurement of insulin. The procedure consisted of adding various amounts of unlabeled insulin to a mixture of radioactive insulin bound with antibody. Increasing quantities of unlabeled insulin would displace bound material in a proportionate fashion: In a similar manner, unknown levels of the protein could be determined using this technique. Because it enabled minute quantities of radiochemicals to be measured accurately, the technique of radioimmunoassay was immensely more sensitive than were conventional means of analysis. The first papers on the application of radioimmunoassay for the measurement of insulin in blood plasma were published by Yalow and Berson in 1959 and 1960.

In the early 1960's, Yalow and Berson extended their research to the study of other hormones within the body. The RIA procedures they had developed proved to be applicable to a wide variety of studies. Meanwhile, Berson became more involved with administrative work, leaving the research area to Yalow. In 1967, the Veterans Administration Hospital became associated with Mt. Sinai School of Medicine. Berson became chairman of the Department of Medicine, and Yalow eventually became chief of Nuclear Medicine Service, formerly the Radioisotope Section. Yalow was also appointed research professor at Mt. Sinai and, in 1974, she became distinguished research professor at the medical school.

In 1972, Berson's unexpected death ended years of joint study. That same year, Yalow became the first woman appointed senior medical investigator at the VA Hospital. At Yalow's request, her laboratory was renamed the Solomon Berson Research Laboratory.

Numerous awards followed. She was elected to the National Academy of Sciences in 1975 and the American Academy of Arts and Sciences in 1978. In 1976, Yalow became the first woman to receive the Albert Lasker Award for basic medical research. Success did not change her. Prior to the party in her honor, Yalow was seen peeling the potatoes for the salad. Yalow also received many other honorary doctorates and awards. In 1977, she was awarded the Nobel Prize in Physiology or Medicine for the development of techniques. Subsequently, Yalow has served on a wide range of advisory committees and prestigious boards, and as a consultant for numerous national and international organizations.

Summary

Rosalyn S. Yalow was certainly not the first prominent American woman scientist. She was, however, among the first scientists to wed the emerging field of nuclear physics to diagnostic medicine, and her success is an example of how far women have progressed in science.

Yalow's parents, though strong supporters of her education, initially preferred for her a career in the "standard" female profession of education. It was to Yalow's credit that she overcame not only such subtle pressure but also the more overt pressure that settling in what was previously an overwhelmingly male scientific field entailed. As Marie Curie was a role model for Yalow, so too is Rosalyn Yalow a role model for women who wish to pursue a career in science.

Yalow's success was not of value only to women. The methodology that she and Berson developed had benefits and applications far beyond the initial area of diabetic research. The RIA technique has subsequently been applied to measurements of most serum proteins, vitamins, drugs, and hundreds of other substances. There is currently no other available technique that can measure minute changes in concentrations of these substances during various biological states.

Perhaps most important as an educational philosophy was Yalow's view on opportunity. She has always spoken out for equal opportunity. It was no accident that a "tongue in cheek" announcement of the Nobel award stated "Bronx Lady Who Cooks Wins Nobel Prize." Yalow readily admitted that the support of her spouse and the division of labor established within their strong marriage were important components of her success. Mobility and success ultimately must depend on what people themselves do, not on what is simply provided for them.

Bibliography

Magill, Frank N., ed. "Rosalyn S. Yalow." In *The Nobel Prize Winners: Physiology or Medicine*. 3 vols. Pasadena, Calif.: Salem Press, 1991. Provides a thorough synopsis of Yalow's work and discusses the acclaim that followed the awarding of the prize. A well-written source for information on Yalow's life and career. Included is a list of the subject's important publications.

Moss, Alfred J., Jr., Glenn V. Dalrymple, and Charles M. Boyd, eds. *Practical Radioimmunoassay*. St. Louis, Mo.: C. V. Mosby, 1976. An early text on RIA procedures. Though written primarily for a scientific audience, it is also useful as an introduction to radioimmunoassay techniques. Provides a relatively concise overview of the subject.

Opfell, Olga S. *The Lady Laureates: Women Who Have Won the Nobel Prize*. Metuchen, N.J.: Scarecrow Press, 1978. A concise account of Yalow's life and career. It emphasizes Yalow's biography rather than her scientific work, but it is nevertheless a fine source regarding her early career.

Shepherd, Linda Jean. *Lifting the Veil: The Feminine Face of Science*. Boston: Shambhala, 1993. With training both in biochemistry and psychology, the author presents an alternative philosophical approach to scientific research. The author's thesis is that certain feminine attributes may be used to observe science from other perspectives. Among these characteristics may be found a sense of intuition and connection, with the innate ability to perceive the consequences of actions associated with experimentation.

Stone, Elizabeth. "Mme. Curie from the Bronx." *The New York Times Magazine*, April 9, 1978, 29-36, 95-104. An excellent description of the personal and scientific life of Yalow. The article contains the subject's views on a variety of topics, including the role of women in science, and views on her own career and marriage.

Included in the story is the background of the research that provided the framework for Yalow's own work.

Richard Adler

KRISTI YAMAGUCHI

Born: June 12, 1971; Hayward, California

Area of Achievement: Sports

Contribution: Yamaguchi's athleticism and artistry earned for her the gold medal in woman's figure skating at the 1990 Olympics in Albertville, France, making her the fifth American woman to win this honor. In 1992, she became the first American woman since Peggy Fleming in 1968 to defend her World Championship title.

Early Life

Kristi Tsuya Yamaguchi was born on July 12, 1971, in Hayward, California, the second of three children of Jim and Carole (Doi) Yamaguchi. Her grandparents and parents, along with 120,000 other Japanese Americans, were detained in internment camps in the United States during World War II. Neither her grandparents nor her parents discussed their ordeal much with Kristi, but they often reminded her that she was extremely fortunate to have had the opportunities that she has been afforded.

Kristi was born with clubfeet and had to wear special casts for one year to straighten them. Her doctor then required her to wear corrective shoes for four additional years to ensure that her feet would remain straight. As a result, she learned to walk while wearing these heavy corrective shoes.

Her father Jim is a dentist and her mother, Carole is a dental assistant. Her older sister Lori and her younger brother Brett share her interest in sports. While growing up, Kristi and Lori especially liked playing together. Before Kristi began first grade, she practiced dancing in her sister's dance classes. Her mother thought that the exercise would help strengthen her feet, and she allowed Kristi to join the class herself. Kristi also practiced ballet, tap dancing, and tumbling. It was not long before Kristi demonstrated a high level of grace and coordination.

One day, when Kristi was four years old, she accompanied her mother to a local shopping mall and was captivated by the ice skating show that was being held there. Although Kristi wanted to learn to skate her mother insisted that she wait until she began school. Almost immediately after Kristi started school, her mother took her to a local skating rink for the first time. Kristi fell in love with skating from the first moment she put on the skates. She returned to the rink once a week until her parents enrolled her in the junior skating program, where she learned to stand up and to skate. It was not long before she also learned to glide across the ice and to spin.

Because of Kristi's insistence and her continued interest in skating, her mother took her to see all the local ice skating shows. Kristi was determined to skate in one of these shows and asked her parents if she could take private lessons to help her achieve this goal. Realizing their daughter's great interest in the sport, they agreed. At the age of five, Kristi began private skating lessons.

Like many other top athletes, Kristi Yamaguchi found it difficult to attend school regularly while she underwent intensive training in her chosen sport. From her very early years in elementary school and throughout her high school years, she received private tutoring and attended school on a part-time basis. Yamaguchi eventually was graduated from Mission High School in Fremont, California, in 1989. After graduation, she enrolled in the University of Alberta, in Edmonton, Alberta, Canada, in order to continue training with her longtime coach, Christy Kjarsgaard.

From the beginning, Yamaguchi's parents and her grandparents were very supportive of her interest in skating. After winning her first competition at age six, her parents enrolled Yamaguchi in a summer camp for skaters in Santa Rosa, California. It was there that she met a camp instructor named Christy Kjarsgaard who quickly became her favorite instructor. After returning from the camp, Yamaguchi informed her parents about this instructor, and they decided to contact Kjarsgaard to ask her to be their daughter's coach. Once Kjarsgaard became Yamaguchi's coach, the two began to meet regularly for a practice schedule that began at four o'clock each morning. Christy Kjarsgaard was a fine skater and an exceptional coach who worked well with Yamaguchi. Unlike many skaters who change coaches regularly, Kjarsgaard and Yamaguchi have remained together beyond Yamaguchi's amateur years to her professional career.

In 1983, at the age of twelve, Yamaguchi teamed with Rudi Galindo, under the direction of coach Jim Hulick, to add pairs competition to her skating program. This additional training increased her practice time and decreased the time she could spend in school and be with other kids her own age. Nevertheless, Yamaguchi was eager to compete in both singles and pairs events.

Life's Work

Kristi Yamaguchi competed at the juniors level in singles and pairs skating competitions from 1985 to 1988. In 1985, she and her partner, Rudi Galindo, placed fifth in the National Junior Championships in Kansas City, Missouri. In 1986, Yamaguchi placed first in the Central Pacific Championships, in the Junior Ladies singles division. Her winning performance qualified her to compete in the National Championships, where she finished fourth. At these same championships, she and Rudi placed first in the pairs competition.

The year 1987 was an extremely important one for Yamaguchi. She repeated as champion in the Central Pacific Championships, placed first in the Merano Spring Trophy, and placed second in the United States National Championships. These performances established Yamaguchi as one of the best young skaters in the United States. Yamaguchi and Galindo also repeated as pairs champions.

In 1988, Yamaguchi captured the Central Pacific Championship for the third straight year, and placed first in the World Junior Championships. She and Galindo also placed first in the World Junior Championships, making her the first person to ever win gold medals in two separate events at the World Junior Championships. Yamaguchi established her claim as the best junior skater in the world, and she and Rudi were recognized as the best junior pairs skaters in the world. The Women's Sports Foundation named Yamaguchi the Up-and-Coming Artistic Athlete of the Year.

Yamaguchi was ready to compete against the seniors.

Yamaguchi's first competition in the Ladies division was at the 1988 United States Nationals. She finished in a very respectable tenth place, behind more experienced American women such as Jill Trenary and Debi Thomas. Although Yamaguchi continued to skate in pairs competition with Galindo, it was becoming clear that singles competition at the senior level would demand Yamaguchi's entire attention if she wished to advance further.

In early 1989, pairs coach Jim Hulick informed Yamaguchi and Galindo that he had cancer. He abandoned all his coaching duties except for his work with them. Hulick spent six weeks in the hospital receiving radiation treatments and underwent a blood transfusion one week before the competition that enabled him to attend the United States National Championships in Baltimore, Maryland. Yamaguchi and Galindo agreed that they should give their coach their best possible performance. During the competition, they performed a triple flip, a difficult maneuver that no other pair in the world had ever done, and executed perfect side-by-side double axles. As a result of this performance, they won the gold medal—something that no one had expected from such a young pair of skaters. Yamaguchi also skated superbly in the singles events and finished a close second behind Jill Trenary. Thus, Yamaguchi became the first woman to win two medals at the National Championships since Margaret Graham had done so in 1954. She and Rudi Galindo qualified for the World Championships in Paris, France, where they finished in fifth place. Yamaguchi finished sixth in singles. She also finished first in the Olympic Festival and in Skate Canada.

Christy Kjarsgaard, Yamaguchi's singles coach, decided to move to Canada and get married. This required Kristi to fly to Edmonton, Canada, every other week for a few practice sessions. In June of 1989, on the day after she graduated from Mission High School, Yamaguchi moved to Edmonton to continue her training and live with Christy and her husband, Andrew Ness. Still, she had to return to Fremont, California, once a month to train with Galindo for pairs competitions. In December of 1989, pairs coach Jim Hulick died of cancer, and five days later Yamaguchi's grandfather died.

These personal losses took a heavy toll on Yamaguchi. At the 1990 World Championships, she and Galindo again finished fifth in the pairs, and she finished fourth in singles. After this event, Yamaguchi took the advice of many others and dropped out of further pairs competition. She and Galindo never competed again as a pair. Although Galindo was devastated by her decision, he realized that their work together had suffered after they had lost their longtime coach.

Yamaguchi took her disappointing finish as a reason to rededicate herself to skating. She began a strenuous weight lifting program to increase her strength. Four months later, she placed first in the Goodwill Games by defeating fellow American Jill Trenary. Later in 1990, Yamaguchi defeated the outstanding Japanese skater Midori Ito to win the gold medal at Skate America. She finished second in the National Championships, fourth in the World Championships, and first in the Nations Cup.

In 1991, Yamaguchi again finished second in the National Championships to Tonya Harding of Portland, Oregon, who had become only the second woman in the world to complete the difficult triple axle. Determined to improve her routine, Yamaguchi later finished first in the World Championships still without the triple axle. Her winning skating routine was one of the most technically difficult in the world—it included seven triple jumps, a feat matched only by Midori Ito—and it was also one of the most artistically beautiful programs.

Yamaguchi's most successful year as an amateur began in 1992. She established herself as the premier singles skater in the world by winning the United States National Championships. As a result, she held two of the premier titles in the world of women's figure skating and had positioned herself as one of the favorites for the gold medal in the upcoming Winter Olympics in Albertville, France. Fellow skaters Tonya Harding and Midori Ito were still the only two female skaters to complete the difficult triple axle jump successfully in competition. Without this jump, Yamaguchi thought it would be difficult, if not impossible, to win the Olympic gold medal.

During the Olympic competition, all of the top six skaters fell, including Yamaguchi, who fell while making the relatively easy triple loop. Except for this minor error, Yamaguchi performed near flawlessly to capture the gold, thus becoming the first female American figure skater since Dorothy Hamill in 1976 to win the Olympic Championship. In her routine, Yamaguchi performed an opening triple lutz jump into a triple toe loop, a combination her coach called as difficult as the triple axle. Yamaguchi's program kept the crowd spellbound, and she received excellent marks from the judges. Out of a perfect score of 6.0, she received five 5.7's and four 5.8's in the technical category and one 5.8 and nine 5.9's in the artistic category. The judges were impressed with the variety of her skating skills as well as her artistry, grace, and speed. Midori Ito finished second and Nancy Kerrigan of the United States finished third. In the following month, Yamaguchi became the first American skater since Peggy Fleming in 1968 to defend her World Championship title and win.

Following these accomplishments, Yamaguchi decided to turn professional and traveled on several ice show tours. Although she did not attempt to defend her gold medal in the 1994 Olympics in Lillehammer, Norway, Yamaguchi has suggested that she may attempt to skate competitively as an amateur once again, possibly in pairs competition. New Olympic regulations allowing professionals to requalify as amateurs have left open the possibility of Yamaguchi competing in events at the 1998 Winter Olympics.

Summary

Kristi Yamaguchi is known both for her technical and her artistic abilities as a figure skater. Yamaguchi's routines were among the most difficult ever performed by a female skater and were notable for their demonstration of Yamaguchi's athleticism and artistry. Her hard work and dedication to her chosen sport has served to inspire a new generation of skaters. She has become one of the best skaters of all time, joining the company of such skating legends as Sonja Henie, Katarina Witt, Peggy Fleming, and Carol Heiss. Yamaguchi has also capitalized on her Olympic success and immense popularity and has signed numerous commercial endorsements. In addition to increasing public awareness of women's achievements in the world of sports, Yamaguchi's endorsements have allowed her to provide financial support for other young women athletes, particularly in the field of figure skating. Her visibility as one of the first notable world-class American athletes of Japanese descent has also served as a beacon of hope in the wake of the bitter legacy of Japanese American internment during World War II.

Bibliography

Deford, Frank. "The Jewel of the Winter Games." *Newsweek* 119 (February 10, 1992): 46-53. A discussion of the showdown between Yamaguchi and Japan's Midori Ito at the 1992 Winter Olympics in Albertville, France. Includes a profile of both skaters, highlighting details about their personal lives.

Donohue, Shiobhan. *Kristi Yamaguchi: Artist on Ice.* Minneapolis, Minn.: Lerner, 1994. Written for the intermediate reader, this juvenile biography serves as a good introduction to Yamaguchi's career as an amateur and a professional figure skater.

Kurashige, Scott. "Kristi Yamaguchi." In *Japanese American History*, edited by Brian Niiya. New York: Facts on File, 1993. This brief entry on Yamaguchi contains the highlights of her skating career and identifies her heritage as a Yonsei, or fourth-generation Japanese American.

Rambeck, Richard. *Kristi Yamaguchi.* Mankato, Minn.: Child's World, 1993. A well-written biography for the young reader, this work provides an informative overview of Yamaguchi's career.

Swift, E. M. "All That Glitters." *Sports Illustrated* 77 (December 14, 1992): 70-80. An informative profile of two pairs of Olympic competitors—skaters Yamaguchi and Ito from the 1992 Winter games and gymnasts Kim Zmeskal and Shannon Miller from the 1992 Summer games—and the important lessons they learned from their victories and their disappointments. Emphasizes the importance of these women in providing encouragement to other young athletic hopefuls.

—————. "Stirring." *Sports Illustrated* 77 (March 2, 1992): 16-21. One sportswriter's paean to the gracefulness and strength exhibited by Yamaguchi during her medal-winning performance at the 1992 Winter Olympics. Swift comments on Yamaguchi's ability to land "her jumps so softly it seemed as if she were skating in her slippers."

Gregory A. Levitt

"BABE" DIDRIKSON ZAHARIAS

Born: June 26, 1914; Port Arthur, Texas
Died: September 27, 1956; Galveston, Texas
Area of Achievement: Sports
Contribution: The most versatile woman athlete in the history of American sport, Babe Didrikson Zaharias created a national consciousness of women in sport and set standards yet to be matched.

Early Life

Mildred Ella Didriksen was born in Port Arthur, Texas, on June 26, 1914. She was the sixth of seven children born to Ole and Hannah Didriksen, who were recent Norwegian immigrants. (She would later change the name to Didrikson.) A former ship's carpenter, her father made his living as a cabinetmaker and woodworker. Her mother Hannah, most at home with chores of motherhood, never mastered English or fully adjusted to life in the United States.

In 1914, Ole settled his family in the roughneck South End of Beaumont, Texas. In her new surroundings, Mildred grew to young womanhood without benefit of social graces. From the beginning, she was a street urchin who rose above conventional femininity (later she would brag of never having worn brassieres) by excelling in fighting, roller-skating, marbles, track, and pick-up baseball. As adults, neighborhood boys would brag that the famous athlete had outfought them with her fists. She taught herself to run hurdles by jumping the neighborhood hedges. Because she was a powerful homerun hitter, she was called "Babe" in honor of Babe Ruth. Like Ruth, she was a scrappy, cocksure extrovert who could play to the crowd and promote herself to greatness.

At Beaumont Senior High School, Babe excelled in volleyball, tennis, swimming, baseball, and basketball. Had the Texas League rules allowed her, she would have kicked for the football team. In the 1920's, basketball was the premier female sport. Unfortunately, few colleges maintained women's programs. Women seeking top-level competition played for semiprofessional teams sponsored by corporations. Employed as office workers, their real value was measured by their skills in sports. Babe Didrikson dropped out of Beaumont Senior High School during her junior year to play basketball for the Golden Cyclone Athletic Club of the Employers Casualty Insurance Company in Dallas.

Life's Work

During her years with Employers Casualty, Babe Didrikson became the most accomplished female athlete in the world. She was an Amateur Athletic Union (AAU) All-American in basketball in 1930, 1931, and 1932. She won the 1932 AAU track and field championship as a one-woman team, finishing eight points ahead of the twenty-two-woman second place team.

Didrikson perfected the fine art of self-promotion, demanding and often receiving special treatment. She was the only woman allowed by the AAU to compete in more than three events. In the summer of 1932, she was twenty-one years old, but claimed to be nineteen in order to increase the miraculous nature of her already incredible feats. On the train to Los Angeles for the 1932 Olympic Games, Didrikson infuriated her teammates by constantly and publicly proclaiming herself to be the greatest athlete of the time. At Los Angeles, she set world records in the javelin and the hurdles. She would have claimed the high jump as well, but the officials judged her winning jump "a dive" and awarded her the silver medal.

In November, after the Olympics, Didrikson appeared in an advertisement endorsing the Dodge coupe. She also began driving such a car, the price of which far outreached her stenographer's salary. As a result, the AAU declared her a professional and suspended her from further competition. Since no real opportunities existed for women professionals, Didrikson was forced to trade on her amateur fame. She appeared in vaudeville, singing, playing the harmonica, and performing athletic feats; she also toured the backroads of America exhibiting her skills in billiards, basketball, and baseball. Didrikson was more of a circus act than an athlete, but she earned more than forty thousand dollars in a three-year period. Most of this money went to her family in Beaumont, who had become increasingly dependent on her support.

Babe Didrikson had always been an outsider. Once she became a professional, she was pictured as the perfect example of everything unladylike in American culture. Her competitive nature was seen as presumption. Her confidence and fun-loving spirit were interpreted as arrogance. The slogan, "Don't be a muscle moll," began appearing on banners in women's gyms.

In 1933, Babe Didrikson turned to golf in earnest. For six months, she worked between eight and ten hours a day, hitting more than a thousand practice balls. When her hands blistered and bled, she covered them with tape and continued.

Didrikson actually had three separate careers in golf. The first was occasioned by her victory in the 1935 Texas Women's Amateur. Golf was a country club sport in Texas, and the ladies of the Texas Women's Golf Association were not anxious to welcome a scrappy muscle moll from the South End of Beaumont. They successfully appealed to the United States Golf Association to ban Didrikson from further amateur competitions. At that time, the Western Open was the only women's golf tournament open to professionals.

As a professional golfer, Didrikson had no choice but to turn herself once again into a circus act. She signed a contract to endorse the golf equipment of Wilson Sporting Goods, and she set about on a barnstorming tour of exhibitions. Throughout 1935 and 1936, she toured with premier male professional Gene Sarazen. Her natural showmanship made her a big draw. She could drive the ball more than 250 yards, farther than most men of that era. In addition, she could entertain on the harmonica, and, most engaging of all, banter with the crowd: "Well, I'm just gonna have to loosen my girdle and let 'er fly!"

During this period, Didrikson became close friends with R. L. and Bertha Bowen, an influential Fort Worth couple. They were immediately protective of the scrappy tomboy and sought to transform her into a gentle and sophisticated woman. Didrikson adopted Nieman Marcus clothes, learned about cosmetics and hair styling, and began to think of herself as a businesswoman. Sportswriters who had extolled her rough edges began to credit her with the looks and casual authority of a professional model.

Babe Didrikson's second golf career was engineered by her husband, George Zaharias. She met Zaharias when they were paired together for the first two rounds of the 1938 Los Angeles Open. (That she was playing in a man's tournament indicates the scarcity of female professional competition.) They were married in December of 1938. Zaharias reasoned that if Didrikson wanted to establish herself as the greatest golfer in the world, she would have to do it as an amateur. He unearthed a clause in the U.S. Golf Association by-laws that allowed players who had not been a professional for more than five years to apply for reinstatement as an amateur if they refrained from accepting endorsement, appearance, or prize money for three years.

Zaharias had become famous as a professional wrestler, and his six-figure income from promoting wrestling matches and other entrepreneurial operations such as real estate was ample enough to support his wife and her ever-dependent family. The hiatus from competition gave Babe Didrikson Zaharias a chance to recast herself in a more feminine role, refining her expertise in growing numerous varieties of roses, designing and sewing her own sweaters and culottes, and decorating her home.

Nevertheless, the essential athlete would not stay inside for long. She dedicated herself to eighteen months of intense tennis practice until she was ready to enter tournaments, but the United States Lawn Tennis Association would not accept her as an amateur. With no hope of ever winning championships, she simply gave up the game. She also took up bowling in her usual disciplined fashion and competed in local leagues, often receiving bowling scores of more than 200 points.

Babe Didrikson Zaharias did not lose sight of her goals in golf. In 1940, she won the Western Open and the Texas Open, although she could not accept the first prize money. World War II made Babe's reinstatement period somewhat more palatable. Major golf championships were suspended, so she did not suffer from missed opportunities. She kept herself before the public as one of a number of celebrities who gave golf exhibitions to sell war bonds.

In 1943, she began an amateur golf career that included numerous large and small championships. From 1946 to 1947, she won a string of thirteen straight championships, but it was not until she captured the United States Women's Amateur in 1946 and the British Women's Amateur in 1947 that she felt she had established herself as the world's greatest woman golfer. After the British triumph, she turned professional again and set about a third golf career.

In 1949 Babe Zaharias, her husband George, and colleague Patty Berg negotiated with Wilson Sporting Goods for $15,000 seed money for a women's professional golf tour. The Ladies Professional Golfer's Association (LPGA) was born. The first year saw nine events; by 1953, there were twenty-four tournaments and $120,000 in prize money.

The tour afforded Zaharias a place to be her cocksure show-business self. The number one draw, she thrilled the crowds not only with her golf but also with her impromptu harmonica and singing concerts and nonstop banter. As a professional and amateur, she won eighty-two golf tournaments, but nothing so embodied the spirit, courage, and outright tenacity that was Babe Didrikson Zaharias than the last two years of her competitive golf life.

In April of 1953, within two weeks of birdieing the final hole to win an LPGA event named in her honor in Beaumont, Zaharias underwent surgery for rectal cancer which included a colostomy. Cautiously, doctors said she might have her strength back within a year, but they publicly feared that the competitive life of the century's greatest female athlete was over.

In August of 1953, she entered the All American Open at Chicago and, after a rocky start, hung on for fifteenth place. The next week she was third in the World Championship. The Babe was back. In 1954, she won five tournaments and was second leading money winner on the LPGA tour. Her crowning achievement, a stunning example for other cancer and colostomy victims, was winning the 1954 U.S. Women's Open by twelve strokes. She added two more tournament victories in early 1955 before cancer sidelined her permanently. After a long and painful battle waged in the only way she knew, with courage and optimism, Babe Didrikson Zaharias died in September of 1956.

Summary

Babe Didrikson Zaharias was voted Woman Athlete of the Year in 1932, 1945, 1946, 1947, 1950 and 1954. In 1949, she was voted the greatest female athlete of the half century. She was without qualification or competition the most naturally talented woman athlete known to history. Yet, her importance to American life far transcends her achievements. An immigrant's tomboy daughter who struggled up from poverty, she fought snobbery and prejudice almost every day of her life, but she proved that people not born to privilege could control the reins of their own destinies. In her lifetime, she may never have proven truly that athletics were "ladylike," but her example went a long way toward proving that "ladies" could excel at athletics. By turning professional at a time when there were no organized opportunities, she proved women could be astute businesspeople and create and manage their own careers. In helping to create the LPGA, she provided a means for other women to earn a living much more easily than she had. Every female golfer who earns her own way owes a great debt to a handful of visionaries, Babe Didrikson Zaharias and Patty Berg foremost among them. Perhaps her greatest contribution comes in that nothing so distinguished her life as her departure from it. Like that scrappy kid from the wrong side of the Beaumont tracks, the woman who was Babe Didrikson Zaharias never stopped believing in the inevitability of victory, never surrendered hope, and knew to the end that courage alone made her larger than life.

Bibliography
Glenn, Rhonda. *The Illustrated History of Women's Golf.* Dallas, Tex.: Taylor, 1991.

A richly detailed look at nearly one hundred years of women's competitive golf, carefully constructed from archives, print sources, and oral histories. Excellent photographs, solid bibliography.

Johnson, William Oscar, and Nancy P. Williamson. *"Whatta-Gal": The Babe Didrikson Story*. Boston: Little, Brown, 1977. The most complete look at the complex history and personality of Babe Didrikson Zaharias. Nonjudgmental, occasionally sentimental rather than analytical. Excellent use of personal letters, print sources, oral histories.

Nickerson, Elinor. *Golf: A Women's History*. Jefferson, N.C.: McFarland, 1987. The first book to concentrate on the role of women in golf's development. A tight rendering of the essential data without the richness of Rhonda Glenn's book.

Roberts, David. "The Babe Is Here." *Women's Sports and Fitness* 12 (November/December 1990): 42-45. An intelligent profile which attempts analysis of Didrikson's competitive contradictions and androgyny, and assesses her ultimate impact on the world of women's athletics.

Wind, Herbert Warren. *The Story of American Golf*. New York: Simon & Schuster, 1956. The most distinguished golf writer in the history of American journalism writes insightfully and lovingly about "the Babe."

Zaharias, Babe Didrikson, as told to Harry Paxton. *This Life I've Led: My Autobiography*. New York: A. S. Barnes, 1955. A richly detailed, but mostly rosy rendering of her life in Babe's "own words." Useful, but provides best insights when read in conjunction with *"Whatta-Gal."*

Dexter Westrum

ELLEN TAAFFE ZWILICH

Born: April 30, 1939; Miami, Florida

Area of Achievement: Music
Contribution: One of America's foremost composers of art music, Zwilich became the first woman to win the Pulitzer Prize in music.

Early Life

Born in Miami, the cultural mecca of Florida, Ellen Taaffe was adopted by Ruth Howard Taaffe and Edward Taaffe. Her surname is Irish in origin, although many of her father's ancestors can be traced to Austria. While neither parent had a musical background, they did own a piano, which immediately attracted Ellen and on which she began to explore the keys at the age of three. By the age of five, she was studying with a neighborhood piano teacher, but she rebelled at having to play the customary children's pieces. When she was seven or eight years old, she heard the Symphony No. 5 in C minor by Ludwig van Beethoven and was deeply impressed by it.

By the age of thirteen, Ellen came under the tutelage of Bower Murphy, who taught her to play the trumpet, to transpose music into different keys, and to perform in chamber ensembles. He also guided her in learning the orchestral repertoire and in devising ways in which to overcome technical problems in trumpet performance.

At Coral Gables High School, Ellen became an accomplished violinist. Soon she was serving as concertmistress of the school orchestra, as principal trumpeter in the band, and as student conductor. In addition, she composed pieces for band and for orchestra. Music was clearly to be her vocation. After graduating from high school, she entered Florida State University in Tallahassee as a music education major. In her sophomore year, she changed her area of emphasis to composition. Her undergraduate years, which culminated in a bachelor's degree in 1960, found her performing as concertmistress in the university orchestra under the direction of the Hungarian composer and pianist, Ernst von Dohnanyi; as first trumpeter in the symphonic band; and as a jazz trumpeter. Violin was her principal instrument, and she had the good fortune to study violin with Richard Burgin, former concertmaster of the Boston Symphony Orchestra, who had joined the Florida State faculty. Her composition teachers were John Boda and Carlisle Floyd. Following graduation, Ellen stayed at Florida State and pursued graduate work in composition. She received her master's degree in 1962.

Life's Work

After a somewhat less than satisfying year of teaching in a small community in South Carolina, Ellen Taaffe arrived in New York City. She resumed her violin studies with Ivan Galamian and his assistant, Sally Thomas. Taaffe also worked as a freelance musician, and in 1965, began a seven-year relationship as a violinist with the American Symphony Orchestra under its founder and conductor, Leopold Stokowski. She gained experience and seasoning by playing under a variety of guest conductors, some of whom were composers; they included Ernest Ansermet, Luciano Berio, Karl Bohn, Eugen Jochum, Hans Werner Henze, Paul Kletzki, Aram Khachaturian, Yehudi Menuhin, Igor Markevitch, Gunther Schuller, and Andre Previn. On June 22, 1969, she married the Hungarian-born violinist Joseph Zwilich, who played with the Metropolitan Opera Orchestra. These years solidified her intention to pursue a career as a composer rather than as a performer, and, indeed, she began to try her hand at the creation of art songs, producing, for example *Einsame Nacht*, a setting of six poems by Herman Hesse, which explore the theme of loneliness; this song cycle is stylistically beholden to the Second Viennese School and exhibits both craftsmanship and expressivity within the parameters of this sometimes restrictive school.

When Stokowski relocated to London in 1972, Ellen Taaffe Zwilich left her orchestral position and entered the doctoral program in composition at the Juilliard School. Her principal teachers there were Roger Sessions and Elliott Carter. During her three years at this esteemed institution, she formed the core of her creative personality, much of which is related directly to her extensive background as a performer. Music, for Zwilich, is a unique form of communication; therefore, its sheer sound and how that sound is perceived by an audience illuminate her approach to composition.

By the time she received the Doctor of Musical Arts degree, the first woman ever to achieve this distinction at Juilliard, Zwilich had created an impressive array of works that established her as a powerful new voice in the world of music. Her Sonata in Three Movements for Violin and Piano, written in 1973 for her husband and performed by him on a European tour that year, won a gold medal at the G. B. Viotti International Composition Competition in 1975. *Symposium for Orchestra* (1973), introduced by Pierre Boulez and the Juilliard Orchestra in Alice Tully Hall in New York's Lincoln Center during the summer of 1975, was declared an official United States entry for the International Society for Contemporary Music "World Music Days" Festival in Paris; it was also performed in 1978 in Carnegie Hall by the American Symphony Orchestra under Kazuyoshi Akiyama. As the title suggests, this twelve-minute work in one movement takes an academic point of view wherein the various members of the orchestra offer musical commentary on the subject (theme) under consideration.

Zwilich's String Quartet (1974), recipient of the Coolidge Chamber Music Prize, was premiered by the New York String Quartet at Jordan Hall in Boston, Massachusetts, on October 31, 1976. It received subsequent renderings at Alice Tully Hall, Carnegie Hall, and in 1977, at the Aspen Music Festival in Colorado. The composition's essential materials are set forth in the first movement, a type of prologue, and are incorporated in diverse manner through each of the four movements, the last of which is to be regarded as a closing epilogue. Zwilich's String Quartet is to be thought of as musical conversation among four equals, the drama of which impels the divergent exchanges of the four strings.

While Ellen Taaffe Zwilich was working on *Chamber* Symphony on a commission from the Boston Musica Vera, conducted by Richard Pittman, in 1979, her husband Joseph died suddenly of a heart attack while he and Ellen were attending a performance by the Stuttgart Ballet in the Metropolitan Opera House shortly after their tenth wedding anniversary. When the young widow resumed composition on the work, the symphony had evolved into one in which long musical lines are derived from shorter ideas. The solo capacities of the individual instruments are contrasted with a fuller sound created by such devices as instrumental doubling. The Boston premiere on November 30, 1979, was followed by performances in major American and European musical centers including one which was shown on television in Sofia, Bulgaria.

Only two years prior to the *Chamber* Symphony, Zwilich was composing a very different type of chamber music: her Clarino Quartet, dedicated to the memory of her high school trumpet teacher, Bower Murphy. In this unusual work, the piccolo trumpet, playing largely in the clarino register, is exploited handsomely along with the peculiar qualities of the D, C, and B-flat trumpets. The premiere, which took place at Hamline University in St. Paul, Minnesota, during March of 1979, featured members of the Minnesota Orchestra's trumpet section; Charles Schlueter played the clarino part on his personally designed valved instrument. The Clarino Quartet received subsequent performances at the Festival of Contemporary Music at Tanglewood in Lenox, Massachusetts, and in Paris, France, by the Pierre Thibaud Ensemble.

Zwilich received a Norlin Foundation Fellowship from the MacDowell Colony in Peterborough, New Hampshire, in 1980, and a Guggenheim Memorial Foundation Fellowship in 1980-1981. These fellowships enabled her to create such works as *Passages*, a setting of six poems by A. R. Ammons, for soprano and chamber ensemble. Commissioned by Boston Musical Vera, the work concerns the various forms of the passage of life and of time. The *Three Movements for Orchestra*, which includes serial techniques as well as traditional tonality, was retitled Symphony No. 1 and was premiered by the American Symphony Orchestra under the baton of Gunther Schuller in New York on May 5, 1982. It was this composition that made musical history when it was awarded the Pulitzer Prize in music in 1983; it competed against seventy-nine other entries. Zwilich was the first woman ever to win this prestigious award in its forty-year history. The symphony was recorded by John Nelson and the Indianapolis Symphony Orchestra in 1986.

During the next decade, Zwilich firmly established herself as one of America's most respected composers. In May of 1991, she received the Ernst von Dohnanyi Citation from her alma mater, Florida State University, and saw her works featured in the university's Festival of New Music. Her productivity continued at a staggering pace throughout the 1980's and included both large and small compositions. The Fantasy for Harpsichord received its first hearing in Linda Kobler's debut recital at Carnegie Hall in 1984. The Double Quartet for strings, commissioned by the Emerson Quartet and the Chamber Music Society of Lincoln Center, was premiered on October 21, 1984. (The two quartets are treated as separate but equal entities competing and cooperating with each other.) In the same year, Zwilich completed the Concerto for Trumpet and Five Players.

Symphony No. 2, known as the *Cello* Symphony because of the prominence given to that section of the orchestra, was introduced by the San Francisco Symphony Orchestra on November 13, 1985. The Piano Concerto, commissioned by the Detroit Symphony Orchestra and the American Symphony Orchestra League, was premiered on June 26, 1986, at Michigan's Meadowbrook Festival. *Tanzspiel*, Zwilich's only ballet, was commissioned by the New York City Ballet in 1987. *Symbalom*, commissioned by the New York Philharmonic and its conductor, Zubin Mehta, was first heard in the city of Leningrad on June 1, 1988, on the Philharmonic's tour of the Soviet Union. Other works include *Trio* for piano, violin, and cello commissioned by the Kalichstein-Laredo-Robinson Trio (1987), Trombone Concerto (1988), Flute Concerto (1990), Oboe Concerto (1991), Bass Trombone Concerto (1993), and Symphony No. 3 (1993). Symphony No. 3 was commissioned by the New York Philharmonic and premiered by that orchestra under the baton of Jahja Ling, who substituted for the indisposed Kurt Masur. This work seems to sum up the principles upon which Zwilich's art is founded. It is a creation whose roots in the Romantic tradition are clearly discernible. The music communicates an oft-told tale, to speak metaphorically, but it does so with such verve and enthusiasm that the listener retains his or her interest throughout. In short, the expressive power that is contained within the confines of traditional symphonic form is such that it holds in its grip an audience that is eager to accept its message.

Summary

Ellen Taaffe Zwilich has had a profound impact upon twentieth century American music and has been a beacon of inspiration for aspiring women composers and young composers in general. Her success continues to breed success, and it allows her to lead her life solely as a composer; she does not supplement her income by teaching in a university or by conducting or by performing (as she had done early in her career). Although she was trained by such "advanced" composers as Roger Sessions and Elliott Carter, she has discovered and cultivated a musical language which is comprehensible to large numbers of people. For that reason, she is very much a part of the world in which she lives, in opposition to the "ivory tower" creator who lives apart from society at large.

Ellen Zwilich's long list of commissions from eminent musicians and organizations is a testament to the impact she has made on both professional musicians and the public. While her earlier efforts show a linkage to such Viennese masters as Alban Berg and Arnold Schoenberg, her more recent compositions seem to meld classical and Romantic traits. Her large-scale works also call to mind composers such as Dmitri Shostakovitch and Carl Nielsen. Inspiration comes to her through a thorough knowledge and command of her craft. Her career is a testament to the rewards that follow on the heels of prodigious talent, discipline, and the recognition that a composer needs to create not in a vacuum but with a view to addressing one's fellow inhabitants on the planet.

Bibliography

Dreier, Ruth. "Ellen Taaffe Zwilich." *High Fidelity* (Musical America edition) 33 (September, 1983): 4. Dreier, a cellist, interviewed Zwilich shortly after she had won the Pulitzer Prize. Zwilich offers her views on the composer's relationship to the community of humankind, her assessment of the influence of performance on her creativity, and her opinion on the state of orchestras in the early 1980's.

Griffiths, Paul. "Zwillich in F-sharp." *The New Yorker* 69 (March 15, 1993): 113-116. A discussion of Zwilich's *Third Symphony* in relation to her previous works, this essay concludes with the view that the composer is perhaps too beholden to the past in her musical expression.

LePage, Jane Weiner. "Ellen Taaffe Zwilich." In *Women Composers, Conductors, and Musicians of the Twentieth Century: Selected Biographies.* 3 vols. Metuchen, N.J.: Scarecrow Press, 1980-1988. In the absence of a book-length work, this article provides the most complete source of biographical information on Zwilich. Traces her life from childhood through the early 1980's and includes excerpts of reviews of her musical works.

Moor, Paul. "Ellen Taaffe Zwilich." *High Fidelity* (Musical America edition) 33 (March, 1989): 16-18. Focuses on Zwilich's ideas concerning the role of women in music in the late twentieth century and in the past. In addition, Zwilich articulates her notions about the relationship between composer and performer.

Page, Tim. "The Music of Ellen Zwilich." *The New York Times Magazine*, July 14, 1985, 26-32. A wide-ranging interview with Zwilich that provides a good overview of her career. Conveys the breadth of her work, the depth of her commitment to musical composition, and the genesis of her musical inspiration.

David Z. Kushner

GREAT LIVES
FROM
HISTORY

BIOGRAPHICAL INDEX

BIOGRAPHICAL INDEX

BIOGRAPHICAL INDEX

AREAS OF ACHIEVEMENT

TIME LINE

Name	Born	Areas of Achievement
Anne Hutchinson	July 17, 1591	Religion
Pocahontas	c. 1596	Diplomacy
Anne Bradstreet	1612 (?)	Literature
Mercy Otis Warren	September 25, 1728	Literature
Ann Lee	February 29, 1736	Religion
Abigail Adams	November 22, 1744	Women's rights
Elizabeth Ann Seton	August 28, 1774	Religion and education
Emma Willard	February 23, 1787	Education
Sacagawea	c. 1788	Exploration
Sarah Josepha Hale	October 24, 1788	Literature and journalism
Sarah Grimké	November 26, 1792	Social reform and women's rights
Lucretia Mott	January 3, 1793	Social reform and women's rights
Sojourner Truth	c. 1797	Social reform
Mary Lyon	February 28, 1797	Education
Catharine Beecher	September 6, 1800	Education and women's rights
Lydia Maria Child	February 11, 1802	Social reform, literature, and women's rights
Dorothea Dix	April 4, 1802	Social reform
Prudence Crandall	September 3, 1803	Education, social reform, and women's rights
Elizabeth Palmer Peabody	May 16, 1804	Education
Angelina Grimké	February 28, 1805	Social reform and women's rights
Fanny Kemble	November 27, 1809	Theater and drama and social reform
Margaret Fuller	May 23, 1810	Journalism and social reform
Harriet Beecher Stowe	June 14, 1811	Social reform and women's rights
Ann Preston	December 1, 1813	Medicine and women's rights
Elizabeth Cady Stanton	November 12, 1815	Women's rights
Amelia Jenks Bloomer	May 27, 1818	Journalism and women's rights
Maria Mitchell	August 1, 1818	Astronomy
Lucy Stone	August 13, 1818	Social reform and women's rights
Lydia Estes Pinkham	February 9, 1819	Business and industry
Julia Ward Howe	May 27, 1819	Literature, women's rights, and social reform
Harriet Tubman	c. 1820	Social reform
Susan B. Anthony	February 15, 1820	Women's rights
Elizabeth Blackwell	February 3, 1821	Medicine
Mary Baker Eddy	July 16, 1821	Religion
Clara Barton	December 25, 1821	Education, nursing, and social reform
Lydia Folger Fowler	May 5, 1822	Medicine and women's rights
Elizabeth Cabot Cary Agassiz	December 5, 1822	Education
Mary Boykin Chesnut	March 31, 1823	Literature

Name	Born	Areas of Achievement
Jessie Benton Frémont	May 31, 1824	Government and politics
Matilda Joslyn Gage	March 25, 1826	Women's rights
Ellen G. White	November 26, 1827	Religion
Mary Harris "Mother" Jones	May 1, 1830	Social reform and trade unionism
Harriet Hosmer	October 9, 1830	Art
Helen Hunt Jackson	October 15, 1830	Literature and social reform
Belva A. Lockwood	October 24, 1830	Law, women's rights, and peace advocacy
Emily Dickinson	December 10, 1830	Poetry
Louisa May Alcott	November 29, 1832	Literature
Charlotte Forten	August 17, 1837	Education, literature, and civil rights
Liliuokalani	September 2, 1838	Government and politics
Frances Willard	September 28, 1839	Social reform and women's rights
Isabella Stewart Gardner	April 14, 1840	Patronage of the arts
Phoebe Apperson Hearst	December 3, 1842	Patronage of the arts
Sarah Winnemucca	c. 1844	Civil rights and social reform
Mary Cassatt	May 22, 1844	Art
Edmonia Lewis	1845 (?)	Art
Carry Nation	November 11, 1846	Social reform
Anna Howard Shaw	February 14, 1847	Women's rights
Sarah Jane Farmer	July 22, 1847	Religion
Alice James	August 7, 1848	Literature
Emma Lazarus	July 22, 1849	Literature and social reform
Sarah Orne Jewett	September 3, 1849	Literature
Frances Xavier Cabrini	July 15, 1850	Religion and social reform
Kate Chopin	February 8, 1851	Literature
Gertrude Käsebier	May 18, 1852	Photography
Cecilia Beaux	1855	Art
Alice Freeman Palmer	February 21, 1855	Education
Martha Carey Thomas	January 2, 1857	Education and women's rights
Fannie Merritt Farmer	March 23, 1857	Education
Williamina Paton Stevens Fleming	May 15, 1857	Astronomy
Gertrude Atherton	October 30, 1857	Literature
Ida Tarbell	November 5, 1857	Journalism
Julia C. Lathrop	June 29, 1858	Government and politics and social reform
Marion Talbot	July 31, 1858	Education, sociology, and women's rights
Fanny Bullock Workman	January 8, 1859	Exploration, geography, and women's rights
Carrie Chapman Catt	February 9, 1859	Women's rights
Katharine Lee Bates	August 12, 1859	Education and literature
Florence Kelley	September 12, 1859	Social reform and women's rights
Charlotte Perkins Gilman	July 3, 1860	Literature and journalism
Annie Oakley	August 13, 1860	Sports

TIME LINE

Name	Born	Areas of Achievement
Jane Addams	September 6, 1860	Social reform
Grandma Moses	September 7, 1860	Art
Juliette Gordon Low	October 31, 1860	Social reform
Henrietta Szold	December 21, 1860	Social reform and education
Loie Fuller	January 15, 1862	Dance
Edith Wharton	January 24, 1862	Literature
Ida B. Wells-Barnett	July 16, 1862	Civil rights, women's rights, and journalism
Annie Jump Cannon	December 11, 1863	Astronomy
Frances Benjamin Johnston	January 15, 1864	Photography
Nellie Bly	May 5, 1864	Journalism and social reform
Susan La Flesche Picotte	June 17, 1865	Medicine and social reform
Antonia Maury	March 21, 1866	Astronomy
Anne Sullivan Macy	April 14, 1866	Education
Emily Greene Balch	January 8, 1867	Peace advocacy, social reform, women's rights, and economics
Lillian D. Wald	March 10, 1867	Nursing and social reform
Frances Densmore	May 21, 1867	Anthropology
Maggie Lena Walker	July 15, 1867	Business and industry and social reform
Maud Powell	August 22, 1867	Music
Amy Marcy Beach	September 5, 1867	Music
Madam C. J. Walker	December 23, 1867	Business and industry
Alice Hamilton	February 27, 1869	Medicine and social reform
Emma Goldman	June 27, 1869	Social reform
Rachel Crothers	December 12, 1870	Theater and drama
Florence Sabin	November 9, 1871	Medicine
Julia Morgan	January 26, 1872	Architecture
Beatrix Jones Farrand	June 19, 1872	Landscape architecture
Willa Cather	December 7, 1873	Literature and journalism
Gertrude Stein	February 3, 1874	Literature
Amy Lowell	February 9, 1874	Literature
Romaine Brooks	May 1, 1874	Art
Dorothy Reed Mendenhall	September 22, 1874	Medicine
Abby Aldrich Rockefeller	October 26, 1874	Patronage of the arts
Gertrude Vanderbilt Whitney	January 9, 1875	Art and patronage of the arts
Mary McLeod Bethune	July 10, 1875	Education and social reform
Elsie Clews Parsons	November 27, 1875	Anthropology
Mary Beard	August 5, 1876	Historiography and social reform
Nellie Tayloe Ross	November 29, 1876	Government and politics
Isadora Duncan	May 26, 1877	Dance
Meta Vaux Warrick Fuller	June 6, 1877	Art
Belle Moskowitz	October 5, 1877	Social reform and government and politics
Grace Abbott	November 17, 1878	Social reform
Ruth St. Denis	January 20, 1879	Dance
Ethel Barrymore	August 16, 1879	Theater and drama

Name	Born	Areas of Achievement
Margaret Sanger	September 14, 1879	Women's rights and social reform
Frances Perkins	April 10, 1880	Government and politics
Jeannette Rankin	June 11, 1880	Government and politics and social reform
Helen Keller	June 27, 1880	Social reform and education
Lois Weber	June 13, 1881	Film
Imogen Cunningham	April 12, 1883	Photography
Sophie Tucker	January 13, 1884	Music and theater and drama
Alice Roosevelt Longworth	February 12, 1884	Government and politics
Sara Teasdale	August 8, 1884	Literature
Eleanor Roosevelt	October 11, 1884	Social reform
Elizabeth Arden	December 31, 1884	Business
Alice Paul	January 11, 1885	Women's rights
Malvina Hoffman	June 15, 1885	Art
Karen Horney	September 16, 1885	Psychology
Louise Bryant	December 5, 1885	Journalism
Ida Rosenthal	January 9, 1886	Business and industry
H. D.	September 10, 1886	Literature
Hazel Hotchkiss Wightman	December 20, 1886	Sports
Ruth Benedict	June 5, 1887	Anthropology
Marianne Moore	November 15, 1887	Literature
Georgia O'Keeffe	November 15, 1887	Art
Frances Marion	November 18, 1887	Film
Anita Loos	April 26, 1888	Literature and film
Perle Mesta	October 12, 1889	Government and politics
Katherine Anne Porter	May 15, 1890	Literature
Elizabeth Gurley Flynn	August 7, 1890	Trade unionism, social reform, and women's rights
Zora Neale Hurston	January 7, 1891	Literature
Laura Gilpin	April 22, 1891	Photography
Fanny Brice	October 29, 1891	Music and theater
Edna St. Vincent Millay	February 22, 1892	Literature
Agnes Smedley	February 23, 1892	Journalism, social reform, and women's rights
Augusta Savage	February 29, 1892	Art
Mary Pickford	April 8, 1892	Film
Djuna Barnes	June 12, 1892	Literature
Pearl S. Buck	June 26, 1892	Literature
Mabel Normand	November 9, 1892	Film
Gordon Hamilton	December 26, 1892	Education and sociology
Hanya Holm	1893	Dance
Lorena Hickok	March 7, 1893	Journalism
Irene Castle	April 7, 1893	Dance
Helen Hokinson	June 29, 1893	Art
Dorothy Thompson	July 9, 1893	Journalism
Mae West	August 17, 1893	Film and theater and drama
Dorothy Parker	August 22, 1893	Literature
Lillian Gish	October 14, 1893	Film and theater and drama
Bessie Smith	April 15, 1894	Music

Name	Born	Areas of Achievement
Martha Graham	May 11, 1894	Dance
Blanche Wolf Knopf	July 30, 1894	Publishing
Dorothea Lange	May 26, 1895	Photography and social reform
Susanne K. Langer	December 20, 1895	Philosophy and education
Helen Merrell Lynd	March 17, 1896	Sociology and education
Mari Sandoz	May 11, 1896	Historiography and literature
Gerty Cori	August 15, 1896	Biochemistry
Ruth Gordon	October 30, 1896	Theater and drama, film, and literature
Dorothy Arzner	January 3, 1897	Film
Marian Anderson	February 27, 1897	Music
Amelia Earhart	July 24, 1897	Aviation
Louise Bogan	August 11, 1897	Literature
Margaret Rudkin	September 14, 1897	Business and industry
Dorothy Day	November 8, 1897	Journalism and social reform
Margaret Chase Smith	December 14, 1897	Government and politics
Ariel Durant	May 10, 1898	Historiography and literature
Berenice Abbott	July 17, 1898	Photography
Edith Head	October 28, 1898 (?)	Film and fashion design
Rachel Fuller Brown	November 23, 1898	Biochemistry and medicine
Louise Nevelson	1899	Art
Eva Le Gallienne	January 11, 1899	Theater and drama
Alice Neel	January 28, 1900	Art
Gracie Allen	July 26, 1900 (?)	Theater, radio, film, and television
Helen Hayes	October 10, 1900	Theater and drama
Helen Gahagan Douglas	November 25, 1900	Theater and government and politics
Ruth Crawford-Seeger	July 3, 1901	Music
Margaret Mead	December 16, 1901	Anthropology
Marlene Dietrich	December 27, 1901	Film
Tallulah Bankhead	January 31 or February 12, 1902	Film and theater
Lillian Hardin Armstrong	February 3, 1902	Music
Barbara McClintock	June 16, 1902	Genetics
Antonia Brico	June 26, 1902	Music
Cheryl Crawford	September 24, 1902	Theater and drama
Diana Vreeland	c. 1903	Fashion
Clare Boothe Luce	April 10, 1903	Journalism and government and politics
Erna Gibbs	March 5, 1904	Medicine
Margaret Bourke-White	June 14, 1904	Photography
Dorothy Fields	July 15, 1904	Music
Alexandra Danilova	November 20, 1904	Dance
Agnes de Mille	1905	Dance
Anna May Wong	January 3, 1905	Film
Oveta Culp Hobby	January 19, 1905	Government and politics
Lillian Hellman	June 20, 1905	Literature and film
Greta Garbo	September 18, 1905	Film
Helen Wills Moody	October 6, 1905	Sports

Name	Born	Areas of Achievement
Josephine Baker	June 3, 1906	Dance, theater, and civil rights
Maria Goeppert Mayer	June 28, 1906	Physics
Hannah Arendt	October 14, 1906	Philosophy and social science
Gertrude Ederle	October 23, 1906	Sports
Grace Murray Hopper	December 9, 1906	Invention and technology
Katharine Hepburn	May 12, 1907	Film
Rachel Carson	May 27, 1907	Biology and literature
Henriette Wyeth	October 22, 1907	Art
Ethel Merman	January 16, 1908	Theatre and drama
Dominique de Menil	March 23, 1908	Patronage of the arts and philanthropy
Bette Davis	April 5, 1908	Film and theater and drama
Lee Krasner	October 27, 1908	Art
Virginia Apgar	June 7, 1909	Medicine
Jessica Tandy	June 7, 1909	Theater and drama and film
Katherine Dunham	June 22, 1909	Dance, anthropology, and education
Jacqueline Cochran	c. 1910	Aviation
Annie Dodge Wauneka	April 10, 1910	Social reform and public health
Mary Lou Williams	May 8, 1910	Music
Margaret Wise Brown	May 23, 1910	Literature
Elizabeth Bishop	February 8, 1911	Literature
Ginger Rogers	July 16, 1911	Film and dance
Lucille Ball	August 6, 1911	Film and television
Mahalia Jackson	October 26, 1911	Music
Louise Bourgeois	December 25, 1911	Art
Barbara Tuchman	January 30, 1912	Historiography
Agnes Martin	March 22, 1912	Art
Chien-Shiung Wu	May 29, 1912	Physics
Mary McCarthy	June 21, 1912	Journalism and literature
Rosa Parks	February 4, 1913	Civil rights
Alice Marble	September 28, 1913	Sports
Muriel Rukeyser	December 15, 1913	Literature
Gypsy Rose Lee	January 9, 1914	Dance and film
"Babe" Didrikson Zaharias	June 26, 1914	Sports
Billie Holiday	April 7, 1915	Music
Mary Kay Ash	May 12, 1915 (?)	Business and industry
Lucy S. Dawidowicz	June 16, 1915	Historiography and education
Carson McCullers	February 19, 1917	Literature
Betty Comden	May 3, 1917	Film, music, and theater and drama
Gwendolyn Brooks	June 7, 1917	Literature
Katharine Graham	June 16, 1917	Publishing and journalism
Gertrude Belle Elion	January 23, 1918	Biochemistry
Ida Lupino	February 4, 1918	Film
Patty Berg	February 13, 1918	Sports
Ella Fitzgerald	April 25, 1918	Music
Rita Hayworth	October 17, 1918	Film
Pearl Primus	November 29, 1919	Dance and anthropology

TIME LINE

Name	Born	Areas of Achievement
Pamela Digby Churchill Harriman	March 20, 1920	Government and politics
Peggy Lee	May 26, 1920	Music
Bella Abzug	July 24, 1920	Government and politics
Marguerite Higgins	September 3, 1920	Journalism
Juanita Kreps	January 11, 1921	Economics, education, and government and politics
Betty Friedan	February 4, 1921	Women's rights
Rosalyn S. Yalow	July 19, 1921	Biochemistry and medicine
Margaret Hillis	October 1, 1921	Music
Yoshiko Uchida	November 24, 1921	Literature
Helen Gurley Brown	February 18, 1922	Publishing
Eileen Ford	March 25, 1922	Business and industry
Jeanne Sauvé	April 26, 1922	Government and politics
Judy Garland	June 10, 1922	Film and music
Mavis Gallant	August 11, 1922	Literature
Diane Arbus	March 14, 1923	Photography
Jean Nidetch	October 12, 1923	Business and industry
Gloria Vanderbilt	February 20, 1924	Fashion and art
Sarah Caldwell	March 6, 1924	Music
Sarah Vaughan	March 27, 1924	Music
Lauren Bacall	September 16, 1924	Film and theater
Geraldine Page	November 22, 1924	Theater and drama and film
Shirley Chisholm	November 30, 1924	Government and politics
Gwen Verdon	January 13, 1925	Dance
Maria Tallchief	January 24, 1925	Dance
Flannery O'Connor	March 25, 1925	Literature
Angela Lansbury	October 16, 1925	Theater and drama and film
Julie Harris	December 2, 1925	Theater and drama and film
Aileen Clarke Hernandez	May 23, 1926	Labor relations, social reform, and women's rights
Elisabeth Kübler-Ross	July 8, 1926	Psychiatry
Jeane Kirkpatrick	November 19, 1926	Diplomacy, government and politics, and women's rights
Leontyne Price	February 10, 1927	Music
Ruth Prawer Jhabvala	May 7, 1927	Literature and film
Althea Gibson	August 25, 1927	Sports
Maya Angelou	April 4, 1928	Literature
Shirley Temple Black	April 23, 1928	Film and diplomacy
Anne Sexton	November 9, 1928	Literature
Helen Frankenthaler	December 12, 1928	Art
Liz Claiborne	March 31, 1929	Fashion
Beverly Sills	May 25, 1929	Music
Jacqueline Kennedy Onassis	July 28, 1929	Government and politics
Joyce Brothers	October 20, 1929	Psychology
Toshiko Akiyoshi	December 12, 1929	Music
Joanne Woodward	February 27, 1930	Film and theater and drama
Sandra Day O'Connor	March 26, 1930	Government and politics and law
Dolores Huerta	April 10, 1930	Trade unionism

Name	Born	Areas of Achievement
Lorraine Hansberry	May 19, 1930	Literature
Toni Morrison	February 18, 1931	Literature
Alice Rivlin	March 4, 1931	Economics and government and politics
Anne Bancroft	September 17, 1931	Film and theater
Barbara Walters	September 25, 1931	Journalism
Dian Fossey	January 16, 1932	Anthropology
Megan Terry	July 22, 1932	Theater and drama
Patsy Cline	September 8, 1932	Music
Jane Cahill Pfeiffer	September 29, 1932	Business and industry
Sylvia Plath	October 27, 1932	Literature
Susan Sontag	January 16, 1933	Literature
Dianne Feinstein	June 22, 1933	Government and politics
Ann Richards	September 1, 1933	Government and politics
Marilyn Horne	January 16, 1934	Music
Gloria Steinem	March 25, 1934	Women's rights and journalism
Jane Byrne	May 24, 1934	Government and politics
Katherine Davalos Ortega	July 16, 1934	Government and politics
Kate Millett	September 14, 1934	Women's rights
Maureen Connolly	September 17, 1934	Sports
Loretta Lynn	April 14, 1935	Music
Geraldine Ferraro	August 26, 1935	Government and politics
Barbara Jordan	February 21, 1936	Government and politics, law, and education
Marge Piercy	March 31, 1936	Literature
Carol Burnett	April 26, 1936	Theater and television
Barbara Mikulski	July 20, 1936	Government and politics
Elizabeth Dole	July 29, 1936	Government and politics
Marva Collins	August 31, 1936	Education
Rosemary Radford Ruether	November 2, 1936	Religion and social reform
JoAnne Akalaitis	June 29, 1937	Theater and drama
Tina Howe	November 21, 1937	Literature
Jane Fonda	December 21, 1937	Film
Janet Reno	July 21, 1938	Law and government and politics
Ellen Taaffe Zwilich	April 30, 1939	Music
Marian Wright Edelman	June 6, 1939	Civil rights, education, and social reform
Judy Chicago	July 20, 1939	Art
Lily Tomlin	September 1, 1939	Theater and drama and film
Margaret Atwood	November 18, 1939	Literature
Tina Turner	November 26, 1939	Music
Cicely Tyson	December 19, 1939 (?)	Theater drama and film
Mary Hatwood Futrell	May 24, 1940	Education
Shirley Muldowney	June 19, 1940	Sports
Wilma Rudolph	June 23, 1940	Sports
Patricia S. Schroeder	July 30, 1940	Government and politics
Maxine Hong Kingston	October 27, 1940	Literature
Martha Stewart	1941 or 1942	Business and industry
Joan Baez	January 9, 1941	Music and peace advocacy

Name	Born	Areas of Achievement
Donna Shalala	February 14, 1941	Education and government and politics
Nora Ephron	May 19, 1941	Journalism and film
Twyla Tharp	July 1, 1941	Dance
Charlayne Hunter-Gault	February 27, 1942	Journalism
Aretha Franklin	March 25, 1942	Music
Barbra Streisand	April 24, 1942	Music, film, and theater and drama
Penny Marshall	October 15, 1942	Film and television
Meredith Monk	November 20, 1942	Dance, music, and theater and drama
Janis Joplin	January 19, 1943	Music
Joni Mitchell	November 7, 1943	Music
Billie Jean King	November 22, 1943	Sports
Alice Walker	February 9, 1944	Literature
Linda Ellerbee	August 15, 1944	Broadcast journalism
Rita Mae Brown	November 28, 1944	Literature and women's rights
Susan Rothenberg	January 20, 1945	Art
Sarah Weddington	February 5, 1945	Law, government and politics, and women's rights
Suzanne Farrell	August 16, 1945	Dance
Jessye Norman	September 15, 1945	Music
Wilma P. Mankiller	November 18, 1945	Government and politics
Catharine A. MacKinnon	1946	Law and women's rights
Dolly Parton	January 19, 1946	Music
Cher	May 20, 1946	Music and film
Linda Ronstadt	July 15, 1946	Music
Martha Coolidge	August 17, 1946	Film
Connie Chung	August 20, 1946	Journalism
Kim Campbell	March 10, 1947	Government and politics
Glenn Close	March 19, 1947	Film and theater and drama
Linda Bloodworth-Thomason	April 15, 1947	Television
Laurie Anderson	June 5, 1947	Performance art and music
Linda Chavez	June 17, 1947	Government and politics
Marsha Norman	September 21, 1947	Literature
Hillary Rodham Clinton	October 26, 1947	Law and government and politics
Diane English	1948	Television
Donna Karan	October 2, 1948	Fashion and business and industry
Meryl Streep	June 22, 1949	Film and theater and drama
Annie Leibovitz	October 2, 1949	Photography
Bonnie Raitt	November 8, 1949	Music
Whoopi Goldberg	November 13, 1949	Theater and drama, television, and film
Le Ly Hayslip	December 19, 1949	Literature and social reform
Cathy Guisewite	September 5, 1950	Journalism and art
Jane Pauley	October 31, 1950	Broadcast journalism
Elizabeth Swados	February 5, 1951	Music and theater and drama
Sally Ride	May 26, 1951	Aeronautics and astrophysics

Name	Born	Areas of Achievement
Amy Tan	February 19, 1952	Literature
Beth Henley	May 8, 1952	Literature
Susan Seidelman	December 11, 1952	Film
Oprah Winfrey	January 29, 1954	Film and television
Louise Erdrich	June 7, 1954	Literature
Amy Eilberg	October 12, 1954	Religion
Chris Evert	December 21, 1954	Sports
Martina Navratilova	October 18, 1956	Sports
Nancy Lopez	January 6, 1957	Sports
Katie Couric	January 7, 1957	Journalism
Geena Davis	January 21, 1957	Film and television
Gloria Estefan	September 1, 1957	Music
Maya Ying Lin	October 5, 1959	Architecture
K. D. Lang	November 2, 1961	Music
Jodie Foster	November 19, 1962	Film
Kristi Yamaguchi	June 12, 1971	Sports